Frank Lloyd Wright : The Early Years : Progressivism : Aesthetics : Cities

Frank Lloyd Wright : The Early Years : Progressivism : Aesthetics : Cities examines Wright's belief that all aspects of human life must embrace and celebrate an aesthetic experience that would thereby lead to necessary social reforms. Inherent in the theory was a belief that reform of nineteenth-century gluttony should include a contemporary interpretation of its material presence, its bulk and space, and its architectural landscape.

This book analyzes Wright's innovative, profound theory of architecture that drew upon geometry and notions of pure design and the indigenous as put into practice. It outlines the design methodology that he applied to domestic and non-domestic buildings and presents reasons for the recognition of two Wright Styles and a Wright School. The book also studies how his design method was applied to city planning and implications of historical and theoretical contexts of the period that surely influenced all of Wright's community and city planning.

Donald Leslie Johnson taught at Flinders University in Adelaide, South Australia, from 1972 until retirement in 1988. He has been an adjunct professor of architectural history at the University of South Australia for twenty years. Previously, he practiced architecture in Seattle, Philadelphia, and Tucson and taught theory and design at Arizona, Washington State, and Adelaide universities. He has written extensively about the architecture of Frank Lloyd Wright, Walter Burley Griffin and Canberra, Australian architectural history, and American and Australian city planning history. He was in Lois I. Kahn's masters class of 1960–61 at the University of Pennsylvania. Johnson was a member of the American Institute of Architects and is an Honorary Fellow of the Australian Institute of Architects.

Frank Lloyd Wright : The Early Years : Progressivism : Aesthetics : Cities

Donald Leslie Johnson

LONDON AND NEW YORK

First published 2017
by Routledge
2 Park Square, Milton Park, Abingdon, Oxon OX14 4RN

and by Routledge
711 Third Avenue, New York, NY 10017

First issued in paperback 2018

Routledge is an imprint of the Taylor & Francis Group, an informa business

© 2017 Donald Leslie Johnson

The right of Donald Leslie Johnson to be identified as author of this work has been asserted by him in accordance with sections 77 and 78 of the Copyright, Designs and Patents Act 1988.

All rights reserved. No part of this book may be reprinted or reproduced or utilized in any form or by any electronic, mechanical, or other means, now known or hereafter invented, including photocopying and recording, or in any information storage or retrieval system, without permission in writing from the publishers.

Trademark notice: Product or corporate names may be trademarks or registered trademarks, and are used only for identification and explanation without intent to infringe.

British Library Cataloguing in Publication Data
A catalogue record for this book is available from the British Library

Library of Congress Cataloging-in-Publication Data
Names: Johnson, Donald Leslie, author.
Title: Frank Lloyd Wright : the early years : progressivism : aesthetics : cities / Donald Leslie Johnson.
Description: New York : Routledge, 2017. | Includes bibliographical references and index.
Identifiers: LCCN 2016009931 | ISBN 9781472458025 (hb : alk. paper) | ISBN 9781315583051 (ebook)
Subjects: LCSH: Wright, Frank Lloyd, 1867–1959—Criticism and interpretation. | Architecture—Philosophy—20th century.
Classification: LCC NA737.W7 J58 2017 | DDC 720.92—dc23
LC record available at https://lccn.loc.gov/2016009931

ISBN 13: 978-1-138-60162-8 (pbk)
ISBN 13: 978-1-4724-5802-5 (hbk)

Typeset in Sabon
by Apex CoVantage, LLC

The letters, writings, and drawings of Frank Lloyd Wright are copyright © 2016 The Frank Lloyd Wright Foundation, Scottsdale, Arizona. All rights reserved. The Frank Lloyd Foundation Archives (The Museum of Modern Art | Avery Architectural & Fine Arts Library, Columbia University).
Book cover image: Library of Congress.

This book is dedicated to the Safeway Studio,

students and staff of the 1960s

from whom I learned so much,

and as a thank you to Bruce Brooks Pfeiffer, Archivist.

Contents

List of illustrations   ix
Acknowledgements   xvi
Biography   xix
Preface   xx
Abbreviations and acronyms to notes and captions   xxi

Conditions   1

1   Reformation and progressivism   3

Conditions 6
Societal lessons 9
Radicals and reformers 14
Wright observes 18
Place and circumstance 20
Burnham et al., 1893–09 24

The aesthetics of progress   35

2   Education   37

J.-J. Rousseau and after 38
Kindergartens 42
Unity Chapel and Silsbee 48
Hillside Home School 51
The Martins and the Coonleys 59
The Fellowship 62

3   Tutelage   71

Teen years at work 71
Reverend Jenkin Lloyd Jones 78
Dankmar Adler 85
Aesthetic inclinations 91
Ruskin and Viollet-le-Duc 92
Primitive and indigenous 98

4 Design generators 111

Conventionalization's limits 111
Pure design 113
Dynamics of the square 123

5 Architectural synthesis 132

The studio, golf clubhouse, and stables 136
Walter and Marion Griffin 144
Analysis 148

6 The Wright School 164

Parallelepipedons 164
Domestic buildings, Silsbee, and plan evolution 176
Wright Styles and the Wright School 188

The city scientific 199

7 Rousseau to professionalism 201

Ledoux, Soria y Mata, Sitte, Howard . . . 201
Professionalism 205

8 Wright's community planning 212

English garden suburbs 212
Quadruplets 214
University Heights 224
Bitter Root town and village 226
Hooker and the city club 232
Drummond's neighborhood unit 245
Evolution 249

9 Contraction 260

Appendices 263

A Visual examination of geometries 265

B Wright's Yesler Avenue Hotel of 1894 266

C Further quadruplets 267

References 279
Index 295

Illustrations

1.1 A Winnebago encampment in Wisconsin in the 1850s, no different than in the 1870s; painting by Seth Eastman, then captain in the US Army. As settlers the Jones family encountered Winnebagos who lived in southern Wisconsin and northern Illinois. Winnebagos surrendered their lands and, in the 1830s, were shunted farther west. Some refused to move and in Wisconsin today name themselves Ho-Chunk. From McKenney/Hall, 1836–44. 20
1.2 "President Grant and the Emperor of Brazil starting the great Corliss engine in Machinery Hall" at the Centennial International Exhibition in Philadelphia in 1876. From Leslie, 1877. 21
1.3 Chicago's Haymarket Square in about 1893, with trolley tracks and police box; none of the buildings exist today. (Note the number of horses and estimate their manure.) From private collection. 22
1.4 Aerial perspective of Chicago's central precinct as proposed in 1909 by Burnham/Bennett showing trees (in black), blocks of commercial buildings, residential apartments, government buildings, and a central, high-domed edifice suffering from giganticism and ominously fronting ceremonial avenues lined with trees shown in black. 26
2.1 Interior of the "Kindergarten Cottage" located beside the Women's Pavilion at the Centennial International Exhibition, Fairmont Park, Philadelphia, 1875–76. (Is Miss Burritt standing at far left and at right a student teacher?) From Leslie, 1877. 43
2.2 On left: a perspective rendering of the Jones family's "Unity Chapel" at Hillside/Helena, Wisconsin, published December 1885, "Jos Silsbee Architect," same as built in 1885–86. Top right: Wright's 1887 rendering that copied Silsbee's perspective angle, drawing style, and caption. From Hasbrouck, 1970. Bottom: Wright's design perspective rendering of a proposal for a "Unitarian Chapel for Sioux City, Iowa," as published June 1887. From Hasbrouck, 1970. 49
2.3 Old postcard of the Jones sisters' Hillside Home School around 1900; wood shingle siding; to the left of the two dormers is Silsbee's design of 1886; to the right are additions organized and constructed post-1887, likely by Thomas Jones in 1889. 54
2.4 Bird's-eye perspective drawing of "Hillside Home School buildings" as built near Spring Green, Wisconsin, 1901–02. From Wright, 1910. 58
2.5 Bottom: pencil drawing of the floor plan, scheme one of 1911 for a proposed kindergarten complex for Mrs Coonley, entry is at bottom of drawing of this formal beaux-arts scheme. Top: frontal sketch perspective view of the project. Both from Pfeiffer, 07–13. Courtesy and © 2016 FLWF. 60
2.6 Garden front of Coonley kindergarten, scheme two photographed ca. 1912. From private collection. 61

x *Illustrations*

3.1	Speculative house for developer Edward B. Smith in Buffalo, New York, Silsbee & Marling, Architects, 1885, designed by Silsbee then practicing in Buffalo and Chicago; some modifications when built. From a journal as published by <jlsilsbee.blogspot.com>.	76
3.2	Presentation pencil drawing of the front elevation of the Henry N. Cooper house, a project of 1887 or 1898 for a site in the La Grange suburb of Chicago. Courtesy and © 2016 FLWF.	77
3.3	Frank Lloyd Wright's house in the Oak Park suburb of Chicago, June 1889–90; photograph ca. 1893. From Riley, 1994.	79
3.4	Portrait of Reverend William Cary Wright in the early 1850s. Original held by the State Historical Society of Iowa, Iowa City, Elizabeth Wright Heller Collection. From Patterson, 2013.	80
3.5	Madison Street entrance to the Schlesinger and Mayer building in 1900, St Louis, Missouri, Louis H. Sullivan, Architect, 1898–99; note Luxfer glass tiles above large clear-glass windows. The building was sold in 1904 to Carson Pirie Scott & Co. and subsequently enlarged. From author's collection.	91
3.6	Top: Papworth's illustration of Durand's typographical plan forms using the square proportion. Bottom: plan of Papworth's "Points of Supports" that defined apartments and spaces following Roman tradition.	97
4.1	Two-dimensional "Line-ideas" composed within a square as drawn by Arthur Wesley Dow; all drawings are variations of pattern No. 17, top left, except the middle three at the top and bottom line of "dynamic" compositions. From Dow, 1899.	115
4.2	Front elevation in 1908 of the George W. Tilton Elementary School in West Garfield Park, Chicago, Dwight Perkins, Board of Education architect, 1907–08. From author's collection.	118
4.3	Perspective of "Proposed commercial high school building, Harrison Street and Plymouth Court" in Chicago, Dwight Perkins, Board of Education architect, 1908. From *Annual Report of the Board*, 1908–09.	119
4.4	Russell C. Allen house in Bonita, near San Diego, California, Gill & Mead Architects, Irving J. Gill designer, 1907–08. From Kamerling, 1993.	120
4.5	Centered above main entries to Midway Gardens in Chicago, 1913–14, were cast concrete sculptures (a sprite) holding a cube titled "Queen of the Gardens"; basic esquisse by Wright, sculptor Alfonso Iannelli. From Kruty, 1998.	121
4.6	Top: Rudolph Arnheim's inferred dynamics of what appears to be a stable form, a square. Bottom: traditional extrapolations using T-square and compass to apply or confirm proportion.	123
4.7	Typical formalities and dynamics apparent in potential proportions and symmetries of a square.	124
4.8	Plan forms of buildings using the square, including Wright's buildings in column three. After March and Steadman, 1971.	126
4.9	World's first Ferris Observation Wheel designed and built by George W. D. Ferris Jr. for the Chicago Exposition of 1893, then rebuilt in Chicago's Lincoln Park in 1895, then rebuilt as shown here for the Louisiana Purchase Exposition in St Louis, Missouri, 1903–04, its final installation and soon demolished. Note the standing man center-left. Dated 19 April 1904, from author's collection.	127
5.1	"Study for a concrete bank building in a small city / Illustrating an article contributed to the *Brickbuilder* [10 August 1901] . . . 'A Village Bank'," first designed in brick; author's notations. From Wright, 1910.	134

5.2	"House for Mr W. H. Winslow in River Forest Illinois"; trace of a photograph; buildings in background repeat roof lines of house. From Wright, 1910.	135
5.3	"Atelier of FLW, Oak Park, Ill" / "An early study in articulation – the various functions featured, individualized and grouped." Space for eight in drafter's room; fireproof vault; eyebrow roofs on four sides of the octagon library are not shown; author's notations. Composite of original plans in Wright, 1910.	136
5.4	Ground-floor plan of FLW's home and office, ca. 1898; author's notations. From Riley, 1994.	137
5.5	River Forest Golf Clubhouse, scheme two as built; photographed shortly after completion in 1899 and before a fire took one half of the building.	139
5.6	River Forest Golf Clubhouse, scheme two as built; floor plan and elevations, 1898. From Hamilton, 1990. Courtesy and © 2016 FLWF.	140
5.7	River Forest Golf Clubhouse, "first version"; floor plan, 1898; author's notations. From Pfeiffer, 98–02, as published in Spencer, 1900.	141
5.8	"Suburban dwelling for George E. Millard in Highland Park, Illinois. A simple wooden house in the woods by a Highland Park ravine"; exterior of horizontal square wood battens; author's annotations. From Wright, 1910.	142
5.9	Lake Mendota boathouse for the Madison Improvement Association, 1893; left: plan at water level on left of center line, entry or second level on right of center line; right: lake-front elevation; author's notations. From Holzhueter, 1990. Courtesy and © 2016 FLWF.	142
5.10	Project for a Lake Monona boathouse for the Madison Improvement Association, 1893; left: plan at water level; bridge from shore to the building set on piles; right: lake-front elevation; author's notations. From Holzhueter, 1990. Courtesy and © 2016 FLWF.	143
5.11	"Stable of the Winslow house, River Forest. Ground plan and perspective"; perspective drawing a trace of a photograph; author's notations. From Wright, 1910.	144
5.12	William H. Emery Jr. house in Elmhurst, Illinois, by architect Walter Burley Griffin, 1902–03; photograph of 1908 by architect William Gray Purcell, one copy in Purcell papers, Northwest Archives. From Kruty (1998a).	146
5.13	Left: schematic analysis of Emery house design. Right: one practical application of the dynamics of a square, a fundamental detail for several of Wright's buildings.	147
5.14	"Front" and "Side" elevations of the "Studio-Residence" project for sculptor Richard Bock of Maywood, Illinois, 1902. From Pfeiffer, 02–06. Courtesy and © 2016 FLWF.	148
5.15	"West Elevation," "House for Mrs Thomas H. Gale," Oak Park, Illinois, 1909; similar to as built. From Pfeiffer, 07–13. Courtesy and © 2016 FLWF.	149
5.16	Developmental pencil drawing of the ground-floor plan of the H. J. Ullman house project of 1904 in Oak Park, Illinois of 1904; also showing lines for constructing a perspective drawing. From Pfeiffer, 02–06. Courtesy and © 2016 FLWF.	150
5.17	Gilmore house in Madison, Wisconsin, 1908. Left: ground-floor plan (based on 0806.09); a three-foot by six-inch grid drawn by Loy Maconi for Menocal, 1992. Right: square proportions by this author.	151

xii *Illustrations*

5.18	Top: photograph ca. 1940 of one of the twin Gale houses of 1892. From Manson, 1958, and Ashbee, 1911a. Bottom: ground-floor plan of the Emmond house, typical of the three houses in 1892; author's notations.	152
5.19	Winslow house ground-floor plan, 1894–05; author's notations. From Wright, 1910.	153
5.20	"House for Mrs Aline Devin. Ground- [and second-floor] plan," project, 1898; two distinct front elevations; author's notations. From Wright, 1910.	154
5.21	Hickox house ground- and second-floor plans, 1900; perspective drawing a trace of a photograph; author's notations. From Wright, 1910.	155
5.22	Rogers (Thomas) house ground- and second-floor plans, 1900; perspective drawing a trace of a photograph; author's notations. From Wright, 1910.	156
5.23	"Hillside Home School building / Built for the Lloyd Jones sisters in 1906," 1901–02; principle floor plan; author's notations. From Wright, 1910.	157
5.24	Willits house ground- and second-floor plans, 1902; author's notations. From Wright, 1910.	157
5.25	D. Martin (Barton) house ground-floor plan, 1902–04; perspective drawing a trace of a photograph; author's notations. From Wright, 1910.	158
5.26	D. Martin house ground-floor plan, 1903–05, and site plan; Martin (Barton) house upper left; author's notations. From Wright, 1910.	159
5.27	Coonley kindergarten ("playhouse") ground-floor plan, 1912; author's notations. From Storrer, 1993, and Ashbee 1911a.	160
5.28	Midway Gardens ground-floor plan, 1913–14; author's notations. From *Wendingen* (4–5 1925).	161
6.1	Perspective of 1903 penultimate facade design of "The Abraham Lincoln Centre" in Chicago, "FLW & Dwight Heald Perkins, Architects." From Siry, 1996, from *All Souls Church Twentieth Annual*, 1903.	167
6.2	Final auditorium third- or balcony-floor plan dated February 1903, The Abraham Lincoln Centre in Chicago, "FLW & Dwight Heald Perkins, Architects"; signed "JLlJ," i.e. Jenkin Lloyd Jones; author's notations. From Pfeiffer, 02–06. Courtesy and © 2016 FLWF.	168
6.3	The Abraham Lincoln Centre, Chicago, Dwight Heald Perkins & FLW, photographed in about 1907. One of the more important buildings of the twentieth century; floor plans and general design Wright and Perkins 1901–03; exterior elevations Perkins and Rev. Jones, 1903–05. At right is the entry vestibule to All Souls Church of 1885, Joseph L. Silsbee, Architect. From private collection.	169
6.4	Principal facade and main entry photograph, ca. 1906, Larkin Administration Building in Buffalo, New York, 1902–05, demolished in 1929. From private collection.	170
6.5	Ground-floor plan, Larkin Administration Building in Buffalo, New York, 1902–05; author's notations. From Wright, 1910.	170
6.6	Drawing traced on a photograph of the interior of the Larkin Administration Building in Buffalo, New York, 1902–05; a grand space for practical office and filing; steel posts and beams hidden by terra cotta and stucco for fireproofing; continuous ceiling skylight. From Wright, 1910.	171
6.7	Ground-floor plan, Beye boathouse project for Madison, Wisconsin, 1905. Composite drawing by author.	172

6.8	Perspective of the Beye boathouse project for Madison, Wisconsin, 1905. From Wright, 1921.	172
6.9	Women's Pavilion "Spring Green Fairground," Wisconsin, 1914; photograph courtesy Franklin Porter as published in Hamilton (1909); conjectural floor plan by author.	173
6.10	Unity Temple and Unity House in Oak Park, Illinois, 1905–08; entry-level floor plan; author's notations.	174
6.11	Photograph 1909 by Henry Fuermann of Unity Temple and Unity House in Oak Park, Illinois, 1905–08. From Ashbee, 1911a.	175
6.12	"Unity Temple / Longitudinal Section"; top left: one half of the temple reflected ceiling plan; top right: one half of the house reflected ceiling plan; drawing dated "Mar 1906." From Wright, 1925.	175
6.13	Plan schematics for non-domestic buildings before 1915.	177
6.14	Plan typologies leading to the Wright Style of domestic architecture.	178
6.15	Application of plan typology number 3b in 6.14: from top left: proposed Helena Valley house for Silsbee, 1889; Wright's own house, 1889; *Ladies Home Journal* project (July 1901); Rogers house, 1900; Willits house, 1902; T. Gale house, 1909; author's notations.	181
6.16	Plan typology number 4 in 6.14: from top left: Cochran house for Silsbee, 1887; Emmond house, 1892; Hickox house, 1901; Henderson house, 1901; *Ladies Home Journal* project (February 1901); author's notations.	182
6.17	Schematic explanation of the evolution from stacked chambers to rather open floor plans and an extended horizontality on the exterior. Author's drawing.	185
6.18	Above: Bradley house, east or principle elevation, 1899–1901; measured drawing by Mario Messer, Philippe Brochart, Jonathan Klocke of house as built. Courtesy HABS, IL-327.9. Below: Darwin Martin house, south or principle elevation, 1903–05; measured drawing by John W. Joseph, 1987, of house as built. Courtesy HABS, NY,15-BUF,5–6. Drawings not to same scale.	186
6.19	South and west elevations of Emil Bach house in Chicago, Illinois, 1911–12; tan brick, light-brown stucco, oak-colored wood trim; measured 1965, drawing by J. William Rudd, 1966. Courtesy HABS, ILL,16-CHIG,83–4.	187
6.20	Project of a studio for N. H. Lowell in Matteawan, New York, 1901; raised window for north light typical for artists' studios. From Twombly, 1979. Courtesy and © 2016 FLWF.	189
6.21	Bradley house living room as built in Kankakee, Illinois, 1900–01; tracing by FLW, probably using a pantograph and prepared for Wright, 1910.	192
8.1	"A plot of village property" for Col. N. Barrett near New Brighton on Staten Island, designed by William H. Ranlett, Architect, 1849. From Ranlett, 1849.	214
8.2	Plan of a major portion of Ladbroke Estate, or Notting Hill, Holland Park, London, 1851–63; six private public parks and two open public gardens are shown in this section of the up market real estate Ordinance Survey map of 1871.	215
8.3	"A Home in a Prairie Town," at top a "Perspective of Quadruple Block Plan" and plot plan for the four houses that was used for all Quadruple Block Plans to follow; perspectives and plans correspond. From Wright, 1901a.	217

xiv   *Illustrations*

8.4	Speculative housing for C. E. Roberts's city block in Ridgeland/Oak Park, Illinois, a project of 1902–03; top: perspective drawing of two houses with alternate fronts to street; bottom: ground- and second-floor plans of houses in the above drawing; the plans fit the left house orientation.	218
8.5	"A small house with lots of room in it" as published in the *Ladies Home Journal* of July 1901; the plan on left fits the perspective orientation; drawings as prepared for Wright, 1910.	219
8.6	"A Fireproof House for $5000" for the *Ladies Home Journal* of April 1907, drawings as prepared for Wright, 1910.	220
8.7	"Village of Bitter Root plan" project for a site north of Stevensville, Montana, for BRIVCo. Courtesy and © 2016 FLWF.	220
8.8	Typical gable-roofed house project for E. C. Waller for unknown sites, ca. 1908; also prepared for Bitter Root village in 1909; wood-batten siding. From Wright, 1910.	221
8.9	Quadruple Block Plan, 1910, with two orientations and erased perspective title; both sets of plans do not fit the perspective; author's notations; as presented in Wright, 1910; author's notations.	222
8.10	Quadruple Block Plan, 1915, with three options for house orientation; pans were redrawn and colored for Wright, 1916. From Levine 1916.	223
8.11	University Heights aerial perspective, 1909, detail of drawing by Marion L. Mahony. From Wright, 1910.	226
8.12	University Heights site plan, 1909, partially built west of Darby, Montana; author's notations. From Wright, 1910.	227
8.13	"Town of Bitter Root, Plan of Development," for a site just north of Stevensville, Montana of 1909; a project for BRVICo. Courtesy and © 2016 FLWF.	228
8.14	"Town of Bitter Root" plan for a site just north of Stevensville, Montana, 1909; a project for BRVICo. Author's notations.	229
8.15	Aerial perspective of "Village of Bitter Root" project; detail of a drawing by Marion L. Mahony in 1909. Courtesy and © 2016 FLWF.	231
8.16	Bitter Root town and village site plans superimposed showing existing conditions in the 1980s. Author's drawing.	232
8.17	"Non-competitive plan for development of quarter section of land competition," with "Key to Plan," as published in Yeomans, 1916.	237
8.18	Diagrams related to the design method applied to Wright's quarter-section plan in Figure 8.17. Author's drawings.	238
8.19	"Bird's-eye View of the Quarter-Section" of suburban land. From Yeomans, 1916.	239
8.20	"Workmen's Row Houses for Larkin Company, Buffalo, New York," 1904, later titled "Workmen's Cottages" for an expensive project for an E. C. Waller River Forest real estate development of 1906; three up, two down with basement. From Wright, 1910.	242
8.21	"Scheme of development" of a quarter-section designed by Dr A. C. Tenney in 1913, assisted by young Chicago architect Oscar B. Marienthal. From Yeomans, 1916.	244
8.22	"A City Area Developed on the 'Neighborhood Unit' Plan," area south of Chicago of a scheme for adjoining "Neighborhood Units" as designed by architect William E. Drummond in 1915. From Yeomans, 1916.	247
8.23	"Bird's-eye View of an Alternative Scheme for [Neighborhood] 'Unit' Development," by William E. Drummond; grey area for typical suburban houses. From Drummond, 1915.	248
8.24	Plan schematics of Wright's community designs from 1909–34; author's drawing.	251

Illustrations xv

Appendices 263

Appendix A Visual examination of geometries, no caption 265
Appendix B No illustration 266
Appendix C 267
  C1 Proposal for a house in Shingle or Queen Anne style with typical nearly-square floor plans of the 1880s, position of the stairs uniquely positioned. From Clark, 1986. 267
  C2 Smith house near Portland, Maine, by architect John Calvin Stevens, 1884–85; ground-floor plan a kin of C1, 3 and 4. Author's collection. 268
  C3 Sketches of ground-floor plans of Wright-designed houses, 1893–1909. All five ground designs for Roberts in 1896 would apply. Author's drawing. 269
  C4 J. G. Melson house in Mason City, Iowa, 1911, Walter Burley Griffin, Architect; ink-on-linen rendering by Marion Griffin in 1912. Author's collection, original in Mary and Leigh Block Museum of Art, Northwestern University. 271
  C5 Aerial perspective drawing of Quadruple "House" project for federal government housing in Pittsfield, Massachusetts, 1941–42. Courtesy and © 2016 FLWF. 274
  C6 Aerial perspective drawing of "Quadruple House" project called Cloverleaf; ground-floor plan lower left quadrant, "mezzanine" lower right, "penthouse" upper right, roof deck upper left; floor plans as prepared in 1941–42 for federal government housing in Pittsfield, Massachusetts. Courtesy and © 2016 FLWF. 275
  C7 "Quadruple Housing" projects for unknown sites, as published in Wright, 1958. Left: revised Quad Plan site plan without stables/garage, each unit to occupy one-half acre, image a reproduction of an original plan entitled "North Carolina Housing," Pfeiffer (51–59), plate 610. Courtesy and © 2016 FLWF. 276

Acknowledgements

An academic cannot satisfactorily conduct historical research without considerable help, not least that offered by many authors and scholars whose dissertations and published works have been a source of knowledge and inspiration to this historian. Many are identified in the references and notes herein. Additionally, it is with great pleasure and gratitude that I acknowledge the generosity, encouragement, or assistance of the following people and organizations.

Over the past three-and-one half decades this research project has been active, several people and organizations assisted in a variety of critical ways by responding to my research, commenting on drafts for books or articles, or assisting in practical ways. First, I'd like to thank Bruce Brooks Pfeiffer for his prodigious effort over six decades to discover and save the Wright papers and drawings. Bruce's work, a single-minded endeavor, preserved precious heritage knowledge for his contemporaries and future generations. He opened that heritage to this historian in the late 1970s. Recently, material artifacts and drawings were transferred to the Avery Architecture & Fine Arts Library at Columbia University in a joint arrangement with the Museum of Modern Art also in New York City. The FLW Foundation retains intellectual and other rights. In the late 1970s, I was granted access to the papers and drawings held in the Wright Archives in Scottsdale. I must also thank Bruce's activator Indira Berndtson, retired archive administrator of historic studies, and more lately Oskar Muñoz and Margo Stipe, each of whom have consistently supported my research.

From 1975 until my retirement in 1985, I received annual research and travel grants from the Flinders University Research Committee. These were supported by grants from the Australian Research Grants Commission, the Australia Council (Design Arts Board and Visual Arts Board), Washington State University's College of Engineering, and since 2001, by the University of South Australia. In 1990, I received a much-needed travel grant from the US National Endowment for the Humanities.

A special debt of gratitude is owed to William Allin Storer for his compilation and illustration of Wright's constructed buildings, herein Storrer 1993.

Ashgate Publishing, in particular publisher Valerie Rose, who in recent years supported my research by producing my book on Wright's *Concrete Adobe* of 2014. She then teased the typescript for this book to acceptance by Ashgate and then by its successor, Routledge where Kate Fornadel and her assistants were patient and professional.

I also must thank:

In Japan, the late Professor Hisiao Koyama, School of Architecture at University of Tokyo, host and counsel during a study visit.

In California, architect Eric Lloyd Wright for access to his and to his father's Lloyd Wright papers at the University of Southern California; Professor Lionel March in Los Angeles; the late architect Jon Lardner in Auburn; and the late Emeritus Professor David Gebhard and Dr Gerald and Marian Groff, each in Santa Barbara.

In New York, Rodney Gorme Obien and Kathleen M. DeLaney at the University Archives, University at Buffalo, for access to the Darwin Martin letters; staff at the Avery Library of Art and Architecture, Columbia University; and the late Edgar Kaufmann Jr.

In Washington State, the late Milton Stricker, Seattle architect and former student at Taliesin, for several interviews; professors J. William Rudd and Samuel Wayne Williams at the

Washington State University School of Architecture; Mrs Betty Wagner, now retired librarian (and my boss back in 1955–57) at the College of Architecture and Urban Planning, now Built Environment, at the University of Washington, Seattle.

In Illinois, Professor Paul Kruty at the University in Champaign, and Emeritus Professor Mati Maldre at Chicago State University.

In Montana, Dale Johnson, archivist in the Mansfield Library, University of Montana; Erma Owings, Henry Grant, and Glenn Wright in Hamilton; Leonard Melnarik, former owner of the University Heights ranch; Ted and Thelma Moody and Debbie Keep in Stevensville near the Bitter Root town site; architect Wally Roberts in Missoula; and William Lang, editor of *Montana*.

In Wisconsin, Rick Pifer and Lee Grady, archivists, and other staff at the Wisconsin Historical Society in Madison, and Emeritus Professor Paul Sprague, formerly at the University of Wisconsin in Milwaukee, now in Florida.

In Texas, Robert E. Fairbanks, University of Texas, Arlington, reader for *Perspectives in Planning*.

In Eliot, Maine, Rosanne Adams and Eric Christian.

In New Jersey, William Allen Storrer.

In Australia, for constant advice and criticism Professor Christopher Vernon at University of Western Australia; architect and historian Peter Freeman; the late Professor Peter Corkery, formerly at University of Adelaide, then University of Canberra; Professor Mads Gaardboe and the late Professor Donald Langmead; and photo and digital specialist Neville Eime in Blackwood, South Australia.

Architects and art, architecture, and planning historians who have read portions large or small of the typescript (other than many referees) and provided useful criticism and/or research direction on particular subjects: Professor Anthony Alofsin, University of Texas, Austin, read a complete early draft; Professor David Van Zanten, Northwestern University; the late Professor Peter Reyner Banham then at University of California at Santa Cruz; Professor Christopher Silver, University of Illinois; Professor Robert McCarter, then University of Florida, Gainsville, read a complete early draft; Professor Robert Freestone, University of New South Wales, Australia; Professor Emeritus Gilbert Herbert, Technion: Israel Institute of Technology, Haifa; Professor Christine Garnaut, University of South Australia; the late Professor Donald Langmead, University of South Australia; Dr Mervyn Miller, independent historian in Herts, England; Professor Richard A. Sundt, University of Oregon; Elisabeth Walton Potter, independent historian in Salem, Oregon; Professor Christopher Vernon, University of Western Australia, late University of Illinois; Professor Emeritus Samuel Wayne Williams, Washington State University; the late Professor Emeritus Norman J. Johnston, University of Washington, Seattle; Professor David Van Zanten, Northwestern University; and Dr Steve Harfield, University of Technology, Sydney.

My first visit to Chicago was in 1949 when on leave from the US Navy. My first visit as an architectural historian was in 1975 when studying the Griffins and Wright. I was ably and warmly assisted by Richard Twiss, Donald G. Kalec, and Tom Fauser.

Staff at the following institutions provided valuable assistance: Oak Park Library; National Library of Australia, Canberra; Art Institute of Chicago; Chicago Historical Society; Wisconsin Historical Society; Library of Congress, Washington, DC; the National Endowment for the Humanities for a travel grant; Getty Center for the History of Art and the Humanities in Santa Monica for facilitating Wright's letters; Flinders University for research grants, as well as the library, whose staff provided excellent service with much patience; Washington State University for research grants; the University of South Australia for varied and needed research assistance; the University of Washington's Department of Architecture for a visiting scholar appointment; Marriott Library, University of Utah; Northwestern University; archivists at the University of Minnesota; Special Collections at the University of Oregon; Bitter Root Valley Museum, Hamilton; Mansfield Library and Archives, University of Montana; Avery Architecture & Fine Arts Library, Columbia University; and the library and archivists at the University of California, Los Angeles.

Acknowledgements

Capable and good-humored research assistants in the early stages of activity were Elizabeth Beck, Alan Feeney now a historian, Bridget Jolly now a professional historian, Professor Christine Garnaut (née Smerdon) now director of the Architecture Museum at the University of South Australia, K. D. Pederson, Mary Gunn, the late Christine Finimore became a heritage advocate, and Anton Johnson now an architect. Assistance with translations was provided by Adelaidians Margaret Chong and Irena Pavlovo.

The comments of anonymous readers or concerned editors about relevant essays and solicited by *Architecture Australia*; *Journal of the Society of Architectural Historians* (United States); *Journal of the Planning Institute* (United States); *Journal of Architectural and Planning Research* (United States/United Kingdom); *Journal of Planning History* (United States); *Planning Perspectives* (United Kingdom); *Fabrications* (Melbourne); *Place* (Adelaide); *Columbia* (Tacoma); and *Pacific Northwest Quarterly* (Seattle) were most valuable, and I thank them for their objectivity.

A special thank you to the people and organizations that generously granted permission to reproduce illustrations and use quotations. They are identified in illustration captions and elsewhere as appropriate. And another special thanx to staff at Ashgate and Taylor and Francis who were involved in creating this book.

The content of this book remains my creation.

To Sonya Hasselberg, wife and weaver extraordinaire (retired), and to our sons Karl and Adam, thank you for all that is worthwhile.

Biography

Named Frank Lincoln Wright at birth, early public schooling was in Wisconsin and Massachusetts, and two courses at the University of Wisconsin (when he adopted the middle name of Lloyd) were followed by a part-time factotum/office job in Madison (1885–86). Wright then apprenticed to Chicago architect Joseph Lyman Silsbee (1887–88), followed by tenure with the architectural firm of Adler & Sullivan (1888–93). He established a private practice in Chicago/Oak Park (1893–1911), then in Spring Green/Madison on family farmland he called Taliesin (1910–59), and in 1939 in Scottsdale, Arizona, as a business-cum-residence known as Taliesin West. He operated temporary offices in Tokyo, Japan (1917–22), and in Los Angeles (1919–24). He and Henry Webster Tomlinson were partners during 1901–02, and later he acted occasionally in association with former employees. Wright married Catherine Lee Tobin in 1889 and then abandoned her and their five children in 1909 to live with Mrs Mamah Borthwick Cheney, who left her family. She and her children were murdered by a servant in 1914. Wright left his second wife Miriam Noel, a morphine addict, in 1924 for Olgivanna Milan Hinzenberg, and they married in 1928.

With the Depression and in urgent need of money, in 1932 Wright formed an apprentice program he called the Taliesin Fellowship. It continues as a professional practice and design school. Two sons became capable architects: (Frank) Lloyd Wright (Jr.) and John (Kenneth) Lloyd Wright. Wright Sr. received national and international honorary degrees, awards, and honors, including gold medals from the Royal Institute of British Architects in 1941 and the American Institute of Architects in 1949.

Five-foot, seven-inches tall, Wright was good looking, with a spare, almost slight, frame, and a deep, resonating voice. He was rather aloof, had a quick temper but a good sense of humor, and loved parties. John described his father as "obsessed" by a craving for greatness, possessing a "colossal ego" matched by a "towering ability."

> I seldom think of my father [John said] without recalling the picture of the vulnerable actor, who, whenever he hears a clap of thunder, strides majestically to the window and proceeds to take a bow. What distinguishes my father from the actor, however, is that even when Dad bows to thunderstorms, a horde of worshipful admirers invariably prostrate themselves before him and fill the air with a deafening applause.

Architectural historian Albert Bush-Brown prepared a eulogy in 1959 and assessed Wright justly, saying in part:

> In his assaults upon taste, Frank Lloyd Wright, the man of the magnificently delayed entrance, the blackthorn cane, the riverboat hat, the white suit, the black cape closed by a gold chain, was an arresting public accusation.... For men inured to committees, afraid to risk an autocratic decision, [Wright's] display of jaunty arrogance, of beguiling self-certainty, of cavalier disrespect, of unshakeable determination was the top showmanship of an idea in an age when publicity agents manufacture stars overnight.

Frank Lloyd Wright, 1867 (Richland Center, Wisconsin)–1959 (Madison, Wisconsin).

Preface

The motivation to undertake this study was a series of discoveries about Frank Lloyd Wright's architecture and community planning and the people and ideas that circled about the man before 1917, when he fidgeted about America while in Tokyo. The presentation is in part a test of Wright's theory that all aspects of human life must embrace and celebrate an aesthetical experience that will ipso facto lead to necessary social reformations. Inherent in that theory was a belief that reform of the gluttonous nineteenth-century city must include a modern interpretation of its material presence, its bulk and space, and its architecture and landscape. In the service of reform, a new aesthetic would provide a visual enhancement, perhaps a fundamental symbol for the new world and righteous nation, his architecture a catalyst.

The general tenants of Progressivism and the acts of reformation as they apply to cities and architecture from the 1890s through 1917 are introduced. Knitted to these is a presentation of Wright's singular thoughts about the city of his early manhood. Since he lived and practiced in the urban and suburban environment of Chicago, it is also necessary to introduce the place he experienced and studied, as well as the significant city planning proposals and events that could have invaded Wright's thoughts during the early developmental period of his career and the maturation of his designs (1892–1909).

That introductory theme is followed by studies of the elements that assembled in Wright's mind to form a theory about the aesthetics of progress and modernism. These included the enormous influence of radical educational theories and practices upon the Wright and Jones families and upon the people who were part of his familial, social, and professional life. (Misinterpretations of Froebelian kindergarten education are corrected.) This is followed by an attempt to tie the intellectual context of Wright's architecture to a strident middle-class society. As well, we look at the aesthetic inclinations that were central to the evolution of his singular designs. The idea of – and proposals for – a new, profoundly universal theory of architecture that drew upon the mysteries and pragmatics of geometry and the notion of the indigenous, as it might exemplify the nation, is analyzed as he put them into practice. Necessarily, then, we outline the design methodology applied to his domestic and non-domestic buildings and find reasons for the Wright School.

Recognizing that a universal design method could be of merit only if it was useful in all of his design activities, the third theme looks at his ideas for city planning, at the implications of historical and theoretical contexts of the period that might have influenced all of his community planning projects, and the use of geometry as a practical methodology. How they may or may not have affected Wright is intimately portrayed. At the same time, we discover perhaps the last hurrah of the Progressives' attempt to persuade the nation as to the value of rational contemporary design and find the one lasting contribution that resulted: the neighborhood unit.

This is a cross-disciplinary study whose components are aesthetics, architectonics, education, sociology, and history, all integrated by the rise of professional city planning. Architecture is an experiential design profession with vision the most critical sense, one relied upon during all phases of the design process; therefore, illustrations are essential evidence. I have visited many extant buildings, city, and community sites at least once during the past seven decades. The results of this research are necessarily condensed for publication.

Abbreviations and acronyms to notes and captions

AIA:	American Institute of Architects, Washington, DC
AForum:	*Architectural Forum*, New York
AmArchitect:	*American Architect and Building News*, Boston
AmCity:	*American City*, New York
ADesign:	*Architectural Design*, London
ARecord:	*Architectural Record*, New York
AReview:	*Architectural Review*, Boston and London
Avery Library:	Avery Architectural & Fine Arts Library, Columbia University
BRV:	Bitter Root Valley Historical Society, Hamilton, Montana
BRVICo:	Bitter Root Valley Irrigation Company
Burnham:	Ryerson and Burnham Libraries, Art Institute of Chicago
CityBull:	*Chicago City Club Bulletin*
DailyT:	*Chicago Tribune. Daily*
DLB:	*Dictionary of Literary Biography*
EandPB:	*Environment and Planning B*. New York/London
Fabrications:	*Fabrications: Journal of the Society of Architectural Historians, Australia and New Zealand*
FLW:	Frank Lloyd Wright
FLWF:	The Frank Lloyd Wright Foundation Archives. The Museum of Modern Art	Avery Architectural & Fine Arts Library, Columbia University, New York City
FLWNews:	*Frank Lloyd Wright Newsletter*, Chicago
HABS:	Historical American Buildings Survey, Library of Congress
Inland Architect:	*Inland Architect and Building News*, after 1887 *Inland Architect and News Record*, Chicago
JAE:	*Journal of Architectural Education*
JAIA:	*Journal of the American Institute of Architects*, later *AIA Journal*, now *Architect*, Washington D.C.
JAIP:	*Journal of the American Institute of Planners*, now *Journal of the American Planning Institute*, Philadelphia
JSAH:	*Journal of the Society of Architectural Historians*, Chicago
JUrban:	*Journal of Urban History*, Beverly Hills
MIT:	Massachusetts Institute of Technology, Cambridge
NMReview:	*National Municipal Review*, Boston
Northwest Archives:	Northwestern Architectural Archives, University of Minnesota, St Paul
Perspecta:	*The Yale Architectural Journal*, New Haven
Purcell papers:	William G. Purcell Papers, 1919–64. Special Collections, University of Oregon Library
PSR:	*Prairie School Review*, Chicago
RecordH:	*Chicago Record-Herald*
SundayT:	*Chicago Tribune. Sunday*
TownPR:	*Town Planning Review*, Liverpool

xxii *Abbreviations and acronyms to notes and captions*

WArchitect:	*Western Architect.* Minneapolis
WHistory:	*Wisconsin Magazine of History*, Madison
Willcox papers:	W.R.B. Willcox Collection, Special Collections, University of Oregon
Woolley Collection:	Taylor Woolley Collection, Marriott Library, University of Utah
Wright Archives:	The Frank Lloyd Wright Foundation Archives, Scottsdale, Arizona, and The Getty Center for the History of Art and the Humanities, History of Art Archives, Santa Monica, California
WrightJr:	Lloyd Wright Papers, Library, University of California Los Angeles.

Conditions

1 Reformation and progressivism

Americans were unaccustomed to urbanization, collectively ill prepared, and many were philosophically opposed to cities. Cities confined people physically while being morally stretched. In the countryside, they were free to action and movement and thought. At least 90 percent of the country's five million Euro American population lived on farms in the year Thomas Jefferson assumed the presidency. By the 1910s, or about 120 years later, the figure was 30 percent, in the 1990s, less than 2 percent. In the absence of social stability, common decency, and legal controls after the Civil War, municipal and commercial corruption became entrenched, political indiscretion de rigueur well before the 1890s, rampant by that decade. That was when Wright launched his independent professional career.

Post-Civil War America optimistically accepted the promise and the means of the industrial revolution as advanced by English enterprise. Americans improved their agriculture, manufacture, and commerce with new engineering technologies and then, on the monetary profits of their extraordinary achievements, the nouveau riche gorged themselves. As observers if not eager participants, Hartford, Connecticut, neighbors Mark Twain and Charles Dudley Warner lampooned the nation's post-Civil War Reconstruction extravagance, dissipation, and gaudy display in a 1873 satirical novel titled *The Gilded Age: A Tale of Today*. Historian Leon Fink observed that . . .

> The Gilded Age, in short, identified a period of rapid economic advance simultaneously associated with shady practices in business and politics. The term *Progressive Era*, in contrast, initially summoned up more positive associations. *Progressive* – a label that urban, middle-class reformers applied to themselves (in preference to *liberal*, *populist*, or *socialist*) in the first decade of the twentieth century – evoked, at least to its defenders, a beneficent and rational reckoning with the excesses of the Gilded Age.[1]

It was America's Gilded Age, *not* British Victorian! It was America's glitter, gorge, and venality.

Born into liberal-minded families, Frank Lincoln Wright was raised during those specious years. He began as a professional architect when various urban reform activities at local and national levels reactively attained urgency and momentum. Twenty five or so years later, he abandoned America to live in Japan, just as the United States sent soldiers to engage in Europe's new family war and just when progressivism's activities had slowed after an initial energetic burst that led to local and national successes. During the intervening personally turbulent years, Wright moved in circles within circles of educationalists, controversialists, socialists, laborites, social workers, communists, novelists, artists, businessmen, Transcendentalists, Social Gospelers, individualists, pragmatists, and other relativists – but especially those committed to excising plutocratic influence, deflating incompetent politicians, reforming city management, and step-by-step improving city life.

The purpose of this book is to present evidence of an aesthetic component to varied transformation programs as advanced by the progressives before 1909, progressive or not, and in which Wright was involved, positively or negatively but mostly passively. Yet,

> because he chose to live a very public life and desperately reached for national and international attention and acclaim (timid, diffident, shy, and fainthearted he was not);

> because he sought an aesthetic resolution to each activity or problem faced and argued rational reasons for artistic expression, his life totally committed to design and art;
> because architecture is a design discipline intimately – almost exclusively – dependent upon society and not a private enterprise or merely an aesthetic object;
> because he created a new architecture, the Wright Style, and it and he were thought to be both radical and progressive; and
> because he engaged in community and city planning and then discoursed on American life, politics, freedoms, economics, and urbanism,

Wright is a wonderful subject for a study of an atypical yet highly public person engaged in the liberal milieu before 1917. He is the catalyst to understanding architectural reforms and the Progressives' city. Therefore, social, city, and architectural histories, as well as design theory and biography, are essential disciplines. Therein are found his creative acts that directed architecture as essential to the artistic revolution that composed one critical component of the Progressives' understanding of cities.

But at the outset, it is important to remember that North Americans were living different phases of civilization. A glaringly high contrast between the co-inhabiting civilizations was marked by episodic violence and epidemic disease. There existed a zone of ethnic and social change, of conflict: incursive to aboriginals, to Euro Americans an advancing frontier; to both lawless. The fullest example was played out during Christmas week in 1890. The last major armed conflict between Native Americans, the traditional landowners, and the US Army was a massacre of 250 Indian women, children, and men beside Wounded Knee Creek. This outrage occurred while Wright was comfortably living with his bride in fashionable Oak Park and conducting soirees, musicals, and kindergartens while helping architects Adler and Sullivan produce designs for large theaters and commercial structures, while he smoked cigars in a men's club, when the company town of Pullman was designed, when rail lines continued to dissect the continental wilderness, when Chicago was chosen to host the World's Colombian Exposition to celebrate Columbus's landings in the West Indies, and while immigrants and laborers battled the politicians' and plutocrats' police in Chicago's factories and on its streets. Yet the last decade of the nineteenth century saw the beginning of two decades . . .

> [of] one of the greatest outpourings of social reform . . . anchored in an environmentalism that assumed a range of forms, including regulating and demolishing slims, building parks and planting trees, devising Beaux Arts city plans, and protecting historic buildings. All were efforts to build . . . [a] rhetoric that all parts of society were bound together – into the landscape of the city . . .[2]

It was natural that architects who held such beliefs would band together.

The Architectural League of America was highly attractive to a minority of professionals, young in age or heart, in centers of the industrial belt from Boston and Chicago to Kansas City and St Louis. Those architects first met at a national convention in Cleveland in 1899 where they shared disappointments with the profession's response to a new technological America, where they expressed deeply felt concerns about the manner of professional development generally, and where they worried about the antique European building styles tendered by elder architects and their clients to a hurriedly modernizing nation.

At the moment when the foundations of Progressivism were being laid, at their second convention in 1900, League members adopted the motto "Progress before Precedent." The motto signaled the intention of those present to reject hegemonic precedents, those antiquated styles, and search for an architecture responsive to and expressive of modern America. The League also considered the devilish problems of a compacting urbanization, and many members became committed reformers. In that pursuit, they suggested the appealing notion that professional efforts should pursue roles both educative and curative.

Wright supported the League and may have assisted in outlining the reformers' intellectual position. Willfully, he then carry on without – or in spite of – them. While energetically developing a high-profile professional presence locally, he became involved in diverse ways with radicals, reformists, and artists who were dedicated to humanizing the city, the workplace, and domestic life. Some were attracted to his reiteration of the proposition that good design demanded an interior functional and philosophical motivation, although less interested in social content. It was in alignment with Progressivism's general position that rejected the dominance of the historicism and vagaries of traditionalism. Wright offered buildings as revolutionary models for society's aesthetic expression. His contribution was a new rationalized design vocabulary that provided a language for, a direction to, a share in those very contemporary desires.

A divided, quickly changing, and highly distressed and despoiled urban society during the three decades before 1900 is grist for critical and theoretical mills targeted by reformist actions. The concern herein, however, is not to present the general urban malaise caused by centralization of industry and commerce, or to rephrase the philosophies that arose as attempts to understand the crises and seeming contradictions, or to reconstruct the urges for reform and the rise of Progressivism. All that has been adequately described and assessed by many others. Unfortunately, they almost always avoided architecture, the city, and other non-literary arts. And they ignored – or, more often than not, misunderstood – Wright's position, at least as publicly presented.

This interdisciplinary pursuit, therefore, focuses on the foundations of his early social, professional, and design experiences during the ferment caused by Americans redefining their culture and intellect, as well as the ideas, contemporary conditions, and personal and professional encounters that influenced Wright's ego and teased his intellectuality as internal to his singular contributions before 1917, when he eschewed an American life for the exotic in Japan.

Clearly, architecture is not a private venture but a social one. It is designed by those within society using a process that is nonetheless both personal and composite. Architects have natural or learned talents, are composed of certain psychological propensities, and react to the full array of environmental conditions in search of an aesthetic response. By their thousands, people use and encounter encounter buildings. As taken from Vitruvius, the words of Henry Wotton in 1624 hold true today:

> In Architecture as in all
> other *Operative* Arts, the
> *end* must direct the *Operation*.
>   *The* end *is to build well*.
> *Well building hath three Conditions*.
> Commoditie, Firmenes, *and* Delight.
>
> – Henry Wotton, as he set them out in
> *The elements of architecture, collected from the best
> authors and examples* (London: John Bill, 1624)

"So too the city!" cried urban reformers.

At the time of the Revolutionary War progress meant happiness. Around the 1890s, and sharing something with the mystical, it was asserted . . .

> that the drive to fulfill human needs alone had power and right to determine truth. At once blatant yet subtle, this was the crux of all revolts against formalism, positivism, and classicism – truth was no fixed absolute, but that which met current human and social need.[3]

Plutocrats had consistently and utterly failed to motivate let alone to provide for "human needs." Shunning conservative resistance to the patently obvious, reformers used progress as an operative word around which American social and political liberals rallied in the cause of improving the human condition, mainly for urbanites.

An agrarian nation before the Civil War, the United States of America was industrially well behind England. But the North's – the Union's – ability to devise and increase the manufacture of products in support of the Civil War was catalytic to future economic success. Postwar America quickly became a creatively endowed industrial power internationally, and soon a competitive exporter of agricultural products. Those developments induced concomitant efficiencies that led to a centralization of production activities and working personnel that in time became dense urban conglomerations bursting with people (by a wide majority they were farm or foreign immigrants – more than one-third of Chicago's population were born overseas),[4] who were coping desperately with immense physical changes that fostered a bevy of psychological, social, technical, and intellectual consequences. Moreover, established residents . . .

> were depressed by the anonymity of the city, confused by its crowding and its noise, astonished and repelled by the blatant exhibition of extremes of wealth and poverty, angered by vice and crime and corruption, ill-concealed, often jubilantly paraded. All this they blamed on the alien and "idolatrous" newcomers.[5]

In rescue, people offered a strange panacea of selfishly motivated advice or ascetic refuge or religious escape or philosophical rationalization, while a few absorbed the shocks and cleverly played the situations.

Historian E. A. Gutkind studied that coarse phenomenon and resolve and said in part that a "confused disunity" led to the ascendancy of "two different lines of action". . .

> there was the line followed by [those] sincerely searching for . . . new and humane solutions . . . This line led reformers to a serious though somewhat confused examination of the existing problems and to suggestions of possible remedies. . . . The other line followed by . . . [those] apostles of laissez-fair, the speculators and industrialists, originated in the vast desert of moral insensibility and dreams of wealth . . . and ended in standardized slums. [In short,] There were [therefore] the dreamers without means but with humanitarian goals, and the realists without social goals but with the means.[6]

Slowly and hesitantly, a few took their intellectual capabilities and moral convictions and, embracing American pragmatism, molded them into a practical response for betterment. Increasingly, therefore, there were reactive gestures to quantify technological problems (like sanitation, water, clean air, rail and road), to seek operable principles for human urban habitation, and to apply the newly described scientific management: Taylorism to some. As for housing, the growing influence of a mix not of the Garden City but of garden suburbs and company towns as set out in England, as well as the concept of zoning laws from Germany, were valuable resources.

Yet, during the two decades before 1914, the only significant attempt to physically rehabilitate American cities was directed not at relieving social evils or physical malformations but at raising grand municipal palaces and places for political pomp and commercial aggrandizement. Cunningly, not for cities comfortable, the guise was for cities beautiful.

Conditions

The preamble to the People's – or more commonly – Populist party platform for the nation's 1892 presidential election was an emotional yet concise summary of reactions to common problems. Targeting economics and morality, it said in part:

> We meet in the midst of a nation brought to the verge of moral, political, and material ruin. Corruption dominates the ballot-box, the legislatures, the [US] Congress, and touches even

the ermine of the bench. The people are demoralized; . . . public opinion silenced; business prostrated; our homes covered with mortgages; labor impoverished; and the land concentrating in the hands of the capitalists. . . . The fruits of the toil of millions are boldly stolen to build up colossal fortunes . . . while their possessors despise the republic and endanger liberty. . . .[7]

Initially, Populists came from the ranks of farmers, ranchers, and country people who had suffered declining produce prices, overproduction of acreage gained by westward colonization, improved transport, and competition with producers worldwide. The majority of homesteaders soon returned to cities but not the Jones family.

Frank Wright's paternal family emigrated from England to Connecticut in the 1600s and became successful farmers and Baptist ministers in the Northeast. Other than sparse information about his father, the Wright family was autobiographically ignored by Frank. His maternal family, the Joneses, were also emigrants, farmers, and Unitarians from Wales who, in the 1850s, settled on undulating prairies west-southwest of Madison, Wisconsin. The subject of farming by four of his mother's brothers, the drudgery of farming, and hard-won teenage joys occupy a few pages of Wright's 1932 autobiography.[8] Frank claimed that the Joneses had a "family crest, the old Druid symbol," composed of three bold vertical lines. Not old or valid, it was published in an eighteenth-century book of purported Druidic philosophy that was soon found in fact to be spurious.[9]

The Jones family's farms prospered until foundering in the 1890s under the weight of bad debts as a result of poor management. Wright's younger sister Maginel remembered that "in 1890 a farmer could get fifty cents a bushel for corn; in 1898 he was lucky to get a quarter [25¢]." Her uncles blamed the intricacies of "something Washington called the 'foreign market'."[10] Indeed, America's devastating 1893 financial collapse seriously entangled world markets. Uncle John Jones "was a Republican of the staunchest Republicans and later," likely when the Populists and Democrats "fused" for the 1896 national election, John Jones "loathed" presidential candidate William Jennings Bryan.[11] With Bryan's defeat, the *New York Tribune* proffered the establishment's and plutocrat's joy: "Good riddance . . . to the foul menace of repudiation and Anarchy against the honor and life of the Republic."[12] But social disharmony and the pros and cons of politics pre-1927 never attracts Wright's autobiographical utterances.

Historian Howard Zinn outlined the dissenter's fundamental problem, one initially put by Charles Beard, that the Constitution was constructed such that "the purpose of the state was to settle upper-class disputes peacefully, control lower-class rebellion, and adopt policies that would further the long-range stability of the system."[13] An active voice of dissension and for correction was Populism, described as "the greatest agrarian movement the nation" had or would know.[14] It was seen by historian Richard Hofstadter as culminating the first episode of reformation prior to the 1960s. The following two were the Progressive Era from 1900–17 and President F. D. Roosevelt's useful New Deal in the 1930s.[15]

The National Grange was organized in the early 1870s. By 1875, there were eight hundred thousand members possessed by a desire to cast off the "tyranny of monopoly" and oligopoly. The Grangers also attempted to bypass distributing systems, such as rail, by establishing buying and selling cooperatives. (The Chicago-based Montgomery Ward mail order company promoted itself in the 1870s as "The Original Wholesale Grange Supply House.") Soon, the Farmers' Alliance assumed ascendancy over the rather inefficient Grangers and became considerably more active. The Alliance managed to unite groups, first in the South and then on midwestern prairies, into a political coalition that evolved into the Populist Party in 1892. Wright's close friend and confidant, the author Hamlin Garland, dedicated his 1891 novel *Jason Edwards*, about a disillusioned sod buster, to the Farmers' Alliance. Wright's farming uncles likely participated in the local Grange and certainly were aware of the Populist platform. It included several planks in support of urban labor (eight-hour workday and restricted immigration), greater democracy (direct election of senators, direct primaries, referendum, the initiative, the secret or Australian ballot), and the endorsement of a graduated income tax. Conservatives labeled these liberal "fantasies."

8   *Conditions*

Populism was a movement directed to solving issues related mainly to the business of farming, its philosophical roots pragmatic.[16] The progressive agenda was philosophical, social, political, and urban, and therein resides the difference to – and extension of – Populism. Progressives took on many of the Populist's programs that were implemented over succeeding decades, some as late as Roosevelt's New Deal in the 1930s. But government, social, and economic reforms had yet to be confronted, let alone rationalized, by 1900.

Progressivism was within one side of what Henry Steele Commager described as "The Watershed of the Nineties." On one side of the 1890s "lies an America predominantly agricultural. . . . On the other side lies the modern America, predominantly urban and industrial. . . ."[17] The Progressive Movement, Hofstadter said,

> may be looked upon as an attempt to develop the moral will, the intellectual insight, and the political and administrative agencies to remedy the accumulated evils and negligence of a period of industrial growth.[18]

Progressives were not combative revolutionaries. Rather – and as much as Fabians advocated an integration of socialist programs – Progressive strategies were for an "orderly social change" and a resolve to work within the existing political framework.[19] Their agenda was radical in the true sense of the word – to roots and origins and to fundamentals.

Reformers were most often middle incomers, Protestant or Jewish (Catholics and others looked inward), young professionals, and independent women who, among a multitude of concerns, sought "to humanize the modern city," to improve housing and schools, and to "provide a better life for the poor and recent immigrants."[20] Progressive coalitions reached widely, even to naturalists. In Chicago, a Special Park Commission was formed in 1899. Its 1904 report to city council, prepared by architect Dwight Perkins, called for greenbelts, forest preserves, native wilderness areas beyond the margins of suburbia, linked parkways, and small neighborhood parks and playgrounds. The commission was composed of bureaucrats, lawyers, landscape and building architects, civil and sanitary engineers, medics, sociologists, and settlement house people. Together with housewives, politicians, artists, teachers, and more, they formed associations and participated in lectures and walks in local and distant native landscapes and forests and worked to preserve them.[21] But indigenous native people, the Indians, were another matter, still seen as a hindrance to America's expansive ambitions and to the "national interest."

The variety of coalitions can be measured by implication in contemporary texts. In his book *The Progressive Movement*, contemporary observer Benjamin Parke de Witt, a lawyer, identified Progressive concerns in politics: corporate control; government control; nomination and election of officials; the initiative, referendum, and recall; and relieving social and economic distress.[22] When Charles A. Beard reviewed de Witt's book, he thought it revealed "the presence of a new ideal in city politics, a determination of the people that the city shall be a clean, healthful, safe, and beautiful place," and it offered an "abiding revolution in American civic standards."[23]

Beard was committed to that "abiding revolution." It was he who warned Americans that governments were not neutral, that they curried to dominant economic interests. An academic economic historian who was also involved practically with the liberal National Municipal League, Beard contributed to its *National Municipal Review* by reporting and analyzing all aspects of Progressive and reform programs and activities related to urbanization, including those blunted by plutocrats and their politicians. First published in 1912, the *Review*'s informative role offered Canadians and Americans solutions to shared troubles and reform activities.

In a 1912 book titled *American City Government*, Beard set out his reading of the Progressives's aspirations.[24] He also outlined the varied *practical* applications made in the previous ten or so years, together with arguments for future resolutions.[25] Beard rounded comments with tentative observations about city planning's synthetic role. Here, the text was influenced by the writings of landscape architect and city planner Frederick Law Olmsted Jr., as well as by Beard's other friends in New York, architect Benjamin Marsh and housing advocate George

B. Ford.[26] "No city begins to be well planned until it has solved its housing problems," Ford had said. Housing was Wright's principal activity.

Even with vigorous opposition by conservatives and protagonists on the political right, by 1915, therefore, and in the words of longtime student of the movement Otis Pease, progressive reformers had...

> probed city slums and had forcibly exposed middle-class Americans to the poverty they found there. They had secured laws to improve the worst conditions of working-class life. They had founded and managed settlement houses and were training the next generation to manage the rudiments of a welfare state. They had induced their fellow citizens to clean up prisons, asylums, and hospitals, and to transform the schools.... [T]hey had taken the lead in reforming the tax structure, riding herd on public utilities and insurance companies, establishing standards of industrial safety and public health, prohibiting child labor, and regulating the conditions of employment for women....
>
> [S]cores of cities [had gained a] degree of legal and political independence from state legislatures... [and] established direct primaries, the popular election of United States senators, and the right of individual citizens to initiate or to disapprove legislation....

Contrary to Jeffersonian tradition, "the Progressive reformers," Pease continued, "were the first Americans to examine the city with both a clear-eyed realism and an enthusiasm for its values and its promises."[27] They shared Frederick C. Howe's vision in 1905 of the city as "the hope of democracy."[28] Wright may have read Howe when, in 1918, he paraphrased "if instead of the expedients of the business men drugged by commercialism we would cling to the practical and to principle, the great hope: democracy...."[29] If he knew Howe, he knew Beard, if only secondhand.

In greater or lesser ways, Wright and his immediate families were involved not with the many reform or Progressive organizations – he and they were not joiners – but in independent contact and action with those people. It was a cultivated association activated during familial social or educational activities or professional engagements.

Societal lessons

During the 1890s, when Wright was attentive to the political ructions of Populists and urban anarchists, the articulate politician William Jennings Bryan succinctly put one pragmatic reality of America's rural contribution: "Burn down your cities and leave our farms, and your cities will grow again as if by magic, but destroy our farms and grass will grow in the streets of every city in the country."[30] In spite of Uncle John's feelings, Wright had attended Bryan's Chicago public lectures.[31] As late as the 1930s, Wright borrowed from Bryan to predict that grass would grow on city streets because people would rush to his decentralized Broadacre villages. And in his Kahn lectures at Princeton University in 1930, Wright reiterated a long-held view when he said with Jeffersonian fervor: "Ruralism as distinguished from Urbanism is American, and truly Democratic." Ruralized instincts pervaded his philosophic queries and pronouncements and even supported what had become a faded Progressivism in agrarian Wisconsin. In 1932, for instance, Wright observed that "The name of La Follette distinguishes our [Wisconsin's] political history.... And I too always speak of Wisconsin as 'progressive'.... Not understanding very well just what the word means...."[32] He feigned ignorance of Progressivism. The opposite was made obvious by the examples of his long friendship with the La Follette family, realist authors like Hamlin Garland and Zona Gale, and social workers and political activists such as Florence Kelley or others at Ellen Starr and Jane Addam's Hull-House; of a sturdy acquaintanceship with Charlotte Gilman and Henry Demarest Lloyd; of association with other Progressive architects, Chicago City clubbers, and Progressive educational its; and of appreciating John Dewey, Henry George, Thomas Carlyle, Peter Kropotkin, and Herbert Spencer, among other diverse thinkers.

Wisconsin was a leader in state and municipal reform before 1917. Under Governor Robert La Follette and his successors, the state established a railroad commission, direct primaries, a state income tax, measures to distribute the tax burden, a pure-food law, and a corrupt-practices act. These and other reforms were called the Wisconsin Idea and were soon taken on by a few other states. Editorially, the Milwaukee *Journal* said conservatives "fight socialism blindly . . . while Progressives fight it intelligently and seek to remedy the abuses and conditions upon which it thrives."[33] La Follette was a known champion of labor, conserving natural resources, and agricultural relief, and he was against monopolies and child labor.

La Follette Senior's sons attended Wright's aunts' Hillside Home School. Son Philip was Wright's attorney beginning in 1927, acting for Wright, Inc. And Robert, along with Zona Gale, Jane Addams, and Wright's uncle, Reverend Jenkin Jones, were active passivists and joined Henry Ford's peace crusade against entering the first World War. Robert's first son, "Young Bob," became a US senator, and Philip succeeded to the governorship of Wisconsin. After breaking from the Republican party, the sons established a state Progressive party and were reelected in 1934.[34] Sherman Booth, Wright's lawyer after returning from Europe and also a client, was raised in a family dedicated to Progressive activities. He and his wife Elizabeth were likewise committed, she a suffragette.

However, those closest to Wright were few and most often clients. "E.C. Waller, Arthur Heurtley, and Hamlin Garland – these are the men who are his [Wright's] friends," said wife Catherine in 1909, adding, "They know his makeup, his disposition, what he had to contend with."[35] Edward Carson Waller was a prominent Chicago real estate developer. From Kentucky, Waller settled in Chicago in 1860 and later cofounded the Central Safety Deposit Company. It built the tall Home Insurance and old Tacoma buildings, two of Chicago's earliest skyscrapers. Waller was Wright's client for more than twenty years, and Waller Jr. was a commissioner of Midway Gardens in 1913, one of Wright's most important buildings. If we include The Rookery office building of which Waller was director and fostered Wright's employment to renovate the lobby interior in 1905, as well as the Cheltenham Beach and Wolf Lake resort projects, at least fourteen commissions are known, a few of major significance: eight were built.[36]

One job was an experiment in model apartments for low-income families that began with Wright's design in early 1895 for Waller Apartments. Planning concentration was on a minimally sized living unit and low construction costs. It was planned as five contiguous units, each containing four one-bedroom apartments. Not a wholly philanthropic venture, Waller expected no more than a 3.5 percent return. External ornament was limited to creative patterns of exterior brickwork: "faced in light yellow-buff face brick with matching terra cotta and grey Bedford limestone trim . . . as sills, string courses, mullion bases, and capitals, and exterior staircases."[37]

Satisfied by the results of the Waller Apartments, Wright was engaged in October 1895 to design an adjacent and much larger apartment block as an addition to the earlier apartments called Francisco Terrace. Then, in 1901, Wright and Waller began planning another larger apartment block known as Lexington Terrace. They worked on the project until 1909, when it was abandoned. These commissions were Wright's first and most successful foray into workers' housing.

Boston-born Arthur B. Heurtley moved to Chicago in 1881 and became secretary of Northern Trust Company, an office he held from 1889–1920. *Oak Leaves* newspaper described Heurtley as "one of Oak Park's most prominent citizens." Like Wright, he was a member of Cliff Dwellers, likely because of the family's "interest in music and the other arts and distinguished artists frequently were their guests."[38] He asked Wright to design what became an interesting two-story house unique in Wright's oeuvre, as well as a summer cottage, both in 1902.

After life in Wisconsin, then Iowa, South Dakota, and Massachusetts, in 1893, Hannibal Hamlin Garland settled in Chicago and soon became one of Wright's closest friends, sharing interests in Indian culture, the colonized West, "the hot and dusty" prairie, and city life. When introduced to readers of *The Craftsman* magazine, Garland was described as "a loyal friend by the Indians."[39] While living in Boston, Garland joined the Anti-Poverty Society, made up of George followers, and began "forming" in his mind "two great literary concepts: that truth was a higher quality than beauty . . . and that to spread the reign of justice should everywhere be the design and intent of the artist."[40] Beauty resides in truth. In Chicago and after, Garland wrote stories and novels mainly about "the barrenness and futility of western farm life" and conditions of the "weary poor" that enjoined the Populist revolt. Garland was a radical individualist whose works reflected . . .

> the most vital intellectual, social, and aesthetic ideas of his time, responding as a zealous reformer to such issues as the rise of Populism, [George's] single tax, Indian rights, the struggle for woman's rights, and evolution; and to such artistic [literary] concepts as local color [or regionalism] and impressionism.[41]

Garland's causes, dedications, and philosophic yearnings were in close conjunction with Wright's. They also shared artistic discourse and celebrity, often at the Cliff Dwellers, a club started by Garland and whose name he took from Henry Blake Fuller's 1893 novel *The Cliff Dwellers*. Garland described its membership as including "most of the leading painters, sculptors, architects, musicians and literary men of the middle West."[42] On one occasion in 1908, Wright, a charter member, "inaugurated a program of events" held at Oak Park's new Unity Church, just completed to his design. He "organized and hosted an evening" attended mostly by members of Cliff Dwellers and open to the local community. Titled "A Symposium of Art,"

> Wright had invited the sculptor Lorado Taft, the poet William Guthrie; the conductor of the Chicago Symphony Orchestra, Frederic W. Stock; the actor Donald Robertson, the newspaper editor Wallace Rice; the German musician Ferdinand Steindel, the painter Charles Francis Brown; . . . choral [director] Clarence Dickinson; and author Hamlin Garland. The evening conveyed Chicago's role as a regional center for the arts. . . .[43]

The 1880s and 1890s witnessed a great output of novels, not just Garland's, about the calamities of industrialized commercial life.[44] Zona Gale was among them.

After returning from Japan in 1922, Wright visited Gale often. He found her "like something exquisitely carved out of ivory," a woman he "just didn't know how to make love to." Moreover, "I hated her environment [her new house a Georgian 'columnar village-palazzo'] as utterly unworthy of her . . . I hadn't met Olgivanna and I thought Taliesin would be a much more appropriate place for the author."[45] But he said nothing about her ideas. Gale was a friend of Wright's mother and her teaching sisters and for shared reasons. Gale vigorously supported causes of pacifism, social welfare (the General Federation of Women's Clubs),[46] women's suffrage, ethic equality, educational reform, political Progressivism (stating in 1936, "I have been a progressive since Progressivism was born"),[47] and fighting for Robert La Follette's programs. In 1913, she wrote *Civic Improvements in the Little Towns*. In 1923, she helped draft the Wisconsin Equal Rights Law and also that year was appointed a regent of the University of Wisconsin. Gale's play *Miss Lulu Bett* (from her book *Lulu Bett*) won the 1921 Pulitzer Prize and was made into a movie by Paramount.

In the 1920s, Gale studied orientalism and mysticism through Gandhi, Rabindranath Tagore, H. P. Blavatsky, and Georgi Gurdjieff. Englishman A. R. Orage (an active acolyte of Gurdjieff) visited Gale in her hometown of Portage, Wisconsin, where a small colony of followers camped in the early 1920s (perhaps 1924) for a "Gurdjieff experience."[48] Wright's third wife Olgivanna was a teacher with Gurdjieff at the time they first met in Chicago in the autumn of 1924. Orage, Gurdjieff, Gale, the Hartmanns, and other Gurdjieff followers were houseguests of the Wrights post-1928.

Influenced by the Social Gospel theology of Wright's uncle, Reverend Jones, the more rational proposals of Kropotkin, and the theosophy of architect Claude Bragdon, Gale promoted the good works of longtime friends, including the socialist and labor advocate Florence Kelley and the humanist Jane Addams. In 1914, Gale promoted a new Spring Green Women's Club building designed by Wright. She was accompanied by California anarchist and leading feminist theorist Charlotte Perkins Gilman.[49] On occasion, the two women participated in Reverend Jones's Tower Hill summer camp devoted to religion and social issues. In her introduction to Gilman's autobiography, Gale described her as "one of the great women of the" century."[50] Gilman visited Wright and Mamah Cheney "a couple of times" early in 1914[51] and Wright in the early 1920s. With Addams, Wright's uncle, Reverend Jones, industrialist Henry Ford, and many others, Gilman was a founder of the Woman's Peace Party in 1915.[52]

Abandoning their families, Wright and Mrs Mamah Cheney had fled to Europe in 1909. After returning to Spring Green in 1911, they continued to live together until her murder in September 1914.[53] Among other philosophic reasons for their publicly expressed lifestyle, Frank and Mamah pleaded a right to free association as argued in the writings of Kropotkin and Ellen Key of Sweden; Mamah met Key in 1910 in Paris. Although they disliked the particulars of one another's views, there was a similarity in Gilman's, Key's, and Mamah's ideas, particularly about the evil of gender bias and social inequality, if not on methods to achieve liberation.[54]

While fictional literature came to realism, photography began with realism, the lens innocently transmitting to film the light before its lens: we need only reflect on Matthew B. Brady's disturbing but visually accurate record of the Civil War. In the late nineteenth century, however, there was a strong movement, satisfying the socially dependent, to imitate "fine art," eschewing the potential of photography as a new art medium. The photographic picture appeared truthful (could the lens deceive?) and therefore became a potent weapon in the war to expose degradations of farm, industrial, and urban life. Photographer Alfred Stieglitz and his wife, the painter Georgia O'Keeffe, were certain that realism was both evidence and art. While O'Keeffe is fawned over, Stieglitz too often is ignored. Critic William Wasserstrom measured the man . . .

> In 1903 Alfred Stieglitz, a man of prodigious power over taste and style not only in photography but also in American painting, drama, and fiction, opened his Photo-Secession Gallery [on 5th avenue, New York City] in order to present works of art that displayed his vision of an "integral society." Stieglitz was certain that American culture would fulfill Whitman's prophecies, would become a "dynamic, organic whole," only when the nation as a whole took its inspiration from a properly accomplished "communal, creative movement" in the arts.[55]

Paintings and small sculptures by European and American modernists shared display space with photography in what in 1905 became Gallery 291.[56] Sharing similar ideas about the role of the arts in society, the two New Yorkers and Wright became friends, likely before the 1920s. O'Keeffe was born and raised in Wisconsin, schooled in Madison, and studied at the Art Institute of Chicago (1905–06) and in New York with Arthur Wesley Dow (1914–15). Years later, O'Keeffe presented one of her oil paintings to Wright.[57]

Of the more popular literary observers, Wright's son John has recounted at some length how "Papa liked to read 'Mr. Dooley' " to the family and Papa would "go into convulsions." Irish Chicago saloon keeper Dooley was the fictional creation of Finley Dunne, a Chicago newspaperman. His Dooley short stories were popular throughout the nation from 1893 to ca. 1908. Mr. Dooley . . .

> shared the reformer's view of the privileged plutocrat ('Niver steal a dure-mat. Iv ye do, ye'll be invistigated, hanged, an' mabe rayformed. Steal a bank, me boy, steal a bank') and the cynic's view of the reformer.[58]

John quoted extensively from Dooley's exposition on "Life at Newport," Rhode Island (" 'Tis the socyal capital iv America . . . Tis like wash'nton, on'y it costs more' ").[59] Mr. Dooley's mixed feelings about reform were conveyed to a friend in these words: "Rayformers, Hinnissy, is in favor iv suppressin' ivryting, but rale pollyticians believes in suppressin' nawthin' but ividence."[60] Dunne was a cynical observer, not a muckraker.

Muckrakers were those who raked up the mud and muck of plutocrats and told readers what was exposed. Now referred to as investigative journalists, muckrakers and their publishers introduced what historian Richard Hofstadter described as a "Revolution in Journalism." The progressive mind, he said with utter clarity,

> was characteristically a journalistic mind, and its characteristic contribution was that of the socially responsible reporter-reformer. The muckraker was a central figure. Before there could be action, there must be information and exhortation. Grievances had to be given specific objects, and these the muckraker supplied.[61]

Graft, corruption, vice, extortion, and their links with business (large and small) and all levels of government were researched and exposed. One of the first and more prominent was Henry Demarest Lloyd, a lawyer (who defended union leader and socialist Eugene V. Debs on charges stemming from the 1894 Pullman strike) and a journalist with the *Chicago Tribune* from 1872–85. He studied the shameful monopolistic practices used by Standard Oil and railroad conglomerates to eliminate competitors. The results were published in *The Atlantic Monthly* in March 1881. This experience led Lloyd to an anti-capitalist position, and he again attacked monopolies in *Wealth Against Commonwealth* in 1894.

Born to wealth, Lloyd devoted himself full time to public affairs after 1885 and became a literate "professional reformer" active at the Hull-House and Chicago Commons settlements. A Populist leader, he – like Wright in each instance – worshipped Emerson and learned from John Ruskin, William Morris, Giuseppe Mazzini, Henry George, and Edward Bellamy.[62] Lloyd's exposé presaged the new category of reportage: muckraking. Matthew Arnold praised it as the New Journalism.[63]

Lloyd had taken into his home and cared for the three children of a divorced compatriot, Florence Kelley. But earlier, in the 1890s, while she worked and lived in Hull-House, the children were boarded with Wright's mother Anna, who then cozily and cloyingly lived next door to Frank and Catherine in Oak Park.[64] Kelley, a lawyer, was described by Supreme Court Justice Felix Frankfurter as having had "probably the largest single share in shaping the social history of the United States during the first thirty years of this century."[65]

Assisted by a ten-year-long correspondence with Friedrich Engels, in 1887, Kelley translated his *The Condition of the Working Class in England in 1884*, the only English-language version until 1958. Inspired by Engels, Kelley led a sociological survey of the area around Hull-House that was published as *Hull-House Maps and Papers* in 1895. It had comparisons with Jacob Riis's study of New York City, *How the Other Half Lives*, of 1890. It was likely Kelley who invited Riis to lecture on housing debacles to the public at Hull-House in 1899. And she headed the National Consumers League for thirty years, focusing on labor legislation for women . . .

> [on] enactment and enforcement of numerous minimum wage, maximum hour, and child labor laws; establishment of the U.S. Children's Bureau; passage of woman suffrage; and arguments, organizations, and networks that transformed much of nineteenth-century philanthropy into the profession of social work.[66]

"Her pen and tongue flayed opponents, she became the Thomas Paine of her generation."[67] Not only was she a close acquaintance of the Wrights, they must have accepted her brazen and impudent pen.

Corruption by businessmen and the malfeasance of politicians were exposed by Lincoln Steffens in 1904 as *The Shame of the Cities* (drawn from his original articles in *McClure's* magazine); by David Graham in *The Treason of the Senate* in 1906; by Upton Sinclair's novel *The Jungle* also in 1906, which described the horrors of Chicago's meat packing industry; by

Frank Norris, who dramatized the railroads' stranglehold on farmers in *The Octopus* in 1900; by *Collier's*, who alerted readers to false advertising and dangerous drugs and patent medicines in 1912; and so on. Then there was the attack by *The New York Times* and *Harpers Weekly* on the democrat's Tammany Hall political machine in New York City, as well as Garland's Populist novel *A Spoils of Office* about state corruption. Following Lloyd's earlier effort, Ida Tarbell's series began in 1893 in *McClure's Magazine* as another exposé of John D. Rockefeller's sometimes cruel practices.

Of course, Wright was aware of these exposures. Some of the authors were members of Cliff Dwellers while others held discourse. But, sticking to crafts and architecture, he made no public comment about them except on two occasions. "No Rockefeller" should "rise to a legitimate point of vantage that would justify the control of such a vast share of the earth's resources, *how unspeakably vulgar and illegitimate . . .*," he exclaimed in 1900.[68] Then in an essay titled "The Art and Craft of the Machine," first prepared in 1901 as an address given to only fifteen or so people at Hull-House, in which he absolved the artist of blame for industry's misuse of the machine to repetitively reproduce ugly decorative arts, arguing that . . .

> [one might] as well blame Richard Croker for the political inequity of America.
> As "Croker is the creature and not the creator" of political evil, so the machine is the creature and not the creator of . . . degradation in the name of the artistic.[69]

Irish emigrant Croker was Tammany boss (1885–1901) and retired to Ireland on the spoils of extortion. Mr. Dooley despised him.

Of course, Wright knew at least something of the protagonists. In a lengthy paper delivered to the Architectural League at the Art Institute of Chicago in 1900, he concluded with reference to a designer's or artist's stylization of nature, specifically of a flower:

> The Socialist would bow his neck in altruistic submission to the "harmonious whole" . . . his flower [conventionalized] with the living character of the flower left out.
> The Anarchist would pluck the flower as it grows and use it as it is for what it is – he is realistic with the essential reality left out.
> The Plutocrat justifies his existence by his ability . . . to appropriate the flower to his own use after the craftsman has given it life . . . and keeps the craftsman too by promising him his flower back – if he behaves well.
> The Aristocrat does virtually the same thing. . . .[70]

Simplistic perhaps, but typical of the way Wright, as a non-verbal designer, verbally responded. Design and art were mediums of diverse potential, illusive in abstraction. But he was an attractive aberration in a socially confused city. His self-propaganda and writings on any subject, but mainly architecture and other design disciplines, were recognized locally when he was made a life member of the Chicago Press Club in July 1913.[71]

Radicals and reformers

Between the financial disaster of 1893 and American participation in the European monarchs' new war, the most active and outspoken radicals and reformers were those with socialistic inclination, and they successfully exploited the "arts." By common consensus, design and art allow, with the trick of metaphors, the apparent liberty of free expression, where ideas can be tested or promoted by imagination. Therefore, fictional literature, cinema, and drama especially, but also painting and photography, were effective propagandistic mediums.

The alliance of design and art and radical politics was obvious at most settlement houses. That is one reason why settlements were attracted to the erratic socialistic theories of William Morris and his movement to revive crafts. Many settlements were directed and administered by Protestants, anarchists, and socialists and sustained by volunteers drawn from supportive ranks. The majority were centrists with a social conscious. Thus, Mrs Catherine Wright not only attended to Frank's family but also found time to participate in Hull-House settlement and argue for woman's suffrage. After Wright's abandonment, she found even more time for such service.[72]

It is to theater that many extroverted if not egocentric personalities were attracted. The Hull-House Players began in 1907 and produced mainly European ethnic plays for immigrant audiences. That same year, the Donald Robertson Players offered drama in and around Chicago. Wright invited Robertson to his "Symposium for Art" at Oak Park Unity Church and wrote in the *Oak Leaves* newspaper about the actor, who was to begin a series of plays for Oak Park in 1908.[73] Before 1909, Catherine was involved with children's puppetry and theater in a room in the Fine Arts Building (the old Studebaker) located beside Chicago's Michigan Avenue. The building contained a coffee shop, bookstore, and halls and theaters; Cliff Dwellers Club on the top floor; and offices and studios for musicians, writers, artists, and architects, including Wright's city office during 1908 and 1910–11.

The English poet and drama producer Maurice Browne and his American wife, actress Ellen Van Volkenburg, both previously active in New York City, began the Chicago Little Theatre in an eighth-floor room with ninety-one seats in the Fine Arts Building. Begun in 1912, it presented poetic drama, used simple settings with mood lighting after Gordon Craig, and offered marionette productions. It was the progenitor of the Little Theatre Movement in America. Wright had designed and built a marionette theater for son Llewellyn in either 1908 or 1912,[74] and in 1918 he recalled the contribution of "Browne's 'Little Theatre'" to Chicago culture.[75] The "star" of the Little Theatre was Kira Markham, who was also a muralist and printmaker and later married Wright's son, Frank Jr. Among those attracted to Hull-House Players and the Little Theatre were Wright's future client Aline Barnsdall and the Lithuanian emigrant and outspoken anarchist Emma Goldman.

Goldman, close to Margaret Anderson (founder of *The Little Review*), Gilman, Lloyd, and Kelley, was a frequent visitor to Hull-House when on a lecture tour. Goldman's "stock in trade," as one of her contemporaries put it, "was to lecture on Philosophic Anarchy to the younger generation."[76] Like Gilman, Hull-House was Goldman's base in Chicago. Unlike most other anarchists, Goldman's conversations were as much concerned with drama and art as sex and revolution. Her book *The Social Significance of Modern Drama* was released in 1914 and, in the words of Alice Friedman, who has studied the relationship between Goldman and Aline Barnsdall, it expressed sentiments that . . .

> endeared Goldman to the Little Theatre group and to other young artists in Chicago, for she outspokenly described the ways in which the arts could confront the issues with which they themselves were grappling: love, sexuality, marriage, the education of children, poverty, class struggle, and not the least, what it meant to be an American.[77]

Barnsdall produced her first plays in 1915, and in that year she commissioned Wright to design a theater for a site yet determined. This required Wright to become even more involved with theater as conceived by Barnsdall and Goldman. But, deciding that an old Chicago had inferior possibilities to a new Los Angeles, Barnsdall moved west in 1916, yet retained Wright. The Chicago theater was not built, but she commissioned him to design another, as well as studio apartments, rental housing, a kindergarten, and her house, all for a new private art colony on Olive Hill in Hollywood. A house and two studios were built (1920–23) but the colony remained a puzzling dream.[78]

Wright acknowledged derivatives of his conditions in 1939 to the Association of Federal Architects when he said, "I have read Henry George, Kropotkin, Gesell, Prudhomme, Marx, Mazzini, Whitman, Thoreau, Veblen and many other advocates of freedom."[79] On the last page of the 1943 edition of his *Autobiography*, they were listed as among authors "long ago consulted and occasionally remembered." Here, he also mentioned "inspirational" authors and included the New England naturists and Transcendentalists James Russell Lowell and

16 *Conditions*

Henry Wadsworth Longfellow, as well as John Greenleaf Whittier, William Cullen Bryant, William Black, Ruskin, Goethe, Carlyle, Victor Hugo, and the poet Robert Browning. Most were favored not only by American followers of Frederick Froebel, but socialists, Transcendentalists, Unitarians, and Wright's parents' families.[80] Lessons from the 1880s and 1890s profoundly stretched Wright's mind and enlivened imagination. None were active post-1920. But there were others with more immediate lessons.

Edelmann et al.

Louis Sullivan acknowledged that it was *not* the architect but the man, John Herman Edelmann, who was a deep influence. Edelmann "lauded Henry George in superlatives" as Sullivan put it in reminiscences of 1924. He also announced that he, Louis, had discovered in Edelmann . . .

> a THINKER, a profound thinker, a man of immense range of reading, a brain of extraordinary keenness, strong, vivid, that ranged in its operations from saturnine intelligence concerning men and their motives, to the highest transcendentalisms of German metaphysics. He [Edelmann] was as familiar with the great philosophers as with the daily newspaper . . . never before or since has Louis met his equal in vitality, in verity, and in perspicacity of thought.[81]

To Sullivan, Edelmann's ideas were natural extensions of an outrageous German–Jewish personality. Raised in Cleveland, where he obtained some apprentice training in architectural drafting, perhaps with Alexander Koehler, Edelmann moved to Chicago immediately after the great fire of 1871 and soon found work as a draftsman with architects Burling & Adler. Then Edelmann, along with part-timer Sullivan, began as draftsmen in William Le Baron Jenny's architectural office in 1873. A year later, Edelmann became a junior partner of architect Joseph S. Johnston, and Sullivan acted as an occasional apprentice. Johnston had worked alone from 1868 into 1873, when he began with Burling & Adler. In July 1874, Sullivan left for Paris. From there, he wrote to his brother Albert that Edelmann's "progress in Architecture has filled me with delight . . . he is one of the smartest and most honorable boys I have ever met. . . ."[82] When the partnership with Johnston dissolved in 1876, Edelmann worked at various tasks in Chicago and Cleveland, which included stints with Koehler, and finally again with Burling & Adler. When Edelmann left Chicago in the spring of 1880, he suggested to Adler that Sullivan replace him. Deciding to reside permanently in New York City, Edelmann became an outspoken anarchist, actively supported Henry George's ideas and political ambitions, and became friends of Kropotkin and Emma Goldman.[83] From 1891–94, he worked for the variable architect Alfred Zucker. For him, Edelmann was allowed to control the design of the tall but thirty-foot-wide Decker Building in New York City, completed in 1893 and, with a slender tower gone, still facing Union Square.[84]

Wright understood Edelmann to be Sullivan's "most respected" teacher,[85] whose sentiments were "expressed with forcible [forceful?] profanity."[86] Was Edelmann the principle source for Sullivan's anti-historicism, unfettered individualism, and later a quasi-Socratic methodology of argument? Perhaps. But when it came to architecture, Edelmann's designs were based on historical precedent and mundane. So too his ornament, the patterns found in many publications. In the absence of primary evidence, it is difficult to know exactly the nature of Edelmann's architectural discourse that so persuaded Sullivan. Perhaps it was distilled in 1892 in the only known published architectural essay by Edelmann. Titled "Pessimism of Modern Architecture" he offered interesting observations:

> [E]motional expression is the very essence of architecture. . . .
> Take a later period – that of the [civil] war and before the "seventies" – with its large, badly constructed, ill-arranged buildings, aping all manner of ancient styles, covered all

over with ill-assorted tawdry detail. . . . Are they not eloquent of a people intoxicated with material wealth finding their emotional expression in lavish vulgar display? . . .

Richardson was undoubtedly the first great American architect. . . . [H]is wholesale store for Marshall, Field, in Chicago, . . . massive, simple, brutal, naive, the true expression of its inward character. . . .

To the present writer it seems that a new master has arisen, not popular as yet. . . . Mr. Louis H. Sullivan has, in my judgment at least, an even deeper insight than Richardson and greater power of expression. . . .

I select the Wainwright Building in St. Louis as the most complete expression of American commercial architecture. . . . The building is treated as one essential and integral growth. Instead of concealing the simplicity of internal function it is emphasized by repetition of parts; instead of minimizing the height by horizontal divisions into three or more fields the height is made the artistic motive. . . . [A] "child's building-block design." . . .

Yet in spite of Wainwright, Edelmann concluded that "from modern commercialism no happy art can spring. If this phase of civilization is to prevail Pessimism must become its final expression and embodiment."[87] Some praise, muddled ordinary thoughts, but the message was, according to historian Lauren Weingarden, plain: "For Edelmann, Sullivan's achievement was a limited one, since a society that considers architecture merely a commodity thwarts artistic originality and cultural growth."[88] Those persuasions were relayed to Wright while in Sullivan's office: John "was quoted to me often," Wright has said, and many of Edelmann's and Sullivan's "venerated" authors became Wright's.[89] If not by his uncle, Reverend Jones, Sullivan may have been Wright's earliest experience with anarchist thought and George's ideas. But Wright would find nothing positive or useful, personally or professionally, in the various anarchisms.

George's treatise *Progress and Poverty: An Inquiry into the Cause of Industrial Depression and of Increase of Want with Increase of Wealth* of 1879 was extremely influential on Populists, Progressives, anarchists, economists, and the religious lay public.[90] A California-raised journalist, George "was driven to explain the persistence of poverty in the midst of great increases in resources, wealth, and income." He concluded that . . .

> the growth of industrial societies created two kinds of wealth: the kind which resulted from the application of labor and skill to privately created capital resources, and the kind which resulted purely from the increment in the value of unimproved or idle land on the edge of urban settlement.[91]

The first belonged mainly to the individual producer. The second was "the product of social growth" and therefore belonged to the people. The idea as cogently explained by Charles Beard was for a "Single-Tax" or real-property tax as more ethical and humanitarian. It would "materially reduce, if not entirely abandon, the tax upon buildings and personal property."[92]

Although typecast as an urban political economist, George was motivated by issues related to environmental declension. He wrote in favor of small-scale, diversified agriculture and against land-degrading monocultures. Historian John L. Thomas has said, "In proceeding from rent and monopoly to the theme of land and the fecundity of nature, George was invoking an agrarian mystique that the great majority of Americans understood," or, more likely, they shared. Simply put, George supported the Jeffersonian agrarian nation that in the late nineteenth century was in violent throes of urbanization. George was a "nationwide attraction, soon worldwide. Linked to the Arts and Crafts, George villages soon began as testaments – or tests – of his ideas: Arden in Pennsylvania, Fairhope in Alabama, Roycroft in New York, New Claireau in Massachusetts."[93]

Wright's monetary proposals and much of his political dialogue post-1927 arose directly out of his understanding of George's theses. Later, he rejected the single-tax idea but included the attractive writings of the Progressive economist and labor historian John R. Commons, a friend

18 Conditions

and professor at the University of Wisconsin in Madison.[94] Wright's views were presented after 1922 and reemerged in his first autobiography released in 1932. However, he said nothing substantial about such issues in print or in known correspondence just before and during the Progressive years.

Edward Bellamy approached reform more generally yet with specific recommendations for curative action in his socialistic utopian novel *Looking Backward* of 1888. Along with Harriet Beecher Stowe's *Uncle Tom's Cabin* in 1852, Bellamy's book was one of the most popular of the nineteenth century – at times sales averaged ten thousand copies a week worldwide. His solution to the problems of political impotence and social inequality was a promise that "through painless evolution technological progress would end in the recovery of idyllically pastoral culture," through nationalization in preference to all else. His panacea was a gigantic trust owned and operated by the national government whose bureaucrats would oversee a highly communalized society blessedly devoid of irrational passions, greed, and other human frailties. Followers established Nationalist Clubs, 160 by the early 1890s, others in Canada and Europe. By 1910, his nationalism had disappeared from America's conscious. Because of Bellamy, however, a heightened awareness of and keenness for socialism and labor's rights did not dissipate in America but steadily increased.

Jay Hubbell, who likely remains America's best historian of its early literature, made the agreeable suggestion that George and Bellamy "relied too much upon their own panaceas." Yet Hubbell also found that, beginning with the Populists,

> [t]he old idea, advocated by Jefferson and Emerson, that the best government is that which governs least, gradually gave way ... to the conviction that the central government must regulate every phase of the nation's life. The new attitude is found in Henry George's *Progress and Poverty* (1879), Edward Bellamy's *Looking Backward* (1888), [William Dean] Howell's *A Traveler from Altruria* (1894) [in support of Bellamy], and in Hamlin Garland's *Main Travelled Roads* (1891).[95]

It was a conviction resting on the principles of right-thinking people, which Wright firmly rejected, then and later. Wright favored individuals operating in anarchic bliss while gently overseen by wise and artistically inclined people, like himself. He could not assign his individuality to others he believed of wayward thought or lesser insight or talent, regardless of their collective weight. He acknowledged economic reform as a necessary partner but only as it might amplify and consolidate an individual's free exercises and association. This did not mature as a public view until his philosophic thoughts during the 1920s evolved to become the theoretical foundation for his panacea, Broadacre City.[96]

During the Progressive years, therefore, Wright was attracted to leftists, liberals, socialists, and reformers. But always he was a passive supporter, not an advocate; an architect, not yet a celebrity. And some of them were in turn drawn to him by dint of personality and new-era designs.

Wright observes

Wright's contribution to those heterogeneous city-focused activities before 1917 was directed to thoughts about the physical character of the city by way of architecture and as manifest in his buildings and landscapes, as well as in his design ideas. Each way was realized not speculatively in words or dream-like projects but as a result of responding to commissions, to a client's specific program and site. But what of his publicly expressed thoughts about the city? Before the 1920s, he gave the city – and the reformist's proposals for it – scant attention publicly or in published form, except on two occasions.

In 1901, he lectured to the Chicago Arts and Crafts Society, of which he was a founding member, at a venue in Hull-House settlement. It was attended by fifteen people: eight from Wright's office, Jane Addams, and six others;[97] hardly the grand affair he later claimed. His subject was the machine as it attracts or repels designers and artists. He believed the "Ideals" of Englishmen William Morris and Ruskin as related to architecture, together with the "teaching of the Beaux Arts of Paris especially," he pronounced, "have so far prevailed in America as to steadily confuse and demoralize."[98] Wright's rambling arguments favored the proposition that "in the Machine lies the only future of art and craft – as I believe, a glorious future; that the Machine is, in fact, the metamorphosis of ancient art and crafts." Near the conclusion of an edited version, suddenly, out of context and while attempting to widen the definition of "machine," he wondered if the city was the greatest machine:

> There beneath, grown up in a night, is the monster leviathan, stretching acre upon acre upon acre into the far distance.... Ten thousand acres of cellular tissue, layer upon layer, the city's flesh, outspread enmeshed by intricate net work of veins and arteries, radiating into the gloom....
> And the heavy breathing, the murmuring, the clangor, and the roar! – how the voice of this monstrous thing, this greatest of machines, a great city, rises to proclaim the marvel of the units of its structure....
> And the texture of the tissue of this great thing ... has been deposited particle by particle, in blind obedience to organic law, the law to which the great solar universe is but an obedient machine.
> Thus is the thing into which the forces of Art are to breathe the thrill of ideality! A SOUL!

Lastly, he described a city's "nerve ganglia! – the peerless Corliss tandems whirling their hundred ton fly-wheels, fed by gigantic rows of water-tube boilers burning...."[99] Here, he referred to the Corliss engine, thirty feet tall, oil burning, steam driven, 1,400 horsepower, which was initially built to power parts of the 1876 Centennial Exhibition in Philadelphia. Soon thereafter, it was purchased by George Pullman to power his new private company town.[100] It was a grand symbol of industrialism, technical achievement, commercial success, and supremacy. It was in extreme contrast to a Winnebago encampment on the frontier (see Figures 1.1 and 1.2). The rather dark description of the "monster leviathan" was romantic prose, not art theoretical and not political or social or reformist, but an artist's expressive document, an impression. Here, Wright leads us to believe, perhaps correctly, that the city is the most technologically organic example imaginable, but he seemingly does not recognize it as also a humanistic social organ. And that psychological lapse will persist with rare exceptions in his writings through the 1940s.

The only other early occasion on which Wright spoke publicly about the city was in descriptions for a model neighborhood from 1913–15 that will be presented later. It was a more practical and sympathetic exposition because it responded to a detailed program set out by reformist colleagues.

In 1923, Wright published an essay titled *Experimenting with Human Lives*. It was written after abandoning the idea of a career in Japan and while attempting to settle professionally in Los Angeles.[101] Learning of the 1922 Tokyo earthquake, he prepared for publication an awkwardly written piece mainly about the evils of skyscrapers and of needless congestion. He mentioned earthquakes generally, obliquely referred to his work in Japan, discussed problems of tall building construction and offered his own concrete block system as a superior construction method, and saw the decentralization of Los Angeles as "creating a competitive confusion having benefits" unnamed, "but far greater waste" unspecified.[102] Clearly, the essay was an attempt to finagle a job to rebuild Tokyo because he sent copies to people in Japan: "I am sending it to Tokyo," he told Louis Sullivan, "to try and head off the propaganda which [if successful] will try to rebuild Tokyo as a modern American city."[103]

From 1887–1917, Wright trained and practiced in Chicago, "the city profitable."[104] Up to 1917, he was obsessively, myopically consumed by self and by association with radicals and reformers, yet pragmatically by displaying his design prowess as it might persuade Chicago's cultural elite. All else was distantly secondary.

Figure 1.1 A Winnebago encampment in Wisconsin in the 1850s, no different than in the 1870s; painting by Seth Eastman, then captain in the US Army. As settlers the Jones family encountered Winnebagos who lived in southern Wisconsin and northern Illinois. Winnebagos surrendered their lands and, in the 1830s, were shunted farther west. Some refused to move and in Wisconsin today name themselves Ho-Chunk. From McKenney/Hall, 1836–44.

Place and circumstance

The Great Lakes were physically joined to the Atlantic Seaboard, foremost at New York City, by completion of the Erie Canal in 1825. Founded in 1833, Chicago soon became a port and began to absorb massive migrations of workers and professionals all willing to participate in its accelerating growth. By the 1850s, Chicago had become the principal midwestern shipping terminus and rail center for one-third of the nation.[105] In the quest for personal achievement that fed a zealous boosterism, the October 1871 fire caused only hesitation to the hurly-burly. Now there was a need to rebuild. Nearly all of Chicago's architects before 1900 were emigrants from eastern and midwestern cities eager to participate in ways to rebuild a fireproof city. But housing the flood of immigrant labor was left to speculators, exploiters, plain hustlers, and the vagaries of uncontrolled money sectors. The Chicago Englishman Steevens experienced was an overly proud city just beginning to evaluate its physical and social condition:

> Chicago! Chicago [in 1893], queen and guttersnipe of cities, cynosure and cesspool of the world! . . . The most beautiful and the most squalid, girdled with a twofold zone of parks and slums; where the keen air from lake and prairie is ever in the nostrils, and the stench

Figure 1.2 "President Grant and the Emperor of Brazil starting the great Corliss engine in Machinery Hall" at the Centennial International Exhibition in Philadelphia in 1876. From Leslie, 1877.

of foul smoke is never out of the throat; the great port a thousand miles from the sea; the great mart which gathers up with one hand the corn and cattle of the West and deals out with the other the merchandise of the East; ... where women ride straddle-wise, and millionaires dine at mid-day on the Sabbath; the chosen seat of public spirit and municipal boodle, of cut-throat commerce and munificent patronage of the art.... the first and only veritable Babel of the age....[106]

22   Conditions

As the century progressed, it became a city of compelling dual – but not conflicting – ambitions. As a regional center in all ways, it was a place of magnetic attraction to those impelled in a search for money. A few were successful, but their "concentrated wealth" was "garishly conspicuous amid the poverty of the down-and-outs, many of them political refugees from repressive regimes."[107] The other ambition was to obtain the outward symbols of culture, highly desired (if only to best a tired Boston, a rejuvenated New York City, and a risen St Louis), and frenetically pursued by the elite.

Culture, always packaged with esteem, was instituted, as expected, by the establishment of museums of natural history, fine art, science, and technology, by music, by a magnificent park system, by libraries, and so forth. The World's Columbian Exposition of 1893, commemorating the four-hundredth anniversary of Columbus's discovery of the West Indies, ratified internal wealth and external appearances and symbolized a confidence that beckoned people who created schools of literature, psychology, sociology, philosophy, and architecture. By the turn of the century, the "creative center of cultural forces" had indeed challenged the northeastern nexus. Journalist and scholar H. L. Mencken once described the city as "the most civilized" and "the most thoroughly American" (see Figure 1.3).[108]

Obtaining the trappings of culture was an obsession, education catalytic. Education was a primary focus shared by reformers among the social elite who sought its signature of social and intellectual sophistication. Chicago and much of the northern Midwest were influenced by Protestants, mainly of German and Scandinavian origin, who respected and fostered book learning and public education. Among a bevy of private colleges established in the region,

Figure 1.3 Chicago's Haymarket Square in about 1893, with trolley tracks and police box; none of the buildings exist today. (Note the number of horses and estimate their manure.) From private collection.

the University of Chicago was revived in 1887 by the Baptist Education Society and opened its doors in 1892. As a private university, its dedication was to graduate research and heavily financed by John D. Rockefeller, a Baptist; $35 million by 1910, $80 million by 1937.[109]

In 1870, Germany's Otto von Bismark wrote to America's General Philip H. Sheridan: "I wish I could go to America if only to see that Chicago."[110] Suffice it to say that published descriptions with comments more or less luridly detailed abound.[111] The greatest attraction was the extraordinary 1893 Exposition and the experience of a notorious city spreading out and up. Immediately, there was a dramatic increase in interest by Europe in American culture, its cities and, mainly because of skyscrapers, its architecture. Many quite rightly wondered if, sans stockyards, 1890s Chicago did foretell of an urbanized twentieth century.

During the 1873 nationwide financial collapse, the plight of the immigrant poor was so critical that the ground floor of city hall "was given over to families who had no other shelters."[112] People insulted policemen or smashed shop windows hoping to be jailed, warmed, and fed. The combination of new foreigners and the influx of southern blacks, each group either unemployed or accepting low wages, provided a dangerous cocktail, one easily mixed with emotional tinder by those of experience or dark motivation. In Philadelphia, draftsman Louis Sullivan was laid off by architect Frank Furness.

The loudest protest voices in Chicago were those of the organized anarchists and bellicose socialists, who had among their midst "ragged Commune wretches," old Chicagoans complained. Most strident were militants who instigated a series of organized demonstrations that culminated in 1886. In protest to police wantonly killing strikers outside the McCormick reaper factory that May, a call was made in Chicago's *Arbeiter-Zeitung* newspaper to join a "great mass meeting" at Haymarket Square. The *lingua universal* on Chicago streets was not English but German, the idiom of the immigrant majority After a few rather inflammatory speeches, police ordered the unruly crowd to disperse. Suddenly, a bomb exploded and gunshots were fired; within five minutes, seven police officers were dead and sixty others wounded, perhaps two hundred other casualties.[113] This violent event occurred while eighteen-year-old Wright was working as an office factotum in small-town Madison.

One self-anointed industry "robber baron" thought he could control the rebellious. George M. Pullman did not wholly believe, as Andrew Carnegie did, that "the millionaire will be but a trustee for the poor."[114] Pullman, who began his railroad sleeping car company in 1867, believed in protecting his accomplishments in the guise of beneficence by relocating his industrial plants and employee housing to a private new town southeast of Chicago's commercial center on the northwestern shore of shallow Lake Calume; construction began in 1881.

Pullman created a physical model as one answer to the problems of high city, corporate, and land taxes as well as volatile laborers. Architect Solon Spenser Beman prepared a rather tidy street- and land-use layout for Pullman's Pullman and designed most buildings. The landscape architect was Nathan F. Barrett. A central market owned by Pullman was relatively close to rental row housing that faced a grid of fairly wide streets, all hierarchically arranged relevant to a resident employee's wages or status. The giant Corliss engine provided power for all facilities. By 1893, there were 12,600 residents, 72 percent foreign born.

The general consensus among first evaluations held that the town would "mould not only a body of employees, but a whole population of workmen and their families to ways of living which would raise their moral, intellectual and social level"[115] and thereby increase productivity. But those determinist comments were premature; paternalistic intimidation ruled:

> [Mr Pullman's] company owned the theater and decided what would be shown, it owned the schools and decided what would be taught, it owned the public library and decided what books would be shelved, it owned the church . . . [E]mployees could not buy property, could not acquire real political rights, could not even express opinions in print.[116]

There was a three dollar per annum library fee, the church was expected to show a profit, and so forth.[117] Saloons and similar indoor leisure facilities were located in popular parasitic slums just beyond Mr Pullman's moralistic control, outside city limits, the other side of rail tracks. While solving "one of the great problems of the immediate present, which is a diffusion of the benefits of concerted wealth among wealth-creators," as economist Richard T. Ely put it in 1885, he also believed "There is repression here."[118]

Pullman's experiment began to shudder ten years later due to the devastating economic turmoil of 1893. When business fell off, Mr Pullman cut workers' wages but did not lower rents; he refused to meet workers' delegations, fired its members, and dispossessed them of their homes. Those who participated were fired. Mr Pullman refused arbitration; thus, in 1894 employees sought out Eugene V. Debs, then in charge of the fledgling national American Railway Union, who suggested a strike. A lockout ensued; state and federal troops guarded industrial facilities and railways; and employees and the union became isolated, defeated. When factories reopened, employees were required to sign a pledge to not join a union.[119] Discredited, Mr Pullman never recovered and, in 1897, died a broken man.[120]

Burnham et al., 1893–09

In 1890, a federal government commission considered submissions from the cities of Chicago, Washington, New York, and St Louis to host a national celebration of the four-hundredth anniversary of Spain's – not the Viking's – discoveries. It was to be a national affair, not local, and a US House of Representatives committee selected Chicago. The 1893 World's Columbian Exposition is best remembered in popular American annals for an architecture style, collectively referred to then and now as the White City. It "touched the deep longing of a national suffering from a loss of continuity with history for visual assurance of maturity and success," as historian Mel Scott put it.[121]

Daniel Burnham was hired as director of works. His architectural business was largest in Chicago, perhaps second in the nation only to the New York City firm of McKim, Mead & White. As such, the Chicagoan was praised and damned, locally and nationally. Typical comments of praise are similar to those by Hamlin Garland who called Burnham "the great builder" of "serene confidence" who "voiced a relentless determination" with a "powerful" personality and so on.[122] Wright found "Uncle Dan," apparently a local nickname, to be powerful, a "handsome, jovial, splendidly convincing" person, "not a very creative architect but he was a great man."[123] However, Louis Sullivan was scathing: Burnham "was obsessed by the feudal idea of power," he was "elephantine, tactless, and blurting," a "colossal merchandiser."[124] In retrospect, historians Burchard and Bush-Brown referred to Burnham as "Titan, the emperor of architecture."[125] Burnham was the business and senior partner of the firm, not the designing architect.

Burnham's office was charged with the physical organization of the entire Exposition, including architecture but excluding preparation of exhibits. Landscape architect Frederick Law Olmsted the Elder prepared a site plan. Burnham also enlisted architect Charles F. McKim of New York. Charles B. Atwood, who had become Burnham's principal designer on the death of John Root, was in charge of coordinating the design of more than sixty buildings.[126] These men determined the Exposition's physical character, selected architects, oversaw technical and aesthetic details, and demanded that all major buildings be pastiche fantasies derivative of Francophilian beaux-arts *classique* styles. When constructed, they were wrought iron cages clothed in stucco and staff (a mix of plaster of Paris and straw), all painted virginal white.

In 1893, the year Wright grudgingly began to practice independently, New York architectural critic Montgomery Schuyler assessed the White City "palaces" as the "most illusive piece of scenic architecture that has ever been produced."[127] Scenic, but the buildings were unassimible. Yet, collectively, they did influence the character of America's civic – and much other – architecture for the next four decades, but only after the first City Beautiful was promoted for Washington, DC.

In 1900, the nation's capitol was to celebrate the one-hundredth anniversary of shifting the seat of government from Philadelphia to Washington. One attraction was to revitalize the existing city. On advice at the national level of the AIA (American Institute of Architects), mainly through its secretary, Glenn Brown, the same people who controlled planning and architecture for the 1893 Exposition were employed in 1900 to advise Congress through its Senate Park Commission: Burnham, the Olmsted firm now controlled by Olmsted Jr., McKim, and sculptor Augustus St Gaudens. The advisors toured western Europe, where they concentrated on seventeenth- and eighteenth-century princely palaces and especially their grand landscapes, each with an imperially hierarchical presence, diagonality mixed with right-angled axial symmetry.[128]

Led by Burnham, the advisor's design proposal was placed and accepted by the Commission in 1902 with a plan of two distinct emphases: transportation and parks. It retained diagonal streets, effectively rationalized rail lines, and superimposed a system of grand parkways and water basins that were loosely based on Louis XIV's palace garden at Versailles. And they agreed that new buildings should clutter the great green mall. As a result of the design's acceptance, the city's difficult street network and building sites were worsened, even for horse and buggy, and its residential, community, and neighborhood conditions ignored. Moreover, the advisors envisaged white stone neoclassical federal buildings placed on axial termini and of grand green parks with reciprocal vistas.[129]

Historian Mel Scott nicely characterized the result: the Commission's plan was "a kind of national civic center in a vernacular city" and "historical artifact," one "immune to the whims of time and chance" but of demanding "immutability."[130] It was a proposal to extend the 1893 White City. It sanctified a past that never existed yet offered a future trapped in the historicism of Imperial Rome and its Baroque successors. It was dichotomous, defeating the fact that the America of native Indians and European immigrants was physically and intellectually home *and* frontier, a nation of ethnic diversity, composed of people who had escaped the belligerence of imperial and religious authoritarianism and to whom the immutable – emphatically revisited in Burnham's symbolism – was abhorrent.

The great majority of Washington's existing land area, however, was not devoted to government and ceremony but overwhelmingly to people's daily exercises. That greater part was disregarded – in fact, portions were rejected.[131] As spokesman for City Beautiful movers, Charles Robinson made clear that Burnham et al. were concerned with "civic art" and could "reasonably assert . . . that civic art need concern itself only with the outward aspects of the houses": facades, not neighborhoods.[132] Planning emphasis was given to glorifying civic and political pomp and commercial circumstance. This was true for the grandest City Beautiful proposal prepared in 1907–08 for Chicago, again Burnham and Co. was directorially involved.

Burnham had promised the "rich people's" Merchant's Club, as it was locally known,[133] to prepare a plan for the renovation of Chicago's disheveled lakefront. After Merchants merged with the Commercial Club, they gave Burnham $85,000 in 1907 (about $2,145,000 in 2015 money) to start work on a project whose program would soon be expanded to include the entire city. He hired Edward H. Bennett as the planning expert. To much fanfare, an exhibition of exquisite colored renderings by artist Jules Guerin was held in 1908 and a book, *The Plan of Chicago*, was released by the club in 1909, $25 a copy or $630 today. Burnham and Bennett were joint authors, the volume edited by Charles Moore.[134]

Biographer Thomas Hines believes that Burnham and Bennett were aiming "to rouse Chicagoans to the cause of planning and to layout in broad strokes an orderly set of proposed improvements." As Burnham elliptically said, "good citizenship is the prime object of good city planning."[135] However, *The Plan of Chicago* offered another visual stage set ordered by Francophilian architectural and planning classicism that by 1908 was de rigueur for the City Beautiful Movement. The abyss in the Burnham and Bennett plan, as with Washington, was a failure to explicitly call for the provision of local community commerce and housing and related infrastructure. *The Plan of Chicago* expressly left these needs to private agencies, philanthropy, charity, and speculators, not to the public purse.

To reformers and most Progressives, the plan was seen as a flagrant attempt to use tax monies for aggrandizing self-serving politicians and aristocratically minded plutocrats, as exemplified by ward bosses and the merchant princes of the Commercial Club itself (see Figure 1.4). Respected New York City housing reformer and social worker Benjamin C. Marsh said to the First National Conference on City Planning in 1909 that the "gigantic cost" for "civic vanity," for mere "external adornment" posed by Burnham, was not acceptable. Such adornments could ignore but not hide the stench of filth, foul air, and disease or the evils of pauperism, degeneracy, and crime.[136] Back in Chicago, the Neighborhood Improvement League of Cook County was formed immediately after publication of *The Plan of Chicago*.

Many citywide organizations, led and maintained mainly by women volunteers, were formed to provide information and focus on political reform and civic betterment. Some were concerned that *The Plan of Chicago* would effect only the central metropolitan area, as it concentrated on the political and commercial precincts, an emphasis that occupied three-quarters of book's textual and pictorial attention.

The pros and cons have been well worn in analyses and rhetoric since 1909. Regardless of its major shortcomings, *The Plan for Chicago*, accepted by city politicians in 1910, was a

Figure 1.4 Aerial perspective of Chicago's central precinct as proposed in 1909 by Burnham/Bennett showing trees (in black), blocks of commercial buildings, residential apartments, government buildings, and a central, high-domed edifice suffering from giganticism and ominously fronting ceremonial avenues lined with trees shown in black.

significant event of great influence;[137] less so opposition to it. Yet after 1910, City Beautiful movers reactively changed their principles and broadened their objectives to embrace some of the reformers' urgent demands. City Beautiful, therefore, was a two-phased movement, a fact seldom acknowledged.[138]

In their day, the city planning efforts of Burnham and his followers were known throughout the nation and are now embedded in historical lore worldwide. It must be emphasized, however, that they represented the then-prevalent conservative – perhaps snobbish – character of the gentlemanly profession of architecture, less so that of landscape architecture in spite of Olmsted Senior's extraordinary influence. Not until midwestern architects, emboldened by the Architectural League of America and Chicago's young designers, was that professional and social elitism openly challenged, albeit with little immediate result. League members rejected the continuation of old-world social, cultural, and professional hegemonies as perpetuated by the wicked old boys in and out of the northeastern states. While many complained of northeastern cultural dominance, not only in Chicago but in the nation, in architecture only Wright would provide practical, theoretical, and aesthetic resolutions that effectively – if not lastingly – challenged historical eclecticism. His method of liberation, his search for "an architecture that would express honestly the circumstances of its very existence,"[139] came to national, European, and Japanese attention primarily through major publications of his work in New York City in 1905 and 1908, in Berlin, Germany, in 1910 and 1911, and in Amsterdam in 1914.

Yet it must be emphasized that, thankfully, Burnham and Bennett's plan for Chicago popularized the idea that aesthetics were necessary to a satisfying, wholesome community, urban or otherwise. Relative, personal, and dependent on taste, beauty tends to superficiality: as it may refer to complex perceptions of architecture and cities, there is no exception. To anti-eclectics, relativists, Darwinians, rationalists, worried Protestants, technologists, and reformers (liberals and radicals), a modern design response would be wrought from fundamental conditions found not judgmentally in fashionable aesthetics alone but in all the circumstances that embody the present and effect the future. Around 1900, the monuments of industrialization and urbanization dominated their thoughts and actions. Mere aesthetics as a principle for progress, for change, were sterile. Style revivals and art nouveau proved this. Before ca. 1928, industrialization was a theoretical fundamental Wright vocally espoused but, as we shall learn, it was *not* a factor crucial to his architectural and community planning designs.

Notes

See Abbreviations and acronyms.
Author (date), such as Roe (1984), refers to the author and publication date as set out in the References.
1 Fink (2001), p.xv, his italic.
2 Steven Conn and Max Page, eds., *Building the Nation* (Philadelphia: University of Pennsylvania Press, 2003), p.309.
3 Roe (1984), pp.2–3; see also David W. Marcell, *Progress and Pragmatism* (Westport: Greenwood, 1974), and compare with Menand (2001).
4 A few statistics of foreign born or one-parent foreign born in 1920, by state and percentages are for the largest "foreign stock": North Dakota, 66 percent from Norway; Minnesota 65 percent, Wisconsin 59 percent, Michigan 52 percent, and Illinois 50 percent, each from Germany; Georgia 1 percent and New York 63 percent, each from Russia.
5 Burchard and Bush-Brown (1961), p.209.
6 E. A. Gutkind, *Urban Development in Western Europe: The Netherlands and Great Britain* (New York: Free Press, London: Collier-Macmillan, 1971), p.278.
7 Preamble to the St Louis platform of February 1892, quoted in Hicks (1931), p.436. The preamble quoted in Gerstle (1996), p.590, is from the Populist's Omaha platform of July 1892. For a good historical summation of the period see Steven Conn, Americans against the City Century (New York: Oxford University Press, 2014), particularly pp. 1–24.
8 Wright (1932), principally pp.3–6, 18–28, 36–47, 61, 119–120; Wright (1943), pp.121–122); and Barney (1965), pp.46–47, 58, 70. On Wright's familial background and heritage see

28 Conditions

  Twombly (1979), pp.1–16; Johnson (1980), pp.5–7; Gill (1987), chapter 2; Secrest (1992), pp.5–77; Alofsin (1992), throughout.
9 Wright (1932), p.4. The symbol was printed on British prisoners' uniforms in the eighteenth and nineteenth centuries.
10 Barney (1965), p.110.
11 Barney (1965), p.83.
12 As quoted in O'Neill (1975), p.7.
13 Zinn (1999), p.258.
14 Grant McConnell, *Private Power and American Democracy* (New York: Random House, 1966), pp.30–31. My appreciation of the Populist movement was further aided by general or particular information and opinion in several studies, including Hicks (1931); Nye (1959); O'Neill (1975); Davis (1994). Wikipedia refers to "People's Party."
15 Hofstadter (1955), p.3.
16 Hicks (1931), p.421.
17 Henry Steele Commager, *The American Mind: An Interpretation of American Thought and Character Since the 1880's* (New Haven: Yale University Press, 1950), a stimulating study of the makers of American culture, although his presentation of architects and their buildings is outdated. Cf. Fink (2001); Charles W. Calhoun, ed., *The Gilded Age: Perspectives on the Origins of Modern America* (Lanham, MD: Rowman & Littlefield, 2007).
18 Hofstadter (1963), introduction, p.3.
19 Hofstadter (1963), p.3. See also Wiebe (1973), pp.425–552; McCarthy (1977), pp.43–54.
20 Davis (1994), p.710; cf. Rice (1977), p.xv.
21 Vernon (2002), pp.xv–xx; *Conservation in the Progressive Era*, David Stradling, ed. (Seattle: University of Washington Press, 2004); Fink (2001), chapter 14; William H. Tishler, ed., *Midwestern Landscape Architecture* (Urbana: University of Illinois Press, 2000); Grese (1992), pp.39–43, 120–125; Michael J. Lacy, "Federalism and National Planning: The Nineteenth-Century Legacy," in Fishman (2000), pp.129–131; Bachin (2004), chapter 3; a popular basic outline is T. H. Wilkins, "Wilderness and the West," in Geoffrey C. Ward, ed., *The West* (New York: West Book Project, London: Weidenfeld & Nicholson, 1996), pp.324–329; on one source of the national park movement see Johnson (2013a).
22 Cf. De Witt (1915).
23 Charles A. Beard, review of de Witt (1915), *NMReview*, 4(October, 1915), pp.682–683. Indeed, aspirations for a "clean, healthful, safe and beautiful place" are contained in de Witt's chapters 15–16.

  Publications about the Progressive Era proliferate. Some of those that assisted in this work included Cranshawe (1978); Fink (2001); Frances (1982); Glaab (1963), chapter 5; Hofstadter (1955); Hays (1957); Howe (1905), and Otis A. Pease's introduction; Mason (1956), especially parts 12 ("Romantic Individualism") and 16 ("Liberal Variations"); May (1959); Nye (1959); Resek (1967); Strauss (1968), parts 12–13; Wiebe (1967); de Witt (1915); Zinn (1999); Zueblin (1903).

  Progressivism in national politics is associated with the presidential campaigns of Theodore Roosevelt, somewhat of a Progressive pretender (1912, aka the Bull Moose Party), the sincere Robert M. LaFollette Sr. (1924); and Henry Wallace (1948) who argued for a change in foreign policy and put less emphasis on domestic policy. Each broke from one of the major parties.
24 Beard (1912) can be compared to Benjamin Clarke Marsh, *An Introduction to City Planning* (New York: The Author, 1909).

  The controversial Beard was a professor of politics at Columbia University (1906–17), a cofounder in 1918 of the New School for Social Research in New York City, and a prolific author. See Ellen Nore, *Charles A. Beard: An Intellectual Biography* (Carbondale: Southern Illinois University Press, 1983), especially chapter 4. On one aspect of Beard's apparent switch to the political right, see Robert E. Spiller, ed., *The Van Wyck Brooks Lewis Mumford Letters* (New York: Dutton, 1970), pp.302–336.
25 Beard (1912), p.ix. Beard envisaged the text as a supplement to his *American Government and Politics* (revised 1914) and drew on the contents of the magazines *AmCity* and *NMReview*, of which he was an editor. An excellent comprehensive study of the period is Ernest S. Griffith, *A History of American City Government: The Progressive Years and Their Aftermath, 1900–1920* (Washington, DC: National Municipal League/University Press of America, 1983); see also David W. Noble, *Historians against History: The Frontier Thesis and the National Covenant in American Historical Writing Since 1830* (Minneapolis: University of Minnesota Press, 1965), Beard is chapter 4.

26 As is quoted in Beard (1912), p.359.
27 Otis A. Pease, introduction to Howe (1905), pp.xvi–xvii, xxvii.
28 Cf. Howe (1905), a lawyer and an inspirational reform author.
29 Wright (1918), p.10.
30 As quoted in Johnson (1990), p.107, in the context of Wright's trip to the USSR in 1937.
31 Twombly (1979), p.79.
32 FLW, "Why I Love Wisconsin," from *Wisconsin Magazine* as quoted in Gutheim (1941), pp.158–159, likely edited.
33 As quoted in Zinn (1999), p.353.
34 Cf. Nye (1959). On Hillside Home School and La Follette, see Twombly (1979), p.92n.9. Lincoln Steffens analysis in 1904 of the La Follette governorship is in his *The Struggle for Self-Government being an Attempt to Trace American Political Corruption to Its Sources . . . to the Czar* (New York: McClure, Phillips, 1906), pp.79–119, reprinted in Pease (1962), pp.131–155. A brief outline of Wright's antiwar position Johnson (1990), p.319; Twombly (1979), pp.294–298.
35 Words of wife Catherine Wright (then estranged from Frank on his departure to Germany with Mrs Mamah Cheney, a client), *DailyT* (17 November 1909), p.4, brought to my attention by Anthony Alofsin.
36 On Waller, see *National Cyclopaedia of American Biography . . .*, vol. 37 (New York: J. T. White, 1951); Kruty (1998), pp.61n17, 85; Obituary, *Chicago Tribune*, 14 January 1931, p.24.; *Book of Chicagoans* (Chicago: Marquis, 1917).
37 Staff Summary, Commission on Chicago Landmarks, *City of Chicago Landmarks Designation Reports* (Chicago: The Commission, 1987), see "Waller Apartment" website accessed July 2014.
38 Obituary, Arthur B. Heurtley, *Oak Leaves* (Oak Park), 20 September 1934. p.13a. Heurtley was a member of Cliff Dwellers, Louis Sullivan became a life member and made it his Chicago residence.
39 Hamlin Garland, "The Red Plowman," *The Craftsman*, 13(November 1907), opposite p.181. His love of Indian lore and frontier life was well known, yet he settled permanently in New York City ca. 1914.
40 Hamlin Garland, *A Son of the Middle Border* (New York: Borealis, 1917), p.374, an autobiography, as quoted in Hubbell (1936), vol. 3, p.186. See Duncan (1964) and Larsar Ziff, "The prairie in literary culture and the prairie style of . . . Wright," in Bolon (1989), especially pp.183–184.
41 Joseph B. McCullough, DLB78, pp.183, 193.
42 Garland (1912), p.558; cf. Henry Regnery, *Cliff Dwellers: The History of a Chicago Cultural Institution* (Chicago: The Club, 1990). There was also the recently popularized Pueblo cliff dwellings.
43 As quoted in Siry (1996), pp.168–169.
44 A current realist novelist in the exposé genre of the 1990s is John Grisham who, in *The Street Lawyer* (New York: Bantam, 1998), for example, exposes the corruption and graft that controls the lives of the homeless in Washington, DC, but he does not name names.
45 Wright (1943), p.507, not in Wright (1932); see also Secrest (1992), p.302.
46 See, for example, Zona Gale, "A Club That 'Studied America'," *AmCity*, 9(June 1913), pp.624–662; and idem., "How Women's Clubs Can Co-operate with the City Officials," ibid., 10(May 914), p.537; see also Eugenie Ladner Birch, "From Civic Worker to City Planner: Women and Planning," in Krueckeberg (1983), pp.396–426.
47 As quoted in John F. Moe, DLB78.
48 August Derleth, *Still Small Voice: The Biography of Zona Gale* (New York: Appleton Century, 1940), pp.45–49, 129–131, 149, 221; on Wright, pp.150–151, 234.
49 Hamilton (1989), p.43; Wright (1943), p.507, not in Wright (1932).
50 Zona Gale, foreword to Charlotte Perkins Gilman, *The Living of Charlotte Perkins Gilman: An Autobiography* (New York: Appleton, 1935), p.xxxvii.
51 Mamah Borthwick to Ellen Key, 20 July 1914, as quoted in Alice T. Friedman, "FLW and Feminism . . .," *JSAH*, 61(June 2002), p.148.
52 See relevant discussion in Mary P. Ryan, *Womanhood in America*, 3rd ed. (New York: Franklin Watts, 1983), pp.210–216; Julien S. Murphy, "Gilman," in Mary Ellen Waithe, ed., *A History of Women Philosophers* (Dordrecht/Boston: Springer Science, 1995), vol. 4; Mary A. Hill, *Charlotte Perkins Gilman: The Making of a Radical Feminist 1860–1896* (Philadelphia: Temple University Press, 1980); Margaret S. Marsh, *Anarchist Women 1870–1920* (Philadelphia: Temple University Press, 1981), pp.49ff, on Key, pp.69–94; Margaret Forster, *Significant Sisters: The Grassroots of Active Feminism 1839–1939* (New York: Secker & Warburg, 1984).

30   Conditions

Zona Gale's Portage family was not related to the Oak Park Gales who were intimately involved with local civic and religious affairs. Edwin O. Gale sold and donated Oak Park land on which Wright's Unity Temple rose. Wright also designed houses for Edwin's son Thomas (in 1892 and 1897), son Walter (in 1893), and Mrs Thomas Gale (in 1907?–09) and also for her three rental cottages (in 1909): see Siry (1996), pp.2, 72, 190, 197, and notes; and Storrer (1993), pp.17, 20. The Portage Gales did not employ Wright.

53 On the murder of Mamah Borthwick, her two children, Ernest Weston (age 13), Emil Brodelle, David Lindblom and Thomas Brunker, Google "The Taliesin Murders," and see Julian Carlton at "Murderpedia" website.

54 The connection is made only contextually in a few other works, see for example, Anthony Alofsin, "Taliesin: 'To Fashion Worlds in Little'," in Narciso G. Menocal, ed., *Wright Studies: Taliesin 1911–1914*. Vol. l (Carbondale: Southern Illinois University Press, 1992), pp.44–65. Key referred to Gilman's approach to social problems as from "an inferior point of view," Ellen Key, *Love and Ethics*, trans. by Mamah Bouton Borthwick (that is, the former Mrs. Cheney) and Frank Lloyd Wright (Chicago: Ralph Fletcher Seymour, 1912), p.47, not in idem., ibid., (New York: G. P. Putnam's, 1912).

On women's practical responses see, for example, Maureen A. Flanagan, *Seeing with their Hearts: Chicago Women and the Vision of the Good City, 1871–1933* (Princeton: Princeton University Press, 2002); Daphne Spain, *How Women Saved the City* (Minneapolis: University of Minnesota Press, 2001); Jeanne Catherine Lawrence, "Chicago's Eleanor Clubs: Housing Working Women in the Early Twentieth Century," in Sally McMurry and Annmarie Adams, eds., *People, Power, Places: Perspectives in Vernacular Architecture*, VII (Knoxville: University of Tennessee Press, 2000), pp.219–247.

55 William Wasserstrom, *The Time of the Dial* (Syracuse: Syracuse University Press, 1963), p.15. *The Dial* changed course in 1918 to become more political and leftish when it moved to New York City.

56 During 1906, Gallery 291 exhibited French, British, German, and Viennese photographers. Between 1908–12, the gallery showed artwork by European modernists Rodin, Matisse, Cèzanne, and Picasso; all before the heralded 1913 Armory Show in New York City. 291 closed in 1917.

57 Sergeant (1976a), p.136, appendices E–F. Apparently Wright invited about 170 people (celebrities) to support his Fellowship; nearly all ignored him.

58 As put by Pease (1962), p.245, see also pp.421–428.

59 Son John quoted Finley Peter Dunne in *Mr. Dooley's Opinions* (New York: R. H. Russell, 1901), parts of pp.13–15, in Wright (1946), pp.30–31.

60 Ibid., Dunne (1901), p.175.

61 Hofstadter (1969), p.185. There are many collections of muckraking literature but see Resek (1967); Hofstadter (1963); Hubbell (1936), vol. 3; Glaab (1963).

62 See Destler (1963); Thomas (1983), pp.280–285, 360; Aaron (1951), chapter 5.

63 Harvey Wish, introduction to Stead (1894), p.15.

64 March (1970), p.582.

65 As quoted in Altman (1993), p.294.

66 Altman (1993), p.294.

67 Altman (1993), p.294; Louise C. Wade, *Notable American Women 1607–1950* (Cambridge, MA: Harvard University Press, 1971), p.319. On those liberals who touched the Jones and Wright families, see Richard Schneirov, *Labor and Urban Politics: Class Conflict and the Origins of Modern Liberalism in Chicago 1864–97* (Urbana: University of Illinois Press, 1998).

68 Wright (1900), *Brickbuilder*, p.126.

69 FLW, "Art and Craft of the Machine," address supposedly to the Arts and Crafts Society in Hull-House 6 March 1901, *Catalogue of the Fourteenth Annual Exhibition of the Chicago Architectural Club . . .*, (Chicago: The Club, 1901), and Collected Writings, vol. 1, p.62. Wright claimed his "thesis" was thereafter supported by the likes of Addams, Lathrop, Oliver Triggs, and Charles Zueblin (Wright 1943, p. 132). It was given again as a public lecture sponsored by the Daughters of the Revolution in University Lecture Hall, Fine Arts Building, and originally titled "Man and the Machine," see *The New Industrialism* (Chicago: National League of Industrial Art, 1902), part III. The lecture program included Reverend Jones, Addams from Hull-House, and Prof. Emil C. Hirsch of Sinai Temple, a close friend of Jones. (The National League had been formed in Chicago in 1898.) It was given again to the Western Society of Engineers on 20 March 1901 and thereafter often edited and often republished.

70 FLW, "A Philosophy of Fine Art," Collected Writings, vol. 1, p.44 and no.2.
71 Press Club of Chicago to Wright, 17 July 1913, Wright Archive.
72 Twombly (1979), pp.114–115; Secrest (1992), pp.137–138, 360.
73 FLW, "Tribute" to Donald Robertson, *Oak Leaves* (Oak Park), 14 December 1907, as cited in Twombly (1979), p.114.
74 Alofsin (1992), pp.47–49.
75 Wright (MS.1918), p.7.
76 Opinion of Lawrence Langner, *The Magic Curtain* (New York: Dutton, 1951), p.84.
77 Friedman (1998), p.39. Cf. Emma Goldman, *The Social Significance of Modern Drama* (Boston: R. G. Badger, 1914).
78 Kathryn Smith, *FLW Hollyhock House and Olive Hill* (New York: Rizzoli, 1992), pp.15–19; Perry R. Duis, "Where's Athens Now? The Fine Arts Building 1898–1918," *Chicago History*, 6(Summer, 1977), pp.67–78.
79 Wright (1939), p.33. See also Wright, "Books That Have Meant Most to Me," *Scholastic*, 21(September 1932), p.11; and Sergeant (1976b), pp.130–132. Giuseppe Mazzini was a nineteenth-century Italian patriot and republican revolutionary.
80 Wright (1943); not in Wright (1932). Wright read Gesell in the late 1920s at the earliest. He may have known Veblen, whose writings had little influence on the architect until the late 1920s.
81 Sullivan (1924), pp.204–206; see also Morrison (1935), p.59.
82 L. Sullivan in Paris to A. Sullivan, 7 December 1874, as quoted in Willard Connely, *Louis Sullivan as He Lived*, as quoted in Gregerson (2013), p.11.
83 Donald D. Egbert and Paul E. Sprague, "In Search of John Edelmann," *AIAJ*, 45(February, 1966), pp.35–41. Edelmann died in 1900. On the Edelmann and Sullivan relationship, see also Twombly (1986), pp.50ff.
84 Alfred Zucker was born in Freiburg, Silesia, in 1852, and studied at the polytechnic school in Breig and Berlin before emigrating to New York in 1872. He practiced in Washington, DC, Texas, Mississippi, and New York. To avoid a malpractice lawsuit, in 1904, he fled to Buenos Aires, Argentina, where he and his wife remained. Many of his drawing are held by the Alexander Architectural Archive at University of Texas in Austin.
85 Wright (1932), pp.102, 107.
86 Wright (1946), p.40.
87 J. H. Edelmann, "Pessimism of Modern Architecture," *Engineering Magazine*, 3(April 1892), pp.44–54; further analyzed in Weingarden (2009), pp.284, 363–365; and Twombly (1986), pp.50–52, 70–85.
88 Weingarden (2009), p.364. Edelmann from 1895–1900 (when he died) published short essays in anarchistic/socialist/communist periodicals on subjects other than architecture.
89 Wright (1946), pp.40, 54.
90 Henry George, *Progress and Poverty, An Inquiry into the Cause of Industrial Depression and of Increase of Want with Increase of Wealth: The Remedy* (the author, 1879), (New York: Appleton's, 1879), four editions or reprints by 1881.
91 As digested by Otis Pease, introduction to Howe (1905), p.xxi.
92 Beard (1912), p.134.
93 See, for example, George E. Thomas, *William L. Price: Arts and Crafts to Modern Design* (New York: Princeton Architectural Press, 2000), pp.80–81.
94 Wright claimed that around 1930 he helped Commons restore his health; "we just put him on good terms with himself," Wright (1943), p.408, not in Wright (1932).
95 Hubbell (1936), vol. 3, introduction, p.4. Bostonian Howell's novel *Altruria* apparently was unnoticed by Wright.
96 Amply discussed and annotated within the themes of Johnson (1990).
97 An affair remembered by sculptor Richard Bock, then in Wright's office, as reported in Pierre (1989), p.89.
98 Wright (1910), p.4.
99 Extracts from Wright (1901a), likely edited and expanded from the original address, as were later talks and publications that used the same general text.
100 For the engine's purpose and advantages to industry, see John Brinckerhoff Jackson, *American Space: The Centennial Years 1865–1876* (New York: W. W. Norton, 1972), p.238.
101 On the Los Angeles concrete block buildings, see Johnson (2013a).
102 Wright's exhortations about certain activities and accomplishments and especially about his concrete block system in the early 1920s is critically examined in Johnson (2013a).

103 Wright to L. Sullivan, 26 September 1923, as published in Pfeiffer (1984), p.39.
104 Flanagan (1996), p.163. For Wright's nationalistic concerns in the wake of the 1929 financial collapse, see Johnson (1990).
   Epigraph George W. Steevens, a journalist with the *London Daily Mail*, "Land of the Dollar" in Sutton (1976), pp.352–362.
105 Condit (1968), pp.120–121.
106 George W. Steevens in 1894 from "Land of the Dollar" as quoted in Sutton, 1976.
107 March (1970), p.581.
108 As quoted in Bulmer (1984), p.14; see also Siry (2002), chapters 1 and 2; Bachin (2004), throughout. For a regional perspective, cf. Teaford (1993).
109 On the University of Chicago and graduate study in northeastern America around 1900, see Menand (2001), passim.
110 As quoted in Dedmon (1953), opposite title page.
111 On Chicago ca. 1890s see, as examples, Paul Bourget, *Outre-Mer: Impressions of America* (New York: 1895), a translation from *Outre-Mer/notes sur l'amérique* (Paris: 1894), quoted in Gifford (1966), pp.577–587; Gustave Kobbé, "Sights at the Fair," in Sutton (1976), pp.160–166; Rudyard Kipling in Cook (1973), pp.37–39; David A. Shannon, ed., *Beatrice Webb's American Diary 1898* (Madison: University of Wisconsin Press, 1963), pp.99–109; Hamlin Garland, *Roadside Meetings* (New York: Macmillan, 1930 printing); and here and there in more general compilations such as Henry Steel Commager, ed., *America in Perspective: The United States Through Foreign Eyes* (New York: Random House, 1948); Robert B. Downs, *[Written] Images of America* (Urbana: University of Illinois Press, 1987); Lewis and Smith (1929), note Oscar Wilde's comments p.177, but cf. Louis Edwards, *Oscar Wilde Discovers America: A Novel* (New York: Scribner, 2003 [1882]).
112 Dedmon (1953), p.149.
113 Zinn (1999), p.272.
114 Andrew Carnegie, "Wealth," *North American Review*, 148(1889), pp.654–664, as quoted in Mason (1956), p.571. The editor believed it the "finest article I have ever published in the Review," p.561.
115 Mayer and Wade (1969), part 3, note p.183.
116 As summarized by Burchard and Bush-Brown (1961), p.273.
117 For a summary of conditions, see Zinn (1999), pp.279–282.
118 Richard T. Ely, "Pullman: A Social Study," *Harper's Magazine*, 70(February 1885), pp.452–466, as published in Conn and Page (2003), pp.328–335. The most influential contemporary analysis that described and then damned social and economic conditions.
119 Stanley Buder, *Pullman: An Experiment in Industrial Order and Community Planning 1880–1930* (New York: Oxford University Press, 1967); idem., "The Model Town of Pullman: Town Planning and Social Control in the Gilded Age," *JAIP*, 33(January 1967), pp.2–10; Dal Co (1980), pp.187–200; Garner (1991a); Gilbert (1991). Debs ran unsuccessfully for US president for the Socialist Party of America (founded 1901) in 1903, 1907, and 1911.
   On Pullman and new factory towns to follow, see Crawford (1995); Reps (1965b), pp.426–438; Spann (1989); on their social and architectural context Burchard and Bush-Brown (161), pp.146–149, 237–240, 271–274.
120 In 1898, courts ordered the Pullman Palace Car Company, then operated by caretaker Robert Todd Lincoln, son of the former president, to divest itself of the town. It was taken over by the City of Chicago.
121 Scott (1969), p.33.
122 Garland (1913), pp.555–556; "Daniel Hudson Burnham: An Appreciation," *ARecord*, 23(August 1912), pp.175–185, Wright's eulogy, p.184; Peter B. Wight, "Daniel Hudson Burnham and His Associates," *ARecord*, 38(July 1915), pp.1–12; William E. Parsons, "Burnham as a Pioneer in City Planning," ibid., pp.13–31; A. N. Rebori, "The Work of Burnham . . .," ibid., pp.33–168.
123 Wright (1932), pp.123–125; also "Frank Lloyd Wright" (sic), (eulogy), *ARecord*, 23 (August 1912), p.184.
124 Sullivan (1924), p.288.
125 Burchard and Bush-Brown (1961), p.296.
126 Atwood's Fine Arts Building was not demolished and not burnt in an 1894 fire but rebuilt in granite in 1931 and soon housed the Rosenwald Museum of Science and Industry.

127 Montgomery Schuyler, "Last Words About the Fair," *ARecord*, 3(1893), quoted in Coles and Reed (1961), p.204. Cf. Scott (1969), pp.1000–1109; Cronon (1991), chapter 8.
128 Cf. Peterson (1985); Gillette (1995), chapters 5–6; Manieri-Elia (1980).
129 In the name of axial symmetry, McKim also blocked Jefferson's grand landscape vista from the steps of the University of Virginia's library with a massive building. McKim's recollections of the McMillan Commission are found in Glenn Brown, "Personal Reminiscences of Charles Follen McKim," *ARecord*, 38(November 1915), pp.575–582, and idem., 38(December 1915), pp.681–689. See also Peterson (1985), pp.135–136, 147; Reps (1965a), chapter 18, where, like many historians, he refers to Burnham's "Hausmannization" of cities.
130 Scott (1969), p.54.
131 Gillette (1995), pp.109–110.
132 Charles Mulford Robinson, *Modern Civic Art, or the City Made Beautiful*, 2nd ed. (New York: G. P. Putnam's, 1904), p.257, as quoted in Gillette (1995), p.110. Wilson (1989) approaches an apologist's view; Manieri-Elia (1980) is a balanced but candid view; see also Gilbert A. Stelter, "Rethinking the Significance of the City Beautiful Movement," an outline in Robert Freestone, ed., *The Twentieth Century Urban Planning Experience* (Sydney: University of New South Wales, 1998), pp.869–872; Cynthia R. Field and Jeffrey T. Tilman, "Creating a Model for the National Mall," *JSAH*, 62(March 2004), pp.52–73.
133 Lewis and Smith (1929), p.312; Siry (2002), pp.124–125.
134 Burnham and Bennett (1909).
135 Hines (1974), p.33; see also Cronon (1991), chapter 8; Scott (1969), pp.100–109. On Bennett's theories, see his talk in David L. A. Gordon, "Introducing a City Beautiful Plan for Canada's Capital, Edward Bennett's 1914 Speech to the Canadian Club," *Planning History Studies* (London), 12(1/2, 1998), pp.13–51, esp. 13, 15.
136 Gilbert, Marsh, and Ford as quoted in Wilson (1989), pp.287–288.
137 Post-1911 events and construction (to the tune of about $300 million) are outlined in Wesley Marx, *The Frail Ocean* (New York: Ballantine, 1967), chapter 12; Thomas J. Schlereth, "Burnham's *Plan* and Moody's *Manual*, City Planning as Progressive Reform," in Krueckeberg (1983), pp.75–99; David B. Brownlee, *Building the City Beautiful* (Philadelphia Museum of Art, 1989). The 1909 reformers' dreams, if that is the right word, were only partly realized, but after 1945. For contemporary reality, see Keating (2005).
138 For a more recent example of misunderstanding the movement's complexity, see Gilbert A. Stelter, "Rethinking the Significance of the City Beautiful Idea," in Robert Freestone, ed., *Urban Planning in a Changing World: The Twentieth Century Experience* (London: E & F N Spon, 2000), pp.98–115.
139 March (1970), p.581.

The aesthetics of progress

2   Education

Beginning in his teen years, Wright was intimately and extensively involved with education. Educational theories and practices of the late eighteenth century up to those of immediate experiences insinuated themselves into his personal and professional lives and his theoretical ideas and design expressions. Education is one key to understanding his personal life, yes, but withal it was an impetus to become a revolutionary and reformist architect. It was education as an act of acquiring knowledge through farming and working with nature's way, through observing educational activities, listening to recitations of family beliefs in Emersonian Transcendentalism and Unitarianism, receiving his father's artistic sensibilities and practices, through Froebel's thoughts on kindergartens, the theology of his uncle Reverend Jenkin Jones, the practical architects Joseph Silsbee and Dankmar Adler, the dedication of Hamlin Garland, the impractical pragmatics of a philosophical Louis Sullivan, through wife Catherine's strong familial and social commitments, and who or what else? Education was not just information or know-how or means but a holistic adventure, intellectually, religiously, and socially driven and satisfying; at least, that was the dream.

Wright's father William, his mother's Jones family, his boss Silsbee, and the others, were among those in the late nineteenth century who enjoyed reading authors who followed Rousseau's call in the 1760s to cherish and learn from nature. Humans had become alienated, his followers complained, from their fundamental associations with nature principally by the persuasive artificiality of urban society, by its social conventions and inherent deceptions. This had encouraged egoism, pride, and ruthlessness, they argued, with the loss of the natural virtues of kindness, decency, and honesty. Society's construct of culture was false, a product of vanity; science and technology encouraged idleness and the counterfeit. Therefore, mechanical and social mechanisms thwarted natural vital forces, human vitalism, and demanded control over human actions and shepherding thought. Humanity is happiest, they said, in tribes –thus, in small rural communities. As it was for the polemicists of the English Picturesque around 1800, the city was a gross simulation, an abomination, filthy.

Anxious poets and authors who glorified the natural world included Samuel Taylor Coleridge, William Wordsworth ("The world is too much with us"), Alfred Tennyson, and John Ruskin in England; the Russian Leo Tolstoy; the Americans William Cullen Bryant, Ralph Waldo Emerson, Henry David Thoreau, and Walt Whitman; in France, Victor Hugo; and Johan Goethe in Germany. After their return from Europe in 1910, Wright's mistress (as then called) Mamah Borthwick Cheney translated what she believed was an obscure poem by Goethe. They had discovered it in a Berlin book shop, but it was in fact very popular. Titled "A Hymn to Nature," one line is:

> Each of her Works has its own individual Being – each of her
> Phenomena the most isolated Conception, yet all in Unity.

Another is:

> We obey her Laws even when we most resist them, we work with her
> even when we wish to work against her.[1]

Around the same time, Thoreau observed that "It is the marriage of the soul with Nature that makes the intellect fruitful, and gives birth to imagination": 1851. Painters included the Europeans John Constable, William Blake, Caspar David Friedrich, Honrè Daumier, Claude Monet and French Impressionists, and the Americans Thomas Cole, Albert Bierstadt, George C. Bingham, George Catlin, and Winslow Homer.

Each author and artist insisted on the necessity of beauty; not as something transcendentally "out there" but as an instructional reality derived from nature. Beauty provides emotional delight and a sense of purpose that engages our insight into and feelings of freedom and openness. The evolution appetite and mundane acts of living are best served when clarified by visions of purpose. Meaning and intelligence, therefore, are found in nature and beauty, not in fickle human abstracts. The converse is ugliness, where the senses find entrapment, dirt, triviality, and a festering boredom. Moral ugliness is potent in gray cities, harbors of the insensible. One must educate in order to overcome the failings of urban society and to find meaning and beauty, and that logically begins with the young. So said Rousseau, Johann Pestalozzi, Tolstoy, Froebel, Parker, and so too the experiences of the Wright and Jones families that composed Frank's inheritance.

J.-J. Rousseau and after

> *God makes all things good; man meddles with them and they become evil. . . .*
> *The natural man lives for himself; he is the unit, the whole, dependent only on himself and on his like. . . .*
> *In the social order where each has his own place a man must be educated for it.*

This epigram might have been penned by Goethe, Thomas Carlyle, Emerson, Froebel, John Dewey, or Wright's Uncle Jenkin. But they are the words of Jean-Jacques Rousseau. They encapsulate his long, repetitive, at times wandering, ill-disciplined yet compelling treatise *Emile, or, On Education*, published in 1762.[2] Maurice Cranston, a Rousseau specialist, has neatly summarized the influence of the Frenchman on Western thought. Marking the end of the so-called Age of Reason, Rousseau announced

> the birth of Romanticism. He propelled political and ethical thinking into new channels. His [proposed] reforms revolutionized taste, first in music, then in the other arts. He had a profound impact on people's way of life; he taught parents to take a new interest in their children and to educate them differently; he furthered the expression of emotion rather than polite restraint in friendship and love. He introduced the cult of religious sentiment among people who had discarded religious dogma. He opened men's eyes to the beauties of nature, and he made liberty an object of almost universal aspiration.[3]

Kenneth Clark was succinct: "Whatever his defects as a human being . . . Rousseau *was* a genius: one of the most original minds of any age."[4] In an introduction to a new printing of *Emile*, the French-literature specialist André Boutet de Monvel was also brief:

> Rousseau's work, in which philosophical speculation is closely interwoven with visionary dreams . . . flows entirely from the propositions . . . on the goodness of nature and the corrupting influence of society.[5]

Although necessary for many reasons, in the latter part of *Emile*, Rousseau placed cities at the extreme opposite of nature. At one point, he said he did "not exhort" people to "live in a town, on the contrary, one of the examples which the good should give to others is that of a patriarchal, rural life, the earliest of man, the most peaceful, the most natural. . .":[6] that of primitive societies.

Nearly the whole of Wright's written works post-1904 in some manner further Rousseau's speculations about individuality, nature, the state, and so forth, including attacks on the vile city and the joys of small towns. Wright was a latter-day Rousseauan in architectural guise. Carlyle, Spencer, Ruskin, Emerson, Froebel, and Viollet-le-Duc were intermediaries. But Rousseau's education of parents about the education of their children also intrigues.

Emile is both a novel and a series of episodic and didactic lectures, sometimes hintingly Socratic, about the education of a rich man's son, that "prig," Dewey called him.[7] The voice is a tutor whose task is to condition the son for the onslaught of society's constructions in preparation for republican citizenship. But Rousseau does not set out an instructor's guide. Rather, by a lengthy series of circumstances encountered by child and tutor, *Emile* offers intuitively drawn explanations that advise on nature's way, preparations for society's vain world, and how to reconcile nature and society.

At all times, a teacher must counteract the societal forces of "vice and error" by "manipulating pressures that will work with nature and not against it."[8] "You think you are teaching him what the world is like; he is only learning the map." Dewey saw this last phrase as describing "the defect of teaching *about* things instead of bringing to pass an acquaintance with the relations of the things themselves."[9] Rousseau prepared the way for subsequent enquiry and experimentation, most usefully for modern Progressive education, that was undertaken by Johann Heinrich Pestalozzi.

Rousseau was not interested in educating the peasantry or rural town folks. Pestalozzi, however, used *Emile* and Rousseau's *The Social Contract* (also 1762) as models for a radically innovative pedagogy that extrapolated the one-on-one dialogue suggested by *Emile*. In the beginning, Pestalozzi abandoned theological studies to farm in native Switzerland. There, he took in poor children in an attempt to prepare them for a trade. An unsuccessful venture, he then focused on the importance of a mother's role in early education, the development of individual faculties to enable independent thought and action, the central role of nature, and of Rousseau's naturalism. Finally, he directed the Yverdon Institute, again a school for children of local workers and the poor.

Pestalozzi believed that a child's innate faculties should evolve to enjoy independent thinking by proceeding from observation to comprehension and only then to the formulation of ideas. Religion-born morality was a preeminent component. Practically, this involved group and participatory activities in writing, singing, drawing, physical exercise, collecting, field trips, and mapmaking. He regarded "education as a fostering of all the potentialities inherent in a human being as a process which must be rooted in natural relationships and conditions."[10] His "method" received Europe-wide attention and attracted foreign pupils and observers.

A few American education reformers were attracted to Prussian education methods. The few included Horace Mann, Calvin E. Stowe, and Henry Barnard, each post-1850. Their interest was not on *gymnasium* but the *volksschule*, or people's schools. They were impressed to find that, in some principalities, schooling was compulsory and state endowed for children age five to fourteen, that the state had special tertiary schools to train teachers (seminaries or normal schools), and that education was "heavily" influenced by – and aptly named – Prussian Pestalozzianism. On returning to America, the three pedagogues wrote widely and attracted national attention. From 1855–82, Barnard edited and largely financed the influential *American Journal of Education*.[11] Two other observers were inspired by Pesstalozzi: the German Friedrich Froebel, who first visited the Swiss in 1805 and then trained with him during 1808–10, and Francis W. Parker from Massachusetts, and later, Chicago.

A resurgence in reform occurred parallel with the introduction of Froebelian education by America's German-speaking preschools beginning in the 1850s. We can trace Pestalozzi's ideas as they flowed in a stream of thought and practice through Mann, Barnard, Stowe, and Parker to the Lloyd Jones sisters – and only then to John Dewey and the whole of the Progressive Education Movement. Pestalozzi rationalized Rousseau's philosophy, then Froebel added practical methods and systems that popularized educational reform.

Rousseau had argued that education must prepare a child to act as an individual in a politically and socially driven society, one that normally devolves to what he referred to as the "general will," all to be managed by the aristocracy, later the Republic. Americans tended to neutralize the issue, but Rousseau, Pestalozzi, Froebel, Mann, and the Boston Unitarians, in their way, also saw general education as a focus for spiritual concentration and sustenance. That focus is clear in Froebel's bible, *The Education of Man*.[12] In 1816, Froebel founded a school in the village of Griesheim that later moved to Keilhau and flourished. He then established an infant school in Blankenburg and, interestingly, called it the Child Nurture and Activity Institute. By happy inspiration, he later renamed it The Kindergarten.

> The mind grows by self-revelation [said Froebel]. In play the child ascertains what he can do, discovers his possibilities of will and thought by exerting his power spontaneously. In work he follows a task prescribed for him . . . in play he reveals [discovers] his own original power.[13]

If one adds the moral authority of Tolstoy, so potently influential before 1918, some thoughts of the anarchistic theorist Peter Kropotkin, and the practice of Francis Parker, the historical foundation of America's Progressive education in its many guises becomes clear: Dewey was to become the principal theoretical motivator. All but Pestalozzi and Rousseau were, like so many of his liberal and/or non-conforming contemporaries before 1930, claimed by Wright's parental families as inspirational authors.

Tolstoy's literary works are renown. Yet before about 1900, his educational ideas were also highly regarded by reformers. What marks Tolstoy's life is a fervent belief in non-violence by encouraging civil disobedience and a controlled simplicity of lifestyle. His writings, therefore, illuminate the gap between what seems in harmony with nature and what seems false in the apparent requirements of (Russian) urban society, so vain, trivial and debased. No wonder that among authors he admired were Emerson, Thoreau, Whitman, and Goethe. Settling on a farm early in life, he keenly observed nature and was devoted to the peasantry, a noble commitment by one who would renounced his inherited nobility. By the time of death in 1910, we are told he had given away most of his land and possessions but not a library of 22,000 books. In any event, his book *Childhood* of 1852 was translated into English in 1862. It "conveyed his view that children already possess the truth about life, that they already sense what is important but that their senses can be easily corrupted by [formal] education and a selfish society."[14] It was a Rousseauan message radicalized.

Tolstoy's example in 1858 was to establish a school for peasant children on his farm where, as a fatherly figure, he allowed children greater freedom than the prevalent coercive European systems he had witnessed on varied tours, the exception Pestalozzi's. Tolstoy's rejection of the authority of the state, church, and military, and of the concept of private property, was favored by followers including Jane Addams, who had visited Tolstoy at his home before developing Hull-House settlement. In short, he promoted a right to individual anarchism. With less personal commitment it was a mode of life to which Wright aspired, initially signaled in 1909 by flight from marriage with Catherine to free association with Mamah.

Kropotkin gave Tolstoy's ideas formality and infused them with notions of social justice. He, too, renounced his Russian aristocratic heritage to live among European radicals dedicated to communist and libertarian causes and, oddly, the brutish form of anarchism. When on lecture tours, he resided in Chicago at Addams' Hull-House and in New York with John Edelmann, or at least on one occasion. At one time, Edelmann and Wright were fellow draftsman in the architectural office of Adler & Sullivan. Kropotkin's idea of "voluntary cooperation," or anarchy, argued for the decentralization of cities; nonpolitical cooperative societies where people could develop their creative faculties (as with Rousseau) without interference from politician, priest, or soldier; goods and services freely distributed; the reward of individual merit; and, much like medieval cities (he said, ignoring the church's role), life would be integrated and organic, deviation unexpected.

Like those who would manage society, Kropotkin held that preparation for a future happy life depended on educating the young. Ideally, schools were meant to cultivate mental and manual skills followed by emphasizing the humanities and basic principles of mathematics (numeric metaphors) and science. That proposal of around 1895 also emphasized the natural world, hands-on doing, and observation. It was a compromise of Rousseauan and mechanistic (material) ideas.

Those recommendations were subsequently widely endorsed (most often without reference to Kropotkin to avoid reactive biases) and can *loosely* compare to Wright's Taliesin Fellowship begun in 1932. Kropotkin's ideas were essential to the Modern School Movement, as were those of Tolstoy, the Americans Henry George, and later the anarchist Josiah Warren. French writer Romain Rolland, another of Wright's favorite authors, said that "Kropotkin lived what Tolstoy only advocated, and Oscar Wilde called him one of the two really happy men he had known."[15]

More pragmatic than Tolstoyan and Kropotkinian ideals was the work of New Hampshire-born Francis Wayland Parker. Like Reverend Jones, he was a Civil War veteran attaining the rank of lieutenant colonel. He had studied in Pestalozzi and Froebel programs firsthand in Europe. As superintendent of schools in Quincy, Massachusetts (1875–80), he developed a curriculum that was tuned by Pestalozzian participation. It was dramatically successful and attracted national attention. In 1883, Parker became principal of Chicago's Cook County Normal School and its practice primary school; it, too, was acclaimed. Dewey sent his son Fred and daughter Evelyn to Parker's practice school. Wright's aunts Jane and Ellen Jones attended Parker's lectures that "instilled a Messianic ardor . . . and endeared him to a generation" of educators.[16] The lively continuum of Rousseau to the Jones sisters is certain, to Wright circumstantial.

No doubt Wright's mother Anna and her sisters Jane and Nell attended the 1893 Chicago Exposition's education exhibits, as did a young lass, a friend of literature's Mr. Dooley. One day, Dooley met teacher Mary Casey en route to attend the "grand pidigogical exhibit." She was "takin' along me note'book," Dooley said she said, "an' I will pick up what bets Petzolootzi, the' gr-reat leader iv our profession, has over-looked."[17] John Wright vividly remembered sitting in the home living room listening to his father laugh as he read aloud Mr. Dooley's exploits and insights.

In 1894, John Dewey became professor of philosophy, psychology, and pedagogy at the newly established University of Chicago: the city an empirical laboratory. Five years later, Dewey wrote *The School and Society*, where he brought together many of the ideas specific or latent within those previously outlined or as revealed in his experimental school founded in 1896 at the university. The 1893, Exposition showcased the raw energy of unrestricted industrialism and commercialism, the results of which presented Dewey's inquiring mind with much fodder. He extended his experience by association with Jane Addams's settlement in a slum area, Hull-House, of which he was a trustee. (His daughter Jane is Addams's namesake.) There, he witnessed the exploitation of urban immigrant and minority people and joined other liberals and radicals in supporting legislation to aid the underprivileged, curtail the power of monopolies, legalize labor unions, and help found the National Association for the Advancement of Colored People.

Dewey's persuasive writing included critical discussions of – and drew on – among others, Locke (who, before Rousseau, had ineffectively written about education of an aristocrat), Rousseau, Pestalozzi, Kant, Froebel, Parker, and William James. Dewey *continued* their "revolt against formalism" and promoted a child-centered philosophy. In the light of his predecessors, Dewey was able to say, "I believe that the individual who is to be educated is a social individual, and that society is an organic union of individuals."[18] He also emphasized that the school community must "*reflect* the life of the larger society," thereby releasing its isolation from reality: Education "is not a preparation for life; it is life." Moreover, and as education historian Lawrence Cremin has observed,

> [the] embryonic community [would] *improve* the larger society by making it more "worthy, lovely, and harmonious." Once again, the school is cast as a lever of social change, [the educator] cast into the struggle for social reform.[19]

Compulsory primary and secondary education was legalized by Massachusetts in 1852, and other states followed, the last in 1918. Anarchists rejected it as state control, but Dewey gave support, believing democratic societies are "committed to change," that they are "intentionally progressive" because they are constantly in flux.[20] As Benjamin Disraeli observed in 1851: "Change is inevitable in a progressive country, change is constant." This places serious responsibilities on education to protect the integrity of the process through universal education where all would be empowered by the same knowledge.

A variety of Progressive educational programs active up to 1915 (supporting their theory of no single road to reform) were carefully described by Dewey and daughter Evelyn in *Schools of To-Morrow*. The book synopsizes education's immediate history toward liberating the child: "Nowhere is the faith and optimism of the Progressive Movement more dramatically conveyed."[21] Obviously, Progressive education predates the American Progressive Era by decades. Equally obvious, its humanitarian foundation did much to form Progressivism's philosophic foundation.

Kindergartens

In 1932, Wright autobiographically recorded that, while attending the 1876 Centennial Exposition in Philadelphia, "mother made a discovery":

> The Kindergarten!
> She had seen the "Gifts." . . . The strips of colored paper, glazed and "matt," remarkably soft brilliant colors. . . . The structural figures to be made with peas and small straight sticks: slender constructions, the joinings accented by the little green pea globes. The smooth shapely maple blocks with which to build, the sense of which never afterward leaves the fingers: so *form* became *feeling*. . . .
> And the exciting cardboard shapes with pure scarlet face – such scarlet! Smooth triangular shapes, white-back, and edges, cut in rhomboids with which to make designs on the flat table top.[22]

One commentator thought Wright's "*form* became *feeling*" aphorism (words from Froebelian literature and italicized by Wright) is the key to understanding the importance of Froebel's gifts. That is to ignore color that also might become feeling: "a world of color and form."[23] But these trivialities are typical of minor, easily overemphasized details placed out of chronological order.

Wright was born and raised in Wisconsin with a single seven-year interlude. In 1871, the family moved to McGregor, Iowa, then Pawtucket, Rhode Island, to remain until December 1873, when they began residence with William's father David in Essex, Connecticut. They then moved in September 1874 to Weymouth, Massachusetts, near Boston and the epicenter of Emersonian Transcendentalism. Wright recalled that, in 1876, his mother travelled to Boston to "take lessons of a teacher of the Froebel method and come home to teach the children."[24] Wright was ten years old when the family returned to the Wisconsin hills in early 1878.[25]

Apparently, Anna Wright had sought those parts of the 1876 exposition devoted to women's affairs and education, and there she watched a kindergarten in action. It was described in a contemporary publication as follows:

> The "Kindergarten"
> Close by the Women's Pavilion . . . is a little cottage, where are shown . . . actual methods of education in use in the infant school system of Froebel, termed the "Kindergarten." Here . . . can be seen on certain days of the week, illustrating its working with eighteen little children from three to six years of age taken . . . [who] go through the regular daily exercises. . . . [T]his school is conducted by Miss [Ruth] Burritt, the furniture and material being contributed by Mr. [E.] Steiger, of New York. . . . The idea involves

a large, well ventilated, will-lighted and pleasant room opening upon a garden. . . . [Figure 2.1 herein]

Froebel . . . devised a number of games and exercises . . . and also *six "gifts"* [emphasis added]. . . . These gifts consist of soft balls of different colors – with strings attached to them – cubes, cylinders, wooden balls, cubes divided for the construction of buildings and other objects . . . the whole being intended to convey the meaning of form, color, size, motion, individual and other qualities to the infant mind.[26]

While there were at least five other kindergarten exhibits at the fair, including a small one by Susan Blow, this was the largest, and pupils met three days a week.[27] It was set up by Philadelphia's Froebel Society and planned by Boston education philanthropist Elizabeth Peabody.

The first American kindergarten was conducted in 1855 (into 1858) by Mrs Carl Schurz (i.e. Margarethe Schurz), for German emigrant children who met at her home in Watertown, Wisconsin. She had studied under Froebel in Germany before emigrating. The first English-language kindergarten was set up in Boston by Peabody. It ran from 1861 into 1867, when she left to study briefly with Schurz and then at the Froebel center in Switzerland.[28]

By 1875, Froebelites had taken their educational system into the early years of primary schools in parts of central Europe and England.[29] But not in the United States, where up to ca. 1890 kindergartens were private enterprises for preschoolers. German immigrant communities established private kindergartens in north central America, including Milwaukee, in 1855. But both sets of Wright's grandparents did not speak German. The first English-speaking kindergarten was opened in Boston by Peabody in 1861 but closed after a couple of years. The first American public school system to offer kindergartens at the preschool level was Carondolet district of St Louis in 1875, under the leadership of Susan Blow, the inspirational pedagogue with whom Wright's aunt Jane Jones studied in the late 1870s. The first kindergarten in

Figure 2.1 Interior of the "Kindergarten Cottage" located beside the Women's Pavilion at the Centennial International Exhibition, Fairmont Park, Philadelphia, 1875–76. (Is Miss Burritt standing at far left and at right a student teacher?) From Leslie, 1877.

Madison was formed by the German emigrant community in 1877. Wisconsin's first two English-speaking kindergartens began in 1880. In 1892, the Chicago Board of Education assumed responsibility for kindergartens.[30] But private kindergartens abounded, including Catherine Wright's. By 1900, there were about 1,400 Froebel kindergartens nationwide.[31]

To support private home instruction, Anna had access to manuals available from Bradley's store where, apparently on an occasion or two, she received advice. The earliest kindergarten publication currently held in the Wright archives is not a teaching manual but a E. Steiger Company sales catalog. It contains descriptions of twenty "Kindergarten gifts and Occupation Material" and dated May 1876. Each gift was available separately and purchased any time after 1878. Gifts three to six were boxes of building blocks naturally finished, without color.[32] Some remnants of Froebel gifts are in the Wright archives and, while their exact dates of purchase are unknown, there is little doubt they were obtained either by Catherine around 1894 or by Frank and Olgivanna ca. 1930.[33]

The gifts

In 1876, the first six gifts were designed for nursery infants. Those numbered seven to twenty were for preschool children. Frank Lincoln was no preschooler but nine-and-one-half years old. He had attended public school for at least two and a half years before being exposed to something like kindergarten activities.[34] Only sister Maginel was of preschool age, apparently she did play with the gifts. Her brother's recollections nearly sixty years after Weymouth, carried on in the third person: "Music he [Frank] adored, and the Gifts. Meantime he was learning to play the piano. Going to his mother's kindergarten [at home]. Learning to paint and draw a little. . . ."[35] Just before death in 1966, Wright's sister Maginel remembered the gifts, the "shapes and colors!" She was certain that "Frank reacted to them exactly as she [mother] had hoped, . . . they were the first outlet for his genius." He was mother's "protége" and "music became his second love."[36]

As William and Anna Wright's marriage faltered irreconcilably into divorce in 1885, daughter Maginel juggled her fading memory and wrote that upon the divorce, her mother . . .

> had no time to waste; she gathered all the strands of her yearning, wove them together, and fastened them once and for all to her son. He [Frank] was more than her child. He was her protègè, her legacy. He would accomplish what she and her husband could not.
> From the start, her devotion to Frank was overwhelming. . . .[37]

In the light of ongoing research into William and Anna's home life, Maginel's use of the word "overwhelming" was correct. Sister Jane surely believed she, too, was second best and no doubt overwhelmed. Maginel then referred to "our mother" but "with qualification: she was my mother, and my older sister Jane's, but most of all she was Frank's."[38] How sad. Maginel's 1965 book of recollection, penned at age eighty-five, was about family but also a full eulogy of her famous brother.

There are, therefore, suggestions that music was to be young Frank's future dedication if not vocation: a pregnant suggestion. F. L. Wright Jr. recalled that his father "would relax at the piano and . . . it was beautiful."[39] Music was Frank's father William's first love and catalytic for more intimate contacts with his children. Moreover, it was through music that Frank Lincoln may have appreciated the inherent structure of art. Music is scientific (harmonics, the rhythm of sound and silence) and artistic (selection, expression, intuition): technology and aesthetics, solid and void (sound, silence), abstraction. Wright put it so in 1908: "Music may be for the architect ever and always a sympathetic friend whose counsels, precepts, and patterns even[,] are available to him and from which he need not fear to draw."[40]

However, it is most likely that Wright became seriously interested in buildings not prenatally or by maternal prompting, or as an aesthetic impulse as so often surmised, but as a result of helping his carpenter uncle Thomas construct and repair farm and school buildings. Also to be counted is the family's association with a fellow Emersonian Unitarian and close friend, the architect Joseph Silsbee. Those physical and social interactions were translated to architecture and only then "music became his second love." Frank and Catherine had six children born from 1890–1903; all took private lessons in music and art and most attended their mother's neighborhood kindergarten and their aunt's private school.

Architect Robert Spencer's important 1900 article about Wright was informative if at times embarrassingly laudatory. Reading between the lines and with greater biographical knowledge, we can safely say that wife Catherine, mother Anna, and Wright had convinced Spencer, a close friend with shared reformative ideas, that a kindergarten education and its gifts were a singular contribution to Frank's design abilities:

> If I were making a plea [Spencer said], for the kindergarten idea in education, I would adduce no better living example of its value as a factor in the development of the artistic faculties than by referring to [Wright] . . . one of a very few in our profession [Spencer must have guessed], who have enjoyed that training.

Anna is said to have recalled that Frank's kindergarten training was the foundation of his "instinctive grasp" of the "niceties of line, form and color." But we shall learn that oft-repeated claim is barely a half truth, dissembling.[41] The essay touched Sullivan's ideas and theories nearly as often as Wright's in an attempt to intimately link the two men, even offering Wright as Sullivan's mentorial successor, a claim Wright often made. For the moment, however, it is the influence of Froebel's idea that draws our attention.

The use of geometry in systematized art education dates from the early sixteenth century in Europe with the establishment of humanistic academies. Closer to and more influential on later educators were neoclassical ideals at the end of the eighteenth century. Some teachers and theorists of art favored simple geometric forms because of their elemental purity, they would have said, and a classicity of shape. Goethe's stone sculpture *Altar of Good Fortune* in 1777 was reportedly composed of a sphere (unity) resting on a cube (order). In architecture, the bold geometrical fantasies of Etienne Boullee and C.-N. Ledoux in France, or the lifeless stone forms of Gottfried Semper in Germany, come to mind. It was also argued that plain solid geometrical forms represented paradigms in nature. Within that understanding, geometry and geometrically pure crystals, and proportional logic and symmetry, for instance, were of natural science and therefore of nature.

Germany was a leader not only in toy making but in "systematizing the practice of drawing for purpose-built geometric solids."[42] One exponent was painter and teacher Peter Schmid, whose work, the four-volume *Das Naturzeichnen fur den schul-und Selbstunterrcht* (Drawing from Nature for School and Self-Instruction), was published in Berlin (1828–32). One part was devoted to the use of plain geometric volumes. A related kit included a boxed set of proportionally related plain wooden blocks. (These should not be confused with other contemporary blocks that were colored and of shapes that, when assembled, formed something like, as an example, a pedimented portico.)[43] Schmid made two relevant points. First, nature and geometry were one, and second, blocks were to be manipulated, if by set instructions, in a manner that exploited their three-dimensionality and proportionality. Included were illustrated architectural subjects and perspective drawings, each to copy.

In spite of the demise of neoclassical naturalism (as we shall call it) and then the rise of rationalism, eclecticism, and then aestheticism (the last exemplified by Ruskin's remark that "All good drawing consists merely of dirtying the paper delicately"),[44] by the mid-nineteenth century, systematized study of geometrical shapes had gained acceptance in northern Europe, England, and isolated places in North America. Frederick Froebel's inclusion of plain geometric forms, therefore, was not unique and alone did not distinguish his system. Yet Froebel blocks, balls, sticks, and so on cannot be ignored simply because Wright mentioned them and, in recent years, others have made much too much of them.[45] But those authors and Wright did not describe how the toys taught how to design. They were not about architectural theory of material, space, and form or the design process, especially one as aesthetically and technically complex as architecture. Therefore, we can say the "occupational" toys – the gifts (the *baden*) – not only did *not* but could *not* infix a design method. Froebel, who studied architecture before switching to education, devised a general system to educate infants.

Things in modules can be repeated and interchanged endlessly to form patterns.[46] As to two-dimensional grids, the most practically universal is loom weaving: a paradigm. Wright used the term "textile" for his concrete blocks of 1923 onward. But he borrowed the term from the National Tile Company's "tex-tile" tiles.[47] Architect and educator Richard MacCormac used the term "tartan" (one never used by Wright) in an essay about the two-dimensional patterns for early buildings. However, in that study, the width between lines could vary, not arithmetically or geometrically but selectively, easily added or subtracted by a reviewer.[48] Regardless, such postmortems are somewhat contrived, unassimable, and almost irrelevant, as they exclude the design process. Of course, Wright used a planning module, but not slavishly, as has been implied. It was a square grid, often on three-foot, six-inch centers at least before the 1920s. He learned that proven method not from toy blocks or loom weaving but from office practice with his first employer, the Madison engineer Allan D. Conover, then with Silsbee and, as it is an essential tool for large buildings, then most usefully with his last employers Dankmar Adler and Louis Sullivan.[49]

Wright's children

In a convoluted talk to the Architectural League of America in June 1900, Wright said to the Chicago audience that the "education of the architect should commence when he is two days old . . . and continue until he passes beyond." Then, mimicking a Sullivan exposition "to the young architect," Wright said in part and rather effusively . . .

> [a] kindergarten's . . . circle of sympathetic discernment" [should be] brought into contact with nature by prophet and seer until abiding sympathy with her is his. He should be a true child of hers, in touch with her moods, discerning her principles and harmonies until his soul overflows with love of nature in the highest and his mind is stored with a technical knowledge of her forms and processes.[50]

The colors, shapes, gridded (checked) table pad, decisions on pattern and color and form; arranging the blocks, their rhythms: those were *not* his experiences as a child in 1876 but those with his first six children from 1895 to about 1907! He did *not* mention kindergartens until 1901. His buildings before 1902 show no indication that the gifts were influential in any manner.

Therefore, at the very moment in 1900 that Wright spoke to the League and that he, along with his wife, mother, and son, talked to Robert Spencer, a kindergarten was in action at Wright's house conducted by Catherine.[51] We can recall that in February 1901, Sullivan began a series of essays of tantalizing theoretical musings he later titled "Kindergarten Chats."[52]

Catherine also helped organize a Montessori summer school around 1907 and was involved with a small theater group located in the Fine Arts Building beside Chicago's Michigan Avenue. She was "a woman of decided views," of spirit, dedicated to Frank and their children, but in misery with Wright's mother always present, living next door in Oak Park. Yet Catherine managed to volunteer at Hull-House for many years.[53] Also and oddly, there was a very belated public showing of some of her children's kindergarten work at the Chicago Architectural Club exhibition of 1914. The catalog described them:

> Education Toys.
> Marionette Theater, made for [Robert] Llewellyn Wright.
> Toy Garden Scheme,
>   worked out by Frank Lloyd Wright, Jr.
> Child's Building Blocks,
>   worked out by John Lloyd Wright.[54]

Wright Junior referred to those exercises as "a la Froebel."[55] The heavy portable marionette theater was constructed of wood to Frank Senior's design.

Iovanna was born in 1925 to Wright's third wife Olgivanna. Again, at the very moment of writing about the gifts for his autobiography in 1930 (age sixty-three), he was engaging Iovanna in the following manner:

> My little five-year-old daughter and I . . . have invented a game. She has many kinds and sizes of blocks, among them a set of well-made cubes about an inch square painted pure bright colors. . . . Some of the cubes are divided on the diagonal in contrasting colors. Who ever deals, deals seven blocks to each, two diagonals. Iovanna's turn to play. She chooses a color-block . . . and places it square on the board floor.[56]

Therefore – and this is crucial – when he and Catherine were enjoying the gifts and other Froebel elements with their children in the 1890s, and he and Olgivanna with daughter Iovanna in 1930, Wright became sensitized to the gifts far beyond his own – and it must be said – limited childhood experiences. His and Spencer's words in 1900 and his in own in 1930 were *not* Wright's recollections of his childhood activity but the result of immediate applications with his children.

In 1953, historian Grant Manson introduced the idea that Wright's childhood experiences with "Froebelian education" played a significant role in determining the architectonic forms of his buildings with emphasis on kindergarten gifts. Manson's presentation relied on interviews with the architect in the 1930s after he had played with daughter Iovanna.[57]

Relative to Froebel's educational program, therefore, the conclusion must be that, around 1896, it helped formulate Wright's romantic, Arcadian ideals so cleanly in parallel with Emersonian reflections. At the critical practical level in the late 1870s, the gifts could not have assisted his visual, design, or constructional training, as his own designs pre-1898 confirm. Maturing philosophic impulses, however, were marginally aided, one must assume, *not* by the gifts but by Froebel's philosophy as a neat fit with the Unitarianism and holism as practiced by the Jones and Wright families and as supported by Catherine, not by Anna, Wright. Froebel's holistic philosophy is exemplified in his poetic prayer:

> Silently cherish young baby's dim thought
> That life in itself is as unity wrought.
> Make paths through which he may feel and may think
> That of this great whole he, too, is a link.[58]

Historian Anthony Alofsin correctly concluded that Wright's "explanation of how he learned the geometry of architecture" through Froebel was "but facile," glib.[59] Wright was certain of the philosophic package's value, even at age ninety when he nicely paraphrased Froebel as follows:

> A child should begin to work with materials just as soon as he is able to hold a ball. By holding a ball, a child gets a sense of the universe and there is a closeness to God. The ball [a sphere] leads the child to other geometric shapes: the cone, the triangle, the cylinder. Now he is on the threshold of nature herself. . . .[60]

Sensory stuff but not that of a process.

It is not surprising that, in the 1950s, Wright warned Manson and others that "direct comparisons of Froebelian color-pattern and plan-forms with ultimate buildings is – while extremely ingenious – only a haphazard guess," without foundation.[61] Yet, some observers, too many not trained in the design of buildings, naively persist with visual comparisons and include his buildings of the 1950s.[62] Architecture is too complex to sustain such puerile notions.

In 1953, Wright told Manson that he was influenced by those "same sources of inspiration that Froebel [and others] . . . received,"[63] that he got them firsthand, not second. They may have been nominal inspirations, perhaps, but the facts explain otherwise.

+ + +

A knowledge of the philosophic preferences, roles, and talents of Wright's parents, of what took place with his children, and of Froebel's Rousseauan and holistic educational concept leads to two logical conclusions. First, the genetic and practical source of Frank's artistic genius and intellectual fervor was his father. Philosophic sustenance was sustained by Emersonian Unitarianism as shared by Wright's father and the Jones family. The drive for fame and immortality was obtained from his mother, perhaps genetically but certainly a result of overweening mixed with a Napoleon complex.

From an empirically and creatively directed education that proclaimed the need for an intimate relationship between humankind and nature as argued by Rousseau and his many followers, the steps to a fresh architectural philosophy (encouraged by Silsbee's sensibilities, Adler's pragmaticism, Sullivan's sensate aestheticism, and Emil Lorch's thoughts on pure design) was not too difficult for a perceptive, intelligent, and chauvinistic Frank Wright. We shall learn that, creatively applied, "pure design" helped direct it into what became yet another new architecture meant to serve Progressivism. For now, there are yet further examples of the search through education and an architectural symbol of progress.

Unity Chapel and Silsbee

Being from distinguished Salem, Massachusetts, generations, Silsbee had to be educated at Phillips Exeter Academy and Harvard University, graduating in 1869. After one year of architectural courses at the Massachusetts Institute of Technology, he worked for Boston architectural firms, thereafter traveling about Europe. In 1873, he was appointed professor of architecture at Syracuse University, founded 1870, and set up a private office that attracted several large commissions. Around 1876, he refused the position of dean of the new school of architecture at Cornell University and in 1878 resigned his professorship to concentrate on private practice. From the Syracuse office, Silsbee sent draftsman Edward Austin Kent to his hometown of Buffalo to set up a third office in 1882. Kent became a junior partner only to return to Syracuse in 1884 for personal reasons. In 1883, Canadian expatriate James H. Marling became Silsbee's partner-in-charge in Buffalo. When Silsbee began to centralize work in Chicago, Kent returned east to open his own Buffalo office in 1887.

Like so many other architects who emigrated to Chicago, Silsbee was seduced by the city's post-fire commercial extravagance and related construction frenzy. In an office near the loop, he employed young men such as Cecil Sherman Corwin as head draftsman, George Grant Elmslie, Elbert Wilcox, George Washington Maher, Harry Hale Waterman, De Witt Taylor Kennard, Irving John Gill, Henry G. Fiddelke, and Wright. Elmslie, Gill, Wright, and Fiddelke would later work for Adler and Sullivan until 1893. Therefore, for a few years, Silsbee had offices simultaneously in Syracuse, Buffalo (where he did not reside), and Chicago.[64]

In the 1880s, the Art Institute of Chicago developed an extensive teaching program that involved lecturers from various professions: Cecil's brother and painter Charles A. Corwin, W.M.R. French (design), J. L. Wallace (perspective), L. J. Millet (ornamental design), Jos L. Silsbee (color in architecture), F. W. Gookin (on pattern designing), and W.L.B. Jenney on elements of architecture.[65] Silsbee was obviously comfortably ensconced in local art and design communities. Further, in 1894, he reported to 1869 classmates that:

> [a] hobby that is worthy of notice is the "moving sidewalk," which was in use at the World's Fair [1893], and for which a medal was awarded there. I have since received the Edward Longstreet medal from the Franklin Institute for this, as one of the two inventors

Education 49

of the system, which will in all probability be in practical use both in Chicago and New York within a year.[66]

But nothing eventuated after the exposition.

Reverend Jones and his siblings decided to build a family and community Unitarian chapel on land central to the family's farms south of Spring Green. Fund-raising for what became Unity Chapel started in early 1885. Reverend Jones immediately prepared his program for Silsbee that included the following:

> A three-roomed church, to hold at minimum one hundred, and at maximum, by unfolding audience-room into the parlor, two hundred, with a kitchen-corner tucked in somewhere, – this cased in a form so simply pretty that it will beautify the hills, not blot them with another stiff church-box, . . . A thousand valleys are waiting for this type of churchlet today, – something homelike within, a grace without, and buyable with very humble means.[67]

By early December, broken ashlar stone foundations to sill height were complete and a notice of construction work done was published in *Unity* below a perspective drawing accompanied by a tiny floor plan. The signature of the delineator reads "J L Silsbee." Perhaps as a lesson in rendering, Wright made a copy of the perspective drawing and signed it, and it was published in Reverend Jones's church annual of 1887, without doubt as a favor to his nephew (see Figure 2.2).[68]

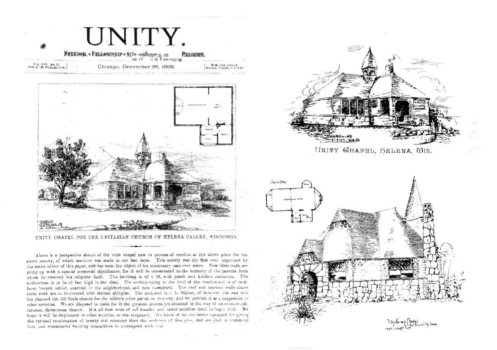

Figure 2.2 On left: a perspective rendering of the Jones family's "Unity Chapel" at Hillside/Helena, Wisconsin, published December 1885, "Jos Silsbee Architect," same as built in 1885–86. Top right: Wright's 1887 rendering that copied Silsbee's perspective angle, drawing style, and caption. From Hasbrouck, 1970. Bottom: Wright's design perspective rendering of a proposal for a "Unitarian Chapel for Sioux City, Iowa," as published June 1887. From Hasbrouck, 1970.

Frank was referred to as "the boy" by Reverend William C. Gannett and most of the Jones family elders, likely because of his boyish facial features and height. "I am 5' 8 1/2" tall," said Wright, but son John and others declared him to be five-foot seven, the same height as Louis Sullivan.[69] Gannett said Wright had "calcimined" the "audience room" and "parlor" walls of the chapel and no more. The parlor and audience room "are wood ceiled . . .; one [room] is calcimined in terra cotta, one [the parlor] in olive green." The "wood-ceil[ing] pine in its own color." And, "if you want one like it," the chapel, then "write to the architect, J.L. Silsbee, Lakeside building, Chicago." The chapel was dedicated August 1886.[70] A pattern of squares by an unknown designer was painted on the ceiling apparently by Wright, their date of execution unknown (Wright made no claim) but obviously after mid-1886. The ceiling remained otherwise unpainted.[71] In 1887, the boy would also copy Silsbee's perspective ink drawing of the Home Building, another similar drawing with the title changed to "Country Residence," and one of All Souls Chicago; his drawing skills only a slight improvement on the chapel perspective.

Reverend Jones envisioned the family chapel serving not only the Jones family but Wyoming Valley folks. It became his summer ministry and was meant to be a prototype meetinghouse for the small Unitarian congregations in the Midwest, especially, but also elsewhere. In the 1880s, and with the guidance of Reverend Jones, the Sioux City congregation was expanding. Young Frank may have been prompted by his uncle to the fact that the First Unitarian Church of Sioux City was organized 11 March 1885, Reverend Mary A. Safford pastor, a church building expected.[72] As an individual's response, Frank proposed to Uncle Jenkin (not to people in Sioux City) his puerile version of Silsbee's rather plain but nicely detailed and elegantly proportioned chapel. Wright's covering letter to his uncle was penned on Conover's stationary and said in part . . .

> I have forwarded to you today [22 August 1885] my preliminary sketches for "Unity Chapel." I have simply made them in pencil on a piece of old paper but the idea is my own and I have copied from nothing. . . . If necessary I will furnish you with more detailed drawings and working plans. Please let me know the faults and short-comings . . . at your earliest convenience.[73]

The pencil drawings and Reverend Jones's response have not survived, but a perspective sketch published two years later in the June 1887 issue of *Inland Architect* was in ink and titled "Unitarian Chapel for Sioux City, Iowa" and signed "Frank L. Wright Archt." In the 1880s, there were no laws structuring the profession of architecture: one could simply hang a shingle or submit a drawing for publication.

Reverend Jones was a man with a sophisticated understanding of art and architecture, as he now and then articulated in lectures and in print; most are still readily available. He would have compared Silsbee's chapel with nephew Frank's perspective version for Sioux City and been disappointed. And why that version was accepted by Chicago's prestigious *Inland Architect* begs understanding.

In post-1930 writings, Wright mentioned Unity Chapel with some fondness and mendacity. For instance, "Every Sunday, spring and summer of these youthful [Madison] years, up to September fifth, the boy [he called himself] would put on his city clothes and go to these chapel gatherings."[74] The fifth was the starting date of the high school academic year and, in this case, two years before the chapel opened. Perhaps not meaning to dissemble, but those pages in his 1932 autobiography were about childhood, pre-high school experiences. Yet he had left for Chicago two months before the chapel was opened and thereafter only regularly returned.[75] Wright further dissembled in his 1943 autobiography when he wrote: "In the little family chapel . . . the old Welsh family stands up. To sing. . . . The boy [Frank], too, sings."[76] And again: "The old chapel walls under the high wooden ceiling of the interior which I had put there when a boy. . . ."[77] "Put there" implies he installed the ceiling, but he did not. Those words are found in "Book Five: Form," a section added to the 1943 edition of his *An Autobiography* that occupies nearly half the book. Including the original first four sections Wright, challenged a reader's belief when he said: "Every word I have written is fact, at least."[78]

Hillside Home School

The secret in education lies in respecting the student.
— Ralph Waldo Emerson

Not surprisingly, the schools of Pestalozzi and Tolstoy, who likely visited Pestalozzi's when studying European facilities, were set in rural environments. When it came into more general use in Europe, England, and America, it was an urban phenomenon that in America evolved into "progressive education." Frank Lincoln Wright became involved with one successful paradigmatic model, the Hillside Home School near Spring Green, Wisconsin. Founded by his spinster aunts Jane (Jennie to family) Lloyd Jones and Elinor (Ellen C. professionally, Nell to family) Lloyd Jones, it opened for autumn enrollment on 10 September 1887. Frank had left for Chicago's streets in February 1887 as a newly hired "tracer" (he said) in Silsbee's office.

In an article-styled advertisement earlier in the year, there was a call for people "of the Liberal Faith" to a new school on "a farm" with "garden, farm – yard and workshop, will give opportunity for manual and domestic training for boys and girls, indoors and outdoors."[79] Founding their school was, as biographer Meryle Secrest correctly observed, yet another "testimonial to the energy and initiative of the Lloyd Jones immigrants, not to mention their liberal, reformist, and humanitarian views."[80] So little has been said about the school that a short history and clarification of Wright's involvement is necessary.

On the death of their father in 1881, the sisters inherited some money and a 140-acre farm and homestead one mile directly south of Spring Green village. Ellen was forty-one, Jane thirty-eight. Both had graduated in 1870 from the normal school that one-hundred years later became the University of Wisconsin – Platteville.[81] Ellen taught geography and history at Wisconsin's River Falls State Normal School, now the University of Wisconsin – River Falls.[82] During the 1879–80 school year, Aunt Jane was a principal and a teacher of grammar at Madison's Second Ward School where Wright attended during the 1878–81 school years.[83] In the early 1880s, the sisters attended Francis Parker's renown Chicago education lectures and also taught at his experimental school.

"At first, the Lloyd Jones sisters planned to use the family's Unity Chapel for their school's classes," historian Joseph Siry has explained, and they did. "Yet by the spring of 1887 they had amassed sufficient funds to build a new structure that would house both bedrooms [for students] and classrooms," and a teachers' cottage. The original farm house, the homestead, built by Thomas in the 1860s, was moved across the road and remodeled for classrooms, again by Thomas. It also became the boarding pupils' residence and called Home Cottage. For the vacated land, architect Joseph L. Silsbee was commissioned to design a new building to fit their educational ideas.[84]

+++

The philosopher Susan Elizabeth Blow was a leading pedagogue in St Louis who, in 1877, opened the first publicly funded kindergarten in the United States. She also ran the kindergarten at Chicago's Hull-House from 1876, where Jane Jones participated. Jane then practiced at a kindergarten training school in St Paul, Minnesota, and remembered that when she "took up the study of early child development as voiced by Froebel and others," she "was astonished to find how very familiar the philosophy seemed."[85] Perhaps this was a consequence of Unitarian principles held by the Joneses; their passion for knowledge matched the Boston Unitarian educators. The description by niece Maginel of her aunts was mellowed by time:

> Aunt Nell, two years older than Aunt Jennie, was the executive one, sterner and less magnetic than her sister, who had glamour and charm beyond anyone in the family, and who was greatly loved by all the students. Aunt Nell's face had been badly scarred by smallpox when she was a girl, and her hair had turned snow white during the illness. . . .

Aunt Jennie, by contrast, was merry and animated. She had a wonderfully mobile face, a wide lovely smile, and iron-gray, curly hair. . . .[86]

Pestalozzi believed that harmony of the universe could be expressed in geometric terms, as did Froebel, Goethe, and Emerson, and that true knowledge could be achieved by studying the "law of forms" – that this method was a component of spiritual liberty – Froebel also agreed, as he, too, was a student of crystallography. But he was more practically oriented to child development. Children should express themselves through play, through "motor-expression," through learning of self and of nature's world. Drawn by the intellectual fervor of mid-nineteenth-century Europe, Froebel naturally exploited the Germanic idealistic philosophies and matched them to Rousseau, Pestalozzi, and his own observations as they favored education. In America, New Englanders, through Transcendentalism, came to education. But they eschewed much of its lofty idealism for those elements that might practically and emotionally assist social experience and later educational reform, for what more generally became pragmatism.

There was, therefore, a close intellectual and social link between Emersonian Transcendentalists and Unitarians to whom the Kindergarten Movement owed much of its initial American development. In Boston, the principle theoreticians and actors were Francis Parker, Horace Mann, Mary Mann and sister Elizabeth Peabody, and John Lowell. Their useful publications were easily assimilated by the Jones family teachers. When sketching out ideas for the school in December 1886, Ellen Jones wrote to her friend, Reverend Gannett, that her school was to be "a permanent good Unitarian school, for that is what it must be in its essence whatever we may call it."[87] On one occasion, it was referred to as "This Family and Farm School."[88]

Wright's mother Anna, who was seven years older than sister Ellen and ten beyond sister Jane, was equally devoted to teaching "but not so fortunate in her training."[89] A promising elementary school pupil, she became a self-taught assistant teacher because, in the 1850s, the family could not afford to support her at normal school. This was not uncommon; most rural schools were conducted by untrained but motivated assistants. Anna's daughter Maginel observed that "Education obsessed her."[90] Brother Frank put the dedication this way: as with Ellen and Jane, education was sister Anna's passion, in fact, "all" of his family were "imbued with the idea of education as salvation." Further,

> Education it was that made man from the brute and saved him from the beast [Wright said]. Education . . . unlocked the stores of Beauty to let it come crowding in on every side at every gate. Although she believed Education the direct manifestation of God to reach it, Sister Anna loved – Beauty. Soon she became a teacher in the country-side. . . .[91]

Wright's reference to education as a "direct manifestation of God" derives not only from Emersonian and Unitarian thought given in weekly doses by senior members of the family but, through Kant and Goethe, Froebel's and Uncle Jenkin's lengthy discussions about the "divine Principle of Unity" and the potent symbolism of a sphere. Wright said of the Unitarian Joneses, "UNITY was their watchword, the sign and symbol that thrilled them, the UNITY of all things!"[92] Moreover, the Unitarian magazine edited by Reverend Jones and Reverend Gannett was titled *Unity*. Uncle Jenkin, senior and paternal in all ways to his sisters and brothers and their children, was likely the most influential intellectual voice during Frank's youth-filled years, more so than his mother and nearly equal to his father.

Frank's father William has been fairly described by historian Mary Hamilton:

> [William was] conspicuously brilliant. He had entered college at fourteen and received a degree from what is now Colgate University. [By 1865,] he had been admitted to the bar, been ordained a Baptist minister, and published one book and several musical compositions. He was a spell binding orator . . . a gifted singer, violinist, pianist, organist, and composer. . . . Almost everyone was drawn to his convivial personality, intrigued by his knowledge, and awed by his abilities. Anna undoubtedly thought he was quite a catch.[93]

He, too, was enthralled by Emerson's words. Frank knew his father as a "music-master," a "musician Circuit rider," a "product of 'Education', one of a family of intellectuals" who was "Going about the countryside . . . teaching folk to sing," playing the fiddle, and giving talks on art, music, and religion.[94] A Baptist minister like many of his New England kin, William married Anna in 1866. Then, around 1884, he switched to Unitarianism and soon thereafter became pastor of a church in nearby Wyoming, Wisconsin. After William received an uncontested divorce in 1885, Anna briefly assisted as a house mother in her younger sisters' school.[95]

Hillside Home School has been passionately portrayed by the author and esteemed university educator Mary Ellen Chase. Her first act upon graduation from the University of Maine was to apply for a teaching position at Hillside. Her description of the job interview in the summer of 1909 is most revealing. The sisters "surprised" Chase by not asking for teaching credentials. Rather, they wanted to know if she "liked the country," if she enjoyed country walks, if "children amused and interested" her, did she know "anything about birds and common flowers," did she like animals and could she ride a horse, what were her favorite books, and did she "love" music. After sharing bedtime milk and crackers, Aunt Jane told Chase she would "do for the" school. Chase encapsulated its eminent position thusly:

> Ten years before [Dewey's famed Laboratory School] and fourteen years before Colonel Francis Parker['s] . . . *child-centered* education [she emphasized], and a full quarter of a century before the progressive school as we know it . . . this school in a remote Wisconsin valley was looking upon each child as an individual and centering all its efforts on his [sic] reasonable growth, activity, and self-expression.[96]

Teaching English and history at Hillside was, for Chase, "accompanied by strenuous duties as a housemother for children from five to twelve years of age."[97] The school's society was like a large farming family dedicated to its children, one third drawn from the local area, nearly two thirds from Madison, including children of university faculty members, and a few from Milwaukee and distant Chicago. Teachers numbered up to around thirteen from 1895–1912 but, in 1888, "the capacity of the school is [was] limited to about twenty."[98]

Former student Florence Fifer Bohrer remembered that the Progressive Wisconsin politician Robert La Follette Sr. lectured and often visited his three sons at Hillside; that dance master F. W. Kehl was from Madison and soon a client of Wright's;[99] that F.W.N. Hugenholtz from the Netherlands was the school's minister and taught Latin, Greek, psychology, and logic and read to students from Henry George's *Progress and Poverty*;[100] that Unitarian ministers Frederick Lucian Hosmer, a poet and hymn composer, William Channing Gannett, a social reformer, and, of course, the sister's brother Jenkin, lectured and joined in hymns; that the countryside – nature – was the principle laboratory; and that the Aunts, as they were affectionately called by all, those "beloved women," were stern, gracious, gentle, disciplined, dignified, and great teachers. The school children – girls and boys, black and white – were "inspired" to "try to pattern [their] lives" after them.[101] Fifer's father was certain that "The whole influence of the school is elevating and ennobling, and highly calculated to build up character and lay the foundations of a useful life."[102]

Wright's son John Kenneth, who attended Hillside, recorded a few lines of a poem by the eminent horticulturalist at Cornell University, Liberty Hyde Bailey, that he believed "guided" his great aunts:

> Voice of the Country-side
>
> I Teach
> The earth and soil
> To them that toil;
> [. . .]
> The plants that grow,
> The winds that blow,

54 *The aesthetics of progress*

> The streams that run,
> In rain and sun
> Throughout the year;
>
> And then I lead
> Through wood and mead,
> Through mould and sod,
> Out unto God,
> With love and cheer,
> I teach.[103]

It fits perfectly with people's intentions, memories, and current knowledge.

Aside from younger sister Maginel, diminutive for Margaret Ellen, and his own children attending Hillside, Wright was involved on the family farms as a teenager and then, to one degree or another, with the construction of seven buildings for the Joneses, four educational and three religious. First was to paint walls for the small family chapel. Second was to watch Silsbee work on the boarding school's Home Building design and detailing. Wright had been working in Silsbee's office for only a month as a factotum and neophyte draftsman. It was by no means Wright's commission *or* design. "When working with [for] architect Silsbee in Chicago," Wright recalled, "and had made the amateurish plans [drawings] for the very first [Hillside Home] school buildings."[104] He design the school's tall wind pump (1896–97) and his third building.[105] The fourth was to watched how All Souls Church Chicago was constructed in 1886. Fifth was his design for additional buildings for his aunts in 1901–02.[106] Sixth was a new church he eventually designed cooperatively with Reverend Jones and architect Dwight Heald Perkins that opened in 1905.

Silsbee's design for the Home Building was a grand, lumpy, wood-shingled building stained green, residential in character (see Figure 2.3). Boys were quartered on the third floor, girls on

Figure 2.3 Old postcard of the Jones sisters' Hillside Home School around 1900; wood shingle siding; to the left of the two dormers is Silsbee's design of 1886; to the right are additions organized and constructed post-1887, likely by Thomas Jones in 1889.

the second, then living room, dining room, and library on the first "furnished with oriental rugs, a grand piano, and Japanese prints."[107] In 1901, the school was known regionally in the following terms:

> Here is located the Hillside Home School. . . . The location . . . removes it from the distractions of the city, and surrounds the pupils with the ennobling influences of Nature. Abundant pure air and water . . ., and such food as the large garden, green house, and well-stocked farm afford, make the conditions such as insure the physical well-being of the family. . . .
> The school aims to inculcate simple habits of life, and an independence to the debilitating conventionalities. It seeks to be devout, but non-sectarian and open in its religious spirit, hospitable to all forms of thought, seeking the underlying unities of faith in diversities of creed and form. It tries to realize that culture which ripens into reverence, and that rationalism which is earnest and helpful. In short, character-building is its aim.[108]

Here, the Jones sisters had moved away from a pedagogical philosophy based on Unitarianism to one heavily influenced by their brother Reverend Jones's noncreedal universalist theology: the search for "unities of faith in diversities of creed and form." Their school was accredited by the universities of Wisconsin, Chicago, Northwestern, and Illinois.

On either side of 1900, the school announced that it was "heartedly endorsed" publicly by the renowned, including Col. Francis W. Parker and Jane Addams, as well as other Chicagoans, such as William R. Manierre (industrialist and Progressive politician), and social reformer Florence Kelley. The late Col. Parker was described as "that lamented guardian of youth."[109] Earlier, he had endorsed the school, closing with "Your beautiful picturesque country home is ideal, and that, combined by your excellent instruction, has . . . made your school the one to recommend. . . ."[110] From 1888 onward, Ellen used the name "Ellen C." She and Jane were identified as "Principals and "proprietors." The usual address for the school was Hillside and nearby was old Helena, an active village until the last years of the nineteenth century.[111]

Three weeks before opening the school, the sisters placed a notice in the *St. Paul Daily Globe* under the heading "Hillside Training School." It continued:

> A department for training kindergarten and primary teachers will be opened in connection with the Hillside Home School, under the supervision of Jane Lloyd Jones, recent supervisor of the Eau Claire Training School [in Minnesota], and teacher of primary methods in the St. Paul Training School [for Teachers]. For particulars . . . .[112]

The sister's training school began with only three students and soon abandoned. It was made clear the "the Principles of Froebel will be faithfully and scientifically applied in a kindergarten thoroughly equipped. . . ."[113] But to emphasize the school's interdenominational character post-1898, "affiliations of the faculty" were made known: "Presbyterians three; Methodists, three; Episcopalians two; Congregational one; liberal Unitarian, four."[114] Not mentioned was one Lutheran, Alfred R. Kent, fresh from Carthage College in Illinois. During the 1888 school year, fourteen "family pupils," or borders, and twenty "day pupils" were taught by five teachers and the sisters.[115] The Wisconsin State Superintendent of Education reported that, in 1896, Hillside had twenty-four male and twenty-eight female students; up to then it had graduated nineteen, and in that year it expected to graduate six. In 1903, there we fifty-three "home pupils" and twenty-three day pupils.[116]

Most of the local Lloyd Jones farming families helped Nell and Jennie set up and operate the school, and they enrolled their children and grandchildren. Their sister and Frank's mother Anna acted as dormitory matrons, at least in the first year, after which she and daughter Maginel moved to Chicago. Maginel's and Frank's sister Jane taught singing and piano for one year. She went on to a position as third-grade teacher in the Oak Park School.[117] From day one, the sister's brother James acted as "Farm Superintendent," while brother Thomas was the first manual training teacher.[118] "Cousin Elsie was physical culture director in the gym," Maginel said, "and Cousin Nell, after two years abroad came back to teach French and German."[119] When appropriate, and quite naturally, Reverend Jones promoted his sisters' school far and wide and initially helped fund it.[120] Cousin Tom, son of settler John, graduated from Hillside in 1892 and then graduated from the university class of 1896. Tom was "assistant principal" of Hillside but left to be superintendent of Wauwatosa schools and then director of University of Wisconsin High School Relations. His sister Mary taught in the Superior, Wisconsin, schools.[121] Grace N. Green of Fulda, Minnesota, and the Wisconsin class of 1895, married young John Lloyd Jones in 1901 while both were teaching at Hillside, she from 1897–1901. Another cousin, Chester Lloyd Jones, son of Enos, studied at Hillside and later became a professor of political science at the university, then a federal government commercial attaché, and later a professor of economics at the university.

Frank's sister Maginel attended Oak Park schools until September 1896, when she spent her final year at Hillside.[122] In 1897, she enrolled at the Art Institute of Chicago's School of Art, entering a new program of illustration. After one year and financially troubled, she obtained employment with the quality lithograph "stereoview" company Barnes-Crosby in Chicago. She went on to be a successful independent illustrator and was able to take her mother Anna on a several-week tour of Europe in 1903.[123] Frank's sister Jennie likely attended Hillside but in the event she became a school teacher. Thomas R. Lloyd Jones's son John completed his final year at Hillside in 1892 and then obtain a degree from the University of Wisconsin in 1896. He taught at Madison High School and later became a professor in education at the university.[124]

The school's student body was indeed diverse. John L. Savage came from country Wisconsin around Cooksville to study at Hillside Home School for two years (1894–96) and finished high school in Madison. After a degree in engineering from the University of Wisconsin, he eventually became a design engineer for the Bureau of Reclamation and supervised the design of such dams as Grand Coulee, Imperial, Hoover, Shasta, and Wheeler.[125] Cecil W. Smith from Clifton, Illinois, was a student at Hillside and, in 1906, prepared a small photographic album of the school and its people. Industrialist and founder of the University of Wisconsin Department of Chemical Engineering in 1905, Charles F. Burgess sent his children Betty and Jack to Hillside in 1914.[126] Mildred Morris and her younger sister Felice, daughters of the well-known London then New York character actor Felix Morris, attended Hillside in the class of 1899.[127] Chicagoan and future Wright client Charles E. Roberts sent his son Chapin to Hillside, and he graduated in 1907, perhaps after four years attendance.[128]

Wisconsin Senator-elect Robert M. La Follette sent sons Robert Jr. and Philip, as well as daughter Mary, to Hillside in January 1902. Bloomingtonian Florence Fifer, Hillside student class of 1895, remembered visits of La Follette Senior. A roommate of Frances was "one colored girl," Mabel Augusta Wheeler, daughter of Chicago attorney Lloyd Garritson Wheeler and a member of Reverend Jones's All Souls Church. Mabel went on to teach in St Louis schools. After marriage, Florence Fifer Bohrer became Illinois's first female state senator.[129]

Margaret and John, two of three children of Florence Kelley, began at Hillside in September 1894. John finally graduated in 1902. Kelley found Margaret "so vastly grown and so well and serene. . . . Surely it is wise care which brings such results as this."[130] During this period, Kelley and children lived with Anna Wright and children Maginel and Llewellyn in Oak Park. Mason City, Iowa, attorney J.E.E. Markley and his wife were Unitarians who looked forward to the one or two occasions each year when Reverend Jones would visit, lecture, and preach. The Markleys sent their two daughters to Hillside; the older child began in 1902. Later, Markley and his law-firm partner James E. Blythe (a Congregationalist) commissioned Wright in 1907 to design a City National Bank and office building, together with the Park Inn Hotel, for a single block-long site in Mason City, both completed in 1909.[131]

Mary Paulding Barnett, who held a degree AB from the University of Kansas (1897), taught Latin and Greek at Hillside in 1899. She went on to obtain an AM degree from Chicago University and, after many tertiary teaching jobs, ended up at Mills College near San Francisco. In the *University of Chicago Magazine*, Dorothea Visher informed alumni classmates of 1904 that, because of an apparent influence of Dewey's ideas, she had accepted a teaching position at Hillside. A student from the Chicago School of Civics and Philanthropy, Helen E. Inglis became "physical director" at Hillside in 1911. Golf, netball, and American rugby were played on lumpy farm fields.

The Jones sisters hired several teachers who had studied at the University of Wisconsin. Among them was Albert C. Ehlman, an instructor of music before taking his degree in 1903, was teaching mathematics and history from 1900–01. He later practiced law in Milwaukee and became a Socialist member of the state assembly. William David Fuller was "headmaster of boys" (1906–09) before obtaining a PhB from the University of Wisconsin. He then became superintendent of schools in Orono, Maine.

Hillside Home School continued to attract students and staff from far afield. After receiving an AM degree from Acadia College in Nova Scotia in 1898, Wylie Churchill Margeson began teaching science that same year at Hillside. He went on to practice law in Michigan. Frederik Willem Nicolaas Hugenholtz was an emigrant from the Netherlands and educated at Harvard University and Meadville Seminary when located in Pennsylvania, Reverend Jones's alma mater. In 1892, Hugenholtz became Unitarian minister at Hillside and taught Greek and Latin until 1896, when he settled in Schiedam near The Hague. After many and varied places of study, including a BS degree from Teachers College at Columbia University, Clarinda Chapman Richards taught hand craft around 1911. L. Irene Buck was from Lansing, Michigan, and taught at Hillside after receiving an art certificate from the Art Institute of Chicago in 1910. Later, she became director of art for Madison Public Schools, a position she held for thirty years.[132] The violinist Etelka Evans from Stockbridge, Massachusetts, was a student who also taught music and then graduated from Hillside in 1902. She went on to study music in Berlin, Germany, and New York City and finally to teach at Southwestern University in Georgetown, north of Austin, Texas.[133]

Reflecting on the students and families just mentioned leads to imagining Reverend Jones traveling about the Northeast and Midwest lecturing, meeting Unitarian preachers or fellow reformers and their flocks, and telling all about his sisters' boarding "home" school. Hillside and Reverend Jones were well known to people at Hull-House, such as Blaine, Parker, Dewey, and their followers, who promoted Progressive education at the University of Chicago. By implication, the intellectual, pedagogical, and mutual connections between the sisters' school and Chicago educators, theorists, and then the Deweyites, is again clear. Equally obvious, the sisters were not disciples of Dewey, as some would have it, including Wright. Rather, Dewey learned from the sisters' practices begun fifteen years earlier! As well, teachers were, for the most part, fresh from normal school or university and eager for the wholesome yet limited experience of Hillside Home School but also eager to expand and find new encounters and make their careers. The tendency, then, was for a teacher to move on after only year or so.

Wright's hillside buildings, 1901–02

The last two buildings were necessary to the Jones sisters' school because of increased enrollments, their design of great significance. In October 1901, Wright was commissioned by his aunts to prepare an architectural "scheme where the efficiency of our work will be very much enhanced," as Aunt Jane put it to Chicago philanthropist Mrs Emmons Blaine, adding that the estimated cost was $8,000. Blaine, in association with Francis Parker, was the financial founder of the School of Education at Chicago University, John Dewey then its director, Parker had been its first.[134] The sisters decided to build "an assembly room (also serving as a chapel), space for a library, manual-training room, a kitchen, an arts and science hall and a gymnasium."[135] By October first, Wright and his aunts resolved the building's program by separating the arts and sciences from rooms devoted to regular classes, assembly, gymnasium, and music. Those grouped functions were connected by an enclosed umbilical corridor. Working drawings were complete 13 October. Figure 2.4 is a bird's-eye view that best explains functional relationships as they influenced form and general character; it is very close to as built. The large form on

58 The aesthetics of progress

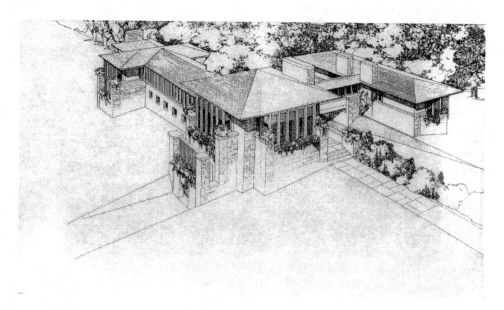

Figure 2.4 Bird's-eye perspective drawing of "Hillside Home School buildings" as built near Spring Green, Wisconsin, 1901–02. From Wright, 1910.

the left was a gym two stories high, and at the gym-floor level a music room was tucked under classrooms with a raised floor that acted as a stage. The larger two-story room on the right contained the square assembly/chapel with a library in a balcony. Not for aesthetic reasons as often assumed, the square floor opening in the upper floor provided four triangular spaces (in plan) for eight study desks. The interior met the sisters' requirement of "a Welsh feel about the room which the material, Druid oak and stone, would make possible."[136]

Exterior walls and interior pillars built of stone quarried on the farm provided a solid, visual base for the lighter wood walls and glazed fenestration. Wood-shingled pitched roofs were in keeping with regional structures. The exterior massing reflected a plan that articulated differing room functions and their size, including general classrooms that ranged between assembly chapel and gym. The roofs recalled local rural forms and materials, yet the buildings were a strikingly new architectonic expression. They proclaimed that the Quincy building scheme was an outdated formula, that schools were unique buildings whose functional parts differ logically, and that fact must be expressed architecturally. Here, form did follow function, and this was expressed by articulated (Wright's word), plain geometrical forms, a clarity of structure, and materials in a natural state.

Completed in 1903, the buildings were very expensive to construct. Wright's client, Susan Dana in Springfield, Illinois, funded the arts and sciences building and loaned another $27,000 to help complete the larger building and meet other costs.[137] The sisters acknowledged the donation and loan: "A beautiful Art and Science hall . . . has been erected through the generosity of Mrs. Susan Lawrence Dana and her mother, Mrs. Mary Lawrence of Springfield, Ill., as a memorial to the father and husband, Mr. Rhuena Lawrence, a man of advanced ideas in education and a keen intellectual and moral insight."[138] Widow Dana was a University of Chicago graduate, taught primary school for a few years, then became active in woman's suffrage and the local woman's club. She donated money for a library at Lawrence School in Springfield that was designed by Wright in 1905. Wright's Dana house of 1902–04 was a "great moment in architecture," in historian Hofmann's view, a house "utterly beyond the quaint realm of Arts and Crafts domesticity."[139] Another client, Charles E. Roberts, loaned the sisters $9000.[140]

Hillside continued to flourish. In 1907, it provided for one hundred souls, teacher and pupil. But because of recent mismanagement of the Jones family farms, whose income had helped sustain the school, and the extraordinarily high cost of Wright's buildings, sizable debts had accrued by 1909. This, together with the frailty of the aging sisters, prompted the school's closure in September 1915.[141]

The Martins and the Coonleys

W. E. Martin was an owner of the E-Z Polish Company of Chicago, maker of polishes for stoves, shoes, and other items. He was an inventive tinkerer and politically rather conservative, while his wife Winnie was rather independent, a suffragette who willingly marched and worked at a public preschool kindergarten in Oak Park. Martin became chairman of the local school board. Through various clubs and in other ways he raised money for good causes, concentrating on the Organic School in Fairhope on the east shore of Alabama's Mobil Bay.[142] Fairhope was a small resort town founded in November 1894 by single-tax disciples of Henry George and its constitution said in part

> to establish and conduct a model community or colony, free from all forms of private monopoly, and to secure to its members therein equality of opportunity, the full reward of individual efforts, and the benefits of co-operation in matters of general concern.[143]

Under the sponsorship of the community, Marietta Pierce Johnson was invited to conduct a free school. From St Paul, Minnesota, her family moved to Fairhope in 1902 and, in 1907, she formed the School of Organic Education. A gifted teacher, Johnson developed a program for kindergarten through high school that Dewey praised as the "living embodiment of Rousseauan pedagogical principles."[144] It borrowed from Dewey's idea, as borrowed from Pestalozzi, that infant education should be based on "activities and occupations intrinsically interesting to young children," then in later years adding more traditional subjects.[145] As a result of Dewey's praise, Johnson became quite active nationally and was a founder of the Progressive Education Movement.[146]

The Martins knew of Wright's liberal tendencies when they approached him to design a new house in 1904. Again in 1905, Martin commissioned Wright to design a factory and office building, but the overly articulated and fussily academic tripartite scheme was impractical and much too expensive, the design altered.

The Martins were Christian Scientists who seemed to be closet Progressives, but not so the Coonleys, who were of the same religion. Avery and Queene Coonley considered themselves liberal and Progressive. Avery inherited a fortune from his mother's family and continued their many businesses. Queene was a daughter of the wealthy and prominent Ferrys of Detroit. Avery's mother Lydia morally and financially helped Addams begin Hull-House settlement. There, a friendship developed between Lydia and Wright's mother, a supporter and volunteer.[147] Queene, who professed an interest in art, craft, and architecture,[148] approached Wright in 1907 asking to prepare plans for a mansion-sized house for a site in Riverside. When completed in 1909, Wright proclaimed it the "most successful of my houses."[149]

Active in the Christian Science Church, Avery was in charge of publications for Illinois, while Queene became a practitioner with an office at home. She actively supported woman's suffrage, a primary goal of Christian Science that attracted many women to the church early in the twentieth century. With the birth of a daughter in 1902, they energetically engaged in educational pursuits. He edited a weekly newsletter for schools and was a member of the local school board. He was also concerned with civic and public health affairs and, as a member of the Chicago City Club's Public Education Committee, gave a talk about proposals for "National Health Legislation."[150]

After graduating from Vassar College, Queene worked for a year, likely in 1898, in the ghetto settlement house Chicago Commons, founded and run by the Dutch Reform clergyman

60 *The aesthetics of progress*

Graham Taylor. She also trained as a kindergarten teacher at the Detroit Normal School, now Wayne State University.[151] Many of her educational activities paralleled the growth of daughter Elizabeth, so she initially conducted prekindergarten classes in their old house.

Believing that education in small groups was preferable, in 1908, Queene opened the Cottage School, beginning with first grade in a comfortable existing wood-shingle-and-stone house. There were games, animals, woodlands, wild flowers, play, carpentry for girls, cooking for boys, self-government, making lunches, weaving, literature, acting out historical narratives, and so on.[152] Her educational practices were studied by John and Evelyn Dewey and found exemplary.[153] The curriculum, in many ways similar to Hillside Home School with which she was familiar, was guided by Tolstoy's "four lines" of activity that she described as:

> *First* – Physical work; something that takes actual muscular effort.
> *Second* – Physical work raised to the point of skill, we call it art.
> *Third* – Some occupation requiring distinct mental concentration.
> *Fourth* – Some activity along altruistic lines, something for humanity and civilization.[154]

Forgiving but not condoning the Wright and Borthwick scandal, in 1911, Queene asked Wright to design a kindergarten and lower primary school on the Coonley estate. It would supplant

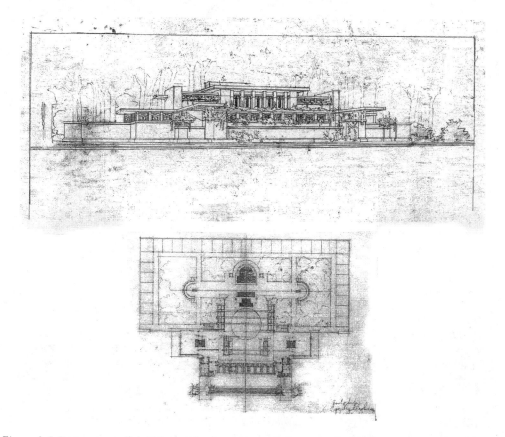

Figure 2.5 Bottom: pencil drawing of the floor plan, scheme one of 1911 for a proposed kindergarten complex for Mrs Coonley, entry is at bottom of drawing of this formal beaux-arts scheme. Top: frontal sketch perspective view of the project. Both from Pfeiffer, 07–13. Courtesy and © 2016 FLWF.

Queene's Cottage School built in 1906 to plans by architect Charles Whittlesey. The client's program was a matter of consensus between architect and client. Wright's first proposal was functionally and aesthetically complex and large yet followed rather faithfully Froebel's suggested layout.[155] Outside was a U-shaped series of square plots for vegetables and flowers arranged about a central place for play, assembly, or whatever (see Figure 2.5). Inside were four small rooms, a larger basement music room, and above an activity space with two small rooms. Its horizontal architectural composition was similar to a second smaller design that was accepted by Queene. There was one commission for a kindergarten, not two. The one Queene accepted was called the Playhouse to emphasize the activity aspect of childhood education.

Completed in 1912 and typical of only a few Wright designs of the period, the Playhouse is an axially formal and brooding building, squat and heavy with flat overhangs implying interlocking planes, deep muntins, a harshly plain exterior stucco finish, and tight interior spaces with bulky detailing about windows and overhead (see Figure 2.6).[156] The result was quite contrary to the expansive spaces and delights of a school as Queene drew it from Tolstoy, Froebel, the Jones sisters, and Dewey, or with the fresh clarity of Wright's 1902 Hillside Home School buildings.

The Coonleys also promoted Progressive education, in one instance by donating land and buildings to nearby Illinois communities. The Brookfield kindergarten was designed by former Wright employee William Drummond, who described it as "built [in 1911] near a brook and in the midst of great natural beauty, [it] seeks to be a fairyland castle, housing many activities in an idealistic manner."[157] Brookfield eventually merged with another school at nearby Downers Grove to become the Avery Coonley Junior Elementary School. Now the Avery Coonley School, it was designed in 1928 by daughter Elizabeth's architect-husband, Waldron Faulkner of Washington, DC. In 1917, the Coonleys had moved to Washington so that Avery might further his Christian Science activities, but he died suddenly in 1920, at age 50. Pestered by

Figure 2.6 Garden front of Coonley kindergarten, scheme two photographed ca. 1912. From private collection.

Wright to help with his "merciless load of debt," a constant of his adult life, Queene became a collector of Wright's Japanese prints.[158]

Queene's most important contribution to education was in 1924 when, with a substantial monetary donation, she helped found the influential national publication *Progressive Education*. A richly illustrated quarterly eagerly read in Europe and North America, it was last produced in 1957. Its demise signaled the formal end to the initial and secondary phases of Progressive education.[159]

The Fellowship

The impact of Wright's 1908 extended treatise published in *Architectural Record* was not openly appreciated in America, but a few Netherlands and German architects responded positively and influentially beginning in 1910.[160] In that year of reinvigoration, Wright announced a decision to devote his life to education of the young.[161] However, between his 1909 flight to Europe with Borthwick and her murder at Taliesin in 1914, Wright made no attempt to teach or establish an educational program or facility. Instead, he built a new house and studio in 1911 he called Taliesin. After the hiatus years, from 1917–22 he was occupied in Japan and then in California until 1924.

During the period understudy, Wright undertook two other commissions related to education. The first, in 1912, was a small two-story proposal for a primary school house in La Grange, Illinois. The floor plans (proportionally exactly two squares long) had four classrooms at ground level and a single room above. Facades were bulky masses in brick with a few windows set in thick stone. Somewhat typical of his work since returning from Europe, it was not built.[162] The second was for a "Women's Building" incorporating a neighborhood kindergarten and clubhouse at the Spring Green fairgrounds in 1914.[163]

Wright's last and greatest educational venture was a private Arts and Crafts school he named The Taliesin Fellowship. Its evolution and influences have been adequately – often emotionally – discussed in many media over recent decades.[164] It is necessary here to provide only an introduction. After obtaining a final divorce from second wife Mariam Noel, Wright immediately married divorcé Olgivanna Hinzenburg. From that moment in 1928, career and social life were joined. With no savings or income ("We had no money. I had no work."),[165] the newlyweds undertook positive actions devised for public/client consumption that might provide an income and announce the reinvented architect. The first action was an autobiography begun in 1928 and released in 1932. Another action was to launch an apprentice scheme in 1925 where young people paid to work for him, the Fellowship. Another was to show America the resolute character of the architect by essays, lecture tours, and exhibitions in parallel with hypothetical projects prepared for publication that included his Broadacre City of 1935. The last action was a public record of his achievements. This was realized in the January 1938 *Architectural Forum* and in a 1940 book by himself and Henry-Russell Hitchcock.

The school's notional curriculum was to also include music and dance, Olgivanna's love. The first intake of fellows discovered that educational practice was found in toil, in the farm fields, cooking and serving meals, scrubbing floors, and chauffeuring, as well as drafting, filing, constructing tents and buildings, being managed by Mrs Wright and, in between, listening to Mr Wright. Over many years, students remodeled the Hillside Home School buildings, abandoned since 1915, and constructed most of the facilities for the Taliesin West enclave outside Scottsdale in Arizona.

The fellows were the "master's comrade," Wright said. Olgivanna preached that a "man takes inspiration from one in whom he has faith," that "All great societies were built by powerful individuals who created new patterns of education, of civilization and culture." Wright was frank: the fellows should "not imagine they were coming to school"; rather, they were "to make themselves as useful to me as they could." The Fellowship was conceptually distant, therefore, from the vibrant holistic philosophy contained in the diverse educational practices of his pre-1917 experiences. Assuredly, it reflected Wright's encounters in the offices of Silsbee, Adler, and Sullivan, where he had been taught by "masters" who paid him a salary.

Notes

1. Goethe, "A Hymn to Nature," translation by "[A] strong man and a strong woman whose lives and whose creations have served the ideals of all humanity in a way that will gain deeper and deeper appreciation," i.e. Wright and Borthwick, editorial introduction to *Little Review*, l(February 1915), pp.30–32.
2. Rousseau (1762), pp.5, 7, 9. Early on, Rousseau was a music copyist and teacher, later a composer and musical theorist, who advanced the idea that music is derived from speech. "French being an unmusical language," he claimed, "the French have no music and never will have any."
3. Cranston (Encyc), p.960, among others Rousseau discarded were original sin, the Trinity, and a risen Christ, as did Tolstoy.
4. Kenneth Clark, *Civilization: A Personal View* (London: Murray, 1969), p.272, his italics. Rousseau and his mistress abandoned their children to a foundling home.
5. De Monvel's introduction to a translation of Rousseau (1762), p.vi. Predecessors to Rousseau's *Emile*, principally Locke and Montaigne, are introduced, p.viii.
6. Rousseau (1762), p.438.
7. Dewey and Dewey (1915), p.45.
8. Cranston (Encyc), p.961.
9. Dewey and Dewey (1915), chapter 10.
10. Lilley (1967), p.18; see also Brosterman (1997), pp.20–22.
11. Kathleen Curran, *The Romanesque Revival* (University Park: Pennsylvania State University Press, 2003), pp.135–138, 240–241.
12. Froebel (1887), "is likely to remain the most useful and faithfully accurate translation", Lilley (1967), pp.18, 26. Joseph Neef opened a Pestalozzi school in 1806 in Philadelphia, and the Scottish industrialist Robert Owen opened another in 1824 at his New Harmony, Indiana, experimental colony, Brosterman (1997), p.154n7.
13. Froebel (1887), p.233.
14. George J. Gutsche (1988), *Contemporary Authors*, no. 123, 1988, p.413.
15. As quoted by Paul Avrich, *Encyclopedia Britannica*. Of particular value is Paul Avrich, *The Modern School Movement: Anarchism and Education in the United States* (Princeton: Princeton University Press, 1980).
    Rolland was a musicologist, author, and biographer (his book about Tolstoy won the family's approval), thoroughly idealistic, an internationalist who later favored Russian communism, a pacifist, and endured a belief in heroes; see Megan Conway in DLB 65.
16. Butts and Cremin (1953), p.135; Menand (2001), chapter 12. Endowed by the philanthropist Anita McCormick Blaine and founded by Parker as principle, the Chicago Institute ran from 1899–1901 when it became the University of Chicago School of Education. Blaine gave more than $10 million in her lifetime in support of education and charities, over $750,000 to the Progressive Party. On some of Parker's programs, see Dewey and Dewey (1915), pp.62–63.
17. Findlay Peter Dunne, *Mr. Dooley's Opinions* (New York: R. H. Russell, 1901), p.137.
18. John Dewey, *My Pedagogic Creed* (Chicago: E. L. Kellog, 1897), p.429, as published in *John Dewey on Education: Selected Writings*, Reginald D. Archambault, ed. (New York: Random House, 1964), pp.427, 430.
19. Butts and Cremin (1953), p.118, their italics.
20. Cremin (1962), p.123; cf. Abigail A. Van Slyck, "'The utmost amount of Effectiv [sic] Accommodation': Andrew Carnegie and the Reform of the American Library," *JSSAH*, 50(December 1991), pp.359–383.
21. Butts and Cremin (1953); Dewey and Dewey (1915), she or he or together visited all schools discussed plus others not presented.
22. Wright (1932), p.11, this portion likely written in 1930, slightly altered in Wright (1943), p.13. See also Wright's comments of 1955 and 1957 as recorded in Peter (1994), pp.112–113.
23. Kaufmann (1981), p.132, reprint in Kaufmann (1989).

64   The aesthetics of progress

24 Wright (1932), p.11, altered Wright (1943), pp.13–14. Social recorder Gill (1987, p.44) believed Wright's comments just quoted are "high falutin rhetoric" or "remote from architecture." Also see Wright (1957), pp.19–20, 220.
25 *The First Half Century of Madison University (1819–1869)* . . . (New York: Sheldon, 1872), p.295, only William could have supplied the information; see also *A General Catalog of Colgate University* (1931), p.16, name change occurred in 1890; Secrest (1992), p.55; Sprague (1990), pp.1–2. On the Wright family lineage, see Secrest (1992), chapters 2–3; Donald Leslie Johnson, "Notes on FLW's Paternal Family," *The FLW Newsletter* (Oak Park), 3(second quarter, 1980), pp.5–7, reprint *Connecticut Nutmegger* (New England Historic and Genealogical Society), 16(1983).
26 *Frank Leslie's Historical Register of the . . . Centennial Exposition 1876* (New York: Frank Leslie, 1876), p.158; the building was also illustrated in James D. McCabe, *Illustrated History of the Centennial Exposition* (Philadelphia: Jones Brothers, 1876), p.215; cf. Johnson (1989b), pp.415–416, that includes letter in reply.
  There was a Woman's Building at the 1893 Chicago Exposition, designed by Boston architect Sophia Hayden (MIT graduate) and supervised by Minerva Parker of Philadelphia (also a competitor), see Margaret Henderson Floyd, *Architectural Education and Boston* . . . (Boston: Boston Architectural Center, 1989); and views in W. H. Jackson, *Jackson's Famous Pictures of the World's Fair* (Chicago: White City Company, 1895), unnumbered plates.
27 Brosterman (1997), p.154n.3, and see colored illustrations of the Froebel gifts; also "FLW Archives," *FLWQ*, 14(1, 2003), p.28.
28 Ann Taylor Allen, "'Let us Live with our Children': Kindergarten Movements in Germany and the United States, 1840–1914," *History of Education Quarterly*, 28(Spring 1988), pp.23–48; Nina C. Vandewalker, "The Place of the Kindergarten in the Wisconsin Public School System," *Milwaukee Normal School Bulletin*, 1(July 1904), pp.1–10; Meike Sophia Baader, "Froebel and the Rise of Educational Theory in the United States," *Studies in Philosophy and Education*, 23(2004), pp.427–444.
  In 1897, after pleadings by the Woman's Club, the Madison public school system implemented a kindergarten program, David V. Mollenhoff, *Madison: A History of the Formative Years* (Madison: University of Wisconsin Press, 2003), p.430n19. The first Wisconsin public schools to offer kindergartens were Milwaukee's in 1882.
29 Evelyn Lawrence, *Friedrich Froebel and English Education* (London: National Froebel Foundation, 1952) for an adequate outline.
30 Pierce (1957), v.3, p.383. Rubin (1989) to be read skeptically.
31 Cf. Michael Wakeford, "Nonprofessional Education," in Ockman and Williamson (2012), pp.364–369.
32 *Kaufmann (1989), pp.21–33. See also Kindergarten Gifts and Occupation Material, May, 1876* (New York: E. Steiger), bound with Matilda H. Kriege, *Friedrich Froebel: A Biographical Sketch* (New York: E. Steiger, 1876), in Library of Congress.
33 Kaufmann (1989), pp.19, 34.
34 As late as Wright to H.-R. Hitchcock, 19 March 1957 (Wright Archives), Wright insisted he was seven in 1876.
35 Wright (1932), p.13, altered Wright (1943), pp.14–15.
36 Barney (1965), pp.64–65.
37 Barney (1965), p.64.
38 Barney (1965), p.58.
39 As quoted in Meehan (1991), p.229; see also Eaton (1972), pp.41–50; Wright (1932), pp.11–13, 29–32.
40 Wright (1908), p.162.
41 Spencer (1900), pp.65–69, Wright's work is illustrated but not Sullivan's.
42 Ashwin (1982), p.155.
43 Other kits can be mentioned: "Improved Mosaic Recreation," England ca. 1850; *Modern Baukunst zur angenehmen Uterhaltung* (Germany ca. 1830), a building block kit that can form a neoclassical building; *Verbesserter Greichischer Baukasten oder Architectonische Unterhaltung* (Germany ca. 1830), similar to previous entry with Doric columns added; *Dr. Richter's Bauvorlagen*, or "Richter's Anchor Stone Building Blocks" in England (Germany ca. 1884), a kit of glazed-fired clay blocks in three colors with architectural pattern books, popular throughout Europe, England, and the northeastern United States.

Education   65

44 As quoted in Ashwin (1982), p.163.
45 Brosterman (1997), pp.138–145; Dudek (1996), pp.55–60; Cronon (1994), pp.15–16; McCarter (1991b), pp.238–289, 300–301; MacCormac (1991), pp.199–123, 296–297; Graf (1991), pp.218–237; cf. Rubin (1989) and Manson (1953). Wright told Manson that part of his article was guesswork while some parts were near "true," letter 18 June 1953 in Letters (1986), pp.114–115. See also Roche (1990); Stiny (1980), pp.409–462; Scully (1980), pp.9–31; Sergeant (1976a and b), pp.l21–224; Wilson (1979), pp.238–241, where the publications referred to were after 1876 (1893 and 1899); Koning and Eizenberg (1981), pp.295–323.
46 A useful comparative analysis is Lionel March, "A Class of Grids," *EandPB*, 8(1981), pp.325–332.
47 Miles Lewis, "Wright, Griffin & Natco," typescript, paper to SAHANZ conference, 1993, revised 1994, Melbourne, an introductory study; Johnson (2013a), throughout.
48 MacCormac (1968, 1974, 1991).
49 Cf. Johnson (1987), pp.22–29, portions now out-of-date.
50 Wright (June 1900), p.538. Beginning in 1985, Froebel blocks were again available through advertisements in art, craft, and architectural journals with words similar to "Wright's favorite childhood toys."
51 Gebhard and von Breton (1971), pp.11–13; on Catherine's Oak Park years, see Secrest (1992), pp.137–138, 190; Pierre (1989), pp.45–99. Catherine lived in Greenville, South Carolina, from 1921–24, where she worked for the Juvenile Protective Association and Red Cross, then in Chicago, where her social work continued and son Robert (b. 1903) lived with her while obtaining a law degree Secrest (1992), p.360.
52 Louis Sullivan, "Kindergarten Chats," *Interstate Architect & Builder* (Chicago), 2–3(16 February 1901–8 February 1902). Published in book form and based on Sullivan's revisions as edited by Claude Bragdon in 1918 (reprint Lawrence, Kansas: Scarab Fraternity Press, 1934).
53 Pierre (1989), p.150, Pierre was sculptor Richard Bock's daughter. She gave a date of 1907, but Montessori began her "children's house" that year in Rome.
54 Chicago Architectural Club, *Book of the Twenty-Seventh Annual Exhibition*, 1914, no pagination. On the complexly sophisticated marionette theater designed by Wright, see Alofsin (1992), pp.47–49; Pfeiffer (2011), p.375, described as a "Puppet Playhouse" dated 1909 only to be demolished. Son John's given middle name was Kenneth, but he preferred Lloyd. His "building blocks" in 1914 formed a house emulating one of his father's designs, illustrated Pfeiffer (2011), p.16.
55 Meehan (1991), pp.222–223.
56 Wright (1932), p.367, altered Wright (1943), pp.371–372.
57 Manson (1953), pp.349–351; reiterated in Manson (1958), pp.5–10.
58 As quoted in Hughes (1905), p.83. Possible ramifications of Froboelian kindergarten education and the gifts on R. Buckminster Fuller's theoretical explorations, structural creations, and possible links to Wright (and Massachusetts and Bradley's store) is discussed in Jolly (MS.1990), pp.34–44.
59 Alofsin (1992), p.359n.69.
60 As quoted in Meehan (1984), p.313. See also Peter (1994), pp.112–113.
61 Wright to Grant Manson, 18 June 1953, Letters (1986), pp.114–115.
62 For examples of exaggeration, see Rubin (1989); Brosterman (1997), pp.138–146; architect Dudek (1996), pp.57–60.
63 Wright to Manson, 18 June 1953, Letters (1986), pp.112–113; see also Wright to Manson, 10 August 1958, *JSAH*, 48(September 1958), p.310.
64 (Silsbee), *Eleventh Report of the Class of 1869* . . . (Cambridge, MA: Riverside Press, 1919), pp.250–256; Withey and Withey (1956), pp.554–555; Susan Karr Sorell, "Silsbee: The Evolution of a Personal Architectural Style," *PSR*, 7(Fourth Quarter 1970), pp.5–13; Thomas J. McCormick, "The Early Work of Joseph Lyman Silsbee," in Helen Searing, ed., *In Search of Modern Architecture: A Tribute to Henry-Russell Hitchcock* (New York/Cambridge, MA: Architectural History Foundation/MIT Press, 1982), pp.172–184; <jlsilsbee.blogspot.com>; Christopher Payne, "The Buffalo Architectural Legacy of J. L. Silsbee," *Western New Heritage* (Buffalo), 5(Winter 2002), pp.8–20. On Kent, see Withey and Whithey (1956), pp.340–341.
65 "The Chicago Art Institute," *Inland Architect*, 7(February 1886), p.26.
66 *Report of the Secretary of the Class of 1869 of Harvard College* (Boston: The College, 1894), p.78. On Silsbee's "moving platform" or the "Multiple Dispatch Railway of Endless Moving

Platforms," see patents of "Max E. Schmidt and Joseph L. Silsbee" for "Railway construction" (filed 2 August 1890, issued 18 November 1890); Joseph L. Silsbee, ibid. (filed 14 February 1891, issued 25 August 1891); idem., ibid. (filed 26 December 1893, issued 28 October 1894), Schmidt was a structural engineer. See also "Moving Platform for New York Subway," *Los Angeles Herald*, 36(22 March 1909), where Silsbee is not mentioned but Schmidt is.
67 As recorded by "W.C.G." (William Channing Gannett), (Notes), *Unity* (Chicago), 15(29 August 1885), p.320, the last line paraphrases Reverend Jones. The meeting rooms as built barely hold fifty people. Reverend Jones likely used similar words in a talk to the Women's Conference of the Western Unitarian Conference held in Cincinnati on 12 May 1886, "Western Unitarian Anniversaries," *The Unitarian* (Boston), 1(May 1886), p.136. At the same conference, J. L. Silsbee gave a paper on "A Needed Reform in Church Architecture," ibid., loc cit.
68 *Fourth Annual All Souls Church, 1887* (Chicago), p.33.
69 Wright (1932), p.141.
70 S.C.Ll.J." (Susan Charlotte Lloyd Jones, Jenkin's wife), [Notes], *Unity*, 16(14 November 1885), p.136; [J. L. Jones], "Unity Chapel for the Unitarian Church of Helena Valley, Wisconsin," *Unity*, 16(26 December 1885), p.1; "Unity Chapel, Helena, Wis," *All Souls Church: Fourth Annual* (Chicago: All Souls Church, 1887), n.p.; W.C.G. [William C. Gannett], "Christening a Country Church," *Unity and the University*, 17(20 August 1886), pp.356–357; Twombly p.29n25, where publications recording construction events are listed.
71 Secrest (1992), p.7; Siry (1996), photograph of chapel interior p.24. Cf. Elizabeth Wright Ingraham, "The Chapel in the Valley," *FLWNews*, 3(2nd quarter, 1980), pp.1–7.
72 siouxcityuu.org, accessed June 1914.
73 Wright to "Uncle" Jenkin, 22 August 1885, Wright Archive; in Letters (1986), p.xiii, Wright mentioned receiving advice from a colleague named "Wise" who was likely in Conover's office. Architect Patrick Pinnell also examined the letter and believes the date could be 1886, not 1885, and links the letter to the Sioux City design, Pinnell (1991), p.294n8.
74 Wright (1932), p.26, altered Wright (1943), p.28; on the chapel familial associations, see Secrest (1992), pp.3–8.
75 Secrest (1992), p.140. Reverend Jones's Tower Hill summer camp meetings occupied the site of the old Helena Shot Tower that produced lead shot from 1832–60. Events described by Wright could not have taken place at Tower Hill cottage because Reverend Jones had not purchased the land (at a tax sale for sixty dollars) or formed the Tower Hill Pleasure Company until 1889, two years after Wright settled in Chicago.
76 Wright (1943), p.301, not in Wright (1932).
77 Wright (1943), p.436, not in Wright (1932).
78 Wright (1943), p.380; the added "Book Five" begins on p.379.
79 "Hillside Home School," *Unity*, 19(4 June 1887); see also Hillside (1890), p.13.
80 Secrest (1992), p.94 and chapters 2–3 on the trials of the immigrant Jones family on arrival in Wisconsin from Wales.
81 Secrest (1992), pp.44, 59, 94–96, 197, which follow the observations of Chase (1956), chapter 4; Barney(1965), chapter 12. Hillside was one of the first coeducational and non-racial private schools in America.
82 Sprague (1990), pp.2, 7.
83 John O. Holzhueter, "FLW's Designs for Robert Lamp," *Wisconsin Magazine of History*, 72(Winter 1988), pp.1, 84, 89n8.
84 Harper (1904) a pamphlet; Barney (1965), p.114; Wright (1932), p.4; Wright (1943), p.6; Siry (1996), p.24.
85 As quoted in Secrest (1992), 59. In Peter (1994, p.113), Wright erroneously refers to Theodore Parker, a nineteenth-century Unitarian minister in Boston. W. N. Hailmann's translation of Froebel's *The Education of Man* was released in America in 1887. According to Wright, the sisters gave their nephew copies of Ruskin's *Stones of Venice* and *Seven Lamps of Architecture* after he had settled in Chicago, Wright (1932), pp.31, 52.
86 Barney (1965), pp.117–118.
87 Ellen Jones to Gannett, 12 Dec 1886, William C. Gannett Papers, Department of Rare Books and Special Collections, University of Rochester Library, as quoted in Siry (1996), p.22.
88 Hillside (1890), p.1.
89 Barney (1965), pp.93, 116; Secrest (1992), p.44.
90 Barney (1965), p.61.

91 Wright (1932), pp.7–8.
92 Wright (1932), p.13.
93 Mollenhoff and Hamilton (1999), p.43.
94 Wright (1932), p.8. For biographical detail on William as well as his relationship with his wife Anna, see Secrest (1992), chapter 2; Mollenhoff and Hamilton (1999), pp.34–37; Johnson (1980), throughout; Gill (1987), chapter 2; Twombly's pioneering study (1979), chapter 1.
95 Sprague (1990), pp.1, 7n.6.
96 Chase (1956), p.94, written while a professor at Smith College in Northampton, Massachusetts. Excerpts about Hillside from Chase's book appeared in *The Milwaukee Journal* newspaper under the tantalizing title of "A School That Taught How to Live," (10 December 1939), p.2c–f, and accompanied by poor-quality portraits of the Jones sisters and dark images of peopled classrooms. The book was selected in 1957 by the US Information Service as "one of a collection of 350 books" about America for distribution worldwide during the Cold War. Wright's 1943 *An Autobiography* was also selected, and some of Chase's text may have been influenced by it. See also Benjamin D. Rhodes, "From Cooksville to Chungking . . .," *WHistory*, 72(Summer 1989), pp.246–248, with illustrations of the school, others of which are also available online through the Wisconsin Historical Society.
97 Helen Kirkpatrick Milbank, "Mary Ellen Chase: Teacher, Writer, Lecturer," *Colby Quarterly*, 6(March 1962), p.6.
98 "The Hillside Home School," *Unity*, 21(2 and 9 June, 1888), p.205.
99 The Kehl School of Dance continues under fourth generation descendants, Mary Jane Hamilton, "The Kehl Dance Academy," *Sprague* (1990), pp.65–68.
100 Hugenholtz, whose father was a minister in the Netherlands, later became a minister of the First Unitarian Holland Church in Grand Rapids, Michigan.
101 Lola Devore, "The Life of Florence Fifer Bohrer: Illinois' First Woman Senator," *Journal of the Illinois State Historical Society*, 93(Autumn 2000), p.305; Bohrer (1955), pp.151–155. Bohrer's father was Joseph W. Fifer, Governor of Illinois; she became a state senator in 1943 and promoted many Progressive causes.
102 Letter Joseph W. Fifer to school, n.d., Hillside (1903), p.35.
103 Wright (1946), p.36, author of poem not cited and the stanzas were arranged differently by John; Gebhard and von Breton (1971), p.16. In 1918, John invented Lincoln Logs and organized the Red Square Toy Company, later J. L. Wright Manufacturing. In 1943, the new company bought the Playskool company, which made toys, mainly of wood. The logs were inducted into the National Toy Hall of Fame in 1999. K'NEX is the current distributor.
104 Wright (1932), p.130; similar Wright (1943), pp.132–137; Barney (1965), p.86. Wright ordered the Home Building demolished in 1950, Pfeiffer (2011), p.19.
105 Wright (1932), pp.130–135, plan p.133, demolished in 1990, reconstructed in 1992 at a cost greater than $150,000. Rather proudly, Wright said relatives had called him the "boy" designer: here again he was conditioning readers to a genius youth, as he might phrase it.
106 Wright (1943), p.410; Barney (1965), pp.85–86, a search has failed to find information about Cramer, but he was likely one of the Milwaukee Cramers.
107 Bohrer (1955), p.154; see also Pinnell (1991); Sorell (1970); Hasbrouck (1969); Twombly (1979), p.29n.29. Often incorrectly referred to as Wright's first design or first commission, it is pure Silsbee, as Wright acknowledged. It has been alleged that some of the program prepared by the sisters was relayed by Wright, Aunt Ellen (in River Falls) to Wright (in Silsbee's office), 9 March 1887, Wright Archives. Other existing farm buildings were remodeled by Thomas for the school, too late for Wright to have helped. On Thomas's role in constructing Hillside buildings, see Barney (1965), pp.77–78, and Aunt Ellen to Wright, 9 March 1887, Wright Archives.
108 *Commemorative Biographical Record of the Counties of Rock, Green, Grant, Iowa, and Lafayette Wisconsin* (Chicago: J. H. Beers, 1901), pp.972–973; a similar presentation was articled in *Kindergarten Magazine*, 10(1897–1898), as found at <www23.us.archive.org/stream/kindergartenmaga16chic/kindergartenmaga16 chic_djvu.txt>
109 See, for example, "The Hillside Home School," *Unity*, 21(1 and 9 June 1888), p.205.
110 Francis Parker to school, Hillside (1903), pp.35–36.
111 Secrest (1992), p.140; Levine (1996), p.446n19.
112 "Hillside Training School," *St. Paul Daily Globe*, 14 August 1887, p.7d.
113 Hillside (1890), p.2.

68 The aesthetics of progress

114 Harper (1904) p.8; *Commemorative Biographical Record*, 1901, loc cit, see end note 106.
115 [Notes], *Unity*, 20(February 1888), p.176; see also "Editorial," ibid., 21(August 1888), p.323.
116 Hillside (1903), pp.27–28.
117 Secrest (1992), pp.95–96; Barney (1965), pp.115, 129.
118 Hillside (1895), p.17.
119 Barney (1965), p.122.
120 Siry (1996), p.42.
121 Obituary, "Thomas Lloyd Jones Is Dead," *Wisconsin State Journal*, 3 September 1931, p.1b.
122 Barney (1965), p.118.
123 Mary Jane Hamilton, "Nantucket in the Art of Maginel Wright," *Historic Nantucket* (Nantucket Historical Association), 56(Summer 2007), pp.10–15; Barney (1965), p.131.
124 *Wisconsin Alumni Magazine*, 3(October 1901), p.34; *Wisconsin State Journal*, 3 September 1931, p.1e, f, g.
125 Benjamin D. Rhodes, "From Cooksville to Chungking: The Dam Designing Career of John L. Savage," *WHistory*, 72(Summer 1989), pp.245–248.
126 Alexander McQueen, *A Romance in Research: The Life of Charles F. Burgess* (Pittsburgh: Instruments Publishing, 1951), p.165.
127 *Who's Who on the Stage* (New York: Walter Browne & F. A. Austin, 1906), p.167; Barney (1965), pp.117–118; Hillside (1895), p.18.
128 Siry (1996), p.261n44, on Roberts's support for school, p.23; on Unity Temple, see Alofsin (1992), pp.72–73, 283–284n90–94. On arrival at the school, student Julian Street announced that he was "from one of the first families of Chicago," Barney (1965), p.117.
129 Judy Ettenhofer, "Passion in the Valley," editorial, *Capital Times* (Madison), 7(September 1902); "La Follette and Party Leave for Washington," *Minneapolis Journal*, 2(January 1906), p.8e; Bohrer (1955), pp.153–154. Philip La Follette acted as Wright's attorney in the 1920s.
130 Hillside (1903), p.38.
131 The Mason City buildings of 1907–09 are well documented, but see also <http://www.steinerag.com/flw/Artifact%20Pages/ParkInn.htm#ParkInn1912> accessed July 2012. The hotel was restored and opened in 2011. During 1913–14, the remarkable Blythe house, located at his and Markley's own Rock Crest-Rock Glen residential real estate development in Mason City, was constructed to a design by architects Walter Burley and Marion Mahony Griffin, see especially Maldre and Kruty (1996), pp.28–29 and related plates: it, too, has been preserved.
132 L. Irene Buck, "Teaching Children Through Art," *Wisconsin State Journal*, 19(May 1946), p.6; Obituary, ibid., 15 February 1953.
133 Information about Hillside students and teachers was taken from numerous and varied sources online and in print too numerous to record here, but see Hillside (1890), p.13, Hillside 1895), p.17, Hillside (1903), pp.24–25, each provides valuable insight into the school and list of people's names.
134 Jane Jones to Blaine, 15 October 1901, as cited in Siry (1996), p.261n43.
135 As quoted in Secrest (1992), p.197. See also Wright (1910), plates Xa, b; Levine (1996), pp.19–20; Siry (1996), pp.22–32; Twombly (1979), pp.96–98.
136 Jane Jones as quoted in Siry (1996), p.29, two interior photos of the assembly room, pp.30–31. On David Timothy, Graham (1983), p.128.
137 Wright (1943), p.383, not in Wright (1932); Hoffmann (1996), pp.11, 106–107.
138 The sisters publicly acknowledged the donation and loan, Hillside (1903), p.2.
139 Hoffmann (1996), p.29. In poor condition, the Lawrence Memorial Library was rebuilt to Wright's plans and reopened in 1993, Storrer (1993), p.70.
140 Wright (1943), p.383, not in Wright (1932); Eaton (1969), p.79. In efforts – from 1933 through the 1950s – to house the Taliesin Fellowship, Wright literally hacked away (vandalized) the interior of many of the school's rooms including, sadly, the chapel.
141 Control of assets were transferred to Wright in May 1915 for one dollar and, as it was incorporated in 1904, other than the sisters, only Susan Dana and Charles Roberts held shares in school that May: Siry (1996), p.261n44; on legal entanglements from 1909–12 see Alofsin (1993), p.350n57.
142 Eaton (1969), pp.79–81; Quinan (1987), pp.170n15; Gill (1987), pp.139–143.
143 Fairhope, Alabama, Wikipedia, accessed August 2013.
144 Dewey and Dewey (1915) vividly describes Johnson's philosophy and teaching methods.

145 Cremin (1961), p.105.
146 Now the Marietta Johnson School of Organic Education, its operations include the original schoolhouse.
147 Destler (1963), p.252, see also pp.216–220, 252–253; Wright (1943), p.387, not in Wright (1932); Turak (1991), pp.144–163, an interview with Queene's daughter Elizabeth.
148 Eaton (1969), pp.82–86; Wright (1932), pp.164, 251.
149 Wright (1932), p.164; Mason (1956), pp.187–197; Kruty (1998), p.214. In the same year, Avery's brother Prentiss and wife Alice asked architect of historical traditions Howard Van Doren Shaw to design a house, Eaton (1969), pp.217–220.
150 *City Club of Chicago 9th Year Book*, 1 May 1912.
151 Secrest (1992), p.236.
152 Sweeney (1978), p.2; Turak (1991), pp.149–150.
153 Dewey and Dewey (1915), pp.66–67, 94–96, 165–166.
154 Queene Ferry Coonley, "The Educational Responsibility of the Mothers," *Vassar Quarterly* (August 1921), p.239, as quoted in Turak (1991), p.150.
155 "Garden for the Children," *Frederick Froebel's Education by Development* (New York: D. Appleton, 1899), an illustration is in Brosterman (1997), p.31.
156 Preliminary of scheme no. 1 in Riley (1994), p.164. Pfeiffer (07-13), pp.28–34, plates 35–37 where, on the first scheme (plate 35), Wright wrote, "early sketch for a Playhouse." See Dewey and Dewey (1915), pp.66ff, for details and illustrations of children's activities, including those with Queene, and chapter 5, on the focus given to group and individual play during this period; see also Turak (1991) and Brosterman (1997), both throughout; Sweeney (1978), pp.2–5. A Coonley garage sympathetic to Wright's house was designed by William Drummond and constructed ca. 1919. The Playhouse has been recently restored by architect John Vinci.

Apparently Wright was not considered for a new Christian Science church in Riverside, Illinois, even though Avery Coonley was chairman of the building committee, Paul Eli Ivey, *Prayers in Stone Christian Science Architecture . . . 1894–1930* (Urbana: University of Illinois Press, 1999), p.178. Wright buildings of similar exterior character were a project for the Pembroke, Ontario (Canada), Carnegie Library, 1913, Pfeiffer (07-13), plate 455; Midway Gardens of 1913–14; and City National Bank, Mason City, Iowa, of 1909–11.
157 Drummond (1916), p.44; Drummond (1915), illustrations; Brooks (1972), pp.179–180, the plan something like Wright's Playhouse for Queene that was based on the Emmond house of 1892.
158 Meech (2001), pp.203–204. Also, in 1910, Queene coaxed her brother Dexter Ferry to approach Drummond to design a large residence. Two proposals resulted, the first a wonderful Wright School design, but neither was built, Brooks (1972), pp.181–187.
159 Cremin (1961), p.247.
160 Langmead and Johnson (2000), throughout but especially introduction.
161 Alofsin (1992), p.54, a long speculative essay; Alofsin (1993), pp.87, 90–100; of less value David Van Zanten, "Frank Lloyd Wright's Kindergarten: Professional Practice and Sexual Roles," reprinted in Christopher Reed, ed., *Not at Home. The Suppression of Domesticity in Modern Art and Architecture* (London: Thames Hudson, 1996), pp.92–97, 279–280.
162 Pfeiffer (07-13), plate 441–443.
163 Letter, Mary Jane Hamilton, *WHistory*, 73(Autumn 1989), pp.42–45, construction was likely unsupervised; the first design Alofsin (1993), pp.97, 350n67.
164 This introduction to the Fellowship was taken from Johnson (1990), pp.38–84; Langmead and Johnson (2000), chapters 10–11, where Henrik Wijdeveld's important contribution is carefully analyzed; Sergeant (1976a), chapter 3; Secrest (1992), chapter 16: each contains citations.

See also Herb Greene, *Mind & Image* (London: Granada, 1962); Edgar Tafel, *Apprentice to Genius: Years with . . .* (New York: McGraw-Hill, 1979, New York: Dover, 1985); idem., *About Wright: An Album of Recollections . . .* (New York: Wiley, 1993); Donald W. Hoppen, *The Seven Ages of . . .* (Santa Barbara: Capra, 1992); Randolph C. Henning, *At Taliesin* (Carbondale: Southern Illinois University Press, 1992); Curtis Besinger, *Working with Mr. Wright: What It Was Like* (New York: Cambridge University Press, 1995); Myron A. Marty and Shirley L. Marty, *FLW's Taliesin Fellowship* (Kirksville, MO: Truman State University Press, 1999); Cornelia Brierly (joined in 1934 and died at Taliesin West in 2012, age 99), *Tales of Taliesin* (Tempe, AZ: Herberger Center for Design Excellence, 2000); Lois Davidson Gottlieb, *A Way of*

Life: An Apprenticeship . . . (Melbourne: Images, 2001); Kamal Aman, *Reflections for the Shinning Brow* (McKinleyville, CA: Fithian Press, 2004); the late Earl Nesbet, *Taliesin Reflections* (Pelatuna, CA: Meridian Press, 2006); Roger Friedland and Harold Zellman, *The Fellowship: The Untold Story of FLW and the Taliesin Fellowship* (Los Angeles: HarperCollins, 2006); and *Journal of the Taliesin Fellows*.

165 "We had no money . . .,"Wright said to Peter (1994), p.121, "we" included Olgivanna.

3 Tutelage

When studying Wright's biography and works, it is an obligation to refer to his autobiography of 1932. However, over intervening years, it has been discovered that it and other writings were either unreliable, particularly when speaking of his early years, or otherwise difficult to to unriddle. This is mainly the result of a peculiar prose style that clouded meaning. One historian and student of Wright of more than a few decades, Gilbert Herbert, has referred to a "cavalier attitude to facts" pointing to the "unreliability" of Wright's "written testimony." It is true that, as people age, their memories play tricks, recollections faint, errors appear. But with Wright, many apparently innocent tricks were perpetuated over decades, leaving a reader to wonder as to motive, particularly when it is apparent that some were intentionally meant to claim unearned credit while others seem to be deliberately self-serving.[1] This is sad because truth better serves Wright: reality always of greater value. Distortions by Wright and the more ardent of his followers led to fantasies, errors, and myths that need the light of clarification or by unbiased examination. Perhaps the most troubling is the late teen years just before marriage at age twenty-one.

Teen years at work

Using credible and competently researched sources and collating new evidence a correct time line of Wright's late juvenile and apprentice working years, 1885–88, or age seventeen to twenty-one, is as follows:

1885   March, he quit high school in his senior year at the end of winter term, not to graduate.
         June, he began halftime as "office man" for the Madison engineering firm of Conover & Porter.
1886   January into March, he was enrolled as a part-time student at the University of Wisconsin in Madison, or UW.
         September into December, he was again a UW part-time student only to quit university at the end of the fall term.
         December, early in the month he was dismissed by Conover & Porter on completion of their new UW Science Hall.
         A maximum of seventeen months halftime employment.
1887   January, he began full-time with architect Joseph Lyman Silsbee in Chicago, interrupted by a couple of weeks working for architect William W. Clay also in Chicago.
1888   February, he began full-time with Adler and Sullivan's architectural firm in Chicago.
         Ten months full-time with Silsbee as factotem then tracer then draftsman, including time with Clay.

Short and uncomplicated supporting evidence follows. It is necessary to recall that, according to his mother, Frank Lincoln Wright was born 8 June 1867 at "about eight o clock" in the morning.[2] Further, released in 1932, his autobiography was begun in 1927 and was likely discontinued in early 1930. The years to publication were darkened by personal insolvency, the Depression, and difficulty finding a publisher, followed by editing issues. The years ca. 1930 to ca. 1941 were more or less included in "Book Five" of the 1943 edition.[3]

1885 March: Architect Joseph Lyman Silsbee designed and construction began immediately on All Souls Church in Chicago for Wright's respected Unitarian uncle, the Reverend Jenkin Jones.

Silsbee's move from staid Syracuse to bustling Chicago occurred in 1882.[4] His father, Reverend William, was a New England Unitarian minister and known to Reverend Jones. Reverend William Channing Gannett, whose Unitarian parish was Hinsdale west of Chicago and who collaborated in many ways with Reverend Jones, introduced architect to potential client in a February 1885 letter to Jones that said, in part, "I enclose Mr Silsbee's note . . . if you care to call on him and interest him in your double-faced church idea, I should not wonder if he could help you well."[5] That would have been an idea for Reverend Jones's first All Souls Church, but "double-faced" was not explained. Probably referred to a social center and church in one ediface.

April: At the end of term in March, Frank quit high school where, because of farm work, he had attended only fall and winter terms each school year as a "special student." During spring term and in summer, he worked on the Jones family farms.[6]

Wright's father, Reverend William Cary Wright, had begun legal action in December 1884 to end his marriage. Grounds for legal separation were "for cruelty, personal violence, and refusal of marital rights." It was found that William had indeed "performed his full duty to the defendant." On 24 April 1885, the marriage was "dissolved," and the house deeded to Anna where she might that she might raise the children.[7] After William's divorce, "The mother was alone now with her son and his two sisters," lamented Wright.[8] Alone with five children, not three. Under the divorce terms, two of Anna's three stepchildren, as well as her own three children by William, remained with Anna. Yet Wright purposely never mentioned his stepsiblings in print.

June: Frank, age eighteen, began working halftime (mornings, he said) as the first office factotum for the Madison engineering firm of Allan Darst Conover and Lew Foster Porter. It was his first paid employment.

After the divorce, "She [mother] found a place for the budding architect with blue-eyed Allen [sic] D. Conover. . . ." More likely, it was Wright's father who talked business neighbor Conover into giving his son a job. Regardless, Wright continued to live in Madison until February 1887. As part of the divorce settlement, Anna's brothers and sisters promised to financially support her and the five children. Practically, if not morally, it was not Wright's role to be the family provider: stepbrother Charles was eldest and living in Milwaukee. Stepbrother George was finishing university while living with Anna, as was stepsister Elizabeth who was still at school, but brother Frank was not.[9]

Architectural plans for a new Dane County Courthouse were prepared in 1883 by noted German-born Milwaukee architect Henry C. Koch. Apparently Koch was too busy to supervise construction, so the county unwisely hired Conover in 1884. The building was completed in 1885 and demolished in 1958. In December 1884, the university's Science Hall and its valuable contents were destroyed by fire. Koch was commissioned to prepare plans for a new building. Conover, a sewage and civil engineer and professor and dean of engineering at UW, played a significant role in programing and consultation. But bids for construction were rejected by university regents. The university unwisely appointed in-house Conover as both contractor and construction supervisor. Emboldened by these appointments, Conover ventured to start a private practice. He persuaded Porter, a UW engineering student who had just completed his junior year and who had some art and architecture training, to join him as a junior partner. Construction and supervisory roles for the UW were the firm's first commission.[10] Koch's Science Hall, completed early December 1887 (when Wright was laid off), steel-framed with a heavy brick-red Richardsonian Romanesque exterior aesthetic and compositionally very similar but superior to Koch's earlier courthouse. Wright would later claim construction experience on Science Hall, not supervision, as implied by him and others, when he said

> At that time Science Hall was being built by a Milwaukee architect out of Professor Conover's office....
> So the young sophomore [sic, freshman] got some actual contact with this construction.
> He was entrusted with the working out of some steel clips to join the apex of the trusses of the main roof....[11]

Office work, not drawing or drafting. Office work was clarified in January 1888 when Conover testified before state legislature that "I had to keep an office and pay my office rent. I had to keep an office man [Wright], a draftsman [named elsewhere in his testimony], and pay all the incidental expenses which come to an office."[12] At the time, "office man" was an entry-level position. (That January, Wright had been unemployed for a month.) As a factotum employee, Wright was not yet an apprentice – and certainly not the "draughtsman" he claimed when forming his entry for the city directory of 1886 – although, perhaps, during the last months of tenure, Wright likely did some supervised tracing or drafting. Obviously, Wright did not in any manner supervise the complex construction of Science Hall.

Why did Frank's family seek out engineer Conover and not a local architect? Three civil engineers and three architects were listed in the Madison directory. Two architects were primarily builders, where they were also listed, who could whip together a modest design. The third was John Nadar. The three engineers were Conover, Dodge McClellan, a capable surveyor and city engineer, and John Nadar. Trained as an engineer in New York, in 1871, the accomplished Nadar was appointed assistant US engineer in charge of the Wisconsin River improvement program headquartered in Portage and, in 1873, he moved headquarters to Madison. When federal funds dried up in 1876, he stayed in Madison and established a private engineering and architecture office. He was city engineer until 1883, when he was reappointed in 1885, and designed several forgettable buildings. Conover moved in social, intellectual, and religious societies also frequented by the extended Jones family and William and Anna Wright. Nadar was active in the Catholic community.[13]

August: Commissioned by Reverend Jones, Silsbee designed and construction began immediately for Unity Chapel on a site central to the Lloyd Jones family farms near Spring Green.

In December 1885, a floor plan and perspective drawing of Silsbee's chapel design was published in Jones's *Unity* magazine. The caption read, "The underpinning to the level of the window-sill is rock-faced broken ashlar... and is now completed."[14] Although of ailing health, construction was supervised by Jones's older brother Thomas, as well as a local builder named Cramer.[15] Reverend Gannett reported that Wright had painted the "audience room" and "parlor" walls. The two rooms were "wood ceiled...; one [room] is calcimined in terra cotta, one [the parlor] in olive green." The "wood-ceil[ing] pine in its own color."[16] Bruce Brooks Pfeiffer, now retired keeper of the Wright Archives in Scottsdale, Arizona, was correct to say that Silsbee was the architect and Wright only painted ceiling designs[17] and a few walls. It is not known who designed the ceiling pattern, but Wright made no claim, so it was likely Silsbee. Clearly, the part-time student working halftime for Conover in distant Madison was *not* involved with the chapel's design, detailing, or construction.

1886 January 6 to March 31: Age eighteen, Frank enrolled part time at UW, Madison, as a "special student" in engineering, the result of not completing high school. Special status was possibly aided by Conover. In any event, Frank was not enrolled in the Engineering School.[18] It is uncertain as to the courses he took, but records indicate he failed to attend French classes, and there is no record of marks for any course. Wright did not enroll for the April–June spring term.

June: In a June, letter Reverend Jones said, "[T]he little Helena [Unity] Chapel, which is being built to house my first missionary movement, my home parish which is fast approaching completion."[19]

August: Unity Chapel was dedicated.

Autobiographically, Wright recounted a visit to Chicago and sighting Silsbee's nearly complete All Souls Church. However, he dated the trip as "late spring, 1887" and used the text as an introduction to a discussion about his first days in the city searching for a job in January 1887. But other details in the text confirm that he was in fact discussing events that took place in August 1886.[20] It was an autobiographical slip up easily made by a distance of forty-five years.

September: All Souls Church in Chicago opened and was dedicated on 11 October.[21]

Unity Chapel and All Souls were constructed concurrently, as Reverend Jones had planned for his growing and expanding ministry.

September 8 to December 22: At age nineteen, Wright again enrolled part time at UW. Records indicate he completed two courses, descriptive geometry and engineering drawing, each awarded average marks.[22]

Therefore, Wright completed only two university trimester-long courses. However, he claimed to have taken courses with "Professor[s] Conover and Storm Bull [a Unitarian] . . . in Stereotomy [descriptive geometry for masonry construction], Graphic-Statistics, Analytical and Descriptive Geometry," mathematics, French, rhetoric, and English. One student drawing he signed "FLlW," so it must be that he became Lloyd Wright during the university term. On another occasion, he claimed to have had "two years of professional training in the Engineering School" and completed three years of university and one term of the fourth year: "So the University training," he said, "Freshman, Sophomore, Junior, and part Senior."[23] Some of the subjects he remembered attending in university were actually undertaken at Madison (now Central) High School. Historian Robert Twombly reported that during Wright's unfinished senior year. September 1884 through March 188.5 his grades were "average" in "rhetoric and botany, both good and poor in physics, and poor to average in algebra which he failed once."[24]

Dissembling continued. Justification to quit university came in autobiographical words such as, "There seemed little meaning in the [university] studies, mathematics excepted . . . taught by Professor [Charles A.] Van Velzer. . .," but mathematics was undertaken in high school.[25] In 1957, at age eighty-nine, Wright repeated words he wrote around 1930: "we [the Jones family] couldn't afford an architectural school. . . . So impatiently I went through nearly four years of engineering school" – that is, at the local university that did not have an architectural program, the nearest in Champaign, Illinois. And again: "several months before I was to receive a degree, I ran away from" the university.[26]

It may be asked why there have been so many questions since 1932 by curious laymen and scholars about Wright's education. The answer is contained in a letter written by architect George Grant Elmslie. He and Wright had shared the drafting room in Silsbee's office during 1887. When Wright went to work for Adler & Sullivan, he said he encouraged them to hire Elmslie. In a letter of 30 October 1932 to Wright about his just-published autobiography, Elmslie was reminded of "times, long ago" and candidly spoke: "I do not understand your reference to your senior year and impending graduation. . . . However, that is not a serious matter except as it relates to a true tale of events," Elmslie's request for truthfulness was repeatedly expressed in the letter.[27]

1887 January: Age nineteen, Wright began full time with Silsbee in Chicago as a "tracer," he said. It was the beginning of his apprenticeship.

Wright was first listed as a member of the parish in the *All Souls Church Fourth Annual* of 6 January 1887.[28] On Frank's arrival in Chicago, Silsbee arranged for him to board with the Waterman family about a block away from All Souls Church. From the Wisconsin town of Oregon and two years younger than Frank, Harry Hale Waterman, a former Northwestern University student, had begun as a draftsman in Silsbee's office in 1886, soon alongside Wright.[29] Waterman left Silsbee in June 1893 to set up his own office that gained clients from throughout the northern Midwest.

A supporting date for beginning with Silsbee is contained in a letter from Wright's Aunt Nell dated 9 March asking, "How is it with you in the great city?" and closing with "I hope you are well, happy, and satisfying Mr. Silsbee." The letter not only confirms that Wright was then with Silsbee formally but also that design of the "new building" for the Hillside school was under way. Nell went on about extensive remodeling and "additions" needed for the "old one" – that is, their old settler's homestead, then a temporary schoolhouse named Home Cottage. She then asked Frank for a "rough sketch" to remodel the old homestead. She did *not* ask for ideas or sketches for a new school building. It remains unknown if Frank replied.[30]

At this time, Silsbee operated a solo Chicago practice after partner Edward Austin Kent returned to Buffalo, New York. Kent, also a Unitarian, earned a degree in civil engineering in 1875 from Yale University, followed by about nine months of architectural studies at the École des Beaux-Arts in Paris. On returning, he entered Silsbee's office in 1877, then quit to serve as a government architect in Washington, DC, for two years to then rejoin Silsbee as a partner: Silsbee & Kent (1882–84), Silsbee alone (1884–1913). Silsbee maintained an office in Syracuse and Buffalo until he became a permanent Chicago resident sometime in 1886.[31] Perhaps Frank was hired upon Silsbee receiving the Jones's Home Building contract, the persuasion of fellow Unitarian Reverend Jones, and Wright's uncle, highly probable.[32] According to Wright, his first personal contact with Silsbee was that January and not before, one of many false autobiographical assertions. Apparently upset over low wages, he left Silsbee around 1 May to work for architect William W. Clay but for only a couple of weeks. He has publicly confessed that the work was beyond his learned capabilities (he was fired), and he returned to an understanding Silsbee.[33]

Wright completed an ink drawing that copied Silsbee's perspective drawing of Unity Chapel, and it was published in the 6 January 1887 issue of *All Souls Church, Fourth Annual*. As previously indicated, it was amateurish, with childlike lettering, and executed sometime late in 1886. Soon thereafter, Wright made two student drawings of All Souls based on copying an exterior photograph of the completed building. Silsbee's own drawing as published also copied the photograph, and Wright's drawings again emulated Silsbee's style. The three twenty-two-inch-wide drawings were not traced over a photograph.[34]

March: Silsbee was commissioned by Wright's maternal maiden aunts Elinor (Nell to family or Ellen or Ellen C. professionally) and Jane (Jen or Jennie to family) Lloyd Jones to design a Home Building for their new Hillside Home School outside Spring Green. Brother Thomas supervised construction and was assisted by a builder named Cramer.

In 1886, Wright listed himself in the *Madison City Directory* as a "draughtsman" at Conover & Porter's address. From 1887–92, he was listed in directories as a "clerk," "archt," "architect" or "designer." For published renderings for Silsbee, he signed as a "Del" [delineator], "arch," "archt," or "architect."[35]

Unfortunately, Silsbee's architectural and construction drawings for the Home Building and Unity Chapel have not survived.[36] Regardless, a confident response to the controversy as to who designed the Home Building can be readily formulated. Wright's only claim of an independent design prior to 1889 was a proposal for a "Unitarian Chapel for Sioux City, Iowa," implying incorrectly that he had the commission: but no commission, no project. Wright may have been prompted by his uncle Jenkin to the fact that the First Unitarian Church of Sioux City was organized 11 March 1885 with Reverend Mary A. Safford pastor, therefore a church building expected. However, the Sioux City chapel was not a wholly independent design. We've noted that the plan and perspective drawing, likely executed during February 1887 while with Silsbee, were published as a plate in the June 1887 issue of Chicago's *Inland Architect and News Record*. The chapel drawing shared the page with a fine ink rendering by architect W. B. Mundie of "A Three Room Village School," a project whose exterior had oversized polygonal stonework.[37] Wright's floor plan mimicked Silsbee's Unity Chapel, as did the elevational scheme of stone below the sill line rising to wood-shingled siding to a constant eve line, then shingled roofs, one a tall cone covering a dinky hemicycle "alcove." The proposed building was naively overelaborate, badly scaled, and ill-proportioned. It too had oversized but plump polgonal stonework.

His drawings as published are that of a neophyte with a rather "clumsy, student hand" and plainly "not the work of an instinctive artist," Secrest rightly observed. His other published

76 *The aesthetics of progress*

renderings for Silsbee were perspectives, some were published in *Inland Architect*, one in 1887, five in 1888. Perspective drawings of two speculative houses for "Helena Valley" implied, again wrongly, that Wright had their commission, he the architect.[38] One was of Silsbee's Home Building more or less as completed. There was his drawing of the front facade of the Falkenau Row Houses of 1888 for Adler & Sullivan where sleek, precisely fit stonework was made to look lumpy. Add to those a set of freehand drawings of 1888, at age twenty, that have survived, all adequately confirm that Wright was correct when, in September years, he once again admitted, "I had never drawn more than a little 'free-hand'. . . my technique condemned me to T-square and triangle."[39] However, it is not just a matter of talent or drawing skill. Rather, it is of architectonic content as indicated by the drawings. Too obviously, those of 1886–87 reveal that he was not a competent two- and three-dimensional planner or designer or detailer of construction materials. Significantly, the Sioux City chapel is not mentioned in the three editions of his autobiography or most other writings.

The Jones sisters program as given to Silsbee for their Home Building was for modest school facilities combined with residences in a single building that must appear homelike. All aspects of the Home Building's exterior, therefore, bear striking similarities to Silsbee's residences of a similar aesthetic. Their residential style was one that Wright and cohorts called Queen Anne (out of Richard Norman Shaw's Bedford Park) and Americans now refer to as Shingle Style. A few exterior designs of Silsbee houses make the point: a speculative house for Edward B. Smith in Buffalo in 1885 with construction of two in 1886, Figure 3.1, Thomas Drummond's house in Chicago in 1885; developer John Lewis Cochran's own house in 1886 and Silsbee's own house in 1889, both in Edgewater, Chicago; and R. A. Waller's house in Buena Park, Chicago, in 1886.[40] Each was a mature, competent, expertly planned, and detailed building.[41]

In responding professionally and honestly to the Jones sisters' Home Building program, did Silsbee, a man professionally proud and of some moral stature, hire an inexperienced Frank Wright and then tell him to mimic or copy aspects of Silsbee's architectural designs to shape the new school building? No. The only reasonable conclusion must fit the evidence, that the Home Building commission was Silsbee's and that he was the architect. Wright was an ambitious

Figure 3.1 Speculative house for developer Edward B. Smith in Buffalo, New York, Silsbee & Marling, Architects, 1885, designed by Silsbee then practicing in Buffalo and Chicago; some modifications when built. From a journal as published by <jlsilsbee.blogspot.com>.

employee but at this time demonstrably still a novice draftsman subject to Silsbee's bidding. And he was not involved when construction begun 13 August 1888 on a Home Building extension, or in 1892 on a separate gymnasium or a new teachers' cottage: he was too busy in Chicago.[42] Photographs of around 1895 suggest a logical scenario where Thomas Jones and Cramer reused Silsbee's working drawings for the extension. Construction of gym and cottage were no doubt the result of Uncle Thomas's talents.

1887 (or 1886 or 1895 or 1898): Presentation drawings of the Henry N. Cooper house, a project for the La Grange suburb of Chicago.[43]

During his tenure with Silsbee, Wright became a competent draftsman with T-square and triangle. But surely he knowingly fibbed when, decades later, he often claimed that a presentation elevation drawing in pencil of the Cooper house was a "Drawing shown to lieber Meister when applying for a job" – to Sullivan or Adler (see Figure 3.2). That would date the drawing mid-1887. The fib began in the 1940s when he wrote on the right side of the sheet: "Dream house – study made in Madison previous to going to Chicago." That would date the drawing as late 1886. That new annotation was written over a partially erased pencil note, "Project. Cooper House, La Grange, Ill. G.C.M," or historian Grant Carpenter Manson, written around 1940 correct.[44] Over Manson's penciled note, someone wrote in red pencil "study made in Madison previous to going to Chicago." The drawing was definitely not done in 1886 or 1887 when it would have been contemporary with his puerile Sioux City exercise! Of the Cooper, drawing the influential historian Henry-Russell Hitchcock's personal view – as differentiated from information directly from Wright – was erringly eulogistic.

> Wright was already a draftsman of exquisite delicacy and precision. He had then had only two [sic] years of professional training in the Engineering School under Dean Conover. . . . [T]hese two years had given him well-rounded introduction to the practice of building, [and] the drawing of the plants, at once so exquisite and so vigorous. . . .[45]

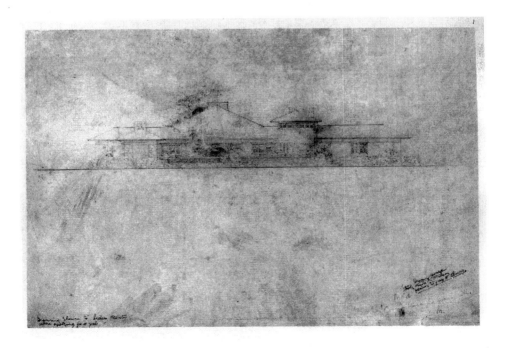

Figure 3.2 Presentation pencil drawing of the front elevation of the Henry N. Cooper house, a project of 1898 for a site in the La Grange suburb of Chicago. Courtesy and © 2016 FLWF.

78 *The aesthetics of progress*

It is reasonable to assume Hitchcock, then working with Wright on a book, was referring to, among other renderings, the Cooper elevation drawing. Was that when Wright inscribed it in an attempt to impress his eminent collaborator, and confuse historians?

Based on a comparison of the Cooper drawings with Wright's Falkenauj Row House drawing of 1888 and his hasty pencil sketches of Rocky Roost Island cottages of ca. 1894,[46] on the style and design of the Cooper presentation drawings, and on Wright's personal architectural formalities and ornamental idiosyncrasies displayed therein, the drawing can be dated sometime after design of the Winslow stables begun in late 1897, therefore 1898. Bruce Brooks Pfeiffer once dated the project 1887, but later on 1890, perhaps to imply "in the 1890s."[47] Yet here's the rub. After forty years of studying drawings out of Wright's office, and in view of this evidence, as well as his confession that he was not a competent renderer, it became obvious to me that his hand was not the only one. It was his unwavering policy from 1893 onward that all presentation drawings, or renderings, were executed by employed out-of-office specialist renderers or a talented employee. It was extremely important that presentation of his designs to clients and the press be of an impressive quality.

1888 February: No longer a teenager at twenty, Wright began employment as a junior draftsman with the Chicago architectural firm of Adler & Sullivan.

Wright implies William Henry Harrison Weatherwax left the firm because of Wright's employment. Rather, Weatherwax left in 1891 to become foreman of the drafting room for the Chicago School Board.[48]

1898: Cooper house.

On 1 June 1 1889, Frank Wright and Catherine Lee Tobin were married in Chicago by Uncle Jenkin in his All Souls Church. On 5 August 1889, Wright purchased one half of corner lot twenty facing Forest Avenue and Chicago Avenue in Oak Park. On 17 May, the deed in trust was placed with Louis Sullivan, who placed it in trust with Henry Warren Austin on 20 August. (Austin died that December.) On 21 August, the other half of lot twenty was purchased by Wright's mother.[49] Wright likely began designing his house in August 1889. It was Wright's *first* independent architectural design and *first* commission, albeit by himself, while working for – and with a hefty loan from – Sullivan (see Figure 3.3). Much altered and enlarged, the original house had standard floor plans and fashionable exterior elevations, including upper floor windows. (He knew the suburb of Lake Forest, there was a window ensemble on the the principle gable front of the Presbyterian Church by architect Henry Ives Cobb completed in 1886.)[50] Wright's small house was well detailed, modestly ornamented, nicely proportioned, and displayed a mature restraint that suggests the young draftsman had received good advice from unmentioned colleagues.

Wright left Adler & Sullivan in June 1893 and that August, via a professional journal, he informed colleagues and the public that in spite of the banking collapse he had active commissions. One was for

> O.S. Goan, at La Grange, a two story basement and attic residence; size 38 by 38 feet; to be of frame construction . . . [with] all the sanitary and modern improvements. Also, making drawings for two boathouses for the city of Madison. . . .[51]

Drawings for the Orrin Goan house are dated 1894. It together with the Lake Momona boathouse remained projects. The Lake Mendota boathouse was built. Orrin's brother also commissioned Wright, and his house was completed.

Reverend Jenkin Lloyd Jones

Wright's father, Reverend William Carey Wright, was born of a New England family and, like many of his male kin, became a Baptist preacher. In 1869, Reverend Wright laid out his

Figure 3.3 Frank Lloyd Wright's house in the Oak Park suburb of Chicago, August 1889–90; photograph ca. 1893. From Riley, 1994.

biography for the "jubilee volume" of Madison University in Hamilton, New York, and it was recorded as follows:

> William C. Wright, son of Rev. David Wright, was born in Westfield, Mass, Jan. 2, 1825. Entered M.U. in '48, and graduated in '49. Married Miss Permelia Holcomb . . . Aug. 4, 1851. Entered the medical profession at first, and was teacher and organist at Utica, N.Y., and Hartford, Conn. In the latter place he studied law, and was admitted to the Bar in '57. In '59 he removed to Lone Rock, Wis., where he practised law for 4 or 5 years. Was licensed to preach by the Baptist Church at Lone Rock. Ordained by the same church, Aug. 5, '63. He filled the office of County Superintendent of Schools in 1864–65. His wife died at Lone Rock, April 6, '64. Organized the Rockland Centre Bap. Ch., Wis., in '66, and married Miss Hannah L. Jones. Served as Home Missionary, '66 to '69. In '69 became paster of the church at McGregor, Iowa, where he still resides.[52]

By all accounts, he was exceedingly well liked.[53] And he adored President Lincoln. With learned biographical insight, Meryle Secrest made this observation of Reverend Wright:

> He was a mesmerizing lecturer. He gave the eulogy for Abraham Lincoln [in 1867 that] "was highly praised by all who heard it." If he gave concerts on the pianoforte, or recitals – he had a fine bass voice – these would be the best anyone had ever heard. When he

wrote waltzes, polkas and govottes in the . . . taste of the day, publishers magically appeared. . . .[54]

William had what might called an artistic temperament attached to a friendly and personable style (see Figure 3.4). As such, he was quite the opposite of his prim and insistent second wife and her stolid farming family.

William and Hanna – or Anna as she and family preferred – Lloyd Jones married in May 1866. Son Frank Lincoln was born 8 June 1867. Reverend Wright left the Baptist ministry in 1878 to become a Unitarian minister, secretary of the Madison congregation when organized in 1879, and then pastor of the Liberal Church in Wyoming, near Spring Green. In considering the switch, the charismatic personality of brother-in-law Reverend Jones must have been mightily persuasive. Frank's mother, an assistant teacher, was not only a committed Jones Unitarian but, as a mother, psychologically and socially demanding and insistently and cloyingly so.[55]

From the outset of marriage Frank's wife Catherine became committed to social and community services. This remained true after Wright abandoned her and their children to take up with Mrs Martha Borthwick Cheney, or Mamah, in 1909. Of course, Mamah gave up her family to become Frank's partner. During their four or so years together in his home Taliesin, Mamah reinforced and stabilized Wright's desire for an anarchic individualism, and they shared other liberal thoughts. Her death in August 1914 was tragic. Taliesin was central to their sharing. Historian Neil Levine was moved to say:

> Few artists have suffered the kind of personal loss Wright did, nor have any perhaps equaled him in fulfilling the modern project of making the artist's persona and individual experience the very ground of authenticity.[56]

Figure 3.4 Portrait of Reverend William Cary Wright in the early 1850s. Original held by the State Historical Society of Iowa, Iowa City, Elizabeth Wright Heller Collection. From Patterson, 2013.

However, this happened well after his fundamental philosophical frame had been instilled by an artistic and community-sensitive father and by the maternal Joneses as clarified by Reverend Jones. Reverend Wright's immediate Wright family remained centered in and around Connecticut and played no role in the performance of his familial and professional life in the upper Midwest. Therefore, it was William alone who transferred certain genetic propensities and performed a significant developmental role in his son's intellectual and artistic life.

We can say with conviction that biographical evidence, notably that collated by Meryle Secrest and Anthony Alofsin, confirms the validity of two observations: that William's temperament and personal character became Frank's, and that the Jones family, certainly his mother and most emphatically Reverend Jones, had a dramatic effect on the thinking of Frank Lincoln.

An ardent religious and social reformer, Reverend Jones was an apolitical "crusading preacher" and grand orator who moved with middle incomer, laborer, Progressive, plutocrat, merchant, unionist, woman's righter, socialist, and those religious, downcast, impoverished, antisocial, pacifistic, and other nontrinitarians. In following a family history of rejecting sectarianism and the dogmatics of the Catholic, Lutheran, and Calvinist churches, he reveled in the intellectual and spiritual freedom offered by Unitarianism. He eventually attempted to extend it by espousing universality. Nationally lauded in life, now he is one of the least appreciated of Chicago's – indeed the nation's – humanitarians, perhaps motivationally second only to his dear friend, the equally charismatic Jane Addams. Wisconsinan August Derleth's description conforms to others:

> He [Reverend Jones] was an intense, earnest, zealous man, a big man physically as well as mentally, with commanding, brooding eyes, a sensuous but determined mouth, and heavy, curved brows. To his head of thick hair he later added a majestic, flowing beard, which made him look more than ever a prophet.[57]

After participating as a volunteer in Civil War battles, Jenkin became a confirmed peace activist and passionate about Lincoln the emancipator, the humanitarian. Leaving his brothers to farm, on completion of theological school at Meadville, Pennsylvania, Jenkin was ordained to the Unitarian ministry in 1870, to serve in Winnetka, Illinois, and then Janesville, Wisconsin. He immediately became involved with mutual improvement societies and cultivated literary, scientific, civic, and philanthropic interests. Again, Secrest was succinct:

> Working with Jane Addams, Susan B. Anthony, Edward Everett Hale, Booker T. Washington, William Jennings Bryan and a host of others, he espoused every progressive liberal position from prohibition, racial justice, education, women's rights, poverty relief and political reform to pacifism and the humane treatment of animals.[58]

Jenkin's missionary zeal was defined by a humanitarian theism that in part held religious participation as a freely private individual act, intermediary priest or clergy unnecessary. Rather, all may engage their god as individuals, and all are divine. Under the banner of the magazine *Unity*, which he helped found in 1878 and co-edited with Reverend Gannett, were these words as a credo: *Freedom, Fellowship and Character in Religion*.[59]

Unity magazine was unashamedly a reformation organ sponsored by the Western Unitarian Conference. In unity, the "spiritual and material were continuous and the processes of one were there processes of the other." Yet his theology slowly but firmly became radical, shifting to an "emphasis upon evolution of man, the mythical analogies and ethical harmony of the great world religions, [and promotion of a] universal religion of ethical theism." His beliefs might be also summed as an "insistence upon ethical rather than theological unanimity as the basis of liberal fellowship."[60] According to biographer Richard Thomas, Reverend Jones "belonged to the liberal-radical wing of the Social Gospel movement" that found the "Gospel in social deed, not creed."[61]

In 1894, Reverend Jones declared for his church a nondenominational status within the American Unitarian Association. That was immediately after the success of the 1893 World's Parliament of Religions, where universality was one of the principle themes. His church, "All Souls, a people's church," then joined the American Congress of Liberal Religious Societies that Jones helped formulate in 1895. An alliance of liberal Jews, Unitarians, Universalists, and Ethical Culturists, their goal was a "church of Humanity, democratic in organization, progressive in thought, . . . [and] open to all new light."[62] Its purpose was to develop a "Church of Humanity" with allegiance to a "Free Church of the Spirit, based on the eternal demands of the Ethical Law alone."[63] His view was plain and utterly simple:

> Jesus wrote no creed [wrote Jones], appointed no bishop, organized no church and taught no trinity. Taking these away, you have instead of Christianity only a blessed humanity left. . . .
> Reverence lies not in the acceptance of dogma bequeathed to you, but in the receptive spirit, the truth-seeking attitude.
> In ethics all religions meet.[64]

And so said Wright on many occasions, if considerably less cogently or effectively.

To meet that commitment, therefore, a new facility across the street from the All Souls Church building was announced by Reverend Jones. With great joy and enthusiasm it was named Abraham Lincoln Center.

> He [Lincoln] is a prophet of religion and morals [Jones proclaimed]. He belongs to humanity because his soul was profoundly religious, in league with justice, dedicated to that love which is not only human but humane.[65]

The new facility would contain an auditorium for religious services, a gymnasium, classrooms for manual training and domestic science, reading and meetings rooms, a kindergarten, and a library together with residents' quarters. Hull-House was the exemplar. Since its function had become that of a social service agency, its founder wanted no nonsense about the way it should look.[66] When completed, Lincoln Center was to Jones's reckoning a "model of function and rectitude." It was a six-story brick box with no ornament and steel-cased windows. After finally opening in 1905, six thousand people attended the center each week (see Figure 6.3).

Like Reverend Jones, Wright was anti-sectarian, anti-creed, yet a religious man who rejected the doctrinal authority of organized churches. Later, he rejected organizations that constrained a person's independence of thought and action. Rather, he followed more closely the Emersonian Transcendentalism of the Jones family in a mix with an ever-refining holism. As Wright put it:

> the "Unitarianism" that had been worked out in the transcendentalism of the sentimental group at Concord: Whittier, Lowell, Longfellow, yes, and Emerson, too. Thoreau? Well, Thoreau had always seemed too smart, made them uncomfortable.[67]

Not all were Concordians. That aside, Reverend Jones's literary gospel was typical of the Jones family: "And now abideth these four: Emerson, Browning, George Eliot, Lowell; and the greatest of these is Emerson."[68] The essence of Reverend Jones's beliefs became Wright's ethical and philosophic standard. Their concordance is found scattered throughout his autobiographical texts, where they arise seemingly out of context.

Jenkin's understanding of and application to architecture was considerably more abstract and rigorous than Wright's when design of Abraham Lincoln Center is considered. As built in 1904–05, its form and appearance without historical or church reference was the result of Reverend Jones's insistence rather than the architects' proposal. Wright played a role early in the design process, but just before construction began, he was dismissed by his uncle. Yet his basic functional arrangement as seen in floor plans, interior details, and proportional system in elevation remained a major contribution besides those of his uncle Jenkin.

Reverend Jones's administration ("busy, ubiquitous") and intelligent theological enthusiasm as an organized general secretary of the World's Parliament of Religions, which he had jointly proposed in 1891, in connection with Chicago's Worlds International Exposition of 1893, brought him national and international attention. There were four thousand attendees who, for the most part, sensed the start of an era of sectarian cooperation. Out of those endeavors, and in a commitment to most aspects of the Social Gospel Movement, came Lincoln Center, "the social agency cum church."[69]

In early teen years, Wright spent summers on the Jones brothers' farms. During 1886 into early 1887, he maintained close contact with Reverend Jones at All Souls while working for the Unitarian architect Joseph Silsbee, who also attended All Souls. He said he met future wife Catherine Lee Clark Tobin (Kitty, still in high school and taller than Frank) at classes studying Victor Hugo's *Les Miserables*.[70] Wright also met some future clients at All Souls or Unity Chapel or Unity Church in Oak Park, including the MacArthur, Bagley, Wooley, Gale, Gannett, Beye, and Roberts families.

Mother Anna and children Frank and Maginel settled in Oak Park in 1887, where they lived with Anna's friend Reverend Augusta Jane Chapin, Universalist and minister at Oak Park's Unity Church (1886–92). In 1893, Lombard University College in Galesburg, Illinois, conferred on her a Doctor of Divinity degree, the first nationally to a woman. She lectured in English literature at the University of Chicago (1892–97) and was a charter member of the American Woman Suffrage Association. Chapin supported the education reformer and author Frances Willard and worked tirelessly for the Woman's Christian Temperance Union. From 1891, she was on committees with Reverend Jones for – and as a chair and lecturer to – the World Parliament of Religions. Maginel remembered her as indeed "august," as "a large imposing woman of solid dignity, with a massive bosom which was upholstered in black satin on weekdays and trimmed with passementeries on Sundays."[71] Of like minds, the three Wrights lived with Reverend Chapin until Frank married Catherine. The bride's family regularly attended Reverend Jones's All Souls religious and social services and literary activities.

In relations with the Jones aunts and uncles, Jenkin, suburban All Souls and rural Unity Chapel, Wright accepted reformers, anarchists, Progressives, liberals, socialists, Emersonians, and Unitarians who moved in circles within circles. For example, Henry Demarest Lloyd and Florence Kelley, both close to Anna Wright, Addams, and Reverend Jones (settlements, unionism, social justice, political activism); Julie C. Lathrop when at Hull-House (civil service, settlements, Chicago School of Civics and Philanthropy, woman's rights); Reverend Jones and Reverend Chapin (Social Gospel, social work, religion, social justice); Addams and Graham Taylor (settlements, unionism, religion, social justice); the Coonley family (education, religion, woman's rights); the Perkins family (education, settlements, architecture, woodland conservation), and so on. And Wright courted those "sensible" businessmen who became clients, often because of their wives' attraction to Wright's personality or shared philosophy of reform.

Settlement houses were administered, staffed, and supported in the main by philanthropy and a volunteer force of Protestant and Jewish middle incomers with or without socialist inclinations. Chicagoans supported several settlements, with Hull-House, Northwestern University, and Chicago Commons (founded 1894) being the more prominent. Jane Addams recorded that "Mrs. Russell [sic] Wright, the mother of Frank Lloyd Wright" was among those to "remain loyal" as a volunteer.[72] (Wright and his mother incorrectly added "Russell" as a middle name. William's brother was named David Russell.) The Helen Heath Neighborhood Settlement in Chicago's south side was begun by Reverend Jones in 1894 as an adjunct to All Souls Church.[73] Its name was changed to Fellowship House, more appropriate to Reverend Jones's expanding philosophy and administered by, among others, Mrs Marion H. Perkins, Dwight's mother.[74] Dwight's sister Myra and niece Marion Lucy Mahony (later Mrs Walter B. Griffin) were active within Fellowship and Hull-House. The Perkinses were keen followers of Reverend Jones as members of All Souls.[75] In 1899, Dwight prepared an unrealized design for the Northwestern University settlement house, and he and wife Lucy also worked at the Chicago Commons, Fellowship House, and Hull-House settlements.[76] Wright and Dwight maintained an awkward relationship onward from 1894, when they shared office space in downtown Chicago. Wright's personality was too much for Lucy; she thought him conceited, a braggart, and tactless.[77]

+ + +

With a knowledge of Reverend Jones's utterances and good works, his severe architectural philosophy as revealed in the chaste design of Abraham Lincoln Center, and Wright's mental and artistic activity, it is clear that Wright's lifestyle, community ideas (but not his practices), and general philosophical beliefs were conditioned by a close educative association with Uncle Jenkin.

Wright often paraphrased his uncle. After all, during the formative years of 1886 to 1908, Wright's life centered on Jenkin's personal and religious families. Wright said little about his uncle, but enough:

> The Unitarianism of the Lloyd-Joneses, a far richer thing, was an attempt to amplify in the confusion of the creeds of their day. . . .
> UNITY was their watchword, the sign and symbol that thrilled them the UNITY of all things! . . .
> But if Uncle Jenkin peached there was the genuine luxury of tears. . . . His sermons always brought them to emotional state – but then – so did readings from the transcendental classics or the singing of the children. . . . Surrender to religious emotion was fervent, sincere. . . .
> The boy's father would play the violin and sing leading the [Jones] uncles and aunts in their favorite hymns. . . . But the hymn-singing – in unison, of course – was the most satisfying feature of the day. . . .[78]

And so forth in autobiographical texts. Indeed, Frank learned much from Uncle Jenk.

The Farm signified a concept where toil with nature was a creative locus, a farming community cozily comprehensible. Historian of the Lloyd Jones family, Thomas Graham provided evidence of – and correctly observed – that

> In all [of Reverend Jones's] work in the city and for the nation at large, it was the soil of rural Wisconsin that nourished his vision and restored his strength. . . . If in the city the higher purposes of human life are worked out, the foundation for those higher purposes is laid by the farm.[79]

The agrarian Populists, most of those associated with the Social Gospel, as well as individualists true to Emerson, Tolstoy, and Froebel, shared "a *rural fundamentalism*, a belief that life on the farm was morally superior to life in the city."[80] It explains Wright's flight from the city back to the Jones family farms in 1911 and again in 1924 and to the Arizona desert in 1937. It is at the heart of more important undertakings, such as the school of artistic fellowship dreamt in 1928 and opened on the family farm in 1932, as well as the 1934 Broadacre City concept of scattered small towns with "Little Farms."[81]

Dankmar Adler

At age twenty, in February 1888, Wright entered the Adler & Sullivan office with an employment record as a office boy and then as a tracer and draftsman, not always full time. He was a competent draftsman with undeveloped skills, not possessed of great technical expertise or yet to display a design virtuosity. The Adler & Sullivan firm was to Wright's reckoning "foremost in Chicago," Burnham and Root "their only rivals."[82] Like any eager young draftsman, Wright would have been attracted to any large and prestigious firm, but he was lucky because the job came fortuitously. Around February 1888, a young representative of a Chicago electrical firm to builders and architects, Walter R. B. Willcox had a desire to be an architect. He learned of an opening in the Adler & Sullivan office and inquired. Sullivan told him they were looking for a more experienced man. Willcox, who was working now and then for Silsbee, told Wright of the opportunity.

Wright recalled that in his initial or second interview with Sullivan he copied "Silsbee's own drawings," or rather he "drew them my own way... So in some few drawings I imitated his style." He called them "imitations of Silsbee." But he also presented onion skin tracings of "Gothic ornament" from Owen Jones's book *Grammar of Ornament*. There was no mention of the Cooper house drawing.[83] Wright was hired to be among the many draftsmen needed to complete construction drawings for the Auditorium Building.[84] Before 1887, Sullivan had published only four short articles, the Auditorium still to rise. His stimulating theoretical utterances were not as yet begun, so he personally was of no particular fascination to Wright, nor was Adler, who was widely admired, and Sullivan was little known.

Born in Stadtlengsfeld, Germany, in 1844, Adler's family emigrated to Detroit, where his father Liebman would serve as a rabbi and cantor. His father apprenticed him to the well-known architect John Schaefer and then to E. Willard Smith. In 1861, the Adlers moved to Chicago so that Liebman could serve as rabbi of the Kehilath Anshe Ma'ariv (K.A.M.) Synagoge. He worked for architect Augustus Bauer until enlisting in the Union Army. After service, he returned to Bauer but, disappointed, soon left to join architect Ozia S. Kinney. On Kinney's death, with his son Ashley J. as principal, Adler became a partner. In early 1871, Adler joined the firm of Edward Burling as a junior partner. Following the Great Fire of 1871, Burling & Adler enjoyed considerable success. With high praise for the Adler's Central Music Hall Block (1878–79, demolished ca. 1901), the partnership was dissolved in 1879 when Adler & Company was formed.[85]

From the 1860s on, Germans were Chicago's largest immigrant population, at nearly one-third the total, Jews a sizable portion. For example, the German Opera Company of Chicago commissioned Adler & Sullivan to design the Schiller Theatre Building, named in respect of Johann Christoph Friedrich von Schiller, German poet, historian, philosopher, and playwright and mentor to Johann Wolfgang von Goethe. The theater was for German-language operas and cultural events and opened in 1892. After the investors withdrew from the project in the late 1890s, it soon acquired the name Garrick Theater after the English playwright. Wright's first professional office was in room 1501 Schiller Building.[86] Many of Wright's colleagues and some clients were influenced by association with German culture and arts. Wright referred to Sullivan as *meister*, not the more common *maestro*. Adler's own designs, when not debased (he might suggest) by excessive ornament, were uncluttered and straightforward in plan, massing, and elevational treatment, with or without classical features.[87] Perhaps an exception would be the First Methodist Church office block of 1872, which was more German than most of his work and done while with Edward Burling.

Sullivan was born in Boston in 1856, after which his parents and brother moved to Chicago. Louis stayed behind and lived with his grandparents. In 1872, Sullivan enrolled in architecture and building classes at the Massachusetts Institute of Technology and attended for less than one academic year. Soon thereafter, he departed for Philadelphia and worked for architect Frank Furness, the son of a Boston Unitarian minister and a close friend of Emerson.

In the wake of the banking crash of 1873 and after barely six months employment, Sullivan was dismissed by Furness. He joined his family in Chicago and began working casually for architect William Le Baron Jenney. There, he met the architect John H. Edelmann, who encouraged Sullivan from the very beginning. Then, after about six months' menial employment, in July 1874, Sullivan left to study in Paris. In October, he was accepted by the École des Beaux-Arts and attended an atelier for only five months, departing in March 1875 and arriving in New York City in May.

On return to Chicago in 1876, Sullivan worked for architects (Joseph S.) Johnston and Edelman. Moreover, he became known citywide for the design of interior fresco-secco decorations, a dried-plaster painting technique. During 1876 and into 1891 he was a freelance design consultant to many architects, including Adler.[88] Sullivan made interior designs in 1876 for the Chicago Avenue Church (aka Moody Church, 1873–76, demolished ca. 1939), the interior by architects Johnston & Edelmann. He also made fresco designs for the Sinai Temple by architects Burling & Adler (1875–76). In 1881, he advertised himself as a "Designer" and surprised colleagues when he was made a partner of Adler & Co.[89] As architectural historians Gilbert Herbert and Mark Donchin correctly summarized,

> Sullivan's practical experience was minimal: part of a year as a junior draughtsman with Furness, half a year with Jenny, a desultory career as a freelance draughtsman working mainly on the decorative aspects of other architects' buildings for some four years. . . .[90]

Sullivan began part time as a draftsman in the spring of 1881 and was made a junior partner in May 1882 and a full partner in April 1883. The partnership ran from 1883–95, when Adler announced to local professionals that he had "retire[d] from the active practice of architecture."[91] By 1895, the firm had completed the design phase for or constructed more than eighty-five buildings, mainly residences, large commercial buildings, and some theaters for which Adler was justly renown. "He was connected with either the erection or remodeling of all but two of the downtown theaters in Chicago [and a] consulting architect in connection with the Carnegie Music Hall" in New York City.[92]

Wright remained with Adler & Sullivan until June 1893. His story was that Sullivan fired him because he obtained clients outside the firm.[93] The two partners no doubt knew of the private work, as most ambitious draftsmen in all firms did likewise. The situation was exacerbated by growing tensions between Sullivan, an alcoholic, and most people, including Wright.[94] George Grant Elmslie emigrated from Scotland in 1884, started with Silsbee in 1887 and, in 1890, began to work beside Wright, sharing the same cubicle in the Adler & Sullivan office. Elmslie stayed with Sullivan for many years following Wright's "exit in disgrace," in Elmslie's words. Sullivan had told Elmslie of Wright's "behavior" and "it [was] not a pleasant story," this said in a candid letter by Elmslie to Wright. Sullivan's "vitriolic comment" on Wright's "ways and means" Elmslie preferred to leave "unsaid." He then told Wright: "But alas, you are not endowed with so human an elements [as 'kindliness'], only with a curious quality of vanity, and a rather vulgar and childish egotism."[95]

As a result of a ruinous nationwide financial panic in May 1893 that instantly destabilized the majority of Chicago's architectural offices, Wright and other employees, including Irving J. Gill, were laid off that spring by a financially strapped Adler. Between that year and 1897, four thousand US banks failed, as did fourteen thousand major businesses. Charles Bebb, English emigrant architect and, beginning in 1888, a superintendent of construction for Adler & Sullivan, wrote to a friend in June 1893 that

> business in Chicago is deplorable. Adler & Sullivan are doing nothing and Mr. Adler told me he could not even make collections of moneys due him, and consequently has had to reduce the office force to three men, and these have nothing to do. I have found that all architects and contractors are in the same or even worse shape.[96]

Wright was not one of the three. Bebb also learned that Adler had been "borrowing from friends each week to pay his pay-roll."[97] That fateful June, Bebb went to Seattle and opened his own practice in 1898.

In early 1894, Adler quit architecture and, in an open letter to the profession, announced that had become a "consulting architect of the Crane Elevator Company, and also to assume supervision and management of the sales department."[98] Dissatisfied, he returned to the profession after one year. Sullivan struggled with an independent practice and was joined by a patient Elmslie. Silsbee's business managed to survive. Apparently making no attempt to gain employment elsewhere, Wright gambled and began an independent practice as did Harry Waterman. Wright and confidant Cecil Sherman Corwin, who had just severed a very brief partnership with George W. Maher, shared office space in the Schiller Building. Both remained independent practitioners.[99] Gill took a lesser risk and moved to burgeoning San Diego, where he immediately found employment and a new career.[100] In 1895, Corwin left for New York to eventually reside in North Carolina. Wright moved in with other young men into a loft of the Steinway Hall office building.

On entering the Adler & Sullivan office, therefore, Wright was not so young and certainly not the fully mature innocent nearly exploding with talent as he and others would have us believe.

Just before the turn of the century, other young architects in the upper Midwest referred to Sullivan as "the master," their referent to master artist. In 1896, Sullivan began to occasionally lecture and publish on architectural theory and education, all directed to young men.[101] Professional adulation began earnestly in 1899, with Sullivan's short paper delivered to the founding convention of the Architectural League of America in Cleveland. Dissatisfied with the limits of fashionable design based on historical precedents as promulgated by Ècole des Beaux-Arts, New England aesthetics, and French pedagogy, the League began as a revolt led in the main by members of the Chicago Architectural Club. "Progress Before Precedent," the League's pragmatic motto, was not only nationalistic and associated with the increasing influence of Progressivism but also, in architecture, aimed directly at Francophilians.

Ill and unable to attend, Sullivan's paper was read by a recent architecture graduate, Henry Webster Tomlinson, soon to be in partnership with Wright during 1901–02. Sullivan proclaimed "his faith in the younger generation . . . to regenerate the art of architecture," that the architect is "a poet and an interpreter of the national life of his time," and he denounced the "fraudulent and surreptitious use of historical documents . . . and unnatural mimicry." If you know your country and the contemporary moment, he said, "you will be understood." His next theoretical utterance was in May 1900 to the League's second convention in Chicago in a paper titled "To The Young Man in Architecture." In reporting on the convention, the New York journal *American Architect* exclaimed that Sullivan was greeted as a hero. Another New York periodical, *Architecture*, was in raptures over the paper.[102] A guru had been identified and found persuasive.

"Chats" was conceptually simple. Sullivan, who preferred office training, imagined "a graduate of one of our [American] architectural schools come to the author for a post-graduate course." During discourse there unfolds "those natural, spontaneous powers which had been submerged and ignored during his [beaux-arts] academic straining." Sullivan's purpose was, he said, "to liberate the mind from serfdom [and] to exhibit man's natural powers in their creative capabilities . . . in the true spirit of democracy," and of America's present.[103]

As inspiring and timely as the Leagues moment seemed, conservative and institutional forces were fearfully wary and successfully responded. A former student of Amherst College, Massachusetts Institute of Technology, and the Paris Ècole, the venerable A.D.F. Hamlin wrote a piece in 1907 about "The Influence of the Ècole des Beaux-Arts." It was a brief history together with some critical and nationalistic comments. It concluded that "the sooner we emancipate our art from dependence upon Paris the sooner will that day come [when] French students will come to America."[104] Avoiding, yet prompted by, the League's ideas, Hamlin argued for a "national style" (of unknown characteristics) and the need for an American beaux-arts center. The AIA's stated policy was oriented to producing, as they put it, "gentlemen of general culture with special architectural ability."[105] By late 1908, League discourse had devolved to a preference for a closer association with the New York Society of Beaux-Arts Architects and its surrogate, the AIA. In a slight gesture to independence, the League did not see the necessity of a European tour.

Wright was fully aware of these machinations and used them to bolster his claims of discipleship to Sullivan. It was first made at the 1900 convention in a tedious paper that was prefaced with the remark "after listening to the master [Sullivan] it hardly seems proper to listen to the disciple."[106] Then, in June 1900, in Spencer's essay about Wright, age thirty-three, two points were made. First, Wright influenced Sullivan ("There must have been between two such natures an interchange of thought and influence not wholly one sided."). Second, Wright was the inheritor of Sullivan's hard-won crown: "I [Spencer] must claim for his [Sullivan's] chief pupil and disciple [Wright] the right to the same appreciation as an *architect*," he emphasized, that has "so justly claimed for the master;" and further, Sullivan and Wright had been "working together as master and trusted pupil."[107] Those were extraordinary assumptions tightly fit to the arrogance Spencer promoted. But he was just warming up. In Wright's next public announcement in 1908, in the "In the cause" essay for *Architectural Record*, he claimed to be Sullivan's rightful successor. It was, Wright said, his "good fortune to be the understudy of a great teacher. . . ."[108] (Understudy: to study in order to replace.) Moreover, around 1900, Wright had said to Elmslie: "How long will it be before the world recognizes me as the Master and Sullivan the man?"[109] And so he pleaded for the next fifty-plus years.

In the connection of disciple and master, there is implied a notional relationship of son and father. Yet in Wrights memory it was Adler, son of a German immigrant rabbi, who approximated a father figure, Sullivan "essentially a lyric poet-philosopher," he said.[110] Wright's description of Adler, "the Big Chief," was of man and character, "A personality, short-built and heavy, like an old Byzantine church." He was "broadly and solidly built, one to inspire others with confidence in his power at once. He walked with deliberate, heavy-legged, flat-footed steps. . . ."[111] "More and more, because of Mr. Sullivan's absences, I was under Dankmar Adler," and, after a year or so, the Big Chief "came to sit and talk with me more often than usual. His generous heart and salty wisdom never seemed dearer and clearer to us all. . . ."[112] Conversely, Sullivan was rather conceited and self-indulgent, somewhat indiscrete, a drunk, and at times verbally volatile.[113] He was an aloof man who found it difficult to hold but a few professional friends while refusing to "let others know who was inside."[114]

Wright acknowledged Alder, twenty-two years his senior, as a "good planner" and a "good critic." Alder was praised in a way Wright was unable to muster for Sullivan, only ten years his senior and the same height. The line of command in the firm was Adler as head, Sullivan next, then Paul Mueller, followed by the twenty remaining staff. Adler's staff referred to him "with respect and affection";[115] Wright remembered that they "All worshipped him," that "He was a great protestant, grey army engineer . . . builder and philosopher."[116] In 1924, Wright recalled Adler as "a fine critic, a master of the plan and of men. His influence on Louis Sullivan . . . was great and good."[117] Later, Wright said that Adler

> was a solid block of manhood, inspiring the confidence of everyone, a terror to any recalcitrant or shifty contractor. His ideas throughout were advanced far beyond his time, . . . and he was known even in those more liberal days (before architecture became obsessed by college degrees) as a liberal, original thinker.[118]

However, in 1900, Sullivan was the young architects' hero, not Adler who died that year, so Wright deliberately aligned himself with the star.

In 1891 the respected Chicago architect John Wellborn Root spoke publicly about Adler:

> Among the highest in all the profession stands Mr. Adler. . . . Of late Mr. Adler has passed the artistic crayon to Mr. Sullivan, but work designed by him [Adler] in the earlier days . . . shows a strength, simplicity, and straight forwardness, together with a certain refinement, which reveal the true architect. No professional man has pursued a more consistent and dignified course than he, and no man is more respected by his confreres.[119]

An artistic crayon was/is not an architect's design tool. But of course Adler recognized what he described as Sullivan's "pre-eminence in the artistic field," knowing, as did others, that it was an eminence gained through Adler's tutelage.[120] Before beginning with Adler, Sullivan wasn't much more than a clever drawing hand.

However, Wright and others made it clear that Sullivan's single-mindedness, egoism, and "a tragic flaw of arrogance," historian David Van Zanten has said, were problems that, as time progressed, client, office personnel, and Adler suffered.[121] As early as 1903, Wright referred to Adler as a "fine broadminded old man, and an excellent critic."[122] In Wright's memory, he appeared not only as a complete architect but also as methodical, practical, kind, wise, and counselor. Not that Sullivan was in some way incomplete or impractical as much as not practical, self-possessed, unreliable.

However, the two senior architects acted pragmatically and were devoted to the profession. They were not concerned with slippery social or reformist issues but with commerce: theirs and their clients'. They (and Wright) did not publicly express concern about political and commercial corruption, social ills, or urban problems. Their utterances concentrated on the craft of construction in relation to the design discipline of architecture. It was a common myopia and here exposed in Sullivan's famous "Kindergarten Chats" essays of 1901–02 and later editions.[123]

Adler did, of course, engage theoretical questions. A public debate on the "form follows function" aphorism exposed serious differences between the partners. Sullivan had published a short Transcendentalist piece on "Emotional Architecture" in 1894 and again in 1896, where he also argued the Greenough principle that "form follows function." Adler responded succinctly in 1896, implying Sullivan was an impractical dreamer, saying in part:

> architecture is not permitted to remain placidly contemplative of the march of events. The architect is not allowed to wait until, seized by an irresistible impulse from within, he gives the world the fruit of his studies and musing. He is of the world as well as in it.[124]

Historian Narciso Menocal's interpretation was that form follows function "meant to Adler the manner in which a master craftsman puts a building together by availing himself of the best planning and technology of his age to solve architectural problems economically, efficiently, and nobly." That function and environment should "determine" form was "to him a truth more important than 'form follows function'."[125] But the word "determine" irritated Sullivan, who asked, "what was left for the creative genius?" Menocal suggested that, to Sullivan,

> the function of architecture was exclusively to express the transcendental essence of a building as eloquently and as characteristically as life is revealed [Sullivan said] in "the sweeping eagle in his flight or the open apple blossom, the toiling work horse, the blithe swan, the branching oak."[126]

For Adler, this was impulsive, unrealistic, too lofty, perhaps haughty, and not properly architectural.

At Adler's urging, America's first architectural engineering curriculum was established a the University of Illinois in 1890. A practical man, yes, but he also enjoyed reading the German theorist and architect Gottfried Semper, who preached a firm Teutonic classicism. In 1860,

Adler wrote that "Every technical product [should be] a resultant of use and material. Style is the conformity of an art object with the circumstance of its origin and the conditions and circumstances of its development."[127] Clearly, Adler preferred Viollet-le-Duc's approach following on from Vitruvius, that architecture was "rational building." Herein, there were many possibilities. Wright's view was, in the beginning, equally prosaic, more like Sullivan's. Each problem is resolved, he said in 1900, with "its common sense fruitfully idealized. That is the heart of the poetry that lives in architecture."[128] But in 1949, he believed that "form and function are one," that "a building can only be functional when integral with environment and so formed in the nature of materials according to purpose and method."[129] Here, he was closer to Adler's interpretation.

And so the two senior architects revealed a most fundamental breach at the theoretical level. Differing opinions were, no doubt, one cause of their professional parting in 1895; that and no commissioned work as a result of the terrible financial crisis. And there was Sullivan's depressing personality. Wright was privy to the content and evolution of these irritations, wrangles, and philosophic positioning. That 1896 debate was Adler's only presentation in the media about democracy, nature, and architecture. Adler directed his enquiries to architectural needs and fundamental solutions with Germanic efficiency and Jewish enthusiasm. Before and after their professional split, he was not overly impressed by the less than pragmatic, mystically transcendental notions of his moody Irish partner.

A study of Adler and Sullivan's architecture is always problematical. As related to this book, one reason becomes obvious: any distinction of or between the two architects' work is blurred by stylistic and aesthetic inconsistencies in their buildings. Even when Sullivan was in command of exterior designs, say after 1886, he remained inconsistent building to building and within building type. As Lewis Mumford correctly observed, "taken together, Sullivan's buildings do not have the unity his doctrine demands (see Figure 3.5)."[130] Perhaps not too firmly, Grant Manson observed, "Unquestionably, Sullivan, as the catalytic agent, had much to do with the materialization of Wright's vision of architecture; but he could have offered little . . . of a specific nature."[131] In similar terms, Allen Brooks believed that Sullivan "offered a manner of thinking" rather than "means."[132] As we shall learn, such opinions give too much to Sullivan and too little to Reverend Jones, Wright's father, Silsbee, or Adler.[133]

Adler was aware of this anomaly and Wright participated. Without doubt, Sullivan's most consistently creative period was post-1905, with the wonderfully ornamented yet resolutely cubic banks and commercial structures.

Wright learned something about constructional and practical aspects initially from Uncle Thomas and Conover and Porter. But lessons about planning, about the design process, came from Silsbee and Adler. He first learned how an architect's office operated from Silsbee, and from Silsbee and Adler he learned how to act for clients and how to plan and build two- and three-dimensionally. From Silsbee and Sullivan, he came to understand not only characteristics but also the intrinsic meaning of architectural styles. He matured, from his reading and from Sullivan, about the poverty and sapping hegemony of historicism. Wright's enjoyment in philosophy was apparently *furthered* by Cecil Corwin and Sullivan. But Corwin, who studied architecture at the Illinois Industrial University in Urbana, could not have offered much architectural fodder, practical or theoretical, to Wright's young radicalized mind. One of Corwin's more important commissions was in 1891–92, a new Laboratory Building for Rush Medical College of Lake Forest University. The building's exterior was in finished stone and to a modest Renaissance revival style with Graeco/Roman classical details, Roman arches, and a quasi-Georgian entrance ensemble.[134]

It was primarily Adler who put buildings together with Germanic efficiency; therefore, the process of planning was Adler's. As Wright observed: "As an architect Louis Sullivan went to school, not the Beaux-Arts but to Dankmar Adler."[135] Wright watched this working process and participated. During early independence, he was, after all, more consummately a practical architect, more involved creatively with designing and building, more "of the world as well as in it," less a verbal theorist or "placidly contemplative." He did not combine architecture and words until confident of his architectural resolutions.[136]

Figure 3.5 Madison Street entrance to the Schlesinger and Mayer building in 1900, St Louis, Missouri, Louis H. Sullivan, Architect, 1898–99; note Luxfer glass tiles above large clear-glass windows. The building was sold in 1904 to Carson Pirie Scott & Co. and subsequently enlarged. From author's collection.

Aesthetic inclinations

As Sullivan's alcoholism became irreducible, so his mind wandered away from building buildings to why build, to philosophy. His most mystifying and therefore irritating thoughts were likely directed to positing that a building's function was both a societal thing and a living thing. Here, he accepts Emerson's organic theory. "Unceasingly the essence of things is taking shape in the matter of things," Sullivan once said. Here, "essence" was spiritual and immaterial, and "matter" implied the physical. If one definition of organic was generally agreed to be a characteristic of, pertaining to, or derived from living organisms, then it follows, Emerson believed, that art must imitate the forms of nature. He then candidly attacked the unnaturalness of the then fashion of neoclassic ornamentation: "outside embellishment is deformity. . . . Our taste in building . . . refuses pilasters and columns that support nothing, and allows the real supporters of the house honestly to show themselves."[137] This was sustenance to those Americans opposed to Gilded Age excesses. In this respect, and following on from Carlyle, the organic theory assumed the practical position that form must be dictated by inner purposes; these words were a harbinger of the twentieth-century theory of functionalism.[138] On Emerson's subjectiveness, in 1914 Wright presented his only useful thoughts on the subject prior to the 1930s. In order to achieve "the integral simplicity of organic nature," he sought

> a serious devotion to the "underneath" in an attempt to grasp the nature of building a beautiful building beautifully, as organically true in itself, to itself and to its purpose, as any tree or flower.

> By organic architecture I mean an architecture that develops from within outward in harmony with the conditions of its being as distinguished from one that is applied from without.[139]

He avoided ambiguities that arose when Sullivan said,

> In seeking now a reasonably solid grasp on the value of the word, organic, we should at the beginning fix in mind the value of the correlated words, organism, structure, function, growth, development, form. All these words imply an initiating pressure of a living force, and a resultant structure or mechanism whereby such *invisible* force is made manifest and operative. Hence the law of function and form discernible throughout nature.[140]

In published essays, Sullivan was of two minds. In one, he thought to infuse a "life force" (his words) *into* an architect's building. In the other, he believed that a properly designed building might *stir* people, users, to find or reinforce their selves, or their intuition, as Emerson would have it. Either way, Sullivan's philosophic motive was unclear, as was Wright's, and for the same reasons. By accepting a functionalist theory for architectonic organization and form, and then the opposite by invoking vitalism's biological imperative, the theoretical result was that a building must be both mechanistic (as a mechanism) and a tease of a person's intuition. Either way, the result, the perception, was an *aesthetic response*. Yet ideas of a hypothetical vitalism (*èlan vital* or life force or energy) could not induce an architectural planning or design methodology. Because it is about arranging matter, architectural theory does not easily accept an invisible essence or life force that in itself is not causative.

The idea of a life force as something with organic potential came to Sullivan via talks with Edelmann, as well as by reading Whitman, Emerson, Thoreau, and Greenough who were indebted to Carlyle, Coleridge, and Ruskin. Emerson's Transcendentalism can be defined as a miscellany of beliefs united by the contention that living processes, human in the main, are not purely mechanistic but energized by an immaterial vitalism, by a vital principle. Then, by self-reliance (individualism) or intuition (an "inner voice"), one can transcend the mundane and find independence by realizing the "integrity of [one's] own mind." Emerson's ca. 1840 essay on self-reliance is individualism's manifesto.[141] But its application to architecture is highly problematic.

However, a pragmatic Alder sought solutions to architectonic problems impressed by industrialization and the cold fact of functional integration. As such, they were planning and construction problems. Sullivan was searching with words for a description of an organic and nationalistic cultural expression, regardless of technological advances or embarrassing social conditions. Wright verbalized an aesthetic response to industrialism that became essential to his role in reformation – he called them protestant or Protestant actions – beginning around 1898 – that is, after he shrugged off the frustrating 1890s, the limits of Adler's practical talent and Sullivan's artistic myopia of grand words that in practice he ignored for an ornamental emphasis.

Yet, while Wright's espousal was for an organic rationalism, his work revealed a continuation of nineteenth-century academic formalism mixed with individuation. The resulting poetical romanticism is why post-1918 Europeans shied away from him and identified the ascetic, non-ethnic, rationalized architecture of post and beam first applied sans ornament to industrial buildings. As well, Europeans could see that, as with Sullivan, Wright's verbalized doctrine was not sustained in architectural productivity; it was too idiosyncratic, fussily ornamented, and ignored technology. And yet it is plain that Wright and Le Corbusier (twenty-five years later) were alike in their rationalistic verbalizations. But their architecture was romantic, individuated, and personal. Their ideas for the city, however, were at opposite poles.

Ruskin and Viollet-le-Duc

The counterposition of some Americans to Ruskin's socialism and to Emerson's individualism and Transcendentalism was by opponents who saw

> [the] extreme danger of making nature – particularly, wild American nature . . . – the standard of judgement. It meant the unleashing of all the forces of nationalism and "sublime"

individualism and the further weakening of ties with Europe . . . [They] seemed to be giving Americans the right to judge art on an individual, even an anarchic, basis.

The concern of some was "for some stabilizing force in American life,"[142] not for individuals defining the nation independent of an implicit European hegemony. As American architect Henry Van Brunt observed in a paper to the Institute of Architects in December 1858, "informed opinion must be that Ruskin was a sound observer of Middle Ages" art, but that is irrelevant to America. It was a popular reaction.[143]

Ruskin

While extremely critical of amoral commercialism and rampant mechanical advances (a Luddite, of course), Ruskin did not look closely at the city because, one might infer, "the city is mechanical, not natural, and therefore does not suggest the nobility and dignity, human and divine, which are the true provinces of art. Only the natural world could do that."[144] In the prose of English literati and gentry and Emersonian followers of Kant, all widely read in America, ruralized nature was seen mystically as "a cure to [urban] society's pathological condition." Additionally, and as summed by Demetri Porphyrios, to Ruskin and followers such as William Morris and his Arts and Crafts followers, the "machine was to become synonymous with inhumanity, standardization, alienation, pleasureless toil; while craft was to be extolled as humanizing, spiritually fulfilling, pleasurable labor."[145]

The debate proceeded as a twofold question: first, "whether, and if so how, industrialized production could be short-circuited": here were A.N.W. Pugin, Ruskin, Morris, and Charles Ashbee. Second, "how it was possible to combine a commitment to craft *and* a dedication to the machine":[146] here were Viollet-le-Duc, the Deutscher Werkbund circle, Wright, and American vocational education. Wright's reconciliation was to accept the machine as a tool for man-the-designer as the conceptual and guiding spirit. That was the essence of Wright's long, tiresome and oft-repeated, and oft-edited paper on the "Art and Craft and the Machine."[147]

Nothing is more obvious than Wright's debt in design, if less so his words, to the Arts and Crafts Movements in England and America, regardless of his occasional criticism. From them, as historian Anthony Alofsin correctly surmised, Wright "absorbed the fundamental principles of simplicity and community":

> Simplicity in design [Alofsin said] provided an antidote to moribund historicizing forms and allowed for the truthful expression of materials and machine technology. . . . In a similar way the Arts and Crafts goal of integrating the everyday life of communities into a harmonious relationship with nature reinforced Wright's views of true American architecture as a democratic architecture, with nature and the individual forming a harmonious community.[148]

That accords with Morris, who would merge and blend city and country to create one national "garden, where nothing is wasted and nothing is spoilt, with the necessary dwellings, sheds, and workshops, scattered up and down the country all trim and neat and pretty."[149] It was George Levine's observation that Morris completed "the redefinition" of Ruskin's art by reference "not to a special skill"

> but to the quality of life which gives it meaning and joy: "the cause of Art is the cause of the people." Art is "the expression by man of his pleasure in labour." By insisting, as did Ruskin, . . . on the connection of art to the ordinary experience of men in the world, he [Morris] moves from sentimentalism to a great new vision of human possibilities.[150]

Wright was closer to Ruskin than he credited, although attempting to emphasize nature as a counter to coldly inert repetitions of industrialism and machine rationalism.[151] Yet all were romantics and/or luddites, not politicians or businessmen.

94 *The aesthetics of progress*

E.-E. Viollet-le-Duc

> (Did you think it was in the white or gray stone? or the lines of the arches or cornices?)
> — Walt Whitman, *A Song for Occupations*, 4.iii

A first reading of the epigraph might appeal, but it is deceptive, saying that architecture is limited to looking at exterior surfaces, a Ruskinian delight or Emersonian place. Delete "when you look upon it" and substitute the inference "when you experience it." Indeed, as with all experiences, a building instructs. That was one implication of E.-E. Viollet-le-Duc's architectural theories so eagerly assimilated by Wright. However, Sullivan "seems to have derived little inspiration from Viollet-le-Duc," a common observation, this by Peter Collins, and he referred to Sullivan's architecture, not his writings.[152]

While Ruskin tantalized people's aesthetic imagination with befuddling, dilettantish ease, it was Viollet who clarified challenges faced by nineteenth-century architects. Ruskin lacked concision, wandered argumentatively, and was a non-practical man of impressions. And he teased. A somber Viollet was thoroughly an architect and rationalist tuned to the century's technical progress. Ruskin pursued the Pugin family and championed Morris and, in their regressiveness, Ruskin was found wanting. As Wright observed in 1910: Ruskin and Morris "have hereto prevailed in America, steadily confusing. . . ."[153]

Viollet-le-Duc's legacy, Donald Egbert correctly noted, was the stimulation of "nearly all of the chief founders of 'modern' architecture."[154] Europhiles Robin Middleton and David Watkins agreed and found that the Frenchman's teachings were given acknowledgement and "interpretation" by turn-of-the-century architects such as Antoni Gaudi in Spain and Victor Horta in Belgium and absorbed by Hendrik Berlage in Holland – and perhaps "the whole school of Russian Constructivism," a big perhaps.[155] Others have added Auguste Perret in Paris, Frank Furness in Philadelphia (strangely, with whom Sullivan had worked), Wright, and later Le Corbusier in Paris.[156]

In his 1932 autobiography, Wright identified but few authors as useful to his education, among them Carlyle, Shelly (Mr), Goethe in English, and William Blake. In design, there was Owen Jones's *Grammar of Ornament* and Viollet's *Habitations of Man in All Ages* and the "'Dictionnaire,' the 'Raissone'," as he described them. Son John recalled that his father presented him with the "Dictionnaire," but it was Viollet-le-Duc's *Discourses on Architecture*, likely the two-volume translation by American architect Henry van Brunt. It was the "only really sensible book on architecture in the world," Wright proclaimed.[157]

Discourses combined education, history, structure, and theory with practice. As an avid rationalist, Viollet's focus was on construction: its methods and building materials. But his ideas about the needs of and forces upon architecture, and his expression of a rather holistic notion about a building's aesthetics, was lucid and inspirational. Also very attractive to Wright, Viollet was a rebel, anti-academic, against the École des Beaux-Arts' unwavering promotion of *classique* but not against all of its pedagogy, against the immutable, and for an architecture that reflected its organic, indigenous culture and geographic regionality. Viollet was independent of mind, philosophically resolute; intransigent perhaps. There was much to attract Wright to that noble Frenchman, and much to emulate.

The writings of Sullivan and Wright were dedicated in part to revitalizing Viollet's arguments in search of an architecture relevant to modern society. The primary evidence for this is found in Wright's words and works of art, and supported, fortunately, in one of son John's memoirs.

The best way to extract from Viollet-le-Duc's vast reservoir those ideas that impressed Wright is to look at what John selected. Architect John Kenneth (Lloyd) Wright stated that Viollet was a teacher his father could never be; in fact, his father was "not a good teacher."[158] That is one reason for father's gift of *Discourses*. The "wholeness of vision" embodied in the two volumes were, as father said to son, "all the architectural school you will ever need."[159] In 1946, John set out extracts he believed influenced his father.[160]

To begin, John noted that Viollet-le-Duc was encouraged by friends and colleagues to establish a private teaching atelier. Some eighty years later, Wright began his own atelier and called it the Fellowship. John quoted from Viollet's preface:

> In my simplicity I did not take into consideration the enmity and opposition to my teachings by certain Professors. . . deeply versed in the study of Greek antiquities [who] were particularly displeased that I drew attention to an art foreign to their studies.

Those professors branded Viollet's teaching as "dangerous dogma." After giving up the professorship, he soon published his lectures where, in part, he said, "my chief object is truth, and if I am liable to any accusation, it is that of not belonging to any school. It is true, that alone is enough to array them all against me. . . ." This corresponds with Wright's expressed radicalism that led to self-imposed isolation. For all of his life, Wright assumed – and that is the right word –society and professional colleagues were against him.

John selected a section that dealt with style. It was important, Viollet said, "to revert to first principles," to study "primitive epochs,"

> [and if a] form is not the immediate expression of a requirement of a certain social condition it is bad form in which there is no style. . . . But what is style? I'm not speaking now of style as applied to the classification of arts by periods, but of style as inherent in the arts of all times. . . .

Viollet's discussion of style was long, often tedious, so John chose the following: "[Style] consists in a marked distinction of form; it is one of the essential elements of beauty, but does not of itself alone constitute beauty." As an example from many analogies, Viollet said of a primitive man making an ordinary pot:

> There must be a means of holding the vessel; the workman therefore attaches handles with revets. But as the vessel must be inverted . . . [to be] drained dry, he makes the handles so that they shall not stand above the level of the top of the vessel. Thus fashioned . . . this vessel has style: first, because it exactly indicates its purpose; second, because it is fashioned in accordance with the material of which this utensil is made, and the use for which it is intended. This vessel has style because human reason indicates exactly the form suitable to it.

A Zen rationalist?

The resource and meaning of many of Wright's analyses and protestations now become clear, like those about his Larkin Administration Building of 1904. Viollet had said: a steam locomotive is "the expression of its power"; therefore, it has style. "Some say it is but an ugly machine. And why ugly? Does it not have the true expression of brutal energy?"[161] (And if so, Ruskinites would retort, so what?) In 1908, Wright commented on his Larkin Administration Building, saying,

> [it was] built to house the commercial engine of the Larkin Company. [It is] a simple working out of certain utilitarian conditions. . . . The machinery . . . is quartered in plan and placed outside the main building. . . . [T]he work may have the same claim to consideration as a "work of art" as an oceanliner, a locomotive or a battleship.[162]

New England beaux-arts architect and critic Russell Sturgis wrote an uncomplimentary review of the Larkin Administration Building, advising on its ugliness. Wright's published reply acknowledged the building "may be ugly" to some "but it is noble." It "has strength and dignity and power. . . . [I]ts high character is a prophecy."[163] Six years later, he said, "[The] work may be severe; it cannot be foolish. It may lack grace; it cannot lack fitness altogether. It may seem ugly; it will not be false."[164] The machine aesthetic. When John's father said at various times that he was not interested in a style but *style* – usually emphasized – he was paraphrasing the Frenchman who said in *Dictionnaire* and with equal emphasis: "There is *style*, there are *the styles*."[165] Theorist M. F. Hearn offered a tidy summary:

> Neither forms nor materials nor technologies should be tied to tradition; a progressive outlook should always be maintained. If . . . principles are adhered to the result will necessarily have style. But the best way to harness these principles, [Viollet-le-Duc] *implied*, is through the use of a guiding metaphor, that of either the machine or the organism.[166]

In the mid- to late nineteenth century, "style" was a popular but vexing question inherently problematic. Its reputation was fixed in 1892 by A.D.F. Hamlin's essay titled "The Battle of the Styles."[167]

The link between primitive people and nature, a link of commonality and virtue as extolled by Rousseau, was another selection by John: "Proceed as nature does in her works," said Viollet, "and you will be able to invest with style all that your brain conceives." Further, "Among primitive peoples . . . the artist can produce nothing but works possessing style, because his mind or imagination proceeds nearly in the same way as nature." That is to say, the primitive mind was artless, the civilized mind erringly sophisticated, perforce corrupted by the demands of social conventions leading to artificiality. As to modern works by modern man, Viollet offered analogies that Wright borrowed in 1908 and 1910, one that son John quoted:

> There is not style but that which is appropriate to the object. A sailing-vessel has style; but a steamer made to conceal its motive power and looking like a sailing-vessel will have none; a gun has style, but a gun made to resemble a crossbow will have none.

In a few years, Viollet-le-Duc abridged this functionalist notion to: "The beautiful is nothing more than the harmony, the exact concordance, between form and function."[168] Horatio Greenough reduced it to "Form Follows Function," Sullivan's preference. As we shall learn, just after the turn of the century, people promoting the "city scientific" used almost those exact words in the cause of a responsible urbanism.

As an intimate witness to his father's musing and preaching, John believed Viollet to be the foundation of his father's theory of architecture and sustenance for his philosophy of life, both ordered by "principles, as opposed to rules."[169] There is no reason to abuse John's belief. Moreover, that was the essence of Wright's utterances that so intrigued Europeans before 1925.

Another example will further illustrate Viollet-le-Duc's influence. In volume one of *Discourses*, Viollet discussed structural articulation and showed in plan the evolution of wall and column articulation from Roman basilica to Romanesque and Gothic churches. In 1898, Wright experimented on his Oak Park Studio with a design that explored articulation, to use his word, of space and volume, less of structure. Yet he did refer to post and lintel, or trabeated construction. Wright employee Charles E. White Jr. mentioned that his boss often did not support an overhead beam on a wall pilaster but rather by an interior post freestanding and clear of its juxtaposed non-bearing wall.[170] The detail in plan had been clearly outlined and illustrated by Viollet (see Figure 3.6, bottom).[171]

The degree to which late nineteenth-century rationalism was promoted in architecture and justified by employing technological advances, mainly to structure, can be measured by another theorist. J.N.-L. Durand's encyclopedic typologies were based on structure defining space enhanced by classical forms, often reduced similar to those of his colleague C.-N. Ledoux and teacher E.-L. Boullé, both neoclassicists. All his recipes of 1802–05 employed a

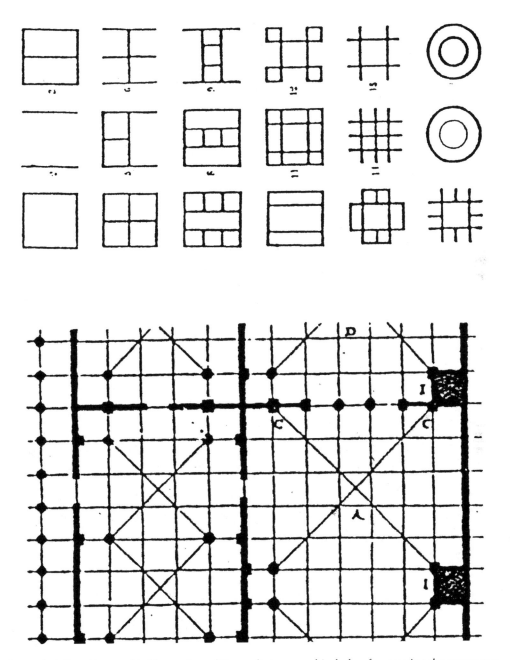

Figure 3.6 Top: Papworth's illustration of Durand's typographical plan forms using the square proportion. Bottom: plan of Papworth's "Points of Supports" that defined apartments and spaces following Roman tradition.

two-dimensional module in plan (see Figure 3.6, top). Of course, design and structural modules were universal in antiquity. As Viollet's said, there is "not an absolute but a relative unit, known as a *module*."[172] Wright's boss, Adler, had said that the "subdivision of space" is determined by function ("the proposed occupation"), structure, and "artistic expression." And he paraphrased Viollet and beaux-arts theorists: "The unit of subdivision will also be the unit of construction and the unit of design."[173] Wright later called his module a "unit system" and implied it contained something new and magical.[174]

Now and then, Viollet-le-Duc discussed the persistently lingering Italian Renaissance, "that setting sun all Europe mistook for dawn," as Victor Hugo said.[175] For simplicity, the prefatory comments of translator Benjamin Bucknall, an English architect, provide a neat summation:

> [Viollet] calls special attention to the notion of "Revival," ... which in its essence is clearly akin to the justly deprecated *Renaissance*. He condemns it as the fundamental error [of] our time ... [and] proves that a reproduction of the mere forms or methods of the past must be devoid of genuine vitality, and that it is to *analysis and the application* of principles, and not to the imitation of *forms*, that we must look for a true revival.[176]

The italics are Bucknall's. Revival was the practical aesthetic discussion of the day and depended on stylistic precedents. In 1881, New York architect Leopold Eidlitz quipped that "American architecture is the art of covering one thing with another thing to imitate a third thing which, if genuine, would not be desirable."[177]

By accepting Viollet-le-Duc's rationalism and Adler's practicalism, Wright was able to carry architecture beyond Sullivan's poetic, emotive, personal, anthropomorphic ideas.[178] Sullivan's architecture gave expression to *given* structural and social (programmatic) conditions enlivened by surface ornament that became sculpted poetic meditations. Perhaps Narciso Menocal put it correctly when he said Sullivan substituted Viollet's "accuracy" for empathy.[179] If so, he was empathetic to art only, not to society or humanistic responsibilities.

Primitive and indigenous

During Europe's century of enlightenment, Linnean nomenclature for categories and hierarchies (Durand was architecture's voice), and Newtonian physics, Gothic was thought barbaric. With Horace Walpole's *The Castle of Otranto: A Gothic Story* of 1785, there began a slow but determined acceptance in theology, architecture, and literature, notably in England but also in France with Victor Hugo's *Notre Dame de Paris* of 1783. By the time of Viollet-le-Duc's first investigations in the 1840s, the reaction had been established and centered on medievalism. In a wonderful alliance, mystery, primitivism, picturesque, pseudo-science (Mary Shelley's *Frankenstein* [1818] or Jules Verne's tales [1860s and 1870s]), the obscure, and nationalism had become collaborators. In architecture, it proved to be a viable counter to Italy's too-long-lived, formalized, restrained Graeco-Roman Renaissance. Within the romantic impulse was fantasy, expressiveness, subjectivity, exoticism, complex symmetry, and especially the unconventional.

In peoples' minds, medievalism was aligned with peasantry, abundant nature, and things indigenous. The word "indigenous" had two meanings. One referred to something original in or characteristic of a particular region or country, something native. The other reference was to something innate, inherent, or natural: exotic the opposite. Also allied was the imperfect idea of primitivism, at least to philistines. While "primitive" can refer to the first or earliest, it can also mean rough and simple. But "primitivism" in part carried the idea that, untainted by the civilizing effects of later societies, primitive art was innately, fundamentally superior to that to follow. From the apparently uncluttered primitive mind would come pure thoughts that would lead to a freedom from the forces of convention. Viollet's "primitive peoples," those first, prime cultures, produced "nothing but works possessing style."

Somewhat similar arrangements were found in Arts and Crafts theories, if aristocratically delicate. Life, sustenance, and labor twined: that was within the cults of picturesque and Ruskinian medievalism. Because medieval people were supposedly closer to nature through life's mundane, sustaining daily work, went the argument, they naturally and intimately exercised a fundamental religiosity, one perforce holistic, natural, and near perfect. Their crafts were noble expressions of functional necessity. This, of course, ignored their drudging, marginal existence, or what Sullivan referred to as "the repressive force of feudalism."[180] In the nineteenth century, it was intellectual nostalgia idealizing human splendors that never existed.

Entwined with those noble yet condescending thoughts was the notion of nature and a consequent ruralism. There is little doubt that Emerson was the Wright and Jones families' favorite author, in their minds a paternal figure. Nearly all members could quote the New Englander at the drop of a hat. And Frank Wright paraphrased Emerson and his poet Walt Whitman, throughout life, finally in August 1958 as an appendix to the third edition of his monograph on "The Disappearing City" titled *The Living City*. There, in support of his decentralized urbanism, he quoted – or rather, by addition or subtraction, misquoted – extracts from Emerson's essay titled "Farming," as in this example:

> The glory of the farmer is that, in the division of labors, it is his part to create. All trade rests at last on his primitive activity. He stands close to Nature; he obtains from the earth the bread and the meat. [. . .] all nobility rests on possession and use of land. . . .[181]

Wright's "living city" was not a city, as I've detailed elsewhere, but a series of villages.[182] Farmers were imputed as naturally frugal, practical, disinterested in profit, healthier, wise, and more resourceful than urbanites.

Although a son of religious and farming families, Wright did not wholly accept those emotive images. But he did imply the essence of their character as it should fit architecture in writings scattered about texts, such as his paper to the Architectural League in 1900, an article for the cause of architecture in 1908, and again in 1910 when, in a clarifying summary of Viollet-le-Duc's call to study "primitive epochs," Wright said,

> the true basis for any serious study of the art of architecture is in those indigenous structures, the more humble buildings everywhere, which are to architecture what folk-lore is to literature or folk-songs are to music. . . . In the aggregate of these lie the traits that make them characteristically German or Italian, French, Dutch, English or Spanish in nature. . . . The traits of these structures are national, of the soil. . . . Their functions are thoughtfully conceived, and rendered directly with natural feeling. They are always instructive and often beautiful.[183]

It was a plea for an organic nationalism extracted from indigenous roots and not from the layers of European sophistications as exported. The notion was within Rousseau's *The Social Contract*, where he extolled the nobility of primal people, in particular the American Southwest Indian.[184]

The term "primitive" is variable and quixotic, in this instance conditioned by European condescension and arrogance. However, as historian Joseph Rykwert convincingly argued:

> The return to origins is a constant of human development. . . . The return to origins always implies a rethinking of what you do customarily, an attempt to renew the validity of your everyday actions, or simply a recall of the natural (or even divine) sanction for your repeating them for a season.

[T]he primitive . . . remains the underlying statement, the irreducible, intentional core. . . .[185]

Yet late nineteenth-century Euro American architects spoke not of primitive but erringly of the highly sophisticated exotic cultures of Egypt, the Muslims, Southeast Asia, Japan, Mesoamerica, and so on.[186] Sullivan provided one useful example in his design for the Transportation Building at the Chicago Exposition of 1893. Its central entry was composed of a gold-colored Mogul arch framed by a Mogul-inspired decorated spandrel set between two Hindu chatri. His source was not tenth-century Saracenic art of Palestine, as often suggested, but Indian buildings similar to the Tomb of Humayun, Delhi, of 1565, or the Taj Mahal, Agra, of 1636–53, each widely published. Yet the arch was not innate, just appealing.

Influenced by Silsbee, by his teaching aunts Jane and Ellen, and a few others, Wright's learning path before the 1890s led to a study of traditional Japanese architecture. He discovered its unaffected qualitative and structural applications, as well as its fit with Arts and Crafts ideas of simplicity of design and the frank use of materials. Two recent studies reveal the extent of those lessons. Julia Meech looked at Wright's interest in collecting Japanese art. Kevin Nute traced the people, including Silsbee, who were the foundation of Wright's third passion, after music. Nute displayed elements of Japanese architecture that he believed influenced Wright. But many of Nute's interpretations were narrowly inferred without reasonable foundation or comparison to other influences. Of course, all aspects of Japanese art were very popular in Europe and North America since the 1860s. American painters James M. Whistler in the 1870s and Mary Cassatt in the 1890s found sustention, while Giacomo Puccini's *Madam Butterfly* of 1904 was a crown.

Of equal value to Wright's learning process was the experience and observation of other cultures, especially American Indians, many of whom inhabited the hills and valleys about Hillside and Spring Green. By the 1880s, their cultures were torn asunder, all things Indian became even more popular with Euro Americans and would remain so. And mythmaking ran culturally deep. By the 1920s, there were about eight hundred fraternal orders that incorporated Indian lore and costumes in their ceremonies. There was, therefore, indelible and high contrast between industrialized, mechanized, and urbanized America and the shifting frontier against the primal, earthbound, yet sophisticated Indian cultures. It was understandable for Europeans and Americans to be curious about those exotic people. To some minds, their existence proved the Spencerian myth of superiority through social evolution. But Wright's interest was ambivalent, as the following anecdotes reveal.

From ca. 1895 to ca. 1915, Wright and author Hamlin Garland were close friends. Garland wrote about plains Indians, Euro Americans in the newly ruralized Mississippi Valley, and the spoiling of the unspoiled West. Both men were besotted by Indian themes and dress, even costuming their families and friends for picnics. Wright used abstracted Indian designs for ornament but mainly after experiences in America's Southwest when traveling to San Diego in 1915. A first major ornamental Indian theme was a painting of ca. 1909 by Charles A. Corwin, Cecil's talented brother, on the wall above the fireplace in Wright's wife's home kindergarten room. More abstract forms then appeared on the German Warehouse of 1915+, the Bogk house of 1916, Barnsdall house of 1919, and so on.[187]

In October 1924 the German architect Eric Mendelssohn spent a week or so with Wright at his Spring Green home and office. Mendelssohn would later recall that, on one afternoon, everyone "had to change" into Indian costume, "Bark shoes, a long staff, gloves and a tomahawk." They then hiked and picnicked on land "abandoned by the redskins," as Mendelssohn phrased it.[188] Incidentally, Garland had left Chicago by 1924. What can be read into what seems now to be a frivolous activity? That aside, Wright and son Lloyd were adamant, the Southern California houses for Aline Barnsdall, Mrs Millard, John Storer, the Freemans, and the Ennises, designed and built from 1919–25, "reflect" Southwest Indian buildings, not Mayan. And father and son referred to Wright's Barnsdall house as a "mesa silhouette" and of "Pueblo

Indians."[189] All houses had been commissioned well after Wright's 1915 travels through Indian lands en route to the West Coast.

+ + +

Much of Viollet-le-Duc's writings post-1870 display, with direct or oblique references, an awareness of evolution theory and a resultant improving of function by experiential habituation and social improvement. Examples are found previously herein and by the truths set out in the following:

> [The] main features of construction [said Viollet] are determined by a consideration of habits [societal traditions], exigencies of climate and situation, the *nature of materials* and the means of execution. . . .[190]

[Had Adler and Wright read this?]

> Nothing is complete.[191]
> Investigate thy beginnings [the indigenous primitive]: thou wilt thus learn thy aptitudes, and wilt be able to pursue that path of true Progress. . . .[192]
> Progress always consists in passing from the known to the unknown. . ., [and] by a series of transitions.[193]

We have seen how the design of a house was subjected to familial, societal, and environmental conditions and thus to change. There can be no absolute form of house, only cultural preference got by history. Further, while advancements in science and technology are linear, art as a non-functional activity is cyclic, always beginning. Viollet's procedure was meant to be a slight modification of scientific methodology. With a nod to Goethe rather than Ruskin, he said in *Learning to Draw*, "There is a distinction to be made between the scientific and the poetic or artistic method."[194] Viollet-le-Duc exemplified a growing reaction to Ruskinian–medieval fantasy, not mystery, and to French baroque and rococo frivolities sucked out of ancient and revived styles. He, like Sullivan, realized that styles do not evolve. Rather, they are contrived elaborations of themselves. As such, there can be no progress, no evolution.

Architecture is a design activity, not one of art.

Notes

1 Emeritus Professor Gilbert Herbert in Haifa to this author, 9 July 2014.
2 Mother Anna in Madison to son Frank in Chicago, 8 June 1887, Wright Archive, wherein she states her letter celebrates his twentieth birthday.
3 Wright (1932) and Wright (1943), see previous explanation and Johnson (1990) on publishing the autobiography. Portions of his text were published earlier now and then beginning in 1927, notable is a series of articles in *Architectural Record* titled "In the cause of architecture," 61(May 1927) to 64(December 1928), and a series of lectures Wright (1932); FLW, *Two Lectures on Architecture* (Chicago: Art Institute, 1931).
4 Secrest (1992), p.89.
5 Gannett to Reverend Jones, 11 February 1885, as quoted in Siry (1996), p.256n8. Reverend William Silsbee graduated from Harvard Divinity School in 1836 and was ordained a Unitarian minister in 1840. He was pastor of a church in Trenton, New York, from 1867 into 1887.
6 Mary Jane Hamilton with Anne E. Biebel and John O. Holzheuter, "FLW's Madison Network" in Sprague (1990), pp.2c, 8n17.
7 Twombly (1979), p.11.
8 Wright (1932), p.51; Wright (1943), pp.51–52.
9 Mollenhoff and Hamilton (1999), pp.1c, 2, 7n12; Wright (1943), p.50, not in Wright (1932).

10 On Conover's appointments see Mollenhoff and Hamilton (1999), p.275n25, where it refers to Jim Feldman, *The Buildings of the University of Wisconsin* (Madison: University of Wisconsin Archives, 1997), pp.52–62; Elizabeth L. Miller, *Landmarks and Landmark Sites Nomination Form, University of Wisconsin Science Hall* (Madison: Madison Landmarks Commission, 1994), p.9. The fist mention of the Conover and Porter firm in a *Madison City Directory* was in 1888–89 under architects; the partners parted in 1899. Porter was from Peru, Illinois, and attended Beloit College before UW. From 1906–17, he was secretary of the state's Capitol Building Commission.
11 Wright (1932), pp.51, 57; slightly altered in Wright (1943), pp.57–58.
12 Mollenhoff and Hamilton (1999), p.275n26, square brackets theirs. Conover's testimony began in January 1888 to a state government hearing on cost overruns for Science Hall.
13 John Nader in *Biographical Review of Dane County, WI* (Chicago: Biographical Review, 1893), pp.215–216.
14 J. L. Jones, ed., "Unity Chapel . . . Helena Valley, Wisconsin," *Unity* (Chicago), 16(26 December 1885), p.1.
15 Barney (1965), pp.85–87; Wright (1943), pp.133–136, it was Wright who mentioned "Cramer," p.133.
16 "S.C. Ll. J." (Susan Charlotte Lloyd Jones, Jenkin's wife), [Notes], *Unity*, 16(14 November 1885), p.136; [J. L. Jones], "Unity Chapel for the Unitarian Church of Helena Valley, Wisconsin," *Unity*, 16(26 December 1885), p.1; "Unity Chapel, Helena, Wis," *All Souls Church Fourth Annual* (Chicago: All Souls Church, 1887), n.p.; W.C.G. [W. C. Gannett], "Christening a Country Church," *Unity and the University*, 17(20 August 1886), pp.356–357; Twombly (1979), p.29n25, where publications recording construction events are listed.
17 Bruce Brooks Pfeiffer, compiler, "FLW Complete List of Works," in McCarter (1997), p.344.
18 Wright and three other men were listed as special students in civil engineering, but he was recorded as only "present during latter part of 1885–86 academic year," *Catalogue of the University of Wisconsin . . . Academic Year 1886–87* (Madison: The University, October 1886), pp.19, 23, 26, 30.
19 Reverend Jones to Samuel Barrows, 3 June 1886, as quoted in Siry (1996), p.259n32.
20 Wright (1932) and Wright (1943), pp.63–65, with thanks to Professor Joseph Siry's letter of 22 August 2013 to this author where the discrepancies are laid out.
21 "The Church of All Souls," *Unity*, 17(18 September 1886), p.102; W.C.G. (William C. Gannett), "Dedication of a Church," *Unity*, 17(23 October 1886), p.98; Siry (1996), pp.13–19.
22 See especially Hines (1967), pp.109–119, reprint without illustrations *JSAH*, 26(December 1967), pp.227–233; Hamilton (1990), p.8n18. Three simple drawing exercises are in the Wright Archive, two illustrated in Pfeiffer (2011), p.18.
23 Wright (1932), pp.51–57; slightly altered in Wright (1943), pp.51–58.
24 Twombly (1979), p.10; Hines (1967); Secrest (1992), p.72.
25 Wright (1932), pp.51–52; slightly altered in Wright (1943), pp.52–53. Van Velser taught at UW.
26 John Peter, *The Oral History of Modern Architecture* (New York: Abrams, 1994), p.114; Wright (1957), p.7; Wright (1932), pp.52–56.
27 G. G. Elmslie to Wright, 30 October 1932, p.5 <organica.org/pegge.htm>, accessed May 2013; see also Elmslie to Wright, 12 June 1936, made public by Mark L. Peisch, *JSAH*, 20(October 1961), pp.140–141.
28 Hasbrouck (1970), p.15n6; Siry (1991a), pp.259–260; Siry (1996), pp.14–15.
29 Wright (1932) and Wright (1943), p.72. On leaving Silsbee in May or June 1893, Waterman immediately set up his own office, Harold T. Wolff, "Waterman A La Modern," Ridge Historical Society (February 2000), p.1.
30 Aunt Nell to Frank, 9 March 1887, Wright Archive, also quoted in Patrick Pinnell, "Academic tradition and the individual talent . . . FLW," in McCarter (1991a), p.23; Secrest (1992), p.83; Wright implies he arrived in Chicago "late Spring, 1887," Wright (1932), p.63, unchanged in Wright (1943), p.63, but he told Hitchcock it was true Hitchcock (1942), p.3.
31 Susan Karr Sorell, "Silsbee: The Evolution of a Personal Architectural Style," *PSR*, 7(Fourth Quarter, 1970), p.5n1–2; Thomas J. McCormick, "The Early Work of Joseph Lyman Silsbee," in Helen Searing, ed., *In Search of Modern Architecture: A Tribute to Henry-Russell Hitchcock* (New York: Architecture History Foundation, Cambridge, MA: MIT Press, 1982), p.180.
32 In January 1886, it was announced that J. L. Silsbee, "J. Ll. Jones," and "Miss M.A. Safford" were among those scheduled to give papers to the Unitarian Western Conference in Cincinnati in May 1886, *The Christian Register*, 15(7 January 1886), p.279a.

33 Mother Anna in Madison to Frank, 24 April [1887], Wright Archive, pp.1–2; Wright (1932), pp.63–70, 106, 130; minor changes in Wright (1943), pp.65–71, 110, 130; Secrest (1992), p.83; Twombly (1979), pp.18–19, reports that the Chicago architectural firm Beers, Clay & Dutton as mentioned by Wright did not form until around 1890. William Wilson Clay was elected a Fellow of the American Institute of Architects in 1888.

34 Wright's exercises were discovered by historian Paul E. Sprague in the Jenkin Lloyd Jones collection at Meadville Lombard Theological School, then in Hyde Park, Hasbrouck (1970), pp.14–16; the school is now in Chicago. In July 1989 Siry could not locate Wright's drawings in the Jones collection, Siry (1996), p.258n23.

In the Wright Archives, there is a fragment of a pencil drawing of ornament attributed to Wright. It is a tracing from a Sullivan sketch of ca. 1888, Weingarden (2009), p.143.

35 Various Madison and Chicago city directories as well as drawings as published; Twombly (1979), pp.18–19; Hines (1967), p.230.

36 Construction of the Home Building was recorded in *The Weekly Home News*, Spring Green, and Reverend Jones's *Unity* from July 1887 to August 1888, Twombly (1979), p.29n29.

37 Mundie was in partnership with William LeBaron Jenney from 1888 into 1905, when Jenney retired. They were responsible for the extravagant Horticultural Building for the 1893 World's Columbian Exhibition in Chicago.

38 *Inland Architect*, 10(August 1987), plate 1 ("Country Residence," Helena Valley, basically Silsbee's Home Building); ibid., 11(February 1988), plate 1 (two views of Home Building, Helena Valley); ibid., 11(March 1888), plate (spec house for J. L. Cochran); ibid., 11(May 1888), plates (row "Houses for William Waller"); ibid., 11(July 1888), plates (spec house for J. L. Cochran); some images also in Manson (1958), p.17ff, as often illustrated, for example, in Sorell (1970), throughout; Secrest (1992), pp.93, 94; Hasbrouck (1970), pp.14–16; Pennell (1991), pp.22–25.

39 Wright (1946), p.55, his parentheses; Nickel and Siskind (2010), p.20, where Wright's Falkenau drawing is positioned beside a photograph of the completed building; for some of his freehand drawings, see Margaret Klinkow, "A Day in the Life of FLW," *Inland Architect*, 33(March/April 1989), pp.26, 70–71; see also Hasbrouck (1970), pp.14–16.

40 Sorell (1970), pp.5–13; idem., "A Catalog of work by J.L. Silsbee," 1883–97, loc cit, pp.17–21, drawing of principle elevation of All Souls, p.18; useful color images in <jlsilsbee.blogspot.com>. On Richard Norman Shaw and the Queen Anne style, see Mark Girouard, *Sweetness and Light: The Queen Anne Movement 1860–1900* (Oxford: Clarendon Press, 1977; New Haven: Yale University Press, 1984); Linda E. Smeins, *Building an American Identity: Pattern Book Homes and Communities, 1870–1900* (Walnut Creek: Altamira Press, 1999), pp.226–247.

41 A good description of the house is in "A Residence at Edgewater, Chicago, IL," *Scientific American*, 20(September 1895), pp.34, 41.

42 "The ground was broken today for an additional building . . . 13 August," M.T.L.G. (Mary Thorn Lewis Gannett), "The Spring Green Assembly," *Unity*, 1(18 August 1888), pp.328, 329; Twombly (1979), pp.29–30n29, 57.

43 Cooper graduated from Union College of Law, now Northwestern University, Chicago, in 1885, took an interest in real estate, and soon formed H. N. Cooper & Company; one of his promotions was the suburb of La Grange; *The Biographical Dictionary and Portrait Gallery. . . .* [Part 2] (Chicago, New York: American Biographical, 1893), pp.675–676; Albert Nelson Marquis, *The Book of Chicagoans* (Chicago: A. N. Marquis, 1917), p.142.

44 "Project: [Lieber Meister] . . . 1887," *FLW: Monograph 1887–1901*, Yokio Futagawa, ed. (Tokyo: A.D.A. Edita, 1986), plate 1; "Project: House for Henry N. Cooper . . . 1890," ibid., plate 3.

45 Hitchcock (1942), p.5, whose later guess for the drawing's date was "not more than a year before 1890, certainly . . . not later than 1893," H.-R. Hitchcock, Review of FLW, Drawings for a Living Architecture, *JSAH*, 3(October 1960), pp.129–131, from Pennell (1991), p.294n15; Bruce Brooks Pfeiffer, *FLW* (Köln: Taschen, 2002), pp.12–13. The Cooper house drawings appeared first in Spencer (1900), p.62, with no explanation. Historian Paul E. Sprague dates the house, therefore the drawing, "second half of 1899," Sprague, "The Evolution of Wright's Long, Narrow Hip Roofs," in Paul Kruty ed., *Prelude to the Prairie Style* (Urbana-Champaign: School of Architecture, University of Illinois, 2005), p.21.

See also Eileen Michels, "The Early Drawings of Frank Lloyd Wright Reconsidered," *JSAH*, 30(December 1971), pp.301–302, and reply, Curtis Besinger, "Comment on 'The Early Drawings . . . [by Michels]," *JSAH*, 31(October 1972), pp.216–220. See also Alberto Izzo and Camillo Gubitosi, *FLW: Three Quarters of a Century of Drawings* (London: Academy editions, 1981),

104   *The aesthetics of progress*

plate 1, "made while at University of Wisconsin," plate 3, and after plate 232, but Mrs Wright was advisor to this project as she was for Bruce Brooks Pfeiffer as editor but "under the supervision of Olgivanna Lloyd Wright," for "The Buildings and Projects of FLW," in Olgivanna Lloyd Wright, ed., *FLW: His Life His Work His Words* (New York: Horizon, 1966/London: Pitman, 1970), pp.205–222. The FLWF Archive number is 9004.1–4, i.e. 1904 and four sheets of drawing.

46   John O. Holzhueter, "FLW's Designs for Robert Lamp," *Wisconsin Magazine of History*, 72(Winter 1988), p.96.
47   Pfeiffer (1997), p.344; Pfeiffer (2011), p.28. The stables are not evident in a photograph dated 1905, Levine (1996), figure 14, p.15.
48   Wright (1932), pp.94–95, 104; edited in Wright (1943), pp.96, 107. Weatherwax held head-of-drafting-room positions for the Chicago Exposition and, after 1894, with expositions in Buffalo, St Louis, Jamestown, and Seattle to then practice in Yakima, Washington, in 1910, Weatherwax's entry in *The History of the Yakima Valley, Washington . . .*, Vol. 2 (Chicago: S. J. Clarke, 1919), pp.527–528.
49   [Wesley Shank], "FLW Residence & Studio," "Written Historical and Descriptive Date," (HABS, Ill.16-Oakpa, [1967]), p.5. On finding the house lot and Wright's association with Austin, Wright (1932), pp.81, 83, 103, slightly altered in Wright (1943), pp.79–81, 71–84, 106.
50   Stuart E. Cohen, *Chicago Architects* (Chicago: Swallow Press, 1976), pp.17, 54.
51   "Synopsis of Building News," *Inland Architect*, 22(August 1893), p.xixa; "Building intelligence," "La Grange," *Engineering Record*, 28(2 September 1893), p.228b.
52   *The First Half Century of Madison University (1819–1869) or the Jubilee Volume. . . .* (New York: Sheldon & Co, 1872), "class of 1849," p.295; *Colgate University General Catalog* (Hamilton: 1905), p.66; cf. *The First Half Century of Madison University: The Jubilee Volume* (Chicago: Bible and Publication Society, 1872). Begun by the Baptist Education Society of New York in 1819 and soon known as Hamilton Literary & Theological Institution, it became Madison University in 1846 and Colgate University in 1900. The best and most sensitive information on William is Secrest (1992), pp.48–58, and Twombly (1979), pp.1–12. See also John Harris Gutterson, "Weymouth Music and Musicians," *History of Weymouth Massachusetts*, vol. 2, *Historical* (Weymouth: Historical Society, 1923), pp.864–865; Clarence W. Fearing, "Ecclesiastical history of Weymouth," ibid., vol. 1, pp.279–280. On confirmation of years 1874–77 as pastor of the Weymouth Baptist Church, see "Weymouth, Mass., Semi-Centennial," *The Watchman: A Baptist Journal*, 86(18 February, 1904), p.23a. Reverend Wright attended Amherst College in Massachusetts from 1839–40, *Biographical Record of the Alumni of Amherst College . . . 1821–1871* (Amherst: 1883), listed as a non-graduate, p.66; he was briefly involved with the Liberal Christian Society as identified in "Directory," *Unity*, 8(1 June 1884), p.148.
53   William's first marriage to Permelia Holcomb (1825–64), a handsome and gentle woman, resulted in five children: Charles William (1856, who became a machinist); George Irving (1858, a lawyer then judge); Elizabeth Amelia (1860, a housewife); and of two stillborn the second claimed Permelia's life. Although the three lived happily with Permelia and miserably with a cold, unforgiving Anna Wright, Frank *never* mentioned them. William died in 1904 in Pittsburgh and Permelia died at age thirty-nine. They are buried together in the Bear Valley Cemetery in Wisconsin, a red granite memorial marks the site.
      On William's musicality, David W. Patterson, "FLW's Musical Origins," *FLWQuarterly*, 24(Fall 3013), pp.32–37, wedding photograph of Permelia and William in 1851 on p.34. A new record company producing William's music is named Permelia.
54   Secrest (1992), pp.49–50.
55   Wright (1932), p.15; Joncas (MS.1991), appendix, containing a list of books remnant of the Jones family, *not* those of Anna alone; Barney (1965), p.66.
56   Levine (1996), p.110b.
57   August Derleth, *The Wisconsin: River of a Thousand Isles* (New York: Farrar & Rinehart, 1942), pp.288–289.
58   Secrest (1992), p.86. Reverend Jones and Agneta Chapin were lecturers at the University of Chicago at least during 1895–96, "Lecture Study Department," *Annual Report 1895–1896* (Chicago: 1896), p.335.
59   "*Unity* (formerly *The Pamphlet Mission*) has been established for the purpose of publishing a . . . series of Liberal Religious pamphlets . . . written by men whose words combines Liberal thought with religious feeling. . . . It is hope the publication will meet the want not only of

persons already connected with Liberal organizations but also, especially, of *isolated Liberals*. . . .," from "Notes and News," *Unity, A Pamphlet Mission* . . ." 2(1 December 1878), p.160; see also Allen Ruff, *"We Called Each Other Comrade": Charles H. Kerr and Company, Radical Publishers* (Urbana: University of Illinois Press, 1977), 2nd ed. (Oakland, CA: PM Press, 2011), pp.25–31, *Unity* was published by the company.

60 C.H. L – e, "Jenkin Lloyd Jones," *Dictionary of American Biography*; also Graham (1983), pp.121–127; Lyttle (1952), chapters 9–11; Siry (1991a, b); Thomas (MS.1967); Samuel A. Eliot, ed., *Heralds of a Liberal Faith* (Boston: Beacon Press, 1952), Vol. 4, pp.164–173; Secrest (1992), pp.21–29, 141–142; George Willis Cooke, *Unitarianism in America* (Boston: American Unitarian Association, 1902), pp.276–279; Stead (1894), pp.388–391.

61 Thomas (MS.1967), p.191; see also Graham (1983), p.124.

62 Tauscher and Hughes (1999), p.4. The American Congress of Liberal Religious Societies, of which Reverend Jones was "Gen'l Sec'y," Selected *Unity* and *The Non-Sectarian* out of St Louis to be its "official organs," *The Non-sectarian*, 5(August 1895), p.v.

63 Lyttle (1952), p.222.

64 As quoted in Tauscher and Hughes (1999), p.4, see also <www.unitychapel.org/jenkin>

65 As quoted in Tauscher and Hughes (1999), p.5.

66 Secrest (1992), p.142; Christensen (1993), p.50.

67 Wright (1932), p.15, but Whittier was a Haverfield Quaker, not a Concord Unitarian.

68 As quoted in Tauscher and Hughes (1999), p.3. See also Barney (1965), pp.44, 80. The children of Reverend Wright and Anna were Frank Lincoln (1867–1959), Mary Jane or Jennie (1869–1953), and Margaret Ellen or Maginel (1877–1966). For a short period, Jane was a teacher and then married accountant Andrew T. Porter. They built a house to Frank's design near Hillside Home School. Maginel married the graphic artist Walter J. Enright in 1904, and they moved from Chicago to New York to Nantucket. Her second husband was Hiram Barney. She became a highly regarded illustrator (more than sixty books plus magazines) after studies from 1897–98 in the School of Art at the Art Institute of Chicago.

69 Graham (1983), p.121.

70 Wright (1932), pp.71–77.

71 Barney (1965), p.127; David M. Sokol, "The Role of Women and the Influence of Universalist and Unitarian Feminist Thought on the Design of FLW's Unity Temple," *SECAC Review*, 12(2, 1992), p.92, includes something on the Sioux City church of 1887. On Chapin, see Ernest Cassara, *Notable American Women 1607–1950* (Cambridge, MA: Harvard University Press, 1971); Siry (1996), pp.52, 203, 271; Wright (1932), pp.78, 80–81; Beverly Bumbaugh, <www.25.uua.org/uuhs/duub/articles/augustajanechapain> accessed May 2010.

72 As quoted in Davis (1973), p.76.

73 Jones withdrew support in 1904, the money saved applied to the new building.

74 Thomas (MS.1967), p.203; Lyttle (1952), p.223; Siry (1996), pp.280n.61, 298n.108.

75 Eleanor Ellis Perkins (daughter), *Eve Among the Puritans: A Biography of Lucy Fitch Perkins* (Boston: Houghton Mifflin, 1956), pp.190–193, 218, 220. Lucy, an illustrator, eventually turned to Christian Science and psychic "research."

76 Brooks (1972), p.33, who directs readers to *Inland Architect* (Chicago), 35(April 1900), plate 3; Wright (1980), pp.114–115.

77 ["poetry exchange"], *The Griffin Newsletter* (Des Moines), 3(Spring 2002), p.3.

78 Wright (1932), pp.14, 25–26, 27, altered in Wright (1943), pp.16, 18, 30.

79 Graham (1983), p.124.

80 Hays (1957), p.82, his emphasis.

81 Cf. Johnson (2004), pp.3–28; Johnson (1990), chapters 8 and 9.

82 Wright (1932), p.89.

83 Wright (1932), p.90, unaltered in Wright (1943), pp.43, 91.

84 Wright (1946), p.45; Robert J. Otto (a close friend of Willcox) to D.L.J., 11 February 1988, with thanks to Special Collections, Knight Library, University of Oregon; and Wright (1932), pp.88–89, altered in Wright(1943), pp.89–92. Apparently Willcox was casually employed by Silsbee. Willcox did become an architect in his home state of Vermont, then in Seattle, and eventually head of the Department of Architecture, University of Oregon, beginning in 1922; see entries in Ochsner (1994); Johnson (1988); Johnson (1990), chapter 11.

85 Twombly (1986), pp.86, 95–97.

86 Wright (1943), pp.119, 123; the building was destroyed in 1960, replaced by a parking structure.

87 Nickel and Siskind (2010), p.11; Herbert and Donchin (2013b), pp.82–85; see also Alofsin (1993), pp.1–11; Roula Mouroudellis Geraniotus, "German Design Influence in the Auditorium Theater," in Garner (1991), pp.43–75; and idem., in Zukowsky (1987); R. M. Geraniotis, "German Architectural Theory and Practice in Chicago, 1850–1900," *Winterthur Portfolio*, 21(Winter 1980), pp.298–305.
88 Elia (1996), pp.18, 80–88, and chapter 4.
89 Elia (1996), pp.20, 178.
90 Herbert and Donchin (2013b), p.88.
91 "An Important Letter from Mr. Dankmar Adler," *Inland Architect*, 25(July 1895), p.61.
92 Biographical information on Adler, Sullivan, and Edelman taken in the main from Nickel and Siskind (2010), pp.11, 12, 329; Herbert and Donchin (2013b), pp.87–89; the Sullivan and Adler roles in planning their various buildings is studied throughout the chapter; "Dankmar Adler" in Herman Eliassof, *The Jews of Illinois*, offprint of *The Reform Advocate* (Chicago), 21(May 1901), p.389. Adler's son A.K. received an engineering degree from the University of Michigan, class of 1894, and became an architect, at one time partner, with S. A. Treat.
93 Wright (1946), p.66. In the 1880s, the established profession was relatively small. See also appropriate sections of Manson (1958); Twombly (1979); Twombly (1986); Gill (1987); Wright (1932).
94 Elia (1996), p.109.
95 Elmslie to Wright, 12 June 1936, *JSAH*, 20(October 1961), p.141; correspondence between Sullivan and Wright from 1918–23, sighted Wright Archive; see also Letters (1984), pp.4–43.
96 C. Bebb to Thomas Burke, 14 June 1893, as quoted in Ochsner and Andersen (1989), p.288. Bebb left permanently for Seattle at the same time as Wright and Gill, mid-1893. Twombly (1986), refers to Rebb, p.256. In 1893, Adler & Sullivan accepted seven small commissions, only two were realized, one in 1894, another in 1895, Twombly (1986), p.451.
97 C. Bebb to Thomas Burke, 19 July 1893, as quoted in Ochsner and Andersen (1989), p.288. Sullivan was dismissed from Philadelphia architect Frank Furness's office with the onset of the 1873 financial crisis, exactly twenty years before Wright's dismissal, Sullivan (1924), p.196.
98 "An Important Letter from Mr. Dankmar Adler," *Inland Architect*, 25(July 1895), p.6.
99 Wright (1932), pp.127–128; Wright (1943), pp.131–133; Twombly, 1979, p.30.
100 On Gill's move to San Diego and thereafter his influence on Wright, see Johnson (2013a).
101 For a list of Sullivan's writings, see Elia (1996), pp.185–186.
102 Both were *New York City Magazines*, see Sullivan (1918), pp.8–9; Twombly (1988), introduction, pp.123–125, 131–144; Brooks (1972), pp.37–39; Wright (June 1900), p.127. "To the young man architecture" was a phrase borrowed by Wright and used often, even beyond 1935.

After lengthy visits in 1900 and later, English architect Charles Ashbee found Sullivan to be a "strange half coherent genius who first struck the light of life into [American] architecture...," from Ashbee's unpublished "Memoirs" as quoted in Twombly (1986), p.397.
103 Proposed foreword penned by Sullivan, 10 July 1918, Sullivan (1918), p.15.
104 [A.D.F.] Hamlin, "The Influence of the Ecole des Beaux-Arts on Our Architectural Education," *ARecord*, 23(April 1908), p.147, reprint *Columbia University Quarterly*, 10(June 1908); In 1896, Hamlin had published the first American-authored book on the subject: *A Text-Book of the History of Architecture* (New York).

For a historical outline of education, see Draper (1987); for more interpretation, Bletter (1981), esp. pp.103–106; for raw data but no analysis, see Noffsinger(1955). These studies can be compared to designs in Hélène Lipstadt, "In the Shadow of the Tribune Tower: American Architecture Competitions, 1922–1960," in idem., ed., *The Experimental Tradition: Essays in Architectural Competitions* (New York: Princeton Architectural Press, 1989).

Counters to total French influence are evaluated in Anthony Alofsin, "Tempering the Ecole: Nathan Ricker at the University of Illinois, Langford Warren at Harvard and Their Followers," in Wright and Parks (1990), pp.73–88. Parallel events in Europe are outlined in Roger-Henri Guerrand, "Introduction" to Frank Russell, ed. *Art Nouveau Architecture* (London: Academy Editions, 1979), pp.9–13. See also Mosravansky, "Educated Evolution: Darwinism, Design Education, and American Influence in Central Europe, 1898–1918," in Martha Pollak, ed. *The Education of the Architect* (Cambridge, MA: MIT Press, 1997), pp.113–127.
105 Paraphrase of Joan Draper in Kostof (1977), p.217.

106 "Connection . . .," *Inland Architect*, 35(June 1900), p.43; cf. "The Annual Convention of the Architectural League of America," *Brickbuilder*, 17(September 1900), p.217.
107 Spencer (1900), p.61.
108 Wright (1908), p.164.
109 A recollection contained in Elmslie to Wright, 12 June 1936, made public by Mark L. Peisch in *JSAH*, 20(October 1961), pp.140–141. In the letter, Elmslie said Wright was "greedy for posthumous honor" in relation to Sullivan. Elmslie worked for Wright part time "to do a bit of drawing" for a few months around 1900.
110 Wright (1935), p.6.
111 Wright (1932), pp.95–96.
112 Wright (1946), pp.47, 51.
113 As put by Twombly (1986), p.viii. On Sullivan's decline as witnessed by friends and employee Elmslie, see Craig Zabel, "George Grant Elmslie and the Glory and Burden of the Sullivan Legacy," in Garner (1991), pp.1–41; idem., "George Grant Elmslie: Turning the Jewel Box into a Bank Home," in idem and Susan Scott Munshower, *American Public Architecture, European Roots and Native Expressions*, Papers in Art History from Pennsylvania State University, vol.5 (University Park, 1989).
114 Wright (1932), pp.104–105.
115 Wright quoted in Herbert and Donchin (2013b), p.88.
116 Wright (1957), p.18. Adler (1844–1900), son of "the revered" rabbi Dr Liebman Adler, learned some engineering while in the Union Army during the Civil War, see Twombly (1986), pp.96–97; Hyman L. Meites, *History of the Jews of Chicago* (Chicago: Chicago Jewish Historical Society, 1924), pp.393–394; Irving Cutler, *The Jews of Chicago* (Urbana: University of Illinois Press, 1996), pp.21–22.
117 FLW, "Louis H. Sullivan – His Work," *ARecord*, 58(July 1924), pp.28–29.
118 Wright (1946), p.43.
119 Root (1891), p.91
120 Taken from Adler's unpublished autobiography, as quoted in Twombly (1988), p.97, on an unspecified occasion.
121 Van Zanten and Robinson (2000), p.6.
122 As quoted by C. E. White in White to Willcox, November 1903, White letters, p.104.
123 Following the June paper and before mid-December 1900, Sullivan arranged to have his "Young Man" paper published and expanded and, during that period, decided to title the new series "Kindergarten Chats," Sullivan (1918), pp.5–10, 243.
124 Dankmar Adler, "The Influence of Steel Construction and Plate Glass Upon Style," *Proceedings of the Thirtieth Annual Convention of the American Institute of Architects*, 1896, pp.58–64. The article was a response to Sullivan's "The Tall Office Building Artistically Considered," *Lippincott's Magazine*, 57(March 1896), 403–409, where he states that "form ever follows function." Wright (1946), p.43, highly praised this article, as did Mumford (1952), pp.243–250. Adler's essay more directly approached the subject of industrialization and predates by four years similar arguments put by Wright in his "Machine" essay (Wright, 1901c), and by five years Sullivan's stylistic "Kindergarten Chats."
125 Menocal (1981), especially pp.43–44; see also Twombly (1986), pp.327–331. Of course, environment is within the notion of function, or, function does not exclude environment.
126 Menocal (1981), pp.43–44.
127 Quote from John Root's translation of Semper's "Development of Architectural Style," *Inland Architect*, 14(7, 1889), p.76.
128 Wright (1900), p.540.
129 Wright (1946), p.109, see also p.146.
130 Lewis Mumford, *The Condition of Man* (New York: Harcourt Brace, 1944), p.408. See also Manson (1955), p.299, unsatisfactorily revised in Manson (1958), p.33; James F. O'Gormann, "Henry Hobson Richardson and Frank Lloyd Wright," *Art Quarterly*, 32(3, 1969), pp.292–315; Gebhard (1960), p.63, quotes George Elmslie, "The Chicago School Its Inheritance and Bequest," *JAIA*, 18(July 1952), p.37; Manson (1953), p.349.

On Sullivan's independent years see, for examples, Sprague (1979); Ronald E. Schmitt, *Sullivanesque: Urban Architecture and Ornamentation* (Urbana: University of Illinois Press, 2002); Robert Twombly and Narciso G. Menocal, *Louis Sullivan: The Poetry of Architecture* (New York: W. W. Norton, 2000); Van Zanten and Robinson (2000); Twombly (1988), introduction;

108 *The aesthetics of progress*

O'Gormann (1973); Theodore Turak, "French and English Sources of Sullivan's Ornament and Doctrine," *PSR*, 11(Fall, 1974), pp.5–31. In declining years, Sullivan now and again designed houses aesthetically a la Wright, a fact further supporting a Wright School.
131 Manson (1958), p.30.
132 Brooks (1972), p.7.
133 Richard P. Adams has presented various literary and philosophical sources that unite in a linear manner certain influences – Coleridge to Greenough to Emerson to Furness to Sullivan to Wright – but excludes the shorter and more direct progression of Emerson to Reverend Jones and family, to Silsbee to Wright; see Adams "Architecture and the Romantic Tradition: Coleridge to Wright," *American Quarterly*, 9(Spring 1957), pp.46–62.
134 "New Laboratory Building," *The Corpuscle*, 3(November 1892), illus. p.30, text pp.58–59.
135 Wright (1935), p.6.
136 Wright was never considered a design collaborator by Adler & Sullivan. He began as a draftsman, and may have become head draftsman, but not above Mueller. Building plans on which Wright could have participated as a draftsman can be assumed by the chronology in Elia (1996), p.179, dates 1887–93 and 1893–94, and chapter 9; and in Nickel and Siskind (2010), pp.361–400. The K.A.M. Synagogue has been the Pilgrim Baptist Church since the 1920s and the birthplace of Gospel music.
137 As quoted in Carpenter (1953), p.99.
138 Carpenter (1953), p.101.
139 Wright (1914). On Wright's thoughts about organic theory after 1935, see Herbert (1959).
140 Sullivan quoted in Herbert (1959), p.22, and in Herbert and Donchin (2013a), p.94, italics added.
141 The discovery of DNA closed the door on vitalism. Those who have studied Emerson's writings allow non-specialists a reasonable understanding of his thoughts, cf. Carpenter (1953); Herbert (1959); Meg Brulatour, "Legacy of Transcendentalism: Religion and Philosophy," *American Transcendentalism*, Web, accessed May 2014; Leo Marx, "Lewis Mumford: Prophet of Organicism," Working Paper Number 2, Program in Science, Technology, and Society, MIT, n.d.; and so on.
142 Studies by and about Ruskin flourish, but see Keith Hanley and Brian Maidment, eds., *Persistent Ruskin, Studies in Influence, Assimilation and Effect* (Farnham: Ashgate 2013); Mark Swenarton, *Artisans and Architects:; The Ruskinian Tradition in Architectural Thought* (New York: St. Martins Press 1989), last chapter on FLW; Roger B. Stein, *John Ruskin and Aesthetic Thought in America 1840–1900* (Cambridge, MA: MIT Press, 1967), p.45; Rebecca Daniels and Geoff Brandwood, eds., *Ruskin & Architecture* (Reading: Spire, Victorian Society, 2003); see also Wilson (1987); Siry (1988), pp.170–192; early issues of *Craftsman*, where much of the literature is devoted to Morris, including Arthur Spencer, "The Relation of the Arts and Crafts to Progress," 2(June 1904), pp.228–233; Elizabeth Cumming and Wendy Kaplan, *The Arts and Crafts Movement* (London: Thames Hudson, 1991); Lears (1981), note pp.185–197, 225–235, 301–322; John Unrau, *Looking at Architecture with Ruskin* (London: Thames Hudson, 1978); Clark (1962); Nikolas Pevsner, *Ruskin and Viollet-le-Duc . . .*, (London: Thames Hudson, 1969).
143 As quoted in Middleton and Watkin (1980), p.380. Van Brunt was close to the Arts and Crafts Movement. Ruskin was widely read in the United States immediately after publication of each work and onward.
144 The observation of Levine (1973), p.502.
145 Porphyrios (1982), p.67.
146 As framed by Porphyrios (1982), p.67.
147 Various published and lectured versions of "The Art and Craft of the Machine," 1894–1930, are outlined in Narciso Menocal, "Frank Lloyd Wright as the Anti-Victor Hugo," *American Public Architecture*, Papers in Art History, vol. 5 (University Park: Penn State University Press, 1989), appendix A.
148 Alofsin (1993), p.22.
149 As quoted in Boris (MS.1981), p.344, Kropotkin would make a similar proposal.
150 Levine (1973), p.510, as taken from various of Morris' writings.
151 Wright and Perkins to Ernest Flagg, 4 March 1901, copy Wright Archive.
152 Collins (1965), p.155, and see supporting comments in Hoffmann (1969), p.174.

153 Wright (1910), introduction, n.p. In a letter of 11 April 1967 to Hoffmann (1969), p.173n1, William Wesley Peters (Wright's closest assistant post-1934) recalled that, to quote Hoffmann, "the only writers on architecture whom (Wright) had respected in his youth were Ruskin and Viollet-le-Duc." The late nineteenth-century conundrum is nicely analyzed in Richard Longstreth, "Academic Eclecticism in American Architecture," *Winterthur Portfolio*, 17(Spring 1982), 55–82.
154 Egbert (1980), p.66.
155 Middleton and Watkin (1980), p.38; see also Middleton (1982); Bressani (1989).
156 Hearn (1990), p.14. Reed (1954), p.27, believed that the ideas of Viollet went to America "from Le Corbusier rather than from Wright," and that Wright was "Le Corbusier's American counterpart."
157 Wright (1932), pp.52, 74, altered in Wright (1943), p.75. Two sons became architects, F.L.W. Jr. (b. 1890) and John Kenneth W. (b.1892).

Wright's childhood reading material was supposedly obtained from Madison libraries (but he did not "know in the least what he read in the [public high] school course," Wright [1932], p.52), and Reverend Jones All Souls Church library in Chicago. Grant Manson (1958), p.21, recorded that it was while in Silsbee's office that Wright began "a serious study of books on architecture" and claimed to have made one hundred "onion-skin tracings from 'The Grammar of Ornament' by Owen Jones and the 'Dictionnaire Raisonné' of Viollet-le-Duc," but not why they were made.
158 Wright (1946), p.136.
159 Wright (1946), p.136, apparently Wright arranged private tutoring in engineering for son John.
160 Wright (1946), pp.136–146. See also Hoffmann (1969) and Hoffmann (1973). Portions of *Dictionnaire raisonné* were published in the 1880s in *Building Budget* (Chicago), translated by Nathan Ricker, soon to be chair of architecture at the University of Illinois. It is likely that Wright read them. Some of Viollet's *Dictionnaire* essays on construction were translated by architect G. M. Huss in a book *Rational Building* (New York, 1895).
161 *Discourses*, VI, in Hearn (1990), p.220.
162 Wright (1908), p.167, slightly revised in Wright (1910), plate 33 description.

The important treatise Wright (1908) took some time to reach the public. In mid-1903, *ARecord* offered Wright the complete January 1904 issue. (Wright's friend, Illinois architect Andrew N. Rebori, had become a consulting editor.) The date was put off but not the offer. Wright thought of asking Russell Sturgis to write the piece but, after meeting Sturgis in Chicago during 1904, Wright became uncertain. The date was reset for July 1904, then Wright postponed it until after returning from Japan in mid-1905. An article about – but not by – him, "Work of FLW, Its Influence," appeared in the July 1905 issue. Finally, Wright wrote the article himself. The date of 1903 reveals an early and serious northeasterners' (the national tastemakers) interest in Wright. See Mary N. Woods, "History in the Early American Architecture Journals," *The Architectural Historian in America*, Elisabeth Blair MacDougall, ed. (Washington: National Gallery of Art, 1990), pp.77–89.
163 As quoted in Quinan (1982), p.168, where appendix K is the Sturgis (1908) essay.
164 Wright (1914), p.413.
165 Viollet-le-Duc (1954–68), tome 8, p.477.
166 Hearn (1990), p.13, his emphasis.
167 A.D.F. Hamlin, "The Battle of the Styles," *ARecord*, 1(January and April 1892), pp.265–275, 405–413, reprint in Roth (1983), pp.402–416. Hoffmann (1969) presented other parts of Viollet's treatises that may have attracted Wright. They are arranged under sections titled nineteenth-century disorder, engineering, reason, axiality, and primitive sources.
168 From Viollet-le-Duc (1879/1881), in Hearn (1990), p.89.
169 Hearn (1990), p.12, in speaking of Viollet-le-Duc's advocacy of a "logical system of principles, as opposed to rules."
170 White letters, p.106.
171 For example, Viollet-le-Duc (1863–72), in Bucknall's translation (1889), pp.209, 264, 267. Reference herein is also to Viollet-le-Duc (1854–68).
172 *Discourses*, X, in Hearn (1990), p.229. Middleton and Watkin (1980), pp.30–36, put Durand in a French context.
173 Adler quoted in Siry (1996), pp.120–122n115–116.

174 White letters, p.105.
175 As quoted in Wright (1932), p.77.
176 Viollet-le-Duc (1863/1872), pp.1–2, of Bucknall's 1889 translation, his italics.
177 Leopold Eidlitz, *The Nature and Function of Art, More Especially of Architecture* (London: Sampson Low, 1881), as quoted in Gifford (1966), p.405.
178 Hertz (1993) believes that, through Hugo and Viollet-le-Duc, Wright was able to "surmount" Sullivan.
179 Menoca (1981), p.89.
180 Sullivan (1905), p.338.
181 Emerson as quoted by Wright in Wright (1958), appendix. For the correct text, see *Essays of Ralph Waldo Emerson* (Garden City: Garden City, 1941), pp.524–529. See also Robert Lee Francis, "The Architectonics of Emerson's *Nature*," *American Quarterly*, 19(Spring 1967), pp.39–52.
182 Cf. Johnson (2004); Johnson (1990).
183 Wright (1910), pp.1, 3.
184 Upton (1998), pp.134–141.
185 Joseph Rykwert, *On Adam's House in Paradise: The Idea of the Primitive Hut in Architectural History* (Cambridge, MA: MIT Press, 1972), p.192. Rykwert's comments refer to Wright's publications *after* 1940, pp.17–19.
186 Cf. Alofsin (1993), pp.101–107; Levine (1996), pp.102, 114, 137–138; to mentioned two.
187 Johnson (2013a), chapters 6–7.
188 Eric Mendelssohn, "A Visit with Wright," cited in Brooks (1981), pp.708.
189 Johnson (2013a), chapters 5–7.
190 Viollet-le-Duc (1875/1971), p.vi, italics added to words that formed the title of a book edited by Hitchcock (1942) and that Wright first proposed in 1928 with the same title. Some of Viollet's illustrations and text speculate on the source of exotic house forms. Darwin's first text, *The Origins of Species by Means of Natural Selection*, was released in 1859.
191 Viollet-le-Duc (1875/1971), p.A (i.e. p.1).
192 Ibid., p.394.
193 *Discourses*, XII.
194 Viollet-le-Duc (1879/1881), in Hearn (1990), p.138. In Viollet's book *Learning to Draw*, the main character is a boy, and the literary method is similar to Rousseau's *Emile*.

4 Design generators

Geometry in nature is a perception but, interpretively, a human reconstruction, a reductive abstract. As applied, plain three-dimensional shapes were the stuff of architecture since the invasion of formalism during antiquity. It is within Egyptian and classical Graeco-Roman forms of pyramid, pediment, and triangle; of sphere, cylinder, and circle; of parallelepiped and rectangle; of cube and square. Each established the aesthetics of a building with, in a search for order, a tendency to axial symmetry and therefor to formality. The neoclassic romanticists of eighteenth-century Europe, together with Thomas Jefferson, among other enlightened Americans, were aware of those abstractions. So were Goethe and Froebel: the stone sculpture of Froebel's grave monument was a progression from sphere upon a cylinder upon a cube, each unadorned. It drew inspiration from Johann Goethe's 1777 stone sculpture he titled *Altar of Good Fortune*, composed of a stone sphere on a stone cube and placed in his garden near Weimar.

In 1881, American architect Leopold Eidlitz reiterated an empirical truth when he said that "Architectural forms, like musical compositions, contain a few elements, but these are capable of a great number of combinations."[1] The *structural* reduction, not an abstract, was reiterated – in H. H. Richardson's wake – by Louis Sullivan as "pier, lintel, arch," ignoring tensile or leaving it to engineers.[2] A proportional attribute, almost a motivator, proposed if not adequately used by Viollet-le-Duc and Berlage, was the triangle as they assumed it from French Gothic. Twentieth-century sculptors and painters also studied fundamental geometric shapes; cubism and abstractionism being two resulting types. But they also took much from traditional Japanese art and the supposedly instinctual responses of aboriginal societies as revealed in artifacts discovered in Southwest Asia, Africa, and Mesoamerica by people engaged in the new social science of archeology. Architects reacted more or less in tandem with those revelations. One practical reforming concoction knitting those potentials was called pure design. Another, resting with ancient traditions, was the revival of artistic conventionalization.

Conventionalization's limits

In 1897, Wright designed the title page of one issue of the new Chicago-based Arts and Crafts magazine *House Beautiful*. It depicts an abstracted tree and nine boys in line, each "stands in profile" resting his right leg, while the left hand balances a cube on his head. Narciso Menocal has fairly interpreted the design as follows:

> Wright intended these figures to be as much like trees as their nature allowed.... The contour line of the bodies ran uninterrupted except at the point where there right foot touches the earth. Presumably it is through that aperture that the youths received the powers of nature. Correspondingly, it is through the gesture of placing a cube on their heads that they transmute that force into intelligence. The square symbolized integrity....
>
> [The tree's] geometrical essence [and] the cube – stand for the basic geometrical essence of the universe, which to Wright was the source from which everything derived.[3]

112 The aesthetics of progress

We've discovered that within Wright's received knowledge the philosophic and spiritual source was the sphere. Nonetheless, the idea of an abstract essence was taken from his uncle, Reverend Jenkin Jones, and by reading authors such as Goethe, Carlyle, Emerson, and Froebel.

Observing Sullivan designing ornament, analyzing the illustrations in Owen Jones's comparative study *The Grammar of Ornament* of 1856, and reading Viollet-le-Duc's treatises ensured Wright's knowledge of conventionalization. There was an "inevitable" route from satisfying an architectural problem as the "highest function in relation to human life," he said in 1908, to possessing "harmony" as a "sure foil for life" in "broad simple surfaces and highly conventionalized forms." Or more practically, he believed conventionalization gives a "quality to style."[4] One needs only to reflect on his leaded colored-glass window designs based on local vegetation or on Sullivan's colored terra cotta or cast-iron ornament and embellished interiors.

Wright more fully appreciated conventionalization's modernizing potential during a stay in Europe from 1909–10. There, he experienced French art nouveau and German and Viennese secession art, design, and architecture. In 1912, therefore, he could say with some conviction, "'conventionalization', that free expression of life-principle which shall make our social living beautiful because [it is] organically true."[5] By then, he had completed his most valuable works, with only Midway Gardens to come. Conventionalization had proven to be but one bent arrow in a quiver that held pure design, "pure form" (to some), and cubic design as more essential to a workable architectonic grammar.

The premise of conventionalization, as passed on from the eighteenth century, was that certain man-made geometric forms represent nature. Faithfully read by Wright, Owen Jones put it so: "Flowers or other natural objects should not be used as ornaments, but [as] conventional representations founded upon them sufficiently suggestive to convey the intended image. . . ."[6] Jones also believed conventionalization would in some tacit way be a "means of arriving at a new style" of architecture.[7] Experiments in art nouveau, the Aesthetic Movement, and art deco have proved otherwise. Conventionalization alone could not induce or support architectural design or planning methodology, let alone a workable concept in an architectonic or structural manner.

The pursuit for a modern expression was complex, but only in the United States did it involve and mature as a consequence of a *combination* of initiatives. The most critically important were:

1   studies of pure geometrical forms and
2   of primitive and native buildings to find first principles,
3   channeling nationalistic fervor toward a suitable modern indigenous art,
4   a search for a means to respond to new technical achievements, and
5   an awareness of and service to human social responsibilities.

Each initiative was within the realm of American Progressive thought. Only one and three were among Sullivan's inspiring exhortations in spite of his fellowship with the anarchist and architect John Edelman. The initiatives were not on Edelmann's list of priorities. One to five were in varying degrees of application internal to Wright's unorganized program. Some of his thoughts were exposed in the tedious 1900 paper to the Architectural League, in his "Arts and Crafts of the Machine" essay of 1901, and in his valuable 1908 treatise "In the cause of architecture," where the first sentence is: "Radical though it be, the work illustrated is dedicated to a cause conservative in the best sense of the word."[8]

The debate on the necessity for or on what a "national style" might be was a hot topic in the 1890s. Typical of the beliefs and feelings of young architects was found in a talk by Robert Spencer published in *Art for America* in May 1898 titled "Is their an American style of domestic architecture?" A few lines show the typicality of dissent:

> Twenty years ago, when the hard times following the civil war had given way to prosperity, and when men of wealth were ready to build . . . members of our profession who had enjoyed the advantages of travel and a liberal training were few, and no particular foreign

or historic style had any marked hold upon the public. . . . commercial architecture was in the cast-iron stage and in a very bad way, and in house building we were at the end of the "Mansard Roof" and "Italian Villa" period, and about ready for the "Queen Anne" trouble.

Of late years the reproduction and imitation on a costly scale of foreign examples has become rife . . . only a few . . . are still doggedly persevering in seeking the way to our architectural salvation on original and logical lines.

Let us hope . . . our trained and capable designers will again become *architects* [he emphasized] instead of imitators. . . .[9]

The cause of the Young Turks was not truly radical as it would conserve by applying first principles devoid of societal idiosyncrasies. Only then would there be evolutionary progress. That so, it became clear to those Turks that conventionalization might aid a designer of decorations, but it would not service architectural design in process and form.

Pure design

Attempts at self-education through Chicago-based societies and clubs were meant for those people who had not attended an architecture school, like Wright. Begun as a discussion group in 1885 and continuing as an informal school around 1895, in 1898, the Chicago Architectural Club began operating ateliers conducted by young architects Robert Spencer, Dwight Perkins, and Max Dunning. Wright, not a member, participated as a critic on a couple of occasions. The club was keen on the political and social arguments put by Arts and Crafts devotees and in their modest designs. It was attractive to some of the most Progressive of young draftsmen well before 1904, when the club opened a suite of meeting rooms downtown. In contrast to the professional associations of older practitioners, the club's "concern was design" where "the solution of social or functional problems by architectural form" was nearly a motto.[10] That architects should concern themselves with stratagems that might help solve social issues was a proposition resisted by most established practitioners. That purpose and the club's concerns for solutions through architectural planning and design cannot be overemphasized. The mode of search could not be within traditional schools of architecture or existing atelier-styled practices or a hide-bound AIA but by education of self and by young draftsmen-teachers. Members included not only the young atelier masters but also volunteers such as Myron Hunt, Webster Tomlinson, Walter Burley Griffin, Allen B. and Irving K. Pond, Thomas Tallmadge, a converted Peter B. Wight, Dwight Perkins, George Dean, Wright, and Louis J. Millet, a designer. In about 1899, the clubbers "proclaim[ed] a new principle that might revolutionize architectural design – a principle named 'pure design'."[11]

Parallel to and supportive of the club, landscape architect William M. R. French of the Art Institute oversaw the introduction in 1893 of what was then referred to as a Chicago School of Architecture. It was offered as multidisciplinary program between the Art Institute and Armour Institute of Technology, now Illinois Institute of Technology. Millet, Sullivan's one-time collaborator, became its founding director. He had studied in Paris for five years at the École des Arts Decoratifs and the École des Beaux-Arts and knew Viollet-le-Duc. At this time Millet and George Healy operated an "interior decoration" firm in Chicago. Then in 1899 French hired Emil Lorch, an MIT graduate who also studied at the Paris École des Beaux-Arts, as assistant director and manager of the Institute's architectural program. With other young architects Lorch mounted exhibitions at the club beginning 1900 in an Arts and Crafts room: Wright's work was displayed separately. Included in their 1901 exhibition catalog was an expanded version of Wright's essay "The Art and Craft of the Machine," and in 1902 his designs were again separately mounted.

Leagues in New York, Philadelphia, Boston, and Cleveland, and associated organizations in Toronto, Washington, Detroit, Pittsburgh, and St Louis, sent representatives to Cleveland in 1899, where they founded the Architectural League of America. In *The Architectural Annual*, Philadelphia architect Albert Kelsey "took the editorial position that Beaux Arts and archeological methods were inimical to true modern design, resulting in an architecture that was

114 *The aesthetics of progress*

'servile' and 'decadent'."[12] "Progress before Precedent" became the League's motto when they constituted themselves "To encourage an indigenous and inventive architecture and to lead architectural thought to modern sources of inspiration." Of course, "Archeological revivalism was the object of their special wrath"; therefore, the AIA was a target.[13] Sullivan was so excited about the League's philosophy and prospects that he rashly resigned from the AIA. Sullivan's encouraging message to the founding convention on "The Modern Phase of Architecture" was read by Webster Tomlinson. It was received as the "event of the meeting." Sullivan immediately became the movement's spiritual leader.[14]

On Millet's departure, early in 1901, Lorch encouraged the Art Institute to sponsor lectures by Bostonian artist and educator Arthur Wesley Dow about his reductive interpretation of two-dimensional composition in Japanese art. Spencer and Lorch followed with papers on pure design to the League's May 1901 convention in Philadelphia. Lorch helped formulate an application to architecture that prompted some controversy.[15] Historian Allen Brooks reduced "the idea of pure design" as follows:

> all architecture is based on an abstract, geometric order. To design a building, therefore, the architect must first analyze the component parts – each of which could be expressed by one or more geometric shapes – and then "compose" these parts so as to establish the basic massing of the building. This initial process was similar to a child's use of building blocks. Once the basic massing was established all subsequent aspects of the design would evolve from the abstract order of the unified parts. The detailing and decoration would be inspired by the abstract shapes that constituted the basis of the design.[16]

The process, therefore, was from massing to form to detail and ornament. But that misunderstood the design process, for it excluded planning. Even around 1900, it was agreed that shapes and volumes must be born of reason and include aesthetics. To most architects, then, the process was backward.

Dow also offered "universal" two-dimensional compositions that attempted to interpret Japanese art, usually as found in woodblock prints. He often used the square as a basic shape. Presented within its borders were possible spatial and linear configurations (see Figure 4.1). Impressed with Dow's ideas and Lorch's direction, the Institute's architectural program switched from a New England-styled beaux-arts curriculum to one that incorporated Lorch's understanding of pure design. Student and historian of pure design and Dow, Kevin Nute said,

> Essentially pure design entailed a reduced emphasis on historical styles in favour of a neutral vocabulary of simple geometric forms, and significantly Dow himself was directly associated [with] this movement. . . . [He] was invited to address the third annual convention of the Architectural League of America held in Philadelphia in May 1901, a conference dominated by the topic of pure design.[17]

Wright found this interesting stuff, even if it did not logically serve architectural planning. But it served him well when designing ornament, as witnessed in his designs for colored-glass windows or light fixtures or, much later, the concrete block houses in Los Angeles of 1923–25.[18] However, relevant to his inspired ink presentation drawings as published by Wasmuth in Germany in 1910–11, he was specific: "Their debt to Japanese ideals, these renderings themselves sufficiently acknowledge," self-evident.[19] Such a statement does not imply that he employed Dow's ideas for the renderings. They do indicate that he, too, had studied Japanese crafts and two-dimensional art.

In March 1901, the Chicago Architectural Club, then housed within the Art Institute's building, sponsored an afternoon's discussion on pure design and on the theory of progress.[20] The seminar took up the question "How can pure design be best studied?" Their understanding was not helped by one of the founders, so to speak, of pure design, Denman W. Ross, who said, "By Design I mean Order in human feeling and thought" and how they are "expressed." And again: "By Pure Design I mean simply Order, that is to say, Harmony, Balance and Rhythm." If

Design generators 115

Figure 4.1 Two-dimensional "Line-ideas" composed within a square as drawn by Arthur Wesley Dow; all drawings are variations of pattern No. 17, top left, except the middle three at the top and bottom line of "dynamic" compositions. From Dow, 1899.

simply order, why the term "pure design"? Like Dow, Ross linked order to music: "Pure Design appeals to the eye just as absolute Music appeals to the ear." But he did not define "absolute Music"[21] but it refers to abstract music i.e. not to a program. Therefore, answers varied. Julius E. Harden from New York offered a bland reconciliation at the end of often-heated debate:

> It is all very well to make demands upon the [architecture] schools. The school itself must have opportunity for healthful life, its own disposition, its own environment. The hereditary disposition of the American school must be the spirit of American . . . inventiveness and progressiveness.[22]

116   The aesthetics of progress

The reply of a Mr Watterson referred to a Mr Marshall's article on the "Education of an Architect" and used words that could have been spoken by many looking for points of departure:

> we must teach our architectural student most emphatically to work in structural forms, . . . we should [also] follow the developments of the past, *i.e.*, that we should endeavor to teach the youth the principles of beauty and how to apply them to structural forms. . . .[23]

In a separate paper published during that March, Robert C. Spencer thought pure design as analogous to abstract design. He then attempted to define pure design as "principles" and "Ideals" found in "various media," chiefly "the field of decorative art." Yet he did not refer to Dow. Only a few months before, Spencer had published in *Architectural Record* a major article about his good friend Frank Wright.[24] Thus, it is not surprising that much of Spencer's piece spoke in a manner suggestive of Wright's and Sullivan's thoughts. For instance, kindergartens are an educational foundation and look to the "unconscious, inevitable, natural obedience to Nature's laws" and to ancient "principles."[25] Lorch was more educationally practical when he advised that

> In architectural design instruction – how to strengthen and draw out the analytical power, the appreciation and invention of the architectural student . . . how to make him not an *adaptive* but a *creative* worker [he emphasized], or an artist-builder – an architect.[26]

From techniques found in Dow's system of two-dimensional lines, patterns, and visual effects, Lorch went on to three-dimensional exercises in the molding of form: cylinder (column), parallelepiped (rectangle), cube (square), and the other geometric and natural and rhythmic conventions that might freely combine into complex compositions. From the record of his work pre-1917, we know this intrigued Wright to a critical level. His elliptical postmortem rationalization was that

> Design is abstraction of nature-elements [in] purely geometric terms – that is what we ought to call "pure design." . . . But – nature-pattern and nature-texture in materials themselves often approach . . . the abstract. . . .[27]

Architect Cass Gilbert gave a talk about "Progress." Like most colleagues, he believed progress was linear: a "few boughs across one stick to another" for shelter to evolve into a house; or from a "dugout" log to a steamship; or the entablature and pediment to be "cast aside as useless"; and so on. Stirring words perhaps, but not practically helpful. However, at one point he said, "The architect deals with two elements of human life, the material and the spiritual; the engineer deals with but one, – the material. Which is the greater of the two?" Is architecture possessed "of undefinable spiritual elements"? Later in Gilbert's piece he offer the following: There was a "time when the broad [Western] prairies had scarcely a house upon them, when there was scarcely a tree, when there was scarcely a road, . . . and yet within our short lifetime those prairies have been developed." He went on to give "thankfulness" for the gift of power over nature.[28] Here, he intones the Christian ethic of nineteenth-century English thought on the perfectibility of nature through man's improvements, on humanity's material development. On this, Wright could not agree because he was imbued with Emersonian beliefs in the eminence of nature, the great teacher.

At their third annual meeting in Philadelphia, encouraged by Lorch, Spencer, and Millet, the League endorsed the principles of progress and pure design, even if the majority of participants were unsure of what they were.[29] After studying Lorch's papers on pure design, historian David Van Zanten believed that pure design "was a pedagogical system to free young artists from adopting ready-made historical solutions because of the lack of a system for thinking design through from first principles." In 1901–02, Sullivan wrote a series of articles on the theory of architecture and on education titled "Kindergarten Chats." They were his contribution to the progress and pure design debates. They achieved their goal of inspiring students, laypeople, teachers, and – possibly – potential clients. But they failed to provide a methodology for the lazy minded.

In 1908, architect Thomas Tallmadge, a disaffected follower of Sullivan and the Wright School, was openly critical, stating that the slogan Progress before Precedent was as "illogical as it was tactless." Tactless? Could progress and precedent "journey together?" But "what is pure design?" he asked, noting that

> [finding] answers filled the columns of the architectural papers for some little time [he said], until it was pretty well demonstrated that nobody knew what it was.... [T]he storm center of [this agitation] was Chicago and its Architectural Club, [and] it is not hard to see that all of the pleading was on one side. Very little interest and no concern was manifested by the East[erners]....[30]

But of course. Sullivan found the slogan "neither valuable nor objectionable." Wright thought it "alliterative" and "trite at best." Architect and historian Russell Sturgis believed progress was "founded" on precedent. William Jenny favored it because – and here he drew from the League constitution – we must "free architecture from vulgar importations." And so on.[31] However, Perkins, Sullivan, Gill, and Wright knew how to apply the geometrical elements inherent in Lorch's pedagogy. Wright was less confusing when, in 1912, he offered a common interpretation, saying in part that

> certain geometric forms have come to symbolize for us and potentially to suggest certain human ideas, moods and sentiments – as for instance: the circle, infinity; the triangle, structural unity; the spire, aspiration; the spiral, organic progress; the square, integrity.... [In] elemental geometric forms, we do sense a certain psychic quality which we may call the "spell-power" of the form, and with which the artist freely plays, as much at home with it as the musician at his keyboard with his notes.[32]

We've seen that to Wright "spell power" meant that metaphysically geometry was a "deep resonant, essential force." This suggests he had a knowledge of vitalism.[33]

As the titled of Sullivan's "Chats" confirm, the new pedagogy was to parallel aspects of kindergarten teaching, an educational program eagerly supported by all Progressive architects. At times, Sullivan's post-Adler buildings were referred to by colleagues as "toy block" architecture. In post-1901 practice, Wright and like-minded architects applied a basic design process that proceeded from functional planning to basic geometric form to detail. Three buildings by architect Dwight Heald Perkins (one jointly with Wright), one by Sullivan, and one by Irving J. Gill add clarification.

Reverend Jones's Abraham Lincoln Center of 1903–05 opened on a street corner across from Jones's Silsbee-designed, wood-shingle-covered All Souls Church of 1886. Words pale before the visual evidence of the two buildings, just seventeen years apart (see Figure 6.3). One exemplifies a highly romantic yet positive break from historicism, the other a cubic abstraction without historical or religious referents. Reverend Jones was a tough, unwavering client who wanted the new church building to, in his words, "[interpret] the spirit in which this Centre is reared, – simple dignity and plain honesty, – for these constitute the first and indispensable elements of good art everywhere."[34] Reverend Jones was no doubt aware of the architectural debates then under way. His plain, unadorned rectilinear block building in red brick overall with chocolate-colored brick string courses that expressed internal floor levels. The windows, all without colored glass, were contained by unfashionable iron sash. We shall return to this building.

In 1905, the Chicago Board of Education was well aware of Perkins's architectural ideas and products. After obtaining a high score for a civil service exam, they hired him for a five-year term as their chief architect. His 1906 design for the John B. Rogers school had an exterior character that, in spite of his published disgust of Reverend Jones's reductive lesson for

118 *The aesthetics of progress*

Lincoln Center of just a couple years earlier, was well learnt. In 1907–08, Perkins proposed a series of school plans that could be repeated on any flat site. Usually, one design was constructed at two sites in opposite corners of the greater Chicago. However, the Alfred Nobel Elementary School was repeated for the Harper, Gary, Corkery, and Cleveland schools. The design for the James H. Brown School was used only once, as was the landmark-designated Carl Schurz Public High School, both from 1908–10. Another design was for the George Tilton and Lyman Trumbull Elementary schools, the latter of 1908. (The Trumbull school was closed in June 1913.)

The Tilton model was designed in 1907, and basic functional parts were plainly expressed in bold rectangular massing unornamented (see Figure 4.2). Small storage rooms that on the exterior look like stair towers were capped by shallow pyramids in high relief. On elevations, they interrupt the stacked boxes of classrooms that surround a large auditorium whose ceiling was of great vaults sheathed in plain plaster. The only exterior embellishments were a few simple pediments at entries and straight brick coursing that alternated light red and cream. Also, and as another nod to pure design, clear glass transom lights above entry doors were composed in lead of two squares with diagonals to corners. Like Lincoln Center, the bottom floor was slightly battered on the exterior.[35]

Of equal interest is a design supervised by Perkins of a "Proposed Commercial High School Building" where the upper four floors were for "administration purposes" of the Board of Education (see Figure 4.3). Floor plans are unknown, but the exterior was dominated by a bold composition of squares and rectangles to form oversized high-relief ornament for two principle facades. The only other ornament was on the surface between widows, Sullivanesque in appearance, on the four upper floors, perhaps indicating the administration's area. The thirteen-story building would have been the ultimate pure-design skyscraper.

Sullivan's National Farmers Bank in Owatonna, Minnesota (1906–08), was composed of two brick boxes united by a base course of terra cotta. While of the period, more useful herein is his Merchants' National Bank in Grinnell, Iowa (1913–14). Clearly a parallelepiped box two

Figure 4.2 Front elevation in 1908 of the George W. Tilton Elementary School in West Garfield Park, Chicago, Dwight Perkins, Board of Education architect, 1907–08. From author's collection.

Figure 4.3 Perspective of "Proposed commercial high school building, Harrison Street and Plymouth Court" in Chicago, Dwight Perkins, Board of Education architect, 1908. From *Annual Report of the Board*, 1908–09.

cubes long, it had wonderful terra cotta and brick ornament on exterior, iron and plaster elements on interior. The entry facade (visually a square) was dominated by a great cream terra cotta square rotated within a square in luscious high relief about a circular window. As with his other banks, the interior preserves the impression of being inside an elaborately decorated box.[36]

The professional paths of Irving John Gill and Wright mingled, socially they crossed. Wright worked in Silsbee's office from 1886–87; Gill during 1890–91. They were together in the

Adler & Sullivan office from 1891 until both were laid of in 1893. Wright immediately set up offices in downtown Chicago and in his Oak Park house; Gill moved to San Diego. While using the precedent of Southwest Native American and the arch of California's colonial Spanish architecture as inspiration, Gill developed a universal theory that was likely suggested by pure design ideas as put by former colleagues. The local climate and flora, so different from the upper Midwest, were no doubt influential. In 1913, artist and "interpreter" Eloise Roorbach reiterated words spoken by the architect when she wrote that

> [Gill] resolved to go back to certain fixed principles like the line, square and cube . . . omitting everything useless [and followed] Schiller's observation that "The artist may be known by what he omits."[37]

Rather romantically, Gill believed that

> There is something very restful and satisfying to my mind [Gill said] in the simple cube house with creamy walls, sheer and plain, rising boldly into the sky, unrelieved by cornices or over-hang of roof, unornamented save for the vines that soften a line.[38]

His 1907 Allen house in Bonita southeast of San Diego was a creamish, flat-roofed stucco box with iron-framed windows without trim and seemingly punched-in walls (see Figure 4.4). Gill now and then employed the Spanish colonial semicircular arch but as a countering geometry, not for sentimental tradition. Consistently, his ascetic interiors were plain and devoid of ornament. As he matured, they became less fussy and homely, with fine wood cabinets of naturally stained wood again unornamented and in contrast to rose-white or cream-white plastered walls. The Simmons house of 1909 was the first of Gill's so-called cube designs.

The influence of the plain cubic architecture of the high plains of the American Southwest Indians became cloyingly popular during this period. Even the large and prestigious Chicago commercial firm of Holabird and Roche was persuaded when they designed the Case Deering holiday house at Waikiki Beach in Honolulu (1914–17).[39] The soft-edged, elemental cubic forms of desert societies were an inspiration not only for Gill and his partner Frank Mead,

Figure 4.4 Russell C. Allen house in Bonita, near San Diego, California, Gill & Mead Architects, Irving J. Gill designer, 1907–08. From Kamerling, 1993.

who had traveled throughout North Africa, but also for one strand of European modernism – notably, Algerian architecture for Le Corbusier fifteen years later.

A cast concrete sculpture titled the "Queen of the Gardens" holds aloft a cube. Designed by Wright in 1913 for Midway Gardens, it was "substantially carried out as he sketched" by sculptor Alfonso Iannelli. That winged sprite was given prominence by being centered over the main entrances inside and out.[40] In fact, plane, line, cube, sphere, and square were everywhere apparent on the building and in sculpted artworks (see Figure 4.5). It and Gill's houses presaged by a more than a decade the modernism developed in Europe. Specifically, Wright said, "The straight line, square, triangle and the circle were set to work in this developing sense of abstraction by now by habit to characterize the architecture, painting and sculpture of the

Figure 4.5 Centered above main entries to Midway Gardens in Chicago, 1913–14, were cast concrete sculptures (a sprite) holding a cube titled "Queen of the Gardens"; basic esquisse by Wright, sculptor Alfonso Iannelli. From Kruty, 1998.

Midway Gardens."[41] When nineteenth-century Parisian architectural editor and theorist César Daly rhetorically asked, "Are there symbols which may be called constant; proper to all races, all societies, and all countries?," English architect William Lethaby's answer was the circle and square.[42] About this time, with modesty, Wright said to Craftsman entrepreneur Elbert Hubbard:

> Not only do I intend to be the greatest architect who has yet lived, but the greatest who will ever live. Yes, I intend to be the greatest architect of all time, and I do hereunto affix "the red square" and sign my name to this warning.[43]

Wright used the square colored red as a personal logo, first in 1893.[44] Originally, a white circle was inscribed inside and tangentially touching four sides of the square, but it was an emblem often used by Arts and Crafts organizations. Like the logo, Wright's Monona boathouse project of 1893 was to be a circular building, with a high conical roof, set within a surrounding lower square building beside docks formed from a square in plan.[45] His "Theatre 1" project for an unknown client, and apparently of 1915, proposed a circular floor plan jammed into a square box. Sight lines and lack of space for backstage functions proved too difficult to resolve. Therefore, when the scheme was revived for Aline Barnsdall around 1918, the box was broken irrationally for what remained an unrealized project.[46]

In the 1950s, Wright said to assembled apprentices:

> when I chose a mark [a logo] – what the Japanese call a "mon" – for my work it would be that red-square. The square stands for integrity and the flame color for life – the color of life every-where you go is red.[47]

In the January 1938 *Architectural Forum*, an issue he was commissioned to write and design, Wright placed the following two quotations beside a red square:

> Chanting the square deific,
> Out of the one advancing out of the sides;
> Out of the old and new,
> Out of the square entirely divine, solid – four
>   sided – all sides needed,
>   I am time, old, modern as any.[48]
>   —Walt Whitman

> The color red is invincible. It is the color not only of blood – it is the color of creation. It is the only life-giving color in nature filling the sprouting plant with life and giving warmth to every-thing in creation. . . .[49]
>
> —Kliment Timiryazev

A metal plaque placed on a wall outside Wright's Oak Park studio in 1898 contained in relief his name and profession, six triangles, and a circle touching tangently a square's sides and centered by a Celtic cross. He reused the cross twenty-five years later for a design in relief for square concrete blocks, notably for the cubic Millard house.[50] In 1912, he believed that

> at the beginning of structure lies always and everywhere geometry. But, in this art, mathematics begins and ends here, as the mathematical begins and ends in music, however organically inherent here as there in the result. . . .
>
> [I]n design, that element which we call its structure is primarily the pure form, an organization in a very definite manner of parts or elements into a larger unity – a vital whole. . . .

[It] is primarily the pure form, ... grouped to "build" the Idea; an idea which must always persuade us of its reasonableness. Geometry is the grammar, so to speak, of the form. It is its architecture principle.[51]

In 1942, Wright rejoiced: "This cube – this square – proportion."[52]

Dynamics of the square

Having discovered why Wright used the square and proportions of it, we must understand how he evolved one aspect of a design method by simple geometry. The geometrical constructions herein were generally understood at the end of the nineteenth century and used on the drawing board.[53] Two essential characteristics of the square are considered in the abstract. We can usefully call these "design generators." The square contains within and on its equal boundaries certain potential linear and spatial dynamics recognized by many cultures. A diagram that was discussed by Rudolph Arnheim in the context of evaluating perceptual judgement,[54] Figure 4.6,

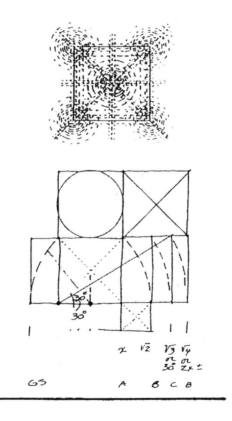

Figure 4.6 Top: Rudolph Arnheim's inferred dynamics of what appears to be a stable form, a square. Bottom: traditional extrapolations using T-square and compass to apply or confirm proportion.

124 *The aesthetics of progress*

top, dramatically illustrates the visual dynamics inherent in what initially appeared to be a stable form. Forms generated by further geometric dynamics were used by Wright more generally after about 1923, see Appendix A.

First, by extracting center lines normal to edges, a new set of dynamics is exposed. With exception of the lines, all spaces, points, and edges in Figure 4.7 are inferred. Therefore, inherent visual dynamics at the internal angles of the intersecting lines, and the implied continuation of parallel lines, results in four equal squares, 2a. Or, the points completing the square can be implied as in 2b1 or more directly by connecting the tips, 2b2, another square. Again, a series of implied spaces can be found by extrapolating the extensions created by the lines, 2c. A second characteristic is created by isolating the cruciform; the preceding comments correspond. In two and three dimensions, the spaces or lines can extend infinitely.[55]

Proportional systems based on squares were traditionally constructed with compass or forty-five-degree or thirty-degree triangles in a manner shown in Figure 4.7 (bottom). Obviously, measurement can be used, but in the early design stages, these methods, or a module, are quick and afford an ample range. GS is the golden section. Example B (from the theorem of Pythagoras) can be elaborated progressively, C,D. There is no evidence that Wright employed elaborations beyond the square root of 2. Each may determine a grid or proportions in plan, for instance, or a wall elevation. These were set out by illustration as early as 1521 in architect Cesar di Lorenzo Cesariano's translation into modern Italian of Vitruvius' treatise *De architectura* and published in Como.

French theorist J.N.-L. Durand attempted to codify, typify, and arrange. Although his relevant publications were begun in 1801 and completed in 1821, his system prevailed well into the

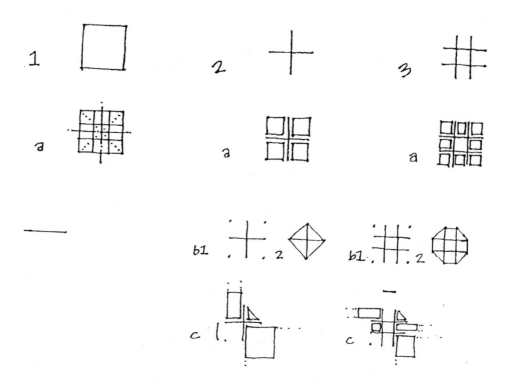

Figure 4.7 Typical formalities and dynamics apparent in potential proportions and symmetries of a square.

first third of the twentieth century.[56] It is, therefore, appropriate to look at a later and reduced permutation, one typical and influential of Wright (up to 1917) and some contemporaries.

A popular pedagogical and practical publication by Joseph Gwilt, *An Encyclopeadia of Architecture*, was first published in New York in 1842. Just when Wright began to seriously study architecture, the fourth edition by Wyatt Papworth was released in 1888. It introduced ideas generated by Durand and Viollet-le-Duc. In the chapter "Principles of Proportion," Durand's systemized planning was presented. One section was devoted to "Subdivisions and Apartments." Here, Durand's system was reduced to its essential grid and configurational patterns, and two illustrations conveyed its usability. The first (Figure 3.6, top) applies the "simple square," where the "thick lines of the diagrams" in plan are "either walls or suits of apartments. In that latter case the open spaces between them may become courts."[57] Another section was on "Points of Supports," and Figure 3.6, bottom, explains how points (like posts for beam or vault) and walls (bearing or partitions) can define apartments and spaces.

Schemes similar to Durand's and Papworth's are tools. They might aid the average architect but can only marginally influence the creative act. They might assist in stabilizing two- or three- dimension designs but exclude reason. In rigidity, they contain inherently fundamental problems, as well as the usual threat of convention, even ritual.[58] Wright was searching for a more responsively elastic methodology than that offered by nineteenth-century formulas and eclecticism. But there was something attractive in the logic of linking space and structure as rigorously delineated by Durand and Viollet-le-Duc. Their words and diagrams made it all clear, simple, and direct.

What about wood blocks and other geometric toys? Froebel's interest in crystallography was extensive; on one occasion he refused a professorship in mineralogy. He devoted considerable attention to the subject in his magnum opus about education. In a complex discussion about planes, energies, and directions (together implying vitalism), biographer Hailmann believed Froebel was attempting "to reduce all forms to one – probably the cube."[59] Crystals were the object of much speculation. Viollet-le-Duc also delved into their mysteries and extrapolated theories to support his view that "the systems of triangulation on which Gothic cathedrals were based as man-made replications of the triangles that composed the dodecahedrons . . . [that] shaped the crust of the planet."[60] To what extent he and Berlage were influenced by the Christian trinity tradition is here irrelevant. Wright shunned ideas that approached teleology. New Yorker and theosophist Claude Bragdon was certain: "I happen to believe that there is a universal canon of proportion, mathematical in its nature, to which the natural world conforms." With considerable conviction, biographer Jonathan Massey argued that, in an attempt to support Sullivan and the Chicago reformers, "Bragdon approached geometry as a symbolic system capable of revealing existential truths." He defined dimensional space "with a theosophical understanding of the fourth dimension as a transcendental space of human spiritual perfection." With less circumspection, Wright was unimpressed: "In this affair of cutting out the head of the drum to see where the sound comes from, Claude Bragdon is an enthusiast without an equal."[61]

+ + +

Prior to 1917, Wright's plans were a conscious result of applying components derived from the dynamics of the square with the resulting two- and three-dimension proportions. They provided the methodological nucleus of a design from the beginning of the process through refinements. Therefore, when used in conjunction with a module, it provided a rational and aesthetic order. Like Greeks, Muslims, Japanese, and Palladio, Wright discovered that the square and cube allowed an integrated system of proportion, aesthetic balance, planning coherence, and visual satisfaction. Once he realized by application in the design process the generative and ordering potentialities of geometry and simple form (simplicity, he echoed his uncle, Reverend Jones), he was – almost suddenly – free of past ways and means. Academic precision and formality were still accepted, but now traditionalism was easily rejected. He was free to explore, articulate,

126 *The aesthetics of progress*

define, and please himself and his audience. Audience participation was essential to the many ways of success for his creative works and national persona.

All of these challenges to theory and aesthetics ceased when, in 1917, he began planning the Imperial Hotel in Tokyo and gorged his mind with extravagant, voluptuous ornament for a recidivistic building.

It was not until 1932, perhaps with the Capital Journal building project for Salem, Oregon, did Wright begin searching for a new architecture.[62] Quite naturally, Wright continued to explore the dynamics of the square and related geometries. Lionel March and Philip Steadman presented some permutations of plan forms (see Figure 4.8). In column one, top to bottom, are plans by Claude-Nicolas Ledoux (Montmorency Palace, De Witt House, Inn St Marceau, Barrier de Picpus, and a House of Entertainment). In column two are two plans by John Soane (Supulchral Church and Kennels). Wright's plans are in column three: Annunciation Greek Orthodox Church of 1956; St Mark's Tower project of 1929; Huntington Hartford

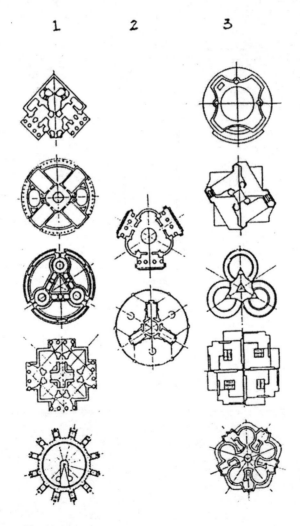

Figure 4.8 Plan forms of buildings using the square, including Wright's buildings in column three. After March and Steadman, 1971.

Clubhouse project of 1947; "Suntop Homes" quadruple house of 1939; and the Daphne Mortuary project of 1945.[63]

Architecture is an experiential art. It is so for the architect when producing his artifact of the drawn plan, of CAD, of model, of detailing, or for the user-audience enjoying the physical environment. Whether by Platonic order, Newtonian laws, Wofflin positivism, Transcendental symbolism, brick laying or carpentry or welding, architecture is created and exists temporally. Many aspects must work harmoniously to make each temporal experience seem rational and aesthetically stimulating such that we, the engager, are pleased. Vision is the most critical sense, proportion one aesthetic tool. As I have noted elsewhere in another context, the whole body, mind, and soul is immersed in an architectural experience. One cannot avoid participation. The architect reveals his ideas of how immersion is to take place at the conceptual level, the constructional process level, and the user's level. It is a personal revelation and process and aesthetic. It cannot be otherwise.[64]

+ + +

The elephant in this room of aesthetics is structure. During the first two decades of Wright's professional career, there arose to a practical level two structural materials that would forever change the man-made—the designed—environment: iron into steel in compression and tension and reinforced concrete in compression and plastic. Some form of metal and concrete had been

Figure 4.9 World's first Ferris Observation Wheel designed and built by George W. G. Ferris Jr. for the Chicago Exposition of 1893, then rebuilt in Chicago's Lincoln Park in 1895, then rebuilt as shown here for the Louisiana Purchase Exposition in St Louis, Missouri, 1903–04, its final installation and soon demolished. Note the standing man center-left. Dated 19 April 1904, from author's collection.

128 The aesthetics of progress

applied in antiquity and since.[65] In late nineteenth century, applied science and engineering refined the usability of those construction materials to such a degree that they became inexpensive enough for direct application, notably by civil engineers. Consider engineer George Washington Gale Ferris's Observation Wheel, designed in 1892 and constructed first in 1893 for the Chicago Exposition as shown in Figure 4.9. It was a bold example of the kind of engineering activity observed in awe by reform architects in North America and Europe. Wright was intrigued by these structural materials and engineering exploits but created a new aesthetic without them. Not until after 1935 did he explore their potential but in limited ways.

Notes

1 Quoted in Gifford (1966), p.409. On Eidlitz, see the valuable O'Gorman (1973). A praiseworthy review on the reissue of Eidlitz's 1881 book *The Nature and Function of Art* appeared in *ARecord*, (February 1915), p.192.
2 Sullivan (1905), p.337.
3 Menocal (1992), pp.79, 80; color illustration Hanks (1989), pp.122–123. Two of the boy figures were used again on either end of the second-floor exterior of the Luxfer Prism elevation for an office building facade of 1898, Pfeiffer (87–01), p.173; the design not for a complete office building as stated in Pfeiffer (2011), p.79.
4 Wright (1908), pp.158, 163; see also Joncas (MS.1991), pp.86–98.
5 Wright (1912), pp.77–78.
6 Own Jones as quoted in Alofsin (1993), p.120.
7 Alofsin (1993), p.120.
8 Wright (1908), p.155.
9 Robert C. Spencer, Jr., "Is There an American Style of Domestic Architecture," paper read before the Architectural Session of the Annual Art Congress, Central Art Association, Chicago, 3–5 May 1898, in *Arts for America*, I7(May–June 1898), pp.570, 572.
10 Van Zanten and Robinson (2000), p.74; see also Hasbrouck (2005), pp.18–62.
11 Van Zanten and Robinson (2000), p.75.
12 As put by George E. Thomas, "William L. Price Arts and Crafts to Modern Design" (New York: Princeton Architectural Press, 2000), pp.115–116, taken from "Expression in Architectural Forms," *The Architectural Annual, 1900* (Boston), p.19.
13 Constitution quoted in Dean (1900), p.92, and presented in "The Constitution of the Architectural League of America," *Architecture*, 1–2(January–December, 1900), pp.248–250; "wrath" in Van Zanten (1989), p.74, together with Van Zanten and Robinson (2000), pp.74–76, sources for much of the outline herein; Hasbrouck (2005), pp.265–271. In 1918, Frenchmen Le Corbusier and Amadée Ozenfant posited "purism" for two-dimensional painting only.
14 Louis Sullivan, "The Modern Phase of Architecture," *Inland Architect*, 33(June 1899), p.40, and *Architectural Annual* (Chicago Architectural Club), 1(1900), p.27. In volume two of 1901 see A. W. Baker, "Louis H. Sullivan, Thinker and Architect," and Charles H. Caffin, "Louis H. Sullivan, Artist Among Architects, American Among Americans," pp.49–68, from Van Zanten and Robinson (2000), p.162n12.
15 Cf. Nute (1993). Arthur Wesley Dow, *Composition* (New York, 1899, 1913, 1929) is a rather crude primer; see also Nute (1993), p.97n.10. Cf. Marie Frank, "The Theory of Pure Design and American Architectural Education in the Early Twentieth Century," *JSAH*, 67(June 2008), pp.248–273; Narciso G. Menocal, "FLW and the Question of Style," *Journal of Decorative and Propaganda Arts*, 2(Summer 1986), pp.4–19; idem., "The Origins of a Metaphor: FLW's Sense of Geometry," *Wisconsin Academy Review: Wisconsin Art History*, 32(March 1986), pp.39–45; Frederick C. Moffatt, "Arthur Wesley Dow and the Ipswich [Massachusetts] School of Art," *The New England Quarterly*, 49(September 1976), pp.339–355; Hasbrouck (2005), pp.287–288; Van Zanten (2013), pp.37–38.

The potential two-dimensionality – and very limited three-dimensionality – of pure design principles is found in the summation of propositions by a man Lorch met in Boston, Denman W. Ross, *A Theory of Pure Design* (Boston: Houghton Mifflin, 1907, reprint New York, 1933). Ross said elliptically: "By Pure Design I mean simply Order, that is to say, Harmony, Balance and Rhythm," pp.1, 5. Ross also lectured in design at Harvard University.

16 Brooks (1972), p.39, who referred to the discussion on pure design in *Inland Architect*, 37(1901), pp.33–35.
17 Nute (1993), p.87.
18 Johnson (2013a), chapter 4 and pp.130–132.
19 Wright (1910), introduction.
20 Announced to profession in [Notes], *Brickbuilder*, 10(March 1901), p.64. On other educational activities of the Architecture Club during 1900–01, see Hasbrouck (2005), pp.260–275.
21 Ross (1907), p.5; Johnson (2013a), p.87.
22 J. E. Harder, "Reply," *Brickbuilder*, 10(June 1901), p.118.
23 Mr. Watterson, "Reply," ibid., p.118.
24 Cf. Spencer (1900).
25 Robert C. Spencer, "Should the Study of Architectural Design and the Historic Styles Follow and be Based Upon a Knowledge of Pure Design?," *Brickbuilder*, 10(June 1901), pp.120–121. Lorch was George Elmslie's brother-in-law.
26 As quoted in Van Zanten and Robinson (2000), p.75.
27 Wright (1932), pp.159–160, his ellipses.
28 Cass Gilbert, "Progress," *Brickbuilder*, 10(June 3 1901), p.123.
29 [Report], *Architecture* (June 1900), p.224.
30 Tallmadge (1908), p.71.
31 Cleveland convention summations in Dean (1900), pp.91–97.
32 A close reiteration in Wright (1932), p.155; see also Wright (1957), p.19.
33 As put by Alofsin (1993), p.122. See also Joncas (MS.1991), pp.19–21. Joncas refers to "pure form" but avoids design processes, chapter 3, to be read cautiously, so, too, on Froebel, pp.40–55.
34 Siry (1996), p.47. On All Souls and Abraham Lincoln Center, see Siry (1991a). The examples in Nute (1993), chapters 5–6, are guesses and would have been rejected by Wright, who warned, we've noted earlier, that similar exercises concerning Froebel blocks were inappropriate.
35 [Tilton School], *Brickbuilder*, 18(November 1909), plate 141; [Trumbull school], *Brickbuilder*, 20(February 1911), p.41; Condit (1973), p.24n10; Brooks (1972), pp.112–114, for the Grover Cleveland Elementary School (1909–10) and the more elaborate Carl Shurz High; "Public School Architecture in Chicago, the Work of Dwight H. Perkins," *ARecord*, 27(January 1910), pp.494–508; *Book of the Twenty First Annual Exhibition of the Chicago Architectural Club* (Chicago: Art Institute, March 1908), n.p.; *Report of the Schoolhouse Commission . . . the District of Columbia* (Washington: GPO, 1908), pp.49–50, a good review of the school with floor plans; John Jones and Fred A. Britten, eds., *A Half Century of Chicago Building* (Chicago: Board of Education, 1910), pp.44, 76–78; Board of Education, *Fifty-Fifth Annual Report . . .*, (Chicago: The Board, 1909), Tilton School plate. Closure of Trumbull school, one of 50 to be closed, <chicagohistoric-schools.wordpress.com/2013/08/lyman-trumbull-elementary-school> accessed July 2014.
36 Van Zanten and Robinson (2000), pp.113–125; Narciso G. Menocal, "Sullivan's Banks: A Reappraisal," in Garner (1991); Lauren S. Weingarden, *Louis H. Sullivan: The Banks* (Cambridge, MA: MIT Press, 1987); Wim de Wit, "The Banks and the Image of Progressive Banking," in de Wit (1986), pp.159–188; Robert R. Warn, "Part II: Louis H. Sullivan . . . 'an Air of Finality'," *PSR*, 10(4, 1973), pp.5–19; Montgomery Schuyler, "The People's Savings Bank . . .," *ARecord*, 31(January 1912), pp.45–56.
37 Based on interviews with Eloise Roorbach, "'Outdoor' Life in California Houses, as Expressed in the New Architecture of Irving J. Gill," *Craftsman*, 24(July 1913), p.437. The Allen house was a Gill and Frank Mead commission. For an account of the relationship of Gill to Wright and Schindler, see Johnson (2013a), chapter 7; see also Thomas S. Hines, *Irving Gill and the Architecture of Reform* (New York: Monacelli Press, 2000); Bruce Kamerling, *Irving J. Gill, Architect* (San Diego: The Museum, 1993); Jordy (1972), pp.246–274.
38 As quoted in Kamerling (1993), p.57; Johnson (2013a), p.150, and on the mutual influence on Wright, Gil, Schindler, Wright Jr., inter alia.
39 Bruegmann (1997), pp.302–303.
40 Kruty (1998), pp.35, 50, plates J, K, L; Hanks (1979), p.120; Alofsin (1993), pp.140–152. For some of Iannelli's sketches, see "The Midway Gardens 1914–1925" (University of Chicago, 1961), pamphlet, figures 6–9. Illustrated in the Chicago Architectural Club's *Book of the Twenty-Seventh Exhibition April 9th to May 3rd 1914* catalog were the following: "Models / 308. Figures Decorating Winter Garden of the Midway Gardens. / A. Ianelli, Sculptor / The Cube / The Sphere / The Triangle / The Hexagon / Sprites."

41 Wright (1932), p.183; altered in Wright (1943), p.181.
42 Lethaby (1892), title page; see also the many designs in William Buchanan, ed., *MacKintosh's Masterwork The Glasgow School of Art* (Glasgow: A & C Black 1989).
43 As quoted in Wright (1946), p.33.
44 *FLW Drawings from 1893–1959* (New York: FLW Foundation, 1983), p.7.
45 Holzheuter (Summer 1989), cover, p.291; illustrated in Pfeiffer (2011), p.41.
46 Smith (1995), pp.18–19, 24–33.
47 As quoted in Pfeiffer (33–59), p.ix. When, in the 1950s, Wright found he could not copyright a square, he used a design of a common running square he first discovered, perhaps not in Japanese art but by reading Viollet-le-Duc (1875), p.87, and, of course, it is found in antiquity. "Mon" is the correct term.
48 Wright (1938), after p.102, poem not identified. In that issue, Wright quoted Whitman often and almost correctly.
49 Perhaps taken from Kliment Arkachievich Timiryazeff, *The Life of the Plant* (London: 1912), translated from Russian. His book on the life of Charles Darwin was widely translated and often reprinted.
50 Cf. Johnson (2013a).
51 Wright (1912), reprint, p.17. See also Menocal (1981), who extends, or rather amplifies, Wright's thoughts to support an iconographical interpretation.
52 Wright (1943), p.157; not in Wright (1932).
53 There are many relevant texts of greater sophistication: George Hersey and Richard Freedman, *Possible Palladian Villas (Plus a Few Instructively Impossible Ones)* (Cambridge, MA: MIT Press, 1992); Graf (1991); Branko Mitravic, "Palladio's Theory of Proportions . . .," *JSAH*, 49(September 1990), pp.279–292; Doczi (1985); Graf (1983); El-Said (1976); Munari (1965); and for vigorous practical applications, see Jonas Lehrman, *Earthly Paradise* (London/Berkeley: Thames & Hudson/University of California Press, 1980), on Mughal India.
54 Relevant studies of similar dynamics of architectonic form include McCarter (1991a); Munari (1965); Kief-Niederwohrmeier (1984); Abercrombie (1984); Graf (1986); less convincing is Douglas Graf, "Strange Siblings . . .," in John Whiteman et al., eds., *Strategies in Architectural Thinking* (Cambridge, MA: MIT Press, 1992); Levine (1982). Cf. Hanks (1979); Graf (1983); for pictorial evidence, see Heinz (1963) and the Pfeiffer series.

 Clark and Pause (1985, 2nd ed., 1996), contains geometric analyses of buildings from antiquity onward and includes some of Wright's buildings. The authors show dynamics noted herein and others. Although titled *Precedents in Architecture*, only geometrical forerunners are offered, not precedents.
55 Arnheim (1977), pp.2–5; Norberg-Schulz (1965), pp.4ff, draws on Arnheim (1977); Graf (1986) draws on Norberg-Schulz.
56 J.N.-L. Durand, *Précis des Leçons d'Architecture*, 2 Vols. (Paris, 1819–21); *Partie Graphique des Cours d'Architecture* (Paris, 1821); and *Recueil et Parallé le des Edificies . . .* (Paris, 1801–09). Useful studies of Durand and his colleagues are found in Middleton and Watkin (1980), pp.30–34; Collins (1965); Péres-Gomez (1983). See also Pevsner (1979), pp.33–34; Rykwert (1982), pp.60–65; Porphyrios (1977), pp.119–133.
57 Joseph Gwilt, *An Encyclopaedia . . .*, 4th edition by Wyatt Papworth, p.940. My copy is the ninth impression of 1903 with 1,443 pages. Editions of 1867 and 1876 were also by Papworth.
58 We are speaking of the period prior to ca. 1924. On Wright's square proportions (but not other dynamics), see McCarter (1991b), pp.258–261. McCarter uses "symmetry" contemporaneously, not as Wright understood it. See also Arnheim (1977), chapter 8; on rotation of the square, see Alofsin (1992), pp.168–175.
59 Froebel (1887), p.173. Froebel's study follows on from work carried out in the eighteenth century – for instance, on geometrical units forming crystals, see René Just Haüy in the 1780s but initially refer to Vidler (1977), pp.95–115; then Rubin (1989) and critical responses in the following issue.
60 As put by Menocal (1981), pp.70–71.
61 The Bragdon and Wright quotations were paired by editors of *AForum*, 70(February 1939), p.133, perhaps at Wright's request. Jonathan Massey, *Crystal and Arabesque: Claude Bragdon, Ornament, and Modern Architecture* (Pittsburgh: University of Pittsburgh Press, 2009), introduction.

Perhaps Wright flirted with theosophy, but surely he would have seen the non-logical – as distinct from illogical – generalities mixed with mysticalities as exemplified in Claude Bragdon's *The Beautiful Necessity* (Rochester: Manas, 1910), but see pp.36–39 on the "law of consonance"; see also Doczi (1981), chapter 8; cf. Eugenia Victoria Ellis, "The Red Square: FLW, Theosophy and Modern Conceptions of Space," *Theosophical History*, 15(April 2011), pp.3–14.
62 Cf. Donald Leslie Johnson, "FLW's Design for the Capital Journal, Salem, Oregon (1932)," *JSAH*, 55(March 1996).
63 March and Steadman (1971), p.59.
64 Cf. Donald Leslie Johnson, "Architecture Today. Two views," *Art and Australia*, 19(2, 1981), p.220.
65 On concrete, see Johnson (2013a), especially pp.10–18.

5 Architectural synthesis

During the first decade of professional independence, Wright's architectural designs were overtly contrived, no doubt in a frantic effort to find his own stylizations. Buildings were at times awkward in plan, massing, and elevation, now and then lapsing into bold display, noticeably for several houses. While working as a draftsman in Wright's office, architect Charles White witnessed the latter stages of those struggles and, in 1904, remarked that Wright

> was trying to break away from Sullivanism, and casting about for methods of self expression. His works of those days . . . [lacked] the stability and refinement of his present work. It was over-elaborated – covered with "ornamented ornament." His tendency of the last two years has been to simplify and reduce to the "lowest elements" (as he says). . . .[1]

In addition, materials were dark in color and used in a way that imparted a brooding massiveness that, together with heavy eave facias, tended to exaggerate a noticeable dumpiness; buildings appeared to press upon the earth. Critic and Wright's contemporary, poet Harriet Monroe, wrote that his "certain boxes" were too "square" and "squat." In a verbose letter in response, Wright hoped they did not "offend" her "dainty love of fleshly curves."[2] Socially, Wright purposely favored radical groups in which Monroe participated. At Hull-House, he met among others: Ashbee, Dewey, Florence Kelley, Julia Lathrop (Jane Addams, "She sympathized with me," said Wright, "as did Julia Lathrop"),[3] and listened to the like-minded people outside commerce; but not musicians of modern music.

A founding member of the Chicago Arts and Crafts Society at Hull-House in 1897, Wright was attracted to the movement's tendency toward leftist political and radical promotions. There was no favored Arts and Crafts style; rather, various products had the character of punk vernacular or of folk craft with an emphasis on materials. George Elmslie remembered that, while in Adler & Sullivan's office, *The Studio* was a magazine eagerly read by staff. It began in London in 1893, just before Wright's dismissal.[4] Another Arts and Crafts magazine, *House Beautiful*, was started in Chicago in 1897. Co-founder Wright was involved at the outset and provided designs for publication. Also of influence were the occasional published visual examples of European art nouveau and secession, but more especially of Japanese traditional designs. After a visit in 1900 to Wright's new studio, English designer and promoter of William Morris's idea of medievalized English Arts and Crafts, Charles Ashbee noticed that "the spell of Japan is on him."[5]

The Roycrofters (king's craftsmen) handicraft shops and press in East Aurora near Buffalo, New York, begun in 1894 (to 1938), attracted Wright, as did its socialist wizard, Elbert Green Hubbard. He was a founder with his brother-in-law John D. Larkin of The Larkin Company wholesale and mail order firm.[6] When Hubbard traveled to Chicago, or Wright to Buffalo to supervise construction of buildings, they often visited. Wright's son John remembered Hubbard: he "was almost as picturesque as was Father – they talked arts, crafts and philosophy by the hour."[7] Wright's furniture, cabinets, and interior decorative products, however, were highly sophisticated in design, use of materials, and joinery in comparison to the lumpy, often crude products of Roycrofters, or Gustave Stickley's United Crafts, later Craftsman

Workshop, or other similarly inspired companies. ("Crude furniture of the Roycroft-Stickley-Mission style . . . was plain [Wright once said], plain as a barn door – but was never simple. . . .")[8] Each based their designs more or less on English precedents, many with occasional Japanese flavors. No longer active in the commercial world, Sullivan now and then prepared short articles for Stickley's magazine *The Craftsman* during the years 1905–09.

Before 1897, Arts and Crafts idioms cannot be found in Wright's architecture. (Interior photographs of Wright's own house in the mid-1890s show a clutter of typical folksy stuff.)[9] But thereafter they permeate all of his designs, including pottery, ironwork, his wife's clothing, sculpture, and leaded glass. They were less an influence after he returned from Europe in 1910 and nearly disappear after 1917. Some earlier buildings may appear craftsman-like but only because they were part of a growing public interest in naturalesque recreational design, his own Lake Mendota and Lake Monona boathouses, for example, or related to the popular wood-shingled buildings, such as Queen Anne, as seen in the professional press or in Silsbee's Unity Chapel or Wright's own house.

Architect Robert Closson Spencer Jr. was a man described by his contemporary and coworker, the sculptor Richard Bock, as "an artistic chap, soaring in the clouds." In the 1900s, Spencer wrote about the theoretical attitudes Wright shared with Arts and Crafts movers and Progressive confederates.[10] Milwaukee born, Spencer earned a degree in mechanical engineering from the University of Wisconsin and, from 1887–88, studied architecture at MIT. Soon after studies, he was awarded the prestigious Rotch Traveling Scholarship. From 1891–93, he traveled about Europe and Britain. While there, he produced some commendable freehand drawings and watercolors. On return, Spencer gained employment in the Chicago office of Boston architects Shepley, Rutan & Coolidge before setting up a solo practice in 1895. With Cecil Corwin's departure to New York City, Spencer became Wright's closest friend. In an article, Spencer mentioned that "Among the decorative things" in Wright's studio/office were

> interesting vessels and flower-holders of sheet copper of Mr Wright's design, always filled with masses of summer bloom or trophies of autumn fields. . . . Casts of sculpture and architectural detail and exquisite examples of the new process of [Luxfer] electro-glazing, give added richness to the interior, through whose leaded windows a varied panorama of boughs or foliage is seen. . . .
>
> Externally the sculpted capitals of the porch and the nude figures crouching upon the [entry] flanking piers. [They take] a quiet fling at the reactionary spirits who dominate the "Arts and Crafts" movement.[11]

In a 1901 talk at Hull-House to the fledgling Chicago Arts and Crafts Society, Wright chastised the movement for intellectual myopia and regressive sentimentality, William Morris's politics aside. Wright's decorative designs, while exquisitely refined, were of that genre, although less cloying, notably his leaded glass and cabinetry for buildings.

Historian Allen Brooks's summation of the influential roles of the Arts and Crafts Movement in America holds true: one, it "helped foster the idea of a regional or national architecture"; two, its "plea for [aesthetic] reform through elimination, simplicity, respect for materials, and inspiration derived from nature" helped in "direction and goals;" three, its "concern for the decorative arts" appealed to layman and architect; four, it was "strongly held only by a small group of younger" people; and five, the angry young Chicago architects promoted its "concepts and ideals."[12]

Around 1898, Wright realized that he had two conflicting aesthetic systems for architectonic responses: domestic and non-domestic. One had deep eaves combined with an upper wall frieze immediately below and set upon a string course, all very horizontal. The other was box-like static forms usually accompanied by an overly inventive plan. He came to see that the second response had been awkwardly applied to houses like McAfee in 1894, Devin in 1896, Heller in 1896, and Husser in 1898. Their static individuated plans were reflected on the exterior by chunky, rather ill-proportioned masses and boldly ornamented fenestration and wall panels.

134 *The aesthetics of progress*

The second system, therefore, more easily fit his non-domestic architecture. As built, it was squarish, often squat, symmetrical in plan and elevation, if also inconsistent one building to the next. It is hard to believe, for instance, that the Monona boathouse of 1894, the Wolf Lake project in 1895, a facade employing Luxfer prisms of 1897, the Mozart Gardens project of 1898, and a village bank project of 1894 and reused in 1901 were by the same designer. Yet each was generated by application of the square in plan and elevation, the bank project of 1901 an example, Figure 5.1. So, too, the tallish Luxfer facade the main proportion of which was 1:√2.

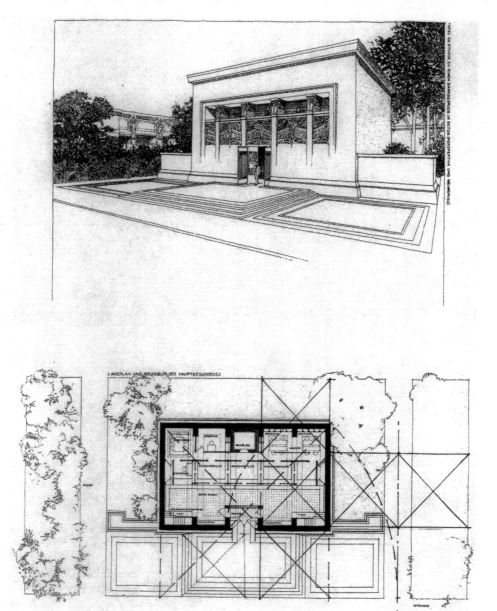

Figure 5.1 "Study for a concrete bank building in a small city / Illustrating an article contributed to the *Brickbuilder* [10 August 1901] . . . 'A Village Bank'," first designed in brick; author's notations. From Wright, 1910.

The Luxfer Prism Company was formed in Chicago in 1896: *lux* Latin for light, *ferre* to carry. Tiny horizontal prisms were in relief on the back side of four-inch, clear-glass square tiles. When a batch is collected together, they direct light deep into a room's interior. In 1897, Wright provided forty-one face designs, all responding to a square, but only his "flower" pattern was manufactured.[13] Historian Anthony Alofsin correctly observed that they "provided a marvelous primer of his basic design motifs."[14] To promote the new product, a competition was announce in January 1898 with aggregate cash prizes of $5000 for the best designs of a office building facade. Luxfer had asked Wright in 1897 to prepare two drawings that were presented with the January announcement and said, "The accompanying studies are suggestions for the use of Luxfer prisms in connection with the steel frame of commercial buildings." Wright describe his number one study in plain terms:

> No attempt at structural elaboration has been made, but the steel frame quietly and consistently covered with terra cotta. The openings are simply *covered* [he stressed] with rich screens of Luxfer iridian prisms set in slightly project frames of ornamental iron. . . . Openings with moveable iron frames for ventilation and filled with plate glass are introduced in the middle of this richly bordered surface of prisms. . . . The openings in the center of the plate which are here shown, about four feet square, are protected by a light canopy filled with prisms. . . .[15]

In April, additional time was given to competitors by jurors D. H. Burnham, W.L.B. Jenny, W. Holabird, physics professor Henry Crew, and Wright. Awards were announced in September 1898, and Robert Spencer got first prize for a complex building dominated by arcades. The front elevation employed square Luxfer glass set in square panels arranged in quadrants, the entire facade devoid of ornament.[16]

Wright's design number one of squares of terra cotta between which was square glass prisms with a smaller prism canopy before square glass was effectively a flush facade, all glass, and unique for the time period, if not prescient. Almost all illustrations of the facade are not of the original drawing but most likely one prepared for exhibition after 1898. Wright's number two facade was not plain but richly ornamental and reminiscent of Sullivan's work.

To return to Wright's house designs, a stylistic lineage is easily identified. He persistently claimed that his first design after leaving Adler & Sullivan was the Winslow house. He insisted it was recognized as designed and built in 1893 and predecessor to all that followed, but it was not. As outlined earlier, his "casting about" is also apparent for the Orrin Goan house of April 1893, so naively Sullivanesque in floor plan and elevation, it is the predecessor to the Winslow house of 1894–95. Yet even with Winslow, massing and elevational treatment were disarranged and inconsistent one facade to the next (see Figure 5.2). Volumetric and elevational

Figure 5.2 "House for Mr W. H. Winslow in River Forest Illinois"; trace of a photograph; buildings in background repeat roof lines of house. From Wright, 1910.

136 *The aesthetics of progress*

parts, such as the port cochere and stair tower, seem added and even disparate. The interior and exterior were an amalgam of Alder's planar attributes, of Sullivan's formal elevational compositions, moldings, and ornament (including a diaper frieze), and of H. H. Richardson in window and door treatment on the front face. The front facade was conceptually a domestic scaled version of Adler & Sullivan's Victoria Hotel in Chicago Heights in late 1892 and Sullivan's entry ensemble to the Charnley house in 1890; Wright had worked on the drawings of both.[17] Importantly, the Winslow plans and exterior appearance were not used again, a design dead end, as was the formal symmetrical entry sequence.

The studio, golf clubhouse, and stables

Wright's studio, 1898 onward

"Studio": it was a beaux-arts and Arts and Crafts word for a workroom and preferred over "office" or "factory" or "rooms" by some architects. Before designing the studio, a square was an organizational part of most floor plans and often determined proportional treatment of elevations. After all, Sullivan used it as the basic frame of his ornament, for instance, and the principal face of his Wainwright building with a proportion $1:\sqrt{2}$, and the Getty Tomb in Chicago of 1890–91, where two facades were square. But that alone could not generate a universally applicable design methodology that in consequence would assist in creating a theoretically related series. It was for the studio addition to Wright's house that experimentation with dynamic aspects of the square was tied to notions of functional articulation and later to pure design (see Figure 5.3).

As Charles White said of his boss in 1904, "Frank Wright hates anything but square bays."[18] Then, a "bay" was known as a portion of a plan or building contained between adjacent piers or columns. In 1910, Wright said that "The studio is merely an early experiment in 'articulation.'" The use of "merely" was not to understate but to indicate simplification. And further,

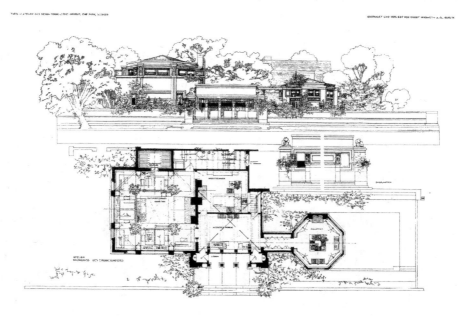

Figure 5.3 "Atelier of FLW, Oak Park, Ill" / "An early study in articulation – the various functions featured, individualized and grouped." Space for eight in drafter's room; fireproof vault; eyebrow roofs on four sides of the octagon library are not shown; author's notations. Composite of original plans in Wright, 1910.

the studio was "an early study in articulation – the various functions featured, individualized and grouped."[19] This idea held firm over the decades. White, who worked on the Unity Temple drawings, commented that "the motif . . . is an evolution of Wright's Studio. An entrance in a link connecting a dominant, and subordinate mass."[20] Wright described the Ennis house of 1923–25, in the Los Feliz district of Los Angles, as "Articulation Emphasized by Texture."[21] The volumes containing bedroom or living/study/dining room or service (kitchen, etc.) had a slightly different concrete block and/or wall pattern on interior and exterior, and each volume differed in size as determined by internal function. Thus, articulation was also emphasized by volume. Later, there was the "zoned house" project of the mid-1930s, and then Ralph Jester's house project of 1938.[22] White offered another valuable observation in 1904:

> The studio is again torn up by the annual repairs and alterations. He [Wright] says he has gotten more education in experimenting on his own premises, that in any other way. [White then mentioned] how everything is in simple square planes in keeping with the horizontal and perpendicular lines of the house, while the angle in the plan, repeats the shape of the roof. . . .[23]

One is confident that those words paraphrased Wright's.

The original house of 1889 was rather plain and wood shingled, its floor plan developed from a square, and typical of the period with some innovations of a minor kind that have been given much undeserved attention.[24] In 1895, Wright expanded the house, top left in (see Figure 5.4), and when, in 1898, it became his main office, Figure 5.3, a drafting room,

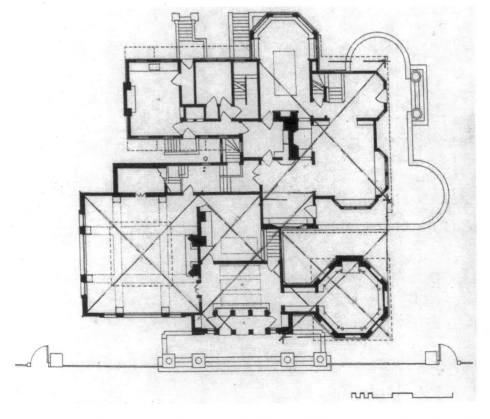

Figure 5.4 Ground-floor plan of FLW's home and office, ca. 1898; author's notations. From Riley, 1994.

study, reception area, and display/library (the octagonal plan at right) were added.²⁵ Open to drafting tables below was a balcony to which surrounding high windows in an octagon offered diffused daylight to the drafting room. "Individualized and grouped functions" were the separate octagon at right, also with high windows, attached by an umbilical to reception and Wright's office that was treated as transitional to the major masses of the drafting room (left) and library. It was a tripartite scheme composed by simple geometry. To the library's exterior, Wright added a shingle-covered parapet and a square eyebrow roof overhang that reiterated the room's geometry in plan and proportionally in elevation. Also, the square eyebrow overhang directly related to the soffit line of the house (see Figure 3.3).

Additionally, the entry, with its symmetrically disposed doors (one in, one out?), was further articulated in plan and frontal elevation with piers defining deep, safe recesses from sidewalk and street traffic. The reception area and Wright's office were rather formally arranged behind the entry. The drafting room and its balcony (the edge hung by chains) were composed about two axes, symmetry obvious.

The question that intrigues an analyst is: How did he aesthetically resolve the "articulations"? As observed by White, it was by application of the square as a design generator. In plan, the position of various rooms (not to be confused with a functional arrangement), walls, and piers, and even site position, were determined by a square and its derivative, $1:\sqrt{2}$. The two-story drafting space and separate library were capped with angled roofs recalling their octagonal interiors and the older house roof, as White described. In elevation, the square was applied sequentially and formally to the two principle volumes and to lines and elevational parts. A minimum of ornament enhanced those relationships, as did materials. Brick on the exterior of the drafting room and library gave way above to wood studs covered externally with cedar shingles, a reference to the house, and cream-colored plaster and dark-stained wood trim inside.

Golf clubhouse, 1898–99, 1901

A prophetic architecture with attributable successors to what became the Wright Style, quickly followed by a Wright School, was initiated with the golf clubhouse and Winslow stables of 1898.²⁶ In Wright's 1942 book *In the Nature of Materials*, historian and joint author Henry-Russell Hitchcock referred to the "maturity of design" of the River Forest Golf Clubhouse. The attending photographs were of the 1898–99 building, Figure 5.5, and the complex 1901 plan that restored and enlarged the fire-damaged original building.

The golf club was formed in July 1898, with a membership of sixty men. Six holes were laid out immediately and, by 1900, when Rollin J. Furbeck was club champion, three more had been added. E. C. Waller was a director, and most of his family were members, as were Wright and sister Maginel. Many of Wright's present and future clients were members, including Furbeck. Wright was likely hired that July to prepare architectural plans for a new clubhouse. It was reported on the front page of the 10 March 1899 issue of the *Oak Park Vindicator* as complete. The formal opening occurred on 30 May 1899, and music was supplied by the Oak Park Banjo Club. In early 1901, a fire partially destroyed one end of the clubhouse. In 1901, "Architects Frank Lloyd Wright & Webster Tomlinson" were engaged to restore and enlarge the house. In 1905, the River Forest Golf Club merged with its westerly neighbor Westward Ho Golf Club, formerly the Oak Park Golf Club. Late in 1905, the River Forest clubhouse was demolished to make room for premises and courts to suit the River Forest Tennis Club's. Some of its members were Wright's clients, and he was commissioned to design their clubhouse.²⁷

Wright's 1898 design would have taken no more that a week to plan and detail the small one-story building (see Figure 5.6). Horizontality was emphasized on the exterior by nailing large

Architectural synthesis   139

Figure 5.5 River Forest Golf Clubhouse, scheme two as built; photographed shortly after completion in 1899 and before a fire took rear-half of the building.

battens, square in section, over wood-board joints; by continuous windows at about shoulder height sitting on a sill course; by a low shall-pitched roof of wood shingles with their inherent horizontal lines; and by an extended sheltering soffit. Wright's employment of a protruded and battered stylobate to visually ease the transition from flat earth to man-made vertical walls was also used on the stables and houses of the period. Horizontality was further emphasized by the locker room's very low eave line that coincided with the circumferential sill course.

Of this building, historian Hitchcock's critical observation in 1942 is too often ignored; it was also correct, even if he did not conflate the clubhouse and stables:

> the River Forest Golf Club represents the beginning of a new architecture. It is not a mere Opus 1, but a First Symphony. If the essential character of its construction and design, so closely integrated to be inseparable can be understood, almost all the work of the first decade of Wright's maturity will fall into place.[28]

White reported that Wright's designs were "suggested by the prairie on which they are built – he is," and here White likely quoted his employer: "he is 'thoroughly saturated with the spirit of the prairie'."[29] In 1910, Wright reiterated that "the horizontal line is the line of domesticity."[30] While not a residence, the clubhouse, like the stables, was situated within a suburban environment and of a comparable size. A mature aesthetic resolution can be seen in Millard's classy residence of 1906 with siding of board and batten (see Figure 5.8).

Wright prepared three different designs for the clubhouse. The second, Figure 5.5 and 5.6, and third were built, but the first was the more theoretically sound, as it clearly expressed functional articulation while maintaining constructional consistency. The main interior space was long and low and separated from a hemicycle lounge by a freestanding, two-sided fireplace with inglenook (see Figure 5.7). Dressing and ancillary rooms were symmetrically disposed on either side. The plan was composed by applying the square.

Although quite different in volume and massing as determined by function, the boathouse and related boat launch beside Lake Mendota in Madison of 1893 had a ground-floor plan whose basic elements were a fore-statement of the clubhouse original and second schemes

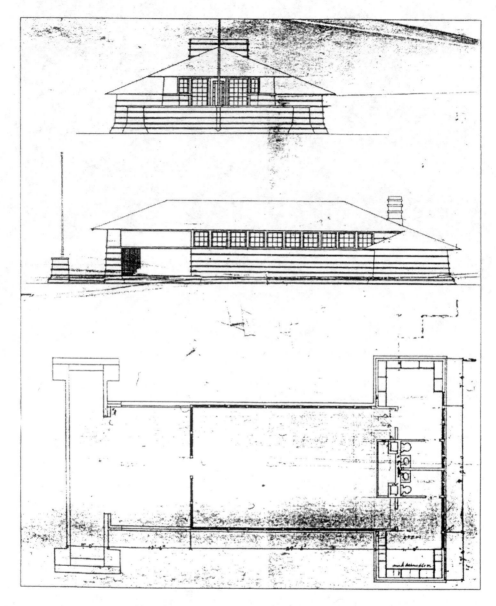

Figure 5.6 River Forest Golf Clubhouse, scheme two as built; floor plan and elevations, 1898. From Hamilton, 1990. Courtesy and © 2016 FLWF.

(see Figure 5.9).[31] The Monona Boathouse project also of 1893 was second of the two and both commissioned by the Madison Improvement Association. Monona was boldly unique, less dependent on the square in elevation, to be clothed with wood shingles and a frieze of stucco punctured by a series of windows. The tall roof was to be held by steel trusses from which steel rods held a balcony floor, the boat level therefore free of columns (see Figure 5.10).

The first two clubhouse designs were aesthetically and economically innovative. Aesthetic principles of the stables and clubhouse were a practical resolution for an appropriate exterior

Architectural synthesis 141

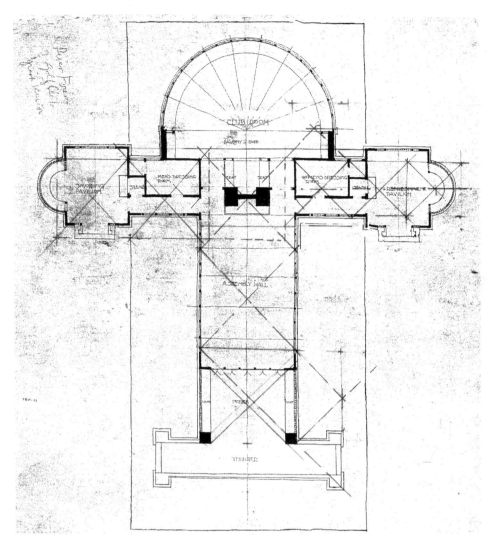

Figure 5.7 River Forest Golf Clubhouse, "first version"; floor plan, 1898; author's notations. From Pfeiffer, 98–02, as published in Spencer, 1900.

expression of domestic architecture and applied immediately thereafter. Houses may or may not have been regarded as regional to the upper Midwest in the use of materials and some planning elements, yet in Wright's mind, appropriate for America. It was his invention, the Wright Style.

Observers can only contemplate what might have eventuated if Wright had proceeded with another 1898 project. In that year, the national Central Art Association asked – commissioned, perhaps the wrong word – George R. Dean, Robert Spencer, and Wright to "design a home which may be considered typical of American Architecture" as an exhibit for the Trans-Mississippi and International Exposition held in Omaha, Nebraska, in 1898.[32] Wright gave two talks, one for fifteen minutes on 28 April, the other more substantial to the Association's congress held in Chicago May fifth, when the three were asked. But the designers never reached the planning stage simply because they had only a month to design and build the house.[33]

Figure 5.8 "Suburban dwelling for George E. Millard in Highland Park, Illinois. A simple wooden house in the woods by a Highland Park ravine"; exterior of horizontal square wood battens; author's annotations. From Wright, 1910.

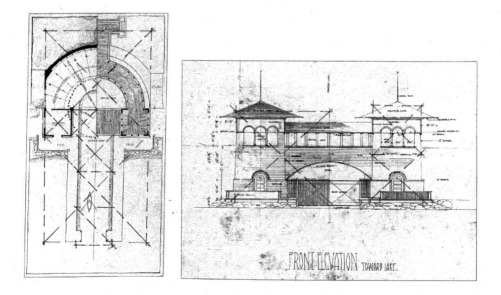

Figure 5.9 Lake Mendota boathouse for the Madison Improvement Association, 1893; left: plan at water level on left of center line, entry or second level on right of center line; right: lakefront elevation; author's notations. From Holzhueter, 1990. Courtesy and © 2016 FLWF.

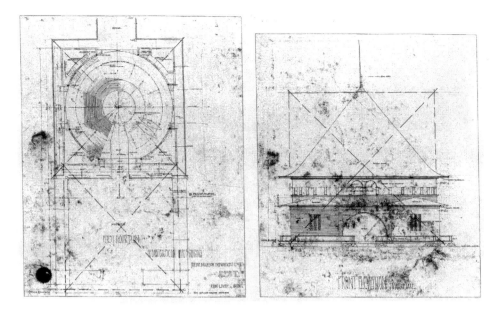

Figure 5.10 Project for a Lake Monona boathouse for the Madison Improvement Association, 1893; left: plan at water level; bridge from shore to the building set on piles; right: lake-front elevation; author's notations. From Holzhueter, 1990. Courtesy and © 2016 FLWF.

Winslow stables, 1898

The stables floor plan was simple and symmetrical, and dynamics of the square were employed (see Figure 5.11). Three-dimensionally, the tops of the gate and fence closing the carriage yard are in line with a string course at sill level and continue about the entire building. It defined a change of materials – Roman brick below, stucco above – that acted as an unembellished frieze. It was normal to and a reflection of a deep soffit. A continuation in front of the second floor on elevation drawing showed what appeared to be a continuous skirt roof. A skirt roof was to become a key factor in developing the strong horizontal lines of Wright's two- and three-story houses.

Sullivan's idioms were not absent. The arched entry to the stables from the yard (the tower proportionally two squares in height) was taken from Adler & Sullivan buildings – for example, the composition below the clock tower face of the Victoria Hotel – while in the spandrel of the stable's arch, the sculptural relief about some windows was also Sullivanesque. Note the lower left and right windows in the frieze were square with an inner leaded-glass circle: an Arts and Crafts idiom and his own emblem. Frontally, roof massing was composed as a shallow pyramid, thereby fitting the classicity of the symmetrically balanced plan. Everything about the stables predicted the exterior character and detail of the prairie houses, of the domestic Wright Style. And they bare no planning or aesthetic relationship to the brick house. Of course, Wright's vanity would not permit admitting publicly that such a mundane building was so important to design evolution. Nonetheless, the stables and clubhouse form a paradigm.[34]

The glaring ambiguities in his first creations, therefore, were resolved by a decision of two parts, first to retain the individuality, subtlety, and aesthetic precision exhibited in the stables and golf clubhouse, and second, to separate conflicting aesthetic systems, identifying one

Figure 5.11 "Stable of the Winslow house, River Forest. Ground plan and perspective"; perspective drawing a trace of a photograph; author's notations. From Wright, 1910.

domestic, the other non-domestic. He emphasized the point by advising readers on the horizontality of the Coonley house so obviously contrasted to the rectilinear bulk of Unity Temple.[35] It would be silly to ponder the question "Which building came first in 1898?" Quite obviously, the stables and clubhouse were on drawing boards simultaneously during the year and in confluence.

Walter and Marion Griffin

Throughout diverse careers as landscape architects, building architects, city planners, community developers, and travelers, Walter Burley and Marion Mahony Griffin reluctantly talked about their experiences while employed by Wright. Most other observations about Walter's roles in Wright's office do little to outline contributions to design. There are, however, valuable sources that enhance our understanding: the words of Mrs Griffin, architectural products by Griffin and Wright, and historian Paul Kruty's notes.

Marion Lucy Mahony was born in 1871, Walter in 1876. Both were raised in families devoted to social reform and Progressive ideals, the Mahonys more active than the Griffins.[36] She obtained an architecture degree from the Massachusetts Institute of Technology in 1894, he from the University of Illinois in 1899. After a few months' employment with her architect cousin Dwight Perkins, Marion began in Wright's office as a drafter and renderer in 1895. During the next fourteen years, she was a constant member of Wright's staff, at times the only member, at times part time, and she became close to Catherine Wright and her

Architectural synthesis 145

children.[37] Walter likely began with Wright in July 1901 and soon became Wright's professional manager and confidant. He left Wright in February 1906, she in mid-1909. Walter and Marion married in June 1911 and almost immediately began work on a design for an international competition for a capital city of Australia, Canberra. They won, and in 1913, were hired to enable their design and subsequently resided in Australia from 1914 until the mid-1930s.[38]

Former apprentice draftsman in Wright's office, Francis Barry Byrne, recalled that

> [Walter's] position was that of general manager of the office. Isabel Roberts assisted him. [Walter] was an unusually agreeable and likable person.... It was evident that Wright held Griffin in specially high regard and, I may say, affection. There was an almost continuous dialogue between them which they both enjoyed and, I am sure it profited both in clarifying such architectural issues as the work in the office presented.[39]

Anders Willatzen, a draftsman who had left Wright in mid-1904, knew that Griffin did everything: client contact, design assistance, chief draftsman, construction supervision, and office management.[40]

Historian Paul Kruty believed the "even-tempered" Walter "was a team player" and, "as Griffin's responsibilities increased during 1903, 1904 and 1905, by any measure he was becoming a [de facto] junior partner." Walter "also introduced landscape gardening to Wright's office." Indeed, in 1913, Walter referred to himself as an "architect and landscape architect" with Wright from 1901–06.[41] Historian Allen Brooks interviewed many of the people in Wright' office or associated with his employees around the century's turn. Brooks thoughtfully weighed Griffin's presence in the following manner:

> [Griffin] increasingly took charge of running the office, and eventually became the office manager and a job superintendent as well.... Wright found him most stimulating, and discussed with him, at length, work that he was designing. This was characteristic of Wright; he would discuss his work with others, accepting or rejecting their views as he saw fit. Griffin therefore, served as a useful critic, a lens through which Wright could re-examine his own ideas. What, if any, influence he had on Wright was largely intangible, being more completely assimilated and less profound than that from more extraneous sources.[42]

Marion, her mother Clara, and aunt Myra Perkins were members of the Church of All Souls in Evanston, formed in 1891 by Unitarian women. Their first service was led by Reverend Jenkin Jones, Wright's uncle.[43] Marion was attracted to Wright and the other "progressive spirits" of young architects, including those known by the *Chicago Inter-Ocean* newspaper as a new "community in architecture" dedicated to "principles of cooperation" and evinced of "a progressive spirit" along "the general lines of social evolution."[44] Marion was also a founding member of the Chicago Arts and Crafts Society in 1897. Sculptor Richard Bock, who worked alongside Marion in Wright's office, believed "[she] was a brilliant intellectual and a match for Wright in debate and argument. She served as a source for practice and criticism for his lecturing in which he became a master."[45]

Marion was in (mostly) and out of Wright's office over a period of about fourteen years. She was present many years before other employees who have offered comments about life in the studio or their own participation, usually short-lived. Barry Byrne recalled that "her dialogues" with Wright, "who, as we all know, is no indifferent opponent in repartee, made such days particularly notable."[46] Marion observed the critical transitional period of 1898–1903, the year before Byrne (a "child" Willatzen once said) entered the office. She therefore witnessed how architectural designs changed in 1897–98 and then as a result of Griffin's presence. There is every reason to accept her views along with, say, White's or Byrne's. Historian Grant Manson did so in 1940 when preparing his doctoral thesis about Wright.[47]

146 *The aesthetics of progress*

In an often bitter, quarrelsome, yet revealing manuscript written in the 1940s and titled *The Magic of America*, Marion referred to Walter's contributions to Wright's architecture that she believed were important. For example, Walter worked on the evolution of the smallish four-square house plan by refining it for the theoretical Quadruple Block Plan of 1903.[48] Here and there in the manuscript, Marion praised Walter's pivotal role in Wright's professional affairs, inside the office and out, with clients and construction contractors.

Nearly coincidental with beginning in Wright's office, Griffin received his first sizable commission, the William H. Emery house at Elmhurst, Illinois (see Figure 5.12).[49] The Emery design of 1902–03 is a simple inline plan composed of squares with two appendages, one for entry on one side, the other for dining (with den above) on the opposite side, each at different floor levels. A schematic plan and section explains the concept, Figure 5.13, left. Four large brick piers are placed at solid corners. Interior spaces flow within the boundary implied by the piers or extend beyond as outgrowths.[50] A line of windows are tucked under the soffit in a rhythm of mullions. On the long axis, the gables extend beyond the lower floor and piers. Of stucco on wood frame for the upper floor, the implication of a light weight gently held by a mass of brick is unmistakable. Setting aside the ill-proportioned elevations, the Emery design was a theoretical tour de force.

Wright did not employ interior spatial juxtapositions indicated by the Emery house or Walter's house for brother Ralph Griffin of 1909. However, embracing corners were employed by Wright on a contemporary building, the chapel/library, of a new building of 1901–02 at

Figure 5.12 William H. Emery Jr. house in Elmhurst, Illinois, by architect Walter Burley Griffin, 1902–03; photograph of 1908 by architect William Gray Purcell, one copy in Purcell papers, Northwest Archives. From Kruty (1998a).

Hillside School that Griffin supervised in Wright's office and in on-site construction work.[51] The bold positive (solid) or negative (recessed) corners allowed a variety of elements to fit between (windows, planters, entry, patios, etc.), and Wright used them regularly. The idea in plan is shown diagrammatically in Figure 5.13, right. Type 2 was seldom used on a floor above plan type 1, thus creating a recess over a solid corner. There are many examples of types 1 and 2 – and their working together – from 1902–13. As suggested, at the cruceform positions A, B, C, and D, any one of several functional elements could be located; entry, patio (such as the Fuller and Martin houses), a block of windows (Heller, Home School gym, Hardy, Hunt, Larkin Administration), bedroom (Stockman, Boynton), or terrace (Horner, Martin, each a pièce de rèsistance). A few Wright School architects applied the parti and others followed, briefly.[52]

Historians Paul Sprague, Narciso Menocal, and the late John Holzhueter agree that the Lamp house of 1903 was executed by Griffin for Wright.[53] Why Wright would assign a commission from a dear friend to an underling bewilders. Although it is an architectonically and aesthetically immature building, implying Wright did not carefully participate, there are intriguing aspects. First, it is almost a perfect cube, wall to wall and earth to roof-garden trellis. Second, when Wright used the Lamp design about three years later for the more elegant concrete house project for *Ladies Home Journal*, he placed the stairs and entry on the edge of the central fireplace wall, not counter to it. Therefore and third, the Lamp house was critical to the maturation of Wright's Quadruple Block Plan, analyzed in Appendix B. Fourth, Wright and Griffin had produced several residences with flat roofs; this the only one with a roof garden. In the 1920s, flat roofs became one potent symbol of European modernism for domestic architecture, much less a concern in the United States.

The evidence presented here is not directed to arguments about who designed a Wright building (the Lamp house aside)[54] but rather to determining the Griffinses' roles. The degree to which advice was effected was a matter for Wright. The Griffinses were a stabilizing factor

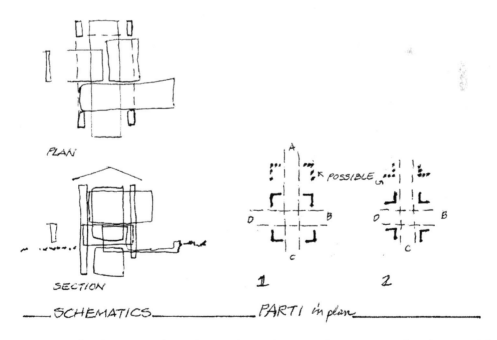

Figure 5.13 Left: schematic analysis of Emery house design. Right: one practical application of the dynamics of a square, a fundamental detail for several of Wright's buildings.

148 *The aesthetics of progress*

during those important spring years when a flighty Wright was creating and formalizing at a fast pace an architectural dialogue of revolutionary importance.

Analysis

In 1908, Wright described a "family resemblance" in his buildings and traced "the 'motif' behind the types within each family." First, "the low-pitched hip roofs, heaped together in pyramidal fashion or presenting quiet, unbroken skylines." Second, "low roofs with simple pediments countering on long ridges." Third, buildings "topped with a simple [flat] slab." Further on he said,

> In laying out the ground plans . . . simple axial law and order and the ordered spacing upon a system of certain structural units definitely established for each structure in accord with its scheme of practical construction and *aesthetic proportion* [italics added], is practiced as an expedient to simplify the technical difficulties of execution, and, although the symmetry may not be obvious[,] always the balance is usually maintained.[55]

"Symmetry" refers to equal balance, a harmonious uniformity in the answer of one part to another, that is the balance of part to part. (Others might refer to eurythmy.) Axial symmetry

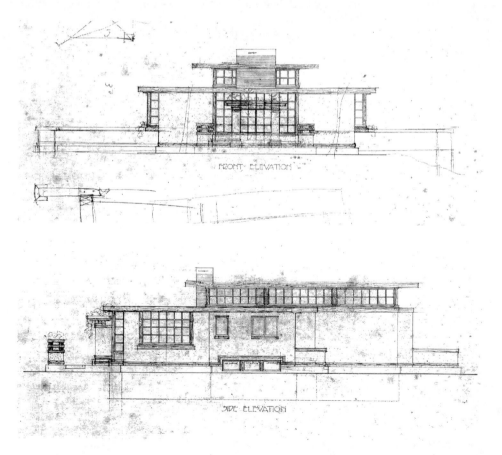

Figure 5.14 "Front" and "Side" elevations of the "Studio-Residence" project for sculptor Richard Bock of Maywood, Illinois, 1902. From Pfeiffer, 02–06. Courtesy and © 2016 FLWF.

("axial law") about a center line is one simple form. Then he referred to modules and placed articulation within functionalism:

> The individuality of the various functions of the various features . . . are complete in themselves and frequently do duty at the same time from within and without as decorative attributes of the whole. This tendency to greater individuality of the parts emphasized by more and more complete articulation will be seen in the plans for Unity Church, the cottage for Elizabeth Stone at Glencoe [1908] and the Avery Coonl[e]y [1908] houses. . . .[56]

Had he added the houses for Dana of 1902 and Martin of 1903, and then asked readers to imagine the gable roofs removed, the appearance of the articulated forms (pier, wall; room, grouped rooms) resemble his non-domestic works, the third roof motif. Yet initially roofs helped identify domestic and non-domestic types.[57] One of the first houses with a flat roof was a 1902 project of a "Studio-Residence for sculptor Richard Bock" in Maywood, Illinois (see Figure 5.14). Perhaps the best known of the period was the "House for Mrs Thomas H Gale" of 1909 in Oak Park, Illinois (see Figure 5.15).

Again, the module defined not only structural points and lines but design construction lines. This is confirmed by inspections of extant plans in the Wright Archives. Only a couple published plans have shown the module and resulting proportionality. One was a preliminary ground-floor plan for Ullman of 1903, where there were sketch lines to find a square and the living/dining room/fireplace space composed of three squares (see Figure 5.16). Other exploratory lines align pier and mullion, and others were used to construct a perspective drawing.[58] Also of value, Narciso Menocal superimposed a three-foot by six-inch grid over a floor plan of Wright's Gilmore house of 1908, and its fit and misfit was revealed (see Figure 5.17).[59] We also discover that the ground-floor plan was three squares wide and one deep.

Wright was not "obsessed with the grid." It was a tool that all building designers since antiquity relied upon, as did builders to construct. But Wright was not controlled by the demands of a two-dimensional module. He used it only where appropriate. For example, the floor plan

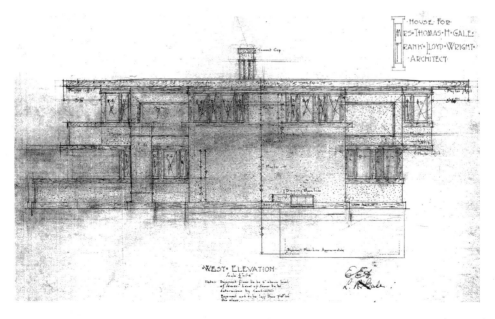

Figure 5.15 "West Elevation," "House for Mrs Thomas H. Gale," Oak Park, Illinois, 1909; similar to as built. From Pfeiffer, 07–13. Courtesy and © 2016 FLWF.

150 *The aesthetics of progress*

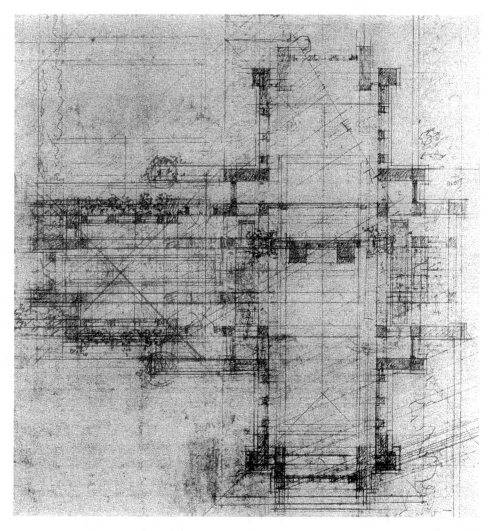

Figure 5.16 Developmental pencil drawing of the ground-floor plan of the H. J. Ullman house project of 1904 in Oak Park, Illinois of 1904; also showing lines for constructing a perspective drawing. From Pfeiffer, 02–06. Courtesy and © 2016 FLWF.

for the Walter Gerts all-timber summer house of 1901 built near Whitehall, Michigan, had grid lines drawn on the first-floor plan in red ink. But the lines do not indicate a module; rather, they were measurements. They were dimension lines that varied from three feet to three feet six inches on centers, with three feet the most common, as, in these early years, they more often than not conformed to prebuilt, in-stock casement windows.[60] This was typical for many of his buildings, including the Coonley house of 1906–09, as were deviations from the square proportion.

To follow are a few other plans that show how Wright did or did not apply the square (see Figures 5.18–5.28).[61] Some buildings were analyzed earlier herein, others later. Most

Architectural synthesis 151

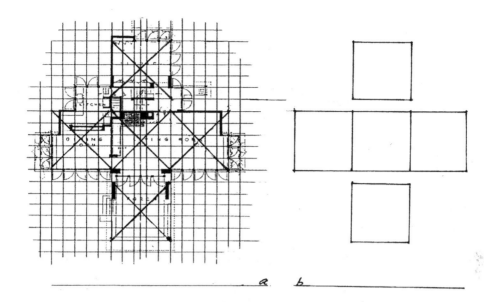

Figure 5.17 Gilmore house in Madison, Wisconsin, 1908. Left: ground-floor plan (based on 0806.09); a three-foot by six-inch grid drawn by Loy Maconi for Menocal, 1992. Right: square proportions by this author.

are from Wright's portfolio *Studies and Executed Buildings* of 1910, the 1919 edition, and for two reasons. First, the drawings are expertly reproduced, if not always correct, when considering as built conditions. Second, Wright was anxious to present clearly his ideas to the European and American audience of fellow professionals. The analytic examinations herein were made directly on photographic reproductions. Some relationships might prove inexact and for two reasons: either he made visual rather than measured determinations, or the result was intentional. Wright continued to use the square into the early 1920s, notably for the concrete buildings for Millard, Storer, and Ennis, as well as for a kindergarten for Alice Barnsdal.[62]

With exceptions, Wright did not present drawings of building elevations to clients or for publication[63] (see Figures 5.6, 5.14 and 5.15). He preferred floor plans and perspectives or, less often, a plaster model. Most perspectives, many made as a tracing over – or by a proportional device on – were from a photograph of a finished building. This allowed for easily understood (by designer and client) three-dimensional compositional elements in space and in landscape.

+ + +

Wright used a geometrical method intuitively. This allowed three events to occur simultaneously. First, an unambiguous three-dimensional organization; second, the evolution of planning goals integrated with aesthetic needs; third, control of the first two by artistic will. The first two were objective events induced by given laws, facts, or empirical evidence. The last,

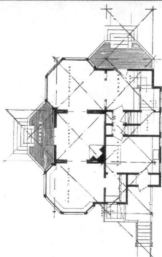

Figure 5.18 Top: photograph ca. 1940 of one of the twin Gale houses of 1892. From Manson, 1958, and Ashbee, 1911a. Bottom: ground-floor plan of the Emmond house, typical of the three houses in 1892; author's notations.

Architectural synthesis 153

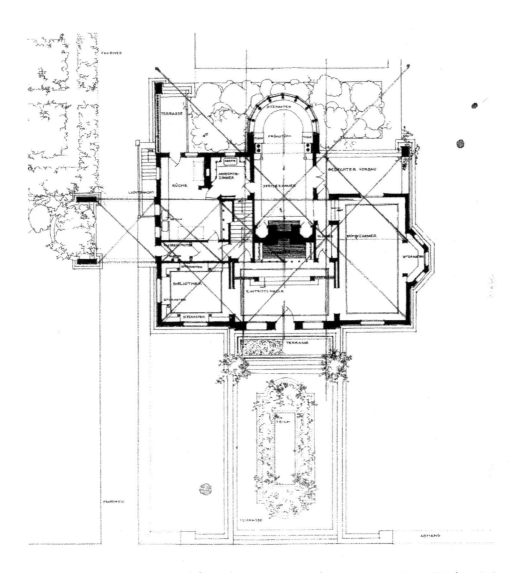

Figure 5.19 Winslow house ground-floor plan, 1894–05; author's notations. From Wright, 1910.

a matter of judgment, was an act extracted from a conscious knowledge of his own Fartistic capacity. The first two were learned, the last was a parental gift. In subprose, Wright ruminated,

> Yes, the "fine thing" is reality. Always reality?
> Realism, the subgeometric, is however the abuse of this fine thing.
> Keep the straight lines clean and significant, the flat plane expressive and clear cut. But let texture of material come into them.
> Reality is spirit . . . essence brooding just behind aspect!

Figure 5.20 "House for Mrs Aline Devin. Ground- [and second-floor] plan," project, 1898; two distinct front elevations; author's notations. From Wright, 1910.

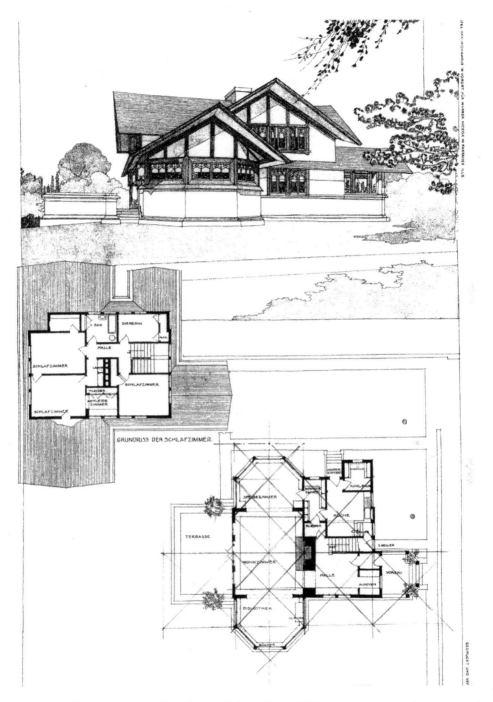

Figure 5.21 Hickox house ground- and second-floor plans, 1900; perspective drawing a trace of a photograph; author's notations. From Wright, 1910.

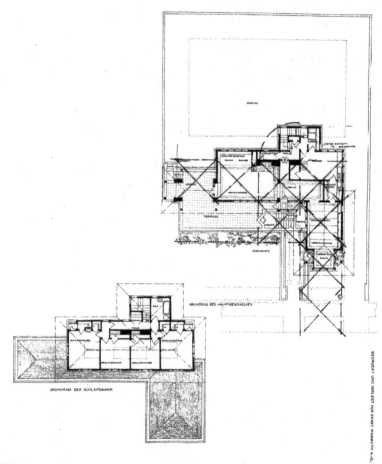

Figure 5.22 Rogers (Thomas) house ground- and second-floor plans, 1900; perspective drawing a trace of a photograph; author's notations. From Wright, 1910.

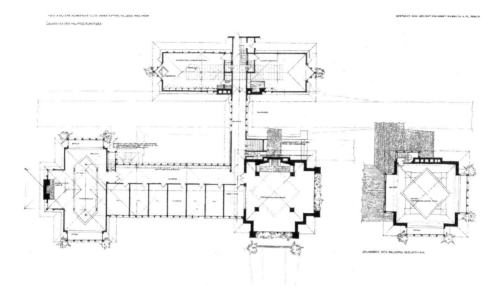

Figure 5.23 "Hillside Home School building / Built for the Lloyd Jones sisters in 1906," 1901–02; principle floor plan; author's notations. From Wright, 1910.

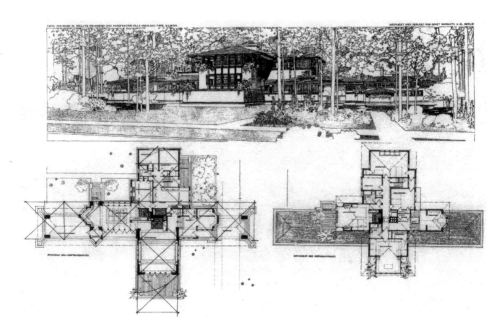

Figure 5.24 Willits house ground- and second-floor plans, 1902; author's notations. From Wright, 1910.

158 *The aesthetics of progress*

Figure 5.25 D. Martin (Barton) house ground-floor plan, 1902–04; perspective drawing a trace of a photograph; author's notations. From Wright, 1910.

Seize it! And . . . after all, reality is supergeometric, casting a spell or a "charm" over any geometry, as such, in itself.[64]

Perception makes reality; human-made reality is less than reality, conventional; Plato's thrice-removed art.

Notes

1 White to Willcox, 13 May 1904, sighted Willcox papers; White letters, p.105. Charles Elmer White Jr studied architecture at MIT, class of 1995, and on marrying Alice became the son-in-law of Charles E. Roberts of Oak Park, Wright's early supporter. White opened his own office in Oak Park in 1903

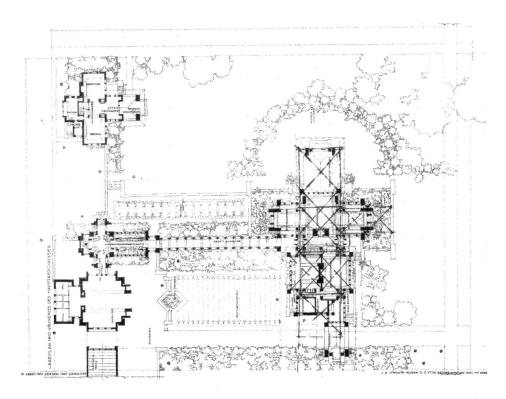

Figure 5.26 D. Martin house ground-floor plan, 1903–05, and site plan; Martin (Barton) house upper left; author's notations. From Wright, 1910.

and incidentally "collaborated" with Vernon S. Watson and Wright on rebuilding the River Forest Tennis Club in 1905 after a fire. See "plaster houses," *AReview* (Boston), n.s.(February 1912) p.19, and n.s.(September 1912), p.103; Charles E. White Jr., "A Fireproof Cottage," *Fireproof Magazine* (edited by Peter B. Wight), 10(April 1907), pp.134–137, and 10(June 1907), pp.209–214, 218. (When, in 1920, the tennis club was forced to move, it was sawn into three sections, carted by horse-drawn wagons and rebuilt on land purchased from E. C. Waller.)

In 1905, White began writing articles about the nuts and bolt of building construction and a series on office practice in 1913–14 for the magazine *Building Progress*, a publication of the Natco Company in Pittsburgh, and for a wide variety of other magazines. He authored several books for good publishers, many illustrated by himself. From 1923–36, he was in partnership in Oak Park with fellow MIT architecture classmate Bertram A. Weber.

2 FLW to H. Monroe, 1907, as published in Duis (1976), p.35, date not cited.
3 Wright (1943), p.132, not in Wright (1932).
4 David Gebhard, "C.F.A. Voysey – To and from America," *JSAH*, 30(December 1971), p.307.
5 C. R. Ashbee, *Memoirs*, as quoted in Robert W. Winter, "American Sheaves from 'C.R.A.' and Janet Ashbee," *JSAH*, 30(December 1971), p.321. Wright recalled that, while Ashbee was visiting Hull-House, Jane Addams suggested he visit Wright in Oak Park, Wright (1943), p.162, not in Wright (1932). *The Studio* ceased publication in 1964. *House Beautiful* was purchased by Hearst Corporation in 1934 and continues.
6 Johnson (1990), pp.47–51.
7 Wright (1946), pp.32–33.
8 Wright (1943), p.144, not in Wright (1932).
9 See, for example, photograph of 1895, Secrest (1992), p.125.
10 Bock (1989), p.67.

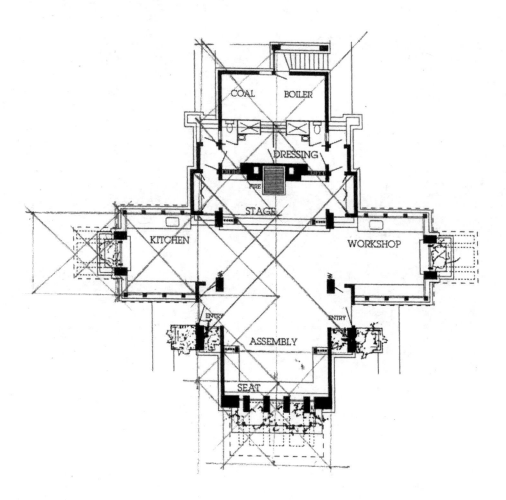

Figure 5.27 Coonley kindergarten ("playhouse") ground-floor plan, 1912; author's notations. From Storrer, 1993, and Ashbee 1911a.

11 Spencer (1900), pp.64–65; the sculptor was Richard Bock. Granger (1899) is much like Spencer (1900).
12 H. Allen Brooks, "Chicago Architecture: Its Debt to the Arts and Crafts," *JSAH*, 30(December 1971), pp.316–317.
    Other valuable works, textual and/or illustrative, are Bowman (1991); Boris (MS.1981); Davey (1980); Dickason (1953); Wendy Kaplan, *The Arts and Crafts Movement* (London: Thames & Hudson, 1991, 2004); Kornwolf (1972); Levine (1973), pp.495–516; Joseph Siry, "FLW's 'The Art and Craft of the Machine': Text and Context," in Martha Pollak, ed., *The Education of the Architect* (Cambridge, MA: MIT Press, 1997), pp.3–35; Mary Ann Smith, *Gustav Stickley, the Craftsman* (Syracuse: Syracuse University, 1983; New York: Dover, 1992); Peter Stansky, *ReDesigning the World: William Morris, the 1880s and the Arts and Crafts* (Princeton: Princeton University Press, 1985); Roger B. Stein, *John Ruskin and Aesthetic Thought in America 1840–1900* (Cambridge, MA: MIT Press, 1967); Wilson (1987).
13 Pfeiffer (2011), pp.60–61 (illustrates thirty designs, including the first "flower"), p.78; Pfeiffer (87–01), p.84, to be corrected.
14 Alofsin (1992), p.353n56.

Architectural synthesis 161

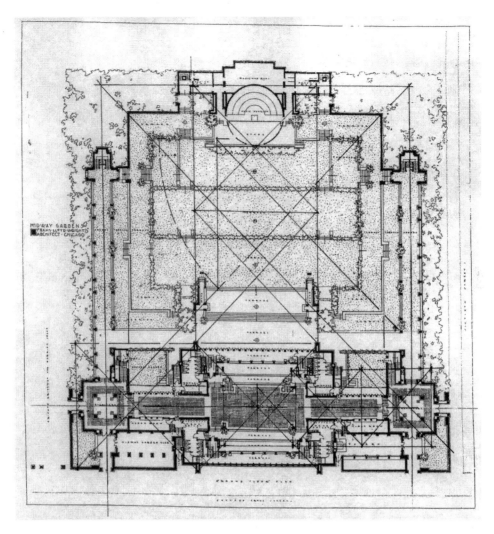

Figure 5.28 Midway Gardens ground-floor plan, 1913–14; author's notations. From *Wendingen* (4–5 1925).

15 "An Interesting Competition," *Inland Architect*, 30(January 1898), pp.63b–64a and plates; see also "Award of Cash Prizes," *AmArchitect*, 41(3 September 1898), p.1a, and other published notices; Dietrich Neumann, " 'The Century's Triumph in Lighting': The Luxfer Prism Companies and Their Contribution to Early Modern Architecture," *JSAH*, 54(March 1995), pp.24–53; Hasbrouck (2005), pp.217–218.
   Wright's friend William Winslow was a major investor in the company when formed in Chicago in 1896. Another investor was Edward C. Waller, who also produced two designs, see the U.S. Patent Office, *Official Gazette*, 7 December 1897.
16 [Competition], *Inland Architect*, 31(May 1898), pp.38b–39a; "Awards in Luxfer Prism Competition," *Inland Architect*, 32(September 1898), pp.15b–16b, and illustrations on unnumbered pages; Van Zanten and Robinson (2000), pp.79–80.
17 Wright claimed the Winslow house was an Adler & Sullivan "contract" that he snared, Pfeiffer (1977), p.22. Spencer (1900) stated the commission came to Wright "in the third year of his independent practice," or 1896. Spencer's manuscript may have been vetted by Wright. Hanks

(1979), p.10, without citing source, dated the design as June 1894, an acceptable date. Other floor plans and additional historical notes in *PSR*, 1(3, 1964), pp.5–14. One of the more coherent analyses is Seligmann (1991), pp.73–85. Drawings of the similar Orrin Goan house, dated 1893, obviously forecast the Winslow house. Peter Goan's house was built 1897 with siding material different to that proposed in 1893.

The Victoria Hotel was destroyed by fire in 1961.

18 White to Willcox, 4 March [1904?], sighted Willcox papers; White letters, p.109.
19 Wright (1910), introduction, and plate VI description.
20 White to Willcox, 4 March [1905?], see note 16.
21 Wright (1928), p.56; Johnson (2013a), chapter 1ff.
22 Outlined in Johnson (1990), chapter 6.
23 White to Willcox, 13 May and 19 May 1904; White letters, pp.106, 107. For photographs on problems of restoration, see Brenner (1986), pp.118–125; for publications since restoration, including Abernathy (1988) and Robert Kronenburg, see "Wright at Home," *Architect's Journal* (London), 186(4 November 1987), pp.40–47.
24 The upper floor window of the front elevation was not taken from any particular building (much as Vincent Scully would like) but was typical of the period; there was a similar window similarly positioned on the Lake Forest Presbyterian Church of 1886 by architect Henry Ives Cobb, as illustrated in Cohen (1976), plates 32–33.
25 The 1898 announcement card for two offices (at Oak Park and in The Rookery Building, Chicago) is illustrated in Bolon (1989), p.100; cf. Granger (1899); FLW Home and Studio Foundation, *The Plan for Restoration and Adaptive Use . . . Studio* (Chicago: The Foundation, 1977); Scully (1971). In 1909, Wright removed small-angled walls and doors that constricted vestibule circulation.
26 Construction dates for the stables have not been verified. After much, searching historian Paul Sprague suggested a date of 1897, but I prefer 1898: Sprague to this author, 31 August 1994, for both of us proof is in its style.
27 Club history taken mostly from *Oak Park Vindicator*, 10(March 1899), p.1, editorial (apparently also reported in the *Chicago Times Herald*), and ibid., 2 June 1899, p.1, editorial; *Outing* (New York), editorial, 19(July1899), p.362; *Golf* (New York), 7(July 1900), p.431, with a photograph of the building; Joseph E. G. Ryan, ed., *Golfers' Greenbook 1901* (Chicago: National Golf Bureau, 1901), p.98, 246–252.
28 Hitchcock (1942), p.30.
29 White to Willcox, 16 November 1903; White letters, 104.
30 Wright (1910), introduction, no pagination.
31 The initial boathouse plan, submitted and won in competition, is in Spencer (1900), p.87, and Pfeiffer (89–02); see especially Holzhueter (1989b), pp.273–287, back cover; Pfeiffer (87–01), plates 88–90; Pfeiffer (2011), p.40. Manson (1958), p.60, suggests the boathouse was the progenitor of the Wolf Lake and Cheltenham Beach projects. Except for building type, their site plans, floor plans, building mass, and elevational treatment are wholly unrelated.
32 [Notices], *The Inter Ocean* (Chicago), 7(May 1898), p.107, the asking at the end of a congress.
33 Fifteen-minute talks were given by Allan Pond, Spencer, Dwight Perkins, and Wright, *Chicago Daily Tribune*, 20 March 1898, p.39b; resumé, *The Inter Ocean* (Chicago), 24(March 1898), p.8a; Wright's 5 May talk was published as "Art in the Home," *Arts for America* (Chicago), 7(June 1898), pp.593–594.
34 Preliminary drawings in Pfeiffer (89–16), plates 22–24.
35 Wright (1928), pp.56–57.
36 Alice T. Friedman, "Girl Talk: Feminism and Domestic Architecture at FLW's Oak Park Studio," in Van Zanten (2011), pp.25–26, 42–43.
37 Marion Griffin to William Purcell, 24 August 1949, p.1, Northwestern Archive.
38 Wright was an unreliable boss. Disappointed with his administration and with wages due, Griffin left in late January 1906, letters to Wright's office to Frank Smith, January and February 1906, Wright Archives. Marion left Wright's employ on his departure to Europe in 1909.

On Griffin's early years and works in the United States, see Christopher Vernon, "'Expressing Natural Conditions with Maximum Possibility': The American Landscape Art (1901–ca. 1912) of Walter Burley Griffin," *Journal of Garden History* 15(April 1995), pp.19–47; idem., "FLW, Walter Burley Griffin, Jens Jensen and the *Jugendstil* Garden in America," *Die Gartenkunst* 7(2, 1995), pp.232–246, on roof gardens, p.240; Paul Kruty, "Walter Burley Griffin and

the University of Illinois," *Reflections* (Urbana), 1993, pp.32–43; Mati Maldre, "Portfolio of the Architecture of Walter Burley Griffin: A Photographic Essay," ibid., pp.44–51; Mati Maldre and Paul Kruty, *Walter Burley Griffin in America* (Urbana: University of Illinois Press, 1988); Kruty (2003), pp.21–25; Brooks (1972), pp.8–83; Monash University, *Walter Burley Griffin – A Review* (Melbourne: Melbourne University Press, 1988); Johnson (2013a), p.53f; Van Zanten (2013), pp.7–13, 23; Van Zanten (2011), inter alia; James Weirick, "Marion Mahony at M.I.T.," *Transition* (Melbourne), 25(Winter 1988), pp.49–54; Watson (1998); less valuable is Johnson (1977).
39 Byrne to Mark Peisch, 22 March 1960, Peisch Papers, Avery Library, as quoted in Kruty (2003), p.29n21,n25; see also Brooks (1972), p.80.
40 Letters by W. Griffin from Wright's office confirm his role. Willatzen worked for Wright for about a year and moved to Seattle in 1907 where, from 1909–13, Barry Byrne was his partner after leaving Wright in August 1908. Sometime during World War I, Willatzen, a Danish immigrant, changed his name to Andrew Willatsen.
41 Kruty (2003), p.221; James Herbert Kelley, ed., *The Alumni Record of the University of Illinois* (Urbana-Champaign: University of Illinois, 1913), p.225.
42 Brooks (1972), p.80.
43 James Weirick, "Spirituality and Symbolism in the Work of the Griffins," in Watson (1998), p.61.
44 As quoted in Kruty (1998), p.12, the influence was of Spencerian social evolution.
45 Bock (1989), p.82.
46 As quoted in Brooks (1972), pp.79–80.
47 Manson interviewed Mahony in the late 1930s, see Grant Carpenter Manson, "The Wonderful World of Taliesin: My Twenty Years on Its Fringes," *WHistory*, 73(Autumn 1989), pp.36; his PhD was approved in 1939 but Manson (1958), p.217, gives 1940.
48 Marion Griffin, "Magic of America," typescript, 1940s, donated in 1949 to the New York Historical Society, confused pagination; letters, M. Griffin to W. Purcell, 7 August 1947?, p.1, and late 1951, various pages, Northwest Archives.
49 Emery final plans were completed in early 1903, so design began in 1902; Maldre and Kruty (1996), pp.80–84, 160, compare with Carter house, pp.85–88, 167. Apparently Wright allowed Walter to accept private commissions.
50 For plan, section, and elevation, see Brooks (1972), pp.72–76.
51 Pfeiffer (89–16), plates 75–83. Preliminary designs for the Beachy house (1902–05) have resemblances to the Emery house.
52 See relevant illustrations in Brooks (1972) and Sprague (1976); cf. Johnson (1977), pp.36–38.
53 Holzhueter (1988), pp.11, 109–114; Pfeiffer (02–06), plates 165–167, but refer to illustrations only.
54 Another clear case was the Wenatchee recreation park project of 1919, designed by R. M. Schindler while Wright was in Japan, see Johnson (1988b) and idem (1989). My employment experiences in architectural firms was typical: for some jobs, I was left alone to complete all the design and detailing, others were closely overseen, for others I was told exactly what to do.
55 Wright (1908), pp.57, 58–59.
56 Wright (1908), pp.160–161.
57 This consistency of volume and structural articulation organized by academic formality is analyzed by Robert McCarter (1991a, pp.238–289) in pen-and-ink drawings for an essay appropriately titled "The Integrated Ideal." The analyses nicely engage McCarter's own sense and purpose of drawing with Wright's, but they are of end products, *not* about how they came to be.
58 Wright (1910), plate XVI; Wright (1955), p.29; Pfeiffer (02–06), plate 219–220, plate 220 has a working grid. A variety of internal ceiling heights is related by Hildebrand (1991) to ideas of "prospect" and "refuge" that were unknown to Wright.
59 Menocal (1981), pp.86–87.
60 Levine (2016), a color illustration of the Gerts floor plan, pp.126, 392n50; Storrer (1993), p.75, and figure 5.16 herein for Wright's search for a proper plan to fit his idea.
61 On authorship of the pre-1913 drawings, see Brooks (1966), note p.202.
62 Johnson (2013a), pp.45–47, illustrations p.46.
63 Wright Archives and various elevational drawings in Pfeiffer (89–16), (87–01), (02–06), (87–59).
64 Wright (1932), p.160, ellipses and emphases are Wright's.

6   The Wright School

school *n. that body of pupils or followers of a master, system, method, etc.*

Parallelepipedons

Before the creation of his revolutionary non-domestic buildings, Wright's designs for multistory structures were of necessity parallelogramatic. Most were for apartments and, of those, a few had commercial space on the ground floor. A couple of early projects in the 1890s need attention.

There are several drawings executed in 1894 for an apartment house project for Giles Belknap's site in Austin, Illinois. During the 1890s decade, Wright tried many aesthetical ideas; none more out of ordinary was the Belknap facades of panels of dark brick outlined by a rectilinear pattern of light-colored stucco, or stone, about twelve- inches wide. The bold pattern formed the only exterior ornament, and rectangular windows were an integral part of the pattern. Floor plans were composed within two exact squares with the same plan in each; each was separated by a narrow passage from sidewalk to entry. Only two floors of apartments were located above commercial spaces.[1] Of that decade, the only other rectilinear pattern devoid of historical referents to come to mind is the unique Luxfer facade number one in the competition of 1898.

Little is known of Wright's flat building "to be built" in 1896 for Robert Ash Perkins, yet its story the most intriguing. Born in Roboro, South Devon, England, in 1837, Perkins arrived in Chicago in 1879 to eventually reside in Berwyn as a real estate developer. He would, on occasion, hire architects to prepare plans for houses, some on speculation, throughout the Chicago area. One architectural firm occasionally employed, at least during 1897–98, was Fowler & Wright. Of interest here is Frank Wright's announcement published in July 1896, as follows:

> Architect F.L. Wright: For R.A. Perkins, a two-story and basement flat building 25 by 70 feet in size; to be built at West Monroe Street; it will have a buff Bedford stone front; oak interior finish, mantels, sideboards, gas fixture, laundry fixtures, steam heating etc.[2]

A small building for a small site. The Frank Lloyd Wright Foundation archives hold one drawing only of what is described as "Robert Perkins Apartment Building" with a date of 1896.[3] It is a perspective of a six-story building with an arched entry ensemble similar to that for Sullivan's Victoria Hotel of 1892–93. The two street facades shown are composed of stacked bow windows at floors two through five and very much in the manner of the seventeen-story Monadnock Building of 1889 designed by Root while with Burnham. While in the perspective drawing the sixth floor appears similar to the Monadnock's top floor, it more closely resembles the top floor of a building also well known to Wright, Adler & Sullivan's Chicago Stock Exchange Building of 1893–94, demolished in 1972. Clearly, the perspective does not fit the description of July 1896. Yet there is another and more probable suggestion.

Shortly after the 1871 fire, German emigrant Charles P. Dose began a real estate and banking business with an office on Lasalle Street in Chicago. Among his promotions were the Chicago Natatorium, much of the Logan Square district and, while Wright was employed, Adler & Sullivan's Schiller Building of 1891–92 for the German Opera House Company. During 1893, Wright encountered Dose, who, as manager of the Schiller Building, accepted rent for office space.[4] Beginning in 1883, Dose also sold real estate in Seattle, Washington Territory, to move there permanently in 1898. In January 1894, he submitted a press release to the *Seattle Post-Intelligencer* (P-I) that said, in part:

> NEW HOTEL BUILDING /. . . / To be Called Yesler Avenue Hotel /. . ./ Plans Now Ready.
> A large six-story hotel is . . . to be erected by C.P. Dose of Chicago. . . . His representative Charles H[erbert] Bebb, architect and engineer, is now in the city and will superintend the construction of the building which will cost $75,000. . . . The plans of the building have been prepared by architect Frank L. Wright of Chicago. . . .[5]

See Appendix B. Bebb had been a supervising architect for Adler & Sullivan before he and fellow employee Wright were laid off in 1893. An English emigrant, Bebb eventually settled in Seattle and managed a long career in architecture. After mentioning the building site was 120 feet square, and that was incorrect, the P-I wrote that the "front will be ornamented with terra cotta in the Romanesque style, the balance of the building in plain brick."[6]

Two weeks later, Dose informed the P-I, who reported on 29 January that progress was "being made on the large building, that construction was about to begin this winter." Also, bids had "been received by C.H. Bebb, superintendent, for excavation for the big Yesler avenue hotel to be built by C. P. Dose, of Chicago. . . . Mr. Dose and his architect F.L. Wright are expected in Seattle in the spring."[7] Then, in February, Wright informed the New York *Engineering Record* of the following: "Seattle, Washington – Plans have been drawn by Frank L. Wright, of Chicago, for a $75,000 hotel."[8]

Not only were there professional connections between Adler, Sullivan, Bebb, Dose, and Wright, but the P-I articles offered meager information. The mention of a ornamental entrance in terra cotta coincides with the Perkins building drawing, as does the mention of a site frontage (on fifth) of sixty-nine feet. Both buildings were to be six stories. Exterior walls were to be "plain pressed brick," the same material that sheathes the Monadnock facades. The double-block front of the Perkins drawing also fits the Dose building facing Fifth Street but only suggestively, as the P-I reported: "there will be no inside rooms, every room in the house having outside windows." These coincidences suggest a Y plan with entry between the arms and off Fifth, a thought that might fit the perspective drawing.

Suffice it to say there is clear evidence that Wright was preparing plans for the hotel, and his colleague Bebb participated. Apparently ground was broken, and this implies that plans had been prepared but to what extent unknown. But it was all for naught. After only one month, in March 1894, the P-I carried Dose's disclosure that "The Yesler Avenue hotel . . . will not be built as a hotel, the plans having been changed into an apartment house. The time when work will begin is yet indefinite."[9] In fact, the proposed building in the perspective could be for a hotel or offices or apartments. The perspective drawing for a so-called Perkins building (9605.01) should be titled as "a perspective sketch" attributed to Wright of a project for a "Yesler Avenue Hotel" for Charles P. Dose, Seattle, 1894.

In 1900 Dose did build what became the Fifth Avenue Hotel; two stories of rooms over shops and constructed of wood studs and beveled clapboard siding. It was demolished after structurally weakened by road construction in 1911 and when named The Frances.[10]

Abraham Lincoln Center, 1897–1905

As early as 1894 Wright told his uncle that, when the time arose to build a new All Souls, he should hire his architect-nephew Frank, which Reverend Jenkin Jones did.[11] He also decided on the name Abraham Lincoln Center for the building to be built across the street corner from All Souls. As far as Jones was concerned, Lincoln was

> the greatest and noblest and dearest of Americans who ever lived, [said Reverend Jones], a man who would represent national and civic interests, and . . . who has already won his place in the hearts of the representatives of all creeds.[12]

Wright's preliminary design of around 1897 was a four-story building, heavily influenced by Sullivan's aesthetics, that attempted to satisfy Jones's own penciled planning diagrams. The floor plans were a reiteration of the then current All Souls building. Over the next few years and to new floor plans, Wright produced one front facade that was delicately Sullivanesque, then another more masculine, then one plain and rather commercial in appearance.[13] In 1898, a concerned building committee controlled by Jones enlisted the assistance of Dwight Heald Perkins, an architect Wright's age then working for D. H. Burnham & Company and a member of All Souls Church in Evanston since 1884. Wright then became principal designer in the collaboration and, in August 1898, the two men responded with a seven-story building.[14]

Late in 1901, it became five stories,[15] of which the building committee obtained opinions from Chicago architect Irving Pond and New York City architect Ernest Flagg, both men much admired by Chicago's League members.[16] Their rather adverse comments jeopardized Wright's position but Reverend Jones supported his nephew, sternly advising him and Perkins to perform radical revisions on the exterior and ensure realistic cost estimates. Jones's final program of February 1902 for All Souls/Lincoln Center was rational, robust, and sermon-like:

> Let me try to outline in a few words, as I see it, this new cathedral. . . .
> I am thinking of a building of modern architecture, gracious though not gorgeous, representing in its lines dignity, hospitality and service, a building with four faces, each honest and clean, . . . it stands there to serve the public, that it is allied to science, in league with literature, free but devout from the street level to the crowning cornice that rims the seventh story.
> The basement and lower stories of this building will be devoted to helping activities. The offices of this department store that deals in spiritual commodities will be a sympathy shop. . . . a reading-room always open, . . . playrooms, night-school rooms, manual training benches and modeling tables. . . .
> [T]he next two floors in the building will be occupied by the auditorium; not large but attractive, not sumptuous but artistic, refined and comfortable. . . . The next floor should be given to class rooms . . . one dedicated to civic, another to the bibles of the world, another to literature. . . . [A] school for domestic science . . . homemaking and house keeping. . . . The next floor should be devoted to the social life of men, women and children, the modern family club refined, elevated and economized. . . .
> The next floor should be devoted to quarters for resident workers. The upper floor will be given to the physical man, gymnasium for women and children, boys and girls, the aged and the invalid; rooms for dancing and banqueting. . . .
> . . .
> And so we venture to call it a "Centre," a "Centre" that shall radiate intelligence, culture, joy, helpfulness, a "Centre" to which will gravitate the lonely, the living, the intellectually hungry, the morally affluent, the spiritually active. . . . We wanted a name . . . a saint of the new order, a martyr of the new day, and such a name we believe "Abraham Lincoln" to be. So we dare Christen . . . this academy of life "The Abraham Lincoln Centre."[17]

(As a young man, Lincoln was a skeptic. Beyond midlife, he became very religious but without connection to an organized church.)

Revisions were completed, and Jones "approved" construction drawings in February 1903 (see Figures 6.1 and 6.2).[18] Frustrated by his uncle's demands after February, particularly for

The Wright School 167

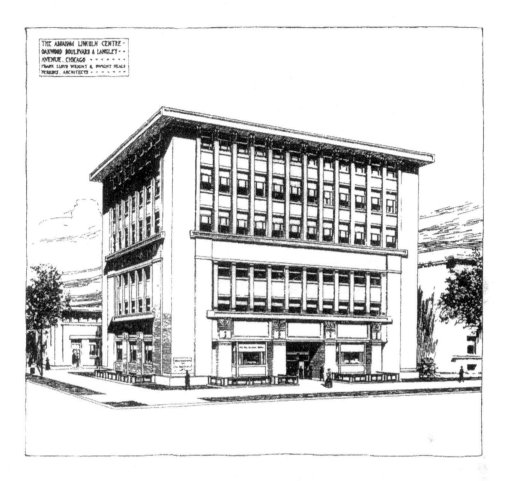

Figure 6.1 Perspective of 1903 penultimate facade design of "The Abraham Lincoln Centre" in Chicago, "FLW & Dwight Heald Perkins, Architects." From Siry, 1996, from *All Souls Church Twentieth Annual*, 1903.

chaste elevations, and by the interference, as Wright saw it, of architects that had been brought in by Jones to evaluate *his* design, Wright quit in June that year.[19] Thus, Perkins became the "constructing architect" and supervisor of construction.

Reverend Jones was very clear about the expressive purpose of the new building. It was not to be domestic in appearance or like other churches. Rather, he declared it must be

> built "four-square," the same material and architectural honesty carried all around. The severest simplicity has been aimed at; no money will be spent on exterior embellishments, because all will be needed to furnish the interior with the tools and life that will justify the expenditure. It is hoped that "the building will be emblematic of the hearty, straightforward ideal of the man for whom it is named. . . .[20]

Perkins initially consented "to serve" as architect because, he said, "Your plea for simple monochrome and for economy, straight forward design in every phase, pleased me."[21] Jones's aesthetic program fit nicely with principles of pure design, and we've seen Perkins's later response for the Tilton and Trumbull schools. Yet, four years, later Perkins became irritated by Jones's

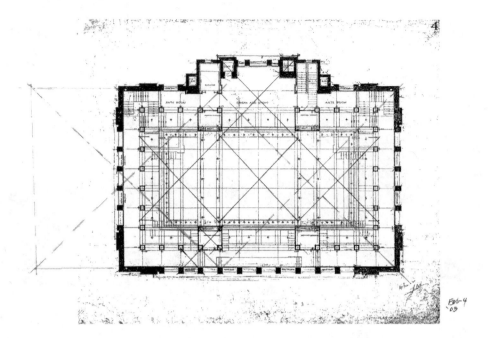

Figure 6.2 Final auditorium third- or balcony-floor plan dated February 1903, The Abraham Lincoln Centre in Chicago, "FLW & Dwight Heald Perkins, Architects"; signed "JLlJ," i.e. Jenkin Lloyd Jones; author's notations. From Pfeiffer, 02–06. Courtesy and © 2016 FLWF.

insistence on "severest simplicity," saying that if he was "compelled to build the center just as Jones wanted . . . [then] this note shall be printed upon every elevation and perspective that is published – *Designed in accordance with specific directions given by Jenkin Lloyd Jones and against the protest of D.H. Perkins.*"[22]

It was not the floor plans or interiors but the appearance of the exterior that offended. Perkins was interviewed in 1939 by historian Grant Manson, who summarized,

> Perkins tried to execute the plans as they then stood [in 1903]; blueprints were made and construction begun. But the client [Jones] continued to find fault with the "elaborateness" of the design and *took pencil in hand* [italics mine] to bring the building into line with his concept of Lincolnesque ruggedness. Confusion reigned. . . .[23]

Wright's elevations in 1903 had three separate ranges of windows, each horizontally defined between piers that, when combined with a deep soffit and fascia, gave the building a squat appearance. The second range expressed the two-story assembly room. Perkins raised the parapet (the front facade then became a square) and Jones's red pencil eliminated all relief and ornamental elements (see Figure 6.3). Windows were not embellished at sill, jamb, or lintel but framed by industrial iron. On the exterior, dark-brown/black brick defined the ground floor. The floors above were encased in a pinkish red brick and flush, dark-brown brick string courses indicated each floor level. The revised exterior faces were Reverend Jones's creation, so to speak.

As completed, the Abraham Lincoln Center was dedicated May 1905, with the Wright/Perkins/Jones floor plans and exterior elevations as modified by Jones and Perkins. The correct attribution must be Wright and Perkins, Associated Architects, as written on their working drawings. It was boldly at the extreme of liberal traditions in Unitarianism, one center of Chicago's Social Gospel Movement, and a remarkably stark statement of Progressive potential, prescient architecturally.

Figure 6.3 The Abraham Lincoln Centre, Chicago, Dwight Heald Perkins & FLW, photographed in about 1907. One of the more important buildings of the twentieth century; floor plans and general design Wright and Perkins 1901–03; exterior elevations Perkins and Rev. Jones, 1903–05. At right is the entry vestibule to All Souls Church of 1885, Joseph L. Silsbee, Architect. From private collection.

Larkin Administration Building, 1902–05

The Larkin Administration Building (1902–05) in Buffalo, New York, can be understood in part as a series of resolutions to latent ideas for and lingering ambiguities in the Abraham Lincoln Center building. Wright's initial Larkin design from winter 1903–04 contained the final parti but the exterior was diminished, as with the initial Lincoln design, by fussy Sullivanesque details and ornamental elements.[24]

The programmatic aesthetical arguments put by Jones were integral to the theory of pure design, of geometric reduction, and for elimination of trappings that might in some way symbolize the wickedness of traditionalism and therefore indolent conformity, church or architecture. After Perkins completed Jones's elevations in late 1903, Wright stripped the Larkin preliminary design of ornament. The major forms were separately articulated and clarified as parallelopipedons (see Figures 6.4 and 6.5). The reductive process, therefore, severely refined the "four square" Larkin building and later Unity Temple. On its completion, Wright described the Larkin and included these words:

> The Larkin Building . . . is a simple working out of certain utilitarian conditions, its exterior a simple cliff of brick whose only "ornamental" feature is the exterior express of the central aisle fashion by means of the sculptured piers at either end of the main block. . . . [M]ost of the critic's "architecture" has been left out. Therefore the work may have the same claim to consideration as a "work of art" as an ocean liner, a locomotive or a battleship.[25]

Figure 6.4 Principal facade and main entry photograph, ca. 1906, Larkin Administration Building in Buffalo, New York, 1902–05, demolished in 1929. From private collection.

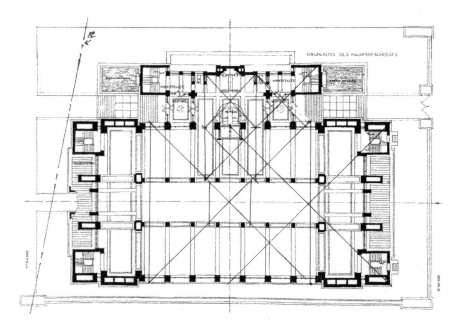

Figure 6.5 Ground-floor plan, Larkin Administration Building in Buffalo, New York, 1902–05; author's notations. From Wright, 1910.

The Wright School   171

With Jones's aesthetic proposals in mind, Wright responded to early published criticism of the building as built:

> [it is] frankly, "a group of bare, square edged, parallelopipedons [sic], uncompromising in their geometrical precision, without delicate light and shade," but fitted to one another organically and with aesthetic intent, and with utter contempt for the fetish so long worshiped that architecture consist . . . in loading their surfaces with irrelevant sensualities.[26]

The Larkin is twice in length as width, and the front elevation precisely square; therefore, it is two cubes long. Although the building used square proportions, it was less obviously experienced inside. The full-height central light well must have felt cramped, Figure 6.6, being narrower than the side spaces, much as the Marshall Field Store in Chicago (of 1902 designed by D. H. Burnham & Company) to which Wright referred Larkin clients. There was a similar central light well within the top three stories of the Lincoln Center.[27]

Beye boathouse, 1905

In November 1905, University of Wisconsin crew commodore Cudworth Beye asked Wright to design a boathouse beside the recently redredged Yahara River channel that connected Madison's two largest lakes and beside Tenney Park. The proposed building was to provide for rowing shells, change rooms, a boat launch, and so on. It was a private commission, and

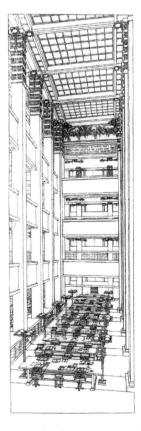

Figure 6.6 Drawing traced on a photograph of the interior of the Larkin Administration Building in Buffalo, New York, 1902–05; a grand space for practical office and filing; steel posts and beams hidden by terra cotta and stucco for fireproofing; continuous ceiling skylight. From Wright, 1910.

172 *The aesthetics of progress*

Beye hoped it would become associated with the university. The result was quite different from Wright's public recreational boathouses of 1893, beside Madison's lakes Monona and Mendota, and more prescient.[28] In this instance, the cantilevered flat roof visually united the building, and its long walls parallel with boat ramps and floats at either end (see Figures 6.7 and 6.8). Wright's written comments to Beye on 19 December 1905 about the just-delivered drawings were minimal:

> The scheme is very simple, – tar and gravel roof, plastered walls and hemlock frame. . . .
> Skylights light the aisles between the shells, so that they may be overhauled there; and provisions has been made for a flue at either end, so that two stoves may be used if heat were necessary.[29]

There is a nice conceptual similarity in plan and section to Wright's Women's Pavilion for the Spring Green Inter-County Fair of October 1914 (see Figure 6.9). The only difference at the fair was a wood-structured pitched roof above clear story windows that covered a central passage

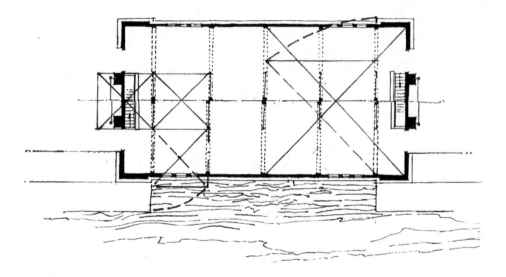

Figure 6.7 Ground-floor plan, Beye boathouse project for Madison, Wisconsin, 1905. Composite drawing by author.

Figure 6.8 Perspective of the Beye boathouse project for Madison, Wisconsin, 1905. From Wright, 1921.

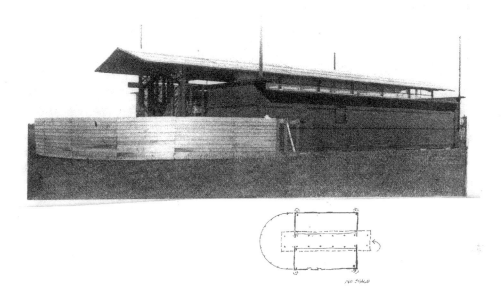

Figure 6.9 Women's Pavilion "Spring Green Fairground," Wisconsin, 1914; photograph courtesy Franklin Porter as published in Hamilton (1909); conjectural floor plan by author.

running lengthwise. It separated two parallel single-story side enclosures built of temporary walls, perhaps canvass. A children's exterior play area was enclosed by a hemicycle of wood siding.[30] Less the fair Pavilion, the proposed Beye building is important in fundamental ways.

The Beye floor plans recall the vertical systems of the contemporary Larkin and Unity Temple designs, where solid corner piers and a series of interior columns defined a central function (space) surrounded by other serving functions. The boathouse was to have a ground floor of clear space for shells. On the floor above were lockers, a meeting room, and viewing decks. The boathouse was a similar plan parti and aesthetic conception to Larkin, from which the Beye end elevations were also derived. The solid corner forms for the boathouse identified interior stairs. So, too, at Larkin in 1902, where solid corner towers contained stairs and expressed other functional parts, such as air circulating systems. And so, too, at Unity Temple in 1904, where the corner walls and volumes were individually expressed, visually obvious; "articulated" was Wright's word.

At this time, Wright produced a few other flat-roofed designs but of small size – for instance, the Gale's cottage in 1905, the Smith bank of 1904–05, the second proposal for Harry Brown's house,[31] the *Ladies Home Journal* concrete house, and Bock's studio project, each of 1906.[32] At this time, the solid corner was effectively applied to the following houses: Little 1902, Walser 1903, Barton 1903, Hoyt 1906, Fuller ca. 1906, Nicholls 1906, Hunt 1907, Stockman 1908, and Evans 1908.

Unity Temple, 1905–08

Wright's preliminary plan and section drawings of 1903 for the Lincoln Center assembly room reveal germinal ideas for the interior of Unity Temple. At the second-floor level, the 1903 proposal had balconies on three sides, a lecture platform on the fourth, corner stairs, a cruceform plan (at least as defined by the four central boxed posts front and rear), an overhead heating

174 The aesthetics of progress

system, lighting in channels, and natural light high on the periphery. These architectonics were more exactly employed for Unity Temple (see Figures 6.10, 6.11, and 6.12). Initially, the temple walls were to have been constructed in brick like Lincoln Center and Larkin. (The temple had a three-foot by six-inch module, while Lincoln was seven feet by six inches.) What prompted the decision to use concrete rather than brick for exterior walls is unclear.

When advising Wright, Reverend Jones insisted Lincoln Center should not exhibit conventional church imagery or historical symbols. This was later supported by Unity Temple's Reverend Rodney F. Johonnot, who recognized Jones as "the dean of local liberal religion," his ideas carefully weighed and opinions valued. Considering interviews and documents, historian Manson compiled a tidy summary of Jones's views for Lincoln Center: "no spires, no stained-glass windows, no trace of ritualistic tradition. The new building must express . . . the down-to-earth directness of his [Jones] gospel."[33] So, too, for Johonnot's Temple. Wright's architectural work for the Jones family and at Oak Park was known by the congregation's building committee. Moreover, Wright's faithful client and close friend, Charles E. Roberts, was chair of that committee. Joseph Siry has written a fine history of the temple and its "architecture for liberal religion." Among corrections of fact, he revealed that Wright was selected as architect in September 1905 over other architects (including Perkins) and the first service was held on 25 October 1908.[34]

Unless one has experienced Unity Temple's interior, it is difficult to appreciate the intensity of daylight and horizontal openness. In the January 1938 issue of *Architectural Forum*, Wright incorrectly referred to the interior as the beginning of the destruction of the box. It was a fictional recount, as many of his pre-1905 houses fully exploited horizontally open spaces. His 1938 target was fellow architects whose current love affair was the neutered European box as imported in the 1930s. In any event, it was not the box-like exterior but the interiors of the temple and its adjacent house where space extended beyond implied boundaries. In Wright's

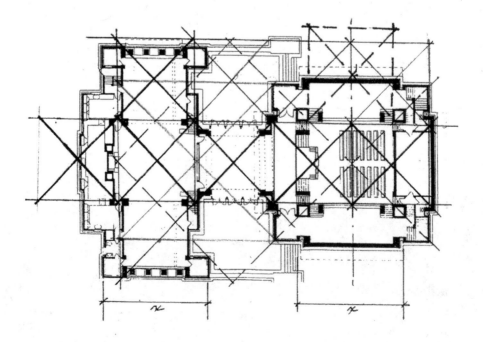

Figure 6.10 Unity Temple and Unity House in Oak Park, Illinois, 1905–08; entry-level floor plan; author's notations.

Figure 6.11 Photograph 1909 by Henry Fuermann of Unity Temple and Unity House in Oak Park, Illinois, 1905–08. From Ashbee, 1911a.

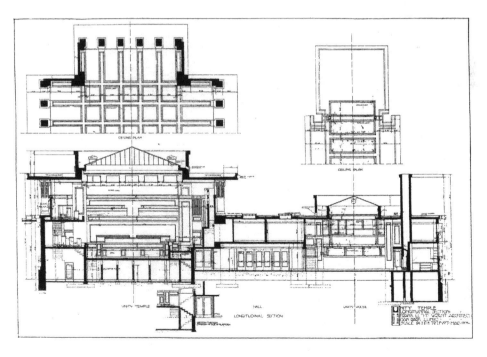

Figure 6.12 "Unity Temple / Longitudinal Section"; top left: one half of the temple reflected ceiling plan; top right: one half of the house reflected ceiling plan; drawing dated "Mar 1906." From Wright, 1925.

residential designs, spatial extension (or spatial flow) was achieved not horizontally through weak corners, as often suggested, even by Wright, but by formal arrangement of fireplace, piers, and walls. At the Temple and House, internal openness was achieved by balconies – that is, vertically displaced horizontal floor planes floating, so to speak, in a large space. Only the temple's basement cloak room was enclosed by four walls.

Four square piers held the temple's concrete roof structure, allowing enclosing exterior walls to be nonstructural screens. The screens were further defined by glass (to receive daylight or transmit nightlight) between roof and walls and vertically as slits between stair and assembly walls. Likely relying on notes prepared by Wright, Reverend Johonnot wrote that the "Temple is a cruceform" plan and it and Unity House

> are lighted mainly from the top through large skylights shielded beneath by glass ceilings. A crown of windows also extends around the Temple beneath the broad protecting roof. . . . With the exception of narrow windows set deeply into recesses between the cruceform mass and the stair chambers, the lowered portion of the Temple is unbroken by doors or windows, save where it opens into the Entrance Hall. . . . At the height of 22 feet the wall of the Temple is recessed to carry columns [collonettes] extending up the roof, thus affording . . . ornamentation and beauty to what would otherwise be [a] too severely simple facade. Behind these columns [colonnettes] is a continuous sweep of windows.[35]

The glazed ceiling emphatically describes the Temple's crown set in a persistent square motif. When inside the assembly room, a person senses he or she is within a cube; indeed, the temple was a cube. Further, the as-built drawings published in Yale University's *Perspecta 22* in 1986 reveal – and Gräf's study in 1983 obsessively informs us – the design of every detail or decoration (leaded glass, lighting fixtures, urns, skylights, or whatever) was based on a square.[36] The entry umbilical was not effectively resolved proportionally and uneasily joined the two major forms, temple and house.

+ + +

Lincoln, Larkin, Beye, and Unity can be conceptually related by simple schematics (see Figure 6.13). Wright loved the square, White said. Wright said Unity Temple's "style," as a qualitative measure, was "due to the way it was made." Surely the way the design was made was also in its style. After all, he also said that the "process of expression is developed, proceeding from generals to particulars," that "each structure is an ordered fabric," that an architectural "revelation" must be "true to the means used to produce it," that during design phases, "little by little . . . the use of significant virile pattern will creep in to differentiate, explain and qualify as a property of the third dimension as poetry."[37]

The spiritual treasures of Unity's ancestors are abundant. It is a classical Greek temple exposed as a jewel on the suburban landscape; an exercise in Roman planer simplicity and structural integrity; a Palladian proportional system in plan, mass, and external treatment; a geometrically pure neoclassical architecture that would have won the admiration of Ledoux;[38] a theoretical exercise that would have teased Goethe or Viollet-le-Duc or Froebel and excited Eidlitz. Therefore, two Wright Styles eventuated.

Domestic buildings, Silsbee, and plan evolution

Silsbee's influence on Wright was enormous, more so than Wright was willing to grant or, as a consequence, historians have hitherto believed. There was Silsbee's picturesque architectural mannerisms and his direct application of materials and ease with three-dimensional forms. Silsbee possessed a collection of Japanese art, craft, and prints that were then so fashionable. More lasting was the conduct of lessons for young Frank about architectural design methodology and

The Wright School 177

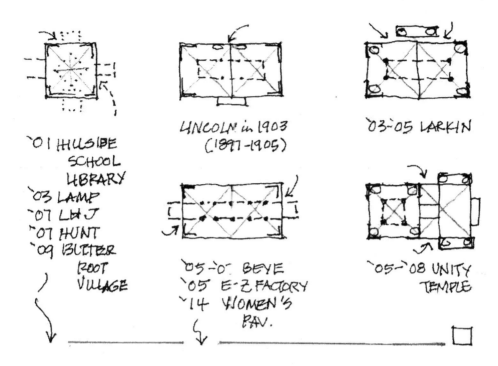

Figure 6.13 Plan schematics for non-domestic buildings before 1915.

procedures leading to planning functions and related three-dimensional form – that is, how to arrange plans, in the main, for domestic architecture. Those ten months of apprenticeship with the affable fellow Unitarian embedded lasting practices.[39]

It will be demonstrated that evolution to the Wright Style house occurred first in the ground-floor plan and then, shedding historicism, three-dimensionally in response to the dynamics of the plan. If stylistic and elevational considerations are ignored for the moment and we study building mass while concentrating on floor plan, evolution will become clear. The "architecture," the elevations, the "expression of the conditions" (i.e. "the stuff architects enjoy," as the late Peter Reyner Banham has said) will easily follow. Not with Conover and Porter but as an employee of Silsbee and Adler & Sullivan, Wright was exposed to three basic house plan types. When in his own office, two proved to be of limited value and were not used other than exceptionally after early experiments.

The first plan to consider, schematically as plan typology Type 1 in Figure 6.14, was used mainly for rather narrow city sites. Main rooms were disposed one or two cells deep along an imprecise axis. Not unique, Wright worked with it on Sullivan's 1891 design of the James Charnley house. Presently known as the Charnley-Persky House Museum Foundation, it is the national headquarters of the Society of Architectural Historians. Wright recalled that he "developed the design in off hours at his Oak Park home, a claim confirmed by statements from the former Adler and Sullivan employees G.G. Elmslie and Paul Mueller." Note that Wright "developed the design," a clear indication that he was dilating and detailing a preliminary design set out by Sullivan. Charnley was a close friend of Sullivan, and they shared vacationland in Mississippi. This approach to preliminary design was – and is – the custom in most

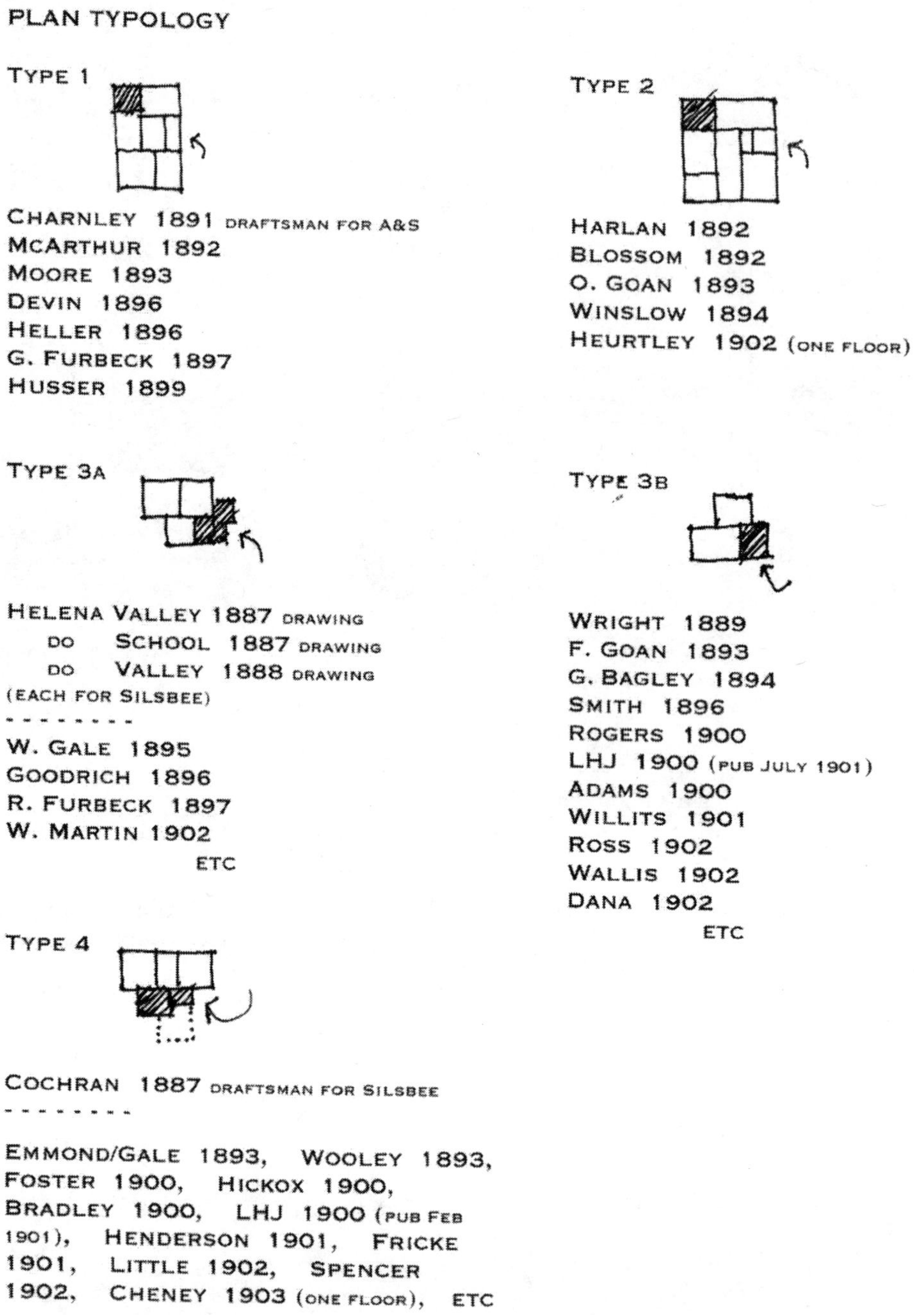

PLAN TYPOLOGY

Type 1

Charnley 1891 draftsman for A&S
McArthur 1892
Moore 1893
Devin 1896
Heller 1896
G. Furbeck 1897
Husser 1899

Type 2

Harlan 1892
Blossom 1892
O. Goan 1893
Winslow 1894
Heurtley 1902 (one floor)

Type 3A

Helena Valley 1887 drawing
  do   School 1887 drawing
  do   Valley 1888 drawing
(each for Silsbee)
- - - - - - - -
W. Gale 1895
Goodrich 1896
R. Furbeck 1897
W. Martin 1902
                ETC

Type 3B

Wright 1889
F. Goan 1893
G. Bagley 1894
Smith 1896
Rogers 1900
LHJ 1900 (pub July 1901)
Adams 1900
Willits 1901
Ross 1902
Wallis 1902
Dana 1902
                ETC

Type 4

Cochran 1887 draftsman for Silsbee
- - - - - - - -
Emmond/Gale 1893, Wooley 1893, Foster 1900, Hickox 1900, Bradley 1900, LHJ 1900 (pub Feb 1901), Henderson 1901, Fricke 1901, Little 1902, Spencer 1902, Cheney 1903 (one floor), ETC

Figure 6.14 Plan typologies leading to the Wright Style of domestic architecture.

architectural offices. The young architect who shared an office room with Wright was Elmslie. He stated that "the first time the design was seen in the office of Adler and Sullivan was when Wright brought the quarter-scale drawings from his home in Oak Park."

Similarly, Mueller, a former chief engineer with the firm, noted that "Wright practically designed the Charnley residence. . . ." In this case, "practically" means an ordinary practical activity, not useful. "Designed" could mean detailing or something more full. It is fairly obvious that, as Nickel and Siskind remarked, "the form and character of the Charnley house reflect a maturity and sophistication not fully evident in Wright's independent work of the same period."[40] Biographer Secrest was also correct when she evaluated the house as "a classical design of almost precocious restraint, clarity and refinement."[41] Indeed, it has a maturity totally inconsistent with buildings designed by Wright alone during the same time.

This learning curve is best revealed by comparing Charnley with Wright's independent designs, especially the McArthur house, whose design was started in 1892, just months after Charnley's. It followed schematically the Charnley plan but, on the long axis, chambers were two deep rather than one. Three-dimensionally, the house was without reference to Charnley. Rather, it was an interpretation of a gambrel-roofed Silsbee exterior form but in stucco, not wood shingles. For McArthur, a series of fussy exterior elements were boldly displayed but without Charnley's polished detail, its proper use of materials, and elegant proportions: restraint is nowhere evident. Except for the complex Tudoresque Moore house of 1895, remodeled by Wright in 1923, the Type 1 plan was not used again. It likely had a minor effect on the long narrow plans of houses for Heller in 1896 and Husser in 1899, less effectively the Young house of 1899 and the contrived mistake for George Furbeck in 1897. Stiffly axial and awkwardly too academic, the experimental Aline Devin house project of 1896 fit no prescribed style in plan, although elevations contained an engorgement of Sullivanesque ornament. Those last houses were one-offs, without evolutionary potential.

Houses designed independently by Wright from 1887–92 while employed by Adler & Sullivan were: none in 1887–88; his own house Oak Park in 1889+ (shingle and typical plan); McArthur house, Chicago, in 1892 (gambrel Silsbee stucco, two floor plans loosely related to Charnley); Blossom house, Chicago, in 1892 (timber, colonial classical, both floor plans similar to Winslow 1894); and Emmond in LaGrange and T. Gale and Parker, each in Oak Park, in 1892 (plans similar, timber, shingle). As those houses were quite dissimilar to Charnley, and as Wright's words connote common office practice, it is safe to believe that for Charnley he did no more than stabilize Sullivan's design and details, who then corrected them, and then Wright and staff prepared construction drawings. Houses built for Adler & Sullivan clients and on which Wright likely did some detailing were the MacHarg house of 1891 (Sullivanesque shingle) and the Harlan house of 1892 or earlier (unique with Sullivanesque ornament), both buildings in Chicago. William Storrs MacHarg graduated from the University of Michigan in mining engineering in 1868 and became a Chicago sanitation and mechanical engineer who provided expertise to Adler & Sullivan for their tall buildings before Wright's employment. Dr Allison Harlan was a dentist and apparently a friend and client of Sullivan's.[42]

Plan Type 2 was also learned by experience in the Adler & Sullivan office and likely began with Sullivan's design for Harlan in 1891 or 1892.[43] The Blossom house of 1892 was Wright's interpretation of classical details in wood as found on one form of colonial residences and possibly at the client's request. The exterior had similarities to houses of the period as well as Silsbee's West Virginia Building of 1891–93 for Chicago's Exposition. When independently practicing, Wright produced a more idiosyncratic design of steep roofs, dormers, and bay windows for Clark's house in La Grange, Chicago, in 1892. For land purchased in 1894 by William Winslow, Wright designed a house that in plan is more rational that those previous, and the street elevation was a study in formalized restraint. He also applied the Sullivan technique for resolving the transition from wall to eave by a band darker than the wall below – a frieze – in which something like tiles or sets of windows could be placed. The front facade shows Wright's mature understanding of Sullivan's treatment of the Charnley house facade of three years earlier and on which he did some drafting. The Winslow rear facade is anomalous. The last of the Type 2 houses was in Oak Park for Goodrich in 1896. The rectangular forms of Types 1 and 2 with restricted perimeters and an apparent need to stack walled chambers were serious limitations.

During those years of independently investigating the mysteries of floor plans and related three-dimensional massing – or of ornamentation – Wright continued to apply a plan type he learned under Silsbee in 1887, Type 3b. He used it on his own house in 1889 and elsewhere into the 1950s. Other examples are Green 1912, Millard 1923, house on a Mesa project 1931, Willey project 1932, Usonian Concrete Block House project 1939, Pew 1938, Obler 1946, Adelman 1954, and Quadruple Housing project 1958. It was the foundation plan for the Wright Style houses built in the Midwest and then in other places.

Young Frank's first exposure to the Type 3a plan was when he made three perspective drawings of two house projects for "Helena Valley" and of his aunt's school Home Building. As previously described, they were drawing exercises set by – and in an ink rendering style of – his boss. Although Wright implies otherwise, they were executed only a month or so after Wright entered the office, their designs complete before he made the drawings. In 1888, Silsbee simplified the plan in a housing scheme for Cochran, and the exterior was no longer shingled, Type 4. Again, Wright prepared a perspective drawing of the house, and Cochran used it in at least one advertisement. The main or ground-floor plan had ancillary rooms, hatched for the illustrations, on one side of a straight inline bifurcation. It was first used by Wright four years later for the Emmond/Gale houses of 1892. Three-dimensionally, the rooms appeared to be stacked vertically. Yet when the plan was applied to the Henderson house early in 1901, horizontality was achieved by the disposition of roofs to a more linear scheme, and the rooms no longer appeared stacked. Beginning about September 1900, he designed a house that was published as a "Home in a Prairie Town" in the February 1901 issue of *Ladies Home Journal* out of Philadelphia. This was followed in 1900 by the Hickox and Bradley houses and in 1901 by the Henderson house.[44]

+ + +

Relying on the forensic evaluations of Paul Kruty, Paul Sprague, Bruce Pfeiffer, and Patrick Cannon, who based their determinations on primary or secondary documents or on the evidence of stylistic evolution, as well as on my own studies, the correct chronology of byways and critical designs leading to formalization of a Wright Style of domestic architecture is now possible (see Figures 6.15 and 6.16).[45]

1889, Wright's house, August; typical floor plans of the period and as experienced in Silsbee's office; shingle style, his first independent design.

1892, Emmond and two Gale houses (Parker was a first resident in one), initial design ca. June; floor plans had developmental potential but three-dimensional aesthetics were Queen Anne; see also 1900 in this list and the similar but clumsy design of the Wooley house of 1893.

1893, Orrin Goan project, ca. April 1893; design likely began just before Wright was laid off by Alder; it was predecessor to the Winslow house of 1894–95; both a theoretical terminus in plan and elevation.

1896, Hillside Home School wind pump; informal commission of Jones family; unique structurally and in detailing of materials for this building type; shingles with intermittent battens; design altered and exterior materials changed in 1938 reconstruction.

1897, Edward C. Waller house project, scheme two; floor plan developed from Emmond house; elevationally a transitional design of unresolved Sullivanesque elements. Commissioned around December as a possible gift for his recently widowed daughter Mrs Robert (Rebecca) Eckart, Waller paid the fees and was Wright's contact; working drawings are dated 1898 and there were none for scheme one.

1897, Heller house, ca. March, and the Waller house project, ca. December; each theoretically impotent and unrelated to future designs.

1897, Wright's studio addition; a miniature beaux-arts scheme with plenty of three-dimensional theoretical potential in the floor plan.

The Wright School 181

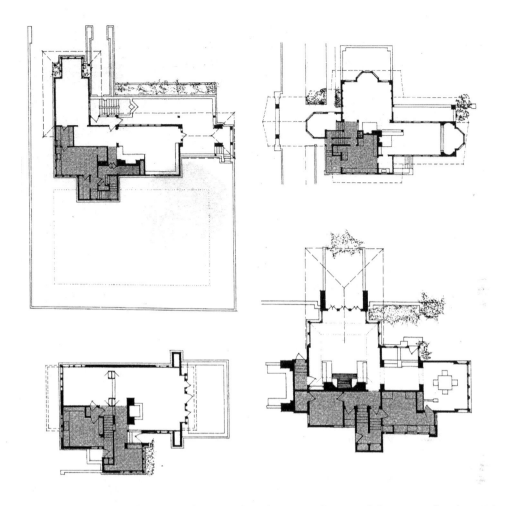

Figure 6.15 Application of plan typology number 3b in 6.14: from top left: proposed Helena Valley house for Silsbee, 1889; Wright's own house, 1889; *Ladies Home Journal* project (July 1901); Rogers house, 1900; Willits house, 1902; T. Gale house, 1909; author's notations.

1898, David T. Devin house project, ca. August 1898; theoretical impotence. Two months after design began, Devin died of a self-inflected gunshot to his abdomen while on a hunting trip at Dead Lake, Minnesota. Mrs Devin carried on and moved to Eliot, Maine. Wright described her as a "fashionable, fastidious client" who commissioned him in 1906 to prepare a "summer cottage" design that was not built.[46]

1898, Golf Clubouse, scheme 1, preferred date is late in the year; high potential aesthetically.

1898, Winslow stables, preferred date is late in the year; near-classical composed floor plan and elevations; exterior aesthetically prescient yet unrelated to house.

1898, Cooper house project, not of 1887 or 1889 or 1893; Paul Sprague suggests the "2nd half of 1899"; floor plan adapted from published sources; theoretical limitations but, aesthetically, the elevations are closely related to Winslow stables.[47]

1899, McAfee house, ca. November, and Husser house earlier in the year; both a theoretical cul-de-sac.

1900, Foster house; published June 1900; a transitional elevational design.

182 The aesthetics of progress

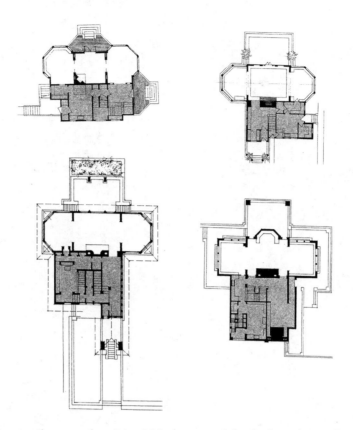

Figure 6.16 Plan typology number 4 in 6.14: from top left: Cochran house for Silsbee, 1887; Emmond house, 1892; Hickox house, 1901; Henderson house, 1901; *Ladies Home Journal* project (February 1901); author's notations.

1900, "Prairie Town," published February 1901 in *Ladies Home Journal*; Hickox house, June 1900; both floor plans based on Emmond house.

1900, "Small House," published June 1901 in *Ladies Home Journal*; the Davenport and Bradley houses both begun in June; floor plans and exterior aesthetics similar.

1901, James C. Rogers house, Oak Park; contemporary with and a scheme similar to "Small House." Commissioned in 1900 by Chicago businessman James Campbell Rogers. He paid Wright's fee and construction costs; he was also Wright's contact and oversaw construction. On completion, the house would be occupied by his newlywed daughter, Susan, and her husband Frank Wright Thomas. For twenty years, the Thomases paid off what was a loan to purchase the house from Rogers; it was not a wedding gift. Surely design began in 1900, before or after a June wedding, and construction began in 1901. In March 1902, Wright referred to "the Metzger house and the Rogers House" as "the work of Frank Lloyd Wright and Webster Tomlinson."[48] Properly, it should be identified hereafter as the James C. Rogers house, otherwise the Thomases known as first residents.

1901, Lowell studio project, 1 January; Arts and Crafts aesthetic, Wright & Tomlinson, Architects, Wright the designer.

1901, Metzger house project, ca. September; and Henderson house, midyear; both an elaboration of the "Prairie Town" house; Wright & Tomlinson, Architects, Wright the designer.[49]

1902, Willits house; an enlarged elaboration of the "Small House"; Wright & Tomlinson, Architects, Wright the designer; linens dated 1 June 1902, revised November 1902 and January 1903.

Pitkin, Scudder, and Adams . . . up North

Wright's neighbor Edward Hand Pitkin was in many ways a typical Oak Park resident and aware of the architect's work and social activities. An Illinois volunteer veteran of the Civil War, in 1872 he and J. W. Brooks founded a crockery and miscellaneous wholesale and retail business in Chicago that, by 1900, had become one of the largest in the nation. His brother Albert Pitkin married Jessie, the sister of Wright's amour, Mamah Borthwick Cheney. A member of the Oak Park Congregational church, Edward was devoted to its Beloit College, of which he was a long-time trustee, and supported local cultural institutions and missionary causes.[50] On 12 September 1900, Pitkin bought eighteen acres of land on the 1,250-meter-long rocky outcrop called Sapper Island, a few hundred feet north of Campement d'Ours Island, which is throwing distance from St Joseph's Island and across St Joseph's Channel (by ferry) to Kensington Point, from there seven kilometers to the small community of Desbarats (the nearest post office to Sapper) in the District of Algoma in south-central Ontario at the northern tip of Lake Huron and a few miles from the international border with Michigan. Shortly thereafter, he asked Wright to design a summer cottage.[51] As with all of his summer cottages, Wright's design was simple and plain. Placed on a large wood platform forty- by forty-eight feet was a room thirteen-feet wide that left a verandah eight-feet wide on three sides and on the front of twelve feet. Behind a rubble stone fireplace were a water closet, tiny kitchen, storage, and stairs up to six bedrooms. All exterior walls were sheathed in board and batten, the first use of that system after the golf clubhouse. A high gable roof with extended soffits appeared chalet-like.[52]

The northern shores and islands of Canadian Lake Huron were summer recreational places for those below the border. Its not surprising that another Chicagoan planned to build a retreat in the area, his site only a few miles from Pitkin's but on Campement d'Ours Island. J. A. Scudder employed Wright, whose September 1904 drawings were not for a cottage but a two-story, three-bedroom cabin sitting on the precipice of a bolder-strewn hill. The walls were single against square upright structural posts at three-foot centers, their material wood boards laid horizontally, in this instance, with milled battens. A hipped roof and the gutter details were based on the Darwin Martin houses of 1902–03. There was nothing unique in a board-and-batten wall. For decades, it had been in common usage throughout North America.[53] Unbuilt, a water-level perspective looking up to the proposed house was imitated in one of many for the 1905 Hardy house that had similar site conditions and floor plans.[54]

Yet another businessman and banker sought Wright's talent. Victor E. Metzger was born in Wisconsin, at one time (1881) a private in the La Crosse Light Guard. He became an insurance agent and banker working and residing in Sault Ste. Marie, Michigan. In early 1901, Metzger commissioned Wright to prepare designs for a family home. The general layout and floor plans were taken from the 1900 project "Home in a prairie town" but enlarged in all respects. Perspective drawings reveal a building sitting awkwardly on a sloping site. When one considers the Bradley and Hickox designs, as well as the two designs for *Ladies Home Journal*, the Metzger design appears regressively overdesigned.[55]

Of interest here is Metzger's relationships with people in Chicago, parts of Wisconsin, and northern Michigan who included Wright's clients. In 1902, the Central Savings Bank of Sault Ste. Marie was organized mainly by the resolve of Robert N. Adams. He was president, Metzger cashier, and, by 1902, vice president. Adams was successful in commerce and banking, involved with civic activities and philanthropy, and had connections throughout the region.[56] In 1902, he personally hired the talented architect Edward Demar. Born in Vermont, Demar studied architecture in Toronto, then trained in offices in Winnipeg and Brandon in Manitoba and in Regina, Saskatchewan, followed by Marquette City and Ishpeming in Michigan, before forming a partnership in 1891 with Andrew Lovejoy in Marquette. After two more short-lived partnerships, in 1901, he settled into a solo practice in Sault Ste. Marie.[57] There, he created three important modern buildings within the span of only three years, each displaying neatly resolved proportions and related details, and each now on the US National Register of Historic Places.

First was the commercial Gowan Block of 1900–01, a unique transitional non-stylistic work and placed on the register in 2010. Gowan Block was contemporary with a synthesis of a drastically stripped Romanesque subtlety fused with early modern plainness for a design of the First United Presbyterian Church of 1901–02. It was placed on the register in 1984. Again proximate, in 1902, Adams wisely employed Demar to design a six-story commercial edifice that was named the Adams Building. It was constructed to a design that showed Wright's influence without mimicry. Demar must have come to know Wright's architecture by experience, in this case, the Francis Apartments of 1895. Provenance obvious, but Demar's was the more elegant, faultless in the use and detailing of materials, and timelessly modern. It was registered in 2010.[58]

+ + +

There is a tendency to fail to understand the importance of the ground-floor plan, its creatively determinant role, its vitality in the design process.[59] As any architect of any culture or century will attest, the principle or ground-floor plan is all. It is the control of and springboard to purpose and intent and evolves three-dimensionally; and it is where all structure is resolved in the earth. It is the architect's private creative instrument, the artifact that reveals to the mind's eye how the design product will be consummated. As such, it is also the constructor's tool. In a floor plan, the architect sees and experiences three-dimensional characteristics and processes much as a musician hears the music revealed by notes of a score.

"A good plan is the beginning and the end," Wright said. In the ground-floor plan is "more beauty" than "in almost any of its ultimate consequences" and "itself will have the rhythms, masses and proportions ... consistent with materials." In the plan, all is seen: "purpose, materials, method, character, style." When developing a plan, he continued, "the concept grows and matures," and with it, "all is won or lost before anything more tangible; begins." A building is conceived in the imagination, and then, working with "triangle and T-square [or CAD program,] should modify or extend or intensify or test the conception – complete the harmonious adjustment of its parts." Of course, elevations "construct" themselves in plan.[60] In 1908, Wright added ... there is a "harmonious relationship between ground plan and elevation, ... the one (elevation) as a solution and the other an expression of the conditions of a problem of which the whole is a project."[61]

In the ground-floor plan, therefore, transformation and evolution will be found. We have noted that factors of building methods and materials, articulation, and "expression" were held in balance by proportions derived by a square and a cube, or a module. Wright recognized that "a certain standardization," he emphasized, would inevitably result but only "at the beginning" of the design process. He suggested that a module was "like a warp in the oriental rug," but he forgot the weft threads! All this was unimportant, he sagely pronounced, in the absence of talent:

> Trained imagination is necessary [he said] to differentiate or syncopate or emphasize, to weave or play upon it consistently.
> Scale is really proportion. Who can teach proportion? Without a sense of proportion, no one should attempt to build. This gift of sense must be the diploma Nature gave to the architect.[62]

(Proportion is an aesthetic determinant totally ignored in modern discourse.) The Darwin Martin house of 1903–05, with an enlarged and theoretically embellished Emmond/Bradley floor plan, was the exemplar of academic excellence. It revealed differentiation, syncopation, and rational structure; and the "sense" proportionally articulates almost every aspect: living room, entry, kitchen, and porch, as well by pier, post, mullion, door, heating radiator, human movement, floor vent, and so forth. Yet Wright was never a slave to the module or square.[63] They always remained a design tool at his will.

As mentioned, Silsbee did not invent the two conceptually simple plans discussed. A flip through the pages of *American Architect* and other publications of the 1880s and 1890s make this clear.[64] Their functional ability was one of Wright's initial experiences as a draftsman. Under Silsbee, he learned by application how the plans could meet a client's needs, how to arrange functional clarity, define it volumetrically, and stylize it three-dimensionally.

Transformation from nineteenth-century bulky forms and cubicle spaces, like the Cochran and Wright's early houses, to open internal spaces and an obvious horizontal exterior spread out and low-profiled, can be explained by speculation as to how Wright likely proceeded during 1898–99. The schematic example in Figure 6.17 again uses hatching lines for ancillary rooms. Normally, the upper floor mounts the lower directly above and the roofs respond to the two-story-high exterior walls. The need to allow horse and carriage (later a car) to meet the entry vestibule and then pass along to stables at the rear is shown by a dark dashed arrow. The ancillary rooms are neatly collected at the rear, together with stairs to bedrooms. Entry to an entertaining terrace (an exterior room) is symmetrically off the living room to the bottom. In the right diagram, a shallow pitched roofs (the outer dashed line) extends beyond the ground floor over exterior spaces left and right, including the entry, and over the living room. The upper floor, indicated by a dotted line, is set back from the street facade and coupled with a skirt roof, the transformation complete.[65] The resolution likely occurred easily during the months 1899 into 1900, the Bradley house a paradigm.

A comparison of houses over a decade leads to four observations. The integration of the block or rectangular designs, such as Larkin or Beye, with horizontally extended houses occurred simultaneously. Horizontal line and form were succeeded by rectangularity and an absence of exterior ornament. Throughout the period, ornamenting house interiors remained a joyful activity. Further, while such an evolution occurred, earlier forms – line and ornament – were not abandoned. And fourth, the first dramatically horizontal house to announce a Wright Style was Bradley's, begun in 1900. The gable roof and slightly flared gable end extends the horizontal ridge line (see Figure 6.18). What Wright might have called organic ornament is in the dark wood window trim (set against white/cream stucco applied to wood studs) and sill line and capstones rigorously highlighting horizontality. This was followed by the Willits house of early 1902 into 1903, whose exterior walls were also stucco. But note that the ridge was no longer extended but that it ended bluntly in a shallow hipped roof and dark wood facia while the reserve and character of exterior and interior follow closely the Winslow stables and Bradley house precedent but lacking its dynamics.

In contrast, Darwin Martin's commission of Wright to design a house for his sister Delta became known by her husband's name, the George Barton house of 1902–04. More correctly, it should be known by its commissioner and as D. Martin's Barton house, whose plan was a

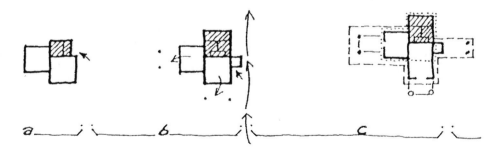

Figure 6.17 Schematic explanation of the evolution from stacked chambers to rather open floor plans and an extended horizontality on the exterior. Author's drawing.

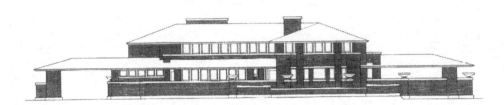

Figure 6.18 Above: Bradley house, east or principle elevation, 1899–1901; measured drawing by Mario Messer, Philippe Brochart, Jonathan Klocke of house as built. Courtesy HABS, IL-327.9. Below: Darwin Martin house, south or principle elevation, 1903–05; measured drawing by John W. Joseph, 1987, of house as built. Courtesy HABS, NY,15-BUF,5–6. Drawings not to same scale.

refinement of the Emmond prototype. It is an academic tour de force in plan, elevation, proportion, and use and detail of materials, notably the Roman brick: architectural ornament would have been ostentatious. Replace the hipped roof with one flat and the building is a brick box. Contemporary with Martin's Barton house, Wright used the same plan with slight revisions to entry but constructed entirely of studs and stucco for the Barnes house project of 1902.[66] The Barnes plan was then overelaborated for the Little residence number one also of 1902 in regular brick, more faithfully for the stud and stucco houses for Walser of 1903, DeRhodes in 1906, and Horner in 1908. Darwin Martin's own house of 1903–05 has been previously discussed herein. As with the Willits and Barton houses, the roof is not gabled but hipped with a shallow pitch, thereby diminishing the ridge's visual impact, emphasis now on the roof and soffit edges. Dark Roman brick walls and planes and gray-white capstones dominate the exterior: all reference to romantic Arts and Crafts set aside.

During the design and construction phases of these buildings, Wright continued to apply the reductive principle to new buildings for Hillside school, the Larkin Soap Company, Unity Temple, and Mr Beye's boathouse.

We recall that Wright used flat roofs for Brock's studio in 1902 and for the T. Gale house in 1909. But material details and elevational treatment were still within Arts and Crafts. A critical residential design transformation began when Wright held hipped roofs back from a flat dark fascia. The visual result was plainly of a flat roof with extended flat soffit, the roof edges read as a flat plane. This was noticeable for the Isabel Roberts house of 1908 in River Forest and next door to William Drummond's own house of 1909 with a flat roof and wide fascia and otherwise influenced by Wright's residential buildings post-1902. (The same held true for Drummond's Ralph S. Baker house of 1909.) There was as well the Oscar Steffens house of 1909 (demolished in the 1950s) and the Frank J. Baker house in Wilmette of 1909, both otherwise appearing much like the Willits's house externally. Finally, in 1911, Wright introduced a flat roof to the Oscar B. Balch house in Oak Park. These buildings were followed by a series of designs for the Coonley playhouse of 1911–12. The paradigm, however, was the Emil Bach house, with plans dated May 1915 (see Figure 6.19). Here, horizontal lines of capstone, sill,

Figure 6.19 South and west elevations of Emil Bach house in Chicago, Illinois, 1911–12; tan brick, light-brown stucco, oak-colored wood trim; measured 1965, drawing by J. William Rudd, 1966. Courtesy HABS, ILL,16-CHIG,83–4.

lintel, and roof were opposed to brick piers, panels, and jambs that held a lighter stuccoed top floor, all above or surrounding a simple four-square (as it is now called) floor plan. The design was undertaken contemporary with the theoretically challenging Midway Gardens of 1913–14, a building so influential on a few European architects.

Historian Paul Kruty correctly remarked that the ill-proportioned and arbitrarily composed William Wood house project of 1917–18 "closes an era just a surely as the first Prairie houses of 1900 had opened it." Now we know it was those of 1898. Anyway, the teens were a time of great drama, personal tragedy, and resurrection.

+ + +

It has been argued that the position of three juxtaposed major spaces used by Wright for the Emmond/Gale floor plan was taken from a traditional religious structure as adapted for Japan's national building at the 1893 Chicago Exposition.[67] Its plan and appearance recalled the Buddhist Byodo-In Temple near Kyoto of 1053. The floor plan had a single central pavilion (Phoenix Hall or Hoodo) whose floor area could be altered by a series of sliding screens.[68] However, the critical incidents in Silsbee's office and immediately thereafter occurred years *before* the Japanese pavilion was opened to the public mid-1893. The degree of its influence was negligible, and for other good reasons. First, potential room divisions in the Japanese central building and other traditional houses and temples had systems not contemplated in America, let alone by Wright. Second, openable walls between rooms, usually sliding paired doors, were generally and not occasionally used by late nineteenth-century American architects and builders. In Wright's immediate experience, for example, there was a relative openness between juxtaposed major rooms in some of Silsbee's plans, and Wright saw other examples in publications. Third, the Emmond/Gale houses were completed in 1892. And fourth, in general terms, Wright denied it.

It should be obvious that traditional Japanese plans and functional arrangements (so intimately cultural) and structural systems did not exist in Wright's work of any period. This does not detract from our knowledge of the inspiration he otherwise received from traditional Japanese two- and three-dimensional crafts, design, and art. As well, he would have noted that the square was a determinant in Japanese design generally and therefore in its architecture.

Wright Styles and the Wright School

If Wright sincerely believed Emerson, Viollet-le-Duc, Uncle Jenkin, and Sullivan, as well as the call of contemporaries, then he had to invent something identifiably his own. English critic, poet, painter, and engraver William Blake, a favorite of Uncle Jenkin and Wright, once said that an artist "must create a system or be enslaved by another man's."

When, in January 1901, the newly formed partnership of Wright and Tomlinson was asked by New England landscape artist Milton H. Lowell to prepare a design for a new studio in Matteawan, New York, they refused. Yet on a one-page letter of reply Wright penned a sketch.[69] It was somewhat similar to Silsbee's Unity Chapel, not only in plan and elevation, but now firmly in Wright's residential style (see Figure 6.20). The chapel and Lowell exterior designs had a stone base capped by a surround string course of wood at windowsill level. Windows were fit between sill and soffit and within a change of material. The effect was a horizontal band – a frieze – around a building's perimeter: like the stables and golf clubhouse. The roof was shallow and the eave deep on the Lowell design, its low-slung bulk and projecting eve emphasized horizontality.[70]

Known as a bright and talented young architect, Henry Webster Tomlinson was taken on to run Wright's business and for his drawing skills. After receiving a bachelor of science in architecture from Cornell University in 1886, Tomlinson moved to Chicago, where he mixed with young radicals. The partnership ceased during 1902. After breaking with Wright, he became a respected architect, active in the AIA and Chicago City Cub to then operate out of Joliet, Illinois.[71]

Former Wright and Griffin employee Barry Byrne correctly observed that

> [Wright's] greatest contributions [were] his incomparable building plans. The value of his exterior massing and details derived from their appearance of inevitability and from the fact of their indisputable rightness as expressions of the plan.

The Wright School 189

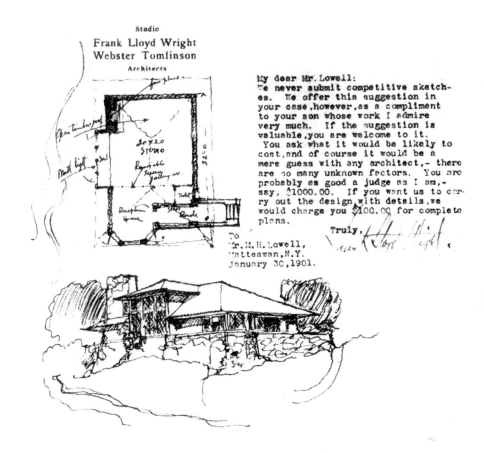

Figure 6.20 Project of a studio for M. H. Lowell in Matteawan, New York, 1901; raised window for north light typical for artists' studios. From Twombly, 1979. Courtesy and © 2016 FLWF.

Further, Byrne believed Wright was "endowed" with "an unerring sense of the third dimension." He was a man who "always arrived at his designs in plan and elevation."[72] The main or ground-floor plan was Wright's functional and structural generator; the square his organizational and aesthetic generator; design motifs large and small were many; a module a conventional tool. Quite plainly and consistent with previous discussions herein, "Art cannot be abstracted from the conditions of art."[73] Aesthetics alone is insufficient. (A proposition certain "postmodern" aestheticians fail to understand.) As Viollet-le-Duc observed in his lecture Discourse 12, "let us frankly adopt the appliances afforded us by our own times, and apply them without the intervention of traditions that have lost their vitality; only thus shall we be able to originate an architecture."[74] Change the last words to "originate an American architecture" and they served Chicago's Progressive young architects. From their ranks, however, it was Wright who created identifiably viable architectonics and styles, potentially national, indigenous.

In 1897, Dwight Perkins believed he was

> the founder of what promises to be a very interesting colony of young architects, who have established themselves in the upper stories of Steinway Hall. Here he established his own office . . . [at] the rear of the eleventh story, which, with the attic above . . . [affords] offices for a number of other architects."[75]

Architects mentioned were Robert C. Spencer, Myron Hunt, "and Frank L. Wright." Wright recalled otherwise. Aware of published gossip, in his last book of 1957, Wright wrote that "No school exists without something to teach." He went on two say that he "was not aware that anything like a 'school' had existed," and then went on trying to prove it had existed. Around 1900, "A small clique soon formed about me, myself naturally enough the leader," he said without modesty. Then he listed his "followers," a group now well known. Architect William Purcell was certain that, in 1911, "young men . . . were following Wright's footsteps."[76] Some remained tied to historical revivalism; others, such as Charles E. White, Gamble Rogers, Hunt, and Byrne, drifted. Nonetheless, most "fell in with the idea" (of a school?), Wright said, and then bragged that "I became original advisory exemplar of the group."[77] Outside the group nationally were only a few followers of the school, most still unidentified.

Mountains, seashores, prairies, and rivers can inspire. Wright believed that only a person "with something to teach" could conduct a school and gain followers. One definition of "school" that he must have preferred was that body of pupils or followers of a master, system, method, and so on. Therefore, there was and is no prairie school. The fact that many, if not most, of his buildings were *not* built on a prairie is relevant. However, there was a Wright School whose teachings and products explored designs for both domestic (regional and non-regional) and non-domestic (non-regional) architecture. Each became a Wright Style as the product of a single mind. Similarly, at the time, there was talk of a prairie style of landscape design, but no school evolved because it was limited to "its horticultural program: the use of plants indigenous to the Middle West."[78]

Wright's architect-sons John and Junior knew what their father had created. From San Diego, they entered a *Brickbuilder* house-design competition in 1914 as "The Lloyd Wright Brothers." Their typical one-sheet ink drawing with a tidy floor plan and a modest perspective drawing imitates their father's style. However, their name and design did not sway judges, and the prizes went to other contestants.

Let it be clear: there is absolutely no doubt young men and women were enthralled and motivated by Sullivan's inspiring prose and the urgings and ideas contained. Soon, they discerned that his thoughts were not obviously translated into his architecture. As well, he seemed to be unmoved by human degradation in cities. He accepted existing social conditions rather than participate in reforms. Unconcerned with technology, he was single-mindedly focused on architectural aesthetics, his designs concentrated on beautiful, idiosyncratically florid ornament placed – sometimes in bold relief – on plain right-angled building forms. Other than his ornament and the placement of it, interior or exterior, and except on rare occasions, his architectural designs were not honored by mimicry. His popular and professional influence suddenly diminished after about 1903 only to rise again with the design of a few brick banks from 1905–19. Moreover, some of his house designs took on Wright Style characteristics. The general view then (and should be now) held that Sullivan was the philosophic motivator, Wright the architectural provider.

For there to be a school, there also must be followers and an identifiable character to the buildings with matching details. Architect J.J.P. Oud in the Netherlands put it unambiguously in 1924 when he observed

> . . . the rise of a "Wright School" in the West of America. . . .
>
> Wright once wrote in a pessimistic mood, [saying] that he grieved to see that the form in which he had expressed his ideas in his works, appeared to have a greater attraction than those ideas themselves. Since those ideas aimed at starting from the function and not from the form, he believed this to be "pernicious." . . .

Oud called those imitations a "Cult of Externals."[79] Oud had discovered that "pessimistic mood" in Wright's testy second paper of 1914 titled "In the cause of architecture" as published in *Architectural Record*. As expected, rather than gracefully accepting the accolade, when former employees or other architects mimicked his houses and non-residential building styles, Wright damned them as philosophically impoverished. And the obviousness of a Wright Style was identified by others in Europe through the writings of, for example, Oud again and Hermann de Fries, both in 1926, architect Curt Behrendt in 1937, and, in 1941, by Sigfried Giedion, who panned the idea of a "prairie style"; each emphasized Wright's Chicago period before 1917.[80]

After publication of Spencer's 1900 article and Wright's of 1905, 1908, and 1910–11, Europe and America saw Wright as the leader of a Midwest revolution. Quite simply, he had created and established an architecture that followers and observers perceived as usefully reformist, potent, and theoretically expandable as later proven by Le Corbusier in France, Willem van Leusden and Theo van Doesburg and Oud in Netherlands, and Mies van der Rohe in Germany, among others.[81] The Wright School had followers nationally and, after his 1908 and 1910 publications, also in Europe, as Oud informed us. In 1908, the national community referred to his "reform houses."[82] By 1914, he and they could refer obliquely to the Wright School, to the "New school" as a "progressive moment," one still evolving. Regression to revival was now impossible.[83] By 1915, he was referred to as a "progressive architect," his school as "Western Progressive."[84]

Based on what had transpired during the decade before 1915, landscape architect and academic Wilhelm Miller coined the term "Prairie School of Architecture" in reference primarily to Sullivan's essays. It was an attempt to link in one region the two design professions. To this suggestion, Wright replied almost immediately that within his knowledge Sullivan "never thought of or cared about the prairie," that while he was the inspiration for men who went on to new inventions, there was no "school." Wright scoffed at the idea of a group (school) holding more importance than the recognized products of the individual creator, in this instance of his Wright Styles.[85]

The Arts and Crafts influence found in Wright's houses (1899–1902), with their diamond-leaded windows, wood carpentry, fussy decoration, and general coziness, gave way to the reductive and plain aesthetic as developed for non-domestic buildings. House floor plans became almost rigidly formal with spaces more open and structure boldly articulated. The exterior, therefore, appeared to be a collection of unornamented piers, stub walls, vertical planes, and verandah and garden walls, all capped with white or cream stone or concrete. Where fenestration was required, it was defined on the brick exterior with a sill and lintel similarly capped, much as done for the Larkin Building, the McArthur flat building project, and the E-Z Factory. More notable house examples were the Little, Martin and Barton houses, the domestically situated assembly room of the Hillside Home School of 1902–03, and houses for Ullman in 1902–05, Heath in 1904, Robie in 1906, May in 1908, Stewart in 1909, Bogk in 1916, and the ornamentally – if not totally – regressive Imperial Hotel of 1917–22.

After his tour of Europe, pitched-roof houses gave way to flat cantilevered roofs for a few residences, as noticed for Esbenshade in 1911 (the exterior so much like Coonley's kindergarten in 1911–12) and Bach in 1915, as well as the 1915 Christian Catholic Church project for Zion, Illinois.[86] Two important exceptions were experiments of the Bock studio of 1902 and the Thomas Gale residence of 1909. Post-1911, it was possible to present an architecture where there was no critical distinction between residential and non-residential, where his theory was sensibly more complete. Yet he felt compelled to return to the pitched roof for houses such as Green in 1912, Kier in 1915, and Allen in 1917. Los Angeles architect Harrison Albright was following rather common talk when, in 1909, he referred to the houses as in a "Wright Style."[87]

The idea of a school was current in 1917 when Charles White rhetorically asked, "Are there two American schools of architecture?" His answer was yes, there was the "Conventional School" of the status quo based on antique European models. This was differentiated from Sullivan's theory of an "Organic Architecture" and from "Prairie Architecture," a creation of "the genuine Wright style so revolutionary in character that its message spread quickly," his "philosophy and feeling molded it into a definite 'style'." White also named it "the 'insurgent' School" as well as the "new school" of the American Midwest.[88]

192   *The aesthetics of progress*

Wright's sense of social responsibility, even if too concentric in social practice and illusive in words, paralleled the Progressives' drive for reform and modernization. He was directed to changing functional and aesthetic components in architecture, believing that good design (as Emerson saw economy) would measurably contribute by example to reform processes – that it was educative. Thus, his houses and community planning had as one aim the demonstration that good design had social value. This is less so for the parallelepipedons. Of course, the San Francisco Call Building project of 1912 and the Imperial Hotel of 1917–22 were aberrations.

For instance, like all architects, Wright's house floor plans clearly separated private functions (like bedrooms) and those public or for entertaining. The kitchen was adjacent and often open to entertaining areas, relieving the semi-isolation of kitchen-bound wives and easing service. Moreover, Wright believed window curtains were unnecessary dirt catchers – glass imparted a sense of cleanliness. Windows allowed air movement and transmitted daylight through lead-trapped colored and clear glass that offered subtle geometric gauze for privacy. He treated them as "metal 'grilles' with glass inserted forming rhythmic arrangement of straight lines, and squares."[89] His houses were more open within, friendly, and with many windows, the interior spaces filled with light and circulating air. They were turn-of-the-century modern for the more affluent modern family in new fresh-air suburbs.

The houses, therefore, were usable and spatially – Sullivan would have said democratically – free. Interior/exterior horizontal spatial relationships usually occurred in entertaining areas where grouped windows or French doors opened the interior to the exterior that was invariably defined by a solid railed porch or partly walled paved area. Emphasis was on an interior room related to an exterior room; Hickox, Bradley, and Gale of 1904 and Willits are exemplars. Otherwise, leaded glass sat on an elbow-high sill (see Figure 6.21). It was an aesthetic engagement with views through leaded colored glass of nature's foliage and sky beyond, as Spencer described in 1900. The interior was not part of the exterior environment but a cozily contained

Figure 6.21 Bradley house living room alcove with leaded windows as built in Kankakee, Illinois, 1900–01; tracing by FLW, probably using a pantograph and prepared for Wright, 1910.

intimate place. If not in their economy, it was the character, quality, and aesthetic component of those relationships that increased their reforming value.

+ + +

However, a survey of architectural activity nationally from, say, 1885–1922, reveals an abundantly rich diversity of design characteristics, some acknowledged to be stylistically repeatable, nearly all based on European historical precedents. Nonetheless, when confronted with this plentiful and varied production nationally, by their numbers in a limited region, the Wright School was a minor participant. It failed to gain acceptance by the commercial, political, and urban elite whose patronage would have ensured greater exposure, acceptance, and longevity. Clients remained among the suburban middle class or the leftish.[90] Yet Wright, not his school, was extremely important on the course of change in twentieth-century architecture nationally and internationally. The school's viability, its acceptance in only a few of North America's regions and by only a few architects, lasted from ca. 1902 to ca. 1922: about two decades. In Europe, acceptance lasted from about 1909, that is after the publication of Wright's buildings, to at least 1932 but mainly within theoretical discourse rather than built productivity. To this day, Wright's words and styles continue to intrigue with little consequence.

Notes

1 Third-floor plan in Pfeiffer (2011), p.52; street elevation and two floor plans in Pfeiffer (87–01), plates 122–124.
2 "Synopsis of building news," *Inland Architect*, 27(July 1896), p.50a. See also "Synopsis . . .," "Architects Fowler & Wright: For R.A. Perkins . . .," ibid., 29(September 1897), p.19a, and same title, ibid., 31(March 1898), p.20b, the architects were George T. Fowler and Harvey Wright; [Obituary], "Robert A. Perkins," *The Inter Ocean* (Chicago), 17(July 1899), p.5d; "Miscellaneous," *The Economist: A Weekly . . .*," (Chicago), 19(19 March 1898), p.330a; [Advertisement], "Robert A. Perkins," ibid., 17(December 1897), p.774b.
3 Pfeiffer (2011), p.79, and the best published illustration.
4 Wright (1932), pp.116–117; Wright (1943), p.119.
5 "New Hotel Buildings," *Seattle Post-Intelligencer*, 10(January 1894), p.5d. On Dose and financing the Schiller Building, see "An Investment Opportunity," an advertisement, *Illinois Staats-Zeitung*, 15 August 1893, "Foreign Language Press Survey" website.
6 "New Hotel Buildings', *Seattle Post-Intelligencer*, 10(January 1894), p.5d.
7 "Progress in Building," *Seattle Post-Intelligencer*, 29(January 1894), p.2b; see also Katheryn H. Kraft, [Gjurasic/Dose Residence], *Landmarks Nomination Form* (Seattle: Preservation Board, 2012), pp.17–18. On Bebb, see T. William Booth and William H. Wilson, *Carl F. Gould: A Life in Architecture and the Arts* (Seattle: University of Washington Press, 1995), pp.3–4, 50, 60–65; on Bebb and partners Louis L. Mendell and later Carl F. Gould, and on Dose, see *Shaping Seattle Architecture: A Historical Guide to the Architects*, Jeffrey Karl Ochsner, ed. (Seattle: University of Washington Press, 1994); see also "Charles P. Dose," *Men of the Pacific Coast 1902–1903* (San Francisco: Pacific Art Company, 1903); "Charles P. Dose," *Handbook of Chicago Biography*, John J. Flinn, ed. (Chicago: Standard Guide Company, 1893).
8 "Public Buildings," "Seattle," *Engineering Record* (New York), 19(10 February 1894), p.181.
9 "New Buildings this Year," *Seattle Post-intelligencer*, 26(March 1894), p.5b.
10 J.R. Sherrard, "The Frances Hotel (aka 5th Avenue regrade," "Seattle Now and Then," at DorpatSherradLomont, web site pauldorpat.com.
11 Wright to Jones, 15 May 1894, as quoted in Meehan (1983), entry B1; Siry (September 1991), p.243. The present essays herein benefited from three studies by Siry (June 1991), (September 1991), and (1996), pp.32–49; cf. Jones (1913); Quinan (1987).
12 As quoted in Siry (September 1991), p.242.
13 Pfeiffer (87–01), plate 224, p.351; Pfeiffer (2011), pp.84, 186–187.
14 Dwight Perkins's association with Wright was announced nationally in *Brickbuilder*, 7(November 1898), p.240a, the men working together "for a new church of especial interest."

The two plans in Spencer (1900), pp.71–72, likely belong to each other. In the same article, the perspective of an eight-story building does not fit either plan. The perspective of a five-story building in Chicago Architecture Club (1902), p.13, has a plan similar to the ground floor in Spencer (1900), but the auditorium plan does not belong to the 1902 perspective. See also the perspective in Architectural Club exhibition, *Inland Architect*, 35(April 1900), plates, Wright and Perkins as architects "Associated"; Manson (1958), p.157; Quinan (1987), pp.23–24, where the illustrations were also misunderstood; Cohen (1976), p.14, plates 7–8. The perspective in the 1902 catalog is of a Sullivanesque building and predates that in Spencer (1900), the plainer. On Perkins and Wright, see Brooks (1972), pp.28ff.

15 Chicago Architecture Club (1902) dated March, n.p.; Siry (September 1991), p.258.
16 Perkins and Wright to Flagg, 4 March and 23 April 1901, Wright Archives; the letters on Wright & Tomlinson letterhead. Ernest Flagg's replies are yet known.
17 Jenkin Lloyd Jones, *The Abraham Lincoln Centre: A Sermon, Delivered at All Souls Church, Chicago, February Second, Nineteen Hundred and Two* (Chicago: The Church, 1902), pp.7, 12–17.
18 Some plans, sections, and elevations are in Pfeiffer (87–01), plates 352–358, on several sheets is written "Approved Feb 4. 03 JLJones," plate 354 shows a reflected ceiling plan superimposed on a floor plan, plate 357 has a left half section opposite direction to the right half. All dates in Pfeiffer (87–01) are confusing.
19 See the valuable Ellen Christensen, "A Vision of Urban Social Reform," *Chicago History*, 22(March 1993), pp.50–61.
20 As quoted in Siry (June 1991), p.266.
21 As quoted in Siry (September 1991), p.258.
22 Siry (September 1991), p.258.
23 Manson (1958), p.158.
24 Quinan (1987), pp.26–29.
25 Wright (1908), pp.64–65.
26 As quoted in Quinan (1987), p.242, source not cited. Wright quotes the negative essay by Russell Sturgis (1908), pp.311ff. For other contemporary comments, see Wright (1906), pp.2–9, reprinted *PSR*, 7(1970), pp.14–19, reprinted Quinan (1987), pp.140–141. See also Pfeiffer (87–01), plate 173, ca. 1895, incorrectly described as a proposed "building" for Luxfer Company.
   On the exhaust of fresh-air distribution systems, see Reyner Banham, "The Services of the Larkin 'A' Building," *JSAH*, 37(October 1978), pp.195–197; Quinan (1987), pp.66–72.
27 Quinan (1987), p.16. On various central light wells in some Chicago buildings from 1881–96, see Daniel Bluestone, "Chicago's Mecca Flat Blues," *JSAH*, 57(December 1998), pp.382–289.
28 Appropriate plates in Wright (1910); Pfeiffer (02–06); Holzhueter (Spring 1989b): until his research the project was called something like "Yahara boathouse" for the University of Wisconsin. A near replicate design was constructed for $5.4 million in Buffalo, New York, for the Westside Rowing Club.
29 Wright to Beye, 19 December 1905, as quoted in Holzhueter (Spring 1989b), p.181.
30 Mary Jane Hamilton to editor of *WHistory*, 73(1, 1989), pp.42–43.
31 Scheme 2 of the Harry E. Brown house of 1906 was to have a "face of blocks" – that is, on the "exterior only" – presumably made of concrete and in two sizes, the interior surfaces plastered, Pfeiffer (02–06), pp.252–253, plates 296–300, 341–347, 463–469; Johnson (2013a), p.49n1.
32 See Wright (1910); Ashbee (1911), here and there.
33 Manson (1958), p.156.
34 Siry (June 1991), p.272; cf. Siry (1996).
35 As quoted in Gill (1987), pp.175–176, apparently taken from Rodney F. Johonnot, *The New Edifice of Unity Church. FLW Architect* (Oak Park: The Church, 1906, reissued 1961).
36 See Graf (1983), throughout, and compare with an equally frenetic geometric analysis of Larkin in Graf (1991), pp.228–237. *Perspecta*, 22, pp.143–187, contains a series of measured drawings by the editors, a few unfortunately cross the journal's gutter. See also Stephen Klausner's drawings in McCarter (1991b), pp.12, 238, 241, 262.
37 Unity Temple and Larkin were shown in Wright (1910) with five different levels in quadrants off center lines of a single-plan drawing, his reason understandable but confusing. Good ideas were lost in a welter of lines saved only by perspective drawings and the photographs in Ashbee (1911, 1911a) where the Larkin ground-floor plan was shown separately.

In January 1988, Unity Temple's congregation agreed to voluntarily protect the church in perpetuity under strict preservation guidelines. It was the first church in the United States to undertake such an agreement; see public announcements in Cheryl Kent, "Unanimity on Unity Temple," *Inland Architect*, 32(March 1988), pp.17–23; Lynn Nesmith, "Unity Temple Granted . . .," *Architecture*, 77(March 1988), 26. See also Wright (1925b), pp.56–57, 62. On developments of concrete construction around 1900, see Siry (1996), pp.108–114; Collins (1957b), particularly pp.62–64, 81–89, 109, 142–143; Johnson (2013a), throughout.

38 That elementary geometry is plain in classical architecture is made clear in Robert Stern's idiosyncratic book *Modern Classicism* (New York: Rizzoli, 1988). Under the impress of classical tradition, pure design advocates tended to produce axially symmetrical designs.

39 This essay is based on Johnson (1987a), pp.23–28, that is now not only out-of-date but riddled with errors.

40 Nickel and Siskind (2010), pp.390–391.

41 Secrest (1992), p.120.

42 The MacHarg house, aka C. H. Berry or Berry-MacHarg house, remodeled by Sullivan in 1903, demolished in 1963, see MacHarg, *The Class of Sixty-Nine in 1887 . . . University of Michigan* (Detroit: Thomas Smith, 1887), p.29; Obituary, *The Michigan Alumnus*, 26(Ann Arbor: Alumni Association, 1910), pp.510–511.

43 Truman W. Brophy, "Dr. Allison Wright Harlan," obituary, *The Bur* (Alumni Association of Chicago College of Dental Surgery), 14(March 1909), pp.35–38. In Wright (1946), he asked, "Had I stolen the Harlan House from the firm?" p.66. It is doubtful that Sullivan would refuse or relinquish the commission.

44 Linen drawings read "James C. Rogers" 14 September 1901. He was a close business friend of Edward C. Waller, also Wright's client. Rogers loaned his newlywed daughter Susan and her husband Frank W. Thomas the money for a new house. It was not a wedding gift, Cannon and Caulfield (2006), p.67. On Waller, see *National Cyclopaedia of American Biography . . .*, vol. 37, p.165.

45 Details from Kruty (2005); Sprague (2005, 2005a); Pfeiffer (33–59, 1997); Cannon and Caulfield (2006); and my own research.

46 Wright (1943), p.177. "David T. Devin Is Dead," *DailyT*, 15 October 1898, p.5b; Kruty (2005), pp.44–48. Devin had recently been dismissed as manager of a financial institution for alleged misuse of funds, but suicide was not considered. Ida Aline Shane married Devin in 1875 and, on her husband's death, carried on as a traveler and society woman. She resided off and on in Eliot, Maine, and Chicago. In 1906, she commissioned Wright to prepare plans for a single-floor "summer cottage" in Eliot. A small two-story house was built before 1911, perhaps in 1908, but not to Wright's plans. Aline called it "Po Ching Tai," a reflection of her avid interest in the orient. Correspondence from Rosanne Adams and Eric Christian, Eliot Historical Society, to this author August 2015, with a 1930s image of the much-altered house; Margaret A. Elliott, *Eliot* (Charleston, SC: Arcadia, 2005), p.108; "Project: Summer Cottage . . .," Pfeiffer (02–06), p.241. See also Aline Shane Devin, "Po Ching Tai, a Chinese House in Maine," *Country Life in America*, 22(May 1912), pp.48, 62, that contains 1911 photographs of the house exterior and interior; idem., "Shall Women be Granted Full Suffrage?," *Illustrated American*, 15(26 May 1894), p.613; idem., "Two Reform Societies of China," *The World To-Day (New York)*, 4(January 1903), pp.466–470; idem., "Housekeeping in a Japanese Buddhist Temple," *Pacific Monthly* (Portland), (June 1909), pp.577–586.

47 Also, the following was published in 1898: For the "Trans-Mississippi Exposition" in Omaha, Nebraska, Geo. R. Dean, Frank L. Wight, and R. C. Spencer Jr. have "been selected by the [Chicago] Central Art Association to design a home which may be considered typical of American architecture," *The Brickbuilder* (New York), 7(April/May 1898), p.107a. Because the idea was put just two months before the exhibition opened in June, the project likely did not proceed.

48 Chicago Architectural Club (1902), p.56.

49 Chicago Architectural Club (1902), n.p.

50 Edward H. Pitkin, "How I Went into Business for Myself," *System* (Chicago), 18(July 1910), pp.54–55; "Edward H. Pitkin, Crockery Man, Is Dead," *Chicago Tribune*, 24(April 1918), p.15; Ron McCrea, "E.H. Pitkin Cottage?" in "Wright Chat" web blog site, 23 August 2013; James Cowan, "Our Only Wright Gem Overlooked," *National Post* (Toronto), 13(November 2004), <canada.com/news>, each accessed May 2015.

51 Property records, land registry office, Sault Ste. Marie, Ontario, as recorded by Frank Dobrovnik, "Last of a Master's Canadian Designs Stands in Algoma," *The Sault Star* (Sault Ste. Marie), 24 July 2010.
52 Pfeiffer (87–01), pp.162–163; Storrer (1993), p.73. Pitkin sold the cottage in 1916 to Chicago engineer and contractor James O. Heyworth; with parts renewed or slightly enlarged, it remains in good condition.
53 For example, see Johnson (1990), pp.16–21.
54 "Summer Lodge for J.A. Scudder, Desbarats [sic], Ontario Canada, 1904," Pfeiffer (02–06), plates 214–217; he was either a Chicago or St Louis Scudder.
55 Kruty (2005), pp.32, 55–57; Wright (1910), plates VIII-IX. Chicagoan O. C. Simonds provided a landscape design; it, too, was not realized.
56 "State Banks of Michigan, No. 269 . . .," *Annual Report of the Commissioner of the Banking Department* (Lansing: The Department, 1903), p.255; "Robert N. Adams" in Alvah Littlefield Sawyer, *A History of the Northern Peninsula of Michigan and its People* . . ., volume 3 (Alger County, MI: Lewis, 1911), pp.1085–1087, 1268. The Adams and Gowan Buildings were sensitively renovated in 2010–11 for apartments and commerce.
57 "Demar, Edward," *Biographical Dictionary of Architects in Canada 1800–1950*, <dictionaryofarchitectsin canada.org>; Adams Building, Goward Block, First Presbyterian United Church, each in Wikipedia; "Copper Country Architects," <social.mtu.edu/CopperCountryArchitects>, each accessed June 2015.
58 "Francis Apartments," <steinerag.com/flw/Artifact%20Pages/Chicago.htm>, accessed May 2015; demolished in 1971, some terra cotta and iron work were saved.
59 Information extrapolated from Wright (1932); Hines (1967); Hasbrouck (1970); Twombly (1979); Clark (1986), chapter 7. The present essay herein evolved from Johnson (June 1987), drafts of which were kindly read by Steve Harfield, the late professors Peter Reyner Banham and Donald Langmead. Comprehensive visual information is Pfeiffer (87–01).

Evidence of historical methodological problems are revealed in many studies that discuss the specific subject of Wright's pre-1911 residential works, such as Nute (1993) on Japan and Alofsin (1993), which is graphic and epistemological; see also McCarter (1991a), where various essays tend to be descriptive postmortems; Koning and Eizenberg (1981), pp.295–323, on computer logic but not on architectural fundamentals or design methodology; likewise Pennell (1991), esp. in diagrams; Seligmann (1991).
60 Wright (1928), p.49.
61 Wright (1908), p.158.
62 Wright (1928), p.57.
63 On the Martin house, see Jack Quinan, *FLW's Martin House: Architecture as Portraiture* (New York: Princeton Architecture Press, 2004); University of Buffalo, *My Dear Mr. Wright . . . Martin Collection* (Buffalo: University of Buffalo, 1997); Marjorie L. Quinlan, *Rescue of a Landmark: . . . Martin House* (Buffalo: Western New York Wares, 1990); Heinrich Klotz, *20th Century Architecture. Drawings . . . Deutschen Architekturmuseums* . . . (New York: Random House, 1989), pp.28–33.
64 See Daniel D. Reif, *Houses from Books . . . 1738–1950* . . . (University Park: Pennsylvania State University Press, 2000), chapter 5; Clark (1986), chapter 3; Guter, Foster and Del Guidice (1992), figures 82, 134–147, 149, 152, as examples; Robert Schweitzer and Michael W. R. Davis, *America's Favorite Homes* (Detroit: Wayne State University Press, 1990), short on plans, but see chapter 12; Blance Cirker, ed., *Victorian House Designs . . . 1885–1894* (New York: Dover, 1996), pp.2, 6, 7, 10, 25; William Comstock, *Country Houses and Seaside Cottages of the Victorian Era* (New York: 1883, Dover, 1989), plates 4, 9, 11, 14, 19, 38; *Radford's Artistic Bungalows* (Chicago: Radford, 1908), pp.22, 207.
65 Pfeiffer (1987), pp.27–28.
66 Morgan and Altberg (2008), pp.8–12.
67 Nute (1993), inter alia, who also documents the Japanese influence upon Silsbee that initially may have lead to Wright's and aunts Ellen and Jane's interest in Japanese prints and crafts.
68 Manson (1958), pp.36–38. The physical enclosure of the central space is illustrated in William Alex, *Japanese Architecture* (London/New York: G. Braziller, 1963), plates 53–58. Cf. Nute (1993); A. L. Sadler, *A Short History of Japanese Architecture* (Sydney: 1941), p.35, plate 38; Lancaster (1983), chapters 8–9. The Kyoto temple was restored in the 1950s.

69 Wright to Lowell in Matteawan, New York, 30 January 1901, on Wright & Tomlinson letterhead, Avery Library, Columbia University, reproduced in Brooks (1984), plate 10.
70 Cohen (1976), pp.16–17, 54–55. For a how-to-do it book, see Guter, Foster and Del Guidice (1992), inter alia. Some of the floor plans had adjacent rooms open to one another or openable with a sliding walls or doors.
71 *Cornell News*, 2(January 1900), p.89.
72 As quoted in Hoffmann (1969), p.26.
73 Dickason (1953), introduction.
74 As quoted in Hearn (1990), below figure 2.
75 "Building Department," *The Economist* (Chicago), 17(13 March 1897), p.287b.
76 As quoted in Vernon (1996), p.139.
77 Wright (1957), pp.34–36; Johnson (2013a), pp.100–101; those paragraphs were an elaboration of a discussion about colleagues he met when, in 1893, he began practice in Chicago, as in Wright (1932), pp.128–129, only slightly altered in Wright (1943), pp.130–131.
78 Christopher Vernon, "Prairie Spirit in Landscape Gardening," in Tishler (2000), pp.185–187, 192n42; see also "Ossian Cole Simonds, Conservative Ethic in the Prairie Style," in ibid., pp.80–98.
79 J.J.P. Oud, "The Influence of FLW on the Architecture of Europe," *Wijdeveld* (1925), p.86.
80 Hermann de Fries, *FLW: Aus dem Lebenswerk* [FLW: From the Life's Work], (Berlin: Ernst Pollak, 1926); Curt Behrendt, *Modern Building* (New York: Harcourt Brace, 1937); Giedion (1956), pp.394–424; see also Jan Wils, "De Dieuwe Booukunst: bij het Work van FLW" [The New Architecture: In the Work of FLW], in *Levende Kunst* [Living Art], 1(November 1918), pp.209–219.
81 Langmead and Johnson (2000), pp.32–36, 55ff.
82 Wright (1908), p.160.
83 Wright (1914), p.410.
84 Anon to *ARecord*, 38(November 1915), p.12; "Narrow Views of Western Progressives," *WArchitect*, (April 1913), pp.33–34.
85 FLW to W. Miller (then in Los Angeles), 24 February 1915; see also Wright to H. P. Berlage (after returning to Amsterdam), 30 November 1922 in Pfeiffer (1984), pp.49–52, 55; Vernon (2002), pp.xxviii,n88.
86 Kruty (1998), pp.200–201.
87 Harrison Albright, "Reinforced Concrete Construction Best," *Cement World*, 3(July 1909) p.360, the Rogers house of 1901 is illustrated.
88 Charles E. White, Jr., "Are there Two American Schools of Architecture?," *The Art World*, (May 1917), pp.179–181; [George R. Dean], "A New Movement in American Architecture. II. Glass," *Brush and Pencil*, 6(April 1900), pp.31–34, illustrated and Dean paraphrases Sullivan.
89 Wright (1908), p.161.
90 Cf. Robert W. Bastian, "The Prairie Style House: Spatial Diffusion in a Minor Design," *Journal of Cultural Geography*, 1(1, 1980), pp.50–65.

The city scientific

7 Rousseau to professionalism

Were Wright's larger, more functionally complex community designs theoretically and practically structured in a manner similar to buildings? Before 1914, his housing commissions included individual or detached, duplex or semi-detached, and multiple living units, such as row houses, apartments, and hotels. Of this group, the largest was the ill-fated Lexington Terraces project begun 1901. However, commissions for large, more functionally complex buildings, those for tourism, entertainment, recreation, and skyscraping, were difficult to acquire after about 1904.[1]

To understand Wright's thoughts about – and designs for – social communities is to place him in a historical context where, as with the earlier discussion about Progressivism's aesthetic component, he was a rather quiet, ill-fitting exemplar in this investigation to outline a possible Progressives' City. Before 1900, the Western city's form and physical character were, like architecture, rooted in historical precedents or in surveyor's tools. Western civilization's first described systemic city planning scheme was developed in Pharaonic Egypt and was orthogonal; so, too, were colonial towns of antique Greece and Rome. Based on cosmological or religio-philosophical ideas, a mix of rigidly but easily applied ideal geometries began in the 1400s to persist into the nineteenth century. A more pertinent inauguration, however, occurred at the end of the eighteenth century with a partially competed town designed by the well-known French architect Claude-Nicholas Ledoux.

Ledoux, Soria y Mata, Sitte, Howard . . .

Something of a radical architectural theorist, Ledoux's contribution to intelligent planning for future community environments was the company town of Chaux, first proposed in 1775. Designed to support an existing salt works, it was in the mode of a traditional central place plan common since the Renaissance but slightly more flexible conceptually than predecessors or successors. As revealed in 1804, and contemporary with Durand, Ledoux's imprecise town geometry was an ellipse with a large central space centered by a director's residence and surrounded by administrative and salt processing buildings. Next were service buildings and kitchen gardens confined by a ring road. Beyond were places for individual buildings on independent sites as needed; general housing somewhere. A few radial roads reached the mines or tentatively into the countryside.

Ledoux was a theoritician whose idealism was inclusive. In public musings, he talked with Rouseauan passion, if rather dreamily, about the private and communal needs of humble employees.

At Chaux, Ledoux desired to harness the vital, religious forces of ordinary people in Arcadian splendor and concurrently "to rediscover the primordial social group."[2] He therefore "broke, once and for all, the thread . . . whose several strands were the teachings of Plato and of Aristotle, astrology, and philosophy in the guise of geometry."[3] The break was to a city not of absolutist rigor bound by geometric exactitude but of individuals magically bonded in nature's settings, acting in concert as Rousseau wished and later as fervently demanded by Tolstoy. Understandably, Ledoux's buildings were tied to *classique* historical precedents.[4]

202 The city scientific

The conceptual imperative had been the central place. Such central places were not only the geometric and spatial center but, as Spiro Kostof has reminded us, the focus of hierarchal power: religious, secular, or military. From the center outward, roads, buildings, and varied functions were located in diminishing order of importance to a fortified border, agriculture and fields were outside. Many were built to military formula. Early Italian Renaissance theoreticians preferred the geometric square, and its revival in the eighteenth century was found in new colonial towns.

The theoretical model that concerns us is that by the artist, engineer, and architect Pietro Cataneo. In 1567, he published an ideal town plan comprised of an equilateral square with a central green space and made of four equilateral square blocks with necessary roads, each with centered green square. Thomas Holme's plan of colonial Philadelphia of 1681 is usually noted as a later use of Cataneo's model. But more faithful examples are two colonial towns in Georgia designed by or for James Oglethorpe in Savannah in 1733 and New Ebenezer in 1747, and there was Radnor by William Bull, surveyor general of South Carolina, and Gother Mann's proposed plan for Toronto's ("Toronto's") harbor and settlement of 1788.[5] In the nineteenth century, the leading example was colonial Adelaide, South Australia, by George Strickland Kingston and William Light. The street plan as first designed in 1835 applied Cataneo's theoretical model. The entire ensemble was surrounded by parklands, a belt of green. Adelaide's parklands comprised the world's first publicly financed and owned municipal park as well as the first botanic garden, both freely accessible to all comers. The town plan and parklands more than adequately responded to aspects of humanitarian reforms so earnestly advanced in Britain in the decade around 1830 by the English member of parliament Charles A. Roebuck and the Scottish landscape gardener John Claudius Loudon.[6]

Loudon's arguments and related radial town plan, and the useful pattern of Adelaide's parklands, carried well into the nineteenth century in the form of widely publicized theoretical projects, such as James S. Buckingham's "Model Town" of 1849, Owenite Robert Pemberton's "Happy Colony" of 1854, Charles Fourier's communal barracks and Peter Kropotkin's similar communes both of the 1880s, Giedion J. Ouseley's proposed Haptapolis in 1884, and Edward Bellamy's popular communalized society in *Looking Backward* of 1888, which recalled Pemberton's idea. Each were square or circular schemes that contained an outer ring of green parklands, an idea taken by Ebenezer Howard. Diagrammatically, Howard's physical plan was very similar to Loudon's, Ouseley's, and Pemberton's, and the political implications and communal land-holding systems of Ouseley and Pemberton were also similar.[7]

The formal schematic geometries of eighteenth- and nineteenth-century theorists were visually ordered as symbolic of higher motivations, supposedly for human salvation: utopia and arcadia. Wright's expansive proposal post-1930 was associated with Arcadian simplicity and wide-eyed optimism. Through Charles Ashbee, Arts and Crafts people locally and from England, and his own reading as can be found in published lists, by Wright's knowledge of – if not familiarity with – William Morris's germinal ideas, and through Wright's reading of George and about Bellamy's theories and probable society and their reference to nineteenth-century theorists, he should have known of Howard's economic and middle-class, semi-Arcadian scheme.

+ + +

The design of cities *ab initio* must involve two major considerations: an accrued natural wholeness or holistic philosophy that, two, embraces and integrates at one geographical place the interdependent functions of collective sustenance and social interaction. Urban growth in the nineteenth century was, generally, of two physical models. One was not so much a product of planning as a hasty *ad-hoc* infusion into an existing fabric, most often at a city's fringe, of flimsy industrial buildings and related workers' housing structures pressing against roadsides. Those additive industrial intrusions were too often crudely executed. Nonetheless, new housing for rural migrants was superior to the dirt-floored hovels they had abandoned. When engulfed by future urban expansion and excessive crowding, they became forbidding, unhealthy, congested, and dark. Therefore, founding decentralized new company towns was preferred and directly influenced later events, especially Titus Salt's Saltaire of 1852, built for employees near Newry, Ireland, or chocolatier Menier's housing colony of 1874 at Noisiel near Paris, or Bourneville near Birmingham, where Cadbury built a new chocolate factory, or the prescient and innovative Port Sunlight of 1886 near Liverpool by the Lever Brother's company, or Pullman's Pullman in Illinois.[8] Two other grand ideas were directed to humanizing the bulk and multitude of a modern city: one by commerce, one by aesthetics.

The concept of a linear city was described in the 1880s by its inventor Arturo Soria y Mata, a Spanish politician, engineer, and entrepreneur, as an urban "ribbon" of limited width on the central axis of which was a road and rail line:

> The most perfect type of city possible, will be that running along a single road, with a width of 500 meters, and that will stretch, if necessary, from Cadiz to St. Petersburg and Peking to Brussels. [Congestion in the] small street, which would run perpendicular to this principal avenue[,] would thus be eased by the rapid movement of people and merchandise by rail.[9]

Therefore, on either side of the main road would be single-family houses placed on individual plots. These disconnected houses would reduce the danger of spreading fires and diseases and allow more light and air to circulate, "thus creating a healthier environment for the city dweller." Soria believed reduced transport costs alone "would be a powerful incentive for further industrial development."[10]

The concept's simplicity, clarity, and modernism ensured recognition, especially by Soviet Union theorists in the early 1930s.[11] It found favor with the political left in England, where architect Berthold Lubetkin reiterated the idea also in the 1930s, and MARS (Modern Architecture Research) used the principle for their greater-London proposal after World War II.[12] (With such interest by the political left, Le Corbusier also borrowed it.) And its basic functional disposition, so similar to Howard's, was used by Wright for Broadacre City's layout in the 1930s.[13] Historian Diana Velez thought Soria believed that an environment

> constructed in harmony with the dominant "form" of an era would mold the very nature of human relations and institutions. Thus, he contended that the "progressive" spirit revealed in the linear city's form could affect the social system. Further, since he believed that changes in the form were reflective of major stages in the development of civilization the growing dominance of the line signified ... the beginning of a new era. ...

Velez added that the "contrast between" modern straight avenues and rail lines with the "meandering streets of earlier towns was for Soria evidence" of the "struggle between progress and tradition." It was Soria's view that older cities "with their filth and inadequate housing, created an intolerable environment," that a "laborer should be able to purchase his home and the land it occupies."[14]

In regions between major centers, Soria believed the linear city would unite "hygienic conditions of country life to the great capital cities."[15] Farms "would have access to the rails and business district by way of the perpendicular streets," and a subsequent increase in market outlets would "stimulate agricultural production." Soria's investors, for it was a commercial venture, saw it partially realized outside Madrid, the railway begun in 1890, all growing slowly, haphazardly, until abandoned after his death in 1920.

As Ledoux, Soria wanted, one, a "union of city and country," two, a "ruralization of urban life the urbanization of the rural," and three, he dreamed

> For each family a house; for each house an orchard.[16]

Wright's often-published paraphrase of those three desires is striking, historical evolution clear. And for his Little Farms and Broadacre City schemes of around 1931, he proposed that each house must sit on an acre of land with a produce garden.[17] One person, however, was interested in learning from existing cities, directing reform energies and accepting aesthetics. Camillo Sitte's quest was for the revival of naturally evolving, thereby beautiful, cities.

After his slim volume on *City Planning According to Artistic Principles* was published in Vienna in 1889, it immediately became the subject of popular and serious debate and influence, and it still is.[18] Sitte studied the varieties of existing European plazas, streets, gardens, and engineering projects; he measured public needs and apathy; and he witnessed a Royal act of vandalism when, for economic profit to few, Vienna's perimeter of centuries-old parklands were destroyed and filled with streets and bulging buildings of imitation Baroque and beaux-arts pomposity.[19]

In the introduction to their translation of Sitte's book,[20] George and Christiane Collins selected comments by the social theorists Percival and Paul Goodman as a neat summation of Sitte's teachings about urban squares. The Goodmans reminded readers that a city

> [is a] social congregation of people. . . . A person is a citizen in the street. A city street is not . . . a machine for traffic to pass through but a square [a plaza] for people to remain within. Without such squares – markets, cathedral places, political forums – . . . there is no city. This is what Sitte is saying. The city aesthetic is the beauty proper to being in or entering such a square; it consists in the right choice and disposition of structures in and around the square. . . .[21]

Sitte's laboratory was the preindustrial city that he described as a social-physical organism whose aesthetic unity derived directly from the activities of its people over time. In all, it is a sensitive study of how old cities can instruct by the experience of artistic and human qualities among historical remnants. Sitte said with emphasis, "The basic idea [was] *to go to school with Nature and the old masters also in matters of town planning.*"[22] His idea spread from Austria to Germany[23] and then to Spain, where Soria incorporated its principles, and then on to England by Garden City people and where Raymond Unwin became a staunch advocate,[24] to France, Russia, Australia, and most of the other British colonies,[25] and to North America: and it persisted. Sitte's analytical and aesthetical methodology was applied by Eliel Saarinen in his book *The City* of 1943, then by G.E. Kidder Smith in his book *Italy Builds* of 1955.

Soria's response was synthetic and pragmatic. He ignored existing cities perhaps in hope that his newly built suburban line would act – by some catalytic means – as a cleansing agent for dirty dramas repeated in foul urban places. Howard's elitist anti-city, the Garden City, held even less regard for existing conditions or offers of amelioration. Yet Wright embraced the idea, claiming it his own. Howard's programmatic test town of Letchworth was physically remote, intellectually and socially aloof. Still, it and Howard's idea have remained teasingly attractive, at least to historians.

Howard's decentralization concept was defined in 1898 as a "Group of Slumless Smokeless Cities." But the word "smokeless" infers no industry because then it was powered by coal. So they were to be bedroom satellites and not agricultural centers. It was a quasi-regional scheme that rejected Soria's formula and Sitte's dynamic model. Howard's general concern has been outlined by historian Daniel Schaffer:

> [Like Soria and Sitte, Howard was] particularly disturbed by his nation's inability to deal with the problem of human misery despite unprecedented growth and prosperity. To overcome this political paralysis, Howard emphasized preplanning, a limited population for each town, the need for green space, unified land ownership and a process of "internal colonization" to create a matrix of clearly defined, self-contained cities.[26]

Peter Batchelor was correct when he found that most of Howard's ideas had been "conceived at some point earlier in history," citing Thomas More, "Bellers, Ledoux, Owen, Pemberton, Buckingham, and Kropotkin who had utilized the fundamental idea of limited population and an agricultural greenbelt." So, too, had Ousley and Soria, but the first greenbelt application had come from the Kingston/Light plan of Adelaide. Those people had also "conceived of their cities as elements in a regional complex." If fundamentals were borrowed, what was Howard's contribution? The core was "the unerring attention to the financial and administrative details."[27] It was to be a carefully managed, non-bureaucratic real estate, a collective of sorts. With simple descriptions and diagrams, his idea was easily understood and seen as a clever, evolutionary synthesis.

Howard's thesis has been amply discussed elsewhere and here taken as read.[28] We can add that he excluded workers' housing, placing it outside, somewhere in the "country." But he proposed a grand avenue to divide "excellently built houses" and fine row houses, all to face a "belt of green," a term invented in the 1830s by Roebuck and Loudon.[29] The belt contained public necessities related to home living, such as schools, playgrounds, and churches. In any event, Wright's Broadacre City mimics almost exactly the Loudon/Pembroke/Buckingham/Howard functional displacement[30] but not his Bitter Root town plan of 1909.

+ + +

Sitte's sensitive reexamination was meant to introduce aesthetics into evaluations that would lead to refurbishment. His words were readily understood by practitioners and theorists in the leading years of the twentieth century. Howard advocated a place elsewhere for the moderate elite and for communal economics. However, along with Cadbury, Lever, Pullman, and Krupp, both men insisted, one directly the other by inference, that the city must be devised equally by practical, technical, and aesthetic endeavors.[31] Following Sitte and adding beaux-arts protocols, Daniel Burnham reminded American's of the artistic necessity.

Professionalism

It is well known that there is a direct line from 1893 Chicago to a vigorous City Beautiful Movement, whose display was opposite of the agreeable reasoning of Soria, Sitte, Howard (more or less), and on occasion, Olmsted Senior. Yet it was America's first movement dedicated to city planning. Richard Wilson summarized its heyday from 1902–11:

> [The movement] involved a cultural agenda [where] aesthetics expressed as beauty, order, system, and harmony, . . . [where] public and semipublic buildings, civic centers, park and boulevard systems, or extension and embellishments of them, were the tokens of the improved environment.

Wilson also paraphrased Burnham by saying it was hoped that "Physical change [would] persuade urban dwellers to become more imbued with civic patriotism and better disposed toward community needs."[32] Regardless, City Beautiful polemics were distant from Sitte's humanistic principles for a beautiful human-scaled city. Only after 1909 did polemics recognize reformers' and sociologists' concerns. A city planning profession evolved from quite diverse American and European collectively impelled sources. Many, if not most, were in natural opposition to the City Beautiful as manifested. Different to European experience, education came to the forefront in America.

Three main influences "made their mark on the idea of education for city planning." First were words and works of the great recreation and landscape planner Frederick Law Olmsted. Second was an assimilation of an increasing knowledge of sociological and health implications. Third was the acceptance of large-scale landscape planning as evidenced by a profusion of splendid municipal parks.[33] By 1909, several American sociologists, engineers, and landscape and building architects were calling themselves city or community planners or consultants. One was Charles Mulford Robinson, who initially advocated Sitte's principles but soon accepted City Beautiful ideas. He then attempted to synthesize the two. In public utterances, he urged visual and spatial forms "with careful notation of European precedents for squares, bridges, canals, parks, street furnishings, and architecture."[34] Robinson's approach, together with most City Beautiful proponents, changed in 1911 when, as president of the National Conference on City Planning (NCCP, who first met in 1909), he called for a "science of city planning."[35] He now settled for a pragmatic approach by reference to engineering and "social benefits" and by addressing tenements, hygiene, and so forth, which explained the growing multiplicity of investigations.

Efficient houses were the concern of many, inspired by the analyses of Catherine E. Beecher in *A Treatise on Domestic Economy for the Use of Young Ladies at Home and at School* (1841), then Harriet Beecher Stowes and Catherine Beecher's book *The American Woman's Home* (1869), followed by E. C. Gardner's *Houses and How to Make Them* (1874). Around 1900, Edward Bok began *Ladies Home Journal* and, significantly, Christine Frederick's *The New Housekeeping: Efficiency Studies in Home Management* appeared in 1914. Functionally efficient floor plans, easily built houses, and labor-saving devices (increasingly electrical) were meant to satisfy physical and psychological needs, all part of the reformers' agenda.[36]

To make management and the workforce more efficient was the focus of Frederick W. Taylor's studies that culminated in an influential book *The Principles of Scientific Management* of 1911, or Taylorism to some.[37] *Brickbuilder* published an article in 1912 about drafting and office efficiencies based on Taylor's published studies and, oddly, on the benefits of profit sharing.[38] Possible city management efficiencies were discussed beginning with a series of articles in the July 1912 issue of *National Municipal Review*.

Budget Meakin's 1905 book about *Model Factories & Villages* was primarily concerned with the social conditions of workers. George M. Price's *The Modern Factory* of 1914 concentrated on technical matters and on safety, sanitation, and welfare as management efficiencies as much as humanitarian concerns, all linked to new factory suburbs or towns.[39] For more factory space and to avoid increasingly higher city taxes, industrialists had begun decentralizing in the 1880s: Pullman outside Chicago; Carnegie Steel to Homestead, Pennsylvania; Doubleday, Page publishers from New York City to Garden City on Long Island; Ford, General Motors, and Chrysler outside Detroit; Gary, Indiana, east of Chicago for US Steel, to mention but a few. A grid of streets defined company towns everywhere. Atypical was the ill-fated town of Tyrone in New Mexico. Built by the Phelps Dodge Copper Company in 1914, its plan and many buildings were designed by architect Bertram Goodhue. By 1919, copper was gone, the town abandoned.[40]

In 1909, the "Boston 1915" campaign was initiated "to promote the city's prosperity as the commercial capital of New England, its social regeneration, and its civic development." Involved were entrepreneur Edward Filene, who was persuaded by Burnham's Chicago example, and New England professionals such as Nolen, Arthur Comey, Olmsted Jr., Benjamin Marsh, George Ford, Robinson, and Werner Hegemann from Germany.[41]

It 1909, Wright began designing his first community and town planning commissions for two sites in a valley of the Montana Rockies; one was uncommon.

In 1911, almost simultaneously, two major city planning schemes were begun elsewhere and received considerable attention. Australia called for designs for a new capital city for the newly federated colonies. Many Americans entered the competition, including the winners, Chicago architects Walter and Marion Griffin. Their design and supporting comments were widely reported, the plan unique, eschewing City Beautiful pomposity and Garden City quaintness in favor of a radial baroque geometry of roads to delineate functional areas and establish physical and hierarchical symbols of a democratic monarchy.[42] And greenswards were proposed and secured.

Also in 1911, Delhi was proclaimed as the Imperial Capital of colonial India. The construction of a new government precinct was also announced, to be built adjacent to the old city and financed by the Colonial Office in London. (Canberra was financed by Australia taxes.) Without a competition and by peculiar means, Englishman Edwin Luytens and South African

Herbert Baker became planners and building architects. Their 1913 new Delhi was a nonfunctional, quasi-city, a rather beaux-arts design with Burnham-like grand boulevards, government palaces and places, and diagonal street patterns.[43] Housing precincts were for the bureaucracy only.

Walter Griffin considered himself primarily a landscape architect, believing buildings and cities were dependent upon nature's physical environment. He and other landscape architects were in the forefront of recreational, community, and industrial town design. Some of those to reach national attention were Nolen, Comey, Olmsted Sr. and Jr., Henry Wright, Jens Jensen, Robert Anderson Pope, and later Harlan Bartholomew and Elbert Peets.[44]

Not a landscape architect, Dwight Perkins was nonetheless prominent among those activists working to protect or preserve woodlands and nature areas. Chicago raised, in 1887 Perkins received a degree from the Massachusetts Institute of Technology, where he taught for a year. In Chicago he worked principally for Burnham and John Wellborn Root Sr., who remained a positive influence. In 1894 Perkins began an architectural practice that continues to this day. His parallel interests included acting as commissioner of Chicago's Special Park Commission from 1899–1909 and the Northwest Park Commission of Evanston from 1911–12. In 1904, he helped form The Prairie Club, whose members were from all walks of life. They were dedicated to empirical studies, therefore in hiking, and successfully lobbied for the conservation of forests, the most successful the sixty-one-square-mile Cook County Forest Reserve. The club's actions and its success with forest reserves exemplify the grassroots component of a national conservation policy soon to become popular and influential.

Immediately after completing Reverend Jenkin Jones's Abraham Lincoln Center in 1905, Perkins became architect for the Chicago Board of Education and completed a few notable schools before his appointment was withdrawn, his "political plum" that was "awarded to the faithful servants of the machine," as historian Carl Condit has put it.[45] Perkins's wife, Lucy Fitch Perkins, was an author and book illustrator, at one time director of art at Pratt Institute in New York City, active in the Woman's Club, Woman's City Club, and Chicago Commons and Hull-House settlements, and supported kindergartens and playground associations.[46] Also, Dwight taught at the Architectural Club where Wright was occasionally a exterior juror but only for a couple of years. While not directly involved with city planning, Dwight and Lucy were typical of young professionals devoted to the ideals of Progressivism and promoting cultural and community welfare through social reform.

Dwight's active commitment to social reform is in sharp contrast to Wright's insular self-aggrandizing mode of professional and social life.

Just as American architecture schools hired French architects to teach beaux-arts *classique* design, the role of European planners was also notable. In 1911, *American City* magazine began a regular foreign department; Werner Hegemann advised on the principles of German zoning and housing; Otto Wagner of Vienna was lauded in America; and from Britain came Garden City/suburb advocates such as Edward Culpin, Raymond Unwin, and Thomas Adams.

The interrelatedness of an ever-increasing number of professions and nongovernmental organizations studying human communities is exemplified in many other ways. There were a growing number of conferences by relevant disciplines on the subject of city renewal: rail, road, construction, municipal bureaucracy, sociology, housing, management, urban recreation, parks, native vegetation, and more: all – consciously or not – working toward some form of comprehensive planning and establishment of a profession. The first convention of the Playground Association of America, for instance, was held in Chicago in 1907. This affiliation included landscape architects, educators, sociologists, woman's clubbers, engineers, architects, civic societies, settlement people, bureaucrats, and representatives of other concerned groups. By 1911, there were 115 associations nationwide.[47]

In fact, the number and kind of conferences held after 1905 throughout the Western world is another measure of the perceived need to control urban growth and for city planning professionalism. Educative exhibits were mounted in Glasgow and Paris beginning in 1900 through to Ghent in 1913, where sociologist Patrick Geddes was still active.[48] The International Congress

208 *The city scientific*

of Architects held sessions on aspects of city planning from 1903–10. City planning exhibits were held in other cities after 1910: Dublin and Liverpool and in San Francisco, Chicago, New York, and Los Angeles.

The Universal City Planning Exhibition was held jointly by Berlin and Dusseldorf in May and June 1910, and American planning was included. Historian Anthony Alofsin's observation was that "Confirming the enthusiastic interest Germany had for American developments, it provided a cultural bridge between the two countries, and between Chicago and Berlin in particular."[49] It can be assumed that Wright knew about it, for he was in Berlin from 1910–11, and his works were known by architects and planners, some of whom were also published by Wasmuth. The Royal Institute of British Architects held an international – mainly Empire – conference in London in October of that year.[50] Wright may have known of the event but that October had returned briefly to Oak Park. An exhibition of American-designed suburban and city plans (including the Griffins' Canberra) and foreign city planning was circulated nationally in 1912–13 by the American City Bureau.[51] In 1913, a National Conference on Housing was held in Chicago that paralleled a call for competitive designs for a model neighborhood in which Wright participated by invitation. The tone of the 1913 conference was set by comments such as those of Robinson, who urged the application of "science." A professionally aggressive though thoughtful John Nolen advised planners to "insist upon asking, 'How do the people live, where do they work, what do they plan?'" The implication was that Burnham did not ask such questions. Earlier, as president of the NCCP in 1910, Olmsted Jr. called for a "new social ideal of unified and comprehensive city planning." Further, inspired by Dewey's pragmatism, he said,

> Any mind with sufficient imagination to grasp it must be stimulated by this conception of the city as one great social organism whose welfare is in part determined by the action of the people, . . . by the collective intelligence and good will that control those actions.[52]

In their many guises, the Progressives and reformers were the intelligent voices of that goodwill and – enmeshed with Protestant churches and Fabian socialists – of those disenfranchised.[53] In 1912, Frederick C. Howe, a Progressive in the city planning movement, argued for the city to be considered "a socializing agency."[54]

All of the actions and thoughts and proposals and demands and worries were whirling around Chicago's intellectual and social atmosphere and, because he could not escape their presence and effect, within Wright's mind. Ascertaining Wright's level of interest in all this is only slightly problematical. He never formerly joined an organization or associated positively with a set of ideas, and he almost never spoke about their beliefs or activities until late his sixties. But they held essential knowledge for all who practiced architecture and who wanted to participate as a known Progressive. Much of it seems to have come as witness to the linear process of historical actions that informed the present – or by osmosis. When opportunity was presented during the critical years of 1908–13, how did he respond?

Notes

1 Tall buildings were the Luxfer facade, Abraham Lincoln Center, and the San Francisco Call project (1913), see Anthony Alofsin, "The Call Building: FLW's Skyscraper for San Francisco," in *Das Bauwerk und die stadt. The Building and the Town. Essays for Eduard F. Sekler*, Wolfgang Bohm, ed. (Vienna: Böhlau, 1994), pp.17–27.

   Residential architecture analyzed were Roloson Apartments and Belknap Apartment project (both in 1894); Francis Apartments (demolished in 1971), Francisco Terrace (a two-story tenement with access to the second-story units from a continuous open balcony ringing a central courtyard, demolished in 1974), and an apartment project for Edward C. Waller, all in 1895; perhaps the robust Perkins apartments (1896). Recreational buildings were Wolfe Lake project (1895); Horseshoe Inn project, Estes Park, Colorado (1908); Lake Geneva Inn (1911–12); Banff Park shelter (1911, demolished in 1939) with Canadian architect Francis C. Sullivan; Bitter Root Inn (burned

Rousseau to professionalism 209

to the ground in 1924), University Heights "clubhouse" (demolished ca. 1945), each in 1909; Midway Gardens (1913–14), demolished in1929.

On apartments from 1890–99 more generally, see Daniel Bluestone, "Chicago's Mecca Flat Blues," *JSAH*, 57(December 1998), pp.382–403.

2 As suggested by Alan Colquhuon, *Essays in Architectural Criticism* (Cambridge, Massachusetts: MIT Press, 1981); see also E. A. Gutkind, *Urban Development in Western Europe: France and Belgium* (New York: Free Press, London: Collier-Macmillan, 1970), p.98 and illustrations.

3 Lang (1952), p.100. For a modern physical form similar to Chaux see Kibbutz Hahalal, Israel, in Kostof (1991), p.158; see also Schwarting (1981), pp.22–47.

4 Cf. Kaufmann (1955); Georges Teyssot, "Neoclassical and 'Autonomous' Architecture: The Formalism of Emil Kaufmann," *ADesign*, 51(June 1981), pp.24–29. At least the principal central buildings were built and at a rather monumental scale.

5 Developments leading to Cataneo's ideal plan and beyond are discussed and illustrated in Johnson (2013b), chapter 3.

6 Johnson (2013b), chapter 10.

7 Buder (1990), pp.34–37. For extracts related to planning from works by George, Kropotkin (a decentralist), and Bellamy, see Weimer (1962).

8 Kostof (1991), inter alia; Sutcliffe (1981); "The Anglo American Suburb," *ADesign*, 51(October 1981), the issue; Gillian Darley, *Villages of Vision* (London: Granada, 1975); Benevolo (1960). On North American utopian thought, see various works of Lewis Mumford; Maren Lock, "The Experimental Utopia in America," in Manuel (1973), pp.183–200, Hayden (1981), and especially Hayden (1976).

For some idea of the variety and number of religious, political, or social utopian communities in North America, see William Alfred Hinds, *American Communities*, 2nd ed. (Chicago, 1908, reprint 1975); see also Dennis Hardy, *Alternative Communities in Nineteenth Century England* (London: Longman, 1979), with a concise bibliography for England and the United States.

9 As quoted in Benevolo (1960), p.361; see Collins (1957a), pp.74–93.

10 Velez (1983), pp.133–134.

11 Anatole Kopp, *Town and Revolution: Soviet Architecture and City Planning, 1917–1935* (New York: George Braziller, 1970), pp.164–186; Gallion (1950), pp.374ff.

12 Thomas Sharp's critical comments against the linear plan are in his *Town Planning* (Harmondsworth: Penguin, 1940), pp.57–62; see also Dennis Sharp, "Concept and Interpretation. The Aims and Principles of the MARS Plan for London," *Perspecta* (13/14, 1971), pp.167–173.

13 Johnson (1990), chapters 8–10.

14 Velez (1983), p.137. Cf. Velez (1983), p.131.

15 Choay (1969), p.100.

16 Velez (1983), p.134.

17 Nicely discussed in Johnson (1990), chapter 10.

18 Sitte was director of the school of applied arts in Vienna. Jane Jacobs (1961), in reaction to the hundreds of ill-conceived "urban renewal" programs of the 1950s, argued for a post-war revival of how to apply Sitte's principles. See also the use of Sitte's analytical and aesthetical methodology by Eliel Saarinen, *The City* (New York: Reinhold, 1943); G. E. Kidder Smith, *Italy Builds* (New York: Reinhold, 1955).

19 Benevolo (1960), vol. 1, pp.82–85.

20 Sitte (1889); see related text in Collins and Collins (1965).

21 Goodman (1960), pp.82–85.

22 Collins and Collins (1965), p.xvi, which is Sitte's introduction to the third "unchanged" 1900 edition of Sitte (1889). Sitte died in 1903.

23 Cf. Franziska Bollerey and Kristiana Hartmann, "A Patriarchal Utopia: The Garden City and Housing Reform in Germany at the Turn of the Century," in Sutcliffe (1980), pp.44–46; Collins and Collins (1965), chapters 8–9.

24 Creese (1960) pays scant attention to Sitte.

25 Cf. Freestone (1989); Freestone (1986).

26 Schaffer (1988), p.22.

27 Batchelor (1969), p.196. Except for Ledoux and Kropotkin, predecessors proposed penal settlements or colonial centers to be located in far-away places.

28 Useful to these essays were Buder (1990); Mumford (1961); Carol Ann Christiansen, "The American Garden City: Concepts and Assumptions," PhD dissertation, University of Minnesota,

1977. Others post-1915 are W. A. Eden, "Ebenezer Howard and the Garden City Movement," *TownPR*, 19(Summer 1947), pp.123–143; Batchelor (1969), pp.184–200; Rockey (1983), pp.83–105; Stephen V. Ward, ed., *The Garden City: Past, Present, and Future* (London: E. & F. Spon, 1992); Lewis (1916), pp.309–316; Standish Meacham, *Regaining Paradise Englishness and the Early Garden City Movement* (New Haven: Yale University Press, 1999); Mervyn Miller, *Raymond Unwin: Garden Cities and Town Planning* (Leicester: Leicester University Press, 1992); Gordon E. Cherry, *Pioneers in British Planning* (London: Architectural Press, 1981); idem., "Bournville, England 1895–1995," *JUrban*, 22(May 1996).
29 Johnson (2013b), pp.28ff.
30 Johnson (1990), pp.115–120.
31 Lang (1952), p.100; Batchelor (1969); Creese (1960); Kornwolf (1972), especially IV.8.
32 Wilson (1989), p.1, emphasis added; William H. Wilson, "The Ideology, Aesthetics and Politics of the City Beautiful Movement," in Sutcliffe (1980), pp.165–198.
33 Collins (1989), pp.74–77.
34 Wilson (1989), p.90.
35 Hancock (1967), p.295. In 1913, Robinson accepted a position to lecture in civic design in what was ostensibly the landscape architecture department at the University of Illinois; Kruty (1993), p.42n32.
36 A useful general discussion is Sigfried Giedion, *Machanization Takes Command* (New York: Oxford University Press, 1948); more specifically, Witold Rybczynski, *Home, a Short History of an Idea* (New York: Viking, 1986), note chapter 7.
37 Begun in the late 1880s, Taylor studied time and motion and industrial shop management, obscure subjects until 1911. See also Samuel Harber, *Efficiency and Uplift: Scientific Management in the Progressive Era 1890–1920* (Chicago: University of Chicago Press, 1964); Philip Gunn, "FLW and the Passage of Fordism," a misleading title, *Capital & Class*, 44(Summer 1991), pp.73–92, supposedly about Broadacre City.
38 William O. Ludlow, "Scientific Management in the Architect's Office," *Brickbuilder*, 21(May 1912), pp.138–139.
39 Cf. Lindy Biggs, *The Rational Factory Architecture, Technology, and Work in America's Age of Mass Production* (Baltimore: Johns Hopkins University Press, 1996); Betsy Hunter Bradly, *The Works: The Industrial Architecture of the United States* (New York: Oxford University Press, 1999).
40 Margret Crawford, "Bertram Goodhue, Walter Douglas and Tyrone, New Mexico," *JAE*, 42(Summer 1989), pp.25–33.
41 Christine Boyer quoted in Collins (1989), p.79.
42 Peter Muller, *The Esoteric Nature of Griffin's Design for Canberra* (Canberra: National Development Commission, 1976), pamphlet, reprint Sydney: the author, 2012; John W. Reps, *Canberra 1912: Plans and Planners of the Australian Capital Competition* (Melbourne: Melbourne University Press, 1997), inter alia.

On Griffin's community and landscape designs, see Vernon (1991), pp.217–229; idem., "FLW, Walter Burley Griffin, Jens Jensen and the Jugenstil Garden in America," *Die Gartenkunst*, 7(2, 1995), pp.232–246; idem., "'Expressing Natural Conditions with Maximum Possibility,' the American Landscape Art (1901–ca.1912) of Walter Burley Griffin," *Journal of Garden History*, 15(Spring 1995), pp.19–47; idem., "The Landscape Art of Walter Burley Griffin," in Watson (1998), pp.86–103; idem., "An 'Accidental' Australian. Walter Burley Griffin's Australian-American Landscape Art," in Jeff Turnbull and Peter Y. Navaretti, eds., *The Griffins in Australia and India* (Melbourne: University of Melbourne Press, 1998), pp.2–15.
43 On the historical relationship of the two capital city designs in Johnson (1977), pp.17–18.

Griffin was offered the headship of the architecture department at the University of Illinois in 1913 but, because he had accepted the position of director of design and construction for Canberra, based in Melbourne, he declined; Kruty (1993), pp.36–40. He was not offered the lectureship in civic design. In 1920, he was ousted as director and his ideas languished until rejuvenated in the 1950s by Canberra planner Peter Harrison.
44 Christopher Vernon, "Wilhelm Miller and *The Prairie Spirit in Landscape Gardening*," in O'Malley and Treib (1995), pp. 271–310; idem., "A Legitimate Art Distinctive . . .," *Landscape Review* (Christchurch), 3(1, 1997), pp.2–277; Robert E. Grese, "The Prairie Gardens of O.C. Simonds and Jens Jensen," in O'Malley and Treib (1995), pp.99–123; then compare with Albert

Fein, "The American City: The Ideal and the Real," in Edgar Kaufmann, Jr. ed., *The Rise of an American Architecture* (New York: Praeger, 1970), pp.51–114.
45 Condit (1973), p.21; Burchard and Bush-Brown (1961), p.282; "Dwight H. Perkins, Father of Today's School Ideas," *AForum*, 97(October 1952), pp.119–125; Perkins is not in *Macmillan* but his son Lawrence is; see also Joan E. Draper, "The Art and Science of Park Planning in the United States, Chicago's Small Parks 1902–1905," in Sies and Silver (1994), chapter 4.
46 For her views on architecture, town planning, and the arts, see Lucy Fitch Perkins, "Municipal Arts," *The Chautauquan*, 36(February 1903), pp.516–527 (available on the web through her name, courtesy John W. Reps); "Imaginative and Pose Drawing," *Pratt Institute Monthly* (Brooklyn), 7(January 1899), pp.57–58.
47 George Gibbs Jr., "Convention, Playground Association of America," *Inland Architect*, 50(July 1907), 7; *Yearbook*, Playground and Recreation Association, 1911, reviewed in *NMR*, 1(April 1912), p.324. Jensen, Griffin, Dwight and Lucy Perkins, and Simmonds were members.
48 Helen Meller, "Cities and Evolution: Patrick Geddes . . . before 1914," in Sutcliffe (1980), pp.199–223. All material for Geddes's exhibition was lost in 1914 on board a ship bound for India that sunk after being shelled by a German cruiser.
49 Alofsin (1993), p.32.
50 Collins (1989), pp.78–80.
51 Scott (1969), pp.149–150; also Lewis (1916), chapter 2; Adams (1932), pp.31–49.
52 As quoted in Hancock (1967), p.295.
53 For a balanced evaluation, see Howard P. Chudacoff, ed., *Major Problems in American Urban History* (Lexington, MA/Toronto: D. C. Heath, 1994), especially chapters 6–9.
54 Frederic C. Howe, "The City as a Socializing Agency: The Physical Basis of the City: The City Plan," *American Journal of Sociology*, 17(March 1912), pp.590–601, the article one indication of sociology's growing research into city life.

8 Wright's community planning

Before 1912, Wright was involved primarily with designing houses, apartments, and recreational facilities for independent land speculators and housing developers. Regardless, if his theoretical notions were to obtain credibility and to be of value, and if his philosophy was to be understood as competent and enduring, he would need to apply the same principles and methodology to all of his creative works.

Rectilinear geometry has been applied to city planning throughout history if for no other reason than roads, spaces, and buildings are easy to lay out with normal 3:4:5 or forty-five degree triangulation or trigonometric survey. This is obvious for workers in villages in Pharoahnic Egypt, for royal precincts in dynastic China, for colonial settlements of ancient Greece and Rome, and, later, worldwide for expansionist Europeans, including Euro-North Americans whose colonial towns scatter on grass prairies and Western mountain slopes. The attention of hundreds of authors to the use of geometry for city planning is plain in the historical record.[1]

We've confirmed that, prior to the 1930s, Wright applied geometry, in particular that derived from the square, to design and construct buildings. We can now demonstrate how geometry defined and enhanced determinants such as land use, spatial configuration, transportation routes, building mass, anticipated social interactions, and aesthetic aspects of his community plans. Other than a new idea for subdivision layout, there are only four: University Heights outside Darby, Montana, in 1909, Bitter Root town north of Stevensville, Montana, in 1909–10, a project for a model neighborhood south of Chicago's southside for exhibitions in 1913–16, and the model Broadacre City and related Little Farms, begun around 1930 for anywhere USA. Schemes of the 1930s have been adequately studied elsewhere, including their design methodology.[2]

English garden suburbs

> *One immense advantage of a suburban residence over one isolated in the country consists of its proximity to neighbors, and the facilities it affords of participating in those sources of instruction and enjoyment which can only be obtained in towns.*
> —John Claudius Loudon, 1838
> *The Suburban Gardener*

Northeastern America in the nineteenth century was culturally and intellectually recycling things British. In tandem, most of America's tastemakers were swayed if not beholden to northeastern thought and action. It is not surprising that Chicago's political and societal leaders were no exception. In the fields of architecture and building, it is valuable to consider only Ruskin's enormous influence or the style then named Queen Anne or the era misnomered Victorian and to further consider suburban housing developments, not for the masses but for the well-to-do.

Historian John Archer convincingly identified "Four British planning types, examples of which many American travelers observed in the 1820s through 1850s, [that] constitute important precedents for American romantic suburbs" – that is, suburbs that attempted to bring the country into the city.[3] They played a significant role in helping to humanize, by romantic and picturesque aesthetics, the place of home beyond the urban fringe. First was Regent's Park, London, begun in 1811 with overall planning by architect John Nash. It was a Crown estate "landscaped in a picturesque manner enclosed by a canal and equally picturesque terrace housing." Its parklands were enclosed and not open to the public until 1841. Second was the private residential developments "at resort towns beginning in the 1820s." One example was Pittville Estate at a spa near Cheltenham, London, begun in 1824. There were a few detached and semidetached houses but mostly terraced row housing. Also set out were two parks beside each other similar in concept to privately subsidized city Georgian squares. The third type was the commuter suburb, and dozens were initiated in the 1830s into the 1850s. In Britain, they usually included some private parks, detached and semidetached, and much terraced housing. One American suburb of this type was Llewellyn Park in Orange, New Jersey, in 1857, designed by architect Alexander Jackson Davis. It was advertised as 'Country Homes for City People" and protected by restrictive covenants. Another prototype was Riverside, nine miles from downtown Chicago and designed by landscape architects Frederick Law Olmsted and Calvert Vaux in 1869. Public parks were proposed along the Des Plaines River, and a commuter railway split what would have been a very large suburb for upmarket clients.

The private "recreational amenities" of Regent's Park, reiterated as *public* lands at Adelaide, South Australia, in 1837 "catalyzed the development of urban parks throughout Britain in the 1840s and after." Perhaps obviously, it was this fourth type that was known to American travelers like Frederick Law Olmsted and William Cullen Bryant, or visits of Britishers to America who discussed urban parks.[4] The rise of architectural journals late in the century provided quick and easy information about all things architectural, including suburban housing.

Two examples support Archer's findings and also connect to Wright. The first to consider was in its day described as a village. In 1846, Col. N. Barrett commissioned architect William H. Ranlett to prepare a plan for a few houses on an eight-acre site just west of new Brighton on Staten Island. A commuter link was by boat to New York City. Practically nothing is known of Barrett except that he was a sometime resident in England. Ranlett was from Maine and, by 1840, was in New York City in partnership with Englishman Joseph C. Wells, who had emigrated in 1839, but the partnership last only one year.[5] A study of Ranlett's own two volume presentation, an early pattern book, confirms his aesthetic impulse for a romantic eclecticism.[6] Wells likely mentioned English suburban planning ideas, but only Ranlett's words were attached to the site plan that he believed "combines, to some extent, the advantages of pleasures of city, and country life."[7] The plan, Figure 8.1, consisted of sixteen plots about 121 feet wide, each for one house, or villa. Front and side gardens were for visual pleasure, while a large kitchen garden beside the stables was at the rear. Ranlett's orderly scheme as published was entirely unique. Therefore, it may or may not have been known to Wright, but as we shall learn, its similarity to Wright's earliest Quadruple Block Plan is striking.

The second example to consider was also something of a model for up-market schemes. The best example is the private development of Ladbroke Estate in Notting Hill, London, first proposed in the 1840s but planned in 1851 into 1863. Rectangular and curved park acres of various sizes were bound by four streets with housing placed on only two sides, Figure 8.2. Housing varied from row houses of various sizes, semidetached with side gardens, and the occasional detached; each type had private gardens. Rather than follow the Georgian Square and Pittville prototypes, communal gardens were large and placed at the rear of house lots. In some instances, row housing had public gardens set between roadside footpaths and house fronts. Communal and public gardens were understood to be for health, recreation, and aesthetic purposes, not for the kitchen.

The two examples adequately exemplify Loudon's prediction in the 1830s that a suburb could, if properly designed, offer certain desirable qualities of country to the city. It was a cause he consistently argued for the entirety of his career, and Americans were avid readers of his prolific writings. Loudon, a Scot, referred to himself and like-employed gentlemen as gardeners.

214 *The city scientific*

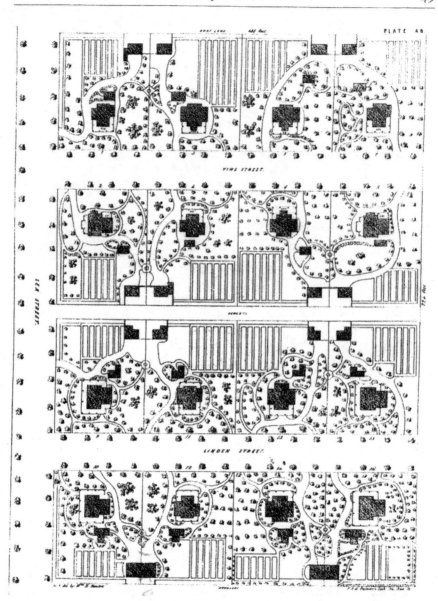

Figure 8.1 "A plot of village property" for Col. N. Barrett near New Brighton on Staten Island, designed by William H. Ranlett, Architect, 1849. From Ranlett, 1849.

Quadruplets

Charles E. Roberts was a neighbor, client, fellow Unitarian, and Wright's promoter. In 1896, Roberts's own Oak Park house and large stables, previously constructed to Daniel H. Burnham designs of 1883, were remodeled to Wright's specifications. Warren Furbeck, Roberts's

Figure 8.2 Plan of a major portion of Ladbroke Estate, or Notting Hill, Holland Park, London, 1851–63; six private public parks and two open public gardens are shown in this section of the up market real estate Ordinance Survey map of 1871.

close friend, commissioned Wright to design a house for each of his sons, George and Rollin Furbeck, in Oak Park, both in 1897. They were very different one to the other, that for George ill-formulated architecturally. George moved out less that two years after completion. Wright designed a house for Mrs Roberts's sister, Mrs Harley Bradley, and for Mrs Roberts's brother, Warren Hickox, both in 1900 for sites beside each other in Kankakee, Illinois. When, in 1901, Wright's aunts Nell and Jane Jones needed funds to construct new buildings for their Hillside Home School, Roberts provided a loan of $9,000. During 1903–04, Roberts was chairman of the Oak Park Unity Temple building committee, where he helped secure the commission for Wright.[8] Equally relevant to the present discussion was a series of earlier commissions.

Wright prepared five preliminary house designs apparently for Roberts in late 1895 for a speculative venture and for sites now unknown. Two plans were similar, the other three resembled one another, and two are dated January 1896. The H. C. Goodrich house in Oak Park may have been one of the five and was designed and constructed in 1896. The G. W. Smith house was likely another 1896 design but constructed in 1898. Around 1897, Roberts requested of Wright another house designed for an unspecified corner lot, but it, too, remained a project.[9] Floor plans were tortuous and overworked, with a complexity equal to the George Furbek house of 1897. The exterior elevations were typical of the period, including a broken roof line (consider the George Furbek, Goodrich, and Smith houses), and have a bulkiness similar to the Heller house of 1896. The front gable end had windows very similar to Wright's own house, including a surmounting arch window that was partially erased on the drawing. There has been a suggestion that it was for a corner site of a city block owned by Roberts in the "village" of Ridgeland, west of Chicago and now part of Oak Park. But drawings indicate the house would be exactly sixty feet square, plus an extension for entry and stairs, much too large for a Ridgeland site with a seventy-five-foot boundary and a twenty-six-foot setback for front garden.[10] Then, in 1899, Wright apparently prepared three house plans for Roberts, described as "germ plans for a block of low cost houses," with no hint of their disposition on unknown building sites.[11] And they were *not* meant for the "community" of houses associated with a quadruple block concept.[12]

The Frank Lloyd Wright Foundation and Archive has preserved a drawing of an outline of an entire city block in Ridgeland. The plan is undated and has a grid in red ink set at eight feet. It has been assumed that the drawing was by Wright's office, but there is no corroborating evidence. It was likely prepared by others, a surveyor, for example, or and engineer or Roberts, and sent to the office. Several hands wrote the few words thereon or drew on the drawing in ink and pencil, and there are erasures. Interestingly, Wright's hand does not appear. One fact is known: Roberts completed purchasing the entire block of land in 1895.[13] This suggests that subdivision, so to speak, was begun late 1895, or 1896 or 1897. On the sheet are some dimensions, lot numbers, and street names (some added) but no written explanations.

Drawn lightly in pencil are what could be allotment boundaries along the four sides. Most are about 128 feet deep, some are 48 feet wide, some 52 feet, and most are about 60 and therefore could be only for houses. The corner sites are about 76 to 80 feet square with a 45-degree and 8-foot wide diagonal access to a central court or garden or building or what? There are 22 peripheral building sites, plus the possibility of one in the center. But the north/south sites are too narrow to receive a house, a fact that relieves Wright of authorship of the drawing. Set in the middle of most sites and at a setback of 26 feet are squares, merely lines, that might represent tiny houses or interior courtyards or what? The supposed central area (210 feet by 102 feet), or garden or garden-with-building or building, has private access from the corner sites and a one-lane entry from the south road. This hints at the prospect of an internal space private to the block of allotments or sites along each street. If so, the presupposed overall plan recalls, if slightly, the valuable president of the highly publicized Ladbrooke Estate and was meant to serve a similar purpose for the same type of clientele. But all this is pure guesswork, information on the drawing slight.

The formalization of a standard city block reconfigured by Wright into quadruple allotments, or sites, came about in discussions with Roberts in 1899 and into 1900, not about "low cost houses" but the middle- to high-income market. Their idea was to erect eight houses, "four on a block, each commanding an entire side."[14] The scheme was first published in the Philadelphia *Ladies Home Journal* in February 1901. In 1895, editor Edward Bok began offering a set of house plans designed to fit behind the facades of popular styles: Elizabethan, Queen Anne, "colonial," or the like. In 1900, he began a new series called Model Suburban Houses, and construction plans were available by mail for five dollars. Wright's February contribution was fifth in the new series. As published, a site plan and an aerial perspective showed a set of four houses identified as a "Quadruple Block Plan," herein called Quad Plan (see Figure 8.3, top). Nothing of theoretical or practical value was said, but the block was to be four-hundred feet square, each house site two hundred square. Wright believed his

> solution of a city man's country home [is] an arrangement of the four houses that secures breadth and prospect to the community as a whole, and absolute privacy both as regards each to the community, and each to each of the four.[15]

A birds-eye perspective showed suggested landscapes with gardens behind street-side solid "privacy" garden walls that connected the four houses.[16] Central stables and garden sheds were arranged pinwheel fashion, with carriageways stretching to the street. However, the house was *not* that planned for Roberts, Figure 8.4, and not a theoretical work because constructions plans were available.[17]

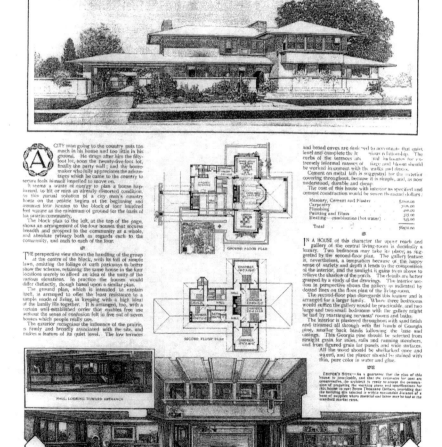

Figure 8.3 "A Home in a Prairie Town," at top a "Perspective of Quadruple Block Plan" and plot plan for the four houses that was used for all Quadruple Block Plans to follow; perspectives and plans correspond. From Wright, 1901a.

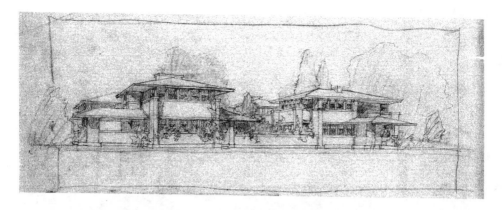

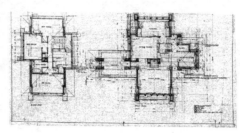

Figure 8.4 Speculative housing for C. E. Roberts's city block in Ridgeland/Oak Park, Illinois, a project of 1902–03; top: perspective drawing of two houses with alternate fronts to street; bottom: ground- and second-floor plans of houses in the above drawing; the plans fit the left house orientation.

A few details of the Quad Plan were published next in the *Chicago Evening Post* in July 1901 but not illustrated. Wright was quoted as saying the site and buildings were integrated "where everything will be in harmony," that this would excite an "architectural surprise." Additionally, there were to be eight houses "built in two blocks on plans [as] outlined in a Philadelphia publication," the *Journal* noted. Each house, "to cost between $6000 and $7000" with exterior walls of stucco on metal lath, was to be "part of an artistic [site] plan" with "no alleys." Each site was to be seventy-one feet by eighty-two feet. Work was to begin "in a few days," and Wright anticipated that, by spring 1902, the "full beauty of a whole neighborhood," he incorrectly advised, ". . . will be unfolded."[18] A week later, on 18 July 1901, the Oak Park *Reporter* repeated the *Post* article if slightly condensed and again without visual information.[19] It is not known if any were constructed, certainly none on a Quad Plan site.

Preparation of documents for the Quad Plan was validated in a letter of September 1900 from Wright to one S. T. Kendall.[20] It confirmed the date of a twenty-four-house scheme, that the Quad Plan was for Roberts, and that the February *Journal* and Quad Plan designs were related, as affirmed in the *Post* article. Plans of 1901 indicate the "colony" was now titled a "Community Project for Twenty Four Dwellings" – that is, for six quadruplets. The Quad Plan scheme was still active with Roberts into 1904 but not thereafter.[21]

That Roberts's project was stopped by local citizens "who objected to it as too radical" seems unlikely.[22] Following that line, and other than economics, Norris K. Smith believed that "members of the classes" who live in "such suburbs are precisely the ones who resist . . . the notion of uniform housing – and for reasons" Wright was "in sympathy with,"[23] as his home was in such a suburb. Yet, in 1901, a typical eight-room, two-story builder's house of brick would have cost around $4,000 when constructed on an average suburban lot forty-five feet wide. That would allow about twelve houses per acre; the Quad Plan proposed five.[24]

The same schematics were displayed at the March 1902 Chicago Architectural Club annual exhibition and fully illustrated in the catalog. The short text mentioned the 1901 *Journal* article.[25] Over the next few years, the concept became even more formal. A normal city block with an alley dividing in one direction (termed a "court") was bisected in the opposite direction by a minor street or pedestrian way. The principal quadrants were again divided to form a set of minor quadrants bound by roads or walks. These became the building lots for one house per site. The square and its symmetry were critical to cultivating the design.

For a second offering to the *Ladies Home Journal* in July 1901, Wright again proposed alternating orientations (see Figure 8.5).[26] The gable ends and eave detail were similar to the Hickox house of 1900 but massing and plans were different. In the July article and the Architectural Club's 1902 exhibition, alternate orientations using the same plan were recommended for normal city block allotments. Obviously not Wright's innovation, it was a modest idea that may have come out of Quad Plan studies. The 1902 text mentioned that "the house is to be built at Riverside Illinois, and finished as here shown," but it did not proceed. A comparison with site plans for Roberts's houses makes the point. Moreover, the perspective drawings of the three published proposals and that for Roberts of 1903 indicated a garden wall connecting neighboring houses of similar design, a fact noted by Wright in the *Post* and consistent with the Quad Plan.

Wright's third and last contribution to Bok's magazine was for the April 1907 issue and titled "A Fireproof House for $5000" (see Figure 8.6). By this time in North America, tens of thousands of buildings had been constructed of concrete.[27] But the design was unique to the general reader because of a flat roof over a tidy square house in plan, the whole nearly a cube. While the Quad Plan was not shown or implied, alternate orientations were illustrated. Wright said the house "may be placed with either the living-room front or the terrace front to the street," as in July 1901.[28]

Alternate orientations were employed in 1909 for a residential section of the proposed Bitter Root village in western Montana. The eight houses were to be in a series with floor plans flipped or opposite hand (see Figure 8.7). These floor plans were the same as Nichols of 1908, the 1907 fireproof house for the *Journal*, Stephen Hunt of 1907, and others. Alternate

Figure 8.5 "A small house with lots of room in it" as published in the *Ladies Home Journal* of July 1901; the plan on left fits the perspective orientation; drawings as prepared for Wright, 1910.

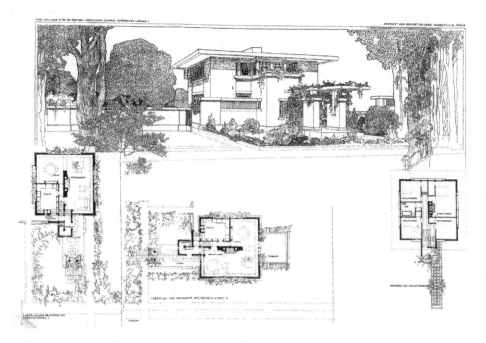

Figure 8.6 "A Fireproof House for $5000" for the *Ladies Home Journal* of April 1907, drawings as prepared for Wright, 1910.

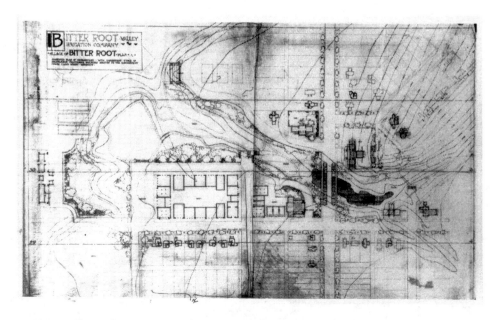

Figure 8.7 "Village of Bitter Root plan" project for a site north of Stevensville, Montana, for BRIVCo. Courtesy and © 2016 FLWF.

orientations appeared again in 1919 for Wright's Monolith Homes scheme for Thomas Hardy's subdivision proposed for Racine, Wisconsin.[29]

The Bitter Root village houses were apparently originally prepared for Edward Waller prior to late 1909, and two remained unbuilt, the "hipped" roofed and "flat" roofed models.[30] The Nichols house of 1906 was a predecessor to the third design called a gable house. Illustrated in 1910 in Wright's *Studies and Executed Buildings* portfolio, they were immediately followed by drawings of University Heights, a project also in Montana. A set of presentation drawings was prepared in 1909 for one of the Bitter Root/Waller houses, Figure 8.8, and titled "Typical house for [BRVICo] Montana."[31] The other two had the same plan but opposite hand.[32]

The twisting course of evolution occurred in 1910 when Wright again published the Quad Plan. The first plate was a redrawing of the house perspective that had appeared in the February 1901 *Ladies Home Journal*. The second plate was in two parts, one the bird's-eye perspective previously used in the 1901 *Journal* with the words "Perspective of Quadruple Block Plan" painted over. The other was two schemes for the disposition and orientation of a quadruplet of houses (see Figure 8.9). In scheme A, the terraces pinwheel, while in B they point inward with backsides to the street.[33] But note: the floor plans and perspectives *do not match*. For unknown reasons, Wright substituted the floor plan for Roberts of 1903 for that of 1901. Also gone were stables and garden sheds.

While the 1903 drawings are undated, the exaggerated articulation of vertical structure indicated in the floor plans and as extended three-dimensionally, and the overall massing in brick and published descriptions, fit 1903 rather than 1900 or 1901.[34] The floor plan is adventuresome, horizontally dynamic, and multileveled. These characteristics are not apparent in the closed, three-dimensional bulkiness of the elevations. The design closely follows the structural articulation and all other architectonics of the 1903 Darwin Martin house. Wright's 1910 description followed previous accounts:

> A typical house intended to form the unit in the group as arranged in the "Quadruple Block Plan."
>
> A new scheme for subdividing property, designed to divide the usual "American block" into two parts by means of a private way through the center, and to group the houses in squads of four on each half. The houses are so placed that a maximum of privacy, and various advantages of position are made possible.[35]

Figure 8.8 Typical gable-roofed house project for E. C. Waller for unknown sites, ca. 1908; also prepared for Bitter Root village in 1909; wood-batten siding. From Wright, 1910.

222 *The city scientific*

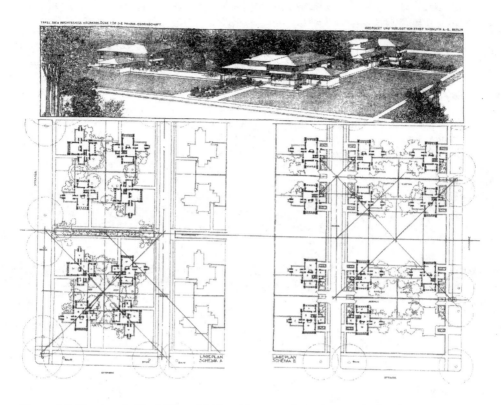

Figure 8.9 Quadruple Block Plan, 1910, with two orientations and erased perspective title; both sets of plans do not fit the perspective; author's notations; as presented in Wright, 1910; author's notations.

The brief descriptions in February 1901, March 1902, and 1910 offer clues as to why he, if not Roberts, favored the idea over normal subdivision practice other than mere difference: privacy, aspect, and a supposedly varied streetscape. Immediately following the Quad Plan illustration in the 1910 publication were plates of the 1907 fireproof house.[36] Its new description was similar to the earlier text:

> A simple house, four sides alike for sake of simplicity in making [concrete] forms with entry added at side, and trellised terrace.
> The chimney supports the floors and carries the water from the roof. An insertion of square colored tiles occur just beneath the soffit of the eaves, certain ones opening for circulation of air in summer. The house may be placed upon the lot in two ways, as shown in schemes A and B.[37]

Previously published illustrations were again redrawn, and a new site plan B was added.

With Wright's words and the visual evidence, the various propositions from 1900–10 for squads of quads and for alternate orientations can be now understood as conceptually related. Later use of the schemes provide additional confirmation and imply a significance for his limited thoughts about communities and their planning. Limited, that is, by the needs of real estate clients.

Application of the Quad Plan was an important component of his submission to the 1913 Chicago City Club exhibition of model designs for a neighborhood community, to be discussed in detail shortly. In 1913, Wright added a further site plan (C, Figure 8.10) in which terraces faced one another. The bird's-eye and ground-level perspectives used in the February 1901 *Journal* were redrawn for 1913 with more garden entourage and the addition of three colors. Floor plans in the site drawings were those of 1900 and 1910, redrawn with color added. Again, perspectives and floor plans *do not match*.[38]

For the 1916 publication of the City Club's 1913 exhibition, Wright prepared a short "Explanation of Alternative Block Arrangements" – that is, the three Quad Plans:

> **A.** Quadruple re-subdivision of city block by means of single cross street and parterres into four sub-blocks. Four houses grouped at center of each sub-block about an interior court enclosed by low walls – 1/4 of the enclosure available to each of the four houses.
> One entrance to one house only on each side of each sub-block. No alleys – houses revolving in plan so that living-rooms and verandas face outward and kitchens inward to courts. A single plan used thus is always presented at a different angle in harmonious groups of four.
> **B.** Same. Single cross-street – no parterres. Houses grouping across the streets increasing interior court gardens and giving direct access from street to all houses with out parterres.
> **C.** Same. Each of the four houses moved to exterior angles of the four lots of the sub-block – grouping uniformly in fours equally distant from each other both ways, garages at center. Each group connected by low walls about eight feet back from public walks. Major area of each lot suited for private use as a garden.
> Schemes might be rhythmically interchanged in some well-balanced arrangements.[39]

Perhaps aware of earlier objections, Wright now promoted the Quad Plan, not the houses, "as valuable for low cost cottages as for luxurious dwellings." Further, it had "picturesque" qualities; was artistically "susceptible of infinite variety of treatment;" and, in skilled hands, "these various treatments could rise to great beauty"; or "the nature of the plan would discipline the average impulse." Wright encouraged "Other rhythms in grouping than those suggested," and here he could have referred to Bitter Root village.[40]

The fact remains, however, that, from 1900–16, Wright did not offer substantive explanations as to how the Quad Plan informed reformers, how it was materially more beneficial or economically viable, or how it was more acceptable sociologically than ordinary block subdivisions: attractiveness aside, he made simple assertions. The Progressive reformers must have found the Quad Plan planning principles ill-conceived and aesthetically questionable,

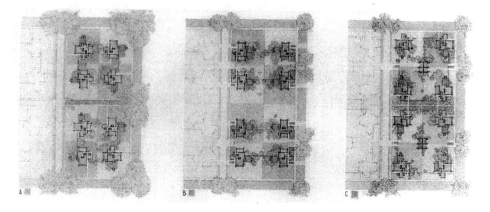

Figure 8.10 Quadruple Block Plans, 1915, with three options for house orientation; pans were redrawn and colored for Wright, 1916. From Levine 1916.

with much too excessive occupation of land, poor economics, and irrelevant. Subdivision developers, including Roberts and Waller, must have held similar views because nothing eventuated. The Quadruple Block Plan was an interesting if capricious real estate scheme. Putting disappointments aside, undeterred Wright explored *quadruplet* schemes for another five decades.[41] See Appendix C. Of course, the Quad Plan was not about community. As well, the concept of the backside of houses enclosing a shared(?) green garden does not equate with a row of houses with wide front gardens. Conceptually, one does not follow or complement the other.

University Heights

The first two communities to study were located in the Bitter Root Valley, a great groove in the Rocky Mountains that embraces the running Bitter Root River. Although lasting about 130 days, the growing season for apples is very dry, so, during the 1890s, developers began constructing irrigation canals and laterals. Then local orchardist Samuel Dinsmore formed an irrigation company in 1900 and, in 1905, sought out financier W. I. Moody. He in turn hired his brother-in-law, Chicagoan Frederick Day Nichols, to superintend works and promotions of the newly formed Bitter Root Valley Irrigation Company, or their abbreviation BRVICo.[42] Work began in 1906 on a "Big Ditch," the principle canal, by enlarging an existing dam named Lake Como and situated at 11,700 foot elevation (3,566 metres) above the southwestern end of the valley to then proceed north along eastern slopes.

Earlier, in 1905, financier Nichols asked Wright to design a summer house for a site near golf courses in fashionable Flossmoor, southeast of Chicago by commuter train. When Nichols moved into the house in 1906, it had no electricity or heat. Floor plans had evolved from the Lamp house of late 1902 and early 1903. The exterior was beveled cedar siding treated with ferric oxide in a similar fashion to many cottages of the period, some with board-and-batten siding. It was through Nichols that Wright was invited to participate in this optimistic enterprise as community planner and architect. His first assignment began in January 1909 with preparation of plans for the summer colony of University Heights. BRVICo then commissioned him to prepare plans for a new town to be located east of the river and six miles north of Stevensville near the Big Ditch. When construction of the town was suddenly abandoned, Wright was asked to provide designs for the buildings of a small village on the same site. BRIVCo had bought the land for $2.50 to $15.00 an acre and sold ten-acre parcels for $400.00 to $1,000.00 an acre.[43] (Four hundred 1909 dollars would be worth about $10,600 in 2014.)

"'University Heights' is the name of a settlement planned" for the Lake Como area west of Darby on a high, projecting bench three miles south of the lake.[44] It was Moody's and Nichols's first scheme to attract "university men and women" or people of "that general type who stand well socially, intellectually, and financially in their eastern communities."[45] The idea was a "summer retreat" for "Members of University Faculties, Famous Authors and Other Noted Men of Effete East. . . ."[46] As investors, they could purchase two or more ten-acre sections of orchard, with profits guaranteed after five years,[47] together with a site at University Heights for a "log or frame cottage."[48] Sometime before April 1908 and nine months before Wright's involvement, the company "issued a pamphlet [that pictured] the cabins in a semi-circle but divided by the clubhouse. An irrigation ditch with rustic bridges is in the foreground."[49] That "picture" and text obviously formed part of the program and influenced Wright.

Wright was likely contacted in January 1909 during a return visit to Chicago by Nichols when he and Moody selected D. C. Bartlett of Oak Park as land agent.[50] In February 1909, Montanans were informed that "one of the most famous architects that America has ever produced – Frank Lloyd Wright" was employed.[51] Elsewhere, it was stated that Wright was in "charge of the buildings and landscape gardening. . . ."[52] From 15 to 19 February 1909, Wright, Bartlett, and other eastern investors visited the site. On return to Oak Park and through March, Wright designed and detailed a site plan, the clubhouse, and all cabins.[53] In March, it was reported that lumber was "being sawed and hauled," that "thirty rustic cabins and a central club house will be erected at University Heights in July," and "The designing . . . is in charge of Frank Lloyd Wright, a noted architect."[54]

Wright's spoke only once about Heights and that was a plate caption in his influential book *Studies and Executed Buildings* of 1910:

> [The colony was] Designed to give accommodation to a group of university men owning adjoining orchards and wishing to live near in summer time. An arrangement of simple wooden cabins with a central clubhouse, where all go for meals, and transients may also be accommodated. . . .

By their number in the 1910 *Studies*, the four plates of Heights shared presentation honors with the Dana house of 1902, Unity Temple of 1905–09, and the Coonley mansion of 1902. By inference, then, in 1910 he believed University Heights was one of his more important – or at least more interesting – works.[55]

Because of axial formality, Figure 8.11, where north is to the right, the grouping may appear rigid and not respond with ease to forest or terrain. But such an observation is stilled by a site visit. The clubhouse was placed on land rising from the water cascade to the crown of the access road in front. Where land was slightly flatter behind the clubhouse, Wright located four tennis courts. Cabins were displaced alternately to receive seasonal south and north winds. The stagger and slope allowed views beyond to the towering Sapphires. The seasonal(?) water "cascade" ended in a pool to be created by expanding an irrigation lateral from nearby Lake Como, not the Big Ditch.

A two-dimensional analysis of the site plan proves geometrical intelligibility (see Figure 8.12). The clubhouse, or inn, was the design center point, while other design lines structured the disposition of boundaries, foci, and edges. Connecting lines extending from some of the internal squares helped locate minor building compositions. (The four corner squares are larger than the central.) In the upper right-hand corner, the primary (or smaller) squares control certain internal axial arrangements, while the secondary (or larger) squares control peripheral axial positions. The outer edge of the secondary squares determine proportionally by an arc off the center line of the tennis courts. The analysis clearly delineates the probable design method. The geometry also would necessarily assist surveyors when laying out building sites and roads. Larger cabins were within the arc of the entry drive or near the cascade. Those medium sized were either side of the tennis courts or otherwise close to the clubhouse and so on. So, there was something of a radiating economic hierarchy. The location of various cabin types on the site plan were Wright's suggestion to investors who, if they wanted, could select a site and cabin plans and modify as desired.[56]

The Heights was conceived as a smallish and simple social community of about 160 individuals, a place where people at leisure might live in physical and blissful social harmony. Wright provided architectural vision and technical knowledge, but Nichols and confederates carried on without Wright's supervision or that of his staff, local BRVICo carpenter talent sufficient.[57] A bird's-eye perspective by Marion Mahony published in 1910 closely matched the final plan.[58] Fourteen buildings were completed by mid-1910, including the clubhouse that nearly followed Wright's floor plan if less the elevations. It was altered in 1923, the verandahs enclosed, the stained timber exterior soon painted a ghostly white.[59] With only two cabins remaining and disinvestments, in the 1930s, the Heights became a private beef ranch.[60] In the 1980s, much of the area was tightly packed with second-growth pine, the clubhouse and orchard rows long gone.

Some say Wright invested in BRVICo schemes.[61] Unfortunately, as early as 1912, the company began experiencing serious financial difficulties. If he did, perhaps that is one reason why thereafter he ignored them. This neglect resulted in the Bitter Root town plan not being published until the 1980s. A sad turn because, for its day, the plan was an extraordinary design document that would have been of stimulating theoretical and practical value to the new profession of city planning.

Figure 8.11 University Heights aerial perspective, 1909, detail of drawing by Marion L. Mahony. From Wright, 1910.

Bitter Root town and village

Wright referred to the town of Bitter Root twice. It was oblique in 1932 when he mentioned an involvement in "the establishment of the Bitter Root Community in Montana," and no more. The other equally terse occurrence was recorded by Wright's co-author Henry Hitchcock in 1942: there were "two projects for a town of Bitter Root on much the same site . . . though neither of them were published."[62] There were two projects but only one for a town.

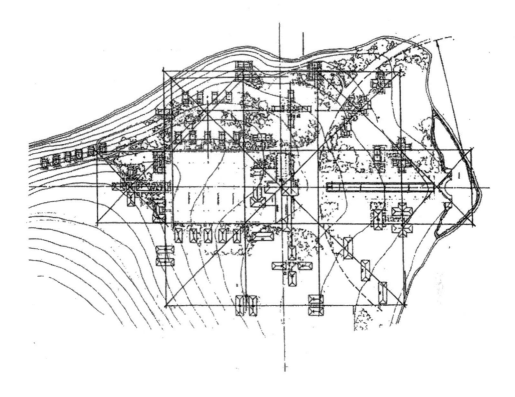

Figure 8.12 University Heights site plan, 1909, partially built west of Darby, Montana; author's notations. From Wright, 1910.

The town

In March 1910, Frederick Nichols explained Wright's role in 1909:

> A competent architect, who designed also the "University Heights" ... was employed to lay out the town and to plan buildings best suited to this mountain valley. Plans of several types of houses are available at the company's offices so that the purchaser may secure the benefit of wise architectural suggestions without excessive cost. Any competent carpenter ... can readily meet the requirements of every new comer who desires to build in harmony with the general architectural ideal.[63]

One of Wright's duties, therefore, was to design easy-to-build houses.

A design for Bitter Root town was requested of Wright no earlier than April 1909. It was his first exercise in city planning and presented to Nichols in mid-June. Figure 8.13, where north is to the left. Again the dynamics of the square organized zoning, building locations, and a street grid that bound square blocks of buildings to more or less fit a very uneven westerly slope (see Figure 8.14).

The street grid recalled traditional plans for thousands of new towns throughout central and western prairies and mountains, including Darby, Stevensville, and Missoula. But it was infused with unique features that collectively would have vitalized the character of a small

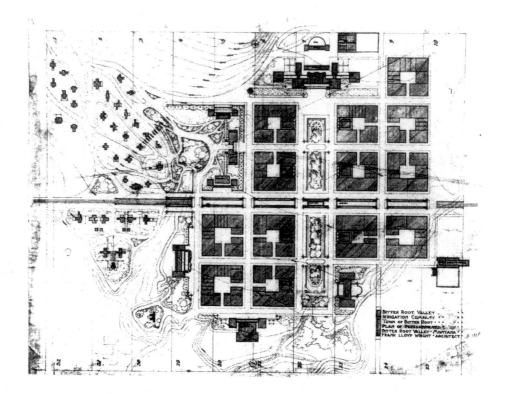

Figure 8.13 "Town of Bitter Root, Plan of Development," for a site just north of Stevensville, Montana of 1909; a project for BRVICo. Courtesy and © 2016 FLWF.

town. Streets were somewhat narrow and city blocks relatively small, while their buildings contained open interior courtyards for service and light. Some buildings were to house normal small-town commercial functions, a restaurant and boutique were mentioned, but there was no indication of multiple-unit housing. Facing the great east–west parkway were community services – telegraph, post office, fire department, utilities – as well as BRVICo's real estate office and a bank; each identified in the plan drawing by a central position and special treatment.

Uniquely, cultural and community functions were located on the grid's periphery. With north to the left in the drawing, therefore in the southwest was a hospital, farthest west a theater with a water fountain or sculpture to the east. In the northeast was a cultural center composed of a museum, school, and library. A city administration building in the northwest was axially opposite the power station to the south. Dominating the east is a spacious hotel, the money spinner, imposing itself from high ground in a formal relationship to the green parkway. On the west, a hospital, theater, and the administrative center sat atop shallow benches that overlooked river lands. These decentralized buildings were symmetrically axial to street or block and themselves axially formal.

Wright isolated suburbia in the northeast along the elongated high mound of Sunnyside Ridge. The formally and symmetrically arranged houses in the northwest (and below the lazy suburban roads) nicely fit the larger organizational grid.

The north–south Eastside highway bisected the town plan, marked a survey division line, and acted as a grand avenue with a two-level transport system: vehicles and pedestrians at

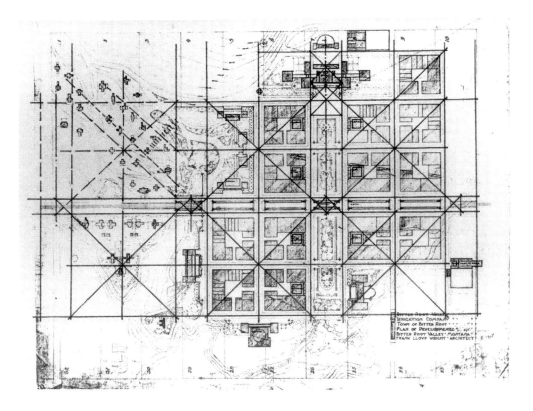

Figure 8.14 "Town of Bitter Root" plan for a site just north of Stevensville, Montana, 1909; a project for BRVICo. Author's notations.

ground level, trains in an open cut. The "subway" (Wright's term) was in a depressed rail line covered only where roads and walkways crossed over. A lower level rail station was centered on the green opposite the hotel accessed by stairs. Over a shallow gully on the northern end, a vehicular bridge connected town and suburb.

But why did Wright include such a grand transportation scheme in that mountain wilderness? During the early months of 1909, there was talk of rail lines connecting eastern Idaho and the Bitter Root Valley and of an electrified rail line from Missoula down the Bitter Root Valley, perhaps as far as Hamilton. By late 1909, it was proposed that the electric line run with Eastside highway to then turn sharply west for a few blocks before returning southward. Its inclusion, therefore, was not an independent decision, although it was likely Wright's idea to place it below grade. His design was a serious preplanned resolution to the impact of auto and rail.

The full range of necessities to classify it as a town or city had been programmed to sustain it: workplace, home, recreation, institutions, commerce, government, and so on, this in spite of Stevensville's close proximity. Sadly, no perspectives or elevations of Wright's plan are extant, although perspective construction lines appear on the drawing.

Wright envisioned solid town blocks tight to sidewalks on each side and set within a grid divisible into major sections and minor quadrants. He disposed cultural functions to the edge of the grid within sylvan areas, positioned community services facing a generous green parkway, and integrated the formal landscape with townscape. He designed separate but combined vehicle, pedestrian, and rail systems, and finally, he strengthened traditional suburban living by placing it in a wooded setting on high ground. All applications were tied by a logical geometrical design tool. There was no precedent for Bitter Root town, and it remained Wright's only commission to design a town or city.[64]

The village

Wright's proposed town plan encroached on orchards recently platted, laterals in place and lots sold, facts likely not received. BRVICo's engineers devised a new street plan for a compact village, Figure 8.7, that extended west rather than south. The prosaic village street plan was *not* Wright's creation as generally held. For unknown reasons, Nichols and BRVICo ignored Wright's town plan and, likely for promotional purposes, asked him to locate village functions and design a few buildings.

North is to the left in the plan, therefore a small school, church, and inn were located east of the bridge. Directly in front of the inn and across the highway was a library and park that extended under a bridge that itself physically separated pedestrian and vehicular traffic. South of the park and in a line progressing west were an opera house and a commercial complex that, with community services, clustered around a large, open service court at the west end of which was a farmer's market. Farthest west was a railroad station attended by apple storage sheds. There was no electrified rail line. The three-dimensional character of the village was portrayed in a bird's-eye perspective of 1909 (see Figure 8.15). A few preliminary pencil sketches for a railroad station suggest that it, the inn, library, school, and church could have been either stuccoed or similar to the inn.

Each rectangular rental unit of the proposed shop buildings (around their large court) stepped with the slope of land and to differing facades and roofs. Perhaps Wright or the renderer was looking for the streetscape variety that occurs normally and spontaneously over many years. In any event, he envisaged "consistent types of inexpensive practicable buildings adapted to the environment:" words in the drawing title block. Obviously, the size of a drawing is irrelevant as long as the building plan and three-dimensional characteristics are clear. All totaled, Wright, or Marion Mahony, made fifty-four independent building designs for the village.

As the Big Ditch approached the village site, BRVICo set up work camps around Stevensville in anticipation of housing the several hundred men hired to survey, clean, plan, cultivate, or set out roads. In about June 1909, Wright prepared preliminary plans for a typical work camp that included a bunk room, mess hall, stables, and a workshop. The camp was not built. Also and as mentioned, a series of designs for the investors' "summer home" was prepared by Wright and based on the cabins he had designed for Heights: window treatment the only noticeable difference. Architectural plans were available from "the company's office."[65]

Of the many preliminary plans and working drawings prepared for Nichols, only the inn was built by BRVICo carpenters, unsupervised. They followed most of the architect's drawings and details but slightly reduced the overall size and excluded stables. It was gable-roofed with board-and-batten siding and a linear T-shape.[66] (Drawings of the inn in Wright's town and village layout and perspective are not as built.)[67]

In October 1909, during the week before the inn opened, the Stevensville *Northwest Tribune* wrote the only clear description:

> The inn is the first building to be erected at the new town which is now being platted....
> The Inn will be modern in every way, having bath rooms, hot and cold water and a sewer system. . . [and] a veranda is full length of the building, and it has a glass front. The dining room will be situated in one end of the building, while the other end will be

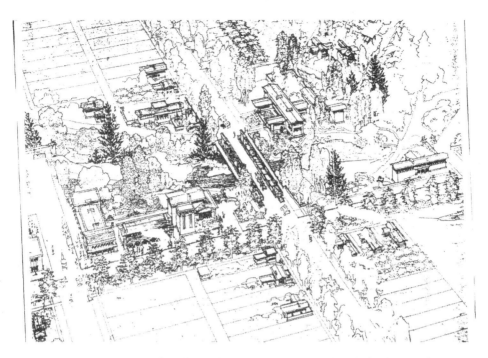

Figure 8.15 Aerial perspective of "Village of Bitter Root" project; detail of a drawing by Marion L. Mahony in 1909. Courtesy and © 2016 FLWF.

the lobby and parlor. . . . The Inn is the architecture of Lloyd Wright of Chicago, one of the most noted landscape artists in the country and who designed the University Heights clubhouse. . . .[68]

That was second and last mention of Wright in local public literature from 1908–10.

Figure 8.16 superimposes information over Wright's first town plan and includes the perimeter of the village plan for comparison. Eastside highway and Three Mile Road (now Rathbone Lane) were determined before 1909, and BRVICo fixed Porter Hill and Camas roads in mid-1909. Supplied by a new water storage tank, some fire hydrants were installed in 1910 or so. The inn, which burned to the ground on 28 July 1924, was located south of Porter Hill Road beside the highway. North of the inn, a Lutheran church was built sometime after 1911 and physically relocated in another town in about 1938. Farther north is a house similar in plan to one beside the highway at the T-junction with Porter Hill Road, nearly opposite the site of the inn. Both houses were of 1912, one of the Wright School, the other a bungalow type.[69]

The electrified line remained a promoter's dream but apparently a golf course located on "bottom land unsuited for orchards" was partly built.[70] A loop of the Northern Pacific was eventually laid about a quarter mile west of the highway. Expectations were high even after Moody and Nichols quit the venture in April 1910.[71] The new entrepreneurs hired Philadelphia architect Guy King, who designed cottages as a specialty. In June 1910, he advertised that fifty cottages were commissioned for Bitter Root and, in February 1912, he called for tenders on the company's infrastructure buildings but nothing resulted.[72] But around 1913, BRVICo schemes began to fall apart, to collapse in 1918.[73]

232 The city scientific

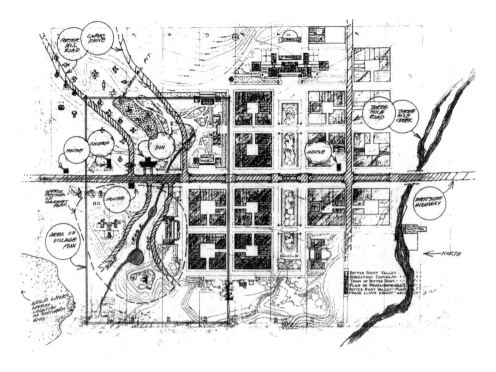

Figure 8.16 Bitter Root town and village site plans superimposed showing existing conditions in the 1980s. Author's drawing.

Hooker and the city club

Soon after Wright's activities in Montana were completed, city reform forces had a brief but resolute focus on Chicago, and Wright was included. The efforts of the City Club of Chicago and its principal spokesman George Ellsworth Hooker played a critical, positive role. In later years, when asked about his profession, the reply was simple: "civic work."[74] He represented those reformers who took the pragmatic route of persuasion, such as Jacob Riis and Benjamin C. Marsh in New York City, Zona Gale from Wisconsin, Frederick C. Howe in Cleveland and New York, and Reverend Jenkin Jones and Mary Simkovitch in Chicago.

Born in Vermont in 1861, Hooker graduated in 1883 from Amherst College and received a law degree in 1885 from Columbia University, to be admitted to the New York bar in 1886. In 1890, he received a bachelor degree from Yale Divinity School and then associated with the American Home Missionary Society as a Congregationalist pastor in eastern Washington State until 1893.[75]

During 1894–95, Hooker traveled to Europe, second of many excursions to follow, and was surprised by Germany's city planning resolutions. As he recalled, after years of frustrating piecemeal reactions to those problems and "bewailing . . . architectural ugliness," he discovered "city planning" and "it seemed like the clearing of a clouded sky."[76] It was likely during this tour he met Sitte and remained America's closest link to the Austrian and his circle. Hooker was named on the masthead of *Der Städtebau*, a magazine collaboratively founded in Vienna by Sitte and Theodor Goecke in 1904 and then published by Wasmuth in Berlin.[77]

Thereafter, Hooker immigrated to a swelling Chicago, where independently he investigated city conditions during 1896–97 and then became secretary to the Special Street Railway Committee of the city council. Soon, he was an editorial writer for Chicago's *Tribune* while its *Record-Herald* published two important articles of his, one about Sitte as a "City Builder," the other on the German "Municipal Movement."[78] Hooker was committed to social welfare, municipal reform, the Settlement House Movement (he resided for nine months in London at Toynbee Hall during a study trip), and resided in Hull-House from 1896 until death in 1937. After formation in 1912, he became a spirited member of the Progressive Party.

Following the lead of the first city club in New York City in 1894, the Chicago City Club evolved out of meetings held in Dwight and Lucy Perkins's living room. Attendees included Charles Zueblin who, in 1891, established the Northwest University settlement house and was president of the American Civic League for Civic Improvement and a popular "civic revival" speaker. Also in attendance was Jens Jensen, Edwin Winston, Louis Post, John Montgomery, and Hooker.[79] When founded in 1903, Hooker became civic secretary of the club, a post held until 1917. Club membership was made up of a wide cross-section of Progressive-minded middle- to upper-middle income people, many of them young landscape and building architects, but not of elected politicians and those plutocrats leading industry and commerce. Wright was not a member but otherwise supported the club because, in the words of David Van Zanten, it "carried on the progressive architectural program in a broad and more focused manner than had been permitted by the framework of the Architectural Club."[80]

Chicago successfully promoted itself as the location of many conventions and conferences where Hooker gained valuable experience. For instance, he was involved in the "civic organizations" section of the International Congress and Exposition of September 1911. It featured a "model city ordinance" and a speech by President William H. Taft. Exhibitors were from America, Canada, and Europe, but apparently city planning was not included.[81] Hooker was also active in the National Conference on City Planning, begun 1909, and the National Housing Conference begun in 1911. As City Club's delegate, in 1910, Hooker attended the Berlin/Düsseldorf city planning conference and visited several central European cities on an itinerary designed to again study planning and model housing in situ, surely visiting the five Krupp garden suburbs around Essen and perhaps Agnetapark in Holland.[82] He likely did not attend the 1910 Royal Institute of British Architects' conference on international – mainly empire – city planning. London transactions were published in 1911, so he no doubt became aware of proceedings.[83] In any event, he was already familiar with the work of Howard, Unwin (who would soon give a paper to the City Club), Culpin, and other Garden City advocates.

German meetings and related planning, zoning, and housing exhibits organized by Werner Hegemann, who Wright likely met in Berlin in 1908, probably fueled Hooker's determination to host an American conference and housing exhibition. To that end, the City Club became a sponsor.[84] The Berlin and London occasions were programmatical. Hooker referred to recent disclosures by "vice commissions, white-slave prosecutions, playground advocates, temperance reformers, and social investigators."[85] The delay from when the proposal was first put in 1911 to realization in 1913 was not excessive but beneficial.[86]

The club's city planning committee, delegated organizers of 1913 celebrations, was chaired by "flamboyant, outspoken" landscape architect Jens Jensen, an advocate of urban playgrounds, recreational parks, and known critic of the City Beautiful Movement.[87] The club's attitude and most other disenchanted critics of the day was echoed by Jensen, who declared Burnham's 1909 *Plan* to be "inhuman, imperialistic, and undemocratic."[88] Jensen had vaguely but correctly observed that the "more formality in design, the less democracy in its feeling and tendency."[89] More specifically, he believed the 1909 *Plan* was a commercial venture, a "show city," a "city of palaces," that to "leave the greatest part of the city in filth and squalor is . . . to put on a false front."[90] Historian Mel Scott reckoned that, like Washington, DC, the Chicago

234 The city scientific

proposal was for "a city of a past that America never knew."[91] Historian Thomas Hines saw a "reverence of the City Beautiful mentality for the culture of the Old World":[92] a natural cultural translocation.

In any event, in an article of 1909, Hooker acknowledged the "new standard of spaciousness" of Burnham's study, but that only approached comprehensiveness.[93] Hooker's colleagues were less sanguine. He was among idealists – they would have said realists – who formed the City Club out of a perceived need

> to keep reform ideas stirred up [and to hold the] frankest and most thoughtful debates on traction [rail ways], public improvements, and civic misdemeanors. "Big Business" was not sacred there; partisan politics got a chilly hearing.[94]

Its "chief function," therefore,

> [was] to promote the acquaintance, the friendly intercourse, the accurate information and personal co-operation of those who are sincerely interested in practical methods of improving the public life and affairs of the community in which we live.[95]

Repeat: accurate information, practical methods.

Under Hooker's guidance, the City Club, often paralleling efforts of settlement houses, sociologists, and women's clubs, established several "task forces" to study existing conditions in housing and relevant regulations, playgrounds, rail transportation, pedestrian and vehicular use of streets, and other sociological and technical research activities. The collective progressive view that urged such studies was reduced by Jensen, who reminded all of the intimate, *domestic* nature of cities: "first of all" a city must be "homelike."

Indeed, the neighborhood, a place of private residences and the heart of family and community social interaction, was becoming a focus of progressive planning by varied professional groups and the lay community, including concerned women. The Chicago Woman's Club (founded in 1876 and, around 1900, headed by Lucy Perkins), the Woman's City Club (founded 1910), and Chicago settlements actively participated in Hooker's 1913 exhibition.[96]

While 1909 is generally considered the high mark of an emphasis on redeveloping city centers as advanced for Washington in 1902, we can now agree that 1909 also signaled a shift in thinking to the city's margins, to the suburbs, and to more humanitarian concerns. The City Club was at the forefront of synthetic thought and willing to agitate and cajole. It, like hundreds of other city clubs, women's clubs, leagues, and civic associations, the National Municipal League (formed 1894), and similarly motivated nongovernmental organizations, were committed to exploring potentialities of reform by investigative and practical resolve directed to law and political administration at one extreme through to improving concomitant domestic circumstances by intelligent design. Hooker's press release put it so: "to encourage land owners and capitalists to promote social welfare by developing ideal suburbs."[97] Thus, the club's quarter-section and neighborhood center national competitions for model plans and a resulting 1916 publication.

To the nation, in December 1912, the City Club invited people to participate in a "Competition with Case Prizes for the producing of a Scheme of Development of a Quarter-Section of Land within the Limits of the City of Chicago, Illinois."[98] National in scope, parochial in detail, the competition was to be accompanied by a housing exhibition. Both events were energized by the forthcoming National Housing Conference to be held in Chicago in May 1913. The conference was subsidized by the Sage Foundation, which allowed Clarence Parry to attend.

The quarter-section competition

The text of the City Club's 1912 competition program expressed a belief that the Burnham and Bennett 1909 *Plan* for Chicago was much too general a "framework," extraordinarily expensive, and that a "long period of time for its execution" obviously left quickly developing areas of the city in jeopardy. The urgent need was not for greater commercial and municipal display but for smaller-scaled, closely detailed plans related to community and "neighborhood institutions."

Perceptively, the program referred to the competition as "a study," preferring to gather a series of designs that would collectively inform on possibilities rather than presume there would be a final solution. When the results were published in 1916 as *City Residential Land Development*, the subtitle was *Studies in Planning*.[99] Yet the suggested reading list was admittedly prescriptive, describing "the progress of the Garden City and Garden Suburb movement, especially in Great Britain and Germany." That emphasis was supported by recent club-sponsored public lectures given by planners the likes of Unwin, Henry Vivian, Ewart G. Culpin, Thomas Adams, and Thomas Mawson, all British and devoted to Garden Cities.[100]

Suggested reading was from Ireland, Germany, and England and dated from 1904–12. By reading Georges Benoit-Lévy's essay, competitors became aware of the extent of Garden Suburb applications in France, Scotland (noting that Andrew Carnegie put $21 million into a Scottish Garden City corporation), the Netherlands, Belgium, Sweden, Switzerland, and Hungary. The only American publication was a pamphlet about ritzy Forest Hills Gardens on New York's Long Island.[101] Many people felt that the Forest Hills suburb was a "spectacular disappointment to social reformers,"[102] that it was, according to Rockwell Kent, one of the most "artistic, most expensive, most exclusive residential parks in the world."[103]

The final and longest part of the club's program was devoted to planning details as prepared by the Illinois Chapter of the AIA. From "building and landscape architects," engineers, and sociologists, the club asked for "the best practice of the present day, for laying out and improving, for residence purposes, areas in Chicago" then unoccupied.[104] On offer was $800 in prizes "for such plans" judged the three best. The program's preamble stated the empirically obvious, that land on "the outskirts of the city" was being

> rapidly built up with homes without that intelligent direction . . . for the good of the city and its population. Recreation centers and parks are not being located until population has made them absolutely necessary, and then at large cost for the requisite land. Nor are the essentials for good housing and for neighborhood institutions being recognized.[105]

The competition's imaginary site eight miles south of central Chicago was flat, empty. (A quarter-section is one-quarter of a mile square and contains 160 acres, about 64.7 hectares.) Chicago and environs had strictly followed quarter-sectional township surveys to such an extent that they had been given names and, in time, political definition.[106] Between the downtown train loop and competition site were located many places of work all served by public transport. Therefore, two necessary ingredients of a city, workplace and transport, were not internal to the design problem, nor was self-government and major infrastructure facilities.

Competitors were required to submit drawings first of their site plan and second of an aerial perspective, together with certain data. Plan requirements specified functional elements, such as street layout, housing lots, business location, commerce, public gardens and open spaces, education and religious facilities, varied recreational activities, and so forth. Jointly, they defined the physical structure of a fully equipped neighborhood. Submissions were due before noon on 3 March 1913.

Many City Club members did not participate in mainstream social or economic activities and were politically left of center. Yet one wonders why concerned professionals, such as landscape architects O. C. Simonds, Nolen, Warren H. Manning, and Harold A. Caparn, or more of the architects of Wright's School, did not participate, although George C. Cone of Simonds's office submitted a design, as did Charles A. Tirrell, "head man" at Jensen's office.[107] Nonetheless, thirty-nine "sets of plans" were juried, all from Americans, except the Swedish husband-and-wife team of Albert and Ingrid Lilienberg, then on a long-term visit to the United States.

236 *The city scientific*

Another woman entrant was Marcia Mead, a principal of a New York City architectural firm with Anna P. Schenck. Twenty-six entries were exhibited at the club's premises.[108] Their designs (i.e. site plans) were predictable, with three notable exceptions: A. C. Tenny's, William Drummond's, and Wright's.

Wright's design

In the introduction to his explanatory notes, Wright accepted the "characteristic aggregation of business buildings, flats, apartments, and formal and informal dwellings for well-to-do and poor[,] natural now to every semi-urban section about Chicago." Consequently, he introduced "only minor modifications in harmony with the nature of this aggregation" (see Figure 8.17).[109] But it is closer to something new than the minor improvements he modestly proclaimed.

The site plan is interesting on two counts. First, he again used geometric precision but in a unique manner.[110] Second, his functional or land-use schema was organically combined with a spatial notion that was in turn integrated with a geometry tied to the existing street pattern. To his mind, the street grid had known historical associations with America's West and was a useful abstraction of communities properly ordered, "the prairie gridiron." A series of sketch diagrams will help describe the process to – and logic of – his design.

Accepting the street pattern on the site's periphery, Figure 8.18, drawing 1, he doubled those east–west. This created a series of internal squares each bound by a street that collectively formed an eight-by-eight block grid that fit his Quadruple Block Plan, or Quad Plan. He then restricted some streets and allowed others to extend from one boundary to its opposite. and they formed the geometric rationale of the plan.

In drawing 2, we see the effect of advancing his grid over an area of more than one quarter-section. The heavier lines indicate the mile square public transport grid as set out in the competition program. The pattern of through streets also established edges that assisted in locating civic functions, drawing 3, and allowed a spatial and functional rationale. This was apparent in Wright's "Key to Plan" where the disposition of functions, or land use, was indicated.

Recognition of a formal architectural solution to volumetric and spatial nodes is clarified in drawing 4. One set of controlling center lines was placed between the lines of the gridded rationale, *axial* in A. Another set defines edges, *spatial* in B. When combined, the axial and spatial geometry are united as in C.

The dominant spatial nodes were large, public, landscape areas juxtaposed to water basins that acted as foci for varied recreational activities. Intersections of the axial system became the figurative centers of semi-open and public functions, such as school, library, art gallery, and so on, and segregate men's and women's apartments. Near one axial intersection and close to parklands were kindergarten and domestic science facilities. Volumetric and spatial integration can be seen in drawing 5. As noted, they also integrated the social functions where, as historian Gwendolyn Wright observed, the "private by no means overshadowed or ostracized the public."[111]

Major tree plantations enhanced both formal design aspects and dominated the aerial perspective (see Figure 8.19). The linear or axial system of streets was tree lined and, from the periphery, connected open landscaped areas, abstracted in 4.5.

Just as public transport followed a one-mile grid, there is an implication that the quarter-section plans could be repeated about the suburbs. Wright implied this by removing one road of the adjacent northern street grid (point **m**, in 4.5) that matched his own plan while retaining or adding streets on the northern periphery. This mirrored match infers that, *if* the plan were repeated, then it would be flipped south to north while in the east–west direction it would be opposite hand. This pattern conforms to the essential requirement of collecting certain commercial, marketing, and cultural functions about transport lines; in other words, a strip development, the dark lines in 4.2 and 4.6, therefore, four quarter-sections would share that functional focus.

Wright's community planning 237

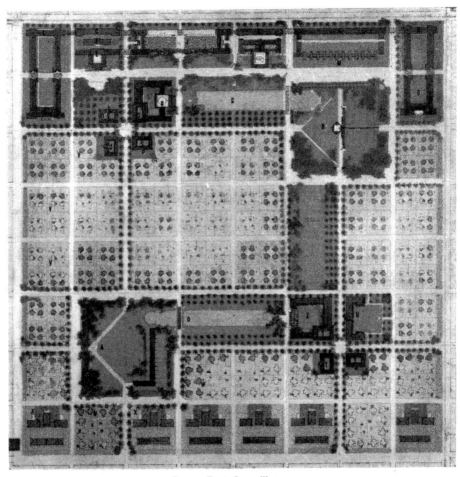

PLAN BY FRANK LLOYD WRIGHT

KEY TO PLAN

A. Park for children and adults. Zoölogical gardens.
B. Park for young people. Bandstand, refectory, etc. Athletic field.
C. Lagoon for aquatic sports.
D. Lagoon for skating and swimming.
E. Theater.
F. Heating, lighting, and garbage reduction plant. Fire department.
G. Stores, 3 and 4 room apartments over.
H. Gymnasium.
I. Natatorium.
J. Produce market.
K. Universal temple of worship, non-sectarian.
L. Apartment building.
M. Workmen's semi-detached dwellings.
N. Four and five room apartments.
O. Stores with arcade.
P. Post Office branch.
Q. Bank branch.
R. Branch library, art galleries, museum, and moving picture building.
S. Two and three room apartments for men.
T. Two and three room apartments for women.
U. Public school.
V. Seven and eight room houses, better class.
W. Two-flat buildings.
X. Two-family houses.
Y. Workmen's house groups.
Z. Domestic science group. Kindergarten.

STATISTICAL DATA

304 Seven and eight room houses.
120 Two-flat buildings, five and six rooms.
18 Four-flat buildings, four and five rooms.
6 Fourteen-family workmen's house groups.
6 Apartment buildings, accommodating 320 families in all.
4 Two and three room apartment buildings for women, accommodating 250 to 300.
Total, 1032 families and 1550 individuals (minimum).

Figure 8.17 "Non-competitive plan for development of quarter section of land competition," with "Key to Plan," as published in Yeomans, 1916.

How did his architecture fit geometry and functional disposition? The bird's-eye perspective reveals little beyond general form, character, and the odd faintly described detail. There were pitched roofs in most instances and an obvious horizontality, except for some bulky buildings along the commercial edge. The commercial, marketing, and cultural functions were along the

238 *The city scientific*

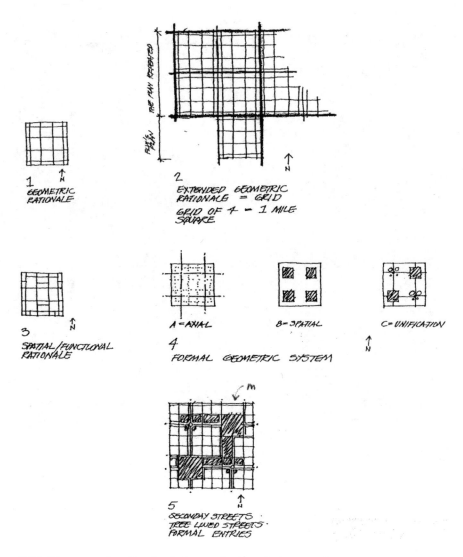

Figure 8.18 Diagrams related to the design method applied to Wright's quarter-section plan in Figure 8.17. Author's drawings.

northern trolley line. The strip was meant to be a continuous two-story building, penetrated at various points by pedestrian and vehicular traffic, the second story to pass over internal north–south streets. At the two northern corners, there was mixed land use with commercial below and apartments over. Elsewhere, the commercial strip contained single uses (outlined or otherwise defined as buildings) or spaces – garden market, central heating plant, a "moving picture building," apartments (for small families or working men and women), recreation, a religious building – all tucked under or behind what can be usefully termed a two-story *stoa*. At the other edges of the site, Wright was ambivalent. Except for a meeting of two streets and two rows of medium-density housing on the southern edge, perhaps as a buffer to internal

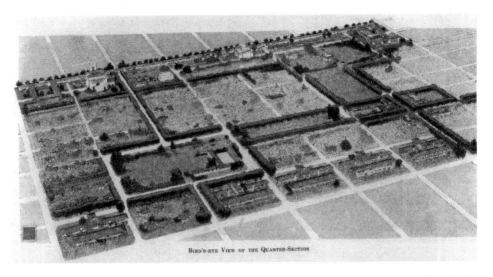

Figure 8.19 "Bird's-eye View of the Quarter-Section" of suburban land. From Yeomans, 1916.

single-family residences, there is no functional or architectural focus. (The small square in the bottom left corner is his logo.)

Of five drawings prepared for the club's publication, three were of the Quad Plan, the center piece. Drawings of 1910 were redone for the 1916 publication. His thesis insisted that it would provide private individuality and "picturesque variety." In any event, repeated many times at the middle of the site, it was close to schools and community recreation and occupied about 50 percent of the total area. For middle to upper income families, two house types were proposed. One was described as "seven and eight room houses, better class" and occupying much of the central land area. Another Quad Plan house type was described only as "two-flat buildings" and here Wright used scheme A as previously described. It is not clear how they would be altered to accommodate flats. The home of blue- and white-collar workers and lower incomers therefore were located on the site's periphery.

Over intervening decades, his quarter-section design has been dated from 1913–17. The Chicago Architectural Club's 1914 exhibition catalog contained a rather large contribution by Wright that included preliminary drawings for the Tokyo Imperial Hotel, the Coonley kindergarten, and others, as well as item 319:

Model Quarter Section Plan.
Plan.
General View
Detail of Typical Block.[112]

The Plan and General View drawings were those requested for the City Club's exhibition, while the Typical Block likely would have been plans A and B as prepared for the 1910 monograph. Also, his 1913 scheme was solicited, described as "non-competitive" and "*Hors concours*," exhibited but not juried.[113]

This is the likely scenario. From mid-January through mid-May 1913, Wright was in Japan attempting to secure the Tokyo Imperial Hotel commission and later developing preliminary design drawings that, as we've just learned, were exhibited one year later.[114] Yet to offer a design to a national affair sponsored by fellow Chicagoans, and to once again place his name before a fairly sophisticated audience, would have demanded his personal attention. Therefore, the designs and three new drawings were finalized early in January 1913 before setting out by train for Seattle and embarking on a steamer bound for Yokohama.[115]

When the City Club was organizing publication of the competition results in 1916, Wright and others were invited to expand on their designs. So he amplified the Quad Plan by redrawing the two theoretical site plans (with no stables) as published in 1910, adding a third with stables (see Figure 8.10).[116] These together with redrawn perspectives, all published in color, accompanied what was likely a freshly edited text. Therefore, he did *not* advance new designs for the 1916 publication. His text, however, is of some interest.

Wright's explanation in 1916 of his 1913 design provides valuable insight into his attitude to the city. He was then considered a revolutionary in the cause of an American architecture with a stature measurable nationally and internationally.[117] The invitation to participate indicated the value that his own and allied professions placed on his views. Reissued, easy accessibility to the essay should encourage intelligent comment.[118] However, the republication does not include the "Key to Plan" and "Statistical Data" or his "Explanation of Alternate Block Arrangement" or the perspective of a typical house, Figure 8.3 herein.

Wright explained how the 1912 program and de facto conditions influenced him (some of it outlined earlier), why he located buildings, sometimes justifying decisions and/or describing one or two aspects. For example, "the small park system are recreation features" and so planned that

> people are attracted to the less quiet portion of the park near the public buildings, the children and more quietly inclined adults to the small park in the opposite direction. . . .
> The division of the small park systems . . . draws the children going and coming from school, kindergarten, and playground in the direction opposite to the business quarter.

Along the north boundary are various "background" buildings that

> are continuously banked against the noisy city thoroughfare, and the upper stories are carried overhead across intervening streets to give further protection from dust and noise, and [provide] a picturesque way, . . . for the combination business and dwelling establishments that cling naturally to the main arteries of traffic.

Wright was and is often accused of being too idealistic or extravagantly impractical. Here, he was pragmatic, drawing from an empirical understanding of people's social, recreational, and commercial habits. But we don't know who he consulted. His essay ended as it began:

> Much has been written, said, and done recently in relation to civic planning all over the world. For the most part, what has happened. . . is what has happened to us in individual buildings: we are obsessed by the old world thing in the old world way with the result that, in this grim workshop, our finer possibilities are usually handed over to fashion and sham. Confusing art with manners and aristocracy. . . .[119]

Indeed, much of what happened was hegemonous. Wright's design was free of such a stigma.

+ + +

Immediate reaction to his explanation, Quad Plan, and quarter-section layout was mixed. Albert Kelsey, the Philadelphia architect keen on the League and "city scientific," was asked by the City Club to review designs "from an aesthetic point." Of Wright's, he said in part that

> [the design] without unsightly alleys, but holding somewhat to the established gridiron plan of Chicago . . . appeals to me mightily in spite of the inconvenient arrangement of its

arterial system. . . . [In] semi-suburban residential districts, as suggested by this design, . . . lots, in smaller and smaller groups, offer many advantages. . . .

[The] use of connecting walls, . . . and the general striving for harmony . . . would not only be individual and artistic but distinctly appropriate if the arterial system were some-what modified. The accompanying perspectives illustrate his intentions . . . while the descriptive text comes from a thoughtful mind. . . .[120]

Kelsey's opinion was free of bias.

Those opposed to Wright's School no doubt agreed with Chicago architect Irving K. Pond. The Pond brothers, Irving and Allen B., were among the young Progressive architects and active in all manner of reform activities. These included remodeling and enlarging Hull-House, where they volunteered, and winning a competition for the design of a new building for the City Club in 1906, which opened 1912.[121] Irving was also asked to review the competition plans. He noted that at least three people contributed plans inspired by the "self-styled American school," not mentioning Wright by name or followers Drummond and the Griffins. Irving Pond went on:

The sociological error underlying these designs inheres in the idea that it is possible to compass the great, varied, pulsing American spirit within . . . the extremely narrow bounds, of a purely local and individual expression. The fundamental psychological error . . . lies not so much in the use of the gridiron plan. . . [but] dwellers thereon repudiate this multiplication of irreconcilable monotony and call for the note of aspiration here and there, the dominant vertical line, the poetical and contrasting curve. It were ungracious, even were it moral, to force the free American spirit to dwell in a depressed and depressing cruciform environment.[122]

Of a similar mind was sociologist Carol Aronovici, who was also asked to comment. Another Philadelphian, he had been general secretary of the Suburban Planning Association to later become director of the Bureau of Social Research and lecture on housing and city planning at the University of Pennsylvania. His comments were wide ranging and drew from experience and study. In one instance, he noted

[that] the gridiron system was almost invariably abandoned [by competitors] . . . That the effect upon the people resulting from the monotony of the straight streets lined with houses without architectural character [such as Wright's] is a social problem worth consideration is easily realized by anyone familiar with American communities.[123]

The wicked gridiron street plan, still a bane to some planners.

These were the only useful contemporary comments about Wright's design, and they occurred in late 1916. By then, his consuming adventures in Japan were under way. The earliest of recent evaluations was Lewis Mumford's of 1953: Wright's "handling of open spaces and the public buildings . . . brilliant."[124]

But what of low-cost housing? For the 1913 exhibition or at anytime prior to 1920 did Wright provide designs of low-cost housing for low incomers? Only once, a row of "Workmens cottages" in 1909 for real estate developer Edward Waller Senior for a site either in Chicago or River Forest, and they were not mentioned in Wright's 1913 plan. The floor plans compare favorably with typical low-income housing in Europe (see Figure 8.20). Their three-dimensional character, however, is singular. A dominant horizontality is enhanced by a roof overhang to the top floor bedrooms and heavy jambs to rows of windows, all relieved by inset entries.

Other designs

The 1912–13 competition jury was composed of Jens Jensen, who looked after City Club affairs as well as analyzing landscape matters; John C. Kennedy, a Canadian "Housing Expert;" John W. Alvord, a consulting engineer (formerly with Chicago's water works); and architects George

242 *The city scientific*

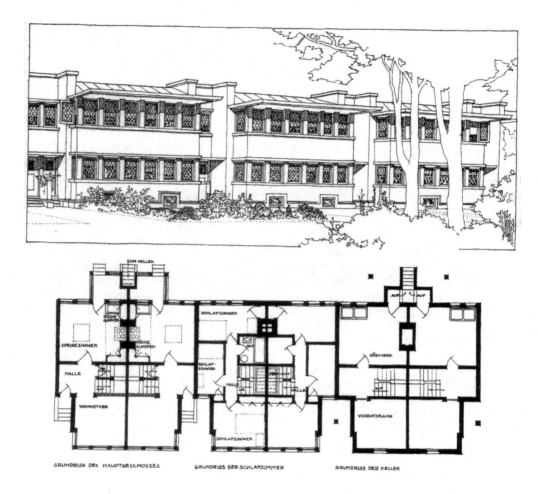

Figure 8.20 "Workmen's Row Houses for Larkin Company, Buffalo, New York," 1904, later titled "Workmen's Cottages" for an expensive project for an E. C. Waller River Forest real estate development of 1906; three up, two down with basement. From Wright, 1910.

W. Maher (one of the young Progressives), and A. W. Waltersdorf, who represented the AIA's Illinois Chapter.[125] Co-opted was Edward H. Bouton, director of Roland Park (1891–1909), a ritzy suburb near Johns Hopkins University in Baltimore,[126] and formerly director of the restricted Forest Hills on Long Island. In 1917, Bouton was a founding member of the American City Planning Institute (now American Planning Association), along with Hooker, Nichols, Arthur Comey, Thomas Adams (English expatriate), and other landscape architects and real estate developers.

The jury's six positive criteria for assessment were economy and practicality; provision for health and sanitation; beauty (including general composition, architecture, and originality); comfort and convenience of residents; provision for social activities, including education and recreation; and commerce.[127]

The jury rejected schemes with large parks or boulevards or public buildings that could not be "maintained by working people," as well as those too monumental; those with business districts distant from public transport; with noisy playgrounds near residences; with a constricted road system; and with "closed courts, or in a sort of cul-de-sac" that were believed to be "defective from the standpoint of ventilation." Although some of the criteria could have been only subjectively weighed, they nevertheless helped define a neighborhood.

Three prizes were awarded. First place of $300 went to Wilhelm Bernhard. He emigrated from Germany in 1912 and began as a draftsman with Wright that year and attended classes at the Chicago Architectural Club.[128] Bernhard's site plan was loosely based on British Garden Suburbs of the immediate past but incorporated torturous streets, awkward intersections, and strange building shapes. When published in 1916, it was accompanied by naively primitive perspective drawings of Germanic-style buildings reminiscent of Forest Hills's principle buildings.

Second place was taken by Boston landscape architect Arthur C. Comey. He studied under Olmsted Jr. at Harvard to later teach at that university and was a consultant of some note. He had placed fifth in the 1911 Canberra competition with a rather disorganized plan.[129] His 1913 site plan was of a similar genre and laxity to Bernhard's but more carefully tuned by Letchworth and Forest Hills in the use of a diagonal street for through traffic and a central Y intersection, the location of community facilities. The Lillienbergs placed third with a symmetrical, rather beaux-arts plan. The Lillienbergs were involved with several Garden City efforts in Sweden: Brooma, Brannkyrka, and some suburbs.[130] The entry of Walter and Marion Griffin and their recently hired structural engineer Edgar H. Lawrence was an attempt to reconcile the tradition of a central space city of Baroque radial roads with a grid of streets.[131]

The second design to consider was radical, not its symmetrical orthogonal plan but its design concept, Figure 8.21, and accompanying text. Both harbor elements of socialist communitarian theory. Perhaps A. C. Tenney, a Chicago homeopathic physician, was persuaded by Charlotte Gilman's ascetic communitarian proposals in the 1890s.[132] Tenney provided only apartment blocks that freed land for two large parks and recreational spaces. Multistoried buildings located on the periphery contain commerce at ground level with living units above. The checkerboard lines near the drawing's corners indicate small cooperative garden allotments and recreation facilities. At the site's center is located a school, church, civic center, and the like. Tenney's tenement buildings, with twenty-seven house units in each, were only one or two cells deep to enable "direct sunshine to every 'living' room, ample air space and circulation." Two diagrams described the desirable height of buildings for best results in relation to sun, shadow, and winds and to latitude and longitude. His housing description and analysis predates architect Walter Gropius's similar and widely publicized investigations by a full seventeen years.[133]

Two entries explored the possibility of extending their plans repetitively over a large geographical area. That of architect Louis H. Boynton, superficially something like the Griffinses', was a formal geometrical pattern of streets and spaces over a mile square and reminds one of two-dimensional mosaic square floor tiles, thereby limiting its value to fascination.[134] The other by William Drummond was prophetic.

The exhibition

When mounted in May 1913, the City Club's housing exhibition contained not only selected competition design. There was an attempt to make it attractive to – and emotionally and intellectually engage – various sections of Chicago society and those attending the housing conference who might seriously respond to other visual and commentary information. A historical section surveyed typical Chicago houses and street scenes since 1830. An examination of building department records determined typical houses constructed in 1912, and they were displayed in photographs accompanied by floor plans. Contrarily, contemporary "squalid homes," dilapidated and overcrowded tenements, and negative effects of no zoning controls were subjects of a photographic exhibit titled "In Darker Chicago" prepared by the Woman's Club and Woman's City Club.[135]

Beside the second city's squalor were placed some "remarkably attractive . . . housing carried out in the Garden suburbs" and other recent European housing schemes. Photographs, maps, and colored plans highlighted developments at Britain's Bournville, Port Sunlight, Letchworth, and Hampstead Heath, as examples, and at Amsterdam, Munich, Essen, and Düsseldorf. Interestingly, those and other European municipalities had received a "special invitation"

244 *The city scientific*

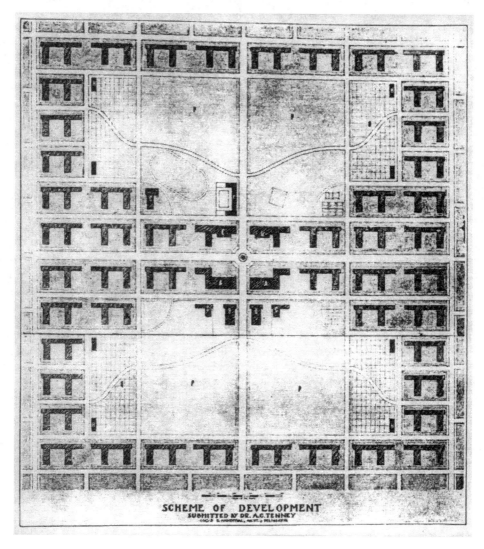

Figure 8.21 "Scheme of development" of a quarter-section designed by Dr A. C. Tenney in 1913, assisted by young Chicago architect Oscar B. Marienthal. From Yeomans, 1916.

to participate when members of the City Club and Chicago's School of Civics and Philanthropy traveled to Europe the previous summer.[136]

Moreover, the exhibition adeptly placed before the public not only the results of its neighborhood competition but also the latest efforts in suburb street layout, housing, landscape, and – by views and maps – the new idea of zoning as applied in Germany. German planning was becoming better known in America mainly through articles published in national magazines, such as those by Hooker, George B. Ford in *American City*, and Frederick C. Howe in *Scribner's Magazine*.[137] Howe also released his book *European Cities at Work* (New York, 1913) about physical structure and government.

It is fairly obvious that the *Tribune* was kept informed of the City Club's various enterprises. Originally scheduled for 17 May, the exhibition officially opened on 23 May. On Monday, 17

May, the *Tribune* published one of its rare boxed editorials, this time devoted to the work of urban reformers, noting particularly the venerable Woman's Club, the City Club, and Women's City Club. The editorial then condemned the "miasmic monster" of the stockyards and its "stink," the railroad and electric "traction" interests who block rationalization, the "baptism of soot" from trains, and the guilty "rich and powerful" who allowed a "city [that] wallows in smoke and slime." The attack was on vested interests, "individual selfishness," and community lethargy.

Not "I Will" but "We Will" was the "battle cry" for a "new Chicago." The editorial demanded "community spirit," the "idea of community welfare," the "neighborhood sense." It called for "municipal efficiency" and the adoption of the "new science of city planning and city management." English and central European planning efforts were an "inspiring story." The corrective spirit of the City Club's exhibition reinvigorated the reform debate in the wake of obvious excesses inherent in Burnham's plan.[138]

Henry Morrow Hyde, former editor of *Technical World Magazine* and member of Cliff Dwellers, was commissioned by the *Tribune* to write a series of daily articles. On the same day, 17 March, he described Chicago as a microcosm of America; of immigrants happily accepted as fodder (not Hyde's word) to rapid industrial and commercial growth powered by electricity and other technologies, coal, and, importantly, greed. Forgotten in the rush were the fodder, the one million residents, and especially those in contact with "germ diseases," rats, and other "filthy human warren." Sociology had shown the "certainty" that slums bred moral degradation. Hyde, no doubt with the approval of the newspaper's owner and director, Robert McCormick, did not stop there.

Hyde argued that attitudes to the urban environment must change. The machine-and-commerce-made city, he suggested, must be seen as an "organic entity," all parts and aspects ecologically (not Hyde's word) and reactively bound: cause and effect. During March 1913 only, Hyde's page-one articles covered issues such as water, fire, waste water, housing (for one article a photograph from the City Club exhibition was published showing separate house structures barely three feet apart and in tandem on a twenty-five by seventy-five-foot city lot),[139] the stockyards, the slow court system disadvantaging the poor, and slum clearances in Europe, a program not begun in the United States until the late 1930s.

A link to the City Club was reinforced by Hyde's essay on 19 March when he made a case for Chicago being robbed as the source of the Garden City concept. It was said that Unwin, likely in 1911, had called Olmsted and Vaux's 1869 plan for Riverside south of Chicago the first Garden City, a comment no doubt offered after consultation with his friend, Howard. Hyde mentioned that the financial panic of 1873 interfered with Riverside's full implementation. English Garden Suburbs and Cities were then discussed and incorrectly likened to Pullman and Gary, Indiana.[140]

Also, for their 1913 meeting, the National Conference on City Planning called for individuals to submit community and housing plans for a hypothetical site. It was not a competition but a request for ideas. The program parroted the Chicago City Club's of 1912, and only nine plans were received, all looking much like Forest Hills or Burnham's proposed civic center for Chicago.

On the weight of evidence, the housing exhibition and quarter-section designs were catalytic. Many other reformist non-government groups participated, the *Tribune* undertook to effectively direct its persuasive and supportive influence. As well, there was positive reaction nationally, some of it by the fledgling profession, and internationally.

Drummond's neighborhood unit

The most substantive and prophetic entry in the City Club's competition was designed by architect William Eugene Drummond, who coined and defined the term "neighborhood unit." He then explored how his ideal units could coexist in a city's physical and social fabric by identifying their relationship to one another, to transport, local activities and commerce, and to parklands, recreational centers, industry, a city's commercial core, and housing. Born in 1876 in Newark, New Jersey, he studied architecture for one year at the University of Illinois, worked briefly for Louis Sullivan and others, and then principally for Wright 1899–1909, where he soon became a central figure, and part time with others. Thereafter, he set up an independent office and, in 1912, formed a partnership with Louis Guenzel.

Drummond's architecture was of the Wright School until around 1912, when his designs took on new characteristics, some borrowed without mimicry from Sullivan and Dwight Perkins, most his own invention. This is noticeable in projects of 1915 for isolated tall buildings related to his scheme for resolving Chicago's railroad termini problem. Three office towers, bold and inventive in form and masculine in character, were to rise above a procession of low buildings along the Chicago River and at a point where all railheads would meet. Drummond's entry in the Chicago *Tribune* tower competition of 1922 was even more robust, not similar to his general work that, by around 1918, had reverted to interesting simplifications of historical styles.[141]

Alfred Beaver Yeomans, a landscape architect and competitor, edited a 1916 book about the City Club's 1912–13 competition. In the preface, he described the volume as consisting "mainly" of plans submitted in competition. Elsewhere, he advised that Drummond's scheme was developed "from a sketch submitted in competition" and further, that competitors had an opportunity to supplement their plan and "bird's-eye view" with "additional drawings or photographs for publication."[142] As a result, a few recent suburban street layouts were included: Bernhard's Shawnee Garden City at Lima, Ohio, and Comey's Billerica, Massachusetts, but not the final plan.[143]

In his competition submission, Drummond proposed a "Neighborhood Unit" (his term) that could be repeated throughout the city (see Figure 8.22). He envisaged "the whole city" ordered by areas "approximately" the size of the quarter-section, each to be "regarded as a unit in the social and political structure of the city." Deriving something from Cooley, a unit was "intended to comprise an area which will permanently exist . . . as a neighborhood or primary social circle [and to have] the usual elementary [school] equipment" together with "intellectual, recreational, and civic requirements" centrally located in a featured "institute" building. Figure 8.23 is an aerial view of two adjoining "units" sharing local "business" centers, left and right, with slightly differing community centers top and bottom. "In a series of [neighborhood] units," Drummond said, there would be "an alternate disposition of centers of activity which would remove as far as possible the operation of one function from that of the other."[144] Using a portion of one area of South Chicago as the example, in plan he explained how neighborhood units might space themselves about a city (located as dark squares or thick crosses in the overall plan, Figure 8.22) while integrating rail lines, small parks, and streets, all imprecisely bound by parklands (the dark gray areas top and bottom). Neighborhoods would be connected by commuter rail to a zoned "Manufacturing Belt." Moreover, he proposed low-rise apartment buildings that were to embrace central recreational areas, an idea taken ten years later to overpraised Radburn, New Jersey, and Baldwin Hills Village, Los Angeles, in 1940–41. But Drummond's theoretical concept of a unit was unique, potent, and provocative. His overall plan also explained its flexibility in form and space.

But the club was not satisfied with just the 1912–13 results. Hooker and his colleagues believed their next competition was a logical component of that in 1912. In 1914, they announced a project "to secure the best architectural expression of a neighborhood center"[145] by drawing on ideas put by the Community Center Movement begun 1911[146] and more practically by the Saint Louis Civic League. Potential competitors were advised that entries were due before 9 November 1914; that there was no specific site; and that quasi-centers "going on" in such a "fragmentary way" indicated a need for "more complete and perfect patterns" that would induce efficiency and create neighborhood "spirit," "attractiveness," and "action."[147]

Jurors were Mary McDowell of the Chicago Woman's City Club; businessman George H. Mead; Wright School follower Robert Spencer and traditionalist Howard van Doren Shaw, both architects in Chicago; and the peripatetic lawyer and planning theorist Charles

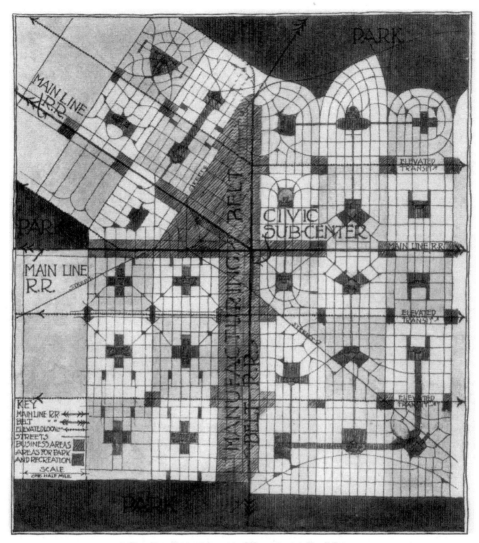

Figure 8.22 "A City Area Developed on the 'Neighborhood Unit' Plan", area south of Chicago of a scheme for adjoining "Neighborhood Units" as designed by architect William E. Drummond in 1915. From Yeomans, 1916.

Mulford Robinson. An exhibition of neighborhood center submissions was held 2 March to 15 April 1915 at City Club premises. First honors went to New York City architects Anna P. Schenck and Marcia Mead, also entrants in the 1912 competition (and close to those involved with Forest Hills), for a resolution of a very odd triangular hillside site in Bronx, New York. Second went to Drummond and Guenzel, and third to architect Joseph Hudnut (then at Alabama Polytechnic Institute) and Carl Berg, Chicago civil engineer and member of the City Club. From only twenty submissions, ten were selected for a second stage. Interestingly, Jens

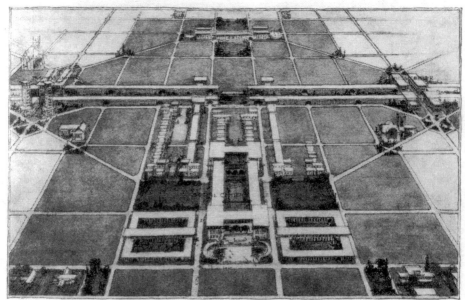

BIRD'S-EYE VIEW OF AN ALTERNATIVE SCHEME FOR "UNIT" DEVELOPMENT

Figure 8.23 "Bird's-eye View of an Alternative Scheme for [Neighborhood] 'Unit' Development," by William E. Drummond; grey area for typical suburban houses. From Drummond, 1915.

Jensen, Bernhard, and Dwight Perkins presented non-competitive designs,[148] while Wright and the Griffins did not participate.

One design may or may not have been entered and was not mentioned at the time. A few months before the competition was announced in 1914, architect Rudolph Schindler had arrived in Chicago from his native Austria in the hope of working for Sullivan or Wright. Schindler's design was rigidly axial in plan and similar in symmetry, massing, and general character to his design thesis of 1913 executed for studio masters under Otto Wagner at the Vienna Academy of Fine Arts. The 1914 design was conceptually of the beaux arts, had elevated walkways over streets and rail lines, and ill-defined but strictly modern buildings reminiscent – perhaps radically superior to – the Viennese *secionists*. There is no community center as such.[149]

Drummond presented several elements from his 1912 and 1914 entries in an article published in February 1915, a month before public announcement of the winners. He illustrated a neighborhood community center, a "Little Capitol," by aerial perspective drawings; two were again published in 1916. He described the neighborhood unit as a scheme "designed to bring about a reconstruction of our social and political urban life." It was, he believed, a solution that promoted the social value of good design and, potentially, both ideal and curative:

> [It] aims at a pronounced "individualization" of neighborhood districts in cities. A whole city ... would be composed of units." Each having a neighborhood center or "little capitol."
>
> [In] neighborhoods, certain streets would be built up with co-related groups of apartment buildings, semi-detached and single dwellings. This arrangement being a "nucleus" or first stage. The remaining areas would be devoted to permanent sites for the more expensive individual dwellings.

The last condition suggests something akin to Wright's housing zones. Drummond was not concerned with how best to exercise eminent domain as it might avoid pitfalls, as he might have seen it, of socialistic centralism. He then advised readers on the essentials set out by the Community Center Movement, the St Louis document, and the City Club's competition program, saying in part,

> the "little capitol" [community center] would have a large public meeting house, school rooms, a library and halls for exhibition and recreation, as well as gymnasia and contiguous park and play space. . . .[150]

Understandably, it was the only community center published in the 1916 book.

From the evidence, we can conclude that Drummond's quarter-section drawings as published in the City Club's report of 1916 were enhancements of entries into the club's 1912 and 1914 competitions and his report therein an elaboration related to those entries. Although the club did not publish the 1914 results, implying they were a disappointment, it did present both of Drummond's designs.

Evolution

Randolph Bourne, the black-caped Greenwich Village habituate and urban affairs critic for *New Republic*, was an advocate of Progressive education as put by John Dewey, of social renewal, and an outspoken pacifist. On these matters he was a highly regarded essayist of the day. His contributions pre-World War I have been outlined as follows:

> Bourne gave voice to other young intellectuals who saw in progressive education, cosmopolitanism, and artistic modernism the means to a radically democratic society . . . [He] insisted on the interdependence of culture and politics and sought in both the enrichment of "the good life of personality lived in the environment of the Beloved Community."

His hopes for the community were "dashed when liberals and other progressives endorsed President Wilson's war effort."[151]

Bourne visited the 1915 exhibition of the 1914 community center competition. His observations likely echoed those of others, pro-reform or pro-laizze faire. At one point, he said,

> The scores of radiant sketches seemed eloquent of a professional belief that for the building-up of the modern American city nothing too fine could be conceived.
>   About these confident designs there was something almost pathetic as one came into them fresh from the pervading architectural crassness. These publicists and town planners, social workers and architects, seemed scarcely out of the magical stage.

Clearly, the City Club's two competitions were not about solving low-cost, low-income housing. They were for middle to high incomers and investors. So Bourne referred to contemporary European planning successes, in particular to the government-sponsored, multiple-unit housing in Holland and Germany he had visited earlier in the year, contrasting them to America's obsession with the private clients' "individual building." After reminding readers that America was yet growing with cities in "constant flux," Bourne continued:

> To preach town-planning in these days of threatened municipal bankruptcy may seem like Utopianism. To emphasize this order and beauty in the face of destitution and unemployment may seem like a case of hyperaesthesia. . . . From the chaos and ugliness of American cities flows too palpably our economic and human waste. . . . Perhaps the road out of bankruptcy for the American city is exactly this Utopia.[152]

The goal of reformers and Progressives was not utopia but the achievement of humane and, as Bourne implied, psychologically safe urban environments. Further, Sophonisba Breckinridge, a director of the Chicago Woman's City Club, together with Edith Abbott, both at the University of Chicago and active at Hull-House, completed an investigation of Chicago's housing. Both women "advocated solving the housing crises not through private enterprise, but through citizen action and reform of the attitudes and, most important, powers of the municipal government." Their work also encouraged the men's and women's City Clubs to offer the 1912 competition. Historians Gwendolyn Wright and Maureen Flanagan reported that Breckinridge, in Flanagan's words,

> acknowledged the problems, shortcomings and corruptions of municipal government, but her advocacy of government-led housing reform reflected the profound belief in the efficacy of democratic government and policy making that characterized much of women's response to environmental issues.[153]

Nonetheless, with such auspicious beginnings, a growing abundance of empirical information, and humanitarian impulses and clarion calls, one might anticipate further study of the neighborhood unit concept. It is true that physical plans for suburban and subdivision developments occurred with increasing regularity from 1909 onward. With new real estate laws and better technology, most were still myopically focused on houses for middle to high incomers. All responded to what was begged as the harsh reality of commerce and economics rather than to solving low-income housing and related humane improvements. Planners supporting Addams, Ford and Marsh, Kelley, Lloyd, Abbot, and Hooker were left deeply worried.

The immediate consequences of the City Club's efforts from 1912–16 on future community planning is less problematical than anticipated, their work known. They had promoted Drummond's formalized neighborhood unit idea, and the competitions' results were widely publicize from 1913–22. And there was an increase in connections with English and German planners from 1905–25. All this has been adequately detailed elsewhere, including the fact that Unwin in 1920 and Clarence Perry in 1929 ingeniously appropriated the idea and detail of neighborhood units without giving credit to Drummond.[154]

One of the first practical responses was contained in a report on the "reconstruction" of New York City's lower east side by landscape architect and planner Harland Bartholomew in 1932. Determined mainly by principle and secondary thoroughfares, Bartholomew set out thirty-eight "more-or-less self-contained" neighborhood units that varied in size from 4.4 (1.78 hectares) to 51.6 acres (20.89 hectares). In 1947 and with pioneer city planner Ladislas Segoe's advice, the city of Detroit set out 150 neighborhood units bound by ribbons of industry, commerce, and service areas as Drummond proposed and without giving credit to him.[155]

+ + +

Some might argue that Wright's 1913–15 plan was the better of the lot. Certainly, its aesthetic components were superior – that is, the logic of the plan, its rationale, and the landscape and building architecture as presented. Except that it may have influenced Drummond when refining his unit scheme, nothing came of it. There is no evidence post-1916 that Wright's quarter-section design influenced anyone. Drummond's conceptual vision proved the more valuable theoretically and practically. In 1963, planning historian Gilbert Herbert enthusiastically described the neighborhood unit as "the most important of all modern town planning theories."[156] Yet time has proven that, with functional, economic, and demographic changes, neighborhoods ad-hoc or as contrived units inevitably alter, often dramatically, and even disappear.

With an awareness of the enormous amount, variety, and quality of transformation activity, with the exception of a forgotten Bitter Root town in 1909 and a 1913 quarter-section, philosophically and practically, Wright's plans for housing were commercially driven and devoid of a moral imperative; his attempts to support city reform appear feeble. Regardless, in design practice, his application of the square as a methodological structure and aesthetic determinant was consistently applied for most of his career (see Figure 8.24).

Wright's community planning 251

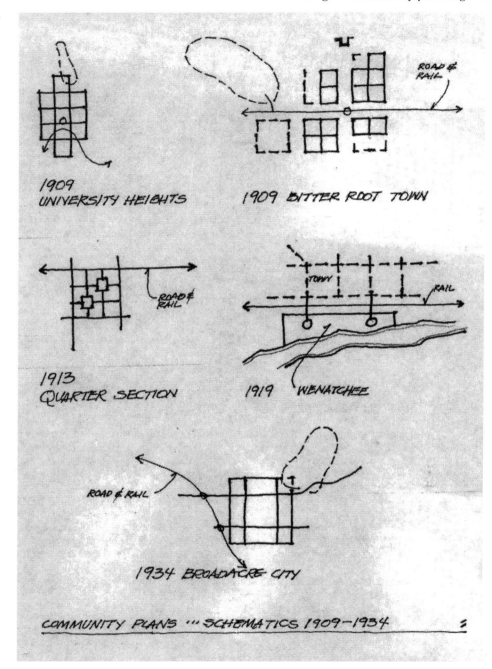

Figure 8.24 Plan schematics of Wright's community designs from 1909–34; author's drawing.

Notes

1 Those hundreds of texts include the reliable and comprehensive city planning and architectural study of this period in America, Ciucci (1979).
2 Those by this author are Johnson (2013a, 2004, 1990, 1988a).

3 Archer (1983), pp.140–141.
4 Archer (1983) whose research introduced the Ranlett and Barett scheme.
5 Wells practiced in New York City from 1839–60 and is credited with designing some of the earliest Gothic Revival houses in New England. He was one of thirteen architects who, in 1857, formed a society to "promote the scientific and practical perfection of its members" and "elevate the standing of the profession": it became the AIA; see Wikipedia.
6 William H. Ranlett, *The Architect*, Vol. 1, (New York: Dewitt & Davenport, 1847), [vol. 2] titled *Cottage & Villa* (ibid., 1849), reprint 1854; reprint Vol. 1 & 2, (New York: Da Capo Press, 1976), reprint as *Early Victorian House Designs* (New York, Dover, 2006). Ranlett produced a second pattern book *The City Architect A Series of Original Designs for Dwelling, Stores, and Public Buildings* (New York: DeWitt & Davenport, 1856), see "New and Important Work," *New York Tribune* (18 January 1856), p.1c, indicating a series of pamphlets.
7 Archer (1983), p.150, not in Ranlett, Vol. 2, see note 7; Hayden (2003), pp.47–50, see also idem., *Architecture and Suburban: From English Villa to American Dream House 1690–2000* (Minneapolis: University of Minnesota Press, 2005). Following the gold rush, Ranlett moved to San Francisco in 1849. Likely in 1857 he and his family resumed residence in New York City, cf. <thehermitage.org/history/history-arch> and follow prompts to "1847–48 Gothic Revival Remodeling"; accessed August 2014.
8 Siry (1996), pp.70–73; also Eaton (1969), pp.77–79; Wright (1932), pp.153, 151. There is no correspondence to/from C. E. Roberts in the Wright Archives, perhaps because they were neighbors. With the information presented in this essay and these notes it is possible to correctly identify and date relevant plates in relevant compilations, particularly Pfeiffer.
9 Pfeiffer (87–01), where the five-house project should be dated 1896, not 1897. Plates 33–35 must be one of the five. It is the more mature and surely not of 1892 as captioned. The other four houses are plates 198–207 with the same floor plan as plate 33, while plates 188–197 are to another plan. Plates 225–227 (titled "Quadruple Block Plan" for Roberts, 1897) show only a single house projected for a corner site, not the Quad Plan. The last paragraph does refer to the Quad Plan, but it is parenthetical and unrelated to plates.
10 Levine (2009), pp.59, 62–64.
11 Spencer (1900), pp.66, 72. For the Roberts schemes, see Pfeiffer (02–06), plates 113–115 (where the houses are detailed with a brick exterior and are therefore 1903 revisions), and plate 116; Pfeiffer (87–01), plates 324, 327–328, the last two plates were redrawn as plate XIIIa for Wright (1910); Pfeiffer (2011), pp.81, 85, 118–121, 204–206.

Plate 325 in Pfeiffer (87–01) is not a project for Roberts but a sketch preliminary plan of the Ullman house project (1904). One thumbnail perspective sketch on the same sheet may be for Ullman, the other is not. Plate 325 was first published in Wright (1959) and there correctly identified.

Ullman can be usefully compared to Beachy house "Scheme II" of 1906, Pfeiffer (89–16), plate 77.
12 Perhaps distracted by its complexity, the Quad Plan is not mentioned in Hitchcock (1942); Farr (1961); Einbender (1986); Twombly (1979); Brooks (1979); Gill (1987); while Manson (1958), p.207, is brief.

Wright (1994), pp.90–91, 105–106, briefly discusses it in a social context, commenting that it "regularized expression while preserving the identity of the individual" (p.105), and included two color reproductions of the 1913 redrawings of the 1901 site plans (plates 394–395) and a perspective of the 1901 houses (plate 41).

Smith (1979), pp.100–102, is short, illusive, and too subjective; Sergeant (1976b), pp.72–75, is a nice outline if slight; it is briefly mentioned in McCarter (1991b), pp.285–286; Levine (1996), pp.30, 33, mentions it in passing and out of context. Various authors in Riley (1994) mention it briefly, pp.64, 90–91, 98, 105–106 and plates 394–395, with incorrect dates. Specific projects were seldom discussed in Wright (1932), so it is not expected and does not appear.
13 Levine (2009), p.72n4, the Ridgeland drawing was brought to public attention by Levine's article; Pfeiffer (2011), p.85.
14 Manson (1958), p.207.
15 Wright (February 1901), p.17. Pfeiffer (87–01) plate 328 is a preliminary aerial perspective sketch with the house design as yet finalized. See also Wright (1910), plates XIII and XIIIb. Plate 329 of Pfeiffer (87–01) is a sketch preliminary elevation while plate 330 is a sketch preliminary study of a single-story house for an unknown client, not for the *LHJ* article. Plate 112 of Pfeiffer (02–06) is of the *LHJ* drawing (not Roberts 1902, as captioned) and some of the text

penned by Wright on the sheet is about the Quad Plan as published by Wright in 1900. Plate 112 was first published in Wright (1959), p.196.

16 A simple site plan with an outline of three of the houses was the basis of the perspective drawing, the construction lines clearly superimposed. It is not a preliminary drawing; Levine (2009), p.66; Aguar and Aguar (2002), p.51. "0309.01" at the bottom of the sheet are archive numbers, not Wright's comment.
17 *Ladies Home Journal* (LHJ) made an attempt to locate houses built to plans offered around 1903, especially Wright's, but without success, "The Ladies' Home Journal House," *the LHJ*, 99(May 1982), p.134. and letter, Lietta Dwork (at LHJ) to this author, 21 October 1985.
18 "New Idea for Suburbs," *Chicago Evening Post* (12 July 1901), p.6(2). The description clearly defined the Quad Plan. Twombly (1979), pp.53–54, believes the Quad Plan was meant to be a "show case" of Wright's Arts and Crafts lecture of 1901, but there is no evidence that he or anyone else believed this. Further, Twombly does not explain the specific relationship among the lecture, Arts and Crafts ideology, and the Quad Plan.
19 "New Idea for Suburbs," *Reporter* (Oak Park) (18 July 1901), p.4(3).
20 Wright to S. T. Kendall, 18 September 1901, Wright Archives.
21 Roberts was unsuccessfully queried about proceeding, Charles White to W.R.B. Willcox, 21 May 1904, White letters, p.107, and Willcox papers. Father-in-law Roberts "is thinking of going ahead with the Wright scheme of twenty houses on his block" in Ridgeland.

Henry Webster Tomlinson and Wright were partners in 1901, the formation announced in *Brickbuilder* (January 1901), p.20. The letter to Kendall (preceding note) was on Wright & Tomlinson letterhead. See also Hitchcock (1942), p.111n., and Manson (1953), pp.137, 216. Their firm should be credited as architects of the 1901 Quad Plan, Wright the designer. The partnership dissolved in March 1902.
22 Manson (1958), p.207, based in part on an interview with Wright.
23 Smith (1979), p.101.
24 A typical small wood-frame single-story house of five or six reasonably sized rooms would have been $1,200 on average (Wright, 1980, p.318n56), or two stories or about $3,000 (Shoppell, 1893). Wright (1910), prefatory notes to references. The book was dedicated to Roberts and clients Francis W. Little and Darwin Martin. The three men had apparently assisted financially in production, one assumes of the Berlin and Chicago editions.
25 Chicago (1902), n.p.
26 Wright (July 1901), p.15, also published in Chicago Architectural Club, *Annual*, 1902, n.p. Pfeiffer (87–01), plates 279–281, the house was no doubt designed in early 1901, not 1900.
27 On Bok and the Quad house see, for example, Wright (1980), pp.136–137, 139–140; Wright (1983), pp.164–165. For a photograph of a house based on Wright's fireproof plans, see E. C. Gutzwiller's design in *A House of Brick of Moderate Cost* (Philadelphia: Brick Association of America, 1910), p.38; Wright (1983), p.165.
28 Wright (1907), p.24.
29 Riley (1994), plate 401.
30 Also in Pfeiffer (07–10), plates 220–231.
31 Floor plans and two elevations, Wright Archives, file 0918, sighted during research visit in July 1990.
32 Curiously, the middle house perspective had a floor plan similar to stables for Darwin Martin of 1903–05. Plans in Woolley Collection are slightly different to those in Wright Archives.
33 Wright (1910), plate XIIIa.
34 Pfeiffer (02–06), plates 113–119.
35 Wright (1910), plate descriptions, n.p.
36 Plates XIV and XIVa in Wright (1910). The initials "M L M" (Marion Lucy Mahony) have been added to one perspective; they were not present when published with a slightly different drawing in 1907.
37 Wright (1910), plate descriptions, n.p. In 1914, Wright prepared plans for "three houses for Honrè-Jaxon" for an unknown site that also had continuous walls to their street fronts and simple floor plans (based on a square, of course), but they do not fit the alternate scheme, Pfeiffer (14–23), plate 14.
38 Wright (1916), pp.96–102. This project was not published in Pfeiffer (07–13) or Pfeiffer (14–23) but listed elsewhere as 1915. It was initially prepared for the 1913 exhibition.

Pfeiffer (02–06) plates 117, 119, are in color and do *not* relate to Roberts, although floor plans are similar. Plate 118 does *not* relate to the Quad Plan or Roberts but is a study showing old-style house plans (Sullivan's, Wright's, and others) and the Walser house plan in repetition along a regular street. Therefore, it is of a date no earlier than 1903. The reason for the drawing exercise is unknown.

See also *Construction News* (Chicago), 22 March 1913, p.1; *Chicago Architectural Club* (Chicago: Art Institute, 1914), n.p., but see Wright entries; Yeomans (1916) where Wright's drawings are in color; McLean (1917), pp.6–8, and plates; H. DeFries, ed., *FLW* (Berlin: Cahiers, 1926).

39 Wright (1916), p.101; FLW, "Explanation of Alternative Block Arrangements," *WArchitect*, 25(January 1917), n.p., plates. These paragraphs by Wright were not published in Pfeiffer (1992), pp.139–143. Plans A and B were published as "habitations a bon marchè?" in *Architecture Vivante* (Paris), 28(1930), part I, p.45.
40 Cf. Wright (1916); Pfeiffer (1992).
41 Cf. Johnson (2004); Aguar and Aguar (2002); Edward Duke Richey, "Montana Eden/Land Use and Change in the Bitterroot Valley, Pre-History to 1930," Thesis (Missoula: University of Montana, 1999); Randall LeCocq, *FLW in Montana; Darby, Stevensville, and Whitefish* (Helena: Drumlummon Institute, 2013), chapter 5.
42 Nichols' sister married Moody; see <stanton-llc.com/genelogy/whitakercampbellfamily/pafg12>; Storrer (1993), p.118, believes he was the father of the architectural historian Frederick Doveton Nichols, but Nichols's only son was a junior; "Who's Who—On the Ballot," *Chicago Alumni Magazine*, Vol. 2 (University of Chicago, March 1908), pp.100–101. For sources of historical background and archival sources see Johnson (2004), p.24n3; Johnson (1987b), notes throughout. There was/is a University Heights district in Madison, Wisconsin, and placenamed in other cities or as towns.

BRIVCo was first called the Bitter Root Irrigation Company. Their Como Orchard Land Co. was incorporated in December 1907 (*Poor's Manual of Industrials, . . .*, New York: Poor's Railroad Manual Co., 1913, p.552). This essay is based on Ludwig (1982); Johnson (1987a), pp.12–15; Johnson (1990), chapter 9; Johnson (2012). BRVICo records held by the BRV Archives begin in 1913. The Wright Archive does not contain relevant correspondence, and most of its other Montana material is duplicates of those in the BRV Archives and copied after 1960.

Beginning with Wright (1910), University Heights, which is the name of the project and the settlement's placename, has been incorrectly called something like "Lake Como Orchards," the name of one large nearby orchard. See D. J. Hawkins, *Map of the Famous Bitter Root Valley* (Hamilton: The Author, 1909), where various orchards are located; and the US Department of the Interior, Bureau of Reclamation, *Bitter Root Project*, map, 1908, both BRV Archives.
43 John B. Wright, *Montana Ghost Dance: Essays on Land and Life* (Austin: University of Texas Press, 2013), p.137.
44 "University Heights," *RavalliR* (24 April 1908), p.1.
45 Nichols (1910), p.26.
46 "A summer retreat . . .," WestN, 22 April 1908, p.1. See also "University Settlement," WestN, 8 May 1908, p.1, a reprint of an article that appeared in the "Chicago Tribune April 26," where, as in other publications at the time, it also stated that "the name of the settlement is University Heights."
47 For example, advertisement "*$5,000 a Year from Ten Acres*" *Country Life in America*, 23(April 1913), p.13.
48 "A Summer Retreat," *WestN* (22 April 1908), p.1. There was/is a district called University Heights near the University of Wisconsin campus in Madison and near to Wright's childhood house, Menocal (1981), p.82.

Chicago Alderman Frank I. Bennett was an investor and became president of BRVICo. Other investors included Philadelphia music critic Phillip Goepp, playwright and author Robert Morss Lovett (he reminisced about the BRVICo and friend Nichols in *The Autobiography of Robert Morss Lovett: All Our Years* [New York: Viking Press, 1948], pp.131–132); Walter Camp ("Famous Athlete of Yale University"), Alexander Du Pont of Dupont Powder Company, and one A. F. Hughes of Hudderford, England. See "Why Things Are Different in the Bitter Root Valley," *Greater Bitter Root*, 1(August 1910), pp.7–8, apparently originally published in the July issue of *National Irrigation*.

On investors from Illinois, Ohio, Minnesota, and Wisconsin, see "A Summer Retreat," WestN (22 April 1908), p.1; *RavalliR* (24 April), p.22, and (27 November 1909), each p.1; George M. Treat, "The Bitter Root Valley," *Overland Monthly* (San Francisco), 53(January 1909), p.66.
49 "University Heights," *RavalliR*, 24 April 1908, p.1.

50 Ibid.
51 "Real Arcadia Will Grace Valley" *Daily Missoulian* (17 February 1909), pp.1g, 4–5.
52 "Returned from Chicago," *RavalliR* (19 February 1909), p.1.
53 Cabin drawings are dated April 1909, construction of the clubhouse began 5 May 1909 ("University Heights," *RavalliR* [May 1909], p.1), although some drawings are dated 13 May. The Wright Archives and Ludwig (1982) are the source for cabins and their types. See also the Harriet R. Wood (from Essex, CT) photo album of 1911 in the Wright Archive.
54 "Personal and Otherwise," *WesternN* (10 March 1909), n.p, [p.5?].
55 Wright (1910), plates XLVI–XLVIIa and plate descriptions. However, the first publication of Heights that Wright allowed after 1910–11 was the site plan and aerial perspective in *Architecture Vivante* (Paris), part 2(1930), p.7.
56 For a sheet of floor plans with construction details for two small cabins, see Pfeiffer (2011), p.340; location of plan types is on an adjacent site plan. Ludwig (1982), p.12, reports (and archive drawings confirm) there were six of type 1, nine type 1-double, three of type 2, two of type 2-variation, two of type 3, two of type 3-A, one of type 3-B, three of type 3-C and four of type 3-D. See also Storrer (1993), pp.145–147, which is based on Ludwig (1982) and Johnson (1987b, 1990). For some comments about the Heights, see Wright (1994), p.91; Smith (1979), pp.102–103; Manson (1958), p.207; Hitchcock (1942), p.55; Robert C. Twombly, "Undoing the City: FLW's Planned Communities," *American Quarterly*, 24(October 1972), p.543, slightly modified in Twombly (1979), pp.224–225, where Bitter Root town is not mentioned. Quite simply, Wright's site plan and building types resulted from the client's brief. Levine (1996) ignored Wright's Montana work. See also "A University Man: Two Remarkable Bitter Root Valley Orchards," *WestN* (May 1910 supplement), p.18, where the "clubhouse" ground-level perspective drawing is pictured.
57 None of the Montana commissions are listed in the 22 September 1909 contract between architect Herman von Holst and Wright (when he left for an extended stay in Europe), see contract description in Alofsin (1993), pp.216, 311–312; Meehan (1983), pp.147–148. It can be safely assumed that Wright was no longer employed by that September.

The cabin just in front and to the right of the clubhouse is a private home and, according to witnesses in the 1920s, the largest and most sturdily built of those constructed (from various interviews during 1980s). See the valuable Grant Hildebrand and Thomas Bosworth, "The Last Cottage of Wright's Como Orchards Complex," *JSAH*, 41(December 1982), pp.325–377, with measured drawings of the two cottages remaining; and photograph, J. A. Phillips, "Beekeeping in the Bitter Root Valley," *Greater Bitter Root* (Hamilton), 1(2, 1911), p.15.
58 Pfeiffer (07–13), plate 165, shows three variations of cabin type 3; plates 166, 169, are the Heights clubhouse, not the inn for Bitter Root town (also incorrectly captioned in Pfeiffer [87–59], plate 49); and the text (p.92) should be read in conjunction with Johnson (1987b).
59 "Improving Ranch," *RavalliR* (1 June 1923), p.3; four good photographs pre-1923 in *Your Opportunity in Montana* (Darby: McIntosh-Morello Orchards, 1924), pp.36ff. On events post-1925, see [B. K. Smith], "Bitter Root Gallery," *Sunday Missoulan* (24 September 1972), p.35.
60 The clubhouse was demolished ca. 1945. Between 1919 and 1970, thirteen cabins were demolished, one burned to the ground. In 1985, two Heights cabins remained. A plan drawing of what was built and extant in the 1980s is in Johnson (1987b), p.18.
61 Eaton (1972), p.167; Manson (1958), p.207.
62 Wright (1932), p.251; Hitchcock (1942), p.55.
63 Nichols (1910), pp.23, 26–27.
64 Some village and other BRVICo buildings for the Stevensville area are illustrated in Pfeiffer (07–13), plates 187–179, but they are not for the town. Plate 169 is not the village inn but the Heights clubhouse.
65 Zeisler (MS.1982), p.62; Stevensville (1971), p.164. The Wright Archives possess three drawings for work camps (n.d.), and working drawings (n.d.) titled "Office for" BRVICo, the design of which is a duplicate of Wright's Cummings Real Estate office, River Forest (1905), see Storrer (1979), item 12. For an idea of how the Bitter Root cottages might have appeared, see the Waller vacation cottage (1909), Storrer (1993), p.168, which is similarly detailed and constructed.
66 Stevensville (1971), p.163; Zeisler (MS.1982), p.60.
67 The inn and three other buildings are shaded on the plan for unknown reasons; only the inn was built. Other illustrations appear in Ludwig (1982). Archival drawings described the building as a "hotel" for BRVICo.

68 *Northwest Tribune* (Stevensville), 1 October 1909. See also *WestN*, 22 September 1909; for a large photograph of the inn Pfeiffer (2011), 336. Storrer (1979), plate 145; photographs of interior and furnishings in *Bitter Root Valley* (Chicago: BRVICo), 1911), p.24.
69 In early 1980s, Ted and Thelma Moody, long-time residents and owners of one of the houses, checked dates at the Ravalli County building records office. Apparently four houses were built ca. 1912 in the area but only two remain.
70 In May 1910, it was reported that "golf links" were being prepared "on the grounds north of the hotel and W.T. Burns, the golfs expert, is recently from London. . . . The links will be ready for use in about two weeks;" they were not; *Northwest Tribune*, 20 May 1910; survey map *Sunnyside Orchards* (Ravalli County: BRVICo, n.d., ca. 1911), BRV Archives.
71 "Moody and Nichols quit ditch co.," *WestN*, 6 April 1910, p.1.
72 "King, Guy," biography from the *American Architects and Buildings* database; "Hamilton, Mont," *American Contractor*, 31(25 June 1910), p.34, and "Fifty Bungalows," p.47c; "Bitter Root Valley (Missoula P.O.)," ibid., 34(1 February 1912), p.32b.
73 LeCocq (2013), pp.16–19.
74 *Who Was Who in America*, the biographical information supplied by Hooker.
75 George E. Hooker, [entry], *Record of the Class of 1883* (Amherst: Amherst College, 1886), pp.16–17; *Class of Eighty-Three Amherst College, Record 1883–1903* (Springfield, MA: F.A. Barette, 1903), p.18; *Chicago Commons*, 1(January 1897), pp.6, 16, 110, 114.
76 As quoted in Handlin (1979), p.180.
77 Collins and Collins (1965, the English translation of Sitte), pp.72, 134n86; Handlin (1981), pp.78–79. The two biographical outlines do not correspond, but Handlin's summarizes Hooker's professional affairs; see also Davis (1967), pp.20, 127.
78 Hooker (1904a), p.6; Hooker (1904b), p.8; Lewis (1923), pp.68–72; Collins and Collins (1965), p.138; Wright (1980), pp.262, 393; Scott (1969), pp.108–109, 130, 150, 164. Also Hooker (1903) and Hooker in references herein.
    Hooker continued to engage in distinguished civic service as trade commissioner with the US Department of Commerce from 1919–21; American labor press correspondent to the League of Nations from 1924–26 and 1928–29, to the World Economic Conference in Geneva in 1927, and to the sixth Pan-American Conference in 1928; he also held several other appointments with the Chicago city council and state of Illinois.
79 Van Zanten and Robinson (2000), p.89.
80 Van Zanten and Robinson (2000), p.88.
81 "Program of the International . . .," *AmCity*, 5(September 1911), p.168.
82 Hooker gave a paper in March 1911 to the City Club titled "The Spirit of Practice of German City Planning," City Club, *Ninth Year Book* (1912), p.63.
    The cover design for the City Club's *Bulletin* (begun in February 1907) has a dark, shadowy, smoky city, but does a peeking sun offer a brighter future? See the illustration in Handlin (1981), p.76.
83 Royal Institute of British Architects, *Town Planning Conference London 10–15 October 1910. Transactions*.
84 Wright (1980), p.262.
85 Hooker (1913), p.89.
86 See the valuable bibliography in Park, Burgess and McKenzie (1925) for an indication of the breadth and complexity of mainly social scientific information.
87 Jensen was followed in the chair by Walter Griffin, also a founding member, for a brief tenure in 1913 after he and wife Marion had won the competition for the design of Canberra. Walter's father George joined the same year, City Club, *Tenth Year Book* (1 July 1913), pp.5, 6. Marion did not join the Woman's City Club.
88 According to Wright (1980), p.263. See also Vernon (1991), pp.221–222, 229. A contemporary view of influence is William E. Parsons, "Burnham as a Pioneer in City Planning," *ARecord*, 38(July 1915), pp.13–31.
89 As quoted in Wright (1980), p.263.
90 Paper of 1910, Jens Jensen to City Club, "Regulating City Building," as quoted in Grese (1992), p.87.
91 Scott (1969), p.108.
92 Hines (1974), p.146.
93 Hooker (1909), pp.778–780.

94 As put by Lewis and Smith (1929), p.329.
95 "Object of the City Club," as set out in 1903, City Club, *Tenth Year Book*, 1 July 1913, pp.28–29.; Garland (1913), pp.557–558; the club was founded by 174 men. On traction, see Lewis (1916), pp.68–72; "The Railway Terminal Problem in Chicago," *CityBull*, 6(23 July), pp.215–220.
96 Wright (1980), p.263, cf. pp.265–267, 280–281.
97 [Press release], "Pick Winners of Housing Prices," *SundayT* (23 March 1913), part I, p.21.
98 Yeomans (1916), p.1.
99 Yeomans (1916), dated December 1916, one assumes distribution began in early 1917.
100 For contemporary American accounts of English predecessors, see J.G.H. Northcroft, "Port Sunlight," *Indoors and Out*, 2(April 1906), pp.1–8, and 2(May 1906), pp.65–74; Samuel Swift, "The Garden City," *Indoors and Out*, 12(November 1905), pp.90–95, and 1(December 1905), pp.37–45; with thanks to the late Jon Lardner. The magazine was absorbed by *House Beautiful* in 1908. A more detailed, equally praiseworthy account is in Hooker (1913).
101 There are many studies of Forest Hills Gardens, but see especially Stilgoe (1988), pp.221–238.
102 Schmitt (1969), pp.178.
103 Rockwell Kent, *Wilderness: A Journal of Quiet Adventure in Alaska* (New York: 1920), as quoted in Schmitt (1969), p.179.
104 Yeomans (1916), pp.1–8.
105 Yeomans (1916), p.1. Prize money was offered by the club's president, Alfred L. Baker, "Chicago's City Planning Competition," *NMReview*, 2(April 1913), p.305; and "Prize-Winning Plans . . . of Urban Land," *AmCity*, 8(April 1913), p.421, descriptions of three winners, pp.421–427.

Results of the competition were also announced in *Construction News* (Chicago), 22 March 1913, p.1; *NMReview*, 2(April 1913), pp.305, 497–499; and *Western Architect*, 19(April 1913), pp.39–40; Nolen (1916), pp.21, 40. Also McLean (1917), pp.6–8, and related plates that include Wright's drawings; Handlin (1981), pp.84–89; Hines (1974), chapter 14; *Book of the . . . Exhibition of the Chicago Architectural Club*, 1913, n.p., item 41 (42 not illustrated), although not a member in 1913, Wright's work was exhibited by the club.
106 Cf. the early chapters of Keating (1988).
107 With thanks to Christopher Vernon for information on Tirrell and Jensen.
108 There is some confusion about the number of entries received. In the index to contributors, Yeomans (1916) mentioned another eleven entries while twenty-six were published. Thirty-three were mentioned in "Cash for Model City Plan," *DailyT* (4 March 1913), p.7. Albert Lilienberg was at the time known to be chief of Goteberg's Town Planning Commission and involved with Swedish Garden Cities.
109 Wright (1916), p.96.
110 A geometrical analysis was first presented tentatively in Johnson (1987b).
111 Wright (1988), p.107.
112 Chicago Architectural Club, *Book of the Twenty-Seventh Annual Exhibition* (Chicago: Art Institute, 1914), n.p.
113 Yeomans (1916), pp.95, 111.
114 Smith (1985), pp.296–310.
115 Smith (1985), pp.300–310; Anders Willatzen to Harry Robinson (in Wright's office), 28 January 1913, Wright Archives.
116 Compare with Pfeiffer (02–06), where plates 117 and 119 are incorrectly dated 1900. Plate 13 in Pfeiffer (1984) is a colored drawing prepared in 1916 for publication (not 1913), so, too, the excellent reproductions in Pfeiffer (2011), pp.460–461.
117 For Wright's introduction to Europe and the role of Dutch architects ca. 1906–13, see Langmead and Johnson (2000).
118 Wright (1916/1992). See analyses in Cranshawe (1978), pp.3–9; Wright (1980), pp.281–290; Wright (1988), pp.105–108; Handlin (1981), pp.78–80.
119 All quotes in Wright (1916), pp.101–102, the essay a discrete part (IV, pp.96–102) of Yeomans (1916).
120 Albert Kelsey, "Aesthetic Review of the Plans," *Yeomans* (1916), p.111.
121 Edward L. Burchard, "Chicago City Club Opening," *NMReview*, 1(April 1912), pp.245–248; Charles A. Beard, "Recent Activities of City Clubs," ibid., 1(July 1912), p.431; Fiske Kimball, "The Social Center. Part II. Philanthropic Enterprises," *ARecord*, 45(June 1919), pp.528–531.

122 Irving K. Pond "Aesthetic Review of the Plans," *Yeomans* (1916), p.116; also Brooks (1972), p.30.
123 Carol Aronovici, "Sociological Review of the Plans," *Yeomans* (1916), p.118. Aronovici's major publications were *The Social Survey* (New York, 1916), and *Housing and the Housing Problem* (Chicago, 1921).

   Robert Anderson Pope, who had entered the competition, provided an "Economic Review" that comprised quantitative data for twenty designs and is of little value here. A landscape architect in the New York City/Philadelphia area, Pope referred to himself as a "Town Planner" and a "Specialist in the Design of Model Communities;" see his "Community Planning with Voluntary Restrictions," *AmCity*, 12(March 1915), pp.241–242, and his magnificent post–World War I housing scheme illustrated in Hayden (1981), p.253.
124 Reprint in Lewis Mumford, *From the Ground Up* (New York: Harcourt, Brace, 1956, p.87; compare with Twombly (1979), p.227.
125 Maher and Wright were together in Silsbee's office in the late 1880s, Wright (1932), p.72.
126 See Harry G. Schalck, "Mini-Revisionism in City Planning. The Planners of Roland Park," *JSAH*, 29(December 1970), pp.347–349; Arthur B. Crawford, "A Suburb ... Roland Park ...," *Brickbuilder*, 13(August 1914), pp.191–194; Oswald C. Hering, *Concrete & Stuccoed Houses* (Boston: 1912), pp.8–9,ix.
127 Yeomans (1916), pp.5–6.
128 McLean (1917), p.8; Alofsin (1993), pp.72, 343n.62.
129 Reps (1997), pp.160–161, 288–294.
130 Creese (1960), p.300. For illustrations of winners and a few other entries and comments, see Wright (1980), pp.281–290; Handlin (1979), pp.158–170; Handlin (1981); Yeomans (1916).

   There is an interesting similarity between the 1913 designs and the presentation of some of those for a municipal housing scheme for Budapest, Hungary, 1900, see Hegemann and Peets (1922), p.272.
131 Because the Griffins were committed to Canberra, the 1913 design was entered under Lawrence's name. A typescript copy of the Griffinses' text was kindly supplied by the late Professor David Gebhard.
132 Hayden (1981), pp.184–193.
133 Siegfried Giedion, *Walter Gropius Work and Teamwork* (New York: Reinhold, 1954), pp.79–81, 201–205.
134 Yeomans (1916), pp.25–26.
135 "City Club Housing Show," *DailyT* (14 March 1913), p.13. See also John Ihlder, "Chicago City Club's Housing Exhibition," *NMReview*, 2(April 1913), pp.497–499; John Nolen, "The Fifth National Conference on City Planning," ibid., pp.496–497.

   Other major exhibitions by the City Club during this period were a "General Civic Exhibit" (opened 8 January 1912), "Chicago's Transportation Problem" (opened 23 May 1912), "Public Health" (opened 30 November 1914), and "Public Properties in Chicago" (opened 3 March 1915).
136 "City Club Housing Show," *DailyT* (14 March 1913), p.13.
137 George B. Ford, "City Planning Exhibition in Berlin," *AmCity*, 3(September 1910), pp.120–124; Frederick C. Howe, "City Building in Germany," *Scribner's Magazine*, 47(May 1910), pp.601–614.
138 Editorial, "We Will," *DailyT* (17 March 1913), p.6.
139 Henry Hyde, "How Jan Sobetski Fought for a Home," *DailyT* (17 March 1913), pp.1, 4.
140 Henry Hyde, "Original Plan by Founders of Riverside Forced to be Abandoned," *DailyT* (28 March 1913), part 1, pp.17, 18.
141 Brooks (1972), pp.79–80, 126–130; Ganschinietz (1969); Hasbrouck (1964), pp.5, 7; Peisch (1964), pp.81–82; Drummond (1915), pp.9–15. Drummond also worked for Richard E. Schmidt (another young Progressive) and Burnham from 1901 to about 1903.

   In 1912, Drummond took on Louis Guenzel as partner to conduct the business of private practice. The firm dissolved in late 1915. Shortly thereafter, Drummond's career was marked by relative obscurity in a quiet solo practice. See, for example, Taylor house, Glen Ellyn, Illinois, in Portland Cement Association (Chicago: The Association, ca. 1919), p.58; William Drummond, *Our National Capitol* (Chicago: The Author, 1946).
142 Drummond (1916), pp.37–44.

143 For Yeomans (1916), Drummond provided photographs of his own buildings. Also included were photographs of houses built at Forest Hills Garden Suburb outside Boston, planned by landscape architect Robert A. Pope, who had entered the 1912 competition, and architects Kilham & Hopkins; see "Two Groups of Houses...," *Brickbuilder*, 22(April 1913), pp.93–96.
Cf. Arthur C. Comey, "Billerica Garden Suburb," *Landscape Architect*, 4(1913–14), pp.145–149; idem., "Plans for an American Garden Suburb," *AmCity*, 11(July 1914), pp.35–37; and idem., *Houston: Plan for Development* (Houston, 1913). Comey wrote an unflattering review of Wright's *When Democracy Builds* (Chicago: University of Chicago Press, 1945), idem., "Some Recent Publications," *Landscape Architect*, 36(October 1945), pp.38–39.
144 Drummond (1916), pp.39–40.
145 Announced nationally in "A Neighborhood Center Competition," *WArchitect*, 20(September 1914), p.103; "Chicago's City Planning Competition," *NMReview*, 2(April 1913), p.305; "Neighborhood Center Competition," *AmCity*, 11(July 1914), p.62.
146 See Arthur Coleman Comey, "Neighborhood Centers," in Nolen (1916), pp.117–128, and note the Froebel School and Recreation Center, Gary, Indiana.
147 "Neighborhood Centers," *NMReview*, 4(July 1915), p.496.
148 Ibid., loc cit; "Competition," *WArchitect*, 21(June 1915), p.48; "The Neighborhood Center Competition," *CityBull*, 8(March 1915), cover, pp.77–78; "The Problem of the Neighborhood," ibid., p.81; "Neighborhood Center," *NMReview*, 4(July 1915), p.496; a good overview in Van Zanten (2013), pp.94–104.
149 Elizabeth A.T. Smith et al., *The Architecture of R. M. Schindler* (Los Angeles: Museum of Contemporary Art; New York: Abrams, 2001), pp.21, 186; Gebhard (1971), pp.16, 26.
150 Drummond (1915), pp.9–15; his aerial perspective is in Hegemann and Peets (1922), p.278.
151 "Bourne," Casey Blake, *Dictionary of Literary Biography 1920–1955* (Detroit: Bruccoli Clark Layman, 1988), no.63, pp.26–27. Bourne died at age thirty-two in the 1918 pandemic influenza.
152 Randolph Bourne, "Our Unplanned Cities," *New Republic*, 3(16 June 1915), pp.202–203, reprinted in idem., *The History of a Literary Radical . . .* (New York: S. A. Russell, 1956), brought to my attention by Wright (1988); however, Bourne had not visited the City Club's 1913 exhibition.
153 Flanagan (1996), pp.177–178, to be read with caution. Uniquely, Breckinridge and Abbot had obtained PhDs from the University of Chicago.
154 Johnson (2002), pp.227–245.
155 Harland Bartholomew [City Plan Engineer], "Toward the Reconstruction of New York's Lower East Side, Part I: An Analysis of the Existing Conditions," *AForum*, 57(July 1932), pp.29–32; June Manning Thomas, *Redevelopment and Race: Planning for Fine City in Postwar Detroit* (Baltimore: Johns Hopkins University Press, 1997), pp.39–43.
156 Herbert (1963), p.166.

9 Contraction

Synthetic, with Drummond prophetic, Chicago City Club's publication in 1916 of the 1912–13 competition may well have been the last hurrah of the Progressives' modeling for cities – that is, until Roosevelt's New Deal promoted real programs. The Arts and Crafts Movement in America came to a symbolic end in 1915 when Gustave Stickley went bankrupt and Elbert Hubbard went down with the *Lusitania*. Also that year, the NCCP began publishing a quarterly journal, *The City Plan*, and books by Graham R. Taylor on *Satellite Cities* and Frederick Howe on *The Modern City* were released. In 1916, the Chicago City Club presented its neighborhood planning studies, and civil engineer Nelson Lewis published his popular manual on *The Planning of the Modern City*. In that year, nine American universities were offering city planning instruction.

The American City Planning Institute was founded in 1917. Citizen planning commissions were becoming popular with municipalities, semi-comprehensive city plans were now and then proposed but seldom acted upon, real estate promoters occasionally employed planners, and so on. Nearly all those people identified Ebenezer Howard's satellite-city co-op management system as inappropriate for American capitalism, let alone its idea of economic democracy. The City Beautiful was seen as a demonstration of political egoism and capitalistic excess in the guise of civic aesthetics. A delayed infusion of humanitarianism and practicality assisted only marginally, in fact nearly dissembled. On the other hand, principles inherent in City Scientific attitudes allowed the emergence of an open-ended flexible methodology. Without a visual, set model for guidance, they encouraged comprehensiveness.

As somber English town planning historian Anthony Suttcliffe summarized, having "clearly passed through its cosmetic phase" (a nice turn of phrase) by 1917, it was nonetheless clear that American "planning was still a collection of ideas, that it had no real administrative existence. Indeed, it would be many years yet before that existence could be firmly established."[1]

Of course, there was no Progressive City, particularly, formally, or typically; no theoretical model or practical construct. Rather, Progressives steadfastly fought for a clean, comfortable, and compassionate city, whatever its physical, administrative, or spiritual components. In pursuit of progress, as well as life, liberty, and happiness, each reformation group described desirable bits and pieces: "a collection of ideas." Yet *The National Municipal Review* and City Club programs were notably comprehensive.

Wright's Bitter Root town plan of 1909 was literally unknown outside the valley and in Missoula. The Griffins' Canberra plan of 1912–14 shined briefly through the teen years. It rejected the Garden City plan form and City Beautiful aesthetic while accepting Anglo-American suburbia. Founded on a rationalism that disposed a wide variety of city and government functions, it carefully studied housing areas, and it responded to – and enhanced experientially – the dramatic landscape. While it closely approached the Progressives' desires for a new, clean, coherent urban place, much of it was realized over the next five decades. As well, the Griffins designed the smaller regional cities of Leeton and Griffiths, built in New South Wales during 1914–17, that also carried to practice some ideals of American Progressives. Being outside the United States and not on European soil but in the antipodes, those three cities were (and are) virtually ignored by observers up North.

Progressives suffered a reaction similar to that of architects. Most reforms were usually promoted by modestly endowed people and carried to fruition by those of means and education – that is, money and language. Their persistent major opposition was greed and power, each controlled by those of equal means if not knowledge or without wisdom. From 1890–1930, nearly all building and landscape architects, as we've learned, and many of those professing city planning expertise, stood aloof from the social, aesthetic, and intellectual ferments of the day. The worldly and prosperous of them were still middle incomers employed by the moneyed and privileged. They included architects Adler, Sullivan, Burnham, and Wright in early career (less in later years, to his dissatisfaction) and landscape architects Nolen, Comey, the Griffins, Bartholomew, Henry Wright, and so on. But they did not effectively influence politicians and their commercial benefactors.

Wright practiced architecture in the city from 1887–1909, then gave up, or as he preferred, the city failed him. He could not abandon his gospel of ungoverned individualism or muster the mental attitude and social graces necessary to compete with normal commercially oriented architectural firms or the demands of their practical, rich clients who, after all, were among the city's multiplicity of controlling factions.

The city is terrifying, stimulating, grandly large, and weirdly complex refuge *and* glass house. Yet, with Rousseau and Carlyle and like the Populists, Arcadians, and Transcendentalists, Wright also found the city without morals, physically and spiritually dirty, incomprehensible, fake, unnatural, and decidedly anti-nature. He complained bitterly to the face of his successful fellow architectural colleagues about what he perceived as their artistic and commercial immorality. His inability to personally cope in business he blamed not on them but on Carlyle's description of urban-born infections and people's – the general population's – complacency.

Nonetheless, before 1917, Bitter Root town was Wright's contribution to developing a reasonable proposition of how best to aesthetically and physically arrange an urbanized society. It was new and would have been theoretically provocative. As with Broad Acre villages, he argued his cause with the intellectual tools of anti-urban nineteenth-century philosophers and theorists. Yet his position cannot be dismissed for that reason alone. Philosophies are debunked not because they are old but only because they are inelastic, less than holistic, biased, and unviable. But they can be temporarily pushed aside by popular appeal or professional myopia.

The Wright School was well represented at the sixteenth Chicago Architectural Club exhibition of 1914. However, by 1917, only two followers of the school were exhibited simply because clients, critics, governments, and press had abandoned them. When architect Thomas Tallmadge, once one of the young Progressives, reviewed the show, he "regretted" the "absence of any evidence . . . [of] the 'Chicago School'," as he called Sullivan's followers, their engineers, and the Wright School, and further,

> Contemporary architecture in the United States . . . is [in] a state of complete eclecticism. . . . [Clients] have turned back to pretty Colonial or the fashionable Italian.
> Where are Sullivan, Wright, Griffin and the others? . . . With the only original note produced in our architecture in the past twenty-five years thus expurgated . . . [there] is a state of complete eclecticism. . . .[2]

Was the rejection foreseeable? Sullivan was ill, alone, and living off handouts at Cliff Dwellers Club. Wright was in Tokyo and Los Angeles, the Griffins in Melbourne and Sydney, Australia, Irving Gill in San Diego and Myron Hunt in Los Angeles, John Dillon in Atlanta, Georgia, and so on. But relocation was not the cause or a symptom. The Wright School had been pushed aside. It was too idiosyncratic, its pervasive conservative "taste" its undoing. Yet the Wright School's theoretical foundation remains solid, universal, and worth *new* constructs. In 1959, architect and historian Albert Bush-Brown provided insight into what he styled as Wright's "honest arrogance":

> He [Wright] believed his social mission was to build beautifully, and when the centers of power failed to seek him, they became in his mind the strongholds of reaction. He clung

> to an idea of primitive democracy at a time when decisions were more commonly made by officials appointed to dole out patronage and organize graft. . . .
> What was truly essential in Wright's work was his capacity to capture space within eccentrically disposed masses; to describe planes that come forward and planes in recession, projections and hollowed places; to balance these as no previous architect had. . . .
> You will find . . . that marvelous development of spatial theme taught the lesson that a building's only memorable function is to be a satisfying work of art. . . . Could a lesser arrogance or a dishonesty have taught as much?[3]

If you asked people "of certain taste," as had Burchard and Bush-Brown in the 1930s, who "had done the most" for current architecture, they likely would have agreed

> that Sullivan had made some imaginative proposals, . . . that Wright had built some interesting houses, . . . that [Ralph] Cram's Gothic churches were excellent, that Cass Gilbert had mastered the Skyscraper [in the Woolworth Building, New York City of 1913] and Paul Cret the problem of government building [the Pan-American Union building in Washington of 1910], . . . [in New York] McKim and his partner Stanford White . . . [in Chicago] the resourceful and indomitable planner . . . "Uncle Dan" Burnham.

For those "right people" of certain taste, it was as if Henry Hobson Richardson and Louis Henry Sullivan and Irving John Gill "had never lived or written or built" or if Unity Temple and the Larkin Administration Building did not exist.[4]

As a single building or as a habitable edge of a city or as a servant to city gnostics and plutocrats, post-1914 architecture entered three decades of regressive "complacency." Designers, including some of those formerly of the Wright School, reverted to cloyingly eclectically applying historical styles, while the French beaux arts, in an elaborate ballooned classicism, regained popularity, especially in architecture schools. The impetus for a technologically driven American modernism was lost to European practicing architects, who carried on with some of Wright's ideas, and to the industrial buildings designed by Albert Kahn and others not necessarily architects. Then, around 1930, as I've discussed elsewhere, European stucco and steel and glass boxes were borrowed unwittingly, it appears, by Americans.[5] A new European hegemony began and eventually dominated design theory and practice, persisting into the 1970s.

In the electronic and overpopulated twenty-first century, there arise similar battles, only different in scale, physical complexity, and language. One struggle is to control the spreading over hill, dale, and marsh of a suburban social and physical wilderness that destroys precious life-sustaining natural environments, all in a race for (again) commercial vanity, excessive profit, and political aggrandizement – and, yes, as well – to exercise unrestricted and uncontrolled so-called individual rights. Unmanaged, they are an abrogation of communal rights and social responsibilities. "Mull it over as you will, the American penchant for fouling the land has no acceptable counterbalance save the hope that lies in education."[6] The hope lies in education.

Notes

1 Suttcliffe (1981), chapter on North America.
2 Thomas E. Tallmadge, "The Thirtieth Annual Architectural Exhibit in Chicago," *WArchitect*, 25(April 1917), p.27.
3 Bush-Brown (1959), pp.25–26.
4 Burchard and Bush-Brown (1961), p.296.
5 Cf. Johnson (1990), (2000), (2013a).
6 Bush-Brown (1959), p.23.

Appendices

Appendix A
Visual examination of geometries

While assisting with this research in the 1980s, Professors Samuel Wayne Williams and Sarah McMillan Reckon investigated possible permutations of compass, triangle, and T-square, making them part of educational projects within the basic architecture design program at Washington State University. The following sketch by Williams was derived from Wright's varieties.

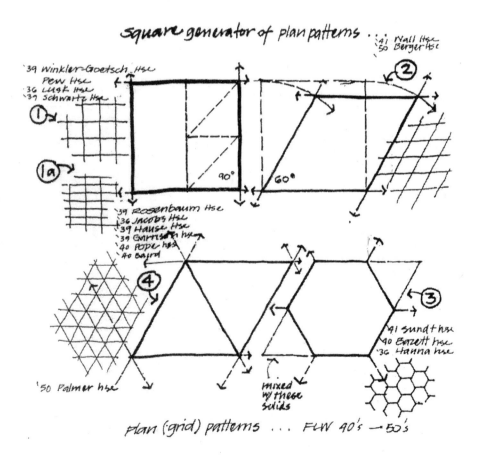

Appendix B
Wright's Yesler Avenue Hotel of 1894[1]

NEW HOTEL BUILDING / A $75,000 Block to Be Begun / Here Immediately / BUILT BY A CHICAGO CAPITALIST / To Be Called Yesler Avenue Hotel, at / the Corner of Yesler and Fifth / – Plans Now Ready.

A large six-story hotel is about to be added to the long list of attractive buildings in Seattle, and the work of construction will begin immediately. It will be called the Yesler Avenue hotel and is to be erected by C.P. Dose of Chicago, who is the owner of considerable real estate here and enthusiastic over the city's prospects. His representative, Charles H[erbert] Bebb, architect and engineer, is now in the city and will superintend the construction of the building, which will cost in the neighborhood of $75,000.

The hotel is to be erected on the north-east corner of Yesler avenue and North Fifth street, occupying ground 120 feet square. The plans of the building have been prepared by Architect Frank L. Wright of Chicago, and contemplate a modern hotel equal to anything in Eastern cities. The noticeable feature is that there will be no inside rooms, every room in the house having outside windows. To accomplish this desirable object advantage is taken of the shape of the lot, one corner of which is cut off by Yesler avenue. The building fronts on three streets, the main front of ninety-six feet being on Yesler avenue. The Fifth street frontage is sixty-nine feet and that on the line of Alder street twenty-eight feet. The angles at the ends of the main front are obtuse. It will be six stories high and contain 120 guest rooms.

The material will be pressed brick and terra cotta, the design being simple and impressive. The Yesler avenue front will be ornamented with terra cotta in the Romanesque style, the balance of the building in plain pressed brick. The interior arrangement will be everything desirable. A closed closet will join each room. There will be fine suites of rooms each on each floor, having a bath attached. The building will have steam heat, electric light, automatic fire alarms, electric calls, etc. It will be built in what is called the slow burning method of construction.

Mr. Dose believes that times will soon be better, and writes that those who move ahead of the procession are always better off than those who follow.

The hotel was not built.

Note

1 From "New Hotel Building," *Seattle Post-Intelligencer*, 10 January 1894, p.5d.

Appendix C
Further quadruplets

A scan through any builder or architectural journal or house plan pattern books of the 1880s and 1890s, or their reprints, will reveal the relative popularity of square ground-floor plans for compact houses. Figure C1 is typical of a nearly square modest builder's house of 1887 in the popular Queen Anne mode. One of the more expensive of the type is the spacious Smith house by John Calvin Stevens in 1884 (see Figure C2). Stevens often used openable rooms/spaces, as did other society architects such as Peabody & Stearns and McKim Mead & White, both in New York City, and Wilson Eyre in Philadelphia.[1] Because the ground-floor plan is common, how did Wright employ it for the majority of his early houses? Only ground-floor plan diagrams are used herein, recognizing that second floors were reserved for bedrooms arranged much as in either figure.

The Peter Goan house of 1893 and built in 1897, Figure C3.1, was Wright's first tentative application. Kitchen, dining, and living rooms arranged about a fireplace with stairs on axis

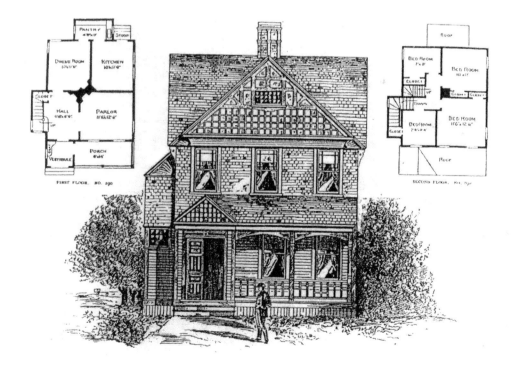

Figure C1 Proposal for a house in Shingle or Queen Anne style with typical nearly-square floor plans of the 1880s, position of the stairs uniquely positioned. From Clark, 1986.

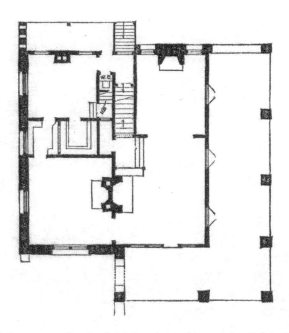

Figure C2 Smith house near Portland, Maine, by architect John Calvin Stevens, 1884–85; ground-floor plan a kin of C1, 3 and 4. Author's collection.

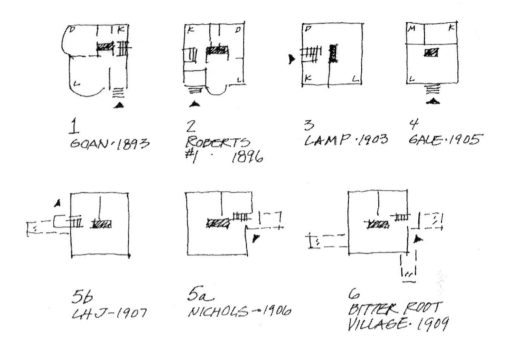

Figure C3 Sketches of ground-floor plans of Wright-designed houses, 1893–1909. All five ground designs for Roberts in 1896 would apply. Author's drawing.

is the key to typicality, as is the limit of three ground-floor chambers.[2] House number one of January 1896, C3.2, was a project for C. E. Roberts. The floor plan was opposite hand to Goan but the rooms were less enclosed, less chambered.[3]

Figures B1–2 follow one of the more popular plans of the 1870s to 1900s and is best explained by reference to the left plan in Figure C1. The lower left quadrant would be entry, hall, stair, vestibule, or porch. A toilet was an outhouse. Dine or kitchen was in the top quadrant with parlor lower right. The wall between parlor and hall or parlor and dine may be openable forming nearly a single space. (The plan could be flipped, not exactly square, and enlarged by elaboration such as Wright's houses for Goodrich in 1896 or Adams in 1900.) Examples abound in the *American Architect* magazine, for example, or in plan books/pamphlets like R.W. Shoppell's in the 1880s and 1890s. Wright's own house of 1889, sans pantry and different stair configuration, was a near duplicate of the ground floor in Figure C1 and for Goan.

Designed by Walter Griffin and with little input by Wright, the ill-proportioned Lamp house of 1902–03 was thoroughly modern and the *first* relatively mature square design from Wright's office (see Figure C3.3). Wright's summer cottage for Thomas Gale in 1905 was in timber throughout and had a maid's room rather than a dining space (see Figure C3.4).[4] It can be usefully compared with the more complex Brown house project also of 1905.[5]

The first mature statement solely by Wright was the Nichols house in 1906 (see Figure C3.5a). It, too, was sheathed in board-and-batten timber.[6] The "Fireproof" proposal of 1907, Figure C3.5b, is the more widely known and offered two street orientations.[7] The slightly larger Hunt house of 1907 used the same plan but construction was plaster on studs.[8] These plans are similar to the aesthetically complex Bach house of 1915 in brick and flying timber cantilevers, or to an untitled project of 1911, or Wright's Melson projects of 1908 and 1910.[9]

Proposed cottages for the Bitter Root town and village of 1909 had alternate entries,[10] as did the projected small houses for Waller (see Figure C3.6).[11] Those compare favorably with the slightly enlarged plan for Stockman in 1908[12] and the compact Elizabeth Gale house plan of 1909.[13]

After 1906, the basic square plan was used, with stair protruding or not, on more than a dozen occasions, built or not. Beyond those mentioned here, there was, for instance, Zeigler (1910, Gerts (1911), Greene (1912), and some of the Ravine Bluffs housing in 1911–15.[14] More rectilinear plans with similar relationships included projects for Melson in 1908 and Larwell in 1909 with almost identical ground-floor plans. A project for a house at Palm Beach, Florida, was one floor with bedrooms in a separate wing attached by a short, enclosed, umbilical corridor to a typical square ground-floor plan.[15]

In 1949, Wright began a new series of house designs that employed an intricate concrete block system, some with embedded clear glass, for houses he called Usonian Automatics.[16] They were an literal reuse of the 1906 Nichols plan type and accompanied by new elevations with recurring solid corners, the Hunt and Stockman houses predecessors. A few houses were built in the 1950s using the new, very expensive construction system but none to the 1949 plan.[17] The most exotic yet academically sound square house was not by Wright but by Walter and Marion Griffin for J. G. Melson in 1912 and of three stories (see Figure C4). It is perched on the topside of a rock-strewn cliff above Willow Creek as it flows through Mason City, Iowa.[18] The wonderful ink-on-linen drawing was by Marion Griffin in 1912.

Jaxon's houses

Wright could have applied alternate orientations to a small scheme of which little is known. Toronto-born William Henry Jackson's life before Chicago in the 1910s and after was committed to social justice issues for aboriginals and laborers in Canada and the United States through the extreme of anarchy. That commitment consumed all aspects of his life until a dismal death in New York City in 1952. Highlights of a few activities include a role in initiating the Canada Indian Northwest Rebellion of 1885; a claim to be a mixed-race Métis; a participant in Coxey's Army March of 1894 to Washington, DC, for an eight-hour day; a supporter of Henry George's radical ideas against private ownership of land; and an organizer of unions. He was a master at promoting himself chameleon-like and, in 1889, accepted the name Honoré Joseph Jaxon. Born in 1861 to Methodists, he converted to Catholicism in 1885 and then to the Bahá'í Faith in 1897, the year he first settled in Chicago. Apparently he and wife Aimée met the Wrights in 1907, perhaps at some function, or maybe Aimée and Catherine as members of the Chicago Women's Civic Club.[19]

On 8 October 1910, Wright again settled with wife Catherine in their Oak Park home to stay three months before he returned in January 1911 to Europe and Mamah Borthwick.[20] In mid-December, Catherine and Frank invited Aimée and Honoré to dinner *en famille*, the evening enjoyed by all. Frank agreed with some of Jaxon's ideas and talked of supporting him. For example, Aimiée and Jaxon, and now Borthwick and Wright, believed, as did most anarchists, that marriage quite simply was "a man-made scheme for the annexing of female slaves."[21] A few months later, Wright loaned Jaxon fifty dollars to attend the anti-racism First Universal Races Congress at the University of London in mid-July 1911.[22] Then, in 1914, Jaxon commissioned or Wright volunteered – although neither seems likely – to prepare a "scheme for layout of a group of three dwellings on fifty foot wide lots." The location of the three 150- by 50-foot sites remains unknown, perhaps hypothetical like the house type. Only a developmental pencil sketch of a ground-floor plan for each two-story house has survived in the Wright Archive. It was very similar to the Emmond (1892)-Barton (1902) prototype and application of a square proportion is obvious.

Wright might have had the Quad Plan schemes of 1910 in mind when he placed a front garden wall, with gate, joining each Jaxon house, implying a common space. Yet a stable/garage was not indicated. Strangely for the architect, living room windows would directly face a neighbor's kitchen window just ten feet away.[23]

Figure C4 J. G. Melson house in Mason City, Iowa, 1911, Walter Burley Griffin, Architect; ink-on-linen rendering by Marion Griffin in 1912. Author's collection, original in Mary and Leigh Block Museum of Art, Northwestern University.

Hogans's houses

Wright's Walter-Griffin floor plans for the Lamp house appeared yet again in 1916 beside William Street in River Forest, Illinois. But those designs were not by Griffin or Wright but by Harry Franklin Robinson. Upon graduation in 1906 with a degree in architectural science from the University of Illinois, Robinson turned down a teaching job at the University of Texas and in June began as a draftsman in Wright's office. Perhaps he replaced Griffin who, over unpaid wages, had quit Wright in January 1906. Two years later in July 1908, Robinson accepted a job as "chief draftsman" and "supervisor of construction" with Griffin. Then, in 1911, he returned to Wright as "office manager" and "supervisor of construction."[24] That second tenure continued until a pay dispute caused him to quit in late 1916 and move to the office of architect-brothers George and Arthur Dean; there he remained until 1923.

During those last years with Wright, Robinson worked steadily on the Booths's Ravine Bluffs speculative housing. Historian Paul Kruty correctly observed that those houses suggested "that Wright himself was no longer able, or willing to give the project his full attention. Indeed, the speculative houses seem to have been largely designed by Robinson."[25] Robinson also accepted residential commissions, a fact surely known to his boss. Among them was one for William B. Heald and another for brother James H. Heald, both in affluent Glen Ellyn, Illinois. Both houses were influenced by Griffin as well as Wright – but they were not by Wright as occasionally reported. Another group of houses was built either side of the 700s of William Street by the developer and builder Henry Hogans. His associate was Ernest Augustus Cummings, who acted as real estate agent.

Hogans emigrated from Norway in 1894 and settled in Oak Park to soon become involved in selling residential properties, eventually within most of Chicago's western suburbs. One architect he occasionally employed after about 1912 was the Wright School emulator John Shellette Van Bergen.[26] Cummings was a respected philanthropist and entrepreneur active in banking and community development as a financial advisor or in real estate. He was credited with developing dozens of subdivisions, including Ridgeland in 1872. To promote a recently purchased 135-acre property, Cummings and friends formed the River Forest Land Association in 1905. That year, Cummings, as the association's principal, commissioned Wright to design a real estate office on a corner of the property at Harlem Avenue and Lake Street. Very symmetrically composed, the office building was constructed of wood and sheathed in stucco, single story, residential in scale, and very much in Wright's style. A sign on one street-side garden wall said "WE WELCOME ALL who would a home acquire."

Cummings and Hogans came to an understanding in 1915 about developing another property on either side of an empty but recently paved William Street. The following appeared in Chicago's weekly *The Economist* in July of that year:

> River Forest
> E.A. Cummings and Co. have sold for the River Forest Land Association to Henry Hogans, 1,300 feet of frontage on both sides of William street between Oak and Chicago avenues, for $25 to $35 a front foot, upon which he [Hogans] has begun the construction of 26 two-story frame and stucco houses to cost 5,000 to $8,000 each.[27]

From this we learn that Cummings acted as agent for the Association, that Hogans would be the owner and builder of each house, that construction had just begun, and that there were no buildings upon the land. To the last point, we note that the *first* house to be listed in the 700s of William Street was for Mr and Mrs Walter A. Scott in 1915. There were *no* listings for 1913–14, implying, therefore, empty land.[28] The earliest William Street building permit granted to Hogans was dated 19 May 1915, the latest 10 December 1916. To further promotions, Cummings and Hogans had an article of explanation placed in a March 1916 issue of Oak Park's newspaper *Oak Leaves* that said in part

> ON WILLIAM STREET
> Beautiful Block of New Houses . . .

... [have] just been made in the construction of a row of beautiful homes ...

The houses have from six to nine rooms, and are all of different architectural design. The straight, simple lines of the California bungalow prevail.

The houses are of the latest design, and represent the last word in construction.

The neighborhood in which the houses have been built has been restricted, and only buildings having certain specifications may be erected. . . .

E.A. Cummings & Co., real estate dealers, have taken charge of the property. The houses are listed at $6,000 and up. . . .

"The buildings . . . [Hogans said] are representative of what is coming in American architecture." . . .

The houses will be ready for occupancy by the middle of April [1916].[29]

California bungalow? If the then famous Frank L. Wright was involved, he most certainly would have been mentioned in promotions, his and theirs. Also, in March 1916, Cummings advertised the William Street houses in *Oak Leaves* and with a nicely detailed perspectives of the houses.[30]

Cummings was familiar with Wright and the entourage of fellow architects. For some reason, the young and affable Robinson ended up with the commission. It may be that he did not supervise all of the houses as built. But Robinson's Rollo M. Givler house, designed and built in 1914 in the suburb Naperville and heavily influenced by Griffin, and the 25 William Street houses show architectonic and aesthetic characteristics found in Robinson's Ravine Bluffs projects and other residences: badly proportioned three-dimensional elevations; poor detailing, especially about fenestration, roof fascias, and interior cabinetry; a strange use of materials in their selection and disposition on a building and in its interior; and floor plans often awkwardly arranged. Yet the proper resolution of these were the very strengths of Wright's architectonics. Clearly, he was not involved at any stage of planning, detailing, or execution of the William Street collection.

A comparison not only with Wright's houses that used the Lamp plan – and all of Robinson's houses on William Street have the same plan – but with other Wright School followers reinforces the correctness of the critical history and architectonics just presented. For example, almost all of Van Bergen's handsome near-copies in and around Oak Park and those of similar character by architects Thomas Eddy Tallmadge and Vernon Watson or those more inventive by William Gray Purcell and George G. Elmslie; or the Harris Brothers's mail-order house number 63, one built on North Willow Street in Elmhurst. In fact an array of housing and commercial designs by many of these and other Wright School architects was published in the January to December 1915 issues of *Western Architect* out of Minneapolis. By comparison, then, none of the William Street houses are outstanding or worthy of the praise that has recently been so zealously but illogically presented: illogical in historical methodology or in plain architectonics as revealed in language.[31]

Importantly, during 1915 Wright was preparing for publication by the City Club of Chicago drawings of his non-competitive design for the subdivision of a quarter section of land, the central part of which was to be quadruple housing with differing orientations. He most certainly would not have rejected the opportunity to finally put into practice his two-orientation scheme. But that likely did not arise.

Quite simply, there is not one iota of primary or secondary documentation that corroborates or even hints at Wright's involvement with William Street. He and sons John and Lloyd never mentioned them yea or nay. Architecture and housing commentators during the period never mentioned them or Wright or Van Bergen or Drummond or Robinson in relation to them. The information presented here supports the generally held scholarly and lay view that the houses in question are attributed to Harry F. Robinson as the designer.

Postscript

The opportunity to apply the two-orientation scheme of 1900 finally arose. For a block of land along West High Street and touching Root River (with a proposed Community Green) and

274 Appendices

opposite to Colonial Park in Racine, Wisconsin, T. P. Hardy commissioned Wright to design a house-for-rental that could be repeated and thereby reduce construction costs. In July 1919, he offered a two-story "Monolith Home" built of monolithic reinforced concrete – that is, poured in place. The plans were to reappear around 1920 but in frame construction as studios/houses for Aline Barnsdall's defunct art colony in Los Angeles. The eighteen Hardy houses were arranged on the site plan with two orientations, as Wright first proposed in 1901.

Some time passed before Wright again gave serious thought to quadruplets. From late 1928 through 1932, Wright searched for patrons willing to finance a private Arts and Crafts school.[32] As part of promotions, he drew architectural plans for remodeling and adding to his aunts' long-abandoned Hillside Home School facilities. Included were studios as well as new staff houses whose floor plans might at first appear taken from the 1903 or 1910 Quad Plan. But they were remarkably similar to his single-story houses for the Richard Company's American System-Built Houses for Milwaukee of 1914–15.[33] "Cottage A" was based on one cabin design project for University Heights in 1909. However, Hillside staff housing projects are somewhat aside.

Quadruples were revived in 1938 in an altered manner that proved more pragmatic if less viable. Called Suntop homes, they were first designed for Otto Tod Mallery's Tod Company in early – likely February – 1938. Mallery thought of Wright as much as an inventor as an architect. He looked to the architect to improve what Mallery believed was an industry "most backward," he said, and a "jumble of anarchy and convention." Wright's proposal was for four two-story houses to share two party walls. Sites for each building of four living units were not as geometrically precise as earlier Quad Plans (see Figure C5). Moreover, each Suntop was to be surrounded by acres of roads that would claim 30 percent of the land area.[34] The name Suntop refers to a open-air roof accessible by stairs, as a "Quadruple House," an uneasy reference to and extension of the Quad Plan concept. Only one Suntop building was constructed in Ardmore near Philadelphia, and only after a longish delay. A few local citizens had concerns; some were relayed to the national architectural press but soon allayed. It was

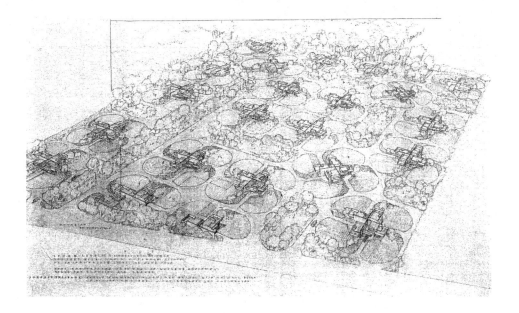

Figure C5 Aerial perspective drawing of Quadruple "House" project for federal government housing in Pittsfield, Massachusetts, in 1941–42. Courtesy and © 2016 FLWF.

Appendix C 275

opened July 1939.[35] Of all proposed house-like quadruplet mutations from 1900–58, only that one Suntop was constructed.

Suntop's predecessor was the twenty-story apartment St Marks Towers, a project for New York City from 1927–29. The basic plan was a square with four external piers supporting in the 1927 version. That of 1929 had an internal structure of walls like the party walls for Suntop. On the presentation drawing of the 1929 version, Wright referred to the structure as a "quadruple arrangement." In each quadrant was a stack of two-story duplex apartments, their floor plans of excessively cramped rooms prey to thirty- or sixty-degree angles and barely space for door swings.[36] The "Grouped Towers" apartment and hotel/office buildings for a site on Lake Shore Drive in Chicago, a project of 1930, had similar floor plans but with a structure like the 1927 St Marks Towers. Also, similar floor plans and structure to the 1929 St Marks was used for the hotel/office building project Crystal Heights (aka Temple Heights and Crystal City) of 1940. Then, from 1952–56, the Harold C. Price Co. Tower of offices and apartments in Bartlesville, Oklahoma, was constructed with equally irrational floor plans and the 1929 quadruple wall structure.

In August 1941, Wright was commissioned by the federal government to prepare designs for one hundred dwellings for workers of a rifle factory in Pittsfield, Massachusetts. By December 1941, preliminary sketches nearly duplicating Suntop were presented, minor changes

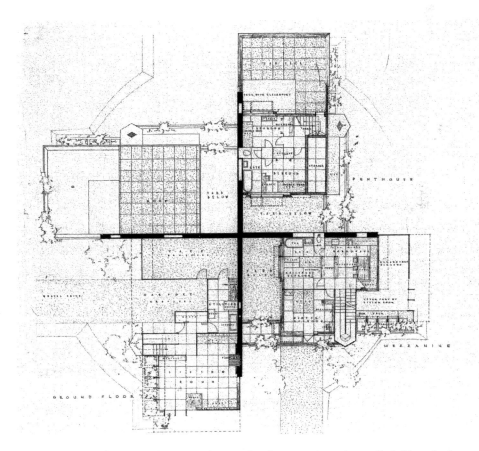

Figure C6 Aerial perspective drawing of "Quadruple House" project called Cloverleaf; ground-floor plan lower left quadrant, "mezzanine" lower right, "penthouse" upper right, roof deck upper left; floor plans as prepared in 1941–42 for federal government housing in Pittsfield, Massachusetts. Courtesy and © 2016 FLWF.

met, and documentation and working drawings commenced. Wright called the new three-story Quad House a Cloverleaf, Figure C6, no doubt picking up on an August 1939 report in *Architectural Forum* that descriptively called a Suntop "a four-leaf clover."

However, in early 1942, local architects and political allies in Washington stopped the project, arguing that, because Wright was not a registered architect in Massachusetts, he could not engage in state-financed work. He and the bureaucrats who had hired him were fired: at least that was the story put out. More likely, the commission was lost as a result of a rumor that Wright be charged with sedition for "obstructing the war" effort – that is, for protesting against the United States entering the new European war and in support of isolation. It is a story best told elsewhere.[37]

In a letter to Wright canceling the Pittsfield contract, federal bureaucrat Baird Snyder said he hoped the Cloverleaf idea would "serve as a guide for project design in other localities." Wright was asked but refused to sell his design to the government. But the Suntop Quad House had already become "a guide." The US Housing Authority's "research," as they put it, in early 1940 produced a lookalike they called a "quatrefoil." It was coupled with a variety of site plans (showing only on-street parking) that deftly joined the quatrefoils. Wright was not mentioned in promotions, and he never again received a federal government commission.

Wright proposed Broadacre City and wrote *The Disappearing City* in 1932. In 1934, he designed the layout of Broadacre and apprentices made a large model that, accompanied by drawings and detailed models of proposed buildings, were first exhibited in New York City in April 1935.[38] The two guises of quadruplets were not part of the scheme. In 1945, he rewrote the treatise and called it *When Democracy Builds* but again did not present the Quad Plan or Quad House. Once more he rewrote the text as a third edition about disappearing cities, the last called *The Living City* of 1958. Here, he included a revised Quad Plan (see Figure C7, left). It followed the 1903 parti but with new floor plans.[39] Each quadruplet was to occupy one acre, thereby fitting his agrarian ideal of partial family subsistence as expressed in publications about Broadacre City. But, in 1958, there were no perspectives or elevations and no sensible conceptual description of the houses.

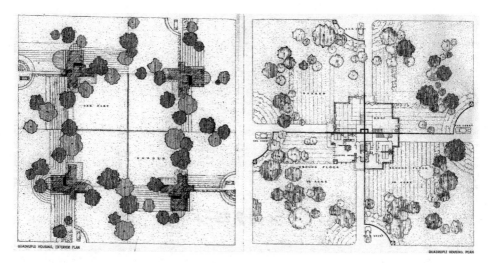

Figure C7 "Quadruple Housing" projects for unknown sites, as published in Wright, 1958. Left: revised Quad Plan site plan without stables/garage, each unit to occupy one-half acre, image a reproduction of an original plan entitled "North Carolina Housing", Pfeiffer (51–59), plate 610. Courtesy and © 2016 FLWF.

During 1956–57, Wright was asked to design housing for Negro families, a paternalistic endeavor for a site in, ironically, Whiteville, North Carolina. He reused the Suntop Quad House site plan and more positively defined site quadrants, each of one-half acre. Again, there were no garages but uncovered parking off peripheral roads. The floor plans were a modification of the Pittsfield project (with one- or two-story options) and elevations were different to – and less satisfactory than – the 1938 and 1941 schemes.[40] A Whiteville site plan was reproduced in *Living City* but not identified (see Figure C7, right).[41] Only with a knowledge of Whiteville do the plans in *Living City* make sense, their commonality with older Quad Plan and newer Quad House made visually clear. In *Living City*, their site plans appeared on facing pages, each quadrant defined by common garden walls, and captions read "Quadruple Housing." A large tip-in fold-out colored *new* site plan of Broadacre City did not locate them, but the text stated that Quad Houses were in the central area.[42]

It is clear that – as Wright and others have done – it is *wrong* to refer to Quad Plans and their expensive kin as relevant to community planning or to the complex ways of urbanism. They were housing schemes for suburban speculators but without community attractions or fundamental communal necessities.

Notes

1 Cooperative Building Plan Association, Architects, *Shoppell's Modern Houses* (New York, series 1880s–1890s), reprinted in part in R. W. Shoppell, et al., *Turn-of-the-Century Houses, Cottages and Villas* (New York: Dover, 1983); see also Scully (1971), figures 88, 92ff.
2 Pfeiffer (87–01), plates 107–111. For buildings that were built, see relevant entries in Storrer (1993).
3 Pfeiffer (87–01), plates 188–193.
4 Pfeiffer (02–06), plates 296–300.
5 Pfeiffer (02–06), plates 288–290.
6 Pfeiffer (02–06), plates 396–398.
7 Pfeiffer (02–06), plates 451–454; see also plate 39 in Pfeiffer (07–13) that perhaps refers to the publish date of April 1907.
8 Pfeiffer (07–13), plate 39.
9 On Bach, Melson, and project houses see Paul Kruty, Postscript to the prairie style: six models of unbuilt houses by FLW: 1911–1918, (Urbana: School of Architecture, University of Illinois, 2010), pp.12ff; Pfeiffer (14–23), plates 87–92; Hitchcock (1942), plates 201–202; Pfeiffer (07–13), plates 160–161.
10 See Johnson (1987b). Pfeiffer (07–13), plates 176–179 were for the village and can be compared with Wright (1910), plate XLVIII. Plate 167 in Pfeiffer (07–13) is the BRVICo plan for the proposed village, not the "town" as captioned, and not designed by Wright. In the lower left center are ground-floor plans for eight square houses.
11 Pfeiffer (07–13), plates 220–232, a modification of plate 167, and compare with Wright (1910), plate XLVIII. The perspectives of "Edward C. Waller, Three Houses" dated 1909 in Pfeiffer (2011), p.374, are not related to the floor plan accompanying but are related to three house types in plate XLVIII.
12 Pfeiffer (07–13), plates 120–125.
13 Ashbee (1911), p.55.
14 Spencer (1979), p.83, where Ravine Bluffs is dated 1911 but the design process proceeded over a couple of years.
15 Pfeiffer (07–13), plates 444–445.
16 Nicely outlined and illustrated in Pfeiffer (42–50), pp.277–281; compare the block system to Johnson (2013a).
17 On the difficulties faced in constructing Wright's new concrete block system and an owner's dedication, see Donald Leslie Johnson, "FLW Houses in the Seattle Area," *Pacific Northwest Quarterly*, 88(1, 1996–97), pp.33–40.
18 Maldre and Kruty (1996), pp.116–121; Brooks (1972), pp.244–246.

19 Smith (2007), pp.141–143; review of Smith (2007), Barbara J. Messamore, *Journal of Historical Biography*, 10(Autumn 2011), pp.134–137; "Speechless" at <oceanflynn.wordpress.com/2009/12/04/william-henry-jackson-honore-joseph-jaxon>, 1861–1952.
20 On activities and dates October 1910 to April 1911, see Alofsin (1993), pp.302–308.
21 As quoted in Will C. van den Hoonaard, *The Origins of the Bahá'í Community in Canada 1889–1948* (Waterloo, Canada: Wilfrid Laurier University Press, 1996), p.21, cf. pp.18–35.
22 Smith (2007), p.145; Alofsin (1993), chronology, pp.307–309.
23 "Three Houses for Honoré Jaxon 1914," Pfeiffer (1914–23), plate 14, no date on drawing.
24 "Robinson," *The Semi-Centennial Alumni Record* . . . (Champaign: University of Illinois, 1918), p.262. On Hogans and Robinson, see Jean Guarino, et al., "Architectural + historical survey, Final Survey Report, August 9, 3013" p.69 at <thelakotagroup.com/riverforest/> (Hogans's son W.J. claimed to be an architect after 1916); "On Robinson see "Harry Robinson," <prairiestyles.com>; cf. James Alexander Robinson, *The Life and Work of Harry Franklin Robinson*, 2nd ed. (Hong Kong: Hilross Development, 1989), it also confirms the existence of drawings for the houses and their addresses, p.6.
25 Kruty (2010) p.13a; cf. pp.6c and 17n6, 9.
26 Van Bergen worked for Wright in 1909. After Wright left for Europe, Van Bergen just locked the office door. On Van Bergen, see Brooks (1972), pp.279–183, the book an excellent seminal outline of the Wright School; Geo. R. Hemingway advertisement for Flori Blondeel's three speculative houses in Oak Park in1913–14, *Oak Leaves*, 19(January 1914), p.17; "John S. Van Bergen" at <en.wikipedia.or/wiki> is a good outline of his life and work.
27 "River Forest," *The Economist: A Weekly*. . . . (Chicago), 53(July 1915), p.1142c.
28 *Chicago Blue Book of Selected Names . . . for the Year Ending 1915* (Chicago: Chicago directory company), p.125; there is no listing of residents for the 700s William Street in 1913, 1914, oddly in 1916, and only one in 1915; Scott is otherwise not mentioned in publications.
29 "On William Street," *Oak Leaves* (Oak Park), 18 March 1916, p.96a, b, each March issue contained full-page advertisements by E. A. Cummings & Co.
30 "One of These . . .," *Oak Leaves* (Oak Park) (4 March 1916), all of p.17. A few renderings including a overall perspective of William Street are held by Robinsons's grandson James and a few are printed in his book. For other designs by Robinson see "Three concrete bungalows," *National Builder* (New York), 52(July 1911), p.33b; "News Siftings," *Cement* (New York) (12 May 1911), pp.60, 124; "Prize Designs for Concrete bungalow," *Cement World* (Chicago) (July 1911), p.28ff.
31 "FLLW UPDATE," "700 William Street Page" at <franklloydwrightinfo.com>; William Allin Storrer, Richard Johnson, and Dominque Watts, *The Anonymous FLW and The 700 William Street, River Forest Project* (Traverse City, MI: Winewright Media, 2014); "New 2-Parter from Storrer," 4 May 2015, in "Wright Chat" web blog site, see also especially protestations of D. D. Watts, 28 March 2015, and reply M. Hertzberg, 29 March 2015.
32 Johnson (1990), chapter 4; Langmead and Johnson (1997), chapter 7.
33 Shirley duFresne McArthur, *FLW American System-Built Homes in Milwaukee* (Milwaukee: North Point Historical Society, 1983).
34 Cf. McArthur (1983); Ludwig (1982); and Johnson (1987b).
35 Wegg (1970); Johnson (1990), chapter 25; and "Usonia comes to Ardmore," *AForum*, 71(August 1939), pp.36, 142–143; Pfeiffer (33–59), plates 143–146; Pfeiffer (37–41), pp.127–134.
36 Bruce Brooks Pfeiffer, "Plates," Krens (2009), p.189, and where buildings for this paragraph are illustrated in full color. The cross-section drawing was a predecessor to the S. C. Johnson & Son Research Tower in Racine, Wisconsin, from 1943–50.
37 Wegg (1970), p.52; "News," *AForum*, 88(January 1948), pp.80–81. The sedition story was outlined by Donald Leslie Johnson, "FLW and the FBI," paper, Australia and New Zealand American Studies Association International Conference, July 1992, and given in more detail in Johnson (2004).
  Ardmore Suntop should be dated 1938 and Pittsfield Cloverleaf 1941. Both were only slightly revised without altering the concept, plans, or elevations and published and/or constructed the year following those dates. See also Storrer (1993), p.256.
38 Cf. Johnson (1988a); Johnson (1990), chapter 7.
39 Wright (1958), p.150. The floor plans are rather blurred by hatching but appear to be new to his oeuvre.
40 Pfeiffer (51–59), plates 608–11.
41 Wright (1958), p.151.
42 Sergeant (1976a), p.75, refers to the later plan in Wright (1958), not that of 1932.

References

To follow are published works referred to more than once in the endnotes or in captions or other works that together form a bibliography: see abbreviations and acronyms.

Wright's autobiographies are effusive, propagandistic, and incomplete. Copies referred to herein are FLW's *An Autobiography* (New York/London: Longmans Green, 1932), as well as the second edition (New York: Duel Sloan & Pearce, 1943), herein Wright (1943). A third edition was released in 1977, eighteen years after his death. Since Wright died in 1959, readers might assume he did not edit or rewrite the third edition, herein Wright (1977), and reprint (Los Angeles: Pomegranate Communications, 2005).

The preferred reference is to *Studies and Executed Buildings*, herein Wright (1910), the American edition of *Ausgefürte Bauten und Entwürfe von Frank Lloyd Wright* (Berlin: Verlag Ernst Wasmuth, A.G., 1910), for the simple reason that the text is in his native language. Reprints (Chicago 1975; New York 1983 and 2002) have altered plate numbers and, in 2002, incorrect plates. A clear and concise history of its publication, "a surprising saga far different from the one traditional history has assumed," is found in Anthony Alofsin's valuable preface to *Studies* (New York: Rizzoli, 1998), which used the 1919 portfolio edition published by Verlag Ernst Wasmuth A. G. in Berlin. The most important publication to European architects, however, was the cheaper, more readily available Ashbee (1911). All 1910–11 publications were financed by Wright, not Wasmuth, and most likely with loans from clients Charles E. Roberts, Francis W. Little, and Darwin D. Martin.

Aaron, Daniel. 1951. *Men of Good Hope: A Story of American Progressives*. New York: Oxford University Press.
Abercrombie, Stanley. 1984. *Architecture as Art: An Esthetic Analysis*. New York: Van Nostrand Reinhold.
Abernathy, Ann. 1988. *The Oak Park Home and Studio of FLW*. Oak Park: FLW Home and Studio Foundation.
Adams, Thomas, James W. R. Adams, and Maxwell Fry. 1932. *Recent Advances in Town Planning*. New York/London: Macmillan.
Aguar, Charles E., and Berdeana Aguar. 2002. *Wrightscapes: FLW's Landscape Designs*. New York: McGraw-Hill.
Alofsin, Anthony. 1992. "Taliesin: 'To Fashion Worlds in Little'." In *Wright Studies*.
———. 1993. *FLW the Lost Years 1910–1922*. Chicago: University of Chicago Press.
Altman, Karen E. 1993. "Florence Kelley. . . ." In Campbell (1993).
Archer, John. 1983. "Country and City in the American Romantic Suburb," *JSAH*, 42(May).
Arnheim, Rudolph. 1977. *The Dynamics of Architectural Form*. Berkeley: University of California Press.
Ashbee, Charles Robert. 1911. *FLW Chicago. Achtes Sonderheft der Architektur des zwanzigsten Jahrhunderts*. Berlin: Wasmuth. Reprinted as *The Early Work of FLW*, New York: Horizon, ca. 1968 and after. Ashbee's essay translated in Roth (1983).
———. 1911a. *FLW. Ausgeführte Bauten*. Berlin: Wasmuth. American edition of Ashbee (1911). (Reprint without Ashbee's Essay, New York: Dover, 1982.)

References

———. 1917. *Where the Great City Stands: A Study in the New Civics*. London: Essex House/B. T. Batsford.
Ashwin, Clive. 1982. "Peter Schmid and *das Naturzeichen*: And Experiment in the Teaching of Drawing." *Art History* (London). Annual, 5(June).
Avarich, Paul. 1984. *The Haymarket Tragedy*. Princeton: Princeton University Press.
Bachin, Robin F. 2004. *Building the South Side: Urban Space and Civic Culture in Chicago 1890–1919*. Chicago: University of Chicago Press.
Banham, Reyner. 1969. *The Architecture of the Well-Tempered Environment*. Chicago: University of Chicago Press.
Barney, Maginel Wright. 1965. *The Valley of the God-Almighty Joneses*. New York: Appleton, Century.
Batchelor, Peter. 1969. "The Origin of the Garden City Concept of Urban Form." *JSAH*. 28(October).
Beard, Charles A. 1912. *American City Government: A Survey of Newer Tendencies*. New York: Century; London: Unwin, 1913.
Bender, Thomas. 1975. *Toward an Urban Vision: Ideas and Institutions in Nineteenth-Century America*. Lexington: University of Kentucky.
Benevolo, Leonardo. 1960. *History of Modern Architecture*. 2 vol. London: Routledge & Keegan Paul.
Bletter, Rosemarie Haag. 1981. "The Interpretation of the Glass Dream: Expressionist Architecture and the History of the Crystal Metaphor." *JSAH*. 40(March).
Bock, Richard W. 1989. *Memoirs of an American Artist*. Los Angeles: CC Publishing.
Bohrer, Florence Fifer. 1955. "The Unitarian Hillside Home School." *WHistory*. 38(Spring).
Bolon, Carol R., Robert S. Nelson, and Linda Seidel, editors. 1989. *The Nature of FLW*. Chicago: University of Chicago Press.
Bourget, Paul. 1895. *Outre-Mer: Impressions of America (1895)*. Whitefish, MT: Kessinger.
Bowman, Leslie Greene. 1991. *American Arts & Crafts: Virtue in Design*. Los Angeles/Boston: Bulfinch Press.
Boyer, M. Christine. 1983. *Dreaming the Rational City*. Cambridge, MA: MIT Press.
Boyer, Paul. 1978. *Urban Masses and Moral Order in America 1820–1920*. Cambridge, MA: Harvard University Press.
Brenner, Douglas. 1986 "Wright at Home Again." *ARecord*. 174(September).
Bressani, Martin. 1989. "Noes on Viollet-le-Duc's Philosophy of History: Dialectics and Technology." *JSAH*. 48(December).
Brooks, H. Allen. 1966. "FLW and the Wasmuth Drawings." *JSAH*. 48(June).
———. 1972. *The Prairie School*. Toronto: University of Toronto Press.
———. 1979. "FLW and the Destruction of the Box." *JSAH*. 38(March).
———. 1981. *Writings on Wright*. Cambridge, MA: MIT Press.
———. 1984. *FLW and the Prairie School*. New York: Braziller.
Brosterman, Norman. 1997. *Inventing Kindergarten*. New York: Harry N. Abrams.
Bruegmann, Robert. 1997. *The Architects and the City: Holabird and Roche of Chicago, 1880–1918*. Chicago: University of Chicago Press.
Buder, Stanley. 1967. "The Model Town of Pullman: Town Planning and Social Control in the Gilded Age." *JAIP*. 33(January).
———. 1990. *Visionaries and Planners: The Garden City Movement and the Modern Community*. New York: Oxford University Press.
Bulmer, Martin. 1984. *The Chicago School of Social Science*. Chicago: University of Chicago Press.
Burchard, John and Albert Bush-Brown. 1961. *The Architecture of America: A Social and Cultural History*. Boston: Atlantic-Little, Brown.
Burg, David F. 1976. *Chicago's White City of 1893*. Louisville: University Press of Kentucky.
Burnham, Daniel H. and Edward H. Bennett. 1909. *Plan of Chicago Prepared Under the Direction of the Commercial Club*. Charles Moore editor. Chicago: The Club.
Bush-Brown, Albert. 1959. "The Honest Arrogance of FLW." *Atlantic Monthly*. 204(August).
Butts, R. Freeman and Lawrence A. Cremin. 1953. A *History of Education in American Culture*. New York: Holt, Rinehart and Winston.

Callow, Alexander B. *American Urban History*. 2nd ed. New York: Oxford University Press.
Campbell, Karlyn Kohrs. 1993. *Women Public Speakers in the United States 1800–1895*. Westport: Greenwood.
Cannon, Patrick E. and James Caulfield. 2006. *Hometown Architect: The Complete Buildings of FLW in Oak Park and River Forest*. Petaluma, CA: Pomegranate.
Carpenter, Frederick Ives. 1953. *Emerson Handbook*. New York: Hendricks House.
Cartwright, William H. and Richard L. Watson, Jr., editors. 1973. *The Reinterpretation of American History and Culture*. Washington: National Council for the Social Studies.
Charney, Wayne Michael. 1978. "The W. I. Clark House, La Grange, Illinois." *FLWNews*. 1(May).
Chase, Mary Ellen. 1956. *A Goodly Fellowship*. New York: Macmillan.
Chicago Architecture Club. 1902. *Annual of the Chicago Architectural Club*. March.
Choay, Françoise. 1969. *The Modern City: Planning in the 19th Century*. New York: Braziller.
Christensen, Ellen. 1993. "A Vision of Urban Social Reform." *Chicago History*. 22(March).
Ciucci, Giorgio, Francesco Dal Co, Mario Manieri Ella, and Manfredo Tafuri. 1979. Trans Barbara Liugia La Penta, *The American City From the Civil War to the New Deal*. Cambridge, MA: MIT Press.
Clark, Clifford Edward, Jr. 1986. *The American Family Home 1880–1960*. Chapel Hill: University of North Carolina Press.
Clark, Kenneth. 1962. *The Gothic Revival: An Essay in the History of Taste*. New York: Harper, Row.
Clark, Roger H. and Michael Pause. 1985. *Precedents in Architecture*. New York: Wiley.
Cleary, Richard, Neil Levine, Mina Marefat, Bruce Brooks Pfeiffer, Joseph M. Siry, and Margo Stipe. 2009. *FLW from within Outward*. New York: Skira Rizzoli.
Coburn, Leslie. 2013. "Considering the People on the Back Streets: Urban Planning at the City Club of Chicago." In Van Zanten (2013a).
Cohen, Stuart E. 1976. *Chicago Architects*. Chicago: Swallow.
Coles, William A. and Henry Hope Reed Jr. 1961. *Architecture in America: A Battle of Styles*. New York: Appleton Century Crofts.
Collected Writings. *FLW Collected Writings*. Bruce Brooks Pfeiffer, editor. Vols. 1–5. New York: 1991–1995.
Collins, Christiane Crasemann. 1989. "A Visionary Disciple: Werner Hegemann and the Quest for the Pragmatic Ideal." *Center*. 5(Austin).
Collins, George R. 1957. "Linear Planning Throughout the World." *JSAH*. 18(October).
Collins, George R. and Christiane Crasemann Collins. 1965a. *Camillo Sitte and the Birth of Modern City Planning*. New York/London: Phaidon Press.
Collins, Peter. 1965. *Changing Ideals in Modern Architecture 1750–1950*. London: Faber & Faber.
Condit, Carl W. 1968. *American Building*. Chicago: University of Chicago Press.
———. 1973. *Chicago 1910–1929. Building, Planning, Urban Technology*. Chicago: University of Chicago Press.
Connors, Joseph. 1988. "Wright and Nature and the Machine." In Bolon (1989).
Cook, Ann, Marilyn Gittell and Herb Mack, editors. 1973. *City Life 1865–1900: Views of Urban America*. New York: Praeger.
Cooley, Charles H. 1909. *Social Organization*. New York: Scribner's & Sons. Reprint 1956.
Cranshawe, Robert. 1978. "FLW's Progressive Utopia." *Architectural Association Quarterly*. London: The Association.
Cranston, Maurice. (Encyc). "Jean-Jacques Rousseau." *Encyclopedia Britannica*.
Crawford, Alan. 1970. "Ten Letters from FLW to Charles Robert Ashbee." *Architectural History*. 13.
———. 1985. *C. R. Ashbee*. New Haven: Yale University Press.
Crawford, Margaret. 1995. *Building the Workingman's Paradise: The Design of American Company Towns*. London: Verso.
Creese, Walter. 1960. *The Search for Environment: The Garden City Before and After*. New Haven: Yale University Press.

Cremin, Lawrence A. 1962. *The Transformation of the School: Progressivism in American Education, 1876–1957.* New York: Alfred A. Knopf.
Cronon, William. 1991. *Nature's Metropolis: Chicago and the Great West.* New York: W. W. Norton.
———. 1994. "In Constant Unity: The Passion of FLW." In Riley (1994).
Dahir, James. 1947. *The Neighborhood Unit Plan: Its Spread and Acceptance.* New York: Sage Foundation.
Dal Co, Francesco. 1980. "From Parks to Region: Progressive Ideology and the Reform of the American City." In Ciucci (1979).
Davey, Peter. 1980. *Arts and Crafts Architecture: The Search for Earthly Paradise.* New York: Rizzoli; London: Architectural Press.
Davis, Allan F. 1967. *Spearheads for Reform: The Social Settlements and the Progressive Movement.* New York: Oxford University Press.
———. 1973. *American Heroine: Jane Addams.* New York: Oxford University Press.
———. 1994. "A Modernizing People, 1900–1945." In Nash (1994).
Dean, George R. 1900. "Progress before Precedent." *Brickbuilder.* 9(May).
Dedmon, Emmett. 1953. *Fabulous Chicago.* New York: Random House.
De Long, David G., editor. 1998. *FLW and the Living City.* Weil am Rhein: Vitra Design Museum.
Destler, Chester McArthur. 1963. *Henry Demarest Lloyd and the Empire of Reform.* Philadelphia: University of Pennsylvania Press.
Dewey, John and Evelyn Dewey. 1915. *Schools of To-Morrow.* New York: E. P. Dutton.
de Witt, Benjamin Parke. 1915. *The Progressive Movement.* New York. Reprint Seattle: University of Washington Press, 1968.
de Witt, Wim. 1986. *Louis Sullivan: The Function of Ornament.* New York: W. W. Norton.
Dickason, David Howard. 1953. *The Daring Young Men. The Story of the American Pre-Raphaelites.* Bloomington: University of Indiana Press. Reprint, New York 1970.
Doczi, Gyorgy. 1981. *The Power of Limits: Proportional Harmonies in Nature, Art and Architecture.* Boulder: Shambhala.
Draper, Joan E. 1987. "Paris by the Lake. Sources of Burnham's Plan of Chicago." In Zukowsky (1987).
Drexler, Arthur. 1962. *The Drawings of FLW.* New York: Horizon.
Drummond, William E. 1915. "The Work of Guenzel and Drummond." *Western Architect.* 21(February). Text reprinted as "On Things of Common Concern." *PSR.* 1(2, 1964).
———. 1916. "Plan of William . . . Developed from a Sketch Submitted in Competition." In Yeomans (1916).
Dudek, Mark. 1996. *Kindergarten Architecture: Space for the Imagination.* New York/London: Spon.
Duis, Perry. 1976. *Chicago: Creating New Traditions.* Chicago: Chicago Historical Society.
Duncan, Hugh Dalziel. 1964. *The Rise of Chicago as a Literary Center from 1885 to 1920.* Totowa, NJ: Bedminster Press.
Dunne, Finely Peter. 1901. *Mr. Dooley's Opinions.* New York: R. H. Russell.
Early, James. 1965. *Romanticism and American Architecture.* New York: Barnes.
Eaton, Leonard K. 1969. *Two Chicago Architects and Their Clients: FLW and Howard Van Doren Shaw.* Cambridge, MA: MIT Press.
———. 1972. *American Architecture Comes of Age.* Cambridge, MA: MIT Press.
Ebner, Michael H. and Eugene M. Tobin, editors. 1977. *The Age of Urban Reform: New Perspective on the Progressive Era.* Port Washington, NY: Kennikat Press.
Egbert, Donald Drew. 1980. *The Beaux-Arts Tradition in French Architecture.* Princeton: Princeton University Press.
Einbinder, Harvey. 1986. *An American Genius: FLW.* New York: Philosophical Library.
Elia, Mario Manieri. 1996. *Louis Henry Sullivan.* New York: Princeton Architectural Press.
El-Said, Issam and Ayse Parmana. 1976. *Geometric Concepts in Islamic Art.* New York: Metropolitan Museum of Art.

References

Elstein, Rochelle S. 1967. "The Architecture of Dankmar Adler." *JSAH*. 26(December).
Estoque, Justin. 1987. "Heating and Cooling Robie House." *APT Bulletin*. 19(2).
Farr, Finis. 1961. *FLW: A Biography*. London: Jonathan Cape.
Fink, Leon, editor. 2001. *Major Problems in the Gilded Age and the Progressive Era*. 2nd ed. Boston: Houghton Mifflin.
Fishman, Robert. 1987. *Bourgeois Utopias: The Rise and Fall of Suburbia*. New York: Basic Books.
———. 2000. *The American Planning Tradition: Culture and Policy*. Washington, DC: Woodrow Wilson Center Press.
Flanagan, Maureen. 1996. "The City Profitable. The City Livable . . . Chicago in the 1910s." *JUrban*. 22(January).
Ford, George B. 1917. *City Planning Progress in the United States*. Washington: American Institute of Architects.
Freestone, Robert F. 1986. "Exporting the Garden City: Metropolitan Images in Australia, 1900–1930." *Planning Perspectives*. 1(January).
———. 1989. *Model Communities: The Garden City Movement in Australia*. Melbourne: Nelson.
Friedman, Alice. 1998. *Women and the Making of the Modern House*. New York: Harry N. Abrams.
Froebel, Friedrich. 1887. *The Education of Man*. Translated W. N. Hailmann. New York: D. Appleton. New York: Dover, 2005.
Gallion, Arthur B. 1950. *The Urban Pattern*. New York: Van Nostrand.
Ganschinietz, Suzanne. 1969. "William Drummond. II. Partnership and Obscurity." *PSR*. 6(2).
Garland, Hamlin. 1912. *A Son of the Middle Border*. New York: Macmillan.
———. 1913. "The New Chicago." *The Craftsman*. 24(September).
Garner, John S., editor. 1991. *The Midwest in American Architecture*. Urbana: University of Illinois Press.
Garner, John S. 1991a. "S. S. Beman and the Building of Pullman." In Garner (1991).
Gebhard, David. 1959. "A Note on the Chicago Fair of 1893 and FLW." *JSAH*. 18(May).
———. 1960. "Louis Sullivan and George Grant Elmslie." *JSAH*. 19(May).
———. 1971. *Schindler*. London: Thames Hudson.
Gebhard, David and Harriet Von Breton. 1971. *Lloyd Wright, Architect*. Santa Barbara: University of California.
Gerstle, Gary. 1996. "The Golden Age." In Murrin et al. (1996).
Giedion, Sigfried. 1956. *Space, Time and Architecture*. 3rd ed. Cambridge: Harvard University Press. First edition 1941.
Gifford, Don, editor. 1966. *The Literature of Architecture*. New York: Dutton.
Gilbert, J. B. 1991. *Perfect Cities: Chicago's Utopias of 1893*. Chicago: University of Chicago Press.
Gill, Brendan. 1987. *Many Masks*. New York: Putnam.
Gillette, Howard. 1983. "The Evolution of Neighborhood Planning." *JUrban*. 9(August).
———. 1995. *Between Justice and Beauty: Race, Planning and the Failure of Urban Policy in Washington, D.C.* Baltimore: Johns Hopkins University Press.
Glaab, Charles N. 1963. *The American City: A Documentary History*. Homewood, IL: Blackwood.
Goodman, Percival and Paul. 1960. *Communitas*. 2nd ed. New York: Vintage.
Graf, Douglas. 1986. "Diagrams." *Perspecta*. 22.
Graf, Otto Antonia. 1983. *Die Kunst des Quadrats zum Werk von FLW*. 2 vol. Vienna: H. Böhlau.
Graf, Otto. 1991. "The Art of the Square: That Most Traditional Architect—FLW." In McCarter (1991a).
Graham, Thomas E. 1983. "Jenkin Lloyd Jones and 'The Gospel of the Farm'." *WHistory*. 67(Winter).
Granger, Alfred. 1899. "An Architect's Studio." *House Beautiful*. 7(December).
Gregersen, Charles E. 2013. *Louis Sullivan and His Mentor, John Herman Edelmann, Architect*. Bloomington, IN: AuthorHouse.
Grese, Robert E. 1992. *Jens Jensen: Maker of Natural Parks and Gardens*. Baltimore: Johns Hopkins University Press.
Groth, Paul. 1981. "Street Grids as Frameworks for Urban Variety." *Harvard Architectural Review*. 2(Spring).

References

Guter, Robert P., Janet W. Foster and Jim Del Guidice. 1992. *Building by the Book: Pattern Book Architecture.* New Brunswick: Rutgers University Press.

Gutheim, Frederick, editor. 1941. *FLW on Architecture.* New York: Grosset & Dunlap.

Hamilton, Mary Jane. 1989. [Letter]. *WHistory.* 73(Autumn).

———. 1990. "The Nakoma Country Club." In Sprague (1990).

Hancock, John L. 1967. "Planners in the Changing American City, 1900–1940." *JAIP.* 33(September).

Handlin, David P. 1979. *The American Home: Architecture and Society, 1815–1915.* Boston: Little Brown.

———. 1981. "The Context of the Modern City." *Harvard Architecture Review.* 2(Spring).

Hanks, David A. 1979. *The Decorative Designs of FLW.* New York: Dutton; New York: Dover, 1999.

———. 1989. *FLW: . . . Decorative Designs from the Domino's Pizza Collection.* New York: E. P. Dutton.

Harper, William Hudson. 1904. *In the Valley of the Clan: The Story of a School* [Pamphlet]. Spring Green: Hillside Home School.

Hasbrouck, Wilbert R. 1969. "The Architectural Firm of Guenzel & Drummond." *PSR.* 6(2).

———. 1970. "The Earliest Work of FLW." *PSR.* 7(4).

———. 2005. *The Chicago Architectural Club: Prelude to the Modern.* New York: Monacelli Press.

Hayden, Dolores. 1976. *Seven American Utopias: The Architecture of Communitarianism 1790–1975.* Cambridge, MA: MIT Press.

———. 1981. *The Grand Domestic Revolution.* Cambridge, MA: MIT Press.

———. 2003. *Building Suburbia: Green Fields and Urban Growth, 1820–1900.* New York: Pantheon.

Hays, Samuel P. 1957. *The Response to Industrialism 1885–1914.* Chicago: University of Chicago Press.

Hearn, M. F., editor. 1990. *The Architectural Theory of Viollet-le-Duc: Readings and Commentary.* Cambridge, MA: MIT Press.

Hegemann, Werner and Elbert Peets. 1922. *The American Vitruvius: An Architects' Handbook of Civic Art.* New York: Architectural Book Publishing, 1922.

Herbert, Gilbert. 1959. "Form and Function: A Study of FLW's Theory of Organic Architecture." In Herbert (1997).

———. 1963. "The Neighborhood Unit Principle and Organic Theory." *Sociological Review.* n.s.11 (July).

———. 1997. *The Search for Synthesis.* Haifa: Technion: Israel Institute of Technology.

Herbert, Gilbert and Mark Donchin. 2013a. *The Collaborators: Interactions in the Architectural Design Process.* Farnham: Ashgate.

———. 2013b. "Speculations on a Black Hole: Adler & Sullivan and the Planning of the Chicago Auditorium Building." In Herbert and Donchin (2013a).

Hertz, David Michael. 1993. *Angels of Reality: Emerson Unfoldings in Wright, Stevens and Ives.* Carbondale: Southern Illinois University Press.

Hicks, John D. 1931. *The Populist Revolt: A History of the Farmers Alliance and the People's Party.* St. Paul: University of Minnesota Press.

Hildebrand, Grant. 1991. *The Wright Space: Pattern and Meaning in FLW's Houses.* Seattle: University of Washington Press.

Hillside. 1890. *Hillside Home School 1890–91.* Pamphlet. Hillside: The School.

———. 1895. *The Hillside Home School, Eighth Year 1895–96.* Pamphlet. Hillside: The School.

———. 1903. *The Hillside Home School, Seventeenth Year 1903–04.* Pamphlet. Hillside: The School.

Hines, Thomas S. 1967. "FLW. The Madison Years, Records versus Recollections." *JSAH.* 26(December).

———. 1974. *Burnham of Chicago: Architect and Planner.* Chicago: University of Chicago Press.

Hitchcock, Henry-Russell. 1942. *In the Nature of Materials.* New York: Hawthorn. Da Capo, 1975.

———. 1944. "FLW and the 'Academic Tradition' of the early Eighteen-Nineties." *Journal of the Warburg and Courtauld Institutes*. 7.
Hoffmann, Donald. 1969. "FLW and Viollet-le-Duc." *JSAH*. 28(October).
———. 1973. *The Architecture of John Wellborn Root*. Baltimore: Johns Hopkins University Press.
———. 1984. *FLW's Robie House*. New York: Dover.
———. 1986. *FLW: Architecture and Nature*. New York: Dover.
———. 1996. *FLW's Dana House*. Mineola: Dover.
Hofstadter, Richard. 1955. *The Age of Reform: From Bryan to F.D.R*. New York: Alfred A. Knopf.
———, editor. 1963. *The Progressive Movement 1900–1915*. Englewood Cliffs, N J: Prentice-Hall.
———. 1969. *Great Issues in American History, Volume 3: From Reconstruction to the Present Day, 1964–1969*. New York: Vintage Books.
Holzhueter, John O. 1988. "FLW's Designs for Robert Lamp." *WHistory*. 72(Winter).
———. 1989a. "FLW's 1893 Boathouse Designs for Madison's Lakes." *WHistory*. 72(Summer).
———. 1989b. "Cudworth Beye, FLW and the Yahara River Boathouse 1905." *WHistory*. l 72(Spring).
———. 1990. "The Lakes Mendota and Monona Boathouses." In Sprague (1990).
Hooker, George E. 1900. "Public Policy Concerning Rapid Transit." National Conference for Good City Government. *Proceedings*.
———. 1903. "German Municipal Exposition." *American Monthly Review of Reviews*. 27.
———. 1904a "Camillo Sitte, City Builder." *RecordH*. 15(January).
———. 1904b. "The German Municipal Movement." *RecordH*. 30(January).
———. 1904c. *Report of the City Council . . . Transportation Develop[ment] in Great Cities*. Chicago: City Council.
———. 1908. "Traffic and the City Plan." *Charities and the Commons* (New York). Later in *Survey*. 19(1 February).
———. 1909. "A Plan for Chicago." *Survey*. 22(4 September). Reprint Still (1974).
———. 1910. "Congestion and Its Causes in Chicago." National Conference on City Planning. *Proceedings*. 2.
———. 1911. "A Strategy of City and Village Improvement" *AmCity*. 5(July).
———. 1912. "Discussion." National Conference on Housing. *Proceedings*. 2.
———. 1913. "Garden Cities." Paper, Third National Housing Conference, Cincinnati, 3 December 1913. *JAIA*. (February 1914). Also *Garden Cities*, offprint, (Washington: American Institute of Architects, 1914).
Howard, Ebenezer. 1902. *Garden Cities of To-morrow*. 2nd ed. London: Faber & Faber. Reprint 1947.
Howe, Frederick C. 1905. *The City: The Hope of Democracy*. New York. Seattle, 1967.
Hubbell, Jay B., editor. 1936. *American Life in Literature*. 4 vol. New York: Harper. Reprint, Washington, 1944.
Hughes, James L. 1905 printing. *Froebel's Educational Laws for All Teachers*. New York: D. Appleton.
Hurtt, Steven. 1983. "The American Continental Grid: Form and Meaning." *Threshold*. New York: School of Architecture, University of Illinois.
Izzo, Alberto and Camillo Gubitosi. 1981. *FLW: Three Quarters of a Century of Drawings*. London: Academy.
Jacobs, Jane. 1961. *The Death and Life of Great American Cities*. New York: Random House.
Johnson, Donald Leslie. 1977. *The Architecture of Walter Burley Griffin*. Melbourne: Macmillan.
———. 1980. "Notes on FLW's Paternal Family." *FLWNews*. 3(2).
———. 1987. "FLW in Moscow: June 1937." *JSAH*. 46(March).
———. 1987a. "Plan Evolution to the Prairie Style: FLW's Debt to Joseph Silsbee." *Architecture Australia*. 76(June).
———. 1987b. "FLW's Architectural Projects in the Bitter Root Valley, 1909–1910." *Montana: The Magazine of Western History*. 37(Summer).

———. 1988a. "Broadacres Geometry: 1934–35." *Architectural Research* (London/Chicago). 5(Summer).

———. 1988b. "FLW in the Northwest: The Show, 1931." *Pacific Northwest Quarterly* (Seattle). 78(July).

———. 1989a. "Wenatchee and FLW: 1919." *Arcade* (Seattle). 9(December).

———. 1989b. "The Froebel-Wright Kindergarten. . . ." *JSAH*. 48(December). Response to Rubin(1989).

———. 1990. *FLW versus America: The 1930s*. Cambridge, MA: MIT Press.

———. 2000. *Architectural Excursion: FLW, Holland and Europe*. Westport: Greenwood.

———. 2002. "Origin of the Neighborhood Unit." *Planning Perspectives* (London). 17(July).

———. 2004. "FLW's Community Planning." *Journal of Planning History* (Thousand Oaks). 3(February).

———. 2012. "Design Espionage: The Griffins, the Taylors, and FLW." *Fabrications* (Melbourne). 21(January).

———. 2013a. *On FLW's Concrete Adobe: Irving Gill, Rudolph Schindler and the American Southwest*. Ashgate: London.

———. 2013b. *Anticipating Municipal Parks: London to Adelaide to Garden City*. Adelaide: Wakefield Press.

Johnson, Donald Leslie and Donald Langmead. 1997. *Makers of 20th Century Modern Architecture*. Westport: Greenwood/London: Fitzroy Dearborn.

Jones, Jenkin Lloyd. 1913. *An Artilleryman's Diary*. Madison: Wisconsin Historical Society.

Jones, Owen. 1856. *Grammar of Ornament*. London: Day and Son.

Jordy, William H. 1972. *American Buildings and their Architects: Progressive and Academic Ideals at the Turn of the Twentieth Century*. Garden City: Doubleday.

Kamerling, Bruce. 1993. *Irving J. Gill, Architect*. San Diego: Historical Society.

Kaufmann, Edgar, Jr. 1955. *An American Architecture*. New York: Horizon.

———. 1981. "'*Form* Became Feeling', a New View of Froebel and Wright." *JSAH*. 40(May). Reprint Kaufmann(1989).

———. 1982. "FLW Mementos of Childhood." *JSAH*. 41(October).

———. 1989. *9 Commentaries of FLW*. Cambridge, MA: MIT Press.

Keating, Ann Durkin. 1988. *Building Chicago: Suburban Developers & the Creation of a Divided Metropolis*. Columbus: Ohio State University Press.

———. 2005. *Chicagoland: City and Suburbs in the Railroad Age*. Chicago: University of Chicago Press.

Kief-Niederwohrmeier, Heidi. 1984. "FLW." *Baumeister*. 81(May).

Koning, H. and J. Eizenberg. 1981. "The Language of the Prairie: FLW's Prairie Houses." *EandPB*. 8.

Kornwolf, James D. 1972. *M. H. Baillie Scott and the Arts and Crafts Movement*. London/Baltimore: Johns Hopkins University Press.

Kostof, Spiro. 1991. *The City Shaped: Urban Patterns and Meanings through History*. London: Bullfinch Press. 2nd ed. New York: Thames & Hudson.

———. 1977. *The Architect: Chapters in the History of the Profession*. New York: Oxford University Press.

Krens, Thomas, Richard Cleary, Neil Levine, Mina Marefat, Bruce Brooks Pfeiffer, Joseph M. Siry, and Margo Stipe. 2009. *FLW from within Outward*. New York: Skira Rizzoli.

Krueckeberg, Donald A., editor. 1983. *The American Planner: Biographies and Recollections*. New Brunswick, NJ: Rutgers University, Center for Urban Policy Research. 2nd ed. 1994.

Kruty, Paul. 1993. "Walter Burley Griffin and the University of Illinois." *Reflections* (Urbana). 9(Spring).

———. 1998. *FLW and Midway Gardens*. Urbana: University of Illinois Press.

———. 1998a. "Chicago 1900: The Griffins Come of Age." In Watson (1998).

———. 2003. "At Work in the Oak Park Studio." *ARRIS*. 14(2003).

———. 2005. "*Prelude to the Prairie Style: Eight Models of Unbuilt Houses by FLW 1893–1901.*" Urbana-Champaign: School of Architecture, University of Illinois.

———. 2011. "Graphic Depictions: The Evolution of Marion Mahony's Architectural Renderings." In Van Zanten (2011).
Lancaster, Clay. 1963. *Japanese Influence in America*. New York: Walton H. Rawls.
———. 1983. *Japanese Influence in America*. New York: Walton H. Rawls.
Langmead, Donald and Donald Leslie Johnson. 2000. *Architectural Excursions: FLW, Holland and Europe*. Westport: Greenwood.
Lang, S. 1952. "The Ideal City from Plato to Howard." *A Review* (London). 112(August).
Lears, T. J. Jackson. 1981. *No Place of Grace: Antimodernism and the Transformation of American Culture 1880–1920*. New York: Pantheon.
LeCocq, Randall. 2013. *FLW in Montana: Darby, Stevensville, and Whitefish*. Helena: Drumlummon Institute.
Leslie. 1877/1974. *Frank Leslie's Historical Register of the . . . Centennial Exposition 1876*. Frank B. Norton, ed. New York: Frank Leslie's Publishing, 1877. Reprint New York: Paddington Press, 1974.
Lethaby, W. R. 1892. *Architecture, Mysticism and Myth*. 2nd ed. London: Shaw & Jackson.
Letters. 1982. *Letters to Apprentices: FLW*. Bruce Brooks Pfeiffer, ed. Fresno: California State University Press.
———. 1984. *Letters to Architects: FLW*. Bruce Brooks Pfeiffer, ed. Fresno: California State University Press.
———. 1986. *Letters to Clients: FLW*. Bruce Brooks Pfeiffer, ed. Fresno: California State University Press.
Levine, George. 1973. "From 'Know-not-Where' to 'Nowhere.' The City in Carlyle, Ruskin, and Morris." In H. J. Dyos and Michael Wolff, ed., *The Victorian City: Images and Realities*. Vol. 2. London: Routledge & Kegan Paul, 1973.
Levine, Neil. 1982. "FLW's Diagonal Planning." In Searing (1982).
———. 1996. *The Architecture of FLW*. Princeton: Princeton University Press.
———. 2009. "Making Community Out of the Grid." In Cleary, 2009.
———. 2016. *The Urbanism of FLW*. Princeton: Princeton University Press.
Lewis, Arnold. 1995. *An Early Encounter with Tomorrow: Europeans, Chicago's Loop, and the World's Columbian Exposition*. Urbana: University of Illinois Press.
Lewis, Lloyd and Henry Justin Smith. 1929. *Chicago: The History of Its Reputation*. New York: Harcourt, Brace.
Lewis, Nelson P. 1916. *The Planning of the Modern City*. New York: John Wiley. Reprint 1922, 2nd ed. 1923.
Lilley, Irene M. 1967. *Friedrich Froebel: A Selection of His Writings*. Cambridge: Cambridge University Press.
Lipman, Jonathan. 1991. "Consecrated Space: The Public Buildings of FLW." In McCarter (1991a).
Ludwig, Delton. 1982. "FLW in the Bitter Root Valley of Montana." *FLWNews*. 5.
Lyttle, Charles H. 1952. *Freedom Moves West: A History of the Western Unitarian Conference 1852–1952*. Boston: Beacon Press.
MacCormac, Richard. 1968. "The Anatomy of Wright's Aesthetic." *AReview* (London). 143 (February).
———. 1974. Froebel's Kindergarten Gifts and the Work of FLW." *EandPB*. 1.
———. 1991. "Froebel's Kindergarten Training and the Early Work of FLW." In McCarter (1991a).
Macmillan Encyclopedia of Architects. 4 vol. New York: Free Press, 1982.
Maldre, Mati and Paul Kruty. 1996. *Walter Burley Griffin in America*. Urbana: University of Illinois Press.
Manieri-Elia, Marion. 1980. "Toward an 'Imperial City': Daniel H. Burnham and the City Beautiful Movement." In Ciucci (1980).
Manson, Grant Carpenter. 1953. "Wright in the Nursery: The Influence of Froebel Education on the Work of FLW." *AReview* (London). 113(June).
———. 1955. "Sullivan and Wright: An Uneasy Union of Celts." *AReview* (London). 118(November).
———. 1958. *FLW to 1910*. New York: Reinhold.

Manuel, Frank E., editor. 1973. *Utopias and Utopian Thought*. London: Penguin.
March, Lionel. 1970. "Imperial City of the Boundless West—Lionel March Describes the Impact of Chicago on the Work of FLW." *Listener* (London). 83(23 April).
March, Lionel and Philip Steadman. 1971. *The Geometry of Environment: An Introduction to Spatial Organization in Design*. London: RIBA.
Mason, Alpheus Thomas, editor. 1956. *Free Government in the Making*. 2nd ed. New York: Oxford University Press.
May, Henry F. 1959. *The End of American Innocence: A Study of the First Years of Our Own Time 1912–1917*. London: J. Cape.
Mayer, Harold M. and Richard C. Wade. 1969. *Chicago: Growth of a Metropolis*. Chicago: University of Chicago Press.
McArthur, Shirley du Fresne. 1983. *FLW American System-Built Homes in Milwaukee*. Milwaukee: North Point Historical Society.
McCarter, Robert, editor. 1991a. *FLW: A Primer on Architectural Principles*. New York: Princeton Architectural Press. 2nd ed. New York: Phaidon.
———. 1991b. "The Integrated Ideal: Ordering Principles in the Architecture of FLW." In McCarter(1991a).
———. 1997. *On and by FLW: A Primer of Architectural Principles*. 2nd ed. New York: Phaidon.
McCarter, Robert, James Steele and Brian Carter. 1999. *FLW*. London: Phaidon.
McCarthy, Michael P. 1977. "Chicago: The Annexation Movement and Progressive Reform." In Ebner and Tobin (1977).
McCormick, Thomas J. 1981. "The Early Work of Joseph Lyman Silsbee." In Searing (1982).
McKenney, Thomas and James Hall, editors. 1836–1844. *History of the Indian Tribes of North America*. Vol. 2. Philadelphia: E. C. Biddle.
McKenzie, R. D. 1921. "The Neighborhood: A Study . . . Columbus, Ohio." *American Journal of Sociology*. 27(1921–1922). Series, see especially number III (November 1921). Expanded in idem., *The Neighborhood: A Study of Local Life in Columbus, Ohio*. Chicago: 1923.
McLean, Robert Craik. 1917. "City Residential Land Development." *WHistory*. 26(January).
Meakin, Budgett. 1905. *Model Factories and Villages: Ideal Conditions of Labour and Housing*. Hampstead: Fisher Unwin.
Meech, Julia. 2001. *FLW and the Art of Japan: The Architect's Other Passion*. New York: Abrams.
Meehan, Patrick J. 1983. *FLW: A Research Guide to Archival Sources*. New York: Garland.
———, editor. 1984. *The Master Architect*. New York: Wiley.
———, editor. 1987. *Truth against the World*. New York: Wiley.
———, editor. 1991. *FLW Remembered*. Washington: Preservation Press.
Menand, Louis. 2001. *The Metaphysical Club*. New York: Farrar, Straus and Giroux.
Menocal, Narciso. 1981. *Architecture as Nature: The Transcendentalist Idea of Louis Sullivan*. Madison: University of Wisconsin Press.
———. 1986. "FLW and the Question of Style." *Journal of Decorative and Propaganda Arts*. 2(Summer).
———. 1992. "Taliesin, The Gilmore House, and the *Flower in the Crannied Wall*." In *Wright Studies*.
Michels, Eileen. 1971. "The Early Drawings of FLW Reconsidered." *JSAH*. 3(December).
Middleton, R. D. 1982. "Viollet-le-Duc." In Macmillan.
Middleton, R. D and David Watkin. 1980. *Neoclassical and Nineteenth Century Architecture*. New York: Abrams.
Mollenhoff, David V. and Mary Jane Hamilton. 1999. *FLW's Monona Terrace: The Enduring Power of a Civic Vision*. Madison: University of Wisconsin Press.
Monroe, Harriet. 1907. "In the Galleries." *Chicago Examiner*. 13(April).
Morgan, Donald and John Altberg. 2008. *The Sutton House McCook, Nebraska*. Hastings, NE: Cornhusker Press.
Morrison, Hugh. 1935. *Louis Sullivan: Prophet of Modern Architecture*. New York: Norton.
Mumford, Lewis. 1952. *Roots of Contemporary American Architecture*. New York: Reinhold.

———. 1954. "The Neighborhood and the Neighborhood Unit." *Town Planning Review*. 24(January).

———. 1961. *The City in History*. New York: Harcourt Brace & World.

Munari, Bruno. 1965. *Discovery of the Square*. New York: George Wittenborn.

Murrin, John M., Paul E. Johnson, James M. McPherson, Gary Gerstle, Emily S. Rosenberg, and Norman L. Rosenberg. 1996. *Liberty, Equality, Power: A History of the American People*. New York: Harcourt Brace.

Nash, Gary B., Julie Roy Jeffrey, John R. Howe, Peter J. Frederick, Allen F. Davis, and Allan M. Winkler, editors. 1994. *The American People: Creating a Nation and a Society*. 3rd ed. New York: HarperCollins.

Nichols, Frederick D. 1910. "The Bitter Root Valley Irrigation Company." *Western News* (Hamilton). May, supplement.

Nickel, Richard and Aaron Siskind. 2010. With John Vinci and Ward Miller. *The Complete Architecture of Adler and Sullivan*. Chicago: Richard Nickel Committee.

Noffsinger, James Philip. 1955. *The Influence of the École des Beaux-Arts on the Architects of the United States*. Washington, DC: Catholic University of America Press.

Norberg-Schulz, Christian. 1965. *Intentions in Architecture*. Cambridge, MA: MIT Press.

———. 1971. *Existence, Space and Architecture*. New York: Praeger.

Nute, Kevin. 1993. *FLW and Japan*. New York: Van Nostrand Reinhold.

Nye, Russell B. 1959. *Midwestern Progressive Politics . . . Origins and Development 1870–1958*. East Lansing: Michigan State University Press.

Ochsner, Jeffrey Karl. 1994. *Shaping Seattle Architecture: A Historical Guide to the Architects*. Seattle: University of Washington Press.

Ochsner, Jeffrey Karl and Dennis Alan Andersen. 1989. "Adler and Sullivan's Seattle Opera House Project." *JSAH*. 48(September).

Ockman, Joan and Rebecca Williamson, editors. 2012. *Architecture School: Three Centuries of Educating Architects in North America*. Cambridge, MA: MIT Press.

O'Gormann, James F. 1973. *The Architecture of Frank Furness*. Philadelphia: Museum of Art/University of Pennsylvania Press.

O'Malley, Therese and Mark Treib, editors. 1995. *Regional Garden Design in the United States*. Washington: Dumbarton Oaks Research Library and Collection.

O'Neill, William L. 1975. *The Progressive Years: America Comes of Age*. New York: HarperCollins College Division.

Park, Robert E., Ernest W. Burgess and Roderick D. McKenzie. 1925. *The City*. Chicago: University of Chicago Press. Reprint 1967.

Patterson, David W. 2013. "FLW"s Musical Origins." *FLW Quarterly*. 24(Fall, no.4).

Pease, Otis, editor. 1962. *The Progressive Years: The Spirit and Achievement of American Reform*. New York: George Braziller.

Peisch, Mark L. 1965. *The Chicago School of Architecture: Early Followers of Sullivan and Wright*. New York: Columbia University Press.

Pennell, Patrick. 1991. "Academic Tradition and the Individual Talent." In McCarter (1991a).

Pérez-Gomez, Alberto. 1983. *Architecture and the Crisis of Modern Science*. Cambridge, MA: MIT Press.

Perry, Clarence A. 1924. "The Relation of Neighborhood Forces . . . from the Social Point of View." National Conference of Social Work. *Proceedings*. Chicago.

———. 1929. "The Neighborhood Unit: A Scheme of Arrangement for the Family Life Community." Monograph in vol. 7. *Regional Survey of New York and Its Environs*. New York: New York Regional Plan.

Peter, John. 1994. *The Oral History of Modern Architecture*. New York: Harry N. Abrams.

Peterson, Jon A. 1976. "The City Beautiful Movement. Forgotten Origins and Lost Meanings." *JUrban*. 2(August).

———. 1985. "The Nation's First Comprehensive Plan." *JAIA*. 51(Spring).

Pevsner, Nikolaus. 1979. *A History of Building Types*. London: Thames & Hudson.

Pfeiffer, Bruce Brooks. 1984–1988. *FLW*. 12 vols. Tokyo: A.D.A. Edita. Each volume is identified by its inclusive dates, e.g. *Monograph 1902–1906* is cited as Pfeiffer (02–06).
———. 1985. *Treasures of Taliesin*. Fresno: California State University Press.
———. 1987. *FLW: His Living Voice*. Fresno: California State University Press.
———, editor. 1992. *FLW Collected Writings. Volume 1. 1894–1930*. New York: Rizzoli.
———. 1997. "FLW Complete List of Works." In McCarter (1997).
———. 2011. *FLW 1885–1916: The Complete Works/das Gesamtwerk/l'oeuvre Complète*. Peter Gössel, editor. Köln/London: Taschen.
Pierce, Bessie Louise. 1957. *A History of Chicago*. vol. 3. *The Rise of a Modern City 1871–1893*. Chicago: University of Chicago Press.
Pierre, Dorathi Bock, editor. 1989. *Memoirs of an American Artist: Sculptor Richard W. Bock*. Los Angeles: C. C. Publishing.
Pinnell, Patrick. 1991. "Academic Tradition and the Individual Talent: Similarity and Difference in the Formation of FLW." In McCarter (1991a).
Porphyrios, Demetri. 1977. "The 'End' of Styles." *Oppositions*. 8.
———. 1982. *Sources of Modern Eclecticism: Studies on Alvar Aalto*. London: Academy Editions.
Price, George M. 1914. *The Modern Factory: Safety, Sanitation, and Welfare*. New York: J. Wiley and Sons.
Quinan, Jack. 1982. "FLW's Reply to Russell Sturgis." *JSAH*. 51(October).
———. 1987. *FLW's Larkin Building: Myth and Fact*. New York: MIT Press. Chicago: University of Chicago Press, 2006.
Reed Henry H. 1954. "Viollet-le-Duc and the USA: A Footnote to History." *Liturgical Arts*. 23(November).
Reps, John W. 1965a. *The Making of Urban America*. Princeton: Princeton University Press.
———. 1965b. "Requiem for Zoning." *Planning 1964*. Chicago: American Society of Planning Officials.
———. 1997. *Canberra 1912: Plans and Planners of the Australian Capital Competition*. Carlton South: Melbourne University Press.
Resek, Carl, editor. 1967. *The Progressives*. Indianapolis: Bobbs-Merrill.
Rice, Bradley Robert. 1977. *Progressive Cities: The Commission Government Movement . . . 1901–1920*. Austin: University of Texas Press.
Riley, Terrance. 1994. *FLW Architect*. New York: Museum of Modern Art.
Robinson, Charles Mulford. 1913. *The Improvement of Towns and Cities or the Practical Basis of Civic Aesthetics*. 4th ed. New York: Putnam.
Roche, John. 1990. "Democratic Space: The Ecstatic Geography of Walt Whitman and FLW." *Walt Whitman Quarterly Review*. 6(Spring).
Rockey, John. 1983. "From Vision to Reality: Victorian Ideal Cities and Model Towns in the Genesis of Ebenezer Howard's Garden City." *Town Planning Review*. 54(January).
Roe, Michael. 1984. *Nine Australian Progressives*. Brisbane: University of Queensland Press.
Root, John. 1891. "Architects of Chicago." *Inland Architect*. 16(January).
Roper, Laura Wood. 1973. *FLO: A Biography of Frederick Law Olmsted*. Baltimore: Johns Hopkins University Press.
Ross, Denman, W. 1907. *A Theory of Pure Design: Harmony, Balance, Rhythm*. Boston: Houghton Mifflin.
Roth, Leland M., editor. 1983. *America Builds*. New York: Harper & Row.
Rousseau, Jean-Jacques. 1762. *Emile, or, On Education*. Paris. Reference herein is to Barbara Foxley, trans., *Emile*. New York/London: Dutton, 1966.
Rubin, Jeanne S. 1989. "The Froebel-Wright Kindergarten Connection: A New Perspective." *JSAH*. 48(March). Critical responses in letters to editor, *JSAH*, 48(December 1989).
Rykwert, Joseph. 1982. *The Necessity of Artifice: Ideas in Architecture*. London: Rizzoli.
Schaffer, Daniel, editor. 1988. *Two Centuries of American Planning*. London: Mansell.
Schmitt, Peter J. 1969. *Back to Nature: The Arcadian Myth in Urban America*. New York: Oxford University Press.

Schultz, Stanley K. 1989. *Constructing Urban Cultures: American Cities and City Planning 1800–1920*. Philadelphia: Temple University Press.
Schwarting, Jon Michael. 1981. "The Lesson of Rome." *Harvard Architecture Review*. 2(Spring).
Scott, Mel. 1969. *American City Planning Since 1890*. Berkeley: University of California Press.
Scully, Vincent J. Jr. 1971. *The Single Style and the Stick Style*. 2nd ed. New Haven: Yale University Press.
———. 1980. "FLW and the Stuff of Dreams." *Perspecta*. 16.
Secrest, Meryle. 1992. *FLW: A Biography*. New York: Knopf.
Seligmann, Werner. 1991. "Evolution to the Prairie House." In McCarter (1991a).
Sergeant, John. 1976a. *FLW's Usonian Houses*. New York: Whitney.
———. 1976b. "Woof and Warp: Spatial Analysis of FLW's Usonian Houses." *EandPB*. 3.
Shoppell, R. W. 1983. Turn-of-the-Century Houses, Cottages, and Villas. New York: Dover. (Each originally published by "The Co-operative Building Plan Association, Architects, New York.")
Silver, Christopher. 1985. "Neighborhood Planning in Historical Perspective." *APA Journal*. 51(Spring).
Siry, Joseph M. 1988. *Carson-Pirie-Scott. Louis Sullivan and the Chicago Department Store*. Chicago: University of Chicago Press.
———. 1991a "FLW's Unity Temple and Architecture for Liberal Religion in Chicago, 1885–1909." *Art Bulletin*. 73(June).
———. 1991b. "The Abraham Lincoln Center in Chicago." *JSAH*. 50(September).
———. 1996. *Unity Temple: FLW and Architecture for Liberal Religion*. New York: Cambridge University Press.
———. 2002. *The Chicago Auditorium Building, Adler and Sullivan's Architecture and the City*. Chicago, University of Chicago Press.
Sitte, Camillo. 1889. *City Planning According to Artistic Principles*. Trans. George R. Collins and Christiana Crasemann Collins. New York: Columbia University Press, 1965. Originally published as *Der Stadtebau nach seinen künstlerischen-Grudsaten*. Vienna. 1889.
Smith, Carl. 1995. *Urban Disorder and the Shape of Belief*. Chicago: University of Chicago Press.
Smith, Donald B. 2007. *Honoré Jaxon: Prairie Visionary*. Regina: Coteau Books.
Smith, Norris Kelly. 1979. *FLW: A Study in Architectural Content*. New York: Prentice-Hall.
Sorell, Susan Karr. 1970. "Silsbee: The Evolution of a Personal Architectural Style." *PSR*. 7(4).
Spann, Edward K. 1989. *Brotherly Tomorrows Movements for a Cooperative Society in America 1820–1920*. New York: Columbia University Press.
Spencer, Brian A., editor. 1979. *The Prairie Style Tradition*. New York: Whitney Library of Design.
Spencer, Robert C. 1900. "The Work of FLW." *AReview* (Boston). 7(June).
Sprague, Paul E. 1976. *Guide to FLW and Prairie School Architecture in Oak Park*. Oak Park: The Municipal Corporation.
———. 1979. *The Drawings of Louis Henry Sullivan*. Princeton: Princeton University Press.
———. 1987. "Review of Twombly (1986)." *JSAH*. 46(December).
———. 1990. *FLW and Madison: Eight Decades of Artistic and Social Interaction*. Madison: Elvehjem Museum of Art, University of Wisconsin.
———. 2005. "The Evolution of Wright's Long, Narrow Hip Roofs." In Kruty (2005).
———. 2005a. "Appendix Documenting the Date of Design of Eight Unbuilt Houses by FLW." In Kruty (2005).
Stead, William T. 1894. *If Christ Came to Chicago*. New York: 1964 reprint.
Stevensville Historical Society. 1971. *Montana Genesis*. Missoula: Mountain Press.
Stilgoe, John R. 1988. *Borderland: Origins of the American Suburb 1820–1935*. New Haven: Yale University Press.
Stiny, G. 1980. "Kindergarten Grammars: Designing with Froebel's Building Gifts." *EandPB*. 7.
Storrer, William Allin. 1979. *The Architecture of FLW*. 2nd ed. Cambridge, MA: MIT Press.
———. 1993. *The FLW Companion*. Chicago: University of Chicago Press.
Strauss, Anselm L. 1968. *The American City: A Sourcebook of Urban Imagery*. Chicago: Aldine Publishing.

Sturgis, Russell. 1908. "The Larkin Building in Buffalo." *ARecord*. 23(April).
Sullivan, Louis. 1905. "Letter to the Editor." *The Craftsman*. 8(July).
———.1918. *Kindergarten Chats and Other Writings*. Isabella Athey, compiler. New York: Wittenborn, Schultz, 1947. New York: Dover, 1979.
———. 1924. *The Autobiography of an Idea*. Washington: A.I.A. New York: Dover reprint, 1956.
Sutcliffe, Anthony. 1980. *The Rise of Modern Urban Planning*. London: Mansell.
———. 1981. *Towards the Planned City*. Oxford: Oxford University Press.
Sutton, Robert P., editor. 1976. *The Prairie State: A Documentary History of Illinois*. . . . Grand Rapids: Erdmans.
Sweeney, Robert L. 1978. *FLW: An Annotated Bibliography*. Los Angeles: Hennessey & Ingalls.
———. 1987a. "The Coonley Playhouse Riverside, Illinois." *FLWNews*. 1(November).
Tallmadge, Thomas. 1908. "The 'Chicago School'." *AReview* (Boston). 15(April).
Tauscher, Cathy and Peter Hughes. 1999. "Jenkin Lloyd Jones." Cambridge, MA: Unitarian Universalist Historical Society Pamphlet.
Teaford, Jon C. 1993. *Cities of the Heartland: The Rise and Fall of the Industrial Midwest*. Bloomington: Indiana University Press.
Thomas, John L. 1983. *Alternative America: Henry George, Edward Bellamy, Henry Demarest Lloyd and the Adversary Tradition*. Cambridge, MA: Harvard University Press.
Tishler, William H., editor. 2000. *Midwestern Landscape Architecture*. Urbana: University of Illinois Press.
Troedsson, Carl B. 1957. *The City, the Automobile, and Man*. Los Angeles/ Sweden: The Author.
Turak, Theodore. 1991. "Mr. Wright and Mrs. Coonley. An Interview with Elizabeth Coonley Faulkner." In Wilson and Robinson (1991).
Twombly, Robert C. 1979. *Frank Lloyd Wright: His Art and His Architecture*. New York: Wiley.
———. 1986. *Louis Sullivan*. Chicago: University of Chicago Press.
———, editor. 1988. *Louis Sullivan: The Public Papers*. Chicago: University of Chicago Press.
Upton, Dell. 1998. *Architecture in the United States*. New York: Oxford University Press.
Van Zanten, David. 1989. "Schooling in the Prairie School: Wright's Early Style as a Communicable System." In Bolon et al. (1989).
———, editor. 2011. *Marion Mahony Reconsidered*. Chicago: University of Chicago Press.
———. 2013. "The Ambition of Reach of Chicago Progressive Architecture." In Van Zanten (2013a)
———, editor. 2013a. *Drawing the Future: Chicago Architecture on the International Stage, 1900–1925*. Evanston, IL: Northwestern University Press.
Van Zanten, David and Cervin Robinson. 2000. *Sullivan's City: The Meaning of Ornament for Louis Sullivan*. New York: W. W. Norton.
Velez, Diana. 1983. "Late Nineteenth-century Spanish Progressivism: Arturo Soria's Linear City." *JUrban*. 9(February).
Vernon, Christopher D. 1991. "Walter Burley Griffin, Landscape Architect." In Garner (1991).
———. 1996. "Berlage in America." In Jan Moleman, editor, *The New Movement in the Netherlands, 1924–1936*. Rotterdam: 010.
———. 2002. Introduction to Wilhelm Miller, *The Prairie Spirit in Landscape Gardening*. Amherst: University of Massachusetts Press, 2002.
Vidler, Anthony. 1977. "The Idea of Type: The Transformation of the Academic Ideal, 1750–1830." *Oppositions*. 8.
Viollet-le-Duc, E.-E. 1854–1868. *Dictionnaire raisonné de l'architecture francaise due XIe au XVIe siécle*. 10 vol. Èdition B. Bance and A. Morel. Reprint, Paris, 1967.
———. 1863/1872. *Entretiens sur l'architecture*. 2 vol. Paris. Trans. Henry Van Brunt as *Discourses on Architecture*. Boston: 1875/1881, and by Benjamin Bucknall as *Lectures on Architecture*, Vol. 1, London: 1877, and *Discourses on Architecture*, Vol. 2, London, 1882.
———. 1873. *Histoire d'une maison*. Paris. Trans. by Benjamin Bucknall as *How to Build a House: An Architectural Novelette*. London: Sampson Low, Marston, Searle, & Rivington, 1874.
———. 1875. *Habitations de l'habitation humaine de puis less temps préhistoriques*. Paris. Trans by Benjamin Bucknall as *The Habitations of Men in All Ages*. London: Sampson Low, Maarston, Searle, & Rivington, 1876, reprint, Ann Arbor: Gryphon Books, 1971.

———. 1881. *Histoire d'un dessinateur*. . . . Paris. Trans by Virginia Champlin as *Learning to Draw or the Story of a Young Designer*. New York: G. P. Putnam, 1881.
Visser, Kristin. 1992. *FLW & the Prairie School in Wisconsin*. Madison: Prairie Oak Press.
Watson, Anne, editor. 1998. *Beyond Architecture: Marion Mahony and Walter Burley Griffin – American, Australia, India*. Sydney: Power Museum.
Wegg, Talbot. 1970. "FLW versus the USA." *AIAJ*. 53(February).
Weimer, David R. 1962. *City and Country in America*. New York: Appleton Century Crofts.
Weingarden, Lauren S. 2009. *Louis H. Sullivan and a 19th-Century Poetics of Naturalized Architecture*. Farham/Burlington: Ashgate.
White, Dana F. 1988. "Frederick Law Olmsted, the Placemaker." In Schaffer (1988).
White letters. Nancy K. Morris Smith, editor. 1971. "Letters, 1903–1906, by Charles E. White, Jr. from the Studio of FLW." *JAE*. 25(Fall 1971).
Wiebe, Robert H. 1967. *The Search for Order 1877–1920*. New York: Hill & Wang.
———. 1973. "The Progressive Years, 1900–1917." In Cartwright/Watson (1973).
Wilson, Richard Guy. 1979. "Architecture, Landscape and City Planning." In idem., *The American Renaissance 1876–1919*. Brooklyn: The Brooklyn Museum, 1979.
———. 1987. "Chicago and the International Arts and Crafts Movements: Progressive and Conservative Tendencies." In Zukovsky (1987).
———. 1989. *The City Beautiful Movement*. Baltimore: Johns Hopkins University Press.
Wilson, Richard Guy and Sidney K. Robinson, editors. 1991. *Architecture in America: Visions and Revisions*. Ames: Iowa State University Press.
Wilson, Stuart. 1967. "The 'Gifts' of Frederick Froebel." *JSAH*. 26(December).
Withey, Henry F. and Elsie Rathburn Withey. 1956. *Biographical Dictionary of American Architects (Deceased)*. Los Angeles: New Age.
Wright, Frank Lloyd. 1900. "The Architect." *Brickbuilder*. 9(9 June). A version in *Construction News*, same title, 10(6 June) and 20(23 June); also condensed as "A Philosophy of Fine Art," In Gutheim (1941).
———. 1901a. "A Home in a Prairie Town." *Ladies Home Journal*. 18(February).
———. 1901b. "A Small House with 'Lots of Room in It'." *Ladies Home Journal*. 18(July).
———. 1901c. "The Art and Craft of the Machine." Chicago Architectural Club. *Catalog of the Fourteenth Annual Exhibition*.
———. 1906. "The New Larkin Administration Building." *The Larkin Idea*. 6.
———. 1907. "A Fireproof House for $5000." *Ladies Home Journal*. 24(April).
———. 1908. "In the Cause of Architecture." *ARecord*. 23(March). Reprint, abridged, *Building* (Sydney), 14 April 1914.
———. 1910. *Studies and Executed Buildings of FLW*. Chicago: Ralph Fletcher Seymour, and Berlin: Verlag Ernst Wasmuth A. B. Preferred reprints Palos Park: Prairie School Press, 1975, and New York: Rizzoli, 1998.
———. 1912. *The Japanese Print. An Interpretation*. Chicago: Ralph Fletcher Seymour. Reprint, New York: Horizon, 1967.
———. 1914. "In the Cause of Architecture. Second Paper." *ARecord*. 35(May).
———. 1916. "Plan by FLW." In Yeomans (1916). Partly republished in Pfeiffer (1992).
———. 1921. FLW. *Wendingen* (Amsterdam). 6(11).
———. 1923. *Experimenting with Human Lives*. Los Angeles: Fine Arts Society. [Chicago: Ralph Fletcher Seymour]
———. 1925a. *The Life-Work of FLW*. Santpoort, Netherlands: C. A. Mees.
———. 1925b. "In the Cause of Architecture: The Third Dimension." *Wendingen* (Amsterdam). 4 & 5.
———. 1928. "In the Cause of Architecture. I. The Logic of the Plan." *ARecord*. 63(January).
———. 1932. *An Autobiography*. New York: Longmans Green. (Reprint 1933, 1938)
———. 1935. "Form and Function." *Saturday Review* (14 December). Review of Hugh Morrison, *Louis Sullivan: Prophet of Modern Architecture*.
———. 1938. "FLW." *Forum* (Supplement). 68(January).

———. 1939. "Speech to the AFA." *Federal Architect*. 9(January).
———. 1943. *An Autobiography*. 2nd ed. New York: Duel Sloan & Pearce. (London: Faber & Faber/Hyperion Press, 1945; *Mon Autobiographie* Paris: Librairie Plon, 1955.)
———. 1955. *An American Architecture*. New York: Horizon.
———. 1957. *A Testament*. New York: Horizon.
———. 1958. *The Living City*. New York: Horizon.
———. 1959. *Drawings for a Living Architecture*. New York: Horizon.
———. 1977. *An Autobiography*. 3rd ed. New York: Horizon. New York: Barnes & Noble, 1998.
Wright, Gwendolyn. 1980. *Moralism and the Model Home*. Chicago: University of Chicago Press.
———. 1983. *Building the Dream: A Social History of Housing in America*. Cambridge, MA: MIT Press.
———. 1988. "Architectural Practice and Social Vision in Wright's Early Designs." In Bolon (1989).
———. 1994. "FLW and the Domestic Landscape." In Riley (1994).
Wright, Gwendolyn and Janet Parks, editors. 1996. *The History of History in American Schools of Architecture 1865-1975*. New York: Princeton Architectural Press.
Wright, John Lloyd. 1946. *My Father Who Is on Earth*. New York: Putnam. Reprint New York: Dover, 1992.
Wright Studies. 1992. *Taliesin 1911–1914*, Vol. l. Narciso G. Menocal, editor. Carbondale: Southern Illinois University Press, 1992.
Yale. 1986. "Drawings and Photographs of Unity Temple." *Perspecta 22: The Yale Architectural Journal*. New York: Rizzoli.
Yeomans, Alfred B. 1916. *City Residential Land Development*. Chicago: University of Chicago Press.
Zinn, Howard. 1999. *A People's History of the United States 1492—Present*. New York: Harper Collins.
Zueblin, Charles. 1903. *American Municipal Progress: Chapters in Municipal Sociology*. New York: Macmillan.
Zukowsky, John, editor. 1987. *Chicago Architecture 1872–1922: Birth of a Metropolis*. Munich: Prestel-Verlag; Chicago: Art Institute of Chicago.

Manuscripts

Boris, Eileen Cynthia. MS.1981. "Art and Labor: John Ruskin, William Morris, and the Craftsman Ideal in America, 1876–1915." PhD dissertation. Brown University.
Donnell, Courtney Graham. MS.1974. "Prairie School Town Planning 1900–1915, Wright, Griffin, Drummond." MA thesis, New York University.
Frances, Ellen E. MS. 1982. "Progressivism and the American House: Architecture as an Agent of Social Reform." MA thesis, University of Oregon.
Griffin, Marion Mahony. MS.1949. "Magic of America." Typescript, New-York Historical Society.
Jolly, Bridget Elizabeth. MS.1990. "Aspects of Eclecticism and Development in the Work of Richard Buckminster Fuller." MA thesis, Flinders University.
Joncas, Richard. MS.1991. " 'Pure form.' The Origins and Development of FLW's Nonrectangular Geometry." PhD dissertation, Stanford University.
Lewis, Dudley Arnold. MS.1962. "Evaluation of American Architecture by European Critics 1875–1900." PhD. dissertation. University of Wisconsin. Refocused in Lewis (1995).
Thomas, Richard Harlan. MS.1967. "Jenkin Lloyd Jones: Lincoln's Soldier of Civic Righteousness." PhD dissertation, Rutgers University.
Wright, Frank Lloyd. MS.1918. "Chicago Culture." Typescript copy, Manuscript Division, Library of Congress. Edited & condensed version Gutheim (1941), pp.85–99; condensed in Collected Writings, vol. 1.
Zeisler, Dorothy J. MS.1982. "The History of Irrigation and the Orchard Industry in the Bitter Root Valley." MA thesis, University of Montana.

Index

Appendices are not indexed.
Numbers in italic **bold** indicate figures.

Abbott, Edith 250
Abraham Lincoln Center 82–2, 165–9, *167*, *168*, 174, 207; cubic abstraction 117; Rev. Jones' influence 117, 165–9; Rev. Jones' program 166; Wright & Perkins Associated (Architects 168, *169*)
Acadia College, Nova Scotia 57
Adams, Richard P. 108n133
Adams, Robert M. 183
Adams, Thomas 207, 235, 242
Adams Building, S.S Marie 183–4
Addams, Jane 9, 10, 11, 41, 55, 83; and Arts & Crafts Society 18–19; and FLW 132; and Lydia Lawrence 59; and Rev. Jones 81
Adelaide, South Australia 202; and public parklands 213
Adelman, Benjamin, house 180
Adler, Dankmar 37, 46, 48, 85–90, 98; father Liebman 85; rational building 90; theory vs Sullivan 88–90
Adler & Sullivan 4, 48, 71, 76, 85–90, 132, 143, 179; and FLW collaborator 108n136; influence 177; and Walter Wilcox 85
aesthetic inclinations 91–2
Aesthetic Movement 112
agrarian movement 7
AIA *see* American Institute of Architects
Alabama Polytechnic Institute 247
Albright, Marrison 191
Alfred Nobel Elementary School 117
Algerian architecture 121
Allen, Russell C. house *120*, 191
All Souls Church, Chicago 54, 72–5, 84, 117, 166, *169*
All Souls Church Fourth Annual 1887 74, 75
Alofsin, Anthony 47, 81, 93, 135, 208
Alvord, John W. 241
American Architect 87
American City 207
American City Bureau 208
American City Government 8
American Civic League for Civic Improvement 233
American Congress of Liberal Religious Societies 82
American Home Missionary Society 232
American Institute of Architects AIA 25, 88, 103n33, 114, 188; Illinois Chapter 235
American Journal of Education 39
American Planning Association 242; founding 242
American Unitarian Association 82
American Woman's Home, The 206
American Womans Suffrage Association 83
Amherst College 87, 232
Amor Institute of Technology 113
anarchism 12
Anti-Poverty Society 10
Arbeiter-Zeitung, Chicago 23
Arcadia 202
Archer, John 212–13
Architect 87
Architectural Annual 113
Architectural Club 207
architectural education: and French architects 207
Architectural *Forum* 62, *122*
Architectural League of America 4, 27, 46, 87, 100, 113–14, 116; city participation 113; foundation 113; Sullivan's papers 1899, 1900 87
Architectural Record 62, 88, 116, 190
architecture: participation 127
Arden, Pennsylvania 17
Arnheim, Rudolph *123*
Arnold, Matthew 13
Aronovici, Carol 241
"Art and Craft of the Machine" 3, 30n69, 93, 100, 112, 113; Wright quotes on city 191
art deco 112
Art for America 112
articulation 96, 136–7, 149
Art Institute of Chicago 12, 14, 48; architectural studies 113; School of Art 56, 57
art nouveau 112

Arts and Crafts/Movement 62, 93, 99, 145, 182, 186; idioms 133; magazines 132
Arts and Crafts Society 207
Ashbee, Charles 106n102, 202; spell of Japan 132
Ashbee, Charles 93
Asia 100; architecture 100
Association of Federal Architects 15
Atlantic Monthly, The 13
Atwood, Charles B. 24, 32n126
Auditorium Building 85
Austin, Henry Warren 78
Austin, Illinois 164
Austin, Texas 57
An Autobiography, FLW: 1932 edition 47, 32, 71; 1943 edition 15, 50
Avery Coonley Junior Elementary School 61
axiality vs asymmetry 184ff

Bach, Emil, house *187*
Bagley, Frederick 83
Bailey, Liberty Hyde: Poem "Voice of the Country-side" 53–4
Baker, Frank J. 186
Baker, Herbert 207
Baker, Ralph, house 186
Balch, Oscar B. 186
Banham, Peter Reyner 177
Baptist Education Society 23
Barnard, Henry 39–40
Barnes-Crosby Co. 56
Barnet, Mary Paulding 56
Barney, Hiram 105n68
Barnsdall, Aline 15, 100; house 151; L.A. theater 122; and Olive Hill, Hollywood 15
Barrett, Nathan F. 23, 213; Barrett/Ranlett "village property" 213–*14*
Bartholomew, Harland 250
Bartlett, D.C. 224
Barton, George 185
Batchelor, Peter 204; on Howard's idea 204
Bauer, Augustus 85
Beard, Charles A. 7, 17, 28n24; *American Government and Politics* 28n25
Bear Valley Cemetery, Wisconsin 104n53
Beau Arts, Paris 19
Bebb, Charles Herbert 86–7, 165; and Adler & Sullivan 165; and C.P. Dose 165, 266
Beecher, Catherine 206
Beers, Clay & Dutton 103n33
Behrendt, Curt 191
Belknap, Giles, project 164
Bellamy, Edward 13, 18; and Nationalist Clubs 18
Beloit College 183
Beman, Solon Spenser 23
Bennett, Edward H. 26
Benoit-Lcvi(y), Georges 235
Berg, Carl 247

Berlaga, Hendrik 94, 111
Berlin, Germany 57, 208
Bernhard, Wilhelm 243, 246, 248; quarter-section competition 243–4
Berwyn, Chicago 164
Beye, Cudworth 171
Beye Boathouse 171–3, *172*, 173, 186; comparisons with previous and (future buildings 173)
Bierstadt, Albert 38
Billerica, Massachusetts 246
Bingham, George C. 38
Bismarck, Otto von 23
Bitter Root/Nichols/Waller village house plan *221*
Bitter Root River 224
Bitter Root town 212, 226–8; analysis 227–8; BRVICo program 227; electric train line 229; town geometry *229*; town plan *228*
Bitter Root Valley 224; Big Ditch 224, 225; description of village/town area 231–2
Bitter Root Valley Irrigation Company (BRIVCo) 224; inn description as built 231; work camps 230
Bitter Root village 219, *220*; bird's eye view *231*; BRIVCo engineer's plan 230; description 230; houses 21, 221; plan of area *232*
Black, William 15
Blaine, Anita McCormick 63n16
Blaine, Mrs Emmons 57
Blake, William 38
Blavatsky, HP. 11
Blossom, George, house: and Silsbee's 179
Blow, Susan 43; and Hull-House 51; and St Louis 51
Blythe, James E. 56
Bock Richard 133, 145; studio-residence *148*, 191
Bogk, F.C. house 100, 191
Bohrer, Florence Fifer 53
Bok, Edward 216; Modern Suburban Houses 216
Booth, Sherman 10
Borthwick, Jessie 183
Borthwick, Mamah, *see* Cheney, Mamah Borthwick
Boston, Massachusetts 41–3, 48; Boston 1915 206
Boston Unitarians 40, 51
Boullè, Etienne 45, 96
Bourne, Randolph 249; city centre competition 249
Bourneville, Birmingham 203
Bouton, Edward H.; Roland Park, Baltimore 242
Boynton, E.E., house 147
Boynton, Louis H. 243

Bradley, B. Harley, house 180, 185, *186*; interior *192*
Brady, Matthew B. 12
Bragdon, Claude 11; FLW's reaction 125; and mathematics 125'
Brandon, Manitoba 183
Brannkyka, Sweden 243
Breckinridge, Sophonisba 249
Brickbulder 190, 206
Brighton, Staten Island, New York 213
Broadacre City 9, 18, 62, 203, 212; Little Farms 84, 203, 212
Brochure, Philippe 186
Bronx, New York 247
Brookfield kindergarten 61
Brooks, H. Allen 90, 133; on pure design 114; on W. Griffin 134
Broome, Sweden 243
Brown, Charles Francis 11
Brown, Glen 25
Browne, Maurice 15
Browning, Robert 15
Brunt, Henry Van 93
Bryan, William Jennings 7, 9
Bryant, William Cullen 15, 37, 213
Buck, L. Irene 57
Buckingham, James S. 202
Bucknall, Benjamin 98
Buena Park, Chicago 76
Buffalo, New York 48, 75, 132, 169
Building Progress 159n1
Bull, Storm 74
Bull, William 202
Bull Moose Party 28n23
Bureau of Social Research 241
Burling & Adler 16, 86
Burnham, Daniel 24, 204–7; commercial venture 233; discussion 233–4; Luxfer competition juror 135; *Plan of* Chicago 1908 25–6, 233
Burnham & Root 85, 207
Burning, Edward 86
Burritt, Ruth 42
Byrne, Francis Barry 145, 188–90; on FLW's floor plans 188

California colonial 120
Campement d"Ours Island, Ontario 183–4
Canada 183
Canberra, Australia: competition 145, 206; finance 206; and W. Griffin 210n43
Caparn, Harold A. 235
Capital Journal buildings 126
Carl Schurz Public High School 118
Carlyle, Thomas 9, 5, 38–9, 91, 112
Carnegie, Andrew 24
Carnegie Music Hall 86
Carondolet, St. Louis 43
Carson Pirie Scott & Co 91

Carthage College, Illinois 55
Case Deering house 120
Cassatt, Mary 100
Castle of Otranto: A Gothic Story, The 98
Catalo, Pietro 202
Catholic community 73
Catlin, George 38
"In the cause of architecture" 1908 88, 109n162, 190
Celtic cross 122
Centennial International Exhibit'n 21, 42
Central Art Association 141
central place town 201–2
Central Safety Deposit Company 10
Chapin, Augusta Jane 83
Charnley, James, house 177, 179
Charnley-Persky House Museum Foundation 177; Society of Architectural Historians 177
Chase, Mary Ellen: on Hillside Home School 53
Chaux, France 201
Cheltenham Beach Resort 10d
Cheney, Mamah Borthwick 12, 37, 62, 80, 183; death 80
Chicago, Illinois 4ff; Arts and Crafts Society 18; Commercial Club 25; Fine Arts Building 1893 32n126; Fire 1871 20, 85; and German as *lingua universal* 23; Merchant's Club 25; population 6; Special Park Commission 1899 207; Special Street Railway Committee 233; Transportation Building 100
Chicago (School) Board of Education 43, 78, 117–18, 207
Chicago Architectural Club 87, 113, 117, 219, 233, 243; and Art Institute 114
Chicago Avenue Church; aka Moody Church 86
Chicago "battle cry" 245
Chicago City Club 232–9; 1913 exhibition 222–3, 234, 243; 1913 National Housing Conference 234; description 243–4; Public Education Committee 59, 188, 222–3; Quarter-Section Competition 234–6 (1912 program 234–5); FLW's plan 234–43 (description 235–40; reaction 240–1); R. Unwin paper 233
Chicago Commons 13, 59, 84, 207
Chicago Evening Post 218
Chicago Inter-Ocean 145
Chicago Little Theatre 15
Chicago Press Club 14
Chicago *Record-Herald* 233
Chicago River 246
Chicago School of Architecture 113
Chicago School of Civics & Philan-thropy 57, 83, 244
Chicago Stock Exchange Building 164
Chicago Tribune 13, 233, 244–6 editorial policy, "new Chicago 245; Hyde's articles

on need for scientific planning 245; Tower competition 246
Chicago Woman's City Club 207, 234; exhibition 1912 243–5
Chicago Woman's Club 234, 243; 1913 exhibition 243–5
Christian Catholic Church 191
Christian Science 59; Church 59
Church of All Souls 145
city, linear 203
city: 19th century 202–4; one type, ad hoc; one, reformed 202–4
city, "one great social organism" 208
City Beautiful Movement 24, 25–7, 205–8
city design *ab initio* 202
City National Bank, Mason City 56
city planning 205–8; British, four types 212–13; education 205–6; international activity 207–8; profession 205–8; "science" of 206
City Planning According to Artistic Principles 204
city renewal, associations 207
City Residential Land Development, Studies in Planing 1916 235
city scientific 96, 203–4, 240; closing thoughts 250
"civic patriotism" 205
civil engineering UW 72–4, 102n18
Civil War 3, 6, 12, 41, 81
Clark, W. Irving, house 179
Clay, William Wilson 71, 75, 103n333
Cleveland, Ohio 4, 16, 87
Cliff Dwellers Club 10, 11, 14, 15, 245
Clifton, Illinois 56
Cobb, Henry Ives 78
Cochran, John Lewis 76, 180
Cole, Thomas 38
Coleridge, Samuel Taylor 37
Colgate University 52
Collier's magazine 14
Collins, Christiane 204
Collins, George 204
Collins, Peter 94
Colonial Office, London 206
colonial town-forms 202
Columbia University 28n24, 57, 232; Teachers College 57
Comey, Arthur 206, 242, 243, 246
Commager, Henry Steele 8
Commoditie, Firmenes, & Delight 5
Commons, John R. 17
communitarian theory 243
Community Centre Movement 246
Concordats (Unitarians) Whittier, Lowell Longfellow, Emerson, Thoreau 82
concrete blocks 45
Condition of the Working Class in England, The 13

Conduit, Carl 207
Cone, George C. 235
Congregationalists 55
Connecticut; Wright family
Conover, Allan Darst 45, 66n73, 71–3
Conover & Porter 71, 75, 177; UW Science Hall 71–3; Wright as "office man" 73
Constable, John 38
constructivism; Russian 94
conventionalisation 111–13
Cook County Forest Reserve 207
Cook County Normal School 41
Cooksville, Wisconsin 56
Coonley, Avery 59–62; house 59, 144, 149, 150, 225
Coonley, Lydia 59; and Hull-House 59
Coonley, Queene 59–62; Cottage School 61; kindergarten Playhouse 59, *60, 61, 160*, 186; and *Progressive Education* 62
Cooper, Henry N. 77; date controversy 77–8, 181
Corliss engine 19, *21*
Cornel University 48, 53, 188
corruption 11–14
Corwin, Cecil Sherman 48, 87, 90, 100, 133
Corwin, Charles A. 48, 100
"Country Homes for City People" 213
countryside 202–94
Craftsman, The 10, *133*
Craftsman Workshop 132
Craig, Gordon 15
Cramer builder 77
Crane Elevator Company 87
Cremin, Lawrence 41
Crew, Henry: Luxfer competition juror 135
Croker, Richard 14
Culpin, Edward 207, 233, 235

Daly, Cèsar 122
Dana, Susan Lawrence 58; Wright's remodelled house 59, 149, 226
Dane Country Courthouse 72
Darby, Montana 212, 227
Daumier, Honrè 38
Davis, Alexander Jackson 213
Dean, George 141
Dear Lake, Minnesota 181
Debs, Eugene V. 13; and American Railway Union 24
decentralisation 204; of manufacturing 206
Decker Building, N.Y. City 16
Demar, Edward 183–4; and National Register 184
Democrats 7
DeRhodes, K.C., house 186
Derleth, August: on Rev. Jones 81
Der Städtebau, Vienna 232
Detroit, Michigan 59, 85

Detroit Normal School now WayneState University 60
Deutscher Werkbund circle 93
Devin, David T. 181
Devin, Mrs. David T. 181; house 133, *154*, 179
Dewey, Evelyn 41
Dewey, Fred 41
Dewey, Jane 41
Dewey, John 9, 38–9, 57, 59; on education 41ff; and Hull-House 41, 132; John & Evelyn 60; Laboratory school 63
design methodology 176–7
D.H. Burnham and Company 166
Dickinson, Clarence 11
Dinsmore, Samuel 224
"Disappearing City", The 99
Discourses on Architecture 94–6
Disraeli, Benjamin; "in a progressive country, change is constant" 42
Doesburg, Theo van 191
Donald Robertson Players 15
Donchin, Mark 86
Dooley, Mr. 12–13, 14; on education 41
Dose, Charles P. 165, 266
Dow, Arthur Wesley 12, 113, *115*
Downers Grove, Illinois 61
"Drawing from Nature of School and Self-Instruction" 45
drawings by FLW 74–5, 78; "imitationms of Silsbee" 85; presentation 78
dreamers 6
Druid 7
Drummond, Thomas house 76
Drummond, William Eugene 61, 236; neighbourhood competition 24, 247; own house 186
Drummond & Guenzel 247
Dublin, Ireland 208
Dunne, Finley 12–13
Dunning,, Max 13
Durand, J.N.-L. 96, *97*, 98, 124, 201; influence of 125
Dusseldorf, Germany 208

Eastman, Seth, captain 20
Eckart, Mrs Robert (Rebecca), house: re E.C. Waller 180
Ècole des Artss Décoratifs 113
Ècole des Beaux-Arts, Paris 75, 87, 113; and Violet-le-Duc 94
Edelmann, John Herman 16, 112; and Henry George 16; and Sullivan 86–6
Edelmann & Johnston 86
Edgewater, Chicago 76; and Kropotkin 40–1; and L. Sullivan 16; "Pessimism of Modern Architecture" 16
education 37ff; hope lies in education 262
Education of Man, The 66n85
Edward Longstreet medal 48

Egbert, Donald 94
Egypt 100
Ehlman, Albert C. 57
Eidlitz, Leopold 111
1893 7, 14, 22–5
Eliot, Maine: re Mrs Devin 181
Elmhurst, Illinois 146
Elmslie, George Grant 48, 177; critical of FLW 74, 86; Wright to Elmslie 88
Ely, Richard T. 24
Emerson, Ralph Waldo 13, 37–40, 45, 85, 91–2, 112, 188; opposition to 92–3; organic theory 91, 99; Wright's view 92
Emery, William H., house *146*; schematics *147*
Emile, or, On Education 38
Emmond, Robert, house *152*, 179, 180
Emmond/Gale floor plan 188
Engineering Record 165
Engles, Friedrich 13
Ennis, Charles, house 137, 151
Enright, Walter J. 105n68
Episcopalians 55
Erie Canal 20
Esbenshade, E.E. 191
Essex, Connecticut 42
Euro American 4, 100
European Cities at Work 244
Evans, Etelka 57, 207
Evanston, Illinois 145
E-Z Polish Company 59, 191

Fabian socialists 208
Fairhope, Alabama 17, 59
Fairmont Park, Philadelphia 43
"family resemblance" FLW buildings 148
Falkenau Row Houses 76, 78
Farmers' Alliance 7
Faulkner, Waldron 61
Fellowship, The 62–3; "Master's comrade" 63
feminism 12
Ferries Observation Wheel 1892 *127*
Ferris Jr., George Washington Gale *127*
Fiddelke, Henry G. 48
Fifer, Florence 56; *see also* Bohrer, F.
Filene, Edward 206
financial panic May 1893 86
Fine Arts building 15, 46
Fink, Leon 3
"Fireproof House for $5000" 219, *220*
First Methodist Church office block 85
First Unitarian Church, Sioux City 75
First United Presbyterian Church 184
Flagg, Ernest 166
floor plan schematics *177*
Flossmoor, Chicago 224
FLW Foundation 164, 216
Ford, George B. 129, 206, 244
Ford, Henry 10
Forest Hills, New York 235, 242, 243

form follows function: by Greenough 96
Foster, S.A. 181
Fourier, Charles 202
Fowler & Wright, architects 164
France 45
Francis Apartments 184
Francisco Terrace apartments 10
Francophilians 87
Frankenstein 98
Frankfurter, Felix 13
Franklin Institute 48
Frederick, Christine 206
French, William M.R. 48, 113
Friedman, Alice 15
Friedrich, Caspar David 38
Fries, Hermann de 191
Froebel, Frederick 15, 37, 38–9, 52; Child Nurture & Activity Inst'e 40; and crystallography 125'; *Education of Man, The* 40ff; Froebel's idea 45; and geometry 111–12; "gifts" 42–4, 46–7, 125; poetic prayer 47
Fulda, Minnesota 56
Fuller, Henry Blake 11
Fuller, R. Buckminster 65n58
Fuller, William David, house 57, 147
functional integration: Adler's view 92
Fur beck, George 215
Furbeck, Rollin J., house 138, 179
Furbeck, Warren 214–15
Furness, Frank 23, 85, 94

Gale, Edwin O. 30n52; Thomas 83; Thomas & Walter Gale 30n52
Gale, Thomas H., house *149*, 179, 186, 191
Gale, Zona 9, 10, 11, 12, 30n52, 232
Galesburg, Illinois 83
Gale "twin" houses *152*, 180; re Parker 180
Gallery 291 30n56
Gannett, William C. 50, 52, 53, 72, 83; and Rev. Jones 81
Garden City 6, 204, 235; advocates 207, 233; European examples 235
garden suburb 212–13, 223, 235; Agnetapark, Netherlands 233; Essen, Germany 233
Gardner, E.C. 206
Garland, Hannibal Hamlin 7, 9, 10, 14, 18, 37, 100; On Burnham 24
Garrick Theatre 85
Gaudi, Antoni 94
Geddes, Patrick 207
geometry 45–6, 150–8; baroque 206; and FLW's geometry ideals 117; in nature 111–12; rectilinear applications 212; square generator patterns 266; 3-D abstractions 111
George, Henry 9, 11, 13, 15, 41; and *Progress and Poverty* 18, 53; and Wright 17
Georgetown, Texas 57
George W. Tilton Elementary School *118*

German "Municipal Movement" 233
German Opera Company of Chicago 85
German Warehouse 100
Germany 16, 22–3, 27, 37, 43–5, 62; German architectural theory 89; Germans & Chicago 86, 164, 165; and toy making 45; zoning 207
Gerts, Walter, house 159
Getty Tomb 136
Ghent, Netherlands 207
Giedion, Sigfried 191
Gilbert, Cass; on pre design/progress 116
Gilded Age 3, 91
Gill, Irving John 48, 86, 117, 118–20; and San Diego 87
Gilman, Charlotte Perkins 9, 15, 243
Gilmore, E.A. *151*
Glasgow, Scotland 207
Goan, Orrin S., house 78, 180
God 52
Goecke, Theodor 232
Goethe, Johann Wolfgang von 15, 37, 52, 101; *Altar of Good Fortune* 45, 111–12; and Schiller
Goldman, Emma 15
Golf Clubhouse see River Forest Golf Clubhouse
Goodie, Bertram 206
Goodman, Paul 204
Goodman, Percival 204
Goodrich, H.C., house 180, 215
Gookin, F.W. 48
Gothic Revival houses 252n5
Gowan Block, S.S Marie 184
Graham, David 13
Graham, Thomas 84
Grammar of Ornament 85, 112
"greatest architect" FLW 122
Green, Grace N. 56
Green, William, house 180, 191
greenbelt, or "belt of green", first application 205; Loudon & Roebuck 205
Greenough, Horatio; form follows function 89
Greenwich Village 249
grid 149–50, *151*
Griffin, Marion Mahony 68n151, 145, 225, 230
Griffin, Ralph 146; and Catherine Wright 144; and *Magic of America* 146
Griffin, Walter Burley 68n151, 113, 162n38, 188
Griffins, the 144–8, 206, 208, 243
Gropius, Walter 243
ground floor plan, role in design 184
Guenzel, Louis 246
Guilt, Joseph 125; *An Encyclopaedia of Architecture* 125
Gurdjieff, Georgi 11

Guthrie, William; Chicago Symphony Orchestra 11
Gutkind, E.A. 6

Habitations of Man in All Age 94
Hailmann, W.N. 66n85, 125
Hamilton, Mary 52
Hamilton, Montana 229
Hamlin, A.D.F. 87, 96
happiness 5
"Happy Colony" 202
Harden, Julius E. 115
Hardy, Thomas P., house 147, 183; Monolith home 221
Harford, Connecticut 3
Harlan, Dr. Allison, house: and Sullivan 179
Harper's Weekly 14
Harvard University 48, 57, 243
Hayden, Sophia 64n26
Haymarket Square, Chicago 22; and 1886 bombing 23
Healy, George 113
Hearn, M.F. 96
Heath, William R. 191
Hegemann, Werner 206, 207
Helena shot tower 66n75
Helena Valley house project 180
Helen Heath Neighbourhood Settlement 84; and Fellowship House 84
Heller, Elizabeth Wright, house 80, 133, 147, 179, 180, 215–16
Henderson, F.B., house 180, 182
Herbert, Gilbert 71, 86
Heurtley, Arthur B. 10; Summer cottage 10
Heurtley house 10
Hickox, Warren, house *155*, 180
Hillside Home School 10, 51ff, *54*, 57–9, 105n68, 180; and C.E. Roberts 215; closure 59; coeducational, nonracial 66n81; Hillside buildings l, 67n107; Home Building *54*, 75–6, 180; Home Cottage 51, 75; [students and teachers] 56–7; wind pump 180
Hillside Home School 1901–02 *58*–9, *62*, *157*, *186*; *chapel/library* 146, 191; gym 147
Hines, Thomas 25, 234
Hinsdale, Chicago 72
Hitchcock, Henry-Russell 62, 77–8, 138
Hofstadter, Richard 7, 8; "Revolution in Journal" 13
Hogans, Henry 272–3
Holabird, W. 120, 135; Luxfer competition juror 135
Holabird & Roche 120
Holcomb, Permelia 79, 104n53
Hollywood 15
Holme, Thomas 202
Holzhueter, John 147
"Home in a Prairie Town" 180, 182, 183, *217*
Home Insurance building, Chicago 10

Homer, Winslow 38
Honolulu 120
Hooker, George Ellsworth 232–4, 242; and Berlin/Dusseldorf exhibitions 232–3; and Sitte 232–3
horizontality 138–9, 144
Horner, I.K., house 147, 186
horse manure 22
Horta, Victor 94
Hosmer, Frederick Lucian 53
House Beautiful 111, 132
house on a mesa 180
Houses and How to Make Them 206
Howard, Ebenezer 202, 204–5, 233
Howe, Frederick C. 9, 208, 232, 244
Howell, William Dean 18; and Bellamy 18
How the Other Half Lives 13
Hubbard, Elbert Green 122, 132
Hubbell, Jay 18
Hudnut, Joseph 247
Hugenholtz, Frederik Willem Nicolaas 57
Hugenholtz F.W.N. 53
Hugo, Victor 15, 37, 98; *Les Miserables* 83
Hull-House Maps and Papers 13
Hull-House Players 15
Hull-House settlement 9, 13, 14, 15, 41, 207; and Arts & Crafts Society 18; and FLW 132; and Hooker 233; remodelling 241; and Rev. Jones 82
Hunt, Myron 113, 190
Hunt, Stephen M.B., house 147
Husser, Joseph, house 133, 179, 181
Hyde, Henry Morrow 245
Hyde Park, Illinois 103n3, 174
"Hymn to Nature, A" Goethe 37

Illinois Institute of Technology 113
Imperial Hotel, Tokyo 191, 192, 239
Indians, *see* Native Americans
indigenous 98
Inglis, Helen E. 57
Inland Architect & New Record 50, 75, 76
international conferences 207–8
International Congress and Exhibition 233; model city ordinance 233
International Congress of Architects 207–8
Iowa, Unitarian Chapel for *49*
Ishpeming, Michigan 183

Jackson, William Henry 270
James H. Brown School 118
Janesville, Wisconsin 81
Japan: architecture 100, 188; FLW's debt 114; national pavilion 1893 188; Prints 55; Tokyo earthquake 1922 19; traditional design 132
Jason Edwards 7
Jaxon, Honorè Joseph 270
Jefferson, Thomas 3, 111; Jeffersonian tradition 9, 17

Jenny, William Le Baron 16, 85; Luxfer competition juror 135; on precedent 117
Jensen, Jens 233, 248; on 1908 Chicago plan 234
Jester, Ralph,house 137
John B. Roers school 117
Johns Hopkins University 242
Johnson, Marietta Pierce 59
Johnston, Joseph S. 16, 86
Johonnnot, Rodney F. 174, 176
Jones, Chester Lloyd 56
Jones, Elinor (Ellen, Nell, Ellen C.) 41, 47–8, 51–2, 56, 75; FLW buildings for 54
Jones, Hanna (Anna), *see* Wright, Hanna
Jones, James 55
Jones, Jane (Jennie) 41, 43, 75
Jones, John [Lloyd] 7, 9, 37
Jones, John Lloyd (Jr.) 7, 9, 37, 56
Jones, Owen 85, 112
Jones, Reverend Jenkin Lloyd 10, 11, 12, 17, 38, 41, 54–5, 82–4, 112, 145, 188, 207, 232; on Abraham Lincoln 82; on Christianity 82; non-creedal theology 55, 74, 82–3; section 78–4; and Silsbee 73–5; and Unity Chapel 49–50
Jones, Thomas 33, 45, 51, 54, 56, 77
Jones family 83, 174
Jones sisters 41, 49, 53, 57, 100, 215; and Maginel 52
Joseph, John W. *186*
Jungle, The 13

Kankakee, Illinois 215
Kant, Emmanuel 41, 52, 93
Kehilath Ashe Ma'ariv (K.A.M.) Synagoge 85
Kehl, F.W. 53
Kelley, Florence 9, 11, 13, 55, 83; and Engles 13; and Hull-House 132
Kelly, John 56
Kelly, Margaret 56
Kelsey, Albert 113, 240
Kendall, S.T., letter from FLW 218
Kennard, De Wit Taylor 48
Kennedy, John C. 241
Kent, Alfred R. 55; and Silsbee 76
Kent, Edward Austin 48d
Kent, Rockwell 235
Key, Ellen 12; free association 12
Kier 191
Kindergarten Chats 87, 89, 116
"Kindergarten Cottage" *43*
Kindergarten Movement 52
kindergarten/s 42, 45, 116
Kingston, George Strckland 202
Kingston/Lightplan, Adelaide 205
Kinney, Ashley J. 85
Kinney, Ozia S. 85
Klocke, Jonathan 186
Koch, Henry C. 72–3

Koehler, Alexander 16
Kostof, Spiro 202
Kropotkin, Peter 9, 11, 12, 15, 16; on city 202; on education 40–1; and Hull-House 40
Kruty, Paul 144, 180, 187; on W. Griffin 145
Kyoto, Japan 188; Byodo-In Temple 188

La Crosse, Wisconsin 183
Ladbroke Estate, Notting Hill, London 213, *214*
Ladies Home Journal 180, 182, 183, 216–21
La Follette, Robert 9, 10, 28n23, 53; Mary La Follett 56; Philip La Follette 10; Robert Jr. 10; Wisconsin Idea 10
La Grange, Chicago 62; primary school 62
Lake Como & Big Dith 224, 225
Lake Forest, Chicago 78; Presbyterian Church 78
Lake Forest University 90; and Cecil Corwin 90
Lake Huron, Michigan
Lake Mendota boathouse 133, 139–43, *142*
Lake Monona boathouse 122, 133, 134, 140–3
Lamp, Robert, house 147, 224
Lansing, Michigan 57
Larkin, John D. 132
Larkin Soap Company 186; Administration Building 95, 147, 169–71, *170–1*, 191; geometry 170–1, *174*; Wright's evaluation 169, 171
Lathrop, Julie C. 83; and Hull-House 132
Lawrence, Edgar H.. 243
Lawrence, Mrs. Mary 58
Lawrence, Rhuena 58
Lawrence School 58
Learning to Draw 101
Le Corbusier vs FLW 92, 94, 121, 191, 203
Ledoux, Claude-Nickolas 45, 96, 126, 201
Letchworth, England 243
Lethaby, William 122
Leusden, Willem van 191
Levine, George 93
Lexington Terrace apartments 10, 201
Light, William 202
Lillienberg, Albert & Ingrid 235, 243
Lincoln, Abraham 79
Lincoln Park, Chicago 127
line ideas 2D *115*
Little, Francis, house 186, 191
Little Theater Movement 15
Liverpool, England 208
"Living City", The 99
Llewellyn, Orange, New Jersey 213
Lloyd, Henry Demarest 9, 14, 83
Lloyd Jones sisters 39
"Lloyd Wright Brothers" 190; in San Diego 190
Loke 41
Lombard University 83
London, lEngland 208

Longfellow, Henry Wadsworth 15
Looking Backward 18
Lorch, Emil 48, 113–14
Los Angeles 15, 19, 208; concrete block houses 114
Loudon, John Claudius 202, 212
Louisiana Purchase Exposition *127*
Lovejoy, Andrew 183
Lowell, James Russell 15
Lowell, John 52
Lowell, M.H., studio 182, *189*
Lubetkin, Behold 203
Lutyens, Edwin 206
Luxfer Prism Company 133, 134,; facade competition 135
Lyman Trumbull Elementary school 118, 167

MacArthur 83
MacCormac, Richard 46
MacHarg, William Stores, house: and Sullivan 179
Maconi, Loy *151*
Madam Butterfly 100
Madison, Wisconsin 12, 44, 46, 53, 71–3; Tenney Park 171; public school system 64n28; Public Schools 57; Second Ward School 51
Madison (now Central) High School 56, 74
Madison University, Hamilton, New York z(single entry) 79
Madison Woman's Club 63n28
Maher, George Washington 48, 87, 242
Mahoney, Clara 145
Mahony, Marion Lucy 84; *see also* Griffin, Marion Mahony
Manierre, William R.: Progressive politician 55
Mann, Gother 202
Mann, Horace 39, 52
Manning, Warren H. 235
Manson, Grant Carpenter 47, 77, 90, 145; and Lincoln Center 168
March, Lionel 126
March & Steadman *126*
Margetson, Wylie Churchill 57
Marienthal, Oscar B.; quarter-section design *244*
Marionette Theater 46
Markham, Kira 15; and Wright, Jr. 15
Markley, J.E.E. 56; Rock Crest, Rock Glen 68n131
Marling, James H 48
Marquette City, Michigan 183
Marsh, Benjamin 8, 206, 232
Marshall Field building 17
Marshall's article "Education of an Architect" 114
Martin, Darwin D., house 147, 149, *159*, 183, *186*, 191, 221; Martin's Barton house *158*, 185–6, *186*

Martin, Delta 185
Martin, W.E. 59; house 59
Martin, Winnie 59
Marx, Karl 15
Mason City, Iowa 56
Massachusetts 42
Massachusetts Institute of Technology (MIT) 113, 133, 144, 159n1, 207
Massey, Jonathan; and Bragdon 125
Mawson, Thomas 235
May, Meyer 191
Maywood, Illinois 149
Mazzini, Giuseppe 13
McAfee, A.C. 133, 181
McArthur, Warren, house 179
McArthur flat building 191
McClellan, Doug 73
McClure's Magazine 13, 14
McDowel, Mary 246
McGregor, Iowa 42
McKim Mead & White 24–5
Mead, Frank 120–1
Mead, George H. 246
Mead, Marcia 236; center commpetition 247
Meadville, Pennsylvania 81
Meadville Lombard Theological School 103n34
Meadville Seminary 57
Meakin, Budget 206
Meech, Julia 100
Meier company 203
Mencken, H.L. 22
Mendelssohn, Eric 100
Menocal, Narciso 89, 147; "geometrical essence" 111
Mesoamerica 100
Messer, Mario 186
Methodists 55
Metzger, Victor, house 182, 183; and "Prairie Town" project 183
Middleton, Robin 94
Midway Gardens, Chicago 10, 112, *163*, 187; Queen of the Gardens *121*–2
Millard, Alice house 100, 122, 161, 180
Miller, Wilhelm 191
Millet, Louis J. 48, 113–14
Mills College 56
Milwaukee, Wisconsin 43, 53, 57, 72
Mississippi Valley 10
Missoula, Montana 227
MIT *see* Massachusetts Institute of Technology
Model Factories & Villages 206
Modern Architecture Research (MARS) 203
Modern Factory, The 206
modern initiatives, American 112
Modern School Movement 41
module 98
Mogul 100
Monadnock Building 164, 165
Monet, Claude 38

304 Index

Monolith Homes 221
monopolies 12–13
Monroe, Harriet 132
Montessori 46
Montgomery, John 233
Montgomery Ward 7
Monvel, Andrè Boutet de 38
Moody, W.I. 224
Moore, Charles 25
Moore, Nathan, house 179
Morris, William 13, 14, 19, 132, 202; a "new vision" 93; and the machine 93
muckraker 13–14
Mueller, Paul 177, 179
Mumford, Lewis 90, 241
Mundie, W.B. 75
Muslim 100

Nadar, John 73
Nash, John 213
Natco Company 159n1
National Association for the Advance-ment of Colored People (NAACP) and Dewey 41
National Conference on City Planning 206, 233, 245
National Conference on Housing: Chicago 208, 233
National Consumers League 13
National Grange 7
National League for Industrial Art 30n69
National Municipal League 8, 234
National Municipal Review 8, 206
National Register of Historic Places 184
National Tile Company; "tex-tile" tiles 46
Native Americans 4, 100, 120
nature 38; opposition to 92–3; vs machine/city 93
In the Nature of Materials 138
Neef, Joseph 63n12
neighbourhood center competition 246; description 258–49; Drummonds description 248–49; short description 246
Neighborhood Unit 245–9, *247*; description 246; "alternative scheme" *248*
Netherlands 53, 57, 62, 190
Newark, New Jersey 246
New Deal 1930s 7–8
New Delhi, India 206; quasi-city 207
New Ebenezer, Georgia 202
New Housekeeping . . . Home Management . . . The 206
Newport, Rhode Island 12
New *Republic* 249
Newry, Ireland 203
New York City 12, 13, 15, 16, 57, 73, 132, 207; and Erie Canal 20; first city club 233; and Henry George 16
New York Society of Beau-Arts Architects 88
New York Times 14
New York Tribune 7

Nichols, Frederick Day 219, 224, 242; Bitter Root Valley (BRIVCo) 227; Nichols/Waller/Bitter Root village plan *221*; prototype house plan? 221
Noel, Mariam 62
Noisier, Paris 203
Nolen, John 206, 208, 235
Norris, Frank 14
Northern Trust Company 10
Northwestern University 55; settlement house 83, 233
Northwest Park Commission 207
Northwest Tribune 230
Notre Dame de Paris 98
Nova Scotia, Canada 57
Nute, Kevin 100; on Lorch & pure design 114

Oak Leaves, Oak Park 10, 15
Oak Park, Illinois 4, 15, 149, 208, 224; kindergarten 59; Oak Park Gales 40n52; School 55
Oak Park Banjo Club 138
Oak Park Congregational church 183
Oak Park Golf Club 138
Oak Park Studio *see* Wright's own house, Oak Park, August 1889'
Oak Park Vindicator 138
Obler, Arch, house 1946 180
Octopus, The 14
Oglethorpe, James 202
O'Keeffe, Georgia 12
Olmsted, Frederick Law 24–5, 27, 205
Olmsted Jr., Frederick Law 8, 206, 213, 243; on "social organism" 208; and Washington D.C. 24, 25
Omaha, Nebraska 141
Orage, A.R. 11
Oregon, Wisconsin 74
organic architecture; Wright's definition 92; Sullivan's ambiguities 82
orientalism 12
ornament; absence on exterior 185; emphasis on interior 185
Orono, Main 57
Oud, J.J.P. 190
Ouseley, Giedion J. 202

Paine, Thomas 13
Papworth, Wyatt *87*, 125
Paris, France 12, 16, 86
Parker, Francis Wayland 39–41ff; and Hillside Home School 55
Parker, Minerva 64n26
Parker, Robert in Emmond house 179
Parker, Theodore 66n85
parklands 202, 204, 213; Georgian squares 213; public 213
Pawtucket, Rhode Island 42
Peabody, Elizabeth 42–3, 52

Pease, Otis 9
Pemberton, Robert 202
People's Party 6
Perkins, Dwight Heald 8, 54, 84, 113, 248; the Perkins 233; on precedent 117, 143–4; school designs 117–18; and Steinway Hall 189; and Lincoln Center 166–9; and woodlands 207
Perkins, Lucy Finch 207, 234
Perkins, Marion H. 84
Perkins, Myra 84, 145
Perkins, Robert A., apartment building 165
Perret, Auguste 94
Perry, Clarence 250
Perspecta 22 176
Pestalozzi, Johann Heinrich 51, 52; on education 39–40ff; and Fairhope, Alabama 69; and Froebel Society 43; Pew, John C., house 180
Pfeiffer, Bruce Brooks 73, 78
Pharaonic Egypt 201
Philadelphia 23, 202, 240, 231; Centennial Exhibition 1876, 21, 42–3
Philips Exeter Academy 48
Photography 12
Photo-Secession Gallery 12
P/picturesque 38
Pitkin, Albert
Pitkin, Edward Hand 183–4; Civil War veteran 183; house 183; and J.W. Brooks 183; and Mamah Borthwick 183
Pittville Estate, Cheltenham, London 213
plan forms, circle/square *126*
planning lessons FLW 90; plan & structure and elevation 184
Plan of Chicago, The 25–6
central precinct *26*
Plan typologies, houses *177*
plan typology number 3b *182*
Playground Association of America 207
Pond, Allen B. 113
Pond, Irving K. 113, 166; American school, self styled 241
Pond brothers 241
Populism 7–9
Populist 7, 11, 13; and George 17
Populist Party 6–7; Peoples Party 93; platform 1892 6
Portage, Wisconsin 11
Porter, Andrew T. 105n68
Porter, Lew Foster 72
Port Sunlight, Liverpool 203
Post, Louis 233
Prairie Club 207
"Prairie School of Architecture" 191
Presbyterians 55
Price, George M. 206
primitive 98–101
Princeton University 9

progress 3
"Progress and Poverty" 17
Progress before Precedent 4, 87, 113
P/progressive 9, 17, 18ff; coalitions 8
Progressive City 201
progressive education 40, 57, 113
Progressive Education 62
Progressive Education Movement 59
Progressive Era 3, 7, 42
Progressive Movement 8, 42; "orderly social change" 8
Progressive Movement, The 8, 42
Progressive Party 233
P/progressivism 3–7, 48, 168, 201
proportion as aesthetic determinant 184
Proposed Commercial High School Building 118, *119*
Protestant 208
Puccini, Giacomo 100
Pueblo Indians 100–1
Pugin, A.N.W 93
Pullman, George M. 19, 23
Pullman, Illinois 4, 203; construction 1881 23; landscape by Barrett 23; site beside Lake Calumet 23
Pullman strike 1894 13, 23–4
Purcell, William Gray *146*, 190
pure design 48, 112–23; FLW's view 116

Quadruple Block Plan 146, 147, 213, 216–19, *218*; 1910 presentation *222*; 1915; presentation *223*; aka Quad Plan herein 216ff; alternative block arrangements 219–23; analysis 216–18, 222–4; and Progressive reformers 223; geometry 221–3, *222*
Queen Anne style 76, 133, 180, 212, *267*
Quincy, Massachusetts 39, 41, 58

Radnor, South Carolina 202
Realists 6
Reckon, Sarah McMillan 265
red square *mon* 122
Red Square Toy Company 67n103
reductive principle 169, 186, 191
Regents Park, London 213
Regina, Saskatchewan 183
Renaissance 201–2; Graeco-Roman 98
Reporter, Oak Park 8, 21
Republicans 7; Republican Party 10
revival 98–9
"revolt against formalism" 41
Rice, William 11
Richards, Clarinda Chapman 57
Richardson, Henry Hobson 111
Ridgeland, Chicago 216; city block plan 216
Riis, Jacob 13, 232
River Forest Golf Clubhouse 138–43; scheme one *141*, 181; scheme two *139*, *140*

Index

River Forest Tennis Club 138, 159n1
Riverside, Chicago 59, 213; public parks, Des Plaines River 213
Roberts, Chapin 56
Roberts, Charles E. 56, 83, 159n1, 174; projets unrealized 215–16, *217*, *218*; Quadruple Block 214–15; Unity Temple building committee 215
Roberts, Isabel, house 145, 186
Roberts, Mrs, sister became Mrs H Bradley 215; Mrs. Roberts brother, Warren Hickox 215
Robertson, Donald 11, 58
Robin, Frederick C. 191
Robinson, Charles 25
Robinson, Charles Mulford 205–6, 247
Robinson, Harry Franklin 272, 273
Roboro, England 164
Rockefeller, John D. 14; and Standard Oil 13; and Baptist Society 23
Rocky Roost cottage 78
Roebuck, Charles A. 202
Rogers, Gamble 190
Rogers, James Campbell house *156*, 182; re Thomas as first resident 181–2
Rohe, Mies van der 191
Rolland, Romain 41, 63n15
Romanticism 37–8
Roobach, Eloise; on Gill 120
roof, gable vs hip 185–6
Rookery, The, building 10
Roosevelt, Franklin D. 7
Roosevelt, Theodore 28n23
Root, John Wellborn 24, 164; on Mr. Adler 89
Rosenwald Museum of Science and Industry 32n126
Ross, Denman W. 114; and pure design 115
Rouseau, John-Jacques 37, 48, 63n2, 96, 201; on education 38ff; and Romanticism 38; *Social Contract, The* 39, 99
Royal Institute of British Architects (RIBA) 208; 1910 conference on empire city planning 233
Roycroft, New York 17, 132
Ranlett, William H. 213
"rural fundamentalism" 84
ruralism 9
Rush Medical College 90
Ruskin, John 13, 15, 19, 37, 66n85, 101, 212; and Romanticism 38–9
Rykwert, Joseph 99

Saarinen, Eliel 204; *The City* 204
Safford, Mary A. 75
St. Louis, Missouri 51, 56, 91, *127*
St. Louis Civic League 246
St. Paul, Minnesota 51, 59
St Paul Daily Globe 55
Salem, Massachusetts 48
Salem, Oregon 126
Salt, Titus 203; Saltier 203
San Francisco, California 208
San Francisco Call building 192
Sapper Island, Ontario 183
Sault Ste. Marie, Michigan 183; Central Savings Bank 183; and Robert N. Adams 183
Savage, John L.: dams designed 56
Savannah, Georgia 202
Schaefer, John 85
Schenck, jAnna P. 236; center competition 247
Schiedan, The Hague, Netherlands 57
Schiller, Johann Christoph Friedrich von 86; on art 120
Schiller Theatre Building 85, 165; for the German Opera House Company 165
Schindler, Rudolph; Sullivan & Wright 248
Schlesinger & Mayer building *91*
Schmid, Peter 45
School of Organic Education 59
school reform 431–42
School vand Society, The 41, 59; by John and Evelyn Dewey 60
Schurz, Mrs. Carl (Margarethe) 43
Schuyler, Montgomery 24
Scott, Mel 25, 233
Scottsdale, Arizona 73
Seattle, Washington (Territory) 87, 165, 266
Seattle Post-Intelligencer (P-I) 165'
secession, Europe 112
Secrest, Meryle 51, 81; on William Wright 79–80
Semper, Gottfried 45, 89
Settlement House Movement 233
settlements 14
Seven Lamps of Architecture 66n85
Shame of the Cities, The 13
Shane, Ida Aline 195n46
Shaw, Howard van Doren 246
Shelley, Mary 98
Shelley, Rutan & Coolidge 133
Sheridan, Phillip H. 23
Shingle Style 76
Scudder, J.A. 183
Silsbee, Joseph Lyman 37, 45, 46, 48, 71–5, 83, 87, 100, 119, 188; and Hillside Home School 53–5, *54*; influence, house plans 176–80; "moving sidewalk" 48; professorship 48; and Unity Chapel 48ff
Silsbee, William 71–3, 101n5
Simkovitch 232
Simonds, O.C. 235
Sinai Temple, Chicago 86
Sinclair, Upton 13
single tax 17
Sioux City, Iowa 50; First Unitarian Church 50
Siry, Joseph 51, 174
Sittte, Camillo 204; "City Builder" 233; "go to school with Nature" 204; influence in

Europe and U.S 204; school of applied arts, Vienna 20
"Small house with lots of rooming it" 219–20, *219*
Smith, Cecil W. 56
Smith, Edward B. house 76
Smith, E. Willard 85
Smith, G.E. Kidder 204; *Italy Builds* 204
Smith, George, house 215
Social Contract 9
Social Gospel 3, 11, 82–3; Movement 83, 168
Social Significance of Modern Drama, The 15
Soria y Mata, Arturo 203
South Australia 213
Southwestern University 57
Soviet Union
Spencer, Herbert 9, 39
Spencer Jr., Robert Classon 45–7, 112–13, 133, 141, 190, 246; 1900 article 88; Luxfer competition 135; on pure design 116; and Rotch Traveling Scholarship 133; on Wright & Sullivan 88
Sprague, Paul E. 103n34, 181
Springfield, Illinois 58
Spring Green 49, 51, 100; and Hillside Home School 52; and Unity Chapel 49–50; Women's Pavilion 62, *173*; and Beye Boathouse 173
Spring Green Women's Club 11, 49
square, dynamics of 123–5, *123*, 136–7, 150, 151
Standard Oil 13
Starr, Ellen 9
Steadman, Phillip 126
Steevens, George W. 20
Steffens, Lincoln 13, 186
Steiger, E. catalog 43–4
Steindal, Ferdinand 11
Steinway Hall office building 87
Stevens, John Calvin 267–*8*
Stevensville, Montana 212, 230
Stewart, George 191
Stickley, Gustave 132–3
Stieglitz, Alfred 12
Sturgis, Russell 95; vs FLW 95–6; on precedent 117
Stock, Frederic W. 11, 66n85
Stockbridge, Massachusetts 57
Stockman, Dr. G.C., house 147
Stone, Elizabeth, house 149
Stones of Venice
Storer, John D., house 151
Stowe, Calvin E. 39
Stowe, Harriet Beecher 18, 206
strutural reduction 111; Sullivan's pier, lintel, arch 11
Studies and Executed Buildings 151, 221, 225
Studio, The 132
style vs *styles* 96

Suburban Planning Association 241
Sullivan, Louis Henry 16, 17, 19, 37, 46, 85–90, 117, 164, 165, 188; and Ashbee 106n012; and Elmslie 87; "Emotional Architecture" 89; and FLW's property 78; and Frank Furness 23; his prose 190; "kindergarten Chats" 46; "Modern Phase of Architecture" 114; on precedent 117; "the master" 87; theory vs Adler 90
Switzerland 39, 43
Symposium for Art 15
A Symposium of Art 11
Syracuse University 48, 75

Tacoma building, Chicago 10
Taft, Lorado 11
Taft, William H. 233
Tagore, Rabindranath 11
Taliesin 62
Taliesin Fellowship 41d
Taliesin West 62
Tallmadge, Thomas 113,; on progress 116
Tammany Hall 14
Taylor, Frederic W. 206
Taylor, Graham 59–60, 83
Taylorism: *Scientific Management* 6, 206
Technical World Magazine 245
teen years FLW 1885–1888 71
Tenney, A.C. 236, 243; quarter-section design *244*
Tennyson, Alfred 37
Tirrell, Charles 235
Theatre 1 project 122
Theosophy 131n61
Thomas, John L. 17
Thomas, Richard; on Rev. Jones 81
Thoreau, Henry David 37, 40
Timiryqazev, Kliment 133
Tolstoy, Leo 37, 51, 201; *Childhood* 40; on education 40ff; "four lines" of activity 60; and Jane Addams 40
Tomlinson, Henry Webster 87, 113, 114, 182, 188
Toronto (Toronto), Canada 202
Tower Hill, Spring Green: summer camp 12, 66n75
Tower Hill Pleasure Company 66n7
town planning reforms 202
Toynbee Hall, London 233
Transcendentalism 3, 15, 42; Emerson 52; New England 15, 52, 82; opposition 92–3; and Sullivan 89
transformation, cubicle to internal space 184, *185*
TransMississippi & International Exposition, Omaha 432
Treason of the Senate, The 13
Treatise on Domestic Economy, A. 206
triangulation in revivals 125

Index

Twain, Mark 3; *The Gilded Age: A Tale of Today* 3
Twombly, Robert 74
Tyrone, New Mexico 206

Ullman, H.J., house *150*, 191
Uncle Tom's Cabin 18
union of city & country 203–204
"Unitarian Chapel for Sioux City, Iowa" *49*, 75
Unitarian/ism 15, 44, 47, 81, 176–7; and FLW & Jones family 884
United Crafts 132
United States; Children's Bureau 13; Senate, Park Commission 25; Bureau of Reclamation 56
"unit system"/module 98
Unity: Freedom, Fellowship and character in Religion magazine 73, 81
Unity Chapel, Spring Green 48–50, *49*, 75, *133*; dedicated 74; FLW paints 50, 73
Unity Church, Oak Park 11, 14; former church 83
Unity Temple 137, 173–6, *174*, *175*, 225; and Unity House *175*, 176, *186*
Universal City Planning Exhibition 208
Universalism 83
university courses FLW 74
University Heights 212, 221, 224–6; analysis 225; clubhouse & cabins 224–5, *226*; FLW employed 224; geometry *227*; summer retreat 224
University of Chicago 23, 41, 55, 56; and Chapin 83; experimental school 41
University of Chicago Magazine 56
University of Illinois 55, 89, 144; and Griffin 210n43; archit'al engineering curriculum 89
University of Kansas 56
University of Main 53
University of Pennsylvania 241
University of Toronto 183
University of Virginia 33n129
University of Wisconsin 18, 55, 56, 57, 133, 171; Platteville 51; River Falls (Normal School) 51; Wright's attendance 72–4
Unwin, Raymond 204, 207, 235
Usonian Concrete Block House project 180

Van Velzer, Charles A. 74
Van Volkenburg, Ellen 15
Van Zanten, David 89, 113, 233; on pure design 116
Vasar College 59
Vaux, Calvert 213
Velez, Diana 203
Versailles gardens 25
Verne, Jules 98
Vienna, Austria 204, 207
Vienna Academy of Fine Arts 248
Victoria Hotel 136, 143, 164

Victorian 3; not American 3, 212
Village Bank *134*
Viollet-le-Duc, E.-E. 90, 92–101, 112, 188; *Discourses on Architecture* 94, 189; FLW's reaction 94–6; influence 94, 125
Visher, Dorothea 56–7
vitalism 38, 92; and DNA 108n141; FLW's readings 92
Vitruvius 5, 90; *De architecture, Cesar di Lorenzo Cesariano's trans* 124
Vivian, Henryi 235

Wagner, Otto 207, 248
Wainwright building, St Louis 17, 136
Wallace, J.L. 48
Wallace, Henry: Progressive 28n23
Waller, Edward Carson 10, 159n1, 221; plan 221, *221*; Waller/Nichols/Bitter Root village; workmen's cottages 241
Waller, R.A., house 76, 180
Waller Apartments 10, 138
Walpole, Horace 98
Walser, J.J., house 186
Waltersdorf, A.W. 242
Warner, Charles Dudley 3; *The Gilded Age: A Tale of Today* 3
warp and weft 184
Warren, Josiah 41
Washington D.C. 24, 61, 75; McMillan Commission's 1902 plan 25, 33n129 (lack of cohesiveness 234; like Chicago 1908 plan 234)
Washington State 232
Washington State University 265
Wasmuth publisher, Berlin 208, 232
Wasserstrom, William 12
Waterman, Henry Hale 48, 74
Watertown, Wisconsin 43
Watkin, David 94
Watson, Vernon S. 273
Wattersson, Mr. 116
Wayne State University 60
Wealth Against Commonwealth 13
Weatherwax, William Henry Harrison 78, 104n48
Weber,, E.C. 159n1
Weingarden, Lauren 17
Wells, Joseph C. 213
Western Unitarian Conference 81
Wester Virginia Building 1893 179
Westward Ho Golf Club 138
Weymouth, Massachusetts 42
Wheeler, Lloyd Garrison 56
Wheeler, Mabel Augusta 56
Whistler, James M. 100
White Jr., Charles Elmer 96, 137, 139, 159n1, 190, 191; on studio 136; and Sullivanism 132
Whitman, Walt 12, 15, 37, 94, 99

Whittier, John Greenleaf 15
Whittlesey, Charles 61
Wight, Peter B. 113
Wilcox, Elbert 48
Wilde, Oscar
Willard, Frances 83
Willatzen, Anders; on W. Griffin 145
Willcox, Walter R.B. 105n84
Willey, Malcomb, house project 180
Williams, Samuel Wayne 265
"Williams Street", On 272–3
Willits, Ward W., house *157*, 183, 186
Wilson, Richard 205
Winnebago tribe 19, 20; encampment *20*; Ho-Chunk 20
Winnetka, Illinois 81
Winnipeg, Manitoba 183
Winslow, William, house *135*–7, *153*; stables 78, 143–*4*, 181
Winston, Edwin 233
Wisconsin 9, 11, 42; Progressivism 9, 12; River improvement 73
Wisconsin State Superintendent of Education 55
Witt, Benjamin Parke De 8
Wolf Lake Resort 10, 134
Woman's Building 1893 64n26
Woman's Christian Temperance Union 83
Woman's Club 207
Woman's Peace Party 12
Woman's Pavilion *173*; comparisons with houses 173
Women's Building 62
Wood, William 187
woodlands 207
Wordsworth, William 37
Workmen's cottages, Waller 241, *242*
Workmen's Row Houses, Larkin/Waller *242*
World's Columbian Exposition 4, 22–4, 41, 83; kindergarten annex 2; U.S. House of Representatives 24; as White City 24; Women's Pavilion 42
World's Parliament of Religions 1893 82–3
Worley, Francis 83
Worley, Francis, house 180
Wotton, Henry 5
Wounded Knee Creek: battle of 4
Wright, Catherine Tobin 13, 14, 15, 37, 80, 83; and Hull-House 46; Juvenile Protective Association 64n5; and kindergarten 44, 46
Wright, Charles William 72, 104n53
Wright, David 42

Wright, Elizabeth 72
Wright, Frank Lincoln 3; and music 44
Wright, Frank Lloyd 5ff; biography xix, 42
Wright, Frank Lloyd, Jr. *See* Lloyd Wright Brothers
Wright, George 72, 104n53
Wright, Hanna (Anna) Lloyd Jones: 42, 44, 45, 56, 83; and education 52; on Frank's birthday 71–2; William's divorce 71–2
Wright Inc 10
Wright, Iovanna Lloyd 47
Wright, John Kenneth (Lloyd) 12, 41, 46, 50, 53, 132; Lincoln Logs 67n103; selection of quotations of Viollet's teachings 95–6
Wright, Lloyd 46–7
Wright, Margaret Ellen 7, 44, 54, 55, 56, 105n68, 138
Wright, Maginel, *see* Wright, Margaret Ellen
Wright, Mary Jane (Jennie) 44, 105n68; and Oak Park School 55
Wright, Olgivanna Hinzenburg 47, 62
Wright, Robert Llewellyn 15, 46, 65n51
Wright, William Carey 37, *80*; Baptist minister 62; Description 52–3, 79–81; divorce 44, 72; and music 44
Wright family 47–8
Wright on Adler and Sullivan 88–9
Wright School 138, 147, 188–93, 246; demise 261, 262
Wright's community designs, schematics *251*
Wright's own house, Oak Park, August 1889 78, *79*, 122, 179, 180; and atelier/studio *136*–7, *137*; articulation 96; purchase of property 78
Wright's reading 94; and tracings 109n157
Wright Style 4, 138, 141, 188–93
'Wright & Tomlinson architects 182–3
Wyoming, Wisconsin 53

Yahara River Channel 171
Yale University 75
Yeoman, Alfred Beaver 246
Yesler Avenue Hotel 266; and FLW 165, 266
Young, H.P., house 179
"Young Man in Architecture" 87

Zinn, Howard 7
Zion, Illinois 191
zoning laws 6; Germany 6
Zucker, Alfred 16, 31n84
Zueblin, Charles 233